Texts in Computer Science

Editors
David Gries
Fred B. Schneider

For further volumes:
http://www.springer.com/series/3191

Krzysztof R. Apt
Frank S. de Boer
Ernst-Rüdiger Olderog

Verification of Sequential and Concurrent Programs

Third, Extended Edition

 Springer

Krzysztof R. Apt
Centrum Wiskunde
& Informatica
Science Park 123
1098 XG Amsterdam
Netherlands
k.r.apt@cwi.nl

Frank S. de Boer
Centrum Wiskunde
& Informatica
Science Park 123
1098 XG Amsterdam
Netherlands
F.S.de.Boer@cwi.nl

Ernst-Rüdiger Olderog
Department für Informatik
Universität Oldenburg
26111 Oldenburg
Germany
olderog@informatik.uni-oldenburg.de

Series Editors

David Gries
Department of Computer Science
Upson Hall
Cornell University
Ithaca, NY 14853-7501, USA

Fred B. Schneider
Department of Computer Science
Upson Hall
Cornell University
Ithaca, NY 14853-7501, USA

ISSN 1868-0941   e-ISSN 1868-095X
ISBN 978-1-4471-2513-6   e-ISBN 978-1-84882-745-5
DOI 10.1007/978-1-84882-745-5
Springer Dordrecht Heidelberg London New York

British Library Cataloguing in Publication Data
A catalogue record for this book is available from the British Library

Printed on acid-free paper

Springer is part of Springer Science+Business Media (www.springer.com)

Endorsements

THE THIRD EDITION is an excellent new version of a valuable book. Enhanced with new material on recursion and object-oriented programs, this book now covers methods for verifying sequential, object-oriented, and concurrent programs using well-chosen sample programming languages that highlight fundamental issues and avoid incidental complications. With growing challenges today to produce correct software systems for the future, this book lets students wisely use a few months now to master concepts that will last them a lifetime.

John C. Mitchell, Stanford University

Verification of programs is the Holy Grail of Computer Science. This book makes its pursuit seem both pleasant and worthwhile. Its unique strength lies in the way the authors have deconstructed the apparently complex subject such that each piece carries exactly one idea. The beauty of the presentation extends from the overall structure of the book to the individual explanations, definitions and proofs.

Andreas Podelski, University of Freiburg

Program verification became an interesting research topic of computing science about forty years ago. Research literature on this topic has grown quickly in accordance with rapid development of various programming paradigms. Therefore it has been a challenge to university lecturers on program verification how to carefully select an easy but comprehensive approach, which can fit in with most programming paradigms and can be taught in a systematic way. The publication of this book is an answer to the challenge, and to my knowledge quite many university lecturers have been influenced by the earlier editions of this book if not chosen them as textbook. Given that the third edition includes verification of object-oriented programs – the most fashionable programming paradigm, and presents it in a way coherent with the approach adopted by the earlier ones, we can expect a further impact of the new edition on university teachings.

Zhou Chaochen, Chinese Academy of Sciences, Beijing

Foreword

THIS BOOK CONTAINS a most comprehensive text that presents syntax-directed and compositional methods for the formal verification of programs. The approach is not language-bounded in the sense that it covers a large variety of programming models and features that appear in most modern programming languages. It covers the classes of sequential and parallel, deterministic and non-deterministic, distributed and object-oriented programs. For each of the classes it presents the various criteria of correctness that are relevant for these classes, such as interference freedom, deadlock freedom, and appropriate notions of liveness for parallel programs. Also, special proof rules appropriate for each class of programs are presented. In spite of this diversity due to the rich program classes considered, there exist a uniform underlying theory of verification which is syntax-oriented and promotes compositional approaches to verification, leading to scalability of the methods.

The text strikes the proper balance between mathematical rigor and didactic introduction of increasingly complex rules in an incremental manner, adequately supported by state-of-the-art examples. As a result it can serve as a textbook for a variety of courses on different levels and varying durations. It can also serve as a reference book for researchers in the theory of verification, in particular since it contains much material that never before appeared in book form. This is specially true for the treatment of object-oriented programs which is entirely novel and is strikingly elegant. I strongly recommend this book to both teachers who wish to train students in the most advanced techniques of verification, and to researchers in this important area.

Amir Pnueli
New York University and the Weizmann Institute of Science, Rehovot

Preface

C OMPUTER PROGRAMS ARE by now indispensable parts of systems that we use or rely on in our daily lives. Numerous examples include booking terminals in travel agencies, automatic teller machines, ever more sophisticated services based on telecommunication, signaling systems for cars and trains, luggage handling systems at airports or automatic pilots in airplanes.

For the customers of travel agencies and banks and for the passengers of trains and airplanes the proper functioning and safety of these systems is of paramount importance. Money orders should reflect the right bank accounts and airplanes should stay on the desired route. Therefore the underlying computer programs should work correctly; that is they should satisfy their requirements. A challenge for computer science is to develop methods that ensure program correctness.

Common to the applications mentioned above is that the computer programs have to coordinate a number of system components that can work concurrently, for example the terminals in the individual travel agencies accessing a central database or the sensors and signals used in a distributed railway signaling system. So to be able to verify such programs we need to have at our disposal methods that allow us to deal with correctness of concurrent programs, as well.

Structure of This Book

The aim of this book is to provide a systematic exposition of one of the most common approaches to program verification. This approach is usually called assertional, because it relies on the use of assertions that are attached to program control points. Starting from a simple class of sequential programs, known as **while** programs, we proceed in a systematic manner in two directions:

- to more complex classes of sequential programs including recursive procedures and objects, and
- to concurrent programs, both parallel and distributed.

We consider here sequential programs in the form of deterministic and nondeterministic programs, and concurrent programs in the form of parallel and distributed programs. Deterministic programs cover **while** programs, recursive programs, and a simple class of object-oriented programs. Nondeterministic programs are used to analyze concurrent programs and the concept of fairness by means of program transformations. Parallel programs consist of several sequential components that can access shared memory. By contrast, distributed programs consist of components with local memory that can communicate only by sending and receiving messages.

For each of these classes of programs their input/output behavior in the sense of so-called partial and total correctness is studied. For the verification of these correctness properties an axiomatic approach involving assertions is used. This approach was initiated by Hoare in 1969 for deterministic programs and extended by various researchers to other classes of programs. It is combined here with the use of program transformations.

For each class of programs a uniform presentation is provided. After defining the syntax we introduce a structured operational semantics as originally proposed by Hennessy and Plotkin in 1979 and further developed by Plotkin in 1981. Then proof systems for the verification of partial and total correctness are introduced, which are formally justified in the corresponding soundness theorems.

The use of these proof systems is demonstrated with the help of case studies. In particular, solutions to classical problems such as producer/consumer and mutual exclusion are formally verified. Each chapter concludes with a list of exercises and bibliographic remarks.

The exposition assumes elementary knowledge of programming languages and logic. Therefore this book belongs to the area of programming languages but at the same time it is firmly based on mathematical logic. All prerequisites are provided in the preparatory **Chapter 2** of Part I.

In Part II of the book we study deterministic programs. In **Chapter 3** Hoare's approach to program verification is explained for **while** programs. Next, we move to the more ambitious structuring concepts of recursive and object-oriented programs. First, parameterless recursive procedures are studied in **Chapter 4**, and then call-by-value parameters are added in **Chapter 5**. These two chapters are taken as preparations to study a class of object-oriented programs in **Chapter 6**. This chapter is based on the work of the second author initiated in 1990, but the presentation is entirely new.

In Part III of the book we study parallel programs with shared variables. Since these are much more difficult to deal with than sequential programs, they are introduced in a stepwise manner in **Chapters 7, 8**, and **9**. We base our presentation on the approach by Owicki and Gries originally proposed in 1976 and on an extension of it by the authors dealing with total correctness.

In Part IV we turn to nondeterministic and distributed programs. Nondeterministic sequential programs are studied in **Chapter 10**. The presentation is based on the work of Dijkstra from 1976 and Gries from 1981. The study of this class of programs also serves as a preparation for dealing with distributed programs in **Chapter 11**. The verification method presented there is based on a transformation of distributed programs into nondeterministic ones proposed by the first author in 1986. In **Chapter 12** the issue of fairness is studied in the framework of nondeterministic programs. The approach is based on the method of explicit schedulers developed by the first and third authors in 1983.

Teaching from This Book

This book is appropriate for either a one- or two-semester introductory course on program verification for upper division undergraduate studies or for graduate studies.

In the first lecture the zero search example in Chapter 1 should be discussed. This example demonstrates which subtle errors can arise during the design of parallel programs. Next we recommend moving on to Chapter 3 on **while** programs and before each of the sections on syntax, semantics and verification, to refer to the corresponding sections of the preparatory Chapter 2.

After Chapter 3 there are three natural alternatives to continue. The first alternative is to proceed with more ambitious classes of sequential programs, i.e., recursive programs in Chapters 4 and 5 and then object-oriented programs in Chapter 6. The second alternative is to proceed immediately to parallel programs in Chapters 7, 8, and 9. The third alternative is to move immediately to nondeterministic programs in Chapter 10 and then to distributed programs in Chapter 11. We remark that one section of Chapter 10 can be studied only after the chapters on parallel programs.

Chapter 12 on fairness covers a more advanced topic and can be used during specialized seminars. Of course, it is also possible to follow the chapters in the sequential order as they are presented in the book.

This text may also be used as an introduction to operational semantics. We present below outlines of possible one-semester courses that can be taught using this book. The dependencies of the chapters are shown in Fig. 0.1.

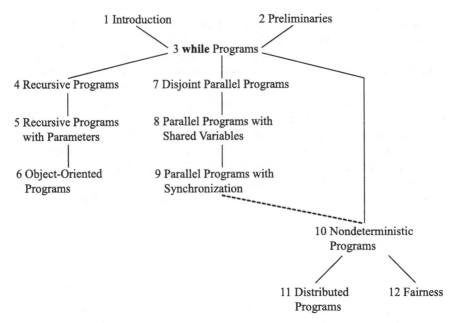

Fig. 0.1 Dependencies of chapters. In Chapter 10 only Section 10.6 depends on Chapter 9.

Changes in the Third Edition

The present, third edition of this book comes with a new co-author, Frank S. de Boer, and with an additional topic that for many years has been at the heart of his research: verification of object-oriented programs. Since this is a notoriously difficult topic, we approach it in a stepwise manner and in a setting where the notational complexity is kept at a minimum. This design decision has led us to add three new chapters to our book.

- In Chapter 4 we introduce a class of recursive programs that extends deterministic programs by parameterless procedures. Verifying such programs makes use of proofs from assumptions (about calls of recursive procedures) that are discharged later on.
- In Chapter 5 this class is extended to the recursive procedures with call-by-value parameters. Semantically, this necessitates the concept of a stack for storing the values of the actual parameters of recursively called procedures. We capture this concept by using a block statement and a corresponding semantic transition rule that models the desired stack behavior implicitly.
- In Chapter 6 object-oriented programs are studied in a minimal setting where we focus on the following main characteristics of objects: they pos-

sess (and encapsulate) their own local variables and interact via method calls, and objects can be dynamically created.

To integrate these new chapters into the original text, we made various changes in the preceding Chapters 2 and 3. For example, in Chapter 3 parallel assignments and failure statements are introduced, and a correctness proof of a program for partitioning an array is given as a preparation for the case study of the *Quicksort* algorithm in Chapter 5. Also, in Chapter 10 the transformation of parallel programs into nondeterministic programs is now defined in a formal way. Also the references have been updated.

Acknowledgments

The authors of this book have collaborated, often together with other colleagues, on the topic of program verification since 1979. During this time we have benefited very much from discussions with Pierre America, Jaco de Bakker, Luc Bougé, Ed Clarke, Werner Damm, Hening Dierks, Edsger W. Dijkstra, Nissim Francez, David Gries, Tony Hoare, Shmuel Katz, Leslie Lamport, Hans Langmaack, Jay Misra, Cees Pierik, Andreas Podelski, Amir Pnueli, Gordon Plotkin, Anders P. Ravn, Willem Paul de Roever, Fred Schneider, Jonathan Stavi and Jeffery Zucker. Many thanks to all of them.

For the third edition Maarten Versteegh helped us with the migration of files to adapt to the new style file. Alma Apt produced all the drawings in this edition.

The bibliography style used in this book has been designed by Sam Buss; Anne Troelstra deserves credit for drawing our attention to it.

Finally, we would like to thank the staff of Springer-Verlag, in particular Simon Rees and Wayne Wheeler, for the efficient and professional handling of all the stages of the production of this book. The TeX support group of Springer, in particular Monsurate Rajiv, was most helpful.

Amsterdam, The Netherlands,   *Krzysztof R. Apt* and *Frank S. de Boer*
Oldenburg, Germany,   *Ernst-Rüdiger Olderog*

Outlines of One-Semester Courses

PREREQUISITES: Chapter 2.

Course on Program Semantics

Class of programs	Syntax	Semantics
while programs	3.1	3.2
Recursive programs	4.1	4.2
Recursive programs with parameters	5.1	5.2
Object-oriented programs	6.1	6.2
Disjoint parallel programs	7.1	7.2
Parallel programs with shared variables	8.1, 8.2	8.3
Parallel programs with synchronization	9.1	9.2
Nondeterministic programs	10.1	10.2
Distributed programs	11.1	11.2
Fairness	12.1	12.2

Course on Program Verification

Class of programs	Syntax	Semantics	Proof theory
while programs	3.1	3.2	3.3, 3.4, 3.10
Recursive programs	4.1	4.2	4.3, 4.4
Recursive programs with parameters	5.1	5.2	5.3
Object-oriented programs	6.1	6.2	6.3, 6.4, 6.5, 6.6
Disjoint parallel programs	7.1	7.2	7.3
Parallel programs with shared variables	8.1, 8.2	8.3	8.4, 8.5
Parallel programs with synchronization	9.1	9.2	9.3
Nondeterministic programs	10.1	10.2	10.4
Distributed programs	11.1	11.2	11.4

Course Towards Object-Oriented Program Verification

Class of programs	Syntax	Semantics	Proof theory	Case studies
while programs	3.1	3.2	3.3, 3.4	3.9
Recursive programs	4.1	4.2	4.3, 4.4	4.5
Recursive programs with parameters	5.1	5.2	5.3	5.4
Object-oriented programs	6.1	6.2	6.3, 6.4	6.8

Course on Concurrent Program Verification

Class of programs	Syntax	Semantics	Proof theory	Case studies
while programs	3.1	3.2	3.3, 3.4	3.9
Disjoint parallel programs	7.1	7.2	7.3	7.4
Parallel programs with shared variables	8.1, 8.2	8.3	8.4, 8.5	8.6
Parallel programs with synchronization	9.1	9.2	9.3	9.4, 9.5
Nondeterministic programs	10.1	10.2	10.4	10.5
Distributed programs	11.1	11.2	11.4	11.5

Course on Program Verification with Emphasis on Case Studies

Class of programs	Syntax	Proof theory	Case studies
while programs	3.1	3.3, 3.4	3.9
Recursive programs	4.1	4.3, 4.4	4.5
Recursive programs with parameters	5.1	5.4	5.4
Object-oriented programs	6.1	6.3–6.5	6.8
Disjoint parallel programs	7.1	7.3	7.4
Parallel programs with shared variables	8.1, 8.2	8.4, 8.5	8.6
Parallel programs with synchronization	9.1	9.3	9.4, 9.5
Nondeterministic programs	10.1, 10.3	10.4	10.5
Distributed programs	11.1	11.4	11.5

Contents

Part II Deterministic Programs

Part I
In the Beginning

1 *Introduction*

P ROGRAM VERIFICATION IS a systematic approach to proving the correctness of programs. Correctness means that the programs enjoy certain desirable properties. For sequential programs these properties are delivery of correct results and termination. For concurrent programs, that is, those with several active components, the properties of interference freedom, deadlock freedom and fair behavior are also important.

The emphasis in this book is on verification of concurrent programs, in particular of parallel and distributed programs where the components communicate either via shared variables or explicit message passing. Such programs are usually difficult to design, and errors are more a rule than an exception. Of course, we also consider sequential programs because they occur as components of concurrent ones.

Krzysztof R. Apt et al., *Verification of Sequential and Concurrent Programs*,
Texts in Computer Science, DOI: 10.1007/978-1-84882-745-5_1,
© Springer-Verlag London Limited 2009

1.1 An Example of a Concurrent Program

To illustrate the subtleties involved in the design of concurrent programs consider the following simple problem, depicted in Figure 1.1.

Problem Let f be a function from integers to integers with a zero. Write a concurrent program $ZERO$ that finds such a zero.

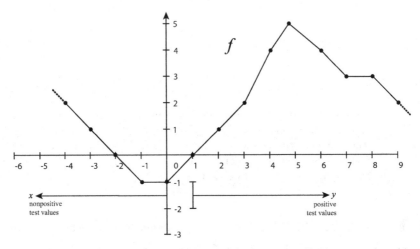

Fig. 1.1 Zero search of a function f : **integer** $\rightarrow$ **integer** split into two subproblems of finding a positive zero and a nonpositive zero.

The idea is to solve the problem by splitting it into two subproblems that can be solved independently, namely finding a positive and a nonpositive zero. Here z is called a *positive zero* of f if $z > 0$ and $f(z) = 0$, and it is called a *nonpositive zero* if $z \leq 0$ and $f(z) = 0$. We are now looking for sequential programs S_1 and S_2 solving the two subproblems such that the parallel execution of S_1 and S_2 solves the overall problem. We write $[S_1 \| S_2]$ for a parallel composition of two sequential programs S_1 and S_2. Execution of $[S_1 \| S_2]$ consists of executing the individual statements of S_1 and S_2 in parallel. The program $[S_1 \| S_2]$ terminates when both S_1 and S_2 terminate.

Solution 1

Consider the following program S_1:

$$S_1 \equiv found := \textbf{false};\ x := 0;$$
$$\textbf{while } \neg found \textbf{ do}$$
$$x := x + 1;$$
$$found := f(x) = 0$$
$$\textbf{od}.$$

S_1 terminates when a positive zero of f is found. Similarly, the following program S_2 terminates when a nonpositive zero of f is found:

$$S_2 \equiv found := \textbf{false};\ y := 1;$$
$$\textbf{while } \neg found \textbf{ do}$$
$$y := y - 1;$$
$$found := f(y) = 0$$
$$\textbf{od}.$$

Thus the program

$$ZERO\text{-}1 \equiv [S_1 \| S_2],$$

the parallel composition of S_1 and S_2, appears to be a solution to the problem. Note that the Boolean variable $found$ can be accessed by both components S_1 and S_2. This shared variable is used to exchange information about termination between the two components.   □

Indeed, once $ZERO\text{-}1$ has terminated, one of the variables x or y stores a zero of f, and $ZERO\text{-}1$ has solved the problem. Unfortunately, $ZERO\text{-}1$ need not terminate as the following scenario shows. Let f have only one zero, a positive one. Consider an execution of $ZERO\text{-}1$, where initially only the program's first component S_1 is active, until it terminates when the zero of f is found. At this moment the second component S_2 is activated, $found$ is reset to **false**, and since no other zeroes of f exist, $found$ is never reset to **true**. In other words, this execution of $ZERO\text{-}1$ never terminates.

Obviously our mistake consisted of initializing $found$ to **false** twice —once in each component. A straightforward solution would be to initialize $found$ only once, outside the parallel composition. This brings us to the following corrected solution.

Solution 2

Let

$$S_1 \equiv x := 0;$$
$$\textbf{while } \neg found \textbf{ do}$$
$$x := x + 1;$$
$$found := f(x) = 0$$
$$\textbf{od}$$

and

$$S_2 \equiv y := 1;$$
$$\quad \textbf{while } \neg found \textbf{ do}$$
$$\qquad y := y - 1;$$
$$\qquad found := f(y) = 0$$
$$\quad \textbf{od}.$$

Then

$$ZERO\text{-}2 \equiv found := \textbf{false}; \; [S_1 \| S_2]$$

should be a solution to the problem.   □

But is it actually? Unfortunately we fooled the reader again. Suppose again that f has exactly one zero, a positive one, and consider an execution of *ZERO-2* where, initially, its second component S_2 is activated until it enters its loop. From that moment on only the first component S_1 is executed until it terminates upon finding a zero. Then the second component S_2 is activated again and so *found* is reset to **false**. Now, since no other zeroes of f exist, *found* is never reset to **true** and this execution of *ZERO-2* will never terminate! Thus, the above solution is incorrect.

What went wrong? A close inspection of the scenario just presented reveals that the problem arose because *found* could be reset to **false** once it was already **true**. In this way, the information that a zero of f was found got lost.

One way of correcting this mistake is by ensuring that *found* is never reset to **false** inside the parallel composition. For this purpose it is sufficient to replace the unconditional assignment

$$found := f(x) = 0$$

by the conditional one:

$$\textbf{if } f(x) = 0 \textbf{ then } found := \textbf{true fi}$$

and similarly with the assignment $found := f(y) = 0$. Observe that these changes do not affect the meaning of the component programs, but they alter the meaning of the parallel program.

We thus obtain the following possible solution.

Solution 3

Let

$$S_1 \equiv x := 0;$$

> **while** $\neg found$ **do**
> $\quad x := x + 1;$
> $\quad$ **if** $f(x) = 0$ **then** $found :=$ **true fi**
> **od**

and

$\quad S_2 \equiv y := 1;$
$\qquad$ **while** $\neg found$ **do**
$\qquad\quad y := y - 1;$
$\qquad\quad$ **if** $f(y) = 0$ **then** $found :=$ **true fi**
$\qquad$ **od.**

Then

$$ZERO\text{-}3 \equiv found := \textbf{false};\ [S_1 \| S_2]$$

should be a solution to the problem.   □

But is it really a solution? Suppose that f has only positive zeroes, and consider an execution of $ZERO\text{-}3$ in which the first component S_1 of the parallel program $[S_1 \| S_2]$ is never activated. Then this execution never terminates even though f has a zero.

Admittedly, the above scenario is debatable. One might object that an execution sequence in which one component of a parallel program is never activated is illegal. After all, the main reason for writing parallel programs is to have components executed in parallel. The problem here concerns the definition of parallel composition. We did not exactly specify its meaning and are now confronted with two different versions.

The simpler definition says that an execution of a parallel program $[S_1 \| S_2]$ is obtained by an arbitrary *interleaving* of the executions of its components S_1 and S_2. This definition does not allow us to make any assumption of the relative speed of S_1 and S_2. An example is the execution of the above scenario where only one component is active.

The more demanding definition of execution of parallel programs requires that each component progress with a positive speed. This requirement is modeled by the assumption of *fairness* meaning that every component of a parallel program will eventually execute its next instruction. Under the assumption of fairness $ZERO\text{-}3$ is a correct solution to the zero search problem. In particular, the execution sequence of $ZERO\text{-}3$ discussed above is illegal.

We now present a solution that is appropriate when the fairness hypothesis is not adopted. It consists of building into the program $ZERO\text{-}3$ a *scheduler* which ensures fairness by forcing each component of the parallel program to eventually execute its next instruction. To this end, we need a new programming construct, **await** B **then** R **end**, allowing us to temporarily suspend the execution of a component. Informally, a component of a parallel program executes an **await** statement if the Boolean expression B evaluates to true.

Statement R is then immediately executed as an indivisible action; during its execution all other components of the parallel program are suspended. If B evaluates to false, then the component executing the **await** statement itself is suspended while other components can proceed. The suspended component can be retried later.

In the following program we use an additional shared variable *turn* that can store values 1 and 2 to indicate which component is to proceed.

Solution 4

Let

$$S_1 \equiv x := 0;$$
$$\quad \textbf{while } \neg found \textbf{ do}$$
$$\qquad \textbf{await } turn = 1 \textbf{ then } turn := 2 \textbf{ end};$$
$$\qquad x := x + 1;$$
$$\qquad \textbf{if } f(x) = 0 \textbf{ then } found := \textbf{true fi}$$
$$\quad \textbf{od}$$

and

$$S_2 \equiv y := 1;$$
$$\quad \textbf{while } \neg found \textbf{ do}$$
$$\qquad \textbf{await } turn = 2 \textbf{ then } turn := 1 \textbf{ end};$$
$$\qquad y := y - 1;$$
$$\qquad \textbf{if } f(y) = 0 \textbf{ then } found := \textbf{true fi}$$
$$\quad \textbf{od}.$$

Then

$$ZERO\text{-}4 \equiv turn := 1; \ found := \textbf{false}; \ [S_1 \| S_2]$$

should be a solution to the problem when the fairness hypothesis is not adopted.   □

To better understand this solution, let us check that it is now impossible to execute only one component unless the other has terminated. Indeed, with each loop iteration, *turn* is switched. As a consequence, no loop body can be executed twice in succession. Thus a component can be activated uninterruptedly for at most "one and a half" iterations. Once it reaches the **await** statement the second time, it becomes suspended and progress can now be achieved only by activation of the other component. The other component can always proceed even if it happens to be in front of the **await** statement. In other words, execution of *ZERO-4* now alternates between the components. But parallelism is still possible. For example, the assignments to x and y can always be executed in parallel.

But is *ZERO*-4 really a solution to the problem? Assume again that f has exactly one positive zero. Consider an execution sequence of *ZERO*-4 in which the component S_1 has just found this zero and is about to execute the statement *found* := **true**. Instead, S_2 is activated and proceeds by one and a half iterations through its loop until it reaches the statement **await** $turn = 2$ **then** $turn := 1$ **end**. Since $turn = 1$ holds from the last iteration, S_2 is now blocked. Now S_1 proceeds and terminates with *found* := **true**. Since $turn = 1$ is still true, S_2 cannot terminate but remains suspended forever in front of its **await** statement. This situation is called a *deadlock*.

To avoid such a deadlock, it suffices to reset the variable *turn* appropriately at the end of each component. This leads us to the following solution.

Solution 5

Let

$$S_1 \equiv x := 0;$$
$$\text{while } \neg found \text{ do}$$
$$\quad \text{await } turn = 1 \text{ then } turn := 2 \text{ end};$$
$$\quad x := x + 1;$$
$$\quad \text{if } f(x) = 0 \text{ then } found := \text{true fi}$$
$$\text{od};$$
$$turn := 2$$

and

$$S_2 \equiv y := 1;$$
$$\text{while } \neg found \text{ do}$$
$$\quad \text{await } turn = 2 \text{ then } turn := 1 \text{ end};$$
$$\quad y := y - 1;$$
$$\quad \text{if } f(y) = 0 \text{ then } found := \text{true fi}$$
$$\text{od};$$
$$turn := 1.$$

Then

$$\text{ZERO-5} \equiv turn := 1; \ found := \text{false}; \ [S_1 \| S_2]$$

is a deadlock-free solution to the problem when the fairness hypothesis is not adopted. □

Can you still follow the argument? We assure you that the above solution is correct. It can, moreover, be improved. By definition, an execution of an **await** statement, **await** B **then** R **end**, temporarily blocks all other components of the parallel program until execution of R is completed. Reducing the execution time of the statement R decreases this suspension time and results in a possible speed-up in a parallel execution. Here such an improvement is possible —the assignments to the variable *turn* can be taken out of the scope of the **await** statements. Thus we claim that the following program is a better solution to the problem.

Solution 6

Let

$$S_1 \equiv x := 0;$$
$$\quad \textbf{while } \neg found \textbf{ do}$$
$$\qquad \textbf{wait } turn = 1;$$
$$\qquad turn := 2;$$
$$\qquad x := x + 1;$$
$$\qquad \textbf{if } f(x) = 0 \textbf{ then } found := \textbf{true fi}$$
$$\quad \textbf{od};$$
$$\quad turn := 2$$

and

$$S_2 \equiv y := 1;$$
$$\quad \textbf{while } \neg found \textbf{ do}$$
$$\qquad \textbf{wait } turn = 2;$$
$$\qquad turn := 1;$$
$$\qquad y := y - 1;$$
$$\qquad \textbf{if } f(y) = 0 \textbf{ then } found := \textbf{true fi}$$
$$\quad \textbf{od};$$
$$\quad turn := 1$$

and let as before

$$ZERO\text{-}6 \equiv turn := 1; \ found := \textbf{false}; \ [S_1 \| S_2].$$

Here **wait** B is an instruction the execution of which suspends a component if B evaluates to false and that has no effect otherwise.   □

The only difference from Solution 5 is that now component S_2 can be activated —or as one says, *interfere*— between **wait** $turn = 1$ and $turn := 2$ of S_1, and analogously for component S_1. We have to show that such an interference does not invalidate the desired program behavior.

First consider the case when S_2 interferes with some statement not containing the variable *turn*. Then this statement can be interchanged with the statement $turn := 2$ of S_1, thus yielding an execution of the previous program $ZERO$-5. Otherwise, we have to consider the two assignments $turn := 1$ of S_2. The first assignment $turn := 1$ (inside the loop) cannot be executed because immediately before its execution $turn = 2$ should hold, but by our assumption S_1 has just passed **wait** $turn = 1$. However, the second assignment $turn := 1$ could be executed. But then S_2 terminates, so $found$ is true and S_1 will also terminate —immediately after finishing the current loop iteration. Just in time —in the next loop iteration it would be blocked!

To summarize, activating S_2 between **wait** $turn = 1$ and $turn := 2$ of S_1 does not lead to any problems. A similar argument holds for activating S_1. Thus Solution 6 is indeed correct.

1.2 Program Correctness

The problem of zero search seemed to be completely trivial, and yet several errors, sometimes subtle, crept in. The design of the final solution proceeded through a disquieting series of trials and errors. From this experience it should be clear that an informal justification of programs constructed in such a manner is not sufficient. Instead, one needs a systematic approach to proving correctness of programs.

Correctness means that certain desirable program properties hold. In the case of sequential programs, where a control resides at each moment in only one point, these properties usually are:

1. *Partial correctness*, that is, whenever a result is delivered it is correct w.r.t. the task to be solved by the program. For example, upon termination of a sorting program, the input should indeed be sorted. *Partial* means that the program is not guaranteed to terminate and thus deliver a result at all.
2. *Termination*. For example, a sorting program should always terminate.
3. *Absence of failures*. For example, there should be no division by zero and no overflow.

In the case of concurrent programs, where control can reside at the same time in several control points, the above properties are much more difficult to establish. Moreover, as observed before, we are then also interested in establishing:

4. *Interference freedom*, that is, no component of a parallel program can manipulate in an undesirable way the variables shared with another component.
5. *Deadlock freedom*, that is, a parallel program does not end up in a situation where all nonterminated components are waiting indefinitely for a condition to become true.

6. Correctness under the *fairness assumption*. For example, the parallel program *ZERO*--3 solves the zero search problem only under the assumption of fairness.

A number of approaches to program verification have been proposed and used in the literature. The most common of them is based on *operational reasoning*, which is the way we reasoned about the correctness of Solution 6. This approach consists of an analysis in terms of the execution sequences of the given program. For this purpose, an informal understanding of the program semantics is used. While this analysis is often successful in the case of sequential programs, it is much less so in the case of concurrent programs. The number of possible execution sequences is often forbiddingly large and it is all too easy to overlook one.

In this book we pursue a different approach based on *axiomatic reasoning*. With this approach, we first need a language that makes it possible to express or *specify* the relevant program properties. We choose here the language of predicate logic consisting of certain *well-formed formulas*. Such formulas serve as so-called *assertions* expressing desirable program states. From logic we also use the concept of a *proof system* consisting of axioms and proof rules that allow us to formally prove that a given program satisfies the desired properties. Such a proof will proceed in a syntax-directed manner by induction on the structure of the program.

The origins of this approach to program verification can be traced back to Turing [1949], but the first constructive efforts should be attributed to Floyd [1967a] and Hoare [1969]. Floyd proposed an axiomatic method for the verification of flowcharts, and Hoare developed this method further to a syntax-directed approach dealing with **while** programs. Hoare's approach received a great deal of attention, and many Hoare-style proof systems dealing with various programming constructs have been proposed since then. In 1976 and 1977, this approach was extended to parallel programs by Owicki and Gries [1976a,1976b] and Lamport [1977], and in 1980 and 1981 to distributed programs by Apt, Francez and de Roever [1980] and Levin and Gries [1981]. In 1991 an assertional proof system was introduced by de Boer [1991a] for a parallel object-oriented language called POOL, developed by America [1987].

In our book we present a systematic account of the axiomatic approach to program verification. It should be noted that the axiomatic approach as described in the above articles has several limitations:

(1) the proof rules are designed only for the a posteriori verification of existing programs, not for their systematic development;
(2) the proof rules reflect only the input/output behavior of programs, not properties of their finite or infinite executions as they occur, for example, in operating systems;
(3) the proof rules cannot deal with fairness.

Overcoming limitation (1) has motivated a large research activity on systematic development of programs *together* with their correctness proofs, initiated by Dijkstra [1976] and extended by many others: see, for example, the books by Gries [1981], Backhouse [1986], Kaldewaij [1990], Morgan [1994], Back and von Wright   [2008], and for parallel programs by Feijen and van Gasteren [1999] and Misra [2001].

The fundamentals of program development are now well understood for sequential programs; we indicate them in Chapters 3 and 10 of this book. Interestingly, the proof rules suggested for the a posteriori verification of sequential programs remain useful for formulating strategies for program development.

Another approach aims at higher-level system development. The development starts with an abstract system model which is stepwise refined to a detailed model that can form a basis for a correct program. An example of such a formal method for modelling and analysis at the system level is Event-B, see Abrial and Hallerstede [2007].

To overcome limitations (2) and (3) one can use the approach based on *temporal logic* introduced by Pnueli [1977]. Using temporal logic more general program properties than input/output behavior can be expressed, for example so-called *liveness properties*, and the fairness assumption can be handled. However, this approach calls for use of location counters or labels, necessitating an extension of the assertion language and making reconciliation with structured reasoning about programs difficult but not impossible. We do not treat this approach here but refer the reader instead to the books by Manna and Pnueli [1991,1995]. For dealing with fairness we use transformations based on explicit schedulers.

1.3 Structure of this Book

This book presents an approach to program verification based on Hoare-style proof rules and on program transformations. It is organized around several classes of sequential and concurrent programs. This structure enables us to explain program verification in an incremental fashion and to have fine-tuned verification methods for each class.

For the classes of programs we use the following terminology. In a *sequential program* the control resides at each moment in only one point. The simplest type of sequential program is the *deterministic program*, where at each moment the instruction to be executed next is uniquely determined. In a *concurrent program* the control can reside at the same time at several control points. Usually, the components of a concurrent program have to exchange some information in order to achieve a certain common goal. This exchange is known as *communication*. Depending on the mode of communication, we distinguish two types of concurrent programs: parallel programs and distributed programs. In a *parallel program* the components communicate by means of *shared variables*. The concurrent programs discussed in Section 1.1 are of this type. *Distributed programs* are concurrent programs with disjoint components that communicate by explicit message passing.

For each class of programs considered in this book the presentation proceeds in a uniform way. We start with its *syntax* and then present an *operational semantics* in the style of Hennessy and Plotkin [1979] and Plotkin [1981,2004]. Next, we introduce Hoare-style *proof rules* allowing us to verify the *partial* and *total correctness* of programs. Intuitively, partial correctness means delivering correct results; total correctness additionally guarantees termination. *Soundness* of proposed proof systems is shown on the basis of the program semantics. Throughout this book correctness proofs are presented in the form of *proof outlines* as proposed by Owicki and Gries [1976a]. *Case studies* provide extensive examples of program verification with the proposed proof systems. For some program classes additional topics are discussed, for example, *completeness* of the proof systems or *program transformations* into other classes of programs. Each of the subsequent chapters ends with a series of *exercises* and *bibliographic remarks*.

In **Chapter 2** we explain the basic notions used in this book to describe syntax, semantics and proof rules of the various program classes.

In **Chapter 3** we study a simple class of deterministic programs, usually called **while** programs. These programs form the backbone for all other program classes studied in this book. The verification method explained in this chapter relies on the use of *invariants* and *bound functions*, and is a prerequisite for all subsequent chapters. We also deal with *completeness* of the proposed proof systems. Finally, we discuss Dijkstra's approach [1976] to a systematic program development. It is based on reusing the proof rules in a suitable way.

In **Chapter 4** we extend the class of programs studied in Chapter 3 by *recursive procedures* without parameters. Verifying such *recursive programs* makes use of proofs from assumptions (about recursive procedure calls) that are discharges later on (when the procedure body is considered).

In **Chapter 5** this class is extended by *call-by-value parameters* of the recursive procedures. Semantically, this necessitates the concept of a stack for storing the values of the actual parameters of recursively called procedures. We capture this concept by using a block statement and an appropriate semantic transition rule that models the desired stack behavior implicitly.

In **Chapter 6** *object-oriented programs* are studied in a minimal setting where we focus on the following main characteristics of objects: objects possess (and *encapsulate*) their own local variables, objects interact via *method* calls, and objects can be dynamically *created*.

In **Chapter 7** we study the simplest form of parallel programs, so-called *disjoint parallel programs*. "Disjoint" means that component programs have only reading access to shared variables. As first noted in Hoare [1975], this restriction leads to a very simple verification rule. Disjoint parallel programs provide a good starting point for understanding general parallel programs considered in Chapters 8 and 9, as well as distributed programs studied in Chapter 11.

In **Chapter 8** we study parallel programs that permit unrestricted use of shared variables. The semantics of such parallel programs depends on which parts of the components are considered *atomic*, that is, not interruptable by the execution of other components. Verification of such programs is based on the test of *interference freedom* due to Owicki and Gries [1976a]. In general, this test is very laborious. However, we also present program transformations due to Lipton [1975] allowing us to enlarge the atomic regions within the component programs and thus reduce the number of interference tests.

In **Chapter 9** we add to the programs of Chapter 8 a programming construct for *synchronization*. Since the execution of these programs can now end in a deadlock, their verification also includes a test of *deadlock freedom*. As typical examples of parallel programs with shared variables and synchronization, we consider solutions to the producer/consumer problem and the mutual exclusion problem, which we prove to be correct.

In **Chapter 10** we return to sequential programs but this time to nondeterministic ones in the form of *guarded commands* due to Dijkstra [1975,1976]. These programs can be seen as a stepping stone towards distributed programs considered in Chapter 11. We extend here Dijkstra's approach to program development to the guarded commands language, the class of programs for which this method was originally proposed. Finally, we explain how parallel programs can be transformed into equivalent nondeterministic ones although at the price of introducing additional control variables.

In **Chapter 11** we study a class of distributed programs that is a subset of *Communicating Sequential Processes* (CSP) of Hoare [1978,1985]. CSP is the kernel of the programming language OCCAM, see INMOS [1984], developed for programming distributed transputer systems. We show that programs in this subset can be transformed into semantically equivalent nondeterministic programs without extra control variables. Based on this program transformation we develop proof techniques for distributed programs due to Apt [1986].

Finally, in **Chapter 12** we consider the issue of fairness. For the sake of simplicity we limit ourselves to the study of fairness for nondeterministic programs, as studied in Chapter 10. Our approach, due to Apt and Olderog [1983], again employs program transformations. More specifically, the proof rule allowing us to deal with nondeterministic programs under the assumption of fairness is developed by means of a program transformation that reduces fair nondeterminism to ordinary nondeterminism.

1.4 Automating Program Verification

In this book we present program verification as an activity requiring insight and calculation. It is meaningful to ask whether program verification cannot be carried out automatically. Why not feed a program and its specification into a computer and wait for an answer? Unfortunately, the theory of computability tells us that fully automatic verification of program properties is in general an undecidable problem, and therefore impossible to implement. Nevertheless, automating program verification is a topic of intense research.

First of all, for the special case of finite-state systems represented by programs that manipulate only variables ranging over finite data types, fully automatic program verification is indeed possible. Queille and Sifakis [1981] and Emerson and Clarke [1982] were the first to develop tools that automatically check whether such programs satisfy specifications written in an assertion language based on temporal logic. In the terminology of logic it is checked whether the program is a model of the specification. Hence this approach is called *model checking*. Essentially, model checking rests on algrorithms for exploring the reachable state space of a program. For further details we refer to the books by Clarke, Grumberg, and Peled [1999], and by Baier and Katoen [2008]. The book edited by Grumberg and Veith [2008] surveys the achievements of model checking in the past 25 years.

The current problems in model checking lie in the so-called *state space explosion* that occurs if many sequential components with finite state spaces are composed in a concurrent program. Moreover, model checking is also considering infinite-state systems, for instance represented by programs where some variables range over infinite data types. One line of attack is here to apply the concept of *abstract interpretation* due to Cousot and Cousot [1977a] in order to reduce the original problem to a size where it can be automatically solved. Then of course the question is whether the answer for the abstract system implies the corresponding answer for the concrete system. To solve this question the approach of *abstraction refinement* is often pursued whereby too coarse abstractions are successively refined, see Clarke et al. [2003] and Ball et al. [2002].

Related to model checking is the approach of *program analysis* that aims at verifying restricted program properties automatically, for instance whether a variable has a certain value at a given control point, see Nielson, Nielson and Hankin [2004]. Program analysis employs static techniques for computing reliable approximate information about the dynamic behavior of programs. For example, *shape analysis* is used to establish properties of programs with pointer structures, see Sagiv, Reps and Wilhelm [2002].

Another attempt to conquer the problem of state space explosion solution is to combine automatic program verification with the application of proof rules controlled by a human user —see for example Burch et al. [1992] and Bouajjani et al. [1992]. This shows that even in the context of automatic program verification a good knowledge of axiomatic verification techniques as explained in this book is of importance.

A second, more general approach to automation is *deductive verification*. It attempts to verify programs by proofs carried out by means of interactive theorem provers instead of state space exploration and thus does not need finite-state abstractions. Deductive verification automates the axiomatic approach to program verification presented in this book. Well-known are the provers Isabelle/HOL, see Nipkow, Paulson and Wenzel [2002], and PVS, see Owre and Shankar [2003], both based on higher-order logic. To apply these provers to program verification both the program semantics and the proof systems are embedded into higher-order logic and then suitable tactics are formalized to reduce the amount of human interaction in the application of the proof rules. As far as possible decision procedures are invoked to check automatically logical implications needed in the premises of the proof rules.

Other theorem provers are based on *dynamic logic*, see Harel, Kozen and Tiuryn [2000], which extends Hoare's logic for sequential programs by modal operators and is closed under logical operators. We mention here the provers KeY that is used to the verification of object-oriented software written in Java, see the book edited by Beckert, Hähnle and Schmitt [2007], KIV (Karlsruhe Interactive Verifier, see Balser et al. [2000]), and VSE (Verification Support Environment, see Stephan et al. [2005]).

1.5 Assertional Methods in Practice

To what extent do the methods of program verification influence today's practice of correct software construction? Hoare [1996] noted that current programming paradigms build to a large extent on research that started 20 years ago. For example, we can observe that the notion of an assertion and the corresponding programming methods appeared in practice only in recent years.

Meyer [1997] introduced the paradigm of *design by contract* for the object-oriented programming language Eiffel. A contract is a specification in the form of assertions (class invariants and pre- and postconditions for each method). The contract is agreed upon before an implementation is developed that satisfies this contract.

Design by contract has been carried over to the object-oriented programming language Java by Leavens et al. [2005]. The contracts are written in the *Java Modeling Language* JML, which allows the user to specify so-called rich interfaces of classes and methods that are not yet implemented. Besides assertions, JML also incorporates the concept of abstract data specified with the help of so-called model variables that have to be realized by the implementation using data refinement.

Checking whether an implementation (a program) satisfies a contract is done either by formal verification using proof rules (as outlined above) or —in a limited way— at runtime. The second approach requires that the assertions in the contracts are Boolean expressions. Then during each particular run of the implementation it is checked automatically whether along this run all assertions of the contract are satisfied. If an assertion is encountered that is not satisfied, a failure or exception is raised.

As an example of a successful application of verification techniques to specific programming languages let us mention ESC/Java (Extended Static Checker for Java) which supports the (semi-)automated verification of annotated Java programs, see Flanagan et al. [2002]. Another example involves Java Card, a subset of Java dedicated for the programming of Smart Cards the programs of which are verified using interactive theorem provers, see van den Berg, Jacobs and Poll [2001], and Beckert, Hähnle and Schmitt [2007].

2 *Preliminaries*

I N THIS CHAPTER we explain the basic concepts and notations used throughout this book. We recommend to the reader to move now to Chapter 3 and consult the individual sections of this chapter whenever needed.

This chapter is organized as follows. In Section 2.1, we list the *standard mathematical notation* for sets, tuples, relations, functions, sequences, strings, proofs, induction and grammars.

Section 2.2 is needed to understand the *syntax* of the programs studied in this book. For the operational *semantics* of all considered classes of programs, Sections 2.3 and 2.4 are needed. For the verification of programs, in particular for the definition of correctness formulas, Sections 2.5 and 2.6 on assertions and Section 2.7 on substitution are needed. The introduction of proof systems for program verification assumes again knowledge of Section 2.4. Finally, to show the soundness of these proof systems the Substitution Lemma introduced in Section 2.8 is needed.

2.1 Mathematical Notation

Sets

We assume the reader is familiar with the notion of a *set*, a collection of elements. Finite sets may be specified by enumerating their elements between curly brackets. For example, {**true**, **false**} denotes the set consisting of the Boolean constants **true** and **false**. When enumerating the elements of a set, we sometimes use "..." as a notation. For example, $\{1, \ldots, n\}$ denotes the set consisting of the natural numbers $1, \ldots, n$ where the upper bound n is a natural number that is not further specified.

More generally, sets are specified by referring to some property of their elements:

$$\{x \mid P\}$$

denotes the set consisting of all elements x that satisfy the property P. For example,

$$\{x \mid x \text{ is an integer and } x \text{ is divisible by 2}\}$$

denotes the infinite set of all even integers.

We write $a \in A$ to denote that a is an *element of* the set A, and $b \notin A$ to denote that b is *not* an element of A. Sometimes it is convenient to refer to a given set A when defining a new set. We write

$$\{x \in A \mid P\}$$

as an abbreviation for $\{x \mid x \in A \text{ and } P\}$.

Some sets have standard names: $\emptyset$ denotes the *empty* set, $\mathbb{N}$ denotes the set of all *natural numbers* $\{0, 1, 2, 3, \ldots\}$, and $\mathbb{Z}$ denotes the set of all *integers* $\{\ldots, -1, 0, 1, 2, \ldots\}$. Connected subsets of integers are called *intervals*. For $k, l \in \mathbb{Z}$ the *closed* interval of integers between k and l is defined by

$$[k : l] = \{i \in \mathbb{Z} \mid k \le i \le l\},$$

and the *open* interval by $(k : l) = \{i \in \mathbb{Z} \mid k < i < l\}$. *Half-open* intervals like $(k : l]$ or $[k : l)$ are defined analogously.

Recall that in a set one does not distinguish repetitions of elements. Thus {**true**, **false**} and {**true**, **false**, **true**} are the same set. Similarly, the order of elements is irrelevant. Thus {**true**, **false**} and {**false**, **true**} are the same set. In general, two sets A and B are *equal* (i.e., the same) if and only if they have the same elements; in symbols: $A = B$.

Let A and B be sets. Then $A \subseteq B$ (and $B \supseteq A$) denotes that A is a *subset* of B, $A \cap B$ denotes the *intersection* of A and B, $A \cup B$ the *union* of A and B, and $A - B$ the *set difference* of A and B. In other words,

$$A \subseteq B \quad \text{if} \quad a \in B \text{ for every } a \in A,$$

$$A \cap B = \{a \mid a \in A \text{ and } b \in B\},$$
$$A \cup B = \{a \mid a \in A \text{ or } b \in B\},$$
$$A - B = \{a \mid a \in A \text{ and } b \notin B\}.$$

Note that $A = B$ if both $A \subseteq B$ and $A \supseteq B$. A and B are *disjoint* if they have no element in common, that is, if $A \cap B = \emptyset$.

The definitions of intersection and union can be generalized to the case of more than two sets. Let A_i be a set for every element i of some other set I. Then

$$\bigcap_{i \in I} A_i = \{a \mid a \in A_i \text{ for all } i \in I\},$$
$$\bigcup_{i \in I} A_i = \{a \mid a \in A_i \text{ for some } i \in I\}.$$

For a finite set A, *card* A denotes the *cardinality*, or the number of elements, of A. For a nonempty finite set $A \subseteq \mathbb{Z}$ let *min* A denote the *minimum* of all integers in A. Finally, for a set A we define $\mathcal{P}(A) = \{B \mid B \subseteq A\}$.

Tuples

In sets the repetition of elements and their order is irrelevant. If these things matter, we use another way of grouping elements: ordered pairs and tuples. For elements a and b, not necessarily distinct, (a, b) is an ordered pair or simply *pair*. Then a and b are called the *components* of (a, b). By definition, two pairs (a, b) and (c, d) are identical if and only if their first components and their second components agree. In symbols: $(a, b) = (c, d)$ if and only if $a = c$ and $b = d$. Sometimes we use angle brackets and write pairs as $< a, b >$.

More generally, let n be any natural number. Then if $a_1, \ldots, a_n$ are any n elements, not necessarily distinct, $(a_1, \ldots, a_n)$ is an *n-tuple*. The element a_i, where $i \in \{1, \ldots, n\}$, is called the *i-th component* of $(a_1, \ldots, a_n)$. An n-tuple $(a_1, \ldots, a_n)$ is *equal* to an m-tuple $(b_1, \ldots, b_m)$ if and only if $n = m$ and $a_i = b_i$ for all $i \in \{1, \ldots, n\}$. For example, the tuples $(1,1)$, $(1,1,1)$, $((1,1),1)$ and $(1,(1,1))$ are all distinct. Note that 2-tuples are the same as pairs. As border cases, we also obtain the 0-tuple, written as (), and 1-tuples (a_1) for any element a_1.

The *Cartesian product* $A \times B$ of sets A and B consists of all pairs (a, b) with $a \in A$ and $b \in B$. The *n-fold Cartesian product* $A_1 \times \cdots \times A_n$ of sets $A_1, \ldots, A_n$ consists of all n-tuples $(a_1, \ldots, a_n)$ with $a_i \in A_i$ for $i \in \{1, \ldots, n\}$. If all the A_i are the same set A, the n-fold Cartesian product $A \times \cdots \times A$ of A with itself is also written as A^n.

Relations

A *binary relation* R between sets A and B is a subset of the Cartesian product $A \times B$; that is, $R \subseteq A \times B$. If $A = B$ then R is called a *relation on* A. For example,

$$\{(a,1),\ (b,2),\ (c,2)\}$$

is a binary relation between $\{a,b,c\}$ and $\{1,2\}$. More generally, for any natural number n an *n-ary relation* R between $A_1, \ldots, A_n$ is a subset of the n-fold Cartesian product $A_1 \times \cdots \times A_n$; that is, $R \subseteq A_1 \times \cdots \times A_n$. Note that 2-ary relations are the same as binary relations. Instead of 1-ary and 3-ary relations one usually talks of *unary* and *ternary* relations.

Consider a relation R on a set A. R is called *reflexive* if $(a,a) \in R$ for all $a \in A$; it is called *irreflexive* if $(a,a) \notin R$ for all $a \in A$. R is called *symmetric* if for all $a,b \in A$ whenever $(a,b) \in R$ then also $(b,a) \in R$; it is called *antisymmetric* if for all $a,b \in A$ whenever $(a,b) \in R$ and $(b,a) \in R$ then $a = b$. R is called *transitive* if for all $a,b,c \in A$ whenever $(a,b) \in R$ and $(b,c) \in R$ then also $(a,c) \in R$.

The *transitive, reflexive closure* R^* of a relation R on a set A is the smallest transitive and reflexive relation on A that contains R as a subset. The *relational composition* $R_1 \circ R_2$ of relations R_1 and R_2 on a set A is defined as follows:

$$R_1 \circ R_2 = \{(a,c) \mid \text{ there exists } b \in A \text{ with } (a,b) \in R_1 \text{ and } (b,c) \in R_2\}.$$

For any natural number n the *n-fold relational composition* R^n of a relation R on a set A is defined inductively as follows:

$$R^\circ = \{(a,a) \mid a \in A\},$$
$$R^{n+1} = R^n \circ R.$$

Note that

$$R^* = \bigcup_{n \in \mathbb{N}} R^n.$$

Membership of pairs in a binary relation R is mostly written in *infix notation*, so instead of $(a,b) \in R$ one usually writes $a\,R\,b$.

Any binary relation $R \subseteq A \times B$ has an *inverse* $R^{-1} \subseteq B \times A$ defined as follows:

$$b\,R^{-1}a \text{ if } a\,R\,b.$$

Functions

Let A and B be sets. A *function* or *mapping* from A to B is a binary relation f between A and B with the following special property: for each element

$a \in A$ there is exactly one element $b \in B$ with afb. Mostly we use prefix notation for function application and write $f(a) = b$ instead of afb. For some functions, however, we use postfix notation and write $af = b$. An example is substitution as defined in Section 2.7. In both cases b is called the *value* of f *applied to the argument* a. To indicate that f is a function from A to B we write

$$f : A \to B.$$

The set A is called the *domain* of f and the set B the *co-domain* of f.

Consider a function $f : A \to B$ and some set $X \subseteq A$. Then the *restriction of f to X* is denoted by $f[X]$ and defined as the intersection of f (which is a subset of $A \times B$) with $X \times B$:

$$f[X] = f \cap (X \times B).$$

We are sometimes interested in functions with special properties. A function $f : A \to B$ is called *one-to-one* or *injective* if $f(a_1) \neq f(a_2)$ for any two distinct elements $a_1, a_2 \in A$; it is called *onto* or *surjective* if for every element $b \in B$ there exists an element $a \in A$ with $f(a) = b$; it is called *bijective* or a *bijection from A onto B* if it is both injective and surjective.

Consider a function whose domain is a Cartesian product, say $f : A_1 \times \cdots \times A_n \to B$. Then it is customary to drop one pair of parentheses when applying f to an element $(a_1, \ldots, a_n) \in A_1 \times \cdots \times A_n$. That is, we write

$$f(a_1, \ldots, a_n)$$

for the value of f at $(a_1, \ldots, a_n)$ rather than $((a_1, \ldots, a_n))$. We also say that f is an *n-ary function*. If $f(a_1, \ldots, a_n) = b$ then b is called the *value* of f when *applied to the arguments* $a_1, \ldots, a_n$.

Consider a function whose domain and co-domain coincide, say $f : A \to A$. An element $a \in A$ is called a *fixed point* of f if $f(a) = a$.

Sequences

In the following let A be a set. A *sequence* of elements from A of *length* $n \geq 0$ is a function $f : \{1, \ldots, n\} \to A$. We write a sequence f by listing the values of f without any sort of punctuation in the order of ascending arguments, that is, as

$$a_1 \ldots a_n,$$

where $a_1 = f(1), \ldots, a_n = f(n)$. Then a_i with $i \in \{1, \ldots, n\}$ is referred to as the *i-th element* in the sequence $a_1 \ldots a_n$. A *finite* sequence is a sequence of any length $n \geq 0$. A sequence of length 0 is called the *empty* sequence and is usually denoted by ε.

We also allow (countably) infinite sequences. An infinite sequence of elements from A is a function $\xi : \mathbb{N} \to A$. To exhibit the general form of an infinite sequence ξ we typically write

$$\xi : a_0 \, a_1 \, a_2 \ldots$$

if $a_i = f(i)$ for all $i \in \mathbb{N}$. Then i is also called an *index* of the element a_i. Given any index i, the finite sequence $a_0 \ldots a_i$ is called a *prefix* of ξ and the infinite sequence $a_i \, a_{i+1} \ldots$ is called a *suffix* of ξ. Prefixes and suffixes of finite sequences are defined similarly.

Consider now relations $R_1, R_2, \ldots$ on A. For any finite sequence $a_0 \ldots a_n$ of elements from A with

$$a_0 \, R_1 \, a_1, \; a_1 \, R_2 \, a_2, \ldots, \; a_{n-1} \, R_n \, a_n$$

we write a *finite chain*

$$a_0 \, R_1 \, a_1 \, R_2 \, a_2 \ldots a_{n-1} \, R_n \, a_n.$$

For example, using the relations $=$ and $\leq$ on Z, we may write

$$a_0 = a_1 \leq a_2 \leq a_3 = a_4.$$

We apply this notation also to infinite sequences. Thus for any infinite sequence $a_0 \, a_1 \, a_2 \ldots$ of elements from A with

$$a_0 \, R_1 \, a_1, \; a_1 \, R_2 \, a_2, \; a_2 \, R_3 \, a_3, \; \ldots$$

we write an *infinite chain*

$$a_0 \, R_1 \, a_1 \, R_2 \, a_2 \, R_3 \, a_3 \ldots .$$

In this book the computations of programs are described using the chain notation.

Strings

A set of symbols is often called an *alphabet*. A *string* over an alphabet A is a finite sequence of symbols from A. For example, $1+2$ is a string over the alphabet $\{1, 2, +\}$. The syntactic objects considered in this book are strings. We introduce several classes of strings: expressions, assertions, programs and correctness formulas.

We write $\equiv$ for the *syntactic identity* of strings. For example, $1+2 \equiv 1+2$ but not $1 + 2 \equiv 2 + 1$. The symbol $=$ is used for the "semantic equality" of objects. For example, if $+$ denotes integer addition then $1+2 = 2+1$.

The *concatenation* of strings s_1 and s_2 yields the string $s_1\, s_2$ formed by first writing s_1 and then s_2, without intervening space. For example, the concatenation of 1+ and 2+0 yields 1+2+0. A string t is called a *substring* of a string s if there exist strings s_1 and s_2 such that $s \equiv s_1 t s_2$. Since s_1 and s_2 may be empty, s itself is a substring of s.

Note that there can be several *occurrences* of the same substring in a given string s. For example, in the string $s \equiv 1 + 1 + 1$ there are two occurrences of the substring 1+ and three occurrences of the substring 1.

Proofs

Mathematical proofs are often chains of equalities between expressions. We present such chains in a special format (see, for example, Dijkstra and Scholten [1990]):

> expression 1
> $=$ {explanation why expression 1 = expression 2}
> expression 2
>
> .
>
> .
>
> .
>
> expression $n - 1$
> $=$ {explanation why expression $n - 1$ = expression n}
> expression n.

An analogous format is used for other relations between assertions or expressions, such as syntactic identity $\equiv$ of strings, inclusion $\subseteq$ of sets, and implications or equivalences of assertions. Obvious explanations are sometimes omitted.

Following Halmos [1985] (cf. p. 403) we use the symbol *iff* as an abbreviation for *if and only if* and the symbol $\square$ to denote the end of a proof, a definition or an example.

For the conciseness of mathematical statements we sometimes use the quantifier symbols $\exists$ and $\forall$ for, respectively, *there exists* and *for all*. The formal definition of syntax and semantics of these quantifiers appears in Sections 2.5 and 2.6.

Induction

In this book we often use inductive definitions and proofs. We assume that the reader is familiar with the *induction principle for natural numbers*. This principle states that in order to prove a property P for all $n \in \mathbb{N}$, it suffices to proceed *by induction on* n, organizing the proof as follows:

- *Induction basis.* Prove that P holds for $n = 0$.
- *Induction step.* Prove that P holds for $n + 1$ from the *induction hypothesis* that P holds for n.

We can also use this induction principle to justify inductive definitions based on natural numbers. For example, consider once more the inductive definition of the n-fold relational composition R^n of a relation R on a set A. The implicit claim of this definition is: R^n is a well-defined relation on A for all $n \in \mathbb{N}$. The proof is by induction on n and is straightforward.

A more interesting example is the following.

Example 2.1. The inclusion $R^n \subseteq R^*$ holds for all $n \in \mathbb{N}$. The proof is by induction on n.

- *Induction basis.* By definition, $R^0 = \{(a, a) \mid a \in A\}$. Since R^* is reflexive, $R^0 \subseteq R^*$ follows.
- *Induction step.* Using the proof format explained earlier, we argue as follows:

$$R^{n+1}$$
$$= \quad \{\text{definition of } R^{n+1}\}$$
$$R^n \circ R$$
$$\subseteq \quad \{\text{induction hypothesis, definition of } \circ\}$$
$$R^* \circ R$$
$$\subseteq \quad \{\text{definition of } R^*\}$$
$$R^* \circ R^*$$
$$\subseteq \quad \{\text{transitivity of } R^*\}$$
$$R^*.$$

Thus $R^{n+1} \subseteq R^*$. □

The induction principle for natural numbers is based on the fact that the natural numbers can be constructed by beginning with the number 0 and repeatedly adding 1. By allowing more general construction methods, one obtains the *principle of structural induction*, enabling the use of more than one case at the induction basis and at the induction step.

For example, consider the set of (fully bracketed) *arithmetic expressions* with constants 0 and 1, the variable v, and the operator symbols $+$ and $\cdot$. This is the smallest set of strings over the alphabet $\{0, 1, v, +, \cdot, (,)\}$ satisfying the following inductive definition:

- *Induction basis.* 0,1 and v are arithmetical expressions.
- *Induction step.* If e_1 and e_2 are arithmetical expressions, then $(e_1 + e_2)$ and $(e_1 \cdot e_2)$ are also arithmetical expressions.

Thus there are here three cases at the induction basis and two at the induction step.

In this book we give a number of such inductive definitions; usually the keywords "induction basis" and "induction step" are dropped. Inductive definitions form the basis for inductive proofs.

Example 2.2. For an arithmetic expression e as above let $c(e)$ denote the number of occurrences of constants and variables in e, and $o(e)$ denote the number of occurrences of operator symbols in e. For instance, $e \equiv ((0 + v) + (v \cdot 1))$ yields $c(e) = 4$ and $o(e) = 3$. We claim that

$$c(e) = 1 + o(e)$$

holds for all arithmetic expressions e.

The proof is by induction on the structure of e.

- *Induction basis.* If $e \equiv 0$ or $e \equiv 1$ or $e \equiv v$ then $c(e) = 1$ and $o(e) = 0$. Thus $c(e) = 1 + o(e)$.
- *Induction step.* Suppose that $e \equiv (e_1 + e_2)$. Then

$$
\begin{aligned}
& c(e) \\
= \quad & \{\text{definition of } e\} \\
& c((e_1 + e_2)) \\
= \quad & \{\text{definition of } c\} \\
& c(e_1) + c(e_2) \\
= \quad & \{\text{induction hypothesis}\} \\
& 1 + o(e_1) + 1 + o(e_2) \\
= \quad & \{\text{definition of } o\} \\
& 1 + o((e_1 + e_2)) \\
= \quad & \{\text{definition of } e\} \\
& 1 + o(e).
\end{aligned}
$$

The case when $e \equiv (e_1 \cdot e_2)$ is handled analogously.   □

These remarks on induction are sufficient for the purposes of our book. A more detailed account on induction can be found, for example, in Loeckx and Sieber [1987].

Grammars

Often the presentation of inductive definitions of sets of strings can be made more concise by using context-free *grammars* in the so-called Backus-Naur format (known as BNF).

For example, we can define an arithmetic expression as a string of symbols $0, 1, v, +, \cdot, (,)$ generated by the following grammar:

$$e ::= 0 \mid 1 \mid v \mid (e_1 + e_2) \mid (e_1 \cdot e_2).$$

Here the letters e, e_1, e_2 are understood to range over arithmetic expressions. The metasymbol ::= reads as "is of the form" and the metasymbol | reads as "or." Thus the above definition states that an arithmetic expression e is of the form 0 or 1 or v or $(e_1 + e_2)$ or $(e_1 \cdot e_2)$ where e_1 and e_2 themselves are arithmetic expressions.

In this book we use grammars to define the syntax of several classes of programs.

2.2 Typed Expressions

Typed expressions occur in programs on the right-hand sides of assignments and as subscripts of array variables. To define them we first define the *types* that are used.

Types

We assume at least two *basic* types:

- **integer**,
- **Boolean**.

Further on, for each $n \geq 1$ we consider the following *higher* types:

- $T_1 \times \ldots \times T_n \to T$, where $T_1, \ldots, T_n, T$ are basic types. Here $T_1, \ldots, T_n$ are called *argument* types and T the *value* type.

Occasionally other basic types such as **character** are used. A type should be viewed as a name, or a notation for the intended set of values. Type **integer** denotes the set of all integers, type **Boolean** the set $\{\textbf{true}, \textbf{false}\}$ and a type $T_1 \times \ldots \times T_n \to T$ the set of all functions from the Cartesian product of the sets denoted by $T_1, \ldots, T_n$ to the set denoted by T.

Variables

We distinguish two sorts of variables:

- simple variables,
- array variables or just *arrays*.

Simple variables are of a basic type. Simple variables of type **integer** are called *integer variables* and are usually denoted by i, j, k, x, y, z. Simple variables of type **Boolean** are called *Boolean variables*. In programs, simple variables are usually denoted by more suggestive names such as *turn* or *found*.

Array variables are of a higher type, that is, denote a function from a certain argument type into a value type. We typically use letters a, b, c for array variables. If a is an array of type **integer** $\rightarrow T$ then a denotes a function from the integers into the value set denoted by T. Then for any k, l with $k \leq l$ the *section* $a[k : l]$ stands for the restriction of a to the interval $[k : l] = \{i \mid k \leq i \leq l\}$. The number of arguments of the higher type associated with the array a is called its *dimension*.

We denote the set of all simple and array variables by *Var*.

Constants

The value of variables can be changed during execution of a program, whereas the value of constants remains fixed. We distinguish two sorts of constants:

- constants of basic type,
- constants of higher type.

Among the constants of basic type we distinguish *integer constants* and *Boolean constants*. We assume infinitely many integer constants: 0,-1,1, -2,2,... and two Boolean constants: **true, false**.

Among the constants of a higher type $T_1 \times \ldots \times T_n \rightarrow T$ we distinguish two kinds. When the value type T is **Boolean**, the constant is called a *relation symbol*; otherwise the constant is called a *function symbol*; n is called the *arity* of the constant.

We do not wish to be overly specific, but we introduce at least the following function and relation symbols:

- $| \ |$ of type **integer** $\rightarrow$ **integer**,
- $+, -, \cdot, min, max, div, mod$ of type **integer** $\times$ **integer** $\rightarrow$ **integer**,
- $=_{int}, <, divides$ of type **integer** $\times$ **integer** $\rightarrow$ **Boolean**,
- *int* of type **Boolean** $\rightarrow$ **integer**,
- $\neg$ of type **Boolean** $\rightarrow$ **Boolean**,
- $=_{Bool}, \vee, \wedge, \rightarrow, \leftrightarrow$ of type **Boolean** $\times$ **Boolean** $\rightarrow$ **Boolean**.

In the sequel we drop the subscripts when using $=$, since from the context it is always clear which interpretation is meant. The value of each of the above constants is as expected and is explained when discussing the semantics of expressions in Section 2.3.

The relation symbols $\neg$ (*negation*), $\vee$ (*disjunction*), $\wedge$ (*conjunction*), $\rightarrow$ (*implication*) and $\leftrightarrow$ (*equivalence*) are usually called *connectives*.

This definition is slightly unusual in that we classify the nonlogical symbols of Peano arithmetic and the connectives as constants. However, their meaning is fixed and consequently it is natural to view them as constants. This allows us to define concisely expressions in the next section.

Expressions

Out of typed variables and constants we construct *typed expressions* or, in short, *expressions*. We allow here only expressions of a basic type. Thus we distinguish *integer expressions*, usually denoted by letters s, t and *Boolean expressions*, usually denoted by the letter B. Expressions are defined by induction as follows:

- a simple variable of type T is an expression of type T,
- a constant of a basic type T is an expression of type T,
- if $s_1, \ldots, s_n$ are expressions of type $T_1, \ldots, T_n$, respectively, and op is a constant of type $T_1 \times \ldots \times T_n \rightarrow T$, then $op(s_1, \ldots, s_n)$ is an expression of type T,
- if $s_1, \ldots, s_n$ are expressions of type $T_1, \ldots, T_n$, respectively, and a is an array of type $T_1 \times \ldots \times T_n \rightarrow T$, then $a[s_1, \ldots, s_n]$ is an expression of type T,
- if B is a Boolean expression and s_1 and s_2 are expressions of type T, then **if** B **then** s_1 **else** s_2 **fi** is an expression of type T.

For binary constants op we mostly use the *infix* notation

$$(s_1 \; op \; s_2)$$

instead of prefix notation $op(s_1, s_2)$. For the unary constant $op \equiv \neg$ it is customary to drop brackets around the argument, that is, to write $\neg B$ instead of $\neg(B)$. In general, brackets (and) can be omitted if this does not lead to any ambiguities. To resolve remaining ambiguities, it is customary to introduce a *binding order* among the binary constants. In the following list the constants in each line bind more strongly than those in the next line:

$$\cdot, \; mod \text{ and } div,$$

$$+ \text{ and } -,$$

$$= \, , \, < \text{ and } \textit{divides},$$

$$\vee \text{ and } \wedge \, ,$$

$$\rightarrow \text{ and } \leftrightarrow .$$

Thus binary function symbols bind more strongly than binary relation symbols. Symbols of stronger binding power are bracketed first. For example, the expression $x + y \; mod \; z$ is interpreted as $x + (y \; mod \; z)$ and the assertion $p \wedge q \rightarrow r$ is interpreted as $(p \wedge q) \rightarrow r$.

Example 2.3. Suppose that a is an array of type **integer** $\times$ **Boolean** $\rightarrow$ **Boolean**, x an integer variable, $found$ a Boolean variable and B a Boolean expression. Then $B \vee a[x + 1, found]$ is a Boolean expression and so is $a[2 \cdot x, a[x, \neg found]]$, whereas $int(a[x, \neg B])$ is an integer expression. In contrast, $a[found, found]$ is not an expression and neither is $a[x, x]$. $\square$

By a *subexpression* of an expression s we mean a substring of s that is again an expression. By $var(s)$ for an expression s we denote the set of all simple and array variables that occur in s.

Subscripted Variables

Expressions of the form $a[s_1, \ldots, s_n]$ are called *subscripted variables*. Subscripted variables are somewhat unusual objects from the point of view of logic. They are called variables because, together with simple variables, they can be assigned a value in programs by means of an assignment statement, which is discussed in the next chapter. Also, they can be substituted for (see Section 2.7). However, they cannot be quantified over (see Section 2.5) and their value cannot be fixed in a direct way (see Section 2.3). Assignments to a subscripted variable $a[s_1, \ldots, s_n]$ model a selected update of the array a at the argument tuple $[s_1, \ldots, s_n]$.

In the following simple and subscripted variables are usually denoted by the letters u, v.

2.3 Semantics of Expressions

In general a semantics is a mapping assigning to each element of a syntactic domain some value drawn from a semantic domain. In this section we explain the semantics of expressions.

Fixed Structure

From logic we need the notion of a *structure*: this is a pair $\mathcal{S} = (\mathcal{D}, \mathcal{I})$ where

- $\mathcal{D}$ is a nonempty set of data or values called a *semantic domain*. We use the letter d as typical element of $\mathcal{D}$.
- $\mathcal{I}$ is an *interpretation* of the constants, that is, a mapping that assigns to each constant c a value $\mathcal{I}(c)$ from $\mathcal{D}$. We say that the constant c *denotes* the value $\mathcal{I}(c)$.

In contrast to general studies in logic we stipulate a fixed structure $\mathcal{S}$ throughout this book. Its semantic domain $\mathcal{D}$ is the disjoint union

$$\mathcal{D} = \bigcup_{T \text{ is a type}} \mathcal{D}_T,$$

where for each T the corresponding semantic domain $\mathcal{D}_T$ is defined inductively as follows:

- $\mathcal{D}_{\textbf{integer}} = \mathbb{Z}$, the set of integers,
- $\mathcal{D}_{\textbf{Boolean}} = \{\textbf{true}, \textbf{false}\}$, the set of Boolean values,
- $\mathcal{D}_{T_1 \times \ldots \times T_n \to T} = \mathcal{D}_{T_1} \times \ldots \times \mathcal{D}_{T_n} \to \mathcal{D}_T$, the set of all functions from the Cartesian product of the sets $\mathcal{D}_{T_1}, \ldots, \mathcal{D}_{T_n}$ into the set $\mathcal{D}_T$.

The interpretation $\mathcal{I}$ is defined as follows: each constant c of base type denotes itself, that is, $\mathcal{I}(c) = c$; each constant op of higher type denotes a fixed function $\mathcal{I}(op)$.

For example, the integer constant 1 denotes the integer number 1 and the Boolean constant **true** denotes the Boolean value **true**. The unary constant $| \, |$ denotes the absolute value function. The unary constant $\neg$ denotes the negation of Boolean values:

$$\neg(\textbf{true}) = \textbf{false} \text{ and } \neg(\textbf{false}) = \textbf{true}.$$

The binary constants *div* and *mod* are written in infix form and denote integer division and remainder defined uniquely by the following requirements:

$$(x \ div \ y) \cdot y + x \ mod \ y = x,$$

$$0 \leq x \ mod \ y < y \text{ for } y > 0,$$

$$y < x \ mod \ y \leq 0 \text{ for } y < 0.$$

To ensure that these functions are total we additionally stipulate

$$x \ div \ 0 = 0 \text{ and } x \ mod \ 0 = x$$

for the special case of $y = 0$.

The binary constant *divides* is defined by

$$x \ divides \ y \ \text{iff} \ y \ mod \ x = 0.$$

The unary constant *int* denotes the function with

$$int(\textbf{true}) = 1 \ \text{and} \ int(\textbf{false}) = 0.$$

States

In contrast to constants, the value of variables is not fixed but given through so-called proper states. A *proper state* is a mapping that assigns to every simple and array variable of type T a value in the domain $\mathcal{D}_T$. We use the letter Σ to denote the set of proper states.

Example 2.4. Let a be an array of type **integer** $\times$ **Boolean** $\rightarrow$ **Boolean** and x be an integer variable. Then each state σ assigns to a a function

$$\sigma(a) : \{..., -1, 0, 1, ...\} \times \{\textbf{true}, \textbf{false}\} \rightarrow \{\textbf{true}, \textbf{false}\}$$

and to x a value from $\{..., -1, 0, 1, ...\}$. For example, $\sigma(a)(5, \textbf{true}) \in \{\textbf{true}, \textbf{false}\}$ and $\sigma(a)(\sigma(x), \textbf{false}) \in \{\textbf{true}, \textbf{false}\}$.   □

Later, in Section 2.6, we also use three *error states* representing abnormal situations in a program execution: $\perp$ denotes divergence of a program, **fail** denotes a failure in an execution of a program and Δ denotes a deadlock in an execution of a program. These error states are just special symbols and not mappings from variables to data values as proper states; they are introduced in Chapters 3, 9 and 10, respectively.

By a *state* we mean a proper or an error state. States are denoted by the letters σ, τ, ρ.

Let $Z \subseteq Var$ be a set of simple or array variables. Then we denote by $\sigma[Z]$ the restriction of a proper state σ to the variables occurring in Z. By convention, for error states we define $\perp[Z] = \perp$, and similarly for Δ and **fail**. We say that two sets of states X and Y *agree modulo* Z, and write

$$X = Y \ \textbf{mod} \ Z,$$

if

$$\{\sigma[Var - Z] \mid \sigma \in X\} = \{\sigma[Var - Z] \mid \sigma \in Y\}.$$

By the above convention, $X = Y \ \textbf{mod} \ Z$ implies the following for error states: $\perp \in X$ iff $\perp \in Y$, $\Delta \in X$ iff $\Delta \in Y$ and **fail** $\in X$ iff **fail** $\in Y$. For singleton sets X, Y, and Z we omit the brackets $\{$ and $\}$ around the singleton element. For example, for proper states σ, τ and a simple variable x,

$$\sigma = \tau \bmod x$$

states that σ and τ agree modulo x, i.e., for all simple and array variables $v \in Var$ with $v \neq x$ we have $\sigma(v) = \tau(v)$.

Definition of the Semantics

The *semantics of an expression* s of type T in the structure $\mathcal{S}$ is a mapping

$$\mathcal{S}[\![s]\!] : \Sigma \to \mathcal{D}_T$$

which assigns to s a value $\mathcal{S}[\![s]\!](\sigma)$ from $\mathcal{D}_T$ depending on a given proper state σ. This mapping is defined by induction on the structure of s:

- if s is a simple variable then

$$\mathcal{S}[\![s]\!](\sigma) = \sigma(s),$$

- if s is a constant of a basic type denoting the value d, then

$$\mathcal{S}[\![s]\!](\sigma) = d,$$

- if $s \equiv op(s_1, \ldots, s_n)$ for some constant op of higher type denoting a function f then
$$\mathcal{S}[\![s]\!](\sigma) = f(\mathcal{S}[\![s_1]\!](\sigma), \ldots, \mathcal{S}[\![s_n]\!](\sigma)),$$

- if $s \equiv a[s_1, \ldots, s_n]$ for some array variable a then

$$\mathcal{S}[\![s]\!](\sigma) = \sigma(a)(\mathcal{S}[\![s_1]\!](\sigma), \ldots, \mathcal{S}[\![s_n]\!](\sigma)),$$

- if $s \equiv$ **if** B **then** s_1 **else** s_2 **fi** for some Boolean expression B then

$$\mathcal{S}[\![s]\!](\sigma) = \begin{cases} \mathcal{S}[\![s_1]\!](\sigma) \text{ if } \mathcal{S}[\![B]\!](\sigma) = \textbf{true}, \\ \mathcal{S}[\![s_2]\!](\sigma) \text{ if } \mathcal{S}[\![B]\!](\sigma) = \textbf{false}, \end{cases}$$

- if $s \equiv (s_1)$ then
$$\mathcal{S}[\![s]\!](\sigma) = \mathcal{S}[\![s_1]\!](\sigma).$$

Since $\mathcal{S}$ is fixed throughout this book, we abbreviate the standard notion $\mathcal{S}[\![s]\!](\sigma)$ from logic to $\sigma(s)$. We extend this notation and apply states also to lists of expressions: for a list $\bar{s} = s_1, \ldots, s_n$ of expressions $\sigma(\bar{s})$ denotes the list of values $\sigma(s_1), \ldots, \sigma(s_n)$.

Example 2.5.
(a) Let a be an array of type **integer** $\to$ **integer**. Then for any proper state σ we have $\sigma(1 + 1) = \sigma(1) + \sigma(1) = 1 + 1 = 2$; so

$$\sigma(a[1+1]) = \sigma(a)(\sigma(1+1)) = \sigma(a)(2) = \sigma(a[2]),$$

thus $a[1+1]$ and $a[2]$ have the same value in all proper states, as desired.
(b) Consider now a proper state σ with $\sigma(x) = 1$ and $\sigma(a)(1) = 2$. Then

$$
\begin{aligned}
& \sigma(a[a[x]]) \\
= \quad & \{\text{definition of } \sigma(s)\} \\
& \sigma(a)(\sigma(a)(\sigma(x))) \\
= \quad & \{\sigma(x) = 1, \ \sigma(a)(1) = 2\} \\
& \sigma(a)(2) \\
= \quad & \sigma(a[2])
\end{aligned}
$$

and

$$
\begin{aligned}
& \sigma(a[\textbf{if } x = 1 \textbf{ then } 2 \textbf{ else } b[x] \textbf{ fi}]) \\
= \quad & \{\text{definition of } \sigma(s)\} \\
& \sigma(a)(\sigma(\textbf{if } x = 1 \textbf{ then } 2 \textbf{ else } b[x] \textbf{ fi})) \\
= \quad & \{\sigma(x) = 1, \text{ definition of } \sigma(s)\} \\
& \sigma(a)(\sigma(2)) \\
= \quad & \sigma(a[2]).
\end{aligned}
$$

$\square$

Updates of States

For the semantics of assignments we need in the sequel the notion of an
update of a proper state σ, written as $\sigma[u := d]$, where u is a simple or
subscripted variable of type T and d is an element of type T. As we shall see
in Chapter 3, the update $\sigma[u := \sigma(t)]$ describes the values of the variables
after the assignment $u := t$ has been executed in state σ. Formally, the update
$\sigma[u := d]$ is again a proper state defined as follows:

- if u is a simple variable then

$$\sigma[u := d]$$

is the state that agrees with σ except for u where its value is d. Formally,
for each simple or array variable v

$$\sigma[u := d](v) = \begin{cases} d & \text{if } u \equiv v, \\ \sigma(v) & \text{otherwise.} \end{cases}$$

- if u is a subscripted variable, say $u \equiv a[t_1, \ldots, t_n]$, then

$$\sigma[u := d]$$

is the state that agrees with σ except for the variable a where the value $\sigma(a)(\sigma(t_1), \ldots, \sigma(t_n))$ is changed to d. Formally, for each simple or array variable v

$$\sigma[u := d](v) = \sigma(v) \text{ if } a \not\equiv v$$

and otherwise for a and argument values $d_1, \ldots, d_n$

$$\sigma[u := d](a)(d_1, \ldots, d_n) = \begin{cases} d & \text{if } d_i = \sigma(t_i) \text{ for } i \in \{1, \ldots, n\}, \\ \sigma(a)(d_1, \ldots, d_n) & \text{otherwise.} \end{cases}$$

Thus the effect of $\sigma[u := d]$ is a selected update of the array variable a at the current values of the argument tuple $t_1, \ldots, t_n$.

We extend the definition of update to error states by putting $\bot[u := d] = \bot$, $\Delta[u := d] = \Delta$ and $\mathbf{fail}[u := d] = \mathbf{fail}$.

Example 2.6. Let x be an integer variable and σ a proper state.
(i) Then

$$\sigma[x := 1](x) = 1,$$

for any simple variable $y \not\equiv x$

$$\sigma[x := 1](y) = \sigma(y),$$

and for any array a of type $T_1 \times \ldots \times T_n \to T$ and $d_i \in \mathcal{D}_{T_i}$ for $i \in \{1, \ldots, n\}$,

$$\sigma[x := 1](a)(d_1, \ldots, d_n) = \sigma(a)(d_1, \ldots, d_n).$$

(ii) Let a be an array of type $\mathbf{integer} \to \mathbf{integer}$. Suppose that $\sigma(x) = 3$. Then for all simple variables y

$$\sigma[a[x+1] := 2](y) = \sigma(y),$$

$$\sigma[a[x+1] := 2](a)(4) = 2,$$

for all integers $k \neq 4$

$$\sigma[a[x+1] := 2](a)(k) = \sigma(a)(k),$$

and for any array b of type $T_1 \times \ldots \times T_n \to T$ and $d_i \in \mathcal{D}_{T_i}$ for $i \in \{1, \ldots, n\}$,

$$\sigma[a[x+1] := 2](b)(d_1, \ldots, d_n) = \sigma(b)(d_1, \ldots, d_n). \qquad \square$$

To define the semantics of parallel assignments, we need the notion of *simultaneous update* of a list of simple variables. Let $\bar{x} = x_1, \ldots, x_n$ be a list of distinct simple variables of types $T_1, \ldots, T_n$ and $\bar{d} = d_1, \ldots, d_n$ a corresponding list of elements of types $T_1, \ldots, T_n$. Then we define for an arbitrary (proper or error) state

$$\sigma[\bar{x} := \bar{d}] \ = \ \sigma[x_1 := d_1] \ldots [x_n := d_n].$$

Thus we reduce the simultaneous update to a series of simple updates. This captures the intended meaning because the variables $x_1, \ldots, x_n$ are distinct.

2.4 Formal Proof Systems

Our main interest here is in verifying programs. To this end we investigate so-called correctness formulas. To show that a given program satisfies a certain correctness formula we need proof systems for correctness formulas. However, we need proof systems even before talking about program correctness, namely when defining the operational semantics of the programs. Therefore we now briefly introduce the concept of a proof system as it is known in logic.

A *proof system* or a *calculus* P over a set Φ of formulas is a finite set of axiom schemes and proof rules. An *axiom scheme* $\mathcal{A}$ is a decidable subset of Φ, that is, $\mathcal{A} \subseteq \Phi$. To describe axiom schemes we use the standard set-theoretic notation $\mathcal{A} = \{ \, \varphi \mid \text{where "..."} \}$ usually written as

$$\mathcal{A}: \qquad \varphi \qquad \text{where "...".}$$

Here φ stands for formulas satisfying the decidable applicability condition "..." of $\mathcal{A}$. The formulas φ of $\mathcal{A}$ are called *axioms* and are considered as given facts. Often the axiom scheme is itself called an "axiom" of the proof system.

With the help of proof rules further facts can be deduced from given formulas. A *proof rule* $\mathcal{R}$ is a decidable $k + 1$-ary relation on the set Φ of formulas, that is, $\mathcal{R} \subseteq \Phi^{k+1}$. Instead of the set-theoretic notation $\mathcal{R} = \{ \, (\varphi_1, ..., \varphi_k, \varphi) \mid \text{where "..."} \}$ a proof rule is usually written as

$$\mathcal{R}: \qquad \frac{\varphi_1, \ldots, \varphi_k}{\varphi} \qquad \text{where "...".}$$

Here $\varphi_1, \ldots, \varphi_k$ and φ stand for the formulas satisfying the decidable applicability condition "..." of $\mathcal{R}$. Intuitively, such a proof rule says that from $\varphi_1, \ldots, \varphi_k$ the formula φ can be deduced if the applicability condition "..." holds. The formulas $\varphi_1, \ldots, \varphi_k$ are called the *premises* and the formula φ is called the *conclusion* of the proof rule.

A *proof* of a formula φ from a set $\mathcal{A}$ of formulas in a proof system P is a finite sequence

$$\varphi_1$$

.

.

.

$$\varphi_n$$

of formulas with $\varphi = \varphi_n$ such that each formula φ_i with $i \in \{1, \ldots, n\}$

- is either an element of the set $\mathcal{A}$ or it
- is an axiom of P or it
- can be obtained by an application of a proof rule $\mathcal{R}$ of P, that is, there are formulas $\varphi_{i_1}, \ldots, \varphi_{i_k}$ with $i_1, \ldots, i_k < i$ in the sequence such that $(\varphi_{i_1}, \ldots, \varphi_{i_k}, \varphi_i) \in \mathcal{R}$.

The formulas in the set $\mathcal{A}$ are called *assumptions* of the proof. $\mathcal{A}$ should be a decidable subset of Φ. Thus $\mathcal{A}$ can be seen as an additional axiom scheme $\mathcal{A} \subseteq \Phi$ that is used locally in a particular proof. Note that the first formula φ_1 in each proof is either an assumption from the set $\mathcal{A}$ or an axiom of P. The length n of the sequence is called the *length of the proof.*

We say that φ is *provable* from $\mathcal{A}$ in P if there exists a proof from $\mathcal{A}$ in P. In that case we write

$$\mathcal{A} \vdash_P \varphi.$$

For a finite set of assumptions, $\mathcal{A} = \{A_1, \ldots, A_n\}$, we drop the set brackets and write $A_1, \ldots, A_n \vdash_P \varphi$ instead of $\{A_1, \ldots, A_n\} \vdash_P \varphi$. If $\mathcal{A} = \emptyset$ we simply write

$$\vdash_P \varphi$$

instead of $\emptyset \vdash_P$. In that case we call the formula φ a *theorem* of the proof system P.

2.5 Assertions

To prove properties about program executions we have to be able to describe properties of states. To this end, we use formulas from predicate logic. In the context of program verification these formulas are called *assertions* because they are used to *assert* that certain conditions are true for states. Assertions are usually denoted by letters p, q, r, and are defined, inductively, by the following clauses:

- every Boolean expression is an assertion,
- if p, q are assertions, then $\neg p, (p \vee q), (p \wedge q), (p \rightarrow q)$ and $(p \leftrightarrow q)$ are also assertions,
- if x is a variable and p an assertion, then $\exists x : p$ and $\forall x : p$ are also assertions.

The symbol $\exists$ is the *existential quantifier* and $\forall$ is the *universal quantifier*. Thus in contrast to Boolean expressions, quantifiers can occur in assertions. Note that quantifiers are allowed in front of both simple and array variables.

As in expressions the brackets (and) can be omitted in assertions if no ambiguities arise. To this end we extend the binding order used for expressions by stipulating that the connectives

$$\rightarrow \text{ and } \leftrightarrow,$$

bind stronger than

$$\exists \text{ and } \forall.$$

For example, $\exists x : p \leftrightarrow q \wedge r$ is interpreted as $\exists x : (p \leftrightarrow (q \wedge r))$. Also, we can always delete the outer brackets.

Further savings on brackets can be achieved by assuming the *right associativity* for the connectives $\wedge$, $\vee$, $\rightarrow$ and $\leftrightarrow$, that is to say, by allowing $A \wedge (B \wedge C)$ to be written as $A \wedge B \wedge C$, and analogously for the remaining binary connectives.

To simplify notation, we also use the following abbreviations:

$$\bigwedge_{i=1}^{n} p_i \quad \text{abbreviates} \quad p_1 \wedge ... \wedge p_n$$

$$s \leq t \quad \text{abbreviates} \quad s < t \vee s = t$$

$$s \leq t < u \quad \text{abbreviates} \quad s \leq t \wedge t < u$$

$$s \neq t \quad \text{abbreviates} \quad \neg(s = t)$$

$$\exists x, y : p \quad \text{abbreviates} \quad \exists x : \exists y : p$$

$$\forall x, y : p \quad \text{abbreviates} \quad \forall x : \exists y : p$$

$$\exists x \leq t : p \quad \text{abbreviates} \quad \exists x : (x \leq t \wedge p)$$

$$\forall x \leq t : p \quad \text{abbreviates} \quad \forall x : (x \leq t \rightarrow p)$$

$$\forall x \in [s : t] : p \quad \text{abbreviates} \quad \forall x : (s \leq x \leq t \rightarrow p)$$

We also use other abbreviations of this form which are obvious.

For lists $\bar{s} = s_1, \ldots, s_m$ and $\bar{t} = t_1, \ldots, t_n$ of expressions, we write

$$\bar{s} = \bar{t}$$

if $m = n$ and $s_i = t_i$ holds for $i = 1, \ldots, n$. In particular, we write $\bar{x} = \bar{y}$ for lists $\bar{x}$ and $\bar{y}$ of simple variables.

The same variable can occur several times in a given assertion. For example, the variable y occurs three times in

$$x > 0 \wedge y > 0 \wedge \exists y : x = 2 * y.$$

In logic one distinguishes different kinds of occurrences. By a *bound occurrence* of a simple variable x in an assertion p we mean an occurrence within a subassertion of p of the form $\exists x : r$ or $\forall x : r$. By a *subassertion* of an assertion p we mean a substring of p that is again an assertion. An occurrence of a simple variable in an assertion p is called *free* if it is not a bound one. In the above example, the first occurrence of y is free and the other two are bound.

By $var(p)$ we denote the set of all simple and array variables that occur in an assertion p. By $free(p)$ we denote the set of all free simple and array variables that have a free occurrence (or *occur free*) in p.

2.6 Semantics of Assertions

The *semantics of an assertion* p in a structure $\mathcal{S}$ is a mapping

$$\mathcal{S}[\![p]\!] : \Sigma \to \{\textbf{true}, \textbf{false}\}$$

that assigns to p a truth value $\mathcal{S}[\![p]\!](\sigma)$ depending on a given proper state σ. Since the structure $\mathcal{S}$ is fixed, we abbreviate the standard notation $\mathcal{S}[\![p]\!](\sigma)$ from logic by writing $\sigma \models p$ instead of $\mathcal{S}[\![p]\!](\sigma) = \textbf{true}$.

When $\sigma \models p$ holds, we say that σ *satisfies* p or that p *holds in* σ or that σ is a *p-state*. This concept is defined by induction on the structure of p. We put

- for Boolean expressions B

$$\sigma \models B, \text{ iff } \sigma(B) = \textbf{true},$$

- for negation

$$\sigma \models \neg p \text{ iff not } \sigma \models p \text{ (written as } \sigma \not\models p),$$

- for conjunction

$$\sigma \models p \wedge q, \text{ iff } \sigma \models p \text{ and } \sigma \models q,$$

- for disjunction

$$\sigma \models p \vee q, \text{ iff } \sigma \models p \text{ or } \sigma \models q,$$

- for implication

$$\sigma \models p \to q, \text{ iff } \sigma \models p \text{ implies } \sigma \models q,$$

- for equivalence

$$\sigma \models (p \leftrightarrow q), \text{ iff } (\sigma \models p \text{ if and only if } \sigma \models q),$$

- for the universal quantifier applied to a simple or an array variable v of type T

$$\sigma \models \forall v : p \text{ iff } \tau \models p \text{ for } \textit{all} \text{ proper states } \tau \text{ with } \sigma = \tau \text{ mod } v \ ,$$

- for the existential quantifier applied to a simple or an array variable v of type T

$$\sigma \models \exists v : p \text{ iff } \tau \models p \text{ for } \textit{some} \text{ proper state } \tau \text{ with } \sigma = \tau \text{ mod } v \ ,$$

By the definition of **mod**, the states σ and τ agree on all variables except v. For simple variables x we can use updates and determine $\tau = \sigma[x := d]$ for a data value d in $\mathcal{D}_T$. See Exercise 2.6 for the precise relationship.

We also introduce the *meaning* of an assertion, written as $[\![p]\!]$, and defined by

$$[\![p]\!] = \{\sigma \mid \sigma \text{ is a proper state and } \sigma \models p\}.$$

We say that an assertion p *is true*, or *holds*, if for all proper states σ we have $\sigma \models p$, that is, if $[\![p]\!] = \Sigma$. Given two assertions p and q, we say that p and q are *equivalent* if $p \leftrightarrow q$ is true.

For error states we define $\perp \not\models p$, $\Delta \not\models p$ and **fail** $\not\models p$. Thus for all assertions

$$\perp, \ \Delta, \ \textbf{fail} \notin [\![p]\!].$$

The following simple lemma summarizes the relevant properties of the meaning of an assertion.

Lemma 2.1. (Meaning of Assertion)

(i) $[\![\neg p]\!] = \Sigma - [\![p]\!]$,
(ii) $[\![p \lor q]\!] = [\![p]\!] \cup [\![q]\!]$,
(iii) $[\![p \land q]\!] = [\![p]\!] \cap [\![q]\!]$,
(iv) $p \to q$ *is true iff* $[\![p]\!] \subseteq [\![q]\!]$,
(v) $p \leftrightarrow q$ *is true iff* $[\![p]\!] = [\![q]\!]$.

Proof. See Exercise 2.7. $\square$

2.7 Substitution

To prove correctness properties about assignment statements, we need the concept of *substitution*. A substitution of an expression t for a simple or subscripted variable u is written as

$$[u := t]$$

and denotes a function from expressions to expressions and from assertions to assertions. First, we define the application of $[u := t]$ to an expression s, which is written in postfix notation. The result is an expression denoted by

$$s[u := t].$$

A substitution $[u := t]$ describes the replacement of u by t. For example, we have

- $max(x, y)[x := x + 1] \equiv max(x + 1, y)$.

However, substitution is not so easy to define when subscripted variables are involved. For example, we obtain

- $max(a[1], y)[a[1] := 2] \equiv max(2, y)$,
- $max(a[x], y)[a[1] := 2] \equiv \text{if } x = 1 \text{ then } max(2, y) \text{ else } max(a[x], y) \text{ fi}$.

In the second case it is checked whether the syntactically different subscripted variables $a[x]$ and $a[1]$ are *aliases* of the same location. Then the substitution of 2 for $a[1]$ results in $a[x]$ being replaced by 2, otherwise the substitution has no effect. To determine whether $a[x]$ and $a[1]$ are aliases the definition of substitution makes a case distinction on the subscripts of a (using the conditional expression **if** $x = 1$ **then** ... **else** ... **fi**).

In general, in a given state σ the substituted expression $s[u := t]$ should describe the same value as the expression s evaluated in the updated state $\sigma[u := \sigma(t)]$, which arises after the assignment $u := t$ has been executed in σ (see Chapter 3). This semantic equivalence is made precise in the Substitution Lemma 2.4 below.

The formal definition of the expression $s[u := t]$ proceeds by induction on the structure of s:

- if $s \equiv x$ for some simple variable x then

$$s[u := t] \equiv \begin{cases} t \text{ if } s \equiv u \\ s \text{ otherwise,} \end{cases}$$

- if $s \equiv c$ for some constant c of basic type then

$$s[u := t] \equiv s,$$

- if $s \equiv op(s_1, \ldots, s_n)$ for some constant op of higher type then

$$s[u := t] \equiv op(s_1[u := t], \ldots, s_n[u := t]),$$

- if $s \equiv a[s_1, \ldots, s_n]$ for some array a, and u is a simple variable or a subscripted variable $b[t_1, \ldots, t_m]$ where $a \not\equiv b$, then

$$s[u := t] \equiv a[s_1[u := t], \ldots, s_n[u := t]],$$

- if $s \equiv a[s_1, \ldots, s_n]$ for some array a and $u \equiv a[t_1, \ldots, t_n]$ then

$$s[u := t] \equiv \textbf{if } \bigwedge_{i=1}^{n} s_i[u := t] = t_i \textbf{ then } t$$
$$\textbf{else } a[s_1[u := t], \ldots, s_n[u := t]] \textbf{ fi},$$

- if $s \equiv \textbf{if } B \textbf{ then } s_1 \textbf{ else } s_2 \textbf{ fi}$ then

$$s[u := t] \equiv \textbf{if } B[u := t] \textbf{ then } s_1[u := t] \textbf{ else } s_2[u := t] \textbf{ fi}.$$

Note that the definition of substitution does not take into account the infix notation of binary constants op; so to apply substitution the infix notation must first be replaced by the corresponding prefix notation.

The most complicated case in this inductive definition is the second clause dealing with subscripted variables, where $s \equiv a[s_1, \ldots, s_n]$ and $u \equiv a[t_1, \ldots, t_n]$. In that clause the conditional expression

$$\textbf{if } \bigwedge_{i=1}^{n} s_i[u := t] = t_i \textbf{ then } \ldots \textbf{ else } \ldots \textbf{ fi}$$

checks whether, for any given proper state σ, the expression $s \equiv a[s_1, \ldots, s_n]$ in the updated state $\sigma[u := \sigma(t)]$ and the expression $u \equiv a[t_1, \ldots, t_n]$ in the state σ are aliases. For this check the substitution $[u := t]$ needs to applied inductively to all subscripts $s_1, \ldots, s_n$ of $a[s_1, \ldots, s_n]$. In case of an alias $s[u := t]$ yields t. Otherwise, the substitution is applied inductively to the subscripts $s_1, \ldots, s_n$ of $a[s_1, \ldots, s_n]$.

The following lemma is an immediate consequence of the above definition of $s[u := t]$.

Lemma 2.2. (Identical Substitution) *For all expressions s and t, all simple variables x and all subscripted variables $a[t_1, \ldots, t_n]$*

(i) $s[x := t] \equiv s$ if s does not contain x,
(ii) $s[a[t_1, \ldots, t_n] := t] \equiv s$ if s does not contain a.   □

The following example illustrates the application of substitution.

Example 2.7. Suppose that a and b are arrays of type **integer** $\to$ **integer** and x is an integer variable. Then

$$a[b[x]][b[1] := 2]$$
$\equiv$ {definition of $s[u := t]$ since $a \not\equiv b$}
$$a[b[x][b[1] := 2]]$$
$\equiv$ {definition of $s[u := t]$}
$$a[\textbf{if } x[b[1] := 2] = 1 \textbf{ then } 2 \textbf{ else } b[x[b[1] := 2]] \textbf{ fi}]$$
$\equiv$ {by the Identical Substitution Lemma 2.2 $x[b[1] := 2] \equiv x$}
$$a[\textbf{if } x = 1 \textbf{ then } 2 \textbf{ else } b[x] \textbf{ fi}]$$ □

The application of substitutions $[u := t]$ is now extended to assertions p. The result is again an assertion denoted by

$$p[u := t].$$

The definition of $p[u := t]$ is by induction on the structure on p:

- if $p \equiv s$ for some Boolean expression s then

$$p[u := t] \equiv s[u := t]$$

  by the previous definition for expressions,
- if $p \equiv \neg q$ then
$$p[u := t] \equiv \neg(q[u := t]),$$

- if $p \equiv q \vee r$ then

$$p[u := t] \equiv q[u := t] \vee r[u := t],$$

  and similarly for the remaining binary connectives: $\wedge$, $\rightarrow$ and $\leftrightarrow$,
- if $p \equiv \exists x : q$ then

$$p[u := t] \equiv \exists y : q[x := y][u := t],$$

  where y does not appear in p, t or u and is of the same type as x,
- if $p \equiv \forall x : q$ then

$$p[u := t] \equiv \forall y : q[x := y][u := t],$$

where y does not appear in p, t or u and is of the same type as x.

In the clauses dealing with quantification, renaming the bound variable x into a new variable y avoids possible clashes with free occurrences of x in t. For example, we obtain

$$(\exists x : z = 2 \cdot x)[z := x + 1]$$
$$\equiv \exists y : z = 2 \cdot x[x := y][z := x + 1]$$
$$\equiv \exists y : x + 1 = 2 \cdot y.$$

Thus for assertions substitution is defined only up to a renaming of bound variables.

Simultaneous Substitution

To prove correctness properties of parallel assignments, we need the concept of *simultaneous substitution*. Let $\bar{x} = x_1, \ldots, x_n$ be a list of distinct simple variables of type $T_1, \ldots, T_n$ and $\bar{t} = t_1, \ldots, t_n$ a corresponding list of expressions of type $T_1, \ldots, T_n$. Then a simultaneous substitution of $\bar{t}$ for $\bar{x}$ is written as

$$[\bar{x} := \bar{t}]$$

and denotes a function from expressions to expressions and from assertions to assertions. The application of $[\bar{x} := \bar{t}]$ to an expression s is written in postfix notation. The result is an expression denoted by

$$s[\bar{x} := \bar{t}]$$

and defined inductively over the structure of s. The definition proceeds analogously to that of a substitution for a single simple variable except that in the base case we now have to select the right elements from the lists $\bar{x}$ and $\bar{t}$:

- if $s \equiv x$ for some simple variable x then

$$s[\bar{x} := \bar{t}] \equiv \begin{cases} t_i \text{ if } x \equiv x_i \text{ for some } i \in \{1, \ldots, n\} \\ s \text{ otherwise.} \end{cases}$$

As an example of an inductive clause of the definition we state:

- if $s \equiv op(s_1, \ldots, s_n)$ for some constant op of higher type then

$$s[\bar{x} := \bar{t}] \equiv op(s_1[\bar{x} := \bar{t}], \ldots, s_n[\bar{x} := \bar{t}]).$$

Using these inductive clauses the substitution for each variable x_i from the list $\bar{x}$ is pursued simultaneously. This is illustrated by the following example.

Example 2.8. We take $s \equiv max(x, y)$ and calculate

$$max(x, y)[x, y := y + 1, x + 2]$$
$$\equiv \quad \{op \equiv max \text{ in the inductive clause above}\}$$
$$max(x[x, y := y + 1, x + 2], y[x, y := y + 1, x + 2])$$
$$\equiv \quad \{\text{the base case shown above}\}$$
$$max(y + 1, x + 2).$$

Note that a sequential application of two single substitutions yields a different result:

$$max(x, y)[x := y + 1][y := x + 2]$$
$$\equiv \quad max(y + 1, y)[y := x + 2])$$
$$\equiv \quad max((x + 2) + 1, x + 2). \qquad \square$$

Note 2.1. The first clause of the Lemma 2.2 on Identical Substitutions holds also, appropriately rephrased, for simultaneous substitutions: for all expressions s

- $s[\bar{x} := \bar{t}] \equiv s$ if s does not contain any variable x_i from the list $\bar{x}$. $\square$

The application of simultaneous subsitution to an assertion p is denoted by

$$p[\bar{x} := \bar{t}]$$

and defined inductively over the structure of p, as in the case of a substitution for a single simple variable.

2.8 Substitution Lemma

In this section we connect the notions of substitution and of update introduced in Sections 2.7 and 2.3. We begin by noting the following so-called coincidence lemma.

Lemma 2.3. (Coincidence) *For all expressions s, all assertions p and all proper states σ and τ*

(i) if $\sigma[var(s)] = \tau[var(s)]$ then $\sigma(s) = \tau(s)$,
(ii) if $\sigma[free(p)] = \tau[free(p)]$ then $\sigma \models p$ iff $\tau \models p$.

Proof. See Exercise 2.8. $\square$

Using the Coincidence Lemma we can prove the following lemma which is used in the next chapter when discussing the assignment statement.

Lemma 2.4. (Substitution) *For all expressions s and t, all assertions p, all simple or subscripted variables u of the same type as t and all proper states σ,*

(i) $\sigma(s[u := t]) = \sigma[u := \sigma(t)](s)$,
(ii) $\sigma \models p[u := t]$ iff $\sigma[u := \sigma(t)] \models p$.

Clause (i) relates the value of the expression $s[u := t]$ in a state σ to the value of the expression s in an updated state, and similarly with (ii).

Proof. (i) The proof proceeds by induction on the structure of s. Suppose first that s is a simple variable. Then when $s \equiv u$, we have

$$\sigma(s[u := t])$$
$$= \quad \{\text{definition of substitution}\}$$
$$\sigma(t)$$
$$= \quad \{\text{definition of update}\}$$
$$\sigma[s := \sigma(t)](s)$$
$$= \quad \{s \equiv u\}$$
$$\sigma[u := \sigma(t)](s),$$

and when $s \not\equiv u$ the same conclusion follows by the Identical Substitution Lemma 2.2 and the definition of an update.

The case when s is a subscripted variable, say $s \equiv a[s_1, \ldots, s_n]$, is slightly more complicated. When u is a simple variable or $u \equiv b[t_1, \ldots, t_m]$ where $a \not\equiv b$, we have

$$\sigma(s[u := t])$$
$$= \quad \{\text{definition of substitution}\}$$
$$\sigma(a[s_1[u := t], \ldots, s_n[u := t]])$$
$$= \quad \{\text{definition of semantics}\}$$
$$\sigma(a)(\sigma(s_1[u := t]), \ldots, \sigma(s_n[u := t]))$$
$$= \quad \{\text{induction hypothesis}\}$$
$$\sigma(a)(\sigma[u := \sigma(t)](s_1), \ldots, \sigma[u := \sigma(t)](s_n))$$
$$= \quad \{\text{by definition of update}, \sigma[u := \sigma(t)](a) = \sigma(a)\}$$
$$\sigma[u := \sigma(t)](a)(\sigma[u := \sigma(t)](s_1), \ldots, \sigma[u := \sigma(t)](s_n))$$
$$= \quad \{\text{definition of semantics}, s \equiv a[s_1, \ldots, s_n]\}$$
$$\sigma[u := \sigma(t)](s)$$

and when $u \equiv a[t_1, \ldots, t_n]$, we have

$$\sigma(s[u := t])$$
$$= \quad \{\text{definition of substitution}, s \equiv a[s_1, \ldots, s_n], u \equiv a[t_1, \ldots, t_n] \}$$
$$\sigma(\textbf{if } \bigwedge_{i=1}^{n} s_i[u := t] = t_i \textbf{ then } t \textbf{ else } a[s_1[u := t], \ldots, s_n[u := t]] \textbf{ fi})$$
$$= \quad \{\text{definition of semantics}\}$$
$$\begin{cases} \sigma(t) & \text{if } \sigma(s_i[u := t]) = \sigma(t_i) \text{ for } i \in \{1, \ldots, n\} \\ \sigma(a)(\sigma(s_1[u := t]), \ldots, \sigma(s_n[u := t])) & \text{otherwise} \end{cases}$$
$$= \quad \{\text{definition of update}, u \equiv a[t_1, \ldots, t_n]\}$$
$$\sigma[u := \sigma(t)](a)(\sigma(s_1[u := t]), \ldots, \sigma(s_n[u := t]))$$
$$= \quad \{\text{induction hypothesis}\}$$
$$\sigma[u := \sigma(t)](a)(\sigma[u := \sigma(t)](s_1), \ldots, \sigma[u := \sigma(t)](s_n))$$
$$= \quad \{\text{definition of semantics}, s \equiv a[s_1, \ldots, s_n]\}$$
$$\sigma[u := \sigma(t)](s).$$

The remaining cases are straightforward and left to the reader.

(ii) The proof also proceeds by induction on the structure of p. The base case, which concerns Boolean expressions, is now implied by (i). The induction step is straightforward with the exception of the case when p is of the form $\exists x : r$ or $\forall x : r$. Let y be a simple variable that does not appear in r, t or u and is of the same type as x. We then have

$$\sigma \models (\exists x : r)[u := t]$$
iff {definition of substitution}
$$\sigma \models \exists y : r[x := y][u := t]$$
iff {definition of truth}
$$\sigma' \models r[x := y][u := t]$$
for some element d from the type associated
with y and $\sigma' = \sigma[y := d]$
iff {induction hypothesis}
$$\sigma'[u := \sigma'(t)] \models r[x := y]$$
for some d and σ' as above
iff {$y \not\equiv x$ so $\sigma'[u := \sigma'(t)](y) = d$,
     induction hypothesis}
$$\sigma'[u := \sigma'(t)][x := d] \models r$$
for some d and σ' as above
iff {Coincidence Lemma 2.3, choice of y}
$$\sigma[u := \sigma(t)][x := d] \models r$$
for some d as above
iff {definition of truth}
$$\sigma[u := \sigma(t)] \models \exists x : r.$$

An analogous chain of equivalences deals with the case when p is of the form $\forall x : r$. This concludes the proof. □

Example 2.9. Let a and b be arrays of type **integer** → **integer**, x an integer variable and σ a proper state such that $\sigma(x) = 1$ and $\sigma(a)(1) = 2$. Then

$$\sigma[b[1] := 2](a[b[x]])$$
= {Substitution Lemma 2.4}
$$\sigma(a[b[x]][b[1] := 2])$$
= {Example 2.7}
$$\sigma(a[\textbf{if } x = 1 \textbf{ then } 2 \textbf{ else } b[x] \textbf{ fi}])$$
= {Example 2.5}
$$= \sigma(a[2]).$$

Of course, a direct application of the definition of an update also leads to this result. □

Finally, we state the Substitution Lemma for the case of simultaneous substitutions.

Lemma 2.5. (Simultaneous Substitution) *Let $\bar{x} = x_1, \ldots, x_n$ be a list of distinct simple variables of type $T_1, \ldots, T_n$ and $\bar{t} = t_1, \ldots, t_n$ a corresponding list of expressions of type $x_1, \ldots, x_n$. Then for all expressions s, all assertions p, and all proper states σ,*

(i) $\sigma(s[\bar{x} := \bar{t}]) = \sigma[\bar{x} := \sigma(\bar{t})](s)$,
(ii) $\sigma \models p[\bar{x} := \bar{t}]$ *iff* $\sigma[\bar{x} := \sigma(\bar{t})] \models p$,

where $\sigma(\bar{t}) = \sigma(t_1), \ldots, \sigma(t_n)$.

Clause (i) relates the value of the expression $s[\bar{x} := \bar{t}]$ in a state σ to the value of the expression s in an updated state, and similarly with (ii).

Proof. Analogously to that of the Substitution Lemma 2.4. $\square$

2.9 Exercises

2.1. Simplify the following assertions:

(i) $(p \vee (q \vee r)) \wedge (q \rightarrow (r \rightarrow p))$,
(ii) $(s < t \vee s = t) \wedge t < u$,
(iii) $\exists x : (x < t \wedge (p \wedge (q \wedge r))) \vee s = u$.

2.2. Compute the following expressions using the definition of substitution:

(i) $(x + y)[x := z][z := y]$,
(ii) $(a[x] + y)[x := z][a[2] := 1]$,
(iii) $a[a[2]][a[2] := 2]$.

2.3. Compute the following values:

(i) $\sigma[x := 0](a[x])$,
(ii) $\sigma[y := 0](a[x])$,
(iii) $\sigma[a[0] := 2](a[x])$,
(iv) $\tau[a[x] := \tau(x)](a[1])$, where $\tau = \sigma[x := 1][a[1] := 2]$.

2.4. Prove that

(i) $p \wedge (q \wedge r)$ is equivalent to $(p \wedge q) \wedge r$,
(ii) $p \vee (q \vee r)$ is equivalent to $(p \vee q) \vee r$,
(iii) $p \vee (q \wedge r)$ is equivalent to $(p \vee q) \wedge (p \vee r)$,
(iv) $p \wedge (q \vee r)$ is equivalent to $(p \wedge q) \vee (p \wedge r)$,
(v) $\exists x : (p \vee q)$ is equivalent to $\exists x : p \vee \exists x : q$,
(vi) $\forall x : (p \wedge q)$ is equivalent to $\forall x : p \wedge \forall x : q$.

2.5.

(i) Is $\exists x : (p \wedge q)$ equivalent to $\exists x : p \wedge \exists x : q$?
(ii) Is $\forall x : (p \vee q)$ equivalent to $\forall x : p \vee \forall x : q$?
(iii) Is $(\exists x : z = x + 1)[z := x + 2]$ equivalent to $\exists y : x + 2 = y + 1$?
(iv) Is $(\exists x : a[s] = x + 1)[a[s] := x + 2]$ equivalent to $\exists y : x + 2 = y + 1$?

2.6. Show that for a simple variable x of type T updates can be used to characterize the semantics of quantifiers:

- $\sigma \models \forall x : p$ iff $\sigma[x := d] \models p$ for *all* data values d from $\mathcal{D}_T$,
- $\sigma \models \exists x : p$ iff $\sigma[x := d] \models p$ for *some* data value d from $\mathcal{D}_T$.

2.7. Prove the Meaning of Assertion Lemma 2.1.

2.8. Prove the Coincidence Lemma 2.3.

2.9.

(i) Prove that $p[x := 1][y := 2]$ is equivalent to $p[y := 2][x := 1]$.
    Hint. Use the Substitution Lemma 2.4.
(ii) Give an example when the assertions $p[x := s][y := t]$ and $p[y := t][x := s]$ are not equivalent.

2.10.

(i) Prove that $p[a[1] := 1][a[2] := 2]$ is equivalent to $p[a[2] := 2][a[1] := 1]$.
    Hint. Use the Substitution Lemma 2.4.
(ii) Give an example when the assertions $p[a[s_1] := t_1][a[s_2] := t_2]$ and $p[a[s_2] := t_2][a[s_1] := t_1]$ are not equivalent.

2.11. Prove Lemma 2.5 on Simultaneous Substitution.

2.10 Bibliographic Remarks

Our use of types is very limited in that no subtypes are allowed and higher types can be constructed only directly out of the basic types. A more extended use of types in mathematical logic is discussed in Girard, Lafont and Taylor [1989], and of types in programming languages in Cardelli [1991] and Mitchell [1990].

For simplicity all functions and relations used in this book are assumed to be totally defined. A theory of program verification in the presence of partially defined functions and relations is developed in the book by Tucker and Zucker [1988]. In Chapter 3 of this book we explain how we can nevertheless model partially defined expressions by the programming concept of failure.

Our definition of substitution for a simple variable is the standard one used in mathematical logic. The definitions of substitution for a subscripted variable, of a state, and of an update of a state are taken from de Bakker [1980], where the Substitution Lemma 2.4 also implicitly appears.

To the reader interested in a more thorough introduction to the basic concepts of mathematical logic we recommend the book by van Dalen [2004].

Part II
Deterministic Programs

3 while *Programs*

I N A DETERMINISTIC program there is at most one instruction to be executed "next," so that from a given initial state only one execution sequence is generated. In classical programming languages like Pascal, only deterministic programs can be written. In this chapter we study a small class of deterministic programs, called **while** programs, which are included in all other classes of programs studied in this book.

We start by defining the syntax (Section 3.1), then introduce an operational semantics (Section 3.2), subsequently study program verification by introducing proof systems allowing us to prove various program properties and prove the soundness of the introduced proof systems (Section 3.3). This

Krzysztof R. Apt et al., *Verification of Sequential and Concurrent Programs*,
Texts in Computer Science, DOI: 10.1007/978-1-84882-745-5_3,
© Springer-Verlag London Limited 2009

pattern is repeated for all classes of programs studied in this book. We introduce here two semantics —partial correctness and total correctness semantics. The former does not take into account the possibility of divergence while the latter does.

The proof theory deals with the correctness formulas. These formulas have the form $\{p\}\ S\ \{q\}$ where p and q are assertions and S is a program. We introduce here two proof systems —one for proving the correctness formulas in the sense of partial correctness and the other for proving them in the sense of total correctness. Then we prove their soundness with respect to the underlying semantics.

Next, in Section 3.4, we introduce a convenient proof presentation, called a proof outline, that allows us to present correctness proofs by giving a program interleaved with assertions at appropriate places. This form of proof presentation is especially important in Chapters 8 and 9 when studying parallel programs.

In Section 3.5 we study completeness of the introduced proof systems, that is, the problem whether all true correctness formulas can be proved in the corresponding proof systems. Then, in Sections 3.6 and 3.7 we study two simple programming constructs that will be useful in the later chapters: the parallel assignment and the failure statement.

Next, in Section 3.8, we introduce auxiliary axioms and proof rules that allow us to organize correctness proofs in a different way. These axioms and proof rules are especially helpful when studying other classes of programs in this book.

In Section 3.9 we prove as a first case study the correctness of the well-known partition program. In Section 3.10 we explain an approach originated by Dijkstra [1976] allowing us to systematically develop programs together with their correctness proofs. Finally, in Section 3.11, as a case study, we develop a small but not so obvious program for computing the so-called minimum-sum section of an array.

3.1 Syntax

A **while** *program* is a string of symbols including the keywords **if, then, else, fi, while, do** and **od**, that is generated by the following grammar:

$$S ::= skip \mid u := t \mid S_1; \ S_2 \mid \textbf{if } B \textbf{ then } S_1 \textbf{ else } S_2 \textbf{ fi} \mid \textbf{while } B \textbf{ do } S_1 \textbf{ od}.$$

Following the conventions of the previous chapter, the letter u stands for a simple or subscripted variable, t for an expression and B for a Boolean expression. We require that in an assignment $u := t$ the variable u and the expression t are of the same type. Since types are implied by the notational conventions of the previous chapter, we do not declare variables in the programs. To avoid repeated qualifications, we assume that *all* programs considered in this book are syntactically correct. Sometimes instead of programs we talk about statements. As an abbreviation we introduce

if B **then** S **fi** $\equiv$ **if** B **then** S **else** *skip* **fi**.

As usual, spaces and indentation are used to make programs more readable, but these additions are not part of the formal syntax. Here and elsewhere, programs are denoted by letters R, S, T.

Although we assume that the reader is familiar with **while** programs as defined above, we recall how they are executed. The statement *skip* changes nothing and just terminates. An *assignment* $u := t$ assigns the value of the expression t to the (possibly subscripted) variable u and then terminates. A *sequential composition* $S_1; \ S_2$ is executed by executing S_1 and, when it terminates, executing S_2. Since this interpretation of sequential composition is associative, we need not introduce brackets enclosing $S_1; \ S_2$. Execution of a *conditional statement* **if** B **then** S_1 **else** S_2 **fi** starts by evaluating the Boolean expression B. If B is true, S_1 is executed; otherwise (if B is false), S_2 is executed. Execution of a *loop* **while** B **do** S **od** starts with the evaluation of the Boolean expression B. If B is false, the loop terminates immediately; otherwise S is executed. When S terminates, the process is repeated.

Given a **while** program S, we denote by $var(S)$ the set of all simple and array variables that appear in S and by $change(S)$ the set of all simple and array variables that *can be modified by* S. Formally,

$$\begin{aligned}
change(S) = \quad & \{x \mid x \text{ is a simple variable that appears in} \\
& \text{an assignment of the form } x := t \text{ in } S\} \\
\cup \ & \{a \mid a \text{ is an array variable that appears in} \\
& \text{an assignment of the form } a[s_1, \ldots, s_n] := t \text{ in } S\}.
\end{aligned}$$

Both notions are also used in later chapters for other classes of programs.

By a *subprogram S* of a **while** program R we mean a substring S of R, which is also a **while** program. For example,

$$S \equiv x := x - 1$$

is a subprogram of

$$R \equiv \textbf{if } x = 0 \textbf{ then } y := 1 \textbf{ else } y := y - x; \; x := x - 1 \textbf{ fi}.$$

3.2 Semantics

You may be perfectly happy with this intuitive explanation of the meaning of **while** programs. In fact, for a long time this has been the style of describing what constructs in programming languages denote. However, this style has proved to be error-prone both for implementing programming languages and for writing and reasoning about individual programs. To eliminate this danger, the informal explanation should be accompanied by (but not substituted for!) a rigorous definition of the semantics. Clearly, such a definition is necessary to achieve the aim of our book: providing rigorous proof methods for program correctness.

So what exactly *is* the meaning or semantics of a **while** program S? It is a mapping $\mathcal{M}[\![S]\!]$ from proper (initial) states to (final) states, using $\perp$ to indicate divergence. The question now arises how to define $\mathcal{M}[\![S]\!]$. There are two main approaches to such definitions: the *denotational* approach and the *operational* one.

The idea of the denotational approach is to provide an appropriate semantic domain for $\mathcal{M}[\![S]\!]$ and then define $\mathcal{M}[\![S]\!]$ by induction on the structure of S, in particular, using fixed point techniques to deal with loops, or more generally, with recursion (Scott and Strachey [1971], Stoy [1977], Gordon [1979],...). While this approach works *well* for deterministic sequential programs, it gets a *lot* more complicated for nondeterministic, parallel and distributed programs.

That is why we prefer to work with an operational approach proposed by Hennessy and Plotkin [1979] and further developed in Plotkin [1981]. Here, definitions remain very simple for all classes of programs considered in this book. "Operational" means that first a *transition relation* $\rightarrow$ between so-called *configurations* of an abstract machine is specified, and then the semantics $\mathcal{M}[\![S]\!]$ is defined with the help of $\rightarrow$. Depending on the definition of a configuration, the transition relation $\rightarrow$ can model executions at various levels of detail.

We choose here a "high level" view of an execution, where a configuration is simply a pair $< S, \sigma >$ consisting of a program S and a state σ. Intuitively, a *transition*

$$< S, \sigma > \; \rightarrow \; < R, \tau > \tag{3.1}$$

means: executing S one step in a proper state σ can lead to state τ with R being the remainder of S still to be executed. To express termination, we allow the *empty program* E inside configurations: $R \equiv E$ in (3.1) means that S terminates in τ. We stipulate that $E;\ S$ and $S;\ E$ are abbreviations of S.

The idea of Hennessy and Plotkin is to specify the transition relation $\rightarrow$ by induction on the structure of programs using a formal proof system, called here a *transition system*. It consists of axioms and rules about transitions (3.1). For **while** programs, we use the following *transition* axioms and rules where σ is a proper state:

(i) $< skip, \sigma > \ \rightarrow \ < E, \sigma >,$

(ii) $< u := t, \sigma > \ \rightarrow \ < E, \sigma[u := \sigma(t)] >,$

(iii) $\dfrac{< S_1, \sigma > \ \rightarrow \ < S_2, \tau >}{< S_1;\ S, \sigma > \ \rightarrow \ < S_2;\ S, \tau >},$

(iv) $< \textbf{if } B \textbf{ then } S_1 \textbf{ else } S_2 \textbf{ fi}, \sigma > \ \rightarrow \ < S_1, \sigma >$ where $\sigma \models B$,

(v) $< \textbf{if } B \textbf{ then } S_1 \textbf{ else } S_2 \textbf{ fi}, \sigma > \ \rightarrow \ < S_2, \sigma >$ where $\sigma \models \neg B$,

(vi) $< \textbf{while } B \textbf{ do } S \textbf{ od}, \sigma > \ \rightarrow \ < S;\ \textbf{while } B \textbf{ do } S \textbf{ od}, \sigma >$
    where $\sigma \models B$,

(vii) $< \textbf{while } B \textbf{ do } S \textbf{ od}, \sigma > \ \rightarrow \ < E, \sigma >$, where $\sigma \models \neg B$.

A transition $< S, \sigma > \ \rightarrow \ < R, \tau >$ is possible if and only if it can be deduced in the above transition system. (For simplicity we do not use any provability symbol $\vdash$ here.) Note that the *skip* statement, assignments and evaluations of Boolean expressions are all executed in one step. This "high level" view abstracts from all details of the evaluation of expressions in the execution of assignments. Consequently, this semantics is a high-level semantics.

Definition 3.1. Let S be a **while** program and σ a proper state.

(i) A *transition sequence of S starting in σ* is a finite or infinite sequence of configurations $< S_i, \sigma_i > \ (i \geq 0)$ such that

$$< S, \sigma > = < S_0, \sigma_0 > \ \rightarrow \ < S_1, \sigma_1 > \ \rightarrow \ \ldots \rightarrow \ < S_i, \sigma_i > \ \rightarrow \ldots .$$

(ii) A *computation of S starting in σ* is a transition sequence of S starting in σ that cannot be extended.

(iii) A computation of S *is terminating in τ* (or *terminates in τ*) if it is finite and its last configuration is of the form $< E, \tau >$.

(iv) A computation of S *is diverging* (or *diverges*) if it is infinite. S *can diverge from σ* if there exists an infinite computation of S starting in σ.

(v) To describe the effect of finite transition sequences we use the transitive, reflexive closure $\rightarrow^*$ of the transition relation $\rightarrow$:

$$< S, \sigma > \ \rightarrow^* \ < R, \tau >$$

holds when there exist configurations $< S_1, \sigma_1 >, \ldots, < S_n, \sigma_n >$ with $n \geq 0$ such that

$$< S, \sigma >=< S_1, \sigma_1 > \to \ldots \to\ < S_n, \sigma_n >=< R, \tau >$$

holds. In the case when $n = 0$, $< S, \sigma >=< R, \tau >$ holds.   □

We have the following lemmata.

Lemma 3.1. (Determinism) *For any* **while** *program S and a proper state σ, there is exactly one computation of S starting in σ.*

Proof. Any configuration has at most one successor in the transition relation $\to$.   □

This lemma explains the title of this part of the book: deterministic programs. It also shows that for **while** programs the phrase "S *can* diverge from σ" may be actually replaced by the more precise statement "S diverges from σ." On the other hand, in subsequent chapters we deal with programs admitting various computations from a given state and for which we retain this definition. For such programs, this phrase sounds more appropriate.

Lemma 3.2. (Absence of Blocking) *If $S \not\equiv E$ then for any proper state σ there exists a configuration $< S_1, \tau >$ such that*

$$< S, \sigma > \to\ < S_1, \tau > .$$

Proof. If $S \not\equiv E$ then any configuration $< S, \sigma >$ has a successor in the transition relation $\to$.   □

This lemma states that if S did not terminate then it can be executed for at least one step. Both lemmata clearly depend on the syntax of the programs considered here. The Determinism Lemma 3.1 will fail to hold for all classes of programs studied from Chapter 7 on and the Absence of Blocking Lemma 3.2 will not hold for a class of parallel programs studied in Chapter 9 and for distributed programs studied in Chapter 11.

Definition 3.2. We now define two input/output semantics for **while** programs. Each of them associates with a program S and a proper state $\sigma \in \Sigma$ a set of output states.

(i) The *partial correctness semantics* is a mapping

$$\mathcal{M}[\![S]\!] : \Sigma \to \mathcal{P}(\Sigma)$$

with

$$\mathcal{M}[\![S]\!](\sigma) = \{\tau \mid < S, \sigma > \to^* < E, \tau >\}.$$

(ii) The *total correctness semantics* is a mapping

$$\mathcal{M}_{tot}[\![S]\!] : \Sigma \to \mathcal{P}(\Sigma \cup \{\bot\})$$

with

$$\mathcal{M}_{tot}[\![S]\!](\sigma) = \mathcal{M}[\![S]\!](\sigma) \cup \{\perp \mid S \text{ can diverge from } \sigma\}. \qquad \Box$$

The reason for this choice of names becomes clear in the next section. The difference between these semantics lies in the way the 'negative' information about the program is dealt with —either it is dropped or it is explicitly mentioned: $\mathcal{M}[\![S]\!](\sigma)$ consists of proper states, whereas $\mathcal{M}_{tot}[\![S]\!](\sigma)$ may contain $\perp$. Thus the negative information consists here of the possibility of divergence.

Observe that, by the Determinism Lemma 3.1, $\mathcal{M}[\![S]\!](\sigma)$ has at most one element and $\mathcal{M}_{tot}[\![S]\!](\sigma)$ has exactly one element.

Let us consider an example to clarify the above concepts.

Example 3.1. Consider the program

$$S \equiv a[0] := 1;\ a[1] := 0;\ \textbf{while } a[x] \neq 0 \textbf{ do } x := x+1 \textbf{ od}$$

and let σ be a proper state in which x is 0.

According to the Determinism Lemma 3.1 there is exactly one computation of S starting in σ. It has the following form, where σ' stands for $\sigma[a[0] := 1][a[1] := 0]$, which is the iterated update of σ:

$$< S, \sigma >$$
$$\rightarrow\ < a[1] := 0;\ \textbf{while } a[x] \neq 0 \textbf{ do } x := x+1 \textbf{ od}, \sigma[a[0] := 1] >$$
$$\rightarrow\ < \textbf{while } a[x] \neq 0 \textbf{ do } x := x+1 \textbf{ od}, \sigma' >$$
$$\rightarrow\ < x := x+1;\ \textbf{while } a[x] \neq 0 \textbf{ do } x := x+1 \textbf{ od}, \sigma' >$$
$$\rightarrow\ < \textbf{while } a[x] \neq 0 \textbf{ do } x := x+1 \textbf{ od}, \sigma'[x := 1] >$$
$$\rightarrow\ < E, \sigma'[x := 1] > .$$

Thus S when activated in σ terminates in five steps. We have

$$\mathcal{M}[\![S]\!](\sigma) = \mathcal{M}_{tot}[\![S]\!](\sigma) = \{\sigma'[x := 1]\}.$$

Now let τ be a state in which x is 2 and for $i = 2, 3, \ldots, a[i]$ is 1. The computation of S starting in τ has the following form where τ' stands for $\tau[a[0] := 1][a[1] := 0]$:

$$< S, \tau >$$
$$\rightarrow \; < a[1] := 0; \; \textbf{while } a[x] \neq 0 \textbf{ do } x := x+1 \textbf{ od}, \tau[a[0] := 1] >$$
$$\rightarrow \; < \textbf{while } a[x] \neq 0 \textbf{ do } x := x+1 \textbf{ od}, \tau' >$$
$$\rightarrow \; < x := x+1; \; \textbf{while } a[x] \neq 0 \textbf{ do } x := x+1 \textbf{ od}, \tau' >$$
$$\rightarrow \; < \textbf{while } a[x] \neq 0 \textbf{ do } x := x+1 \textbf{ od}, \tau'[x := \tau(x) + 1] >$$

$$\dots$$

$$\rightarrow \; < \textbf{while } a[x] \neq 0 \textbf{ do } x := x+1 \textbf{ od}, \tau'[x := \tau(x) + k] >$$

$$\dots$$

Thus S can diverge from τ. We have $\mathcal{M}[\![S]\!](\tau) = \emptyset$ and $\mathcal{M}_{tot}[\![S]\!](\tau) = \{\bot\}$.

$\square$

This example shows that the transition relation $\rightarrow$ indeed formalizes the intuitive idea of a computation.

Properties of Semantics

The semantics $\mathcal{M}$ and $\mathcal{M}_{tot}$ satisfy several simple properties that we use in the sequel. Let Ω be a **while** program such that for all proper states σ, $\mathcal{M}[\![\Omega]\!](\sigma) = \emptyset$; for example, $\Omega \equiv \textbf{while true do } skip \textbf{ od}$. Define by induction on $k \geq 0$ the following sequence of **while** programs:

$$
\begin{aligned}
(\textbf{while } B \textbf{ do } S \textbf{ od})^0 \quad &= \Omega, \\
(\textbf{while } B \textbf{ do } S \textbf{ od})^{k+1} &= \textbf{if } B \textbf{ then } S; \; (\textbf{while } B \textbf{ do } S \textbf{ od})^k \\
&\qquad\quad \textbf{else } skip \textbf{ fi}.
\end{aligned}
$$

In the following let $\mathcal{N}$ stand for $\mathcal{M}$ or $\mathcal{M}_{tot}$. We extend $\mathcal{N}$ to deal with the error state $\bot$ by

$$\mathcal{M}[\![S]\!](\bot) = \emptyset \text{ and } \mathcal{M}_{tot}[\![S]\!](\bot) = \{\bot\}$$

and to deal with sets of states $X \subseteq \Sigma \cup \{\bot\}$ by

$$\mathcal{N}[\![S]\!](X) = \bigcup_{\sigma \in X} \mathcal{N}[\![S]\!](\sigma).$$

The following lemmata collect the properties of $\mathcal{M}$ and $\mathcal{M}_{tot}$ we need.

Lemma 3.3. (Input/Output)

(i) $\mathcal{N}[\![S]\!]$ is monotonic; that is, $X \subseteq Y \subseteq \Sigma \cup \{\bot\}$ implies $\mathcal{N}[\![S]\!](X) \subseteq \mathcal{N}[\![S]\!](Y)$.

(ii) $\mathcal{N}[\![S_1; \; S_2]\!](X) = \mathcal{N}[\![S_2]\!](\mathcal{N}[\![S_1]\!](X))$.

(iii) $\mathcal{N}[\![(S_1;\ S_2);\ S_3]\!](X) = \mathcal{N}[\![S_1;\ (S_2;\ S_3)]\!](X)$.

(iv) $\mathcal{N}[\![\textbf{if } B \textbf{ then } S_1 \textbf{ else } S_2 \textbf{ fi}]\!](X) =$
$\mathcal{N}[\![S_1]\!](X \cap [\![B]\!]) \cup \mathcal{N}[\![S_2]\!](X \cap [\![\neg B]\!]) \cup \{\bot \mid \bot \in X \text{ and } \mathcal{N} = \mathcal{M}_{tot}\}$.

(v) $\mathcal{M}[\![\textbf{while } B \textbf{ do } S \textbf{ od}]\!] = \bigcup_{k=0}^{\infty} \mathcal{M}[\![(\textbf{while } B \textbf{ do } S \textbf{ od})^k]\!]$.

Proof. See Exercise 3.1. ☐

Clause (iii) of the above lemma states that two possible parsings of an ambiguous statement $S_1;\ S_2;\ S_3$ yield programs with the same semantics. This justifies our previous remark in Section 3.1 that the sequential composition is associative.

Note that clause (v) fails for the case of $\mathcal{M}_{tot}$ semantics. The reason is that for all proper states σ we have $\mathcal{M}_{tot}[\![\Omega]\!](\sigma) = \{\bot\}$ and consequently $\bot \in \bigcup_{k=0}^{\infty} \mathcal{M}_{tot}[\![(\textbf{while } B \textbf{ do } S \textbf{ od})^k]\!](\sigma)$ holds for every program **while** B **do** S **od**. On the other hand for some programs **while** B **do** S **od** and proper states σ we have $\bot \notin \mathcal{M}_{tot}[\![\textbf{while } B \textbf{ do } S \textbf{ od}]\!](\sigma)$.

Lemma 3.4. (Change and Access)

(i) For all proper states σ and τ, $\tau \in \mathcal{N}[\![S]\!](\sigma)$ implies

$$\tau[Var - change(S)] = \sigma[Var - change(S)].$$

(ii) For all proper states σ and τ, $\sigma[var(S)] = \tau[var(S)]$ implies

$$\mathcal{N}[\![S]\!](\sigma) = \mathcal{N}[\![S]\!](\tau) \text{ mod } Var - var(S).$$

Proof. See Exercise 3.2. ☐

Recall that Var stands for the set of all simple and array variables. Part (i) of the Change and Access Lemma states that every program S changes at most the variables in $change(S)$, while part (ii) states that every program S accesses at most the variables in $var(S)$. This explains the name of this lemma. It is used often in the sequel.

3.3 Verification

Informally, a **while** program is correct if it satisfies the intended input/output relation. Program correctness is expressed by so-called *correctness formulas*. These are statements of the form

$$\{p\}\ S\ \{q\}$$

where S is a **while** program and p and q are assertions. The assertion p is the *precondition* of the correctness formula and q is the *postcondition*. The precondition describes the set of initial or input states in which the program S is started and the postcondition describes the set of desirable final or output states.

More precisely, we are interested here in two interpretations: a correctness formula $\{p\}\ S\ \{q\}$ is true in the sense of partial correctness if every terminating computation of S that starts in a state satisfying p terminates in a state satisfying q. And $\{p\}\ S\ \{q\}$ is true in the sense of total correctness if every computation of S that starts in a state satisfying p terminates and its final state satisfies q. Thus in the case of partial correctness, diverging computations of S are not taken into account.

Using the semantics $\mathcal{M}$ and $\mathcal{M}_{tot}$, we formalize these interpretations uniformly as set theoretic inclusions.

Definition 3.3.

(i) We say that the correctness formula $\{p\}\ S\ \{q\}$ is true in the sense of *partial correctness*, and write $\models \{p\}\ S\ \{q\}$, if

$$\mathcal{M}[\![S]\!]([\![p]\!]) \subseteq [\![q]\!].$$

(ii) We say that the correctness formula $\{p\}\ S\ \{q\}$ is true in the sense of *total correctness*, and write $\models_{tot} \{p\}\ S\ \{q\}$, if

$$\mathcal{M}_{tot}[\![S]\!]([\![p]\!]) \subseteq [\![q]\!]. \qquad \square$$

In other words, since by definition $\perp \notin [\![q]\!]$, part (ii) indeed formalizes the above intuition about total correctness. Since for all proper states σ $\mathcal{M}[\![S]\!](\sigma) \subseteq \mathcal{M}_{tot}[\![S]\!](\sigma)$ holds, $\models_{tot} \{p\}\ S\ \{q\}$ implies $\models \{p\}\ S\ \{q\}$.

The uniform pattern of definitions in (i) and (ii) is followed for all semantics defined in the book. We can say that each semantics fixes the corresponding correctness notion in a standard manner.

Example 3.2. Consider once more the program

$$S \equiv a[0] := 1;\ a[1] := 0;\ \textbf{while}\ a[x] \neq 0\ \textbf{do}\ x := x + 1\ \textbf{od}$$

from Example 3.1. The two computations of S exhibited there show that the correctness formulas

$$\{x = 0\}\ S\ \{a[0] = 1 \wedge a[1] = 0\}$$

and

$$\{x = 0\}\ S\ \{x = 1 \wedge a[x] = 0\}$$

are true in the sense of total correctness, while

$$\{x = 2\}\ S\ \{\textbf{true}\}$$

is false. Indeed, the state τ of Example 3.1 satisfies the precondition $x = 2$ but $\mathcal{M}_{tot}[\![S]\!](\tau) = \{\perp\}$.

Clearly, all three formulas are true in the sense of partial correctness. Also

$$\{x = 2 \land \forall i \geq 2 : a[i] = 1\} \ S \ \{\textbf{false}\}$$

is true in the sense of partial correctness. This correctness formula states that every computation of S that begins in a state which satisfies $x = 2 \land \forall i \geq 2 : a[i] = 1$, diverges. Namely, if there existed a finite computation, its final state would satisfy **false** which is impossible.   □

Partial Correctness

As we have seen in Examples 3.1 and 3.2, reasoning about correctness formulas in terms of semantics is not very convenient. A much more promising approach is to reason directly on the level of correctness formulas. Following Hoare [1969], we now introduce a proof system, called *PW*, allowing us to prove *partial* correctness of **while** programs in a *syntax-directed* manner, by induction on the program syntax.

PROOF SYSTEM *PW* :
This system consists of the group
of axioms and rules 1–6.

AXIOM 1: SKIP

$$\{p\} \ skip \ \{p\}$$

AXIOM 2: ASSIGNMENT

$$\{p[u := t]\} \ u := t \ \{p\}$$

RULE 3: COMPOSITION

$$\frac{\{p\} \ S_1 \ \{r\}, \{r\} \ S_2 \ \{q\}}{\{p\} \ S_1; \ S_2 \ \{q\}}$$

RULE 4: CONDITIONAL

$$\frac{\{p \land B\} \ S_1 \ \{q\}, \{p \land \neg B\} \ S_2 \ \{q\}}{\{p\} \ \textbf{if} \ B \ \textbf{then} \ S_1 \ \textbf{else} \ S_2 \ \textbf{fi} \ \{q\}}$$

RULE 5: LOOP

$$\frac{\{p \land B\} \ S \ \{p\}}{\{p\} \ \textbf{while} \ B \ \textbf{do} \ S \ \textbf{od} \ \{p \land \neg B\}}$$

RULE 6: CONSEQUENCE

$$\frac{p \to p_1, \{p_1\}\ S\ \{q_1\}, q_1 \to q}{\{p\}\ S\ \{q\}}.$$

We augment each proof system for correctness formulas, in particular PW, by the set of all true assertions. These assertions are used as premises in the consequence rule which is part of all proof systems considered in this book. Using the notation of Section 2.4 we write $\vdash_{PD} \{p\}\ S\ \{q\}$ for provability of the correctness formula $\{p\}\ S\ \{q\}$ in the augmented system PW.

Let us now discuss the above axioms and proof rules. The *skip* axiom should be obvious. On the other hand, the first reaction to the assignment axiom is usually astonishment. The axiom encourages reading the assignment "backwards"; that is, we start from a given postcondition p and determine the corresponding precondition $p[u := t]$ by *backward substitution*. We soon illustrate the use of this axiom by means of an example.

Easy to understand are the composition rule where we have to find an appropriate intermediate assertion r and the conditional rule which formalizes a case distinction according to the truth value of B.

Less apparent is the loop rule. This rule states that if an assertion p is preserved with each iteration of the loop **while** B **do** S **od**, then p is true upon termination of this loop. Therefore p is called a *loop invariant*.

The consequence rule represents the interface between program verification and logical formulas. It allows us to strengthen the preconditions and weaken the postconditions of correctness formulas and enables the application of other proof rules. In particular, the consequence rule allows us to replace a precondition or a postcondition by an equivalent assertion.

Using the proof system PW we can prove the input/output behavior of composite programs from the input/output behavior of their subprograms. For example, using the composition rule we can deduce correctness formulas about programs of the form $S_1; S_2$ from the correctness formulas about S_1 and S_2. Proof systems with this property are called *compositional*.

Example 3.3.

(i) Consider the program

$$S \equiv x := x + 1;\ y := y + 1.$$

We prove in the system PW the correctness formula

$$\{x = y\}\ S\ \{x = y\}.$$

To this end we apply the assignment axiom twice. We start with the last assignment. By backward substitution we obtain

$$(x = y)[y := y + 1] \equiv x = y + 1;$$

so by the assignment axiom

$$\{x = y + 1\}\; y := y + 1\; \{x = y\}.$$

By a second backward substitution we obtain

$$(x = y + 1)[x := x + 1] \equiv x + 1 = y + 1;$$

so by the assignment axiom

$$\{x + 1 = y + 1\}\; x := x + 1\; \{x = y + 1\}.$$

Combining the above two correctness formulas by the composition rule yields

$$\{x + 1 = y + 1\}\; x := x + 1;\; y := y + 1\; \{x = y\},$$

from which the desired conclusion follows by the consequence rule, since

$$x = y \rightarrow x + 1 = y + 1.$$

(ii) Consider now the more complicated program

$$S \equiv x := 1;\; a[1] := 2;\; a[x] := x$$

using subscripted variables. We prove that after its execution $a[1] = 1$ holds; that is, we prove in the system PW the correctness formula

$$\{\mathbf{true}\}\; S\; \{a[1] = 1\}.$$

To this end we repeatedly apply the assignment axiom while proceeding "backwards." Hence, we start with the last assignment:

$$\{(a[1] = 1)[a[x] := x]\}\; a[x] := x\; \{a[1] = 1\}.$$

By the Identical Substitution Lemma 2.2 we have $1[a[x] := x] \equiv 1$. Thus the substitution in the above correctness formula can be evaluated as follows:

$$\{\mathbf{if}\; 1 = x\; \mathbf{then}\; x\; \mathbf{else}\; a[1]\; \mathbf{fi} = 1\}\; a[x] := x\; \{a[1] = 1\}.$$

For the precondition we have the equivalence

$$\mathbf{if}\; 1 = x\; \mathbf{then}\; x\; \mathbf{else}\; a[1]\; \mathbf{fi} = 1 \leftrightarrow (x = 1 \lor a[1] = 1).$$

Since

$$x = 1 \rightarrow (x = 1 \lor a[1] = 1),$$

we can strengthen the precondition by the rule of consequence as follows:

$$\{x = 1\}\; a[x] := x\; \{a[1] = 1\}.$$

Next, consider the second assignment with the postcondition being the precondition of the above correctness formula. We have

$$\{(x = 1)[a[1] := 2]\} \; a[1] := 2 \; \{x = 1\},$$

which by the Identical Substitution Lemma 2.2 gives

$$\{x = 1\} \; a[1] := 2 \; \{x = 1\}.$$

Finally, we consider the first assignment:

$$\{\textbf{true}\} \; x := 1 \; \{x = 1\}.$$

Combining the final correctness formulas obtained for each assignment by two applications of the composition rule, we get the desired result.   □

Let us see now how the loop rule rule can be used. We choose here as an example the first program (written in a textual form) that was formally verified. This historic event was duly documented in Hoare [1969].

Example 3.4. Consider the following program DIV for computing the quotient and remainder of two natural numbers x and y:

$$DIV \equiv quo := 0; \; rem := x; \; S_0,$$

where

$$S_0 \equiv \textbf{while} \; rem \geq y \; \textbf{do} \; rem := rem - y; \; quo := quo + 1 \; \textbf{od}.$$

We wish to show that

> if x, y are nonnegative integers and DIV terminates,
> then quo is the integer quotient and rem is the   (3.2)
> remainder of x divided by y.

Thus, using correctness formulas, we wish to show

$$\models \{x \geq 0 \wedge y \geq 0\} \; DIV \; \{quo \cdot y + rem = x \wedge 0 \leq rem < y\}. \qquad (3.3)$$

Note that (3.2) and (3.3) agree because DIV does not change the variables x and y. Programs that may change x and y can trivially achieve (3.3) without satisfying (3.2). An example is the program

$$x := 0; \; y := 1; \; quo := 0; \; rem := 0.$$

To show (3.3), we prove the correctness formula

$$\{x \geq 0 \wedge y \geq 0\} \; DIV \; \{quo \cdot y + rem = x \wedge 0 \leq rem < y\} \qquad (3.4)$$

in the proof system PW. To this end we choose the assertion

$$p \equiv quo \cdot y + rem = x \land rem \geq 0$$

as the loop invariant of S_0. It is obtained from the postcondition of (3.4) by dropping the conjunct $rem < y$. Intuitively, p describes the relation between the variables of DIV which holds each time the control is in front of the loop S_0.

We now prove the following three facts:

$$\{x \geq 0 \land y \geq 0\} \; quo := 0; \; rem := x \; \{p\}, \qquad (3.5)$$

that is, the program $quo := 0; \; rem := x$ establishes p;

$$\{p \land rem \geq y\} \; rem := rem - y; \; quo := quo + 1 \; \{p\}, \qquad (3.6)$$

that is, p is indeed a loop invariant of S_0;

$$p \land \neg(rem \geq y) \rightarrow quo \cdot y + rem = x \land 0 \leq rem < y, \qquad (3.7)$$

that is, upon exit of the loop S_0, p implies the desired assertion.

Observe first that we can prove (3.4) from (3.5), (3.6) and (3.7). Indeed, (3.6) implies, by the loop rule,

$$\{p\} \; S_0 \; \{p \land \neg(rem \geq y)\}.$$

This, together with (3.5), implies, by the composition rule,

$$\{x \geq 0 \land y \geq 0\} \; DIV \; \{p \land \neg(rem \geq y)\}.$$

Now, by (3.7), (3.4) holds by an application of the consequence rule.

Thus, let us prove now (3.5), (3.6) and (3.7).

Re: (3.5). We have

$$\{quo \cdot y + x = x \land x \geq 0\} \; rem := x \; \{p\}$$

by the assignment axiom. Once more by the assignment axiom

$$\{0 \cdot y + x = x \land x \geq 0\} \; quo := 0 \; \{quo \cdot y + x = x \land x \geq 0\};$$

so by the composition rule

$$\{0 \cdot y + x = x \land x \geq 0\} \; quo := 0; \; rem := x \; \{p\}.$$

On the other hand,

$$x \geq 0 \land y \geq 0 \rightarrow 0 \cdot y + x = x \land x \geq 0;$$

so (3.5) holds by the consequence rule.

Re: (3.6). We have

$$\{(quo + 1) \cdot y + rem = x \wedge rem \geq 0\} \; quo := quo + 1 \; \{p\}$$

by the assignment axiom. Once more by the assignment axiom

$$\{(quo + 1) \cdot y + (rem - y) = x \wedge rem - y \geq 0\}$$
$$rem := rem - y$$
$$\{(quo + 1) \cdot y + rem = x \wedge rem \geq 0\};$$

so by the composition rule

$$\{(quo + 1) \cdot y + (rem - y) = x \wedge rem - y \geq 0\}$$
$$rem := rem - y; \; quo := quo + 1$$
$$\{p\}.$$

On the other hand,

$$p \wedge rem \geq y \rightarrow (quo + 1) \cdot y + (rem - y) = x \wedge rem - y \geq 0;$$

so (3.6) holds by the consequence rule.

Re: (3.7). Clear.

This completes the proof of (3.4).   □

The only step in the above proof that required some creativity was finding the appropriate loop invariant. The remaining steps were straightforward applications of the corresponding axioms and proof rules. The form of the assignment axiom makes it easier to deduce a precondition from a postcondition than the other way around; so the proofs of (3.5) and (3.6) proceeded "backwards." Finally, we did not provide any formal proof of the implications used as premises of the consequence rule. Formal proofs of such assertions are always omitted; we simply rely on an intuitive understanding of their truth.

Total Correctness

It is important to note that the proof system PW does not allow us to establish termination of programs. Thus PW is not appropriate for proofs of total correctness. Even though we proved in Example 3.4 the correctness formula (3.4), we cannot infer from this fact that program DIV studied there terminates. In fact, DIV diverges when started in a state in which y is 0.

Clearly, the only proof rule of PW that introduces the possibility of non-termination is the loop rule, so to deal with total correctness this rule must be strengthened.

We now introduce the following refinement of the loop rule:

RULE 7: LOOP II

$$\{p \wedge B\} \ S \ \{p\},$$
$$\{p \wedge B \wedge t = z\} \ S \ \{t < z\},$$
$$p \ \rightarrow t \geq 0$$

$$\overline{\{p\} \ \textbf{while} \ B \ \textbf{do} \ S \ \textbf{od} \ \{p \wedge \neg B\}}$$

where t is an integer expression and z is an integer variable that does not appear in p, B, t or S.

The two additional premises of the rule guarantee termination of the loop. In the second premise, the purpose of z is to retain the initial value of z. Since z does not appear in S, it is not changed by S and upon termination of S z indeed holds the initial value of t. By the second premise, t is decreased with each iteration and by the third premise t is nonnegative if another iteration can be performed. Thus no infinite computation is possible. Expression t is called a *bound function* of the loop **while** B **do** S **od**.

To prove total correctness of **while** programs we use the following proof system TW:

PROOF SYSTEM TW:
This system consists of the group
of axioms and rules 1–4, 6, 7.

Thus TW is obtained from PW by replacing the loop rule (rule 5) by the loop II rule (rule 7).

To see an application of the loop II rule, let us reconsider the program DIV studied in Example 3.4.

Example 3.5. We now wish to show that

if x is nonnegative and y is a positive integer, then
S terminates with quo being the integer quotient
and rem being the remainder of x divided by y. (3.8)

In other words, we wish to show

$$\models_{tot} \{x \geq 0 \wedge y > 0\} \ DIV \ \{quo \cdot y + rem = x \wedge 0 \leq rem < y\}. \quad (3.9)$$

To show (3.9), we prove the correctness formula

$$\{x \geq 0 \wedge y > 0\} \ DIV \ \{quo \cdot y + rem = x \wedge 0 \leq rem < y\} \quad (3.10)$$

in the proof system *TW*. Note that (3.10) differs from correctness formula
(3.4) in Example 3.4 by requiring that initially $y > 0$. We prove (3.10) by a
modification of the proof of (3.4). Let

$$p' \equiv p \wedge y > 0,$$

be the loop invariant where, as in Example 3.4,

$$p \equiv quo \cdot y + rem = x \wedge rem \geq 0,$$

and let

$$t \equiv rem$$

be the bound function. As in the proof given in Example 3.4, to prove (3.10)
in the sense of total correctness it is sufficient to establish the following facts:

$$\{x \geq 0 \wedge y > 0\} \ quo := 0; \ rem := x \ \{p'\}, \tag{3.11}$$

$$\{p' \wedge rem \geq y\} \ rem := rem - y; \ quo := quo + 1 \ \{p'\}, \tag{3.12}$$

$$\{p' \wedge rem \geq y \wedge rem = z\}$$
$$rem := rem - y; \ quo := quo + 1 \tag{3.13}$$
$$\{rem < z\}.$$

$$p' \rightarrow rem \geq 0, \tag{3.14}$$

$$p' \wedge \neg(rem \geq y) \rightarrow quo \cdot y + rem = x \wedge 0 \leq rem < y. \tag{3.15}$$

By the loop II rule, (3.12), (3.13) and (3.14) imply the correctness formula
$\{p'\} \ S_0 \ \{p' \wedge \neg(rem \geq y)\}$, and the rest of the argument is the same as in
Example 3.4. Proofs of (3.11), (3.12) and (3.15) are analogous to the proofs
of (3.5), (3.6) and (3.7) in Example 3.4.

To prove (3.13) observe that by the assignment axiom

$$\{rem < z\} \ quo := quo + 1 \ \{rem < z\}$$

and

$$\{(rem - y) < z\} \ rem := rem - y \ \{rem < z\}.$$

But

$$p \wedge y > 0 \wedge rem \geq y \wedge rem = z \rightarrow (rem - y) < z,$$

so (3.13) holds by the consequence rule.

Finally, (3.14) clearly holds.

This concludes the proof.   □

Decomposition

Proof system *TW* with loop rule II allows us to establish total correctness of **while** programs directly. However, sometimes it is more convenient to decompose the proof of total correctness into two separate proofs, one of partial correctness and one of termination. More specifically, given a correctness formula $\{p\}\ S\ \{q\}$, we first establish its partial correctness, using proof system *PW*. Then, to show termination it suffices to prove the simpler correctness formula $\{p\}\ S\ \{\textbf{true}\}$ using proof system *TW*.

These two different proofs can be combined into one using the following general proof rule for total correctness:

RULE A1: DECOMPOSITION

$$\frac{\begin{array}{l}\vdash_p \{p\}\ S\ \{q\}, \\ \vdash_t \{p\}\ S\ \{\textbf{true}\}\end{array}}{\{p\}\ S\ \{q\}}$$

where the provability signs $\vdash_p$ and $\vdash_t$ refer to proof systems for partial and total correctness for the considered program S, respectively.

In this chapter we refer to the proof systems *PW* and *TW* for **while** programs. However, the decomposition rule will also be used for other classes of programs. We refrain from presenting a simpler correctness proof of Example 3.5 using this decomposition rule until Section 3.4, where we introduce the concept of a proof outline.

Soundness

We have just established:

$$\vdash_{PW} \{x \geq 0 \wedge y \geq 0\}\ DIV\ \{quo \cdot y + rem = x \wedge 0 \leq rem < y\}$$

and

$$\vdash_{TW} \{x \geq 0 \wedge y > 0\}\ DIV\ \{quo \cdot y + rem = x \wedge 0 \leq rem < y\}.$$

However, our goal was to show

$$\models \{x \geq 0 \wedge y \geq 0\}\ DIV\ \{quo \cdot y + rem = x \wedge 0 \leq rem < y\}$$

and

$$\models_{tot} \{x \geq 0 \wedge y > 0\}\ DIV\ \{quo \cdot y + rem = x \wedge 0 \leq rem < y\}.$$

This goal is reached if we can show that provability of a correctness formula in the proof systems PW and TW implies its truth. In the terminology of logic this property is called *soundness* of a proof system.

Definition 3.4. Let G be a proof system allowing us to prove correctness formulas about programs in a certain class C. We say that G is *sound for partial correctness of programs in C* if for all correctness formulas $\{p\}\ S\ \{q\}$ about programs in C

$$\vdash_G \{p\}\ S\ \{q\} \text{ implies } \models \{p\}\ S\ \{q\},$$

and G is *sound for total correctness of programs in C* if for all correctness formulas $\{p\}\ S\ \{q\}$ about programs in C

$$\vdash_G \{p\}\ S\ \{q\} \text{ implies } \models_{tot} \{p\}\ S\ \{q\}.$$

When the class of programs C is clear from the context, we omit the reference to it.   □

We now wish to establish the following result.

Theorem 3.1. (Soundness of PW and TW)

   (i) The proof system PW is sound for partial correctness of **while** *programs.*
   (ii) The proof system TW is sound for total correctness of **while** *programs.*

To prove this theorem it is sufficient to reason about each axiom and proof rule of PW and TW separately. For each axiom we show that it is true and for each proof rule we show that it is sound, that is, that the truth of its premises implies the truth of its conclusion. This motivates the following definition.

Definition 3.5. A proof rule of the form

$$\frac{\varphi_1, \ldots, \varphi_k}{\varphi_{k+1}}$$

is called *sound for partial (total) correctness* (of programs in a class C) if the truth of $\varphi_1, \ldots, \varphi_k$ in the sense of partial (total) correctness implies the truth of φ_{k+1} in the sense of partial (total) correctness.

If some of the formulas φ_i are assertions then we identify their truth in the sense of partial (total) correctness with the truth in the usual sense (see Section 2.6).   □

We now come to the proof of the Soundness Theorem 3.1.

Proof. Due to the form of the proof systems PW and TW, it is sufficient to prove that all axioms of PW (TW) are true in the sense of partial (total) correctness and that all proof rules of PW (TW) are sound for partial (total) correctness. Then the result follows by the induction on the length of proofs.

We consider all axioms and proof rules in turn.

SKIP
Clearly $\mathcal{N}[\![skip]\!]([\![p]\!]) = [\![p]\!]$ for any assertion p, so the skip axiom is true in the sense of partial (total) correctness.

ASSIGNMENT
Let p be an assertion. By the Substitution Lemma 2.4 and transition axiom (ii), whenever $\mathcal{N}[\![u := t]\!](\sigma) = \{\tau\}$, then

$$\sigma \models p[u := t] \quad \text{iff} \quad \tau \models p.$$

This implies $\mathcal{N}[\![u := t]\!]([\![p[u := t]\!]\!]) \subseteq [\![p]\!]$, so the assignment axiom is true in the sense of partial (total) correctness.

COMPOSITION
Suppose that
$$\mathcal{N}[\![S_1]\!]([\![p]\!]) \subseteq [\![r]\!]$$
and
$$\mathcal{N}[\![S_2]\!]([\![r]\!]) \subseteq [\![q]\!].$$
Then by the monotonicity of $\mathcal{N}[\![S_2]\!]$ (the Input/Output Lemma 3.3(i))

$$\mathcal{N}[\![S_2]\!](\mathcal{N}[\![S_1]\!]([\![p]\!])) \subseteq \mathcal{N}[\![S_2]\!]([\![r]\!]) \subseteq [\![q]\!].$$

But by the Input/Output Lemma 3.3(ii)

$$\mathcal{N}[\![S_1;\ S_2]\!]([\![p]\!]) = \mathcal{N}[\![S_2]\!](\mathcal{N}[\![S_1]\!]([\![p]\!]));$$

so
$$\mathcal{N}[\![S_1;\ S_2]\!]([\![p]\!]) \subseteq [\![q]\!].$$
Thus the composition rule is sound for partial (total) correctness.

CONDITIONAL
Suppose that
$$\mathcal{N}[\![S_1]\!]([\![p \wedge B]\!]) \subseteq [\![q]\!]$$
and
$$\mathcal{N}[\![S_2]\!]([\![p \wedge \neg B]\!]) \subseteq [\![q]\!].$$
By the Input/Output Lemma 3.3(iv)

$$\mathcal{N}[\![\text{if } B \text{ then } S_1 \text{ else } S_2 \text{ fi}]\!]([\![p]\!])$$
$$= \mathcal{N}[\![S_1]\!]([\![p \wedge B]\!]) \cup \mathcal{N}[\![S_2]\!]([\![p \wedge \neg B]\!]);$$

so

$$\mathcal{N}[\![\text{if } B \text{ then } S_1 \text{ else } S_2 \text{ fi}]\!]([\![p]\!]) \subseteq [\![q]\!].$$

Thus the conditional rule is sound for partial (total) correctness.

LOOP
Suppose now that for some assertion p

$$\mathcal{M}[\![S]\!]([\![p \wedge B]\!]) \subseteq [\![p]\!]. \tag{3.16}$$

We prove by induction that for all $k \geq 0$

$$\mathcal{M}[\![(\text{while } B \text{ do } S \text{ od})^k]\!]([\![p]\!]) \subseteq [\![p \wedge \neg B]\!].$$

The case $k = 0$ is clear. Suppose the claim holds for some $k > 0$. Then

$$\mathcal{M}[\![(\text{while } B \text{ do } S \text{ od})^{k+1}]\!]([\![p]\!])$$
$= \quad \{\text{definition of } (\text{while } B \text{ do } S \text{ od})^{k+1}\}$
$\quad \mathcal{M}[\![\text{if } B \text{ then } S; (\text{while } B \text{ do } S \text{ od})^k \text{ else } skip \text{ fi}]\!]([\![p]\!])$
$= \quad \{\text{Input/Output Lemma 3.3(iv)}\}$
$\quad \mathcal{M}[\![S; (\text{while } B \text{ do } S \text{ od})^k]\!]([\![p \wedge B]\!]) \cup \mathcal{M}[\![skip]\!]([\![p \wedge \neg B]\!])$
$= \quad \{\text{Input/Output Lemma 3.3(ii) and semantics of } skip\}$
$\quad \mathcal{M}[\![(\text{while } B \text{ do } S \text{ od})^k]\!](\mathcal{M}[\![S]\!]([\![p \wedge B]\!])) \cup [\![p \wedge \neg B]\!]$
$\subseteq \quad \{(3.16) \text{ and monotonicity of } \mathcal{M}[\![(\text{while } B \text{ do } S \text{ od})^k]\!]\}$
$\quad \mathcal{M}[\![(\text{while } B \text{ do } S \text{ od})^k]\!]([\![p]\!]) \cup [\![p \wedge \neg B]\!]$
$\subseteq \quad \{\text{induction hypothesis}\}$
$\quad [\![p \wedge \neg B]\!].$

This proves the induction step. Thus

$$\bigcup_{k=0}^{\infty} \mathcal{M}[\![(\text{while } B \text{ do } S \text{ od})^k]\!]([\![p]\!]) \subseteq [\![p \wedge \neg B]\!].$$

But by the Input/Output Lemma 3.3(v)

$$\mathcal{M}[\![\text{while } B \text{ do } S \text{ od}]\!] = \bigcup_{k=0}^{\infty} \mathcal{M}[\![(\text{while } B \text{ do } S \text{ od})^k]\!];$$

so

$$\mathcal{M}[\![\text{while } B \text{ do } S \text{ od}]\!]([\![p]\!]) \subseteq [\![p \wedge \neg B]\!].$$

Thus the loop rule is sound for partial correctness.

CONSEQUENCE
Suppose that
$$p \rightarrow p_1, \ \mathcal{N}[\![S]\!]([\![p_1]\!]) \subseteq [\![q_1]\!], \text{ and } q_1 \rightarrow q.$$

Then, by the Meaning of Assertion Lemma 2.1, the inclusions $[\![p]\!] \subseteq [\![p_1]\!]$ and $[\![q_1]\!] \subseteq [\![q]\!]$ hold; so by the monotonicity of $\mathcal{N}[\![S]\!]$,

$$\mathcal{N}[\![S]\!]([\![p]\!]) \subseteq \mathcal{N}[\![S]\!]([\![p_1]\!]) \subseteq [\![q_1]\!] \subseteq [\![q]\!].$$

Thus the consequence rule is sound for partial (total) correctness.

LOOP II
Suppose that
$$\mathcal{M}_{tot}[\![S]\!]([\![p \wedge B]\!]) \subseteq [\![p]\!], \tag{3.17}$$

$$\mathcal{M}_{tot}[\![S]\!]([\![p \wedge B \wedge t = z]\!]) \subseteq [\![t < z]\!], \tag{3.18}$$

and

$$p \rightarrow t \geq 0, \tag{3.19}$$

where z is an integer variable that does not occur in p, B, t or S. We show then that

$$\bot \notin \mathcal{M}_{tot}[\![T]\!]([\![p]\!]), \tag{3.20}$$

where $T \equiv \textbf{while } B \textbf{ do } S \textbf{ od}$.

Suppose otherwise. Then there exists an infinite computation of T starting in a state σ such that $\sigma \models p$. By (3.19) $\sigma \models t \geq 0$, so $\sigma(t) \geq 0$. Choose now an infinite computation ξ of T starting in a state σ such that $\sigma \models p$ for which this value $\sigma(t)$ is minimal. Since ξ is infinite, $\sigma \models B$; so $\sigma \models p \wedge B$.

Let $\tau = \sigma[z := \sigma(t)]$. Thus τ agrees with σ on all variables except z to which it assigns the value $\sigma(t)$. Then

$$\tau(t)$$
$$= \quad \{\text{assumption about } z, \text{ Coincidence Lemma 2.3(i)}\}$$
$$\sigma(t)$$
$$= \quad \{\text{definition of } \tau\}$$
$$\tau(z);$$

so $\tau \models t = z$. Moreover, also by the assumption about z, $\tau \models p \wedge B$, since $\sigma \models p \wedge B$. Thus

$$\tau \models p \wedge B \wedge t = z. \tag{3.21}$$

By the monotonicity of $\mathcal{M}_{tot}$, (3.17) and (3.18) imply

$$\mathcal{M}_{tot}[\![S]\!][\![p \wedge B \wedge t = z]\!] \subseteq [\![p \wedge t < z]\!],$$

since $[\![p \wedge B \wedge t = z]\!] \subseteq [\![p \wedge B]\!]$. Thus by (3.21) for some state σ_1

$$< S, \tau > \to^* < E, \sigma_1 > \tag{3.22}$$

and

$$\sigma_1 \models p \wedge t < z. \tag{3.23}$$

Also, by (3.21) and the definition of semantics $< T, \tau > \to < S; T, \tau >$; so by (3.22) $< T, \tau > \to^* < T, \sigma_1 >$. But by the choice of τ and the Change and Access Lemma 3.4(ii) T diverges from τ; so by the Determinism Lemma 3.1 it also diverges from σ_1.

Moreover,

$$\sigma_1(t)$$
$$< \quad \{(3.23)\}$$
$$\sigma_1(z)$$
$$= \quad \{(3.22), \text{Change and Access Lemma 3.4(i) and}$$
$$\qquad \text{assumption about } z\}$$
$$\tau(z)$$
$$= \quad \{\text{definition of } \tau\}$$
$$\sigma(t).$$

This contradicts the choice of σ and proves (3.20).

Finally, by (3.17) $\mathcal{M}[\![S]\!]([\![p \wedge B]\!]) \subseteq [\![p]\!]$; so by the soundness of the loop rule for partial correctness $\mathcal{M}[\![T]\!]([\![p]\!]) \subseteq [\![p \wedge \neg B]\!]$. But (3.20) means that

$$\mathcal{M}_{tot}[\![T]\!]([\![p]\!]) = \mathcal{M}[\![T]\!]([\![p]\!]);$$

so

$$\mathcal{M}_{tot}[\![T]\!]([\![p]\!]) \subseteq [\![p \wedge \neg B]\!].$$

Thus the loop II rule is sound for total correctness.   □

Our primary goal in this book is to verify programs, that is, to prove the truth of certain correctness formulas. The use of certain proof systems is only a means of achieving this goal. Therefore we often apply proof rules to reason directly about the truth of correctness formulas. This is justified by the corresponding soundness theorems.

Thus, in arguments such as: "by (the truth of) assignment axiom we have

$$\models \{x + 1 = y + 1\} \ x := x + 1 \ \{x = y + 1\}$$

and

$$\models \{x = y + 1\} \ y := y + 1 \ \{x = y\};$$

so by (the soundness of) the composition and consequence rules we obtain

$$\models \{x = y\}\ x := x + 1;\ y := y + 1\ \{x = y\},\text{"}$$

we omit the statements enclosed in brackets.

3.4 Proof Outlines

Formal proofs are tedious to follow. We are not accustomed to following a line of reasoning presented in small formal steps. A better solution consists of a logical organization of the proof with the main steps isolated. The proof can then be seen on a different level.

In the case of correctness proofs of **while** programs, a possible strategy lies in using the fact that they are structured. The proof rules follow the syntax of the programs; so the structure of the program can be used to structure the correctness proof. We can simply present the proof by giving a program with assertions interleaved at appropriate places.

Partial Correctness

Example 3.6. Let us reconsider the integer division program studied in Example 3.4. We present the correctness formulas (3.5), (3.6) and (3.7) in the following form:

$$\{x \geq 0 \land y \geq 0\}$$
$$quo := 0;\ rem := x;$$
$$\{\textbf{inv} : p\}$$
$$\textbf{while } rem \geq y \textbf{ do}$$
$$\qquad \{p \land rem \geq y\}$$
$$\qquad rem := rem - y;\ quo := quo + 1$$
$$\textbf{od}$$
$$\{p \land rem < y\}$$
$$\{quo \cdot y + rem = x \land 0 \leq rem < y\},$$

where

$$p \equiv quo \cdot y + rem = x \land rem \geq 0.$$

The keyword **inv** is used here to label the loop invariant. Two adjacent assertions $\{q_1\}\{q_2\}$ stand for the fact that the implication $q_1 \rightarrow q_2$ is true.

The proofs of (3.5), (3.6) and (3.7) can also be presented in such a form. For example, here is the proof of (3.5):

$$\{x \geq 0 \land y \geq 0\}$$
$$\{0 \cdot y + x = x \land x \geq 0\}$$
$$quo := 0$$
$$\{quo \cdot y + x = x \land x \geq 0\}$$
$$rem := x$$
$$\{p\}. \hspace{8cm} \square$$

This type of proof presentation is simpler to study and analyze than the one we used so far. Introduced in Owicki and Gries [1976a], it is called a *proof outline*. It is formally defined as follows.

Definition 3.6. (Proof Outline: Partial Correctness) Let S^* stand for the program S interspersed, or as we say *annotated*, with assertions, some of them labeled by the keyword **inv**. We define the notion of a *proof outline for partial correctness* inductively by the following formation axioms and rules.

A *formation axiom* φ should be read here as a statement: φ is a proof outline (for partial correctness). A *formation rule*

$$\frac{\varphi_1, \ldots, \varphi_k}{\varphi_{k+1}}$$

should be read as a statement: if $\varphi_1, \ldots, \varphi_k$ are proof outlines, then φ_{k+1} is a proof outline.

(i) $\{p\}$ *skip* $\{p\}$

(ii) $\{p[u := t]\}\ u := t\ \{p\}$

(iii) $\dfrac{\{p\}\ S_1^*\ \{r\}, \{r\}\ S_2^*\ \{q\}}{\{p\}\ S_1^*;\ \{r\}\ S_2^*\ \{q\}}$

(iv) $\dfrac{\{p \land B\}\ S_1^*\ \{q\}, \{p \land \neg B\}\ S_2^*\ \{q\}}{\{p\}\ \textbf{if}\ B\ \textbf{then}\ \{p \land B\}\ S_1^*\ \{q\}\ \textbf{else}\ \{p \land \neg B\}\ S_2^*\ \{q\}\ \textbf{fi}\ \{q\}}$

(v) $\dfrac{\{p \land B\}\ S^*\ \{p\}}{\{\textbf{inv} : p\}\ \textbf{while}\ B\ \textbf{do}\ \{p \land B\}\ S^*\ \{p\}\ \textbf{od}\ \{p \land \neg B\}}$

(vi) $\dfrac{p \rightarrow p_1,\ \{p_1\}\ S^*\ \{q_1\},\ q_1 \rightarrow q}{\{p\}\{p_1\}\ S^*\ \{q_1\}\{q\}}$

(vii) $\dfrac{\{p\}\ S^*\ \{q\}}{\{p\}\ S^{**}\ \{q\}}$

where S^{**} results from S^* by omitting some annotations of the form $\{r\}$. Thus all annotations of the form $\{\textbf{inv} : r\}$ remain.

A proof outline $\{p\}\ S^*\ \{q\}$ for partial correctness is called *standard* if every subprogram T of S is preceded by exactly one assertion in S^*, called $pre(T)$, and there are no other assertions in S^*. $\hspace{3cm} \square$

Thus, in a proof outline, some of the intermediate assertions used in the correctness proof are retained and loop invariants are always retained. Note that every standard proof outline $\{p\}\ S^*\ \{q\}$ for partial correctness starts with exactly two assertions, namely p and $pre(S)$. If $p \equiv pre(S)$, then we drop p from this proof outline and consider the resulting proof outline also to be standard.

Note that a standard proof outline is not minimal, in the sense that some assertions used in it can be removed. For example, the assertion $\{p \wedge B\}$ in the context $\{\mathbf{inv} : p\}$ **while** B **do** $\{p \wedge B\}\ S$ **od** $\{q\}$ can be deduced. Standard proof outlines are needed in the chapters on parallel programs.

By studying proofs of partial correctness in the form of standard proof outlines we do not lose any generality, as the following theorem shows. Recall that $\vdash_{PD}$ stands for provability in the system PW augmented by the set of all true assertions.

Theorem 3.2.

(i) Let $\{p\}\ S^*\ \{q\}$ be a proof outline for partial correctness. Then $\vdash_{PD} \{p\}\ S\ \{q\}$.

(ii) If $\vdash_{PD} \{p\}\ S\ \{q\}$, there exists a standard proof outline for partial correctness of the form $\{p\}\ S^*\ \{q\}$.

Proof. (i) Straightforward by induction on the structure of the programs. For example, if $\{p\}\ S_1^*;\ S_2^*\ \{q\}$ is a proof outline then for some r both $\{p\}\ S_1^*\ \{r\}$ and $\{r\}\ S_2^*\ \{q\}$ are proof outlines. By the induction hypothesis $\vdash_{PD} \{p\}\ S_1\ \{r\}$ and $\vdash_{PD} \{r\}\ S_2\ \{q\}$; so $\vdash_{PD} \{p\}\ S_1;\ S_2\ \{q\}$ by the composition rule. Other cases are equally simple to prove.

(ii) Straightforward by induction on the length of the proof. For example, if the last rule applied in the proof of $\{p\}\ S\ \{q\}$ was the conditional rule, then by the induction hypothesis there are standard proof outlines for partial correctness of the forms $\{p \wedge B\}\ S_1^*\ \{q\}$ and $\{p \wedge \neg B\}\ S_2^*\ \{q\}$, where S is **if** B **then** S_1 **else** S_2 **fi**. Thus there exists a standard proof outline of the form $\{p\}\ S^*\ \{q\}$. Other cases are equally simple to prove. $\qquad\square$

Also, the proof outlines $\{p\}\ S^*\ \{q\}$ enjoy the following useful and intuitive property: whenever the control of S in a given computation starting in a state satisfying p reaches a point annotated by an assertion, this assertion is true. Thus the assertions of a proof outline are true at the appropriate moments.

To state this property we have to abstract from the operational semantics the notion of program control. To this end we introduce the notation $\mathbf{at}(T, S)$. Informally, $\mathbf{at}(T, S)$ is the remainder of S that is to be executed when the control is at subprogram T. For example, for

$$S \equiv \mathbf{while}\ x \geq 0\ \mathbf{do}\ \mathbf{if}\ y \geq 0\ \mathbf{then}\ x := x - 1\ \mathbf{else}\ y := y - 2\ \mathbf{fi}\ \mathbf{od},$$

and

$$T \equiv y := y - 2,$$

the following should hold: $\mathbf{at}(T, S) \equiv \mathbf{at}(y := y-2, S) \equiv y := y-2; S$ because once T has terminated, loop S must be reiterated.

More precisely, we introduce the following definition.

Definition 3.7. Let T be a subprogram of S. We define a program $\mathbf{at}(T, S)$ by the following clauses:

(i) if $S \equiv S_1;\ S_2$ and T is a subprogram of S_1, then $\mathbf{at}(T, S) \equiv \mathbf{at}(T;\ S_1)$; S_2 and if T is a subprogram of S_2 then $\mathbf{at}(T, S) \equiv \mathbf{at}(T, S_2)$;

(ii) if $S \equiv$ **if** B **then** S_1 **else** S_2 **fi** and T is a subprogram of S_i, then $\mathbf{at}(T, S) \equiv \mathbf{at}(T, S_i)$ $(i = 1, 2)$;

(iii) if $S \equiv$ **while** B **do** S' **od** and T is a subprogram of S', then $\mathbf{at}(T, S) \equiv \mathbf{at}(T, S');\ S$;

(iv) if $T \equiv S$ then $\mathbf{at}(T, S) \equiv S$.   □

We can now state the desired theorem.

Theorem 3.3. (Strong Soundness) *Let* $\{p\}\ S^*\ \{q\}$ *be a standard proof outline for partial correctness. Suppose that*

$$< S, \sigma > \rightarrow^* < R, \tau >$$

for some state σ *satisfying p, program R and state* τ. *Then*

- *if* $R \equiv \mathbf{at}(T, S)$ *for a subprogram T of S, then* $\tau \models pre(T)$,
- *if* $R \equiv E$ *then* $\tau \models q$.

Proof. It is easy to prove that either $R \equiv \mathbf{at}(T, S)$ for a subprogram T of S or $R \equiv E$ (see Exercise 3.13). In the first case, let r stand for $pre(T)$; in the second case, let r stand for q. We need to show $\tau \models r$. The proof is by induction on the length of the computation. If its length is 0 then $p \rightarrow r$ and $\sigma = \tau$; so $\tau \models r$ since $\sigma \models p$.

Suppose now the length is positive. Then for some R' and τ'

$$< S, \sigma > \rightarrow^* < R', \tau' > \rightarrow < R, \tau > .$$

We have now to consider six cases depending on the form of the last transition. We consider only two representative ones.

(a) Suppose the last transition consists of a successful evaluation of a Boolean expression B in a conditional statement **if** B **then** S_1 **else** S_2 **fi**. Then $R' \equiv \mathbf{at}(T', S)$ where $T' \equiv$ **if** B **then** S_1 **else** S_2 **fi** and $R \equiv \mathbf{at}(T, S)$ where $T \equiv S_1$. By the definition of a proof outline

$$pre(T') \wedge B \rightarrow r.$$

By the induction hypothesis $\tau' \models pre(T')$. But by the assumption $\tau' \models B$ and $\tau = \tau'$; so $\tau \models pre(T') \wedge B$ and consequently $\tau \models r$.

(b) Suppose the last transition consists of an execution of an assignment statement, say $u := t$. Then $R' \equiv \mathbf{at}(u := t, S)$. By the definition of a proof outline $pre(u := t) \rightarrow p'[u := t]$ and $p' \rightarrow r$ for some assertion p'. Thus

$$pre(u := t) \rightarrow r[u := t].$$

But by the induction hypothesis $\tau' \models pre(u := t)$; so $\tau' \models r[u := t]$. Also, $\mathcal{M}[\![u := t]\!](\tau') = \{\tau\}$; so by the truth of the assignment axiom in the sense of partial correctness, $\tau \models r$.   □

Total Correctness

So far we have only discussed proof outlines for partial correctness. To complete the picture we should take care of the termination of loops. We introduce the following definition.

Definition 3.8. (Proof Outline: Total Correctness) Let S^* and S^{**} stand for program S annotated with assertions, some of them labeled by the keyword **inv**, and integer expressions, all labeled by the keyword **bd**. The notion of a *proof outline for total correctness* is defined as for partial correctness (cf. Definition 3.6), except for formation rule (v) dealing with loops, which is to be replaced by

(viii)

$$
\begin{array}{c}
\{p \wedge B\}\ S^*\ \{p\}, \\
\{p \wedge B \wedge t = z\}\ S^{**}\ \{t < z\}, \\
p \rightarrow t \geq 0 \\
\hline
\{\mathbf{inv} : p\}\{\mathbf{bd} : t\}\ \mathbf{while}\ B\ \mathbf{do}\ \{p \wedge B\}\ S^*\ \{p\}\ \mathbf{od}\ \{p \wedge \neg B\}
\end{array}
$$

where t is an integer expression and z is an integer variable not occurring in p, t, B or S^{**}.

Standard proof outlines $\{p\}\ S^*\ \{q\}$ for total correctness are defined as for partial correctness.   □

The annotation $\{\mathbf{bd} : t\}$ represents the bound function of the loop **while** B **do** S **od**. Observe that we do not record in the proof outline the termination proof, that is, the proof of the formula $\{p \wedge B \wedge t = z\}\ S\ \{t < z\}$. Usually this proof is straightforward and to reconstruct it, exhibiting the bound function is sufficient. By formation rule (vii) of Definition 3.6 no annotation of the form {**inv** : p} or {**bd** : t} may be deleted from a proof outline for total correctness.

Example 3.7. The following is a proof outline for total correctness of the integer division program *DIV* studied in Example 3.4:

$$\{x \geq 0 \land y > 0\}$$
$$quo := 0; \ rem := x;$$
$$\{\textbf{inv} : p'\}\{\textbf{bd} : rem\}$$
$$\textbf{while } rem \geq y \textbf{ do}$$
$$\qquad \{p' \land rem \geq y\}$$
$$\qquad rem := rem - y; \ quo := quo + 1$$
$$\qquad \{p'\}$$
$$\textbf{od}$$
$$\{p' \land rem < y\}$$
$$\{quo \cdot y + rem = x \land 0 \leq rem < y\},$$

where

$$p' \equiv quo \cdot y + rem = x \land rem \geq 0 \land y > 0.$$

This proof outline represents the proof given in Example 3.4. It includes the bound function *rem*, but it does not include the verification of the last two premises of the loop II rule corresponding to the correctness formulas (3.13) and (3.14) in Example 3.5.

We now apply the decomposition rule A1 to *DIV* and split the proof of total correctness into a proof of partial correctness and a proof of termination. To prove

$$\{x \geq 0 \land y > 0\} \ DIV \ \{quo \cdot y + rem = x \land 0 \leq rem < y\} \qquad (3.24)$$

in the sense of partial correctness, let

$$\{x \geq 0 \land y \geq 0\} \ DIV^* \ \{quo \cdot y + rem = x \land 0 \leq rem < y\}$$

denote the proof outline shown in Example 3.6. We strengthen the precondition by an initial application of the consequence rule, yielding the proof outline

$$\{x \geq 0 \land y > 0\}$$
$$\{x \geq 0 \land y \geq 0\}$$
$$DIV^*$$
$$\{quo \cdot y + rem = x \land 0 \leq rem < y\},$$

which proves (3.24) in the sense of partial correctness. To show termination we prove

$$\{x \geq 0 \wedge y > 0\} \; DIV \; \{\textbf{true}\} \qquad (3.25)$$

in the sense of total correctness by the following proof outline with a simpler loop invariant than p':

$\{x \geq 0 \wedge y > 0\}$
$quo := 0; \; rem := x;$
$\{\textbf{inv} : rem \geq 0 \wedge y > 0\}\{\textbf{bd} : rem\}$
while $rem \geq y$ **do**
$\qquad \{rem \geq 0 \wedge y > 0 \wedge rem \geq y\}$
$\qquad rem := rem - y; \; quo := quo + 1$
$\qquad \{rem \geq 0 \wedge y > 0\}$
od
$\{\textbf{true}\}.$

Together, (3.24) and (3.25) establish the desired total correctness result for DIV.   □

Proof outlines are well suited for the documentation of programs because they allow us to record the main assertions that were used to establish the correctness of the programs, in particular the invariants and bound functions of loops.

3.5 Completeness

A natural question concerning any proof system is whether it is strong enough for the purpose at hand, that is, whether every semantically valid (i.e., true) formula can indeed be proved. This is the question of *completeness* of a proof system. Here we are interested in the completeness of the proof systems PW and TW. We introduce the following more general definition.

Definition 3.9. Let G be a proof system allowing us to prove correctness formulas about programs in a certain class C. We say that G is *complete for partial correctness of programs in C* if for all correctness formulas $\{p\} \, S \, \{q\}$ about programs S in C

$$\models \{p\} \, S \, \{q\} \text{ implies } \vdash_G \{p\} \, S \, \{q\}$$

and that G is *complete for total correctness of programs in C* if for all correctness formulas $\{p\} \, S \, \{q\}$ about programs S in C

$$\models_{tot} \{p\} \, S \, \{q\} \text{ implies } \vdash_G \{p\} \, S \, \{q\}. \qquad □$$

Thus completeness is the counterpart of soundness as defined in Definition 3.4.

There are several reasons why the proof systems PW and TW could be incomplete.

(1) There is no complete proof system for the assertions used in the rule of consequence.
(2) The language used for assertions and expressions is too weak to describe the sets of states and the bound functions needed in the correctness proofs.
(3) The proof rules presented here for **while** programs are not powerful enough.

Obstacle (1) is indeed true. Since we interpret our assertions over a fixed structure containing the integers, Gödel's *Incompleteness Theorem* applies and tells us that there cannot be any complete proof system for the set of all true assertions. We circumvent this problem by simply adding all true assertions to the proof systems PW and TW. As a consequence, any completeness result will be in fact a completeness relative to the truth of all assertions.

Obstacle (2) is partly true. On the one hand, we see that all sets of states needed in correctness proofs can be defined by assertions. However, we also observe that the syntax for expressions as introduced in Chapter 2 is not powerful enough to express all necessary bound functions.

Thus our question about completeness of the proof systems PW and TW really address point (3). We can show that the axioms and proof rules given in these proof systems for the individual program constructs are indeed powerful enough. For example, we show that together with the consequence rule the loop II rule is sufficient to prove all true total correctness formulas about **while** programs.

First let us examine the expressiveness of the assertions and expressions. For this purpose we introduce the notion of weakest precondition originally due to Dijkstra [1975].

Definition 3.10. Let S be a **while** program and Φ a set of proper states. We define
$$wlp(S, \Phi) = \{\sigma \mid \mathcal{M}[\![S]\!](\sigma) \subseteq \Phi\}$$
and
$$wp(S, \Phi) = \{\sigma \mid \mathcal{M}_{tot}[\![S]\!](\sigma) \subseteq \Phi\}.$$
We call $wlp(S, \Phi)$ the *weakest liberal precondition* of S with respect to Φ and $wp(S, \Phi)$ the *weakest precondition* of S with respect to Φ.   □

Informally, $wlp(S, \Phi)$ is the set of all proper states σ such that whenever S is activated in σ and properly terminates, the output state is in Φ. In turn, $wp(S, \Phi)$ is the set of all proper states σ such that whenever S is activated in σ, it is guaranteed to terminate and the output state is in Φ.

It can be shown that these sets of states can be expressed or *defined* by assertions in the following sense.

Definition 3.11. An assertion p *defines* a set Φ of states if the equation $[\![p]\!] = \Phi$ holds. □

Theorem 3.4. (Definability) *Let S be a* **while** *program and q an assertion. Then the following holds.*

(i) There is an assertion p defining $wlp(S, [\![q]\!])$, i.e. with $[\![p]\!] = wlp(S, [\![q]\!])$.
(ii) There is an assertion p defining $wp(S, [\![q]\!])$, i.e. with $[\![p]\!] = wp(S, [\![q]\!])$.

Proof. A proof of this theorem for a similar assertion language can be found in Appendix B of de Bakker [1980] (written by J. Zucker). We omit the proof details and mention only that its proof uses the technique of *Gödelization*, which allows us to code computations of programs by natural numbers in an effective way. Such an encoding is possible due to the fact that the assertion language includes addition and multiplication of natural numbers. □

By the Definability Theorem 3.4 we can express weakest preconditions syntactically. Hence we adopt the following convention: for a given **while** program S and a given assertion q we denote by $wlp(S, q)$ some assertion p for which the equation in (i) holds, and by $wp(S, q)$ some assertion p for which the equation in (ii) holds. Note the difference between $wlp(S, q)$ and $wlp(S, \Phi)$. The former is an assertion whereas the latter is a set of states; similarly with $wp(S, q)$ and $wp(S, \Phi)$. Note that $wlp(S, q)$ and $wp(S, q)$ are determined only up to logical equivalence.

The following properties of weakest preconditions can easily be established.

Lemma 3.5. (Weakest Liberal Precondition) *The following statements hold for all* **while** *programs and assertions:*

(i) $wlp(skip, q) \leftrightarrow q$,
(ii) $wlp(u := t, q) \leftrightarrow q[u := t]$,
(iii) $wlp(S_1; \ S_2, q) \leftrightarrow wlp(S_1, wlp(S_2, q))$,
(iv) $wlp(\textbf{if } B \textbf{ then } S_1 \textbf{ else } S_2 \textbf{ fi}, q) \leftrightarrow$
        $(B \land wlp(S_1, q)) \lor (\neg B \land wlp(S_2, q))$,
(v) $wlp(S, q) \land B \to wlp(S_1, wlp(S, q))$,
        where $S \equiv \textbf{while } B \textbf{ do } S_1 \textbf{ od}$,
(vi) $wlp(S, q) \land \neg B \to q$,
        where $S \equiv \textbf{while } B \textbf{ do } S_1 \textbf{ od}$,
(vii) $\models \{p\} S \{q\}$ iff $p \to wlp(S, q)$.

Proof. See Exercise 3.15. □

Note that for a given loop $S \equiv \textbf{while } B \textbf{ do } S_1 \textbf{ od}$ the clauses (v) and (vii) imply

$$\models \{wlp(S, q) \land B\} \ S_1 \ \{wlp(S, q)\}.$$

In other words, $wlp(S, q)$ is a loop invariant of S.

Lemma 3.6. (Weakest Precondition) *The statements (i)–(vii) of the Weakest Liberal Precondition Lemma 3.5 hold when wlp is replaced by wp and* $\models$ *by* $\models_{tot}$.

Proof. See Exercise 3.16.   □

Using the definability of the weakest precondition as stated in the Definability Theorem 3.4 we can show the completeness of the proof system *PW*. For the completeness of *TW*, however, we need the additional property that also all bound functions can be expressed by suitable integer expressions.

Definition 3.12. For a loop $S \equiv$ **while** B **do** S_1 **od** and an integer variable x not occurring in S consider the extended loop

$$S_x \equiv x := 0; \ \textbf{while } B \textbf{ do } x := x + 1; \ S_1 \textbf{ od}$$

and a proper state σ such that the computation of S starting in σ terminates, that is, $\mathcal{M}_{tot}[\![S]\!](\sigma) \neq \{\bot\}$. Then $\mathcal{M}_{tot}[\![S_x]\!](\sigma) = \{\tau\}$ for some proper state $\tau \neq \bot$. By $iter(S, \sigma)$ we denote the value $\tau(x)$, which is a natural number.   □

Intuitively, $iter(S, \sigma)$ is the number of iterations of the loop S occurring in the computation of S starting in σ. For a fixed loop S we can view $iter(S, \sigma)$ as a partially defined function in σ that is defined whenever $\mathcal{M}_{tot}[\![S]\!](\sigma) \neq \{\bot\}$ holds. Note that this function is computable. Indeed, the extended loop S_x can be simulated by a Turing machine using a counter x for counting the number of loop iterations.

Definition 3.13. The set of all integer expressions is called *expressive* if for every **while** loop S there exists an integer expression t such that

$$\sigma(t) = iter(S, \sigma)$$

holds for every state σ with $\mathcal{M}_{tot}[\![S]\!](\sigma) \neq \{\bot\}$.   □

Thus expressibility means that for each loop the number of loop iterations can be expressed by an integer expression. Whereas the assertions introduced in Chapter 2 are powerful enough to guarantee the definability of the weakest preconditions (the Definability Theorem 3.4), the integer expressions introduced there are too weak to guarantee expressibility.

Using the function symbols $+$ and $\cdot$ for addition and multiplication, we can represent only polynomials as integer expressions. However, it is easy to write a terminating **while** loop S where the number of loop iterations exhibit an exponential growth, say according to the function $iter(S, \sigma) = 2^{\sigma(x)}$. Then $iter(S, \sigma)$ cannot be expressed using the integer expressions of Chapter 2.

To guarantee expressibility we need an extension of the set of integer expressions which allows us to express all partially defined computable functions and thus in particular $iter(S, \sigma)$. We omit the details of such an extension.

We can now prove the desired theorem.

Theorem 3.5. (Completeness)

(i) *The proof system PW is complete for partial correctness of* **while** *programs.*

(ii) *Assume that the set of all integer expressions is expressive. Then the proof system TW is complete for total correctness of* **while** *programs.*

Proof.

(i) *Partial correctness.* We first prove that for all S and q,

$$\vdash_{PD} \{wlp(S, q)\} \, S \, \{q\}. \tag{3.26}$$

We proceed by induction on the structure of S. To this end we use clauses (i)–(vi) of the Weakest Liberal Precondition Lemma 3.5.

Induction basis. The cases of the *skip* statement and the assignment are straightforward.

Induction step. The case of sequential composition is easy. We consider in more detail the case of the conditional statement $S \equiv$ **if** B **then** S_1 **else** S_2 **fi**. We have by the Weakest Liberal Precondition Lemma 3.5(iv)

$$wlp(S, q) \wedge B \to wlp(S_1, q) \tag{3.27}$$

and

$$wlp(S, q) \wedge \neg B \to wlp(S_2, q). \tag{3.28}$$

By the induction hypothesis,

$$\vdash_{PD} \{wlp(S_1, q)\} \, S_1 \, \{q\} \tag{3.29}$$

and

$$\vdash_{PD} \{wlp(S_2, q)\} \, S_2 \, \{q\}. \tag{3.30}$$

Using now the consequence rule applied respectively to (3.27) and (3.29), and (3.28) and (3.30), we obtain

$$\vdash_{PD} \{wlp(S, q) \wedge B\} \, S_1 \, \{q\}$$

and

$$\vdash_{PD} \{wlp(S, q) \wedge \neg B\} \, S_2 \, \{q\},$$

from which (3.26) follows by the conditional rule.

Finally, consider a loop $S \equiv$ **while** B **do** S_1 **od**. We have by the induction hypothesis

$$\vdash_{PD} \{wlp(S_1, wlp(S, q))\} \, S_1 \, \{wlp(S, q)\}.$$

By the Weakest Liberal Precondition Lemma 3.5(v) and the consequence rule

$$\vdash_{PD} \{wlp(S, q) \wedge B\} \, S_1 \, \{wlp(S, q)\};$$

so by the loop rule

$$\vdash_{PD} \{wlp(S,q)\} \ S \ \{wlp(S,q) \wedge \neg B\}.$$

Finally, by the Weakest Liberal Precondition Lemma 3.5(vi) and the consequence rule

$$\vdash_{PD} \{wlp(S,q)\} \ S \ \{q\}.$$

This proves (3.26). With this preparation we can now prove the completeness of PW. Suppose

$$\models \{p\} \ S \ \{q\}.$$

Then by the Weakest Liberal Precondition Lemma 3.5(vii)

$$p \rightarrow wlp(S,q);$$

so by (3.26) and the consequence rule

$$\vdash_{PD} \{p\} \ S \ \{q\}.$$

(ii) *Total correctness.*We proceed somewhat differently than in (i) and prove directly by induction on the structure of S that

$$\models_{tot} \{p\} \ S_1 \ \{q\} \text{ implies } \vdash_{TD} \{p\} \ S_1 \ \{q\}.$$

The proof of the cases *skip*, assignment, sequential composition and conditional statement is similar to that of (i) but uses the Weakest Precondition Lemma 3.6 instead of the Weakest Liberal Precondition Lemma 3.5.

The main difference lies in the treatment of the loop $S \equiv$ **while** B **do** S_1 **od**. Suppose $\models_{tot} \{p\} \ S \ \{q\}$. It suffices to prove

$$\vdash_{TD} \{wp(S,q)\} \ S \ \{q\} \tag{3.31}$$

because —similar to (i) and using the Weakest Precondition Lemma 3.6(vii) and the consequence rule— this implies $\vdash_{TD} \{p\} \ S_1 \ \{q\}$ as desired. By the Weakest Precondition Lemma 3.6(vii)

$$\models_{tot} \{wp(S_1, wp(S,q))\} \ S_1 \ \{wp(S,q)\};$$

so by the induction hypothesis

$$\vdash_{TD} \{wp(S_1, wp(S,q))\} \ S_1 \ \{wp(S,q)\}.$$

Thus by the Weakest Precondition Lemma 3.6(v)

$$\vdash_{TD} \{wp(S,q) \wedge B\} \ S_1 \ \{wp(S,q)\}. \tag{3.32}$$

We intend now to apply the loop II rule. In (3.32) we have already found a loop invariant, namely $wp(S,q)$, but we also need an appropriate bound function. By the assumption about the expressiveness of the set of all integer expressions there exists an integer expression t such that $\sigma(t) = iter(S, \sigma)$ for all proper states σ with $\mathcal{M}[\![S]\!](\sigma) \neq \{\bot\}$. By the definition of $wp(S, q)$ and t,

$$\models_{tot} \{wp(S, q) \wedge B \wedge t = z\}\ S_1\ \{t < z\}, \tag{3.33}$$

where z is an integer variable that does not occur in t, B and S, and

$$wp(S, q) \rightarrow t \geq 0. \tag{3.34}$$

By the induction hypothesis (3.33) implies

$$\vdash_{TD} \{wp(S, q) \wedge B \wedge t = z\}\ S_1\ \{t < z\}. \tag{3.35}$$

Applying the loop II rule to (3.32), (3.35) and (3.34) yields

$$\vdash_{TD} \{wp(S, q)\}\ S\ \{wp(S, q) \wedge \neg B\}. \tag{3.36}$$

Now (3.31) follows from (3.36) by the Weakest Precondition Lemma 3.6(vi) and the consequence rule.   □

Similar completeness results can be established for various other proof systems considered in subsequent chapters. All these proofs proceed by induction on the structure of the programs and use intermediate assertions constructed by means of the weakest (liberal) precondition or similar semantics concepts. However, as the proof systems become more complicated, so do their completeness proofs.

In fact, for parallel and distributed programs the proofs become quite involved and tedious. We do not give these proofs and concentrate instead on the use of these proof systems for verifying programs, which is the main topic of this book.

3.6 Parallel Assignment

An assignment $u := t$ updates only a single or subcripted variable u. Often it is convenient to update several variables in parallel, in one step. To this end, we introduce the *parallel assignment* which updates a list of variables by the values of a corresponding list of expressions. For example, using a parallel assignment we can write

$$x, y := y, x$$

to express that the values of the variables x and y are swapped in a single step. With ordinary assigments we need an additional variable, say h, to temporarily store the value of x. Then, the sequential composition

$$h := x; \; x := y; \; y := h$$

of assignments has the same effect as the parallel assignment above, except for the variable h. This shows the usefulness of the parallel assignment. Later in Chapter 5, we use it to model the semantics of the call-by-value parameter mechanism in recursive procedures.

In this section, we briefly introduce syntax, semantics, and an axiom for the verification of parallel assignments.

Syntax

We extend the syntax of **while** programs S by the following clause for parallel assignments:

$$S \; ::= \; \bar{x} := \bar{t},$$

where $\bar{x} = x_1, \ldots, x_n$ is a non-empty list of distinct simple variables of types $T_1, \ldots, T_n$ and $\bar{t} = t_1, \ldots, t_n$ a corresponding list of expressions of types $T_1, \ldots, T_n$.

Semantics

The operational semantics of a parallel assignment is defined by the following variant of the transition axiom (ii) for ordinary assignments, stated in Section 3.2:

(ii') $\quad < \bar{x} := \bar{t}, \sigma > \; \to \; < E, \sigma[\bar{x} := \sigma(\bar{t})] >$

Thus semantically, a parallel assignment is modelled by a simultaneous update of the state. Just as the ordinary assignment, a parallel assignment terminates in one transition step.

As in Section 3.2 we define the input-output semantics of partial and total correctness, referring to the above transition axiom in the case of a parallel assignment. In particular, we have

$$\mathcal{N}[\![\bar{x} := \bar{t}]\!](\sigma) = \{\sigma[\bar{x} := \sigma(\bar{t})]\}$$

for both $\mathcal{N} = \mathcal{M}$ and $\mathcal{N} = \mathcal{M}_{tot}$.

Example 3.8. Now we can make precise the semantic relationship between the two programs for the swap operation:

$$\mathcal{N}[\![x, y := y, x]\!](\sigma) = \mathcal{N}[\![h := x; \; x := y; \; y := h]\!](\sigma) \; \mathbf{mod} \; \{h\} \qquad (3.37)$$

for both $\mathcal{N} = \mathcal{M}$ and $\mathcal{N} = \mathcal{M}_{tot}$. In the following we prove this relationship. By the semantics of parallel assignments, the left-hand side of (3.37) yields

$$\mathcal{N}[\![x, y := y, x]\!](\sigma) = \{\sigma_{x,y}\},$$

where $\sigma_{x,y} = \sigma[x, y := \sigma(y), \sigma(x)]$. By definition, the simultaneous update can be serialized as follows:

$$\sigma_{x,y} = \sigma_x[y := \sigma(x)],$$
$$\sigma_x = \sigma[x := \sigma(y)].$$

In turn, the sequential composition of the three assignments of the right-hand side of (3.37) yields

$$\mathcal{N}[\![h := x; \; x := y; \; y := h]\!](\sigma) = \{\sigma_{h,x,y}\},$$

where we use the following abbreviations:

$$\sigma_{h,x,y} = \sigma_{h,x}[y := \sigma_{h,x}(h)],$$
$$\sigma_{h,x} = \sigma_h[x := \sigma_h(y)],$$
$$\sigma_h = \sigma[h := \sigma(x)].$$

Thus to prove (3.37), it suffices to show the following three claims:

1. $\sigma_{x,y}(x) = \sigma_{h,x,y}(x)$,
2. $\sigma_{x,y}(y) = \sigma_{h,x,y}(y)$,
3. $\sigma_{x,y}(v) = \sigma_{h,x,y}(v)$ for all simple and array variables v different from x, y and h.

The proofs of these claims use the Coincidence Lemma 2.3 and the definition of an update of a state.

Re: 1. We calculate:

$$\sigma_{x,y}(x) = \sigma_x(x) = \sigma(y) = \sigma_h(y) = \sigma_{h,x}(x) = \sigma_{h,x,y}(x).$$

Re: 2. We calculate:

$$\sigma_{x,y}(y) = \sigma(x) = \sigma_h(h) = \sigma_{h,x}(h) = \sigma_{h,x,y}(y).$$

Re: 3. We calculate:

$$\sigma_{x,y}(v) = \sigma(v) = \sigma_{h,x,y}(v).$$

This completes the proof of (3.37). □

Verification

The assignment axiom introduced in Section 3.3, axiom 2, can be easily
adapted to parallel assignment, using simultaneous substitution:

AXIOM 2′: PARALLEL ASSIGNMENT

$$\{p[\bar{x} := \bar{t}]\} \; \bar{x} := \bar{t} \; \{p\}$$

This axiom is sound for both partial and total correctness. We call the
corresponding proof systems PW' and TW', that is, PW and TW extended
by axiom 2′, respectively. Definitions 3.6 and 3.8 of proof outlines for partial and total correctness, respectively, carry over to programs with parallel
assignments in a straightforward way.

Example 3.9. For the program $S \equiv x, y := y, x$ we prove the correctness
formula

$$\{x = x_0 \wedge y = y_0\} \; S \; \{x = y_0 \wedge y = x_0\}$$

in the proof system PW'. Here the fresh variables x_0 and y_0 are used to
express the *swap property* of S. In the precondition x_0 and y_0 freeze the
initial values of the variables x and y, respectively, so that these values can
be compared with the new values of these variables in the postcondition. We
see that the values of x and y are swapped.

We represent the correctness proof in PW' as a proof outline:

$$\{x = x_0 \wedge y = y_0\}$$
$$\{y = y_0 \wedge x = x_0\}$$
$$S$$
$$\{x = y_0 \wedge y = x_0\}.$$

The initial application of the consequence rule exploits the commutativity
of logical conjunction. Then axiom 2′ is applied to S with the substitution
$[x, y := y, x]$. □

3.7 Failure Statement

In this section we introduce a simple statement the execution of which can
cause a *failure*, also called an *abortion*. The computation of a program with
such a statement can either yield a final state, diverge or, what is new, terminate in a failure.

Syntax

We extend the syntax of **while** programs by the following clause for a *failure statement*:

$$S \ ::= \ \textbf{if } B \rightarrow S_1 \ \textbf{fi},$$

where B is a Boolean expression, called the *guard* of S, and S_1 a statement. We refer to the resulting programs as *failure admitting programs*.

The statement **if** $B \rightarrow S$ **fi** is executed as follows. First the guard B is evaluated. If B is true, S is executed; otherwise a failure arises. So the execution of the statement **if** $B \rightarrow S$ **fi** crucially differs from that of **if** B **then** S **fi**. Namely, if B evaluates to false, the latter statement simply terminates.

The fact that the failure statement fails rather than terminates if its guard evaluates to false allows us to program checks for undesired conditions. For example, to avoid integer division by 0, we can write

$$\textbf{if } y \neq 0 \rightarrow x := x \ div \ y \ \textbf{fi}.$$

In case of $y = 0$ this program raises a failure. By contrast, the conditional statement

$$\textbf{if } y \neq 0 \ \textbf{then } x := x \ div \ y \ \textbf{fi}$$

always properly terminates and does not raise any exception.

In the same way, we may use the failure statement to check whether an array is accessed only within a certain section. For example, executing

$$\textbf{if } 0 \leq i < n \rightarrow x := a[i] \ \textbf{fi}$$

raises a failure if the array a is accessed outside of the section $a[0 : n-1]$. Thus the failure statement can be used to model bounded arrays.

As a final example consider the problem of extending the parallel assignment to the subscripted variables. A complication then arises that some parallel assignments can lead to a contradiction, for example $a[s_1], a[s_2] := t_1, t_2$, when s_1 and s_2 evaluate to the same value while t_1 and t_2 evaluate to different values. The failure statement can then be used to catch the error. For example, we can rewrite the above problematic parallel assignment to

$$\textbf{if } s_1 \neq s_2 \vee t_1 = t_2 \rightarrow a[s_1], a[s_2] := t_1, t_2 \ \textbf{fi}$$

that raises a failure in the case when the parallel assignment cannot be executed.

Semantics

The operational semantics of a failure statement is defined by the following two transition axioms:

(iv') $< \text{if } B \to S \text{ fi}, \sigma > \; \to \; < S, \sigma >$ where $\sigma \models B$,

(v') $< \text{if } B \to S \text{ fi}, \sigma > \; \to \; < E, \textbf{fail} >$ where $\sigma \models \neg B$,

that should be compared with the transition axioms (iv) and (v) concerned with the conditional statement **if** B **then** S **fi**.

Here **fail** is a new exceptional state representing a runtime detectable failure or abortion. It should be contrasted with $\bot$, representing divergence, which in general cannot be detected in finite time. Note that configurations of the form $< S, \textbf{fail} >$ have no successor in the transition relation $\to$.

Definition 3.14. Let σ be a proper state.

   (i) A configuration of the form $< S, \textbf{fail} >$ is called a *failure*.
  (ii) We say that a failure admitting program S can *fail* from σ if there is a computation of S that starts in σ and ends in a failure.   □

Note that the Absence of Blocking Lemma 3.2 does not hold any more for failure admitting programs because failures block the computation.

The partial correctness semantics of $\mathcal{M}[\![S]\!]$ of the failure admitting program S is defined as before. However, the total correctness semantics is now defined by taking into account the possibility of a failure. Given a proper state σ we put

$$
\begin{aligned}
\mathcal{M}_{tot}[\![S]\!](\sigma) = \quad & \mathcal{M}[\![S]\!](\sigma) \\
& \cup \; \{\bot \mid S \text{ can diverge from } \sigma\} \\
& \cup \; \{\textbf{fail} \mid S \text{ can fail from } \sigma\}.
\end{aligned}
$$

This definition suggests that a failure admitting program can yield more than one outcome. However, this is obviously not the case since the Determinism Lemma 3.1 still holds and consequently $\mathcal{M}_{tot}[\![S]\!](\sigma)$ has exactly one element, like in the case of the **while** programs.

Verification

The notions of partial and total correctness of the failure admitting programs are defined in the familiar way using the semantics $\mathcal{M}$ and $\mathcal{M}_{tot}$. For example, total correctness is defined as follows:

$$
\models_{tot} \{p\} \; S \; \{q\} \text{ if } \mathcal{M}_{tot}[\![S]\!]([\![p]\!]) \subseteq [\![q]\!].
$$

Note that by definition, **fail**, $\perp \notin [\![q]\!]$ holds; so $\models_{tot} \{p\}\ S\ \{q\}$ implies that S neither fails nor diverges when started in a state satisfying p.

To prove correctness of the failure admitting programs we introduce two proof rules. In the following proof rule for partial correctness we *assume* that the guard B evaluates to true when S is executed.

RULE 4′: FAILURE
$$\frac{\{p \wedge B\}\ S\ \{q\}}{\{p\}\ \textbf{if}\ B \rightarrow S\ \textbf{fi}\ \{q\}}$$

In contrast, in the following proof rule for total correctness we also have to show that the precondition p implies that the guard B evaluates to true, thus avoiding a failure.

RULE 4″: FAILURE II

$$\frac{p \rightarrow B, \{p\}\ S\ \{q\}}{\{p\}\ \textbf{if}\ B \rightarrow S\ \textbf{fi}\ \{q\}}$$

We have the following counterpart of the Soundness Theorem 3.1.

Theorem 3.6. (Soundness)

   (i) *The proof system PW augmented by the failure rule is sound for partial correctness of failure admitting programs.*
   (ii) *The proof system TW augmented by the failure II rule is sound for total correctness of failure admitting programs.*

Proof. See Exercise 3.6.   □

We shall discuss other statements that can cause a failure in Chapters 6 and 10.

3.8 Auxiliary Axioms and Rules

Apart from using proof outlines the presentation of correctness proofs can be simplified in another way —by means of *auxiliary* axioms and rules. They allow us to prove certain correctness formulas about the same program separately and then combine them. This can lead to a different organization of the correctness proof.

In the case of **while** programs these axioms and rules for combining correctness formulas are not necessary, in the sense that their use in the correctness proof can be eliminated by applying other rules. This is the consequence of the Completeness Theorem 3.5. That is why these rules are called auxiliary rules.

Apart from the decomposition rule A1 introduced in Section 3.3, the following auxiliary axioms and rules are used in proofs of partial and total correctness for all classes of programs considered in this book.

AXIOM A2: INVARIANCE

$$\{p\}\ S\ \{p\}$$

where $free(p) \cap change(S) = \emptyset$.

RULE A3: DISJUNCTION

$$\frac{\{p\}\ S\ \{q\}, \{r\}\ S\ \{q\}}{\{p \vee r\}\ S\ \{q\}}$$

RULE A4: CONJUNCTION

$$\frac{\{p_1\}\ S\ \{q_1\}, \{p_2\}\ S\ \{q_2\}}{\{p_1 \wedge p_2\}\ S\ \{q_1 \wedge q_2\}}$$

RULE A5: ∃-INTRODUCTION

$$\frac{\{p\}\ S\ \{q\}}{\{\exists x : p\}\ S\ \{q\}}$$

where x does not occur in S or in $free(q)$.

RULE A6: INVARIANCE

$$\frac{\{r\}\ S\ \{q\}}{\{p \wedge r\}\ S\ \{p \wedge q\}}$$

where $free(p) \cap change(S) = \emptyset$.

RULE A7: SUBSTITUTION

$$\frac{\{p\}\ S\ \{q\}}{\{p[\bar{z} := \bar{t}]\}\ S\ \{q[\bar{z} := \bar{t}]\}}$$

where $(\{\bar{z}\} \cup var(\bar{t})) \cap change(S) = \emptyset$.

Here and elsewhere $\{\bar{z}\}$ stands for the set of variables present in the sequence $\bar{z}$ and $var(\bar{t})$ for the set of all simple and array variables that occur in the expressions of the sequence $\bar{t}$. (So alternatively we can write $var(\bar{z})$ for $(\{\bar{z}\}$.)

Axiom A2 is true for partial correctness for all programs considered in this book and rules A3–A7 are sound for both partial and total correctness for all programs considered in this book. To state this property we refer below to an arbitrary program S, with the understanding that semantics $\mathcal{N}[\![S]\!]$ of such a program S is a function

$$\mathcal{N}[\![S]\!] : \Sigma \rightarrow \mathcal{P}(\Sigma \cup \{\bot, \mathbf{fail}, \Delta\})$$

that satisfies the Change and Access Lemma 3.4. This lemma holds for all programs considered in this book and any semantics.

Theorem 3.7. (Soundness of Auxiliary Axioms and Rules)

(i) Axiom A2 is true for partial correctness of arbitrary programs.

(ii) Proof rules A3–A7 are sound for partial correctness of arbitrary programs.

(iii) Proof rules A3–A7 are sound for total correctness of arbitrary programs.

Proof. See Exercise 3.17. □

Clearly, other auxiliary rules can be introduced but we do not need them until Chapter 11 where some new auxiliary rules are helpful.

3.9 Case Study: Partitioning an Array

In this section we investigate the problem of partitioning an array. It was originally formulated and solved by Hoare [1962] as part of his algorithm *Quicksort*, which we shall study later in Chapter 5. Consider an array a of type **integer** → **integer** and integer variables m, f, n such that $m \leq f \leq n$ holds. The task is to construct a program $PART$ that permutes the elements in the array section $a[m : n]$ and computes values of the three variables pi, le and ri standing for *pivot*, *left* and *right* elements such that upon termination of $PART$ the following holds:

- pi is the initial value of $a[f]$,
- $le > ri$ and the array section $a[m : n]$ is *partitioned* into three subsections of elements,

    - those with values of at most pi (namely $a[m : ri]$),
    - those equal to pi (namely $a[ri + 1 : le - 1]$), and
    - those with values of at least pi (namely $a[le : n]$),

    see Figure 3.1,
- the sizes of the subsections $a[m : ri]$ and $a[le : n]$ are strictly smaller than the size of the section $a[m : n]$, i.e., $ri - m < n - m$ and $n - le < n - m$.

To illustrate the input/output behaviour of $PART$ we give two examples.

1. First consider as input the array section

$$a[m : n] = (2, 3, 7, 1, 4, 5, 4, 8, 9, 7)$$

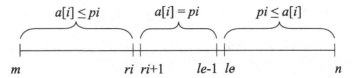

Fig. 3.1 Array section $a[m:n]$ partitioned into three subsections.

with $m = 1$, $n = 10$ and $f = 7$. Then $PART$ computes the values $le = 6$, $ri = 4$ and $pi = 4$, and permutes the array section using the pivot element pi into $a[m:n] = (2, 3, 4, 1, 4, 5, 7, 8, 9, 7)$. Thus the array section is partitioned into $a[m:ri] = (2, 3, 4, 1)$, $a[ri+1:le-1] = (4)$, and $a[le:n] = (5, 7, 8, 9, 7)$.

2. Second consider as input the array section $a[m:n] = (5, 6, 7, 9, 8)$ with $m = 2$, $n = 6$ and $f = 2$. Then $PART$ computes the values $le = 2$, $ri = 1$ and $pi = 5$, and in this example leaves the array section unchanged as $a[m:n] = (5, 6, 7, 9, 8)$ using the pivot element pi. In contrast to the first example, $ri < m$ holds. So the value of ri lies outside the interval $[m:n]$ and the subsection $a[m:ri]$ is empty. Thus the array section is partitioned into $a[m:ri] = ()$, $a[ri+1:le-1] = (5)$, and $a[le:n] = (6, 7, 9, 8)$.

To formalize the permutation property of $PART$, we consider an array β of type **integer** $\rightarrow$ **integer** which will store a bijection on N and an interval $[x:y]$ and require that β leaves a unchanged outside this interval. This is expressed by the following *bijection property* that uses β and the integer variables x and y as parameters:

$$bij(\beta, x, y) \; \equiv \; \beta \text{ is a bijection on } N \; \wedge \; \forall i \notin [x:y] : \beta[i] = i,$$

where β is a bijection on N if β is surjective and injective on N, i.e., if

$$(\forall y \in N \; \exists x \in N : \beta(x) = y) \wedge \forall x_1, x_2 \in N : (x_1 \neq x_2 \rightarrow \beta(x_1) \neq \beta(x_2)).$$

Note that the following implications hold:

$$bij(\beta, x, y) \;\rightarrow\; \forall i \in [x:y] : \beta[i] \in [x:y], \tag{3.38}$$

$$bij(\beta, x, y) \;\wedge\; x' \leq x \;\wedge\; y \leq y' \;\rightarrow\; bij(\beta, x', y'). \tag{3.39}$$

Implication (3.38) states that β permutes all elements of interval $[x:y]$ only *inside* that interval. Implication (3.39) states that the bijection property is preserved when the interval in enlarged.

We use β to compare the array a with an array a_0 of the same type as a that freezes the initial value of a. By quantifying over β, we obtain the desired *permutation property*:

$$perm(a, a_0, [x : y]) \equiv \exists \beta : (bij(\beta, x, y) \wedge \forall i : a[i] = a_0[\beta[i]]). \quad (3.40)$$

Altogether, the program $PART$ should satisfy the correctness formula

$$\{m \leq f \leq n \wedge a = a_0\}$$
$$PART \qquad\qquad\qquad\qquad\qquad\qquad (3.41)$$
$$\{perm(a, a_0, [m : n]) \wedge$$
$$pi = a_0[f] \wedge le > ri \wedge$$
$$(\forall i \in [m : ri] : a[i] \leq pi) \wedge$$
$$(\forall i \in [ri + 1 : le - 1] : a[i] = pi) \wedge$$
$$(\forall i \in [le : n] : pi \leq a[i]) \wedge$$
$$ri - m < n - m \wedge n - le < n - m\}$$

in the sense of total correctness, where $m, f, n, a_0 \notin change(PART)$.

The following program is from Foley and Hoare [1971] except that for convenience we use parallel assigments.

$$
\begin{aligned}
PART \equiv \ & pi := a[f]; \\
& le, ri := m, n; \\
& \textbf{while } le \leq ri \textbf{ do} \\
& \quad \textbf{while } a[le] < pi \textbf{ do} \\
& \quad\quad le := le + 1 \\
& \quad \textbf{od}; \\
& \quad \textbf{while } pi < a[ri] \textbf{ do} \\
& \quad\quad ri := ri - 1 \\
& \quad \textbf{od}; \\
& \quad \textbf{if } le \leq ri \textbf{ then} \\
& \quad\quad swap(a[le], a[ri]); \\
& \quad\quad le, ri := le + 1, ri - 1 \\
& \quad \textbf{fi} \\
& \textbf{od}
\end{aligned}
$$

Here for two given simple or subscripted variables u and v the program $swap(u, v)$ is used to *swap* the values of u and v. So we stipulate that the correctness formula

$$\{x = u \wedge y = v\} \ swap(u, v) \ \{x = v \wedge y = u\}$$

holds in the sense of partial and total correctness, where x and y are fresh variables.

To prove (3.41) in a modular fashion, we shall first prove the following partial correctness properties **P0–P4** separately:

P0 $\{a = a_0\}\ PART\ \{pi = a_0[f]\}$,

P1 $\{\textbf{true}\}\ PART\ \{ri \leq n \wedge m \leq le\}$,

P2 $\{x' \leq m \wedge n \leq y'\ \wedge\ perm(a, a_0, [x' : y'])\}$
   $PART$
   $\{x' \leq m \wedge n \leq y'\ \wedge\ perm(a, a_0, [x' : y'])\}$,

P3 $\{\textbf{true}\}$
   $PART$
   $\{\ le > ri\ \wedge$
   $(\forall i \in [m : ri]:\ a[i] \leq pi)\ \wedge$
   $(\forall i \in [ri + 1 : le - 1]:\ a[i] = pi)\ \wedge$
   $(\forall i \in [le : n]:\ pi \leq a[i])\}$,

P4 $\{m \leq f \leq n\}\ PART\ \{m < le \wedge ri < n\}$.

Property **P0** expresses that upon termination pi holds the initial values of the array element $a[f]$. Property **P1** states bounds for ri and le. We remark that $le \leq n$ and $m \leq ri$ need not hold upon termination. Note that property **P2** implies by the substitution rule A7 with the substitution $[x', y' := m, n]$ and the consequence rule

$$\{perm(a, a_0, [m : n])\}\ PART\ \{perm(a, a_0, [m : n])\}.$$

Since $a = a_0 \rightarrow perm(a, a_0, [m : n])$, a further application of the consequence rule yields

$$\{a = a_0\}\ PART\ \{perm(a, a_0, [m : n])\}.$$

Thus $PART$ permutes the array section $a[m : n]$ and leaves other elements of a unchanged. The more general formulation in **P2** will be helpful when proving the correctness of the *Quicksort* procedure in Chapter 5. Property **P3** formalizes the partition property of $PART$. Note that the postcondition of property **P4** is equivalent to

$$ri - m < n - m \wedge n - le < n - m,$$

which is needed in the termination proof of the *Quicksort* procedure: it states that the subsections $a[m : ri]$ and $a[le : n]$ are strictly smaller that the section $a[m : n]$.

By the conjunction rule, we deduce (3.41) in the sense of partial correctness from **P0**, the above consequence of **P2**, **P3**, and **P4**. Then to prove termination of $PART$ we show that

T $\{m \leq f \leq n\}\ PART\ \{\textbf{true}\}$

holds in the sense of total correctness. By the decomposition rule A1, this yields (3.41) in the sense of total correctness, as desired.

Thus it remains to prove **P0–P4** and **T.**

Preparatory Loop Invariants

We first establish some invariants of the inner loops in $PART$. For the first inner loop

- any assertion p with $le \notin free(p)$,
- $m \le le$,
- $A(le) \equiv \exists i \in [le : n] : pi \le a[i]$

are invariants. For the second inner loop

- any assertion q with $ri \notin free(q)$,
- $ri \le n$,
- $B(ri) \equiv \exists j \in [m : ri] : a[j] \le pi$

are invariants. The claims about p and q are obvious. The checks for $m \le le$ and $ri \le n$ are also straightforward. The remaining two invariant properties are established by the following two proof outlines for partial correctness:

$$\begin{array}{ll}
\{\textbf{inv} : A(le)\} & \{\textbf{inv} : B(ri)\} \\
\textbf{while } a[le] < pi \textbf{ do} & \textbf{while } pi < a[ri] \textbf{ do} \\
\quad \{A(le) \wedge a[le] < pi\} & \quad \{B(ri) \wedge pi < a[ri]\} \\
\quad \{A(le+1)\} & \quad \{B(ri-1)\} \\
\quad le := le + 1 & \quad ri := ri - 1 \\
\quad \{A(le)\} & \quad \{B(ri)\} \\
\textbf{od} & \textbf{od} \\
\{A(le)\} & \{B(ri)\}
\end{array}$$

Note that the implications

$$A(le) \rightarrow le \le n \quad \text{and} \quad B(ri) \rightarrow m \le ri \qquad (3.42)$$

hold. Thus $A(le) \wedge B(ri) \rightarrow ri - le \ge m - n$.

Further, for both inner loops the assertion

$$I3 \equiv a[m : le - 1] \le pi \le a[ri + 1 : n], \qquad (3.43)$$

which is a shorthand for

$$\forall i \in [m : le - 1] : a[i] \le pi \wedge \forall i \in [ri + 1 : n] : pi \le a[i],$$

is an invariant, as the following proof outline for partial correctness shows:

> {**inv** : *I3*}
> **while** $a[le] < pi$ **do**
> $\quad$ {$I3 \wedge a[le] < pi$}
> $\quad$ {$a[m : le] \le pi \le a[ri + 1 : n]$}
> $\quad le := le + 1$
> $\quad$ {$I3$}
> **od**;
> {**inv** : *I3*}
> **while** $pi < a[ri]$ **do**
> $\quad$ {$I3 \wedge pi < a[ri]$}
> $\quad$ {$a[m : le - 1] \le pi \le a[ri : n]$}
> $\quad ri := ri - 1$
> $\quad$ {$I3$}
> **od**
> {$I3$}

From these invariants further invariants can be obtained by conjunction.

Proof of Property P0

Clearly, the inital assignment satisfies

$$\{a = a_0\} \; pi := a[f] \; \{pi = a_0[f]\}.$$

Since there are no further assigments to the variable pi in $PART$, and $a_0 \notin$ $change(PART)$, the correctness formula

$$\{a = a_0\} \; PART \; \{pi = a_0[f]\}$$

holds in the sense of partial correctness. This proves property **P0**.

Proof of Property P1

The initial parallel assignment to le and ri in $PART$ establishes the assertions $ri \le n$ and $m \le le$. We noticed already that $ri \le n$ and $m \le le$ are invariants of the inner loops of $PART$. Also the final **if** statement of $PART$ with its parallel assignment to le and ri preserves $ri \leq n$ and $m \leq le$. These informal arguments can be easily combined into a formal proof of property **P1**.

Proof of Property P2

By a *global invariant* of a program S we mean an assertion GI for which there exists a standard proof outline

$$\{p\}\ S^*\ \{q\}$$

for partial correctness such that for every used assertion r (including p and q) the implication

$$r \rightarrow GI$$

holds. Thus the assertions used in the proof outline are equivalent or stronger than GI. This may be needed to establish GI inside the proof outline.

Consider now the *permutation property*, i.e., that $PART$ permutes the elements of the array a but leaves a unchanged outside an interval $[x' : y']$ containing $[m : n]$. Its definition uses the assertion $perm(a, a_0, [x' : y'])$ defined in (3.40):

$$GI \equiv x' \leq m \wedge n \leq y' \ \wedge\ perm(a, a_0, [x' : y']).$$

Since $le, ri \notin var(GI)$, we conclude by the previous results on loop invariants that GI and hence $m \leq le \wedge ri \leq n \wedge GI$ are invariants of both inner loops. Thus the proof outline presented in Figure 3.2 shows that GI is a global invariant of $PART$. Thus we have verified property **P2** in the sense of partial correctness.

Proof of Property P3

To show the *partition property* **P3** we consider the assertion (3.43), i.e.,

$$I3 \ \equiv\ a[m : le - 1] \leq pi \leq a[ri + 1 : n].$$

The proof outline for partial correctness given in Figure 3.3 shows that

$$\{\textbf{true}\}\ PART\ \{I3 \wedge le > ri\}$$

holds. Note that after the initialization $I3$ is trivially satisfied because the two intervals $[m : le - 1]$ and $[ri + 1 : n]$ are empty for $le = m$ and $ri = n$, and consequently, the two universal quantifications in the expanded definition

$\{GI\}$

$pi := a[f];$

$\{GI\}$

$le, ri := m, n;$

$\{\mathbf{inv} : m \leq le \wedge ri \leq n \wedge GI\}$

while $le \leq ri$ **do**

    $\{\mathbf{inv} : m \leq le \wedge ri \leq n \wedge GI\}$

    while $a[le] < pi$ **do**

    $le := le + 1$

    od;

    $\{\mathbf{inv} : m \leq le \wedge ri \leq n \wedge GI\}$

    while $pi < a[ri]$ **do**

    $ri := ri - 1$

    od;

    $\{m \leq le \wedge ri \leq n \wedge GI\}$

    if $le \leq ri$ **then**

        $\{m \leq le \wedge ri \leq n \wedge GI \wedge le \leq ri\}$

        $\{m \leq le \leq n \wedge m \leq ri \leq n \wedge GI\}$

        $swap(a[le], a[ri]);$

        $\{m \leq le \wedge ri \leq n \wedge GI\}$

        $\{m \leq le + 1 \wedge ri - 1 \leq n \wedge GI\}$

        $le, ri := le + 1, ri - 1$

        $\{m \leq le \wedge ri \leq n \wedge GI\}$

    fi

    $\{m \leq le \wedge ri \leq n \wedge GI\}$

od

$\{m \leq le \wedge ri \leq n \wedge GI\}$

Fig. 3.2 Proof outline establishing property P2 of *PART*.

of (3.43) are vacuously true. Further note that $I3 \wedge le > ri$ implies the postcondition of **P3**. This proves **P3**.

$\{\textbf{true}\}$

$pi := a[f];$

$\{\textbf{true}\}$

$le, ri := m, n;$

$\{le = m \wedge ri = n\}$

$\{\textbf{inv} : I3\}$

while $le \leq ri$ **do**

  $\{\textbf{inv} : I3\}$

  while $a[le] < pi$ **do**

   $le := le + 1$

  od;

  $\{\textbf{inv} : I3 \wedge pi \leq a[le]\}$

  while $pi < a[ri]$ **do**

   $ri := ri - 1$

  od;

  $\{I3 \wedge a[ri] \leq pi \leq a[le]\}$

  if $le \leq ri$ **then**

    $\{I3 \wedge a[ri] \leq pi \leq a[le]\}$

    $swap(a[le], a[ri]);$

    $\{I3 \wedge a[le] \leq pi \leq a[ri]\}$

    $\{a[m : le] \leq pi \leq a[ri : n]\}$

    $le, ri := le + 1, ri - 1;$

    $\{I3\}$

  fi

  $\{I3\}$

od

$\{I3 \wedge le > ri\}$

Fig. 3.3 Proof outline establishing property P3 of $PART$.

Proof of Property P4

To prove property **P4** and to prepare ourselves for the termination proof of $PART$ we need to establish more loop invariants. Define

$$I1 \equiv \ m \leq n \wedge m \leq le \wedge ri \leq n,$$
$$I \equiv \ I1 \wedge A(le) \wedge B(ri),$$

where we recall that

$$A(le) \equiv \exists i \in [le : n] : pi \leq a[i],$$
$$B(ri) \equiv \exists j \in [m : ri] : a[j] \leq pi.$$

Then we have the following proof outlines for partial correctness.

(1) For the initial part of $PART$ we prove:

$$\{m \leq f \leq n\}$$
$$pi := a[f];$$
$$\{m \leq f \leq n \wedge pi = a[f]\}$$
$$le, ri := m, n;$$
$$\{m \leq f \leq n \wedge pi = a[f] \wedge le = m \wedge ri = n\}$$
$$\{I\}$$

(2) For the two inner loops of $PART$ we notice by the previous results on loop invariants that I and $I \wedge pi \leq a[le]$ are invariants of the first and second inner loop, respectively:

$$\{\mathbf{inv} : I\}$$
$$\mathbf{while}\ a[le] < pi\ \mathbf{do}$$
$$\quad le := le + 1$$
$$\mathbf{od};$$
$$\{\mathbf{inv} : I \wedge pi \leq a[le]\}$$
$$\mathbf{while}\ pi < a[ri]\ \mathbf{do}$$
$$\quad ri := ri - 1$$
$$\mathbf{od}$$
$$\{I1 \wedge A(le) \wedge B(ri) \wedge a[ri] \leq pi \leq a[le]\}$$

(3) For the case $le < ri$ of the body of the final **if** statement of $PART$ we prove:

$$\{le < ri \wedge I1 \wedge A(le) \wedge B(ri) \wedge a[ri] \leq pi \leq a[le]\}$$
$$swap(a[le], a[ri]);$$
$$\{le < ri \wedge I1 \wedge A(le) \wedge B(ri) \wedge a[le] \leq pi \leq a[ri]\}$$
$$\{I1 \wedge A(le + 1) \wedge B(ri - 1)\}$$
$$le, ri := le + 1, ri - 1$$
$$\{I1 \wedge A(le) \wedge B(ri)\}$$
$$\{I1 \wedge ((A(le) \wedge B(ri)) \vee m \leq le - 1 = ri + 1 \leq n)\}$$

(4) For the case $le = ri$ of the body of the final **if** statement of $PART$ we prove:

$$\{le = ri \wedge I1 \wedge A(le) \wedge B(ri) \wedge a[ri] \leq pi \leq a[le]\}$$
$$\{m \leq le = ri \leq n \wedge I1\}$$
$$swap(a[le], a[ri]);$$
$$\{m \leq le = ri \leq n \wedge I1\}$$
$$le, ri := le + 1, ri - 1$$
$$\{m \leq le - 1 = ri + 1 \leq n \wedge I1\}$$
$$\{I1 \wedge ((A(le) \wedge B(ri)) \vee m \leq le - 1 = ri + 1 \leq n)\}$$

(5) Combining (3) and (4) with the disjunction rule A3, we establish the following correctness formula:

$$\{le \leq ri \wedge I1 \wedge A(le) \wedge B(ri) \wedge a[ri] \leq pi \leq a[le]\}$$
$$swap(a[le], a[ri]);$$
$$le, ri := le + 1, ri - 1$$
$$\{I1 \wedge ((A(le) \wedge B(ri)) \vee m \leq le - 1 = ri + 1 \leq n)\}$$

(6) From (5) we obtain for the **if** statement:

$$\{I1 \wedge A(le) \wedge B(ri) \wedge a[ri] \leq pi \leq a[le]\}$$
if $le \leq ri$ **then**
$$\{le \leq ri \wedge I1 \wedge A(le) \wedge B(ri) \wedge a[ri] \leq pi \leq a[le]\}$$
$$swap(a[le], a[ri]);$$
$$le, ri := le + 1, ri - 1$$
$$\{I1 \wedge ((A(le) \wedge B(ri)) \vee m \leq le - 1 = ri + 1 \leq n)\}$$
fi
$$\{I1 \wedge ((A(le) \wedge B(ri)) \vee m \leq le - 1 = ri + 1 \leq n)\}$$

Note that by the following chain of implications

$$I1 \wedge A(le) \wedge B(ri) \wedge a[ri] \leq pi \leq a[le] \wedge le > ri$$
$$\rightarrow \quad I1 \wedge A(le) \wedge B(ri)$$
$$\rightarrow \quad I1 \wedge ((A(le) \wedge B(ri)) \vee m \leq le - 1 = ri + 1 \leq n),$$

the implicit **else** branch is properly taken care of.

(7) Finally, we show that

$$le > ri \wedge ((m \leq le - 1 = ri + 1 \leq n) \vee (m \leq le \leq n \ \wedge \ m \leq ri \leq n))$$

implies the postcondition of **P4**, i.e.,

$$m < le \wedge ri < n.$$

If $m \leq le - 1 = ri + 1 \leq n$ we have the implications

$$m \leq le - 1 \rightarrow m < le \quad \text{and} \quad ri + 1 \leq n \rightarrow ri < m$$

If $m \leq le \leq n \ \wedge \ m \leq ri \leq n$ we calculate

$$
\begin{array}{ccc}
m & & ri \\
< \ \{m \leq ri\} & & < \ \{le > ri\} \\
-ri & \text{and} & le \\
\leq \ \{le > ri\} & & \leq \ \{le \leq n\} \\
le & & n.
\end{array}
$$

Now we combine (1), (2) and (6) with (3.42) and (7) to arrive at the overall proof outline for $PART$ given in Figure 3.4. Thus we have verified property **P4** in the sense of partial correctness.

Termination

To prove the termination property

$$\textbf{T} \quad \{m \leq f \leq n\} \ PART \ \{\textbf{true}\}$$

we reuse the invariants established for the three loops in the proof outline of Figure 3.4 and add appropriate bound functions. For the first and second inner loops we take

$$t_1 \equiv n - le \quad \text{and} \quad t_2 \equiv ri - m,$$

respectively, and for the outer loop we choose

$$t \equiv ri - le + n + 2 - m.$$

Let us first consider the two inner loops. Recall that $I \equiv I1 \wedge A(le) \wedge B(ri)$. By (3.42), we obtain $I \rightarrow t_1 \geq 0$ and $I \rightarrow t_2 \geq 0$. Thus it remains to be shown that each iteration of the inner loops decreases the value of the bound functions. But this is obvious since le is incremented and ri is decremented, respectively, whereas m and n do not change.

More subtle is the argument for the outer loop. Note that

$$I1 \wedge ((A(le) \wedge B(ri)) \vee m \leq le - 1 = ri + 1 \leq n) \rightarrow t \geq 0$$

because on the one hand $A(le) \wedge B(ri)$ implies $ri - le \geq m - n$ and thus $t \geq 2$, and on the other hand $I1 \wedge m \leq le - 1 = ri + 1 \leq n$ implies $t = n - m \geq 0$.

$\{m \leq f \leq n\}$
$pi := a[f];$
$le, ri := m, n;$
$\{I1 \wedge A(le) \wedge B(ri)\}$
$\{inv : I1 \wedge ((A(le) \wedge B(ri)) \vee m \leq le - 1 = ri + 1 \leq n)\}$
while $le \leq ri$ **do**
  $\{I1 \wedge A(le) \wedge B(ri) \wedge le \leq ri\}$
  $\{inv : I1 \wedge A(le) \wedge B(ri)\}$
  while $a[le] < pi$ **do**
  $le := le + 1$
  od;
  $\{inv : I1 \wedge A(le) \wedge B(ri) \wedge pi \leq a[le]\}$
  while $pi < a[ri]$ **do**
  $ri := ri - 1$
  od;
  $\{I1 \wedge A(le) \wedge B(ri) \wedge a[ri] \leq pi \leq a[le]\}$
  if $le \leq ri$ **then**
  $swap(a[le], a[ri]);$
  $le, ri := le + 1, ri - 1$
  fi
  $\{I1 \wedge ((A(le) \wedge B(ri)) \vee m \leq le - 1 = ri + 1 \leq n)\}$
od
$\{I1 \wedge ((A(le) \wedge B(ri)) \vee m \leq le - 1 = ri + 1 \leq n) \wedge le > ri\}$
$\{le > ri \wedge ((m \leq le - 1 = ri + 1 \leq n) \vee (m \leq le \leq n \ \wedge \ m \leq ri \leq n))\}$
$\{m < le \wedge ri < n\}$

Fig. 3.4 Proof outline establishing property P4 of $PART$.

To see that the value of t decreases in each iteration of the outer loop, we first give an informal argument. If upon termination of the two inner loops the condition $le \leq ri$ holds, the value of t decreases thanks to the parallel assignment $le, ri := le + 1, ri - 1$ inside the conditional statement. If $le > ri$ holds instead, one of the inner loops must have been executed (because at the entrance of the outer loop body $le \leq ri$ was true), thus incrementing le or decrementing ri.

Formally, we use the following proof outline for total correctness for the first part of the body of the outer loop:

$$\{t = z \wedge le \leq ri \wedge I\}$$

$\{t = z \wedge z \geq n + 2 - m \wedge I\}$

$\{\textbf{inv} : t \leq z \wedge z \geq n + 2 - m \wedge I\}$ $\{\textbf{bd} : t_1\}$

while $a[le] < pi$ **do**

$\quad \{t \leq z \wedge z \geq n + 2 - m \wedge I \wedge a[le] < pi\}$

$\quad le := le + 1$

$\quad \{t \leq z \wedge z \geq n + 2 - m \wedge I\}$

od;

$\{\textbf{inv} : t \leq z \wedge z \geq n + 2 - m \wedge I\}$ $\{\textbf{bd} : t_2\}$

while $pi < a[ri]$ **do**

$\quad \{t \leq z \wedge z \geq n + 2 - m \wedge I \wedge pi < a[ri]\}$

$\quad ri := ri - 1$

$\quad \{t \leq z \wedge z \geq n + 2 - m \wedge I\}$

od;

$\{t \leq z \wedge z \geq n + 2 - m\}$

For the subsequent **if** statement we distinguish the cases $le \leq ri$ and $le > ri$. In the first case we continue with the following proof outline:

$\{le \leq ri \wedge t \leq z \wedge z \geq n + 2 - m\}$

if $le \leq ri$ **then**

$\quad \{t \leq z\}$

$\quad swap(a[le], a[ri])$;

$\quad \{t \leq z\}$

$\quad le, ri := le + 1, ri - 1$

$\quad \{t < z\}$

else

$\quad \{le \leq ri \wedge t \leq z \wedge z \geq n + 2 - m \wedge le > ri\}$

$\quad \{\textbf{false}\}$

$\quad skip$

$\quad \{t < z\}$

fi

$\{t < z\}$

For the clarity of the argument we made the **else** branch of the **if** statement visible. In the second case we use the following proof outline:

$\{le > ri \wedge t \leq z \wedge z \geq n + 2 - m\}$

$\{le > ri \wedge t < n + 2 - m \leq z\}$

if $le \leq ri$ **then**

$\quad \{le > ri \wedge t < n + 2 - m \leq z \wedge le \leq ri\}$

$\{\textbf{false}\}$

$swap(a[le], a[ri]);$

$\{\textbf{false}\}$

$le, ri := le + 1, ri - 1$

$\{t < z\}$

else

$\{t < z\}$

$skip$

$\{t < z\}$

fi

$\{t < z\}$

The disjunction rule A3 applied to the above cases yields

$$\{t \leq z \wedge z \geq n + 2 - m\} \text{ if } \ldots \text{ fi } \{t < z\},$$

which by the composition rule completes the proof that the value of t decreases in each iteration of the outer loop. To summarize, the proof outline in Figure 3.5 establishes the total correctness result $\textbf{T}$.

3.10 Systematic Development of Correct Programs

We now discuss an approach of Dijkstra [1976] allowing us to develop programs together with their correctness proofs. To this end, we make use of the proof system TW to guide us in the construction of a program. We follow here the exposition of Gries [1982]. All correctness formulas are supposed to hold in the sense of total correctness.

The main issue in Dijkstra's approach is the development of loops. Suppose we want to find a program R of the form

$$R \equiv T; \textbf{ while } B \textbf{ do } S \textbf{ od}$$

that satisfies, for a given precondition r and postcondition q, the correctness formula

$$\{r\} \ R \ \{q\}. \tag{3.44}$$

To avoid trivial solutions for R (cf. the comment after (3.3) in Example 3.4), we usually postulate that some variables in r and q, say $x_1, \ldots, x_n$, may not be modified by R. Thus we require

$$x_1, \ldots, x_n \notin change(R).$$

$\{m \le f \le n\}$
$pi := a[f];$
$le, ri := m, n;$
$\{\textbf{inv} : I1 \wedge ((A(le) \wedge B(ri)) \vee m \le le - 1 = ri + 1 \le n)\}\{\textbf{bd} : t\}$
while $le \le ri$ **do**
    $\{\textbf{inv} : I\}\{\textbf{bd} : t_1\}$
    while $a[le] < pi$ **do**
      $le := le + 1$
    od;
    $\{\textbf{inv} : I\}\{\textbf{bd} : t_2\}$
    while $pi < a[ri]$ **do**
      $ri := ri - 1$
    od;
    if $le \le ri$ **then**
      $swap(a[le], a[ri]);$
      $le, ri := le + 1, ri - 1;$
    fi
od
$\{\textbf{true}\}$

Fig. 3.5 Proof outline establishing the termination property T of *PART*.

To prove (3.44), it is sufficient to find a loop invariant p and a bound function t satisfying the following conditions:

1. p is initially established; that is, $\{r\}\ T\ \{p\}$ holds;
2. p is a loop invariant; that is, $\{p \wedge B\}\ S\ \{p\}$ holds;
3. upon loop termination q is true; that is, $p \wedge \neg B \to q$;
4. p implies $t \ge 0$; that is, $p \to t \ge 0$;
5. t is decreased with each iteration; that is, $\{p \wedge B \wedge t = z\}\ S\ \{t < z\}$ holds where z is a fresh variable.

Conditions 1–5 can be conveniently presented by the following proof outline for total correctness:

$\{r\}$
$T;$
$\{\textbf{inv} : p\}\{\textbf{bd} : t\}$
while B **do**
    $\{p \wedge B\}$
    S

$$\{p\}$$
od
$$\{p \wedge \neg B\}$$
$$\{q\}$$

Now, when only r and q are known, the first step in finding R consists of finding a loop invariant. One useful strategy is to generalize the postcondition q by replacing a constant by a variable. The following example illustrates the point.

Summation Problem

Let N be an integer constant with $N \geq 0$. The problem is to find a program SUM that stores in an integer variable x the sum of the elements of a given section $a[0 : N-1]$ of an array a of type **integer** $\rightarrow$ **integer**. We require that $a \notin change(SUM)$. By definition, the sum is 0 if $N = 0$. Define now

$$r \equiv N \geq 0$$

and

$$q \equiv x = \Sigma_{i=0}^{N-1} a[i].$$

The assertion q states that x stores the sum of the elements of the section $a[0 : N-1]$. Our goal is to derive a program SUM of the form

$$SUM \equiv T; \textbf{while } B \textbf{ do } S \textbf{ od}.$$

We replace the constant N by a fresh variable k. Putting appropriate bounds on k we obtain

$$p \equiv 0 \leq k \leq N \wedge x = \Sigma_{i=0}^{k-1} a[i]$$

as a proposal for the invariant of the program to be developed.

We now attempt to satisfy conditions 1–5 by choosing B, S and t appropriately.

Re: 1. To establish $\{r\} T \{p\}$, we choose $T \equiv k := 0; \ x := 0$.

Re: 3. To establish $p \wedge \neg B \rightarrow q$, we choose $B \equiv k \neq N$.

Re: 4. We have $p \rightarrow N - k \geq 0$, which suggests choosing $t \equiv N - k$ as the bound function.

Re: 5. To decrease the bound function with each iteration, we choose the program $k := k + 1$ as part of the loop body.

Re: 2. Thus far we have the following incomplete proof outline:

$\{r\}$
$k := 0;\ x := 0;$
$\{\textbf{inv} : p\}\{\textbf{bd} : t\}$
while $k \neq N$ **do** $\{p \wedge k \neq N\}$
$\qquad\qquad S_1;$
$\qquad\qquad \{p[k := k + 1]\}$
$\qquad\qquad k := k + 1$
$\qquad\qquad \{p\}$
od
$\{p \wedge k = N\}$
$\{q\}$

where S_1 is still to be found.

To this end, we compare now the precondition and postcondition of S_1. The precondition $p \wedge k \neq N$ implies

$$0 \leq k + 1 \leq N \wedge x = \Sigma_{i=0}^{k-1}\, a[i]$$

and the postcondition $p[k := k + 1]$ is equivalent to

$$0 \leq k + 1 \leq N \wedge x = (\Sigma_{i=0}^{k-1}\, a[i]) + a[k].$$

We see that adding $a[k]$ to x will "transform" one assertion into another. Thus, we can choose

$$S_1 \equiv x := x + a[k]$$

to ensure that p is a loop invariant.

Summarizing, we have developed the following program together with its correctness proof:

$$SUM \equiv k := 0;\ x := 0;$$
$$\qquad\qquad \textbf{while}\ k \neq N\ \textbf{do}$$
$$\qquad\qquad\qquad x := x + a[k];$$
$$\qquad\qquad\qquad k := k + 1$$
$$\qquad\qquad \textbf{od}.$$

3.11 Case Study: Minimum-Sum Section Problem

We now systematically develop a less trivial program. We study here an example from Gries [1982]. Consider a one-dimensional array a of type **integer** $\rightarrow$ **integer** and an integer constant $N > 0$. By a *section* of a we mean a fragment of a of the form $a[i : j]$ where $0 \leq i \leq j < N$. The *sum* of a section $a[i : j]$ is the expression $\Sigma_{k=i}^{j} a[k]$. A *minimum-sum section* of $a[0 : N-1]$ is a section $a[i : j]$ such that the sum of $a[i : j]$ is minimal among all subsections of $a[0 : N - 1]$.

For example, the minimum-sum section of $a[0 : 4] = (5, -3, 2, -4, 1)$ is $a[1 : 3] = (-3, 2, -4)$ and its sum is -5. The two minimum-sum sections of $a[0 : 4] = (5, 2, 5, 4, 2)$ are $a[1 : 1]$ and $a[4 : 4]$.

Let $s_{i,j}$ denote the sum of section $a[i : j]$, that is,

$$s_{i,j} = \Sigma_{k=i}^{j} \, a[k].$$

The problem now is to find a program *MINSUM* such that $a \notin change(MINSUM)$ and the correctness formula

$$\{N > 0\} \; MINSUM \; \{q\}$$

holds in the sense of total correctness, where

$$q \equiv sum = min \; \{s_{i,j} \mid 0 \leq i \leq j < N\}.$$

Thus q states that sum is the minimum of all $s_{i,j}$ with i and j varying, where $0 \leq i \leq j < N$ holds.

So the above correctness formula states that *MINSUM* stores in the variable sum the sum of a minimum-sum section of $a[0 : N - 1]$.

First we introduce the following notation, where $k \in \{1, \ldots, n\}$:

$$s_k = min \; \{s_{i,j} \mid 0 \leq i \leq j < k\}.$$

Thus s_k is the sum of a minimum-sum section of $a[0 : k - 1]$. Then we have $q \equiv sum = s_N$.

We begin as in the previous example and try to find the invariant p by replacing the constant N in the postcondition q by a fresh variable k and by putting appropriate bounds on k:

$$p \equiv 1 \leq k \leq N \wedge sum = s_k.$$

As before, we now attempt to satisfy conditions 1–5 of Section 3.10 choosing B, S and t in an appropriate way.

Re: 1. To establish $\{N > 0\} \, T \, \{p\}$, we choose as initialization $T \equiv k := 1; \; sum := a[0]$.

Re: 3. To establish $p \wedge \neg B \rightarrow q$, we choose $B \equiv k \neq N$.

Re: 4. Because $p \rightarrow N - k \geq 0$, we choose $t \equiv N - k$ as the bound function.

Re: 5. To decrease the bound function with each iteration, we put $k := k + 1$ at the end of the loop body.

Re: 2. So far we have obtained the following incomplete proof outline for total correctness:

$\{N > 0\}$
$k := 1;\ sum := a[0];$
$\{\mathbf{inv} : p\}\{\mathbf{bd} : t\}$
while $k \neq N$ **do** $\{p \wedge k \neq N\}$
   $S_1;$
   $\{p[k := k+1]\}$
   $k := k+1$
   $\{p\}$
od
$\{p \wedge k = N\}$
$\{q\},$

where S_1 is still to be found. To this end, as in the previous example, we compare the precondition and postcondition of S_1. We have

$$p \wedge k \neq N \rightarrow 1 \leq k+1 \leq N \wedge sum = s_k$$

and

$$
\begin{aligned}
&p[k := k+1] \\
&\leftrightarrow\ 1 \leq k+1 \leq N \wedge sum = s_{k+1} \\
&\leftrightarrow\ 1 \leq k+1 \leq N \wedge sum = min\ \{s_{i,j} \mid 0 \leq i \leq j < k+1\} \\
&\leftrightarrow\quad \{\{s_{i,j} \mid 0 \leq i \leq j < k+1\} = \\
&\qquad\qquad \{s_{i,j} \mid 0 \leq i \leq j < k\} \cup \{s_{i,k} \mid 0 \leq i < k+1\} \\
&\qquad \text{and}\ \ min(A \cup B) = min\ \{minA, minB\}\} \\
&1 \leq k+1 \leq N \wedge sum = min(s_k, min\ \{s_{i,k} \mid 0 \leq i < k+1\}).
\end{aligned}
$$

Using the abbreviation

$$t_k \equiv min\ \{s_{i,k-1} \mid 0 \leq i < k\}$$

for $k \in \{1, \ldots, n\}$ we obtain

$$p[k := k+1] \leftrightarrow 1 \leq k+1 \leq N \wedge sum = min(s_k, t_{k+1}).$$

It is easy to check that the assignment

$$S_1 \equiv sum := min(sum, t_{k+1}) \tag{3.45}$$

transforms the precondition $1 \leq k+1 \leq N \wedge sum = s_k$ into the postcondition $1 \leq k+1 \leq N \wedge sum = min(s_k, t_{k+1})$. In (3.45) the expression t_{k+1} still needs to be computed. We discuss two possible solutions.

Solution 1: Direct Computation. If we just expand the definition of t_{k+1} we arrive at the program

$$k := 1; \; sum := a[0];$$
while $k \neq N$ **do**
$$\quad sum := min(sum, t_{k+1});$$
$$\quad k := k+1$$
od

with

$$t_{k+1} \equiv min \; \{s_{i,k} \mid 0 \leq i < k+1\}.$$

The computation of t_{k+1} needs a number of steps proportional to k. Since the **while** loop is executed for $k = 1, \ldots, N$, the whole program needs a number of steps proportional to

$$\Sigma_{k=1}^{N} \; k = \frac{N \cdot (N+1)}{2},$$

that is, proportional to N^2.

Solution 2: Efficient Computation. To develop a more efficient program we introduce a new variable x which should store the value of t_{k+1} just before executing the assignment (3.45) to sum. For this purpose we strengthen the invariant p. Since at the beginning of the kth iteration only the sums $s_{i,j}$ with $i \leq j < k$ have been investigated, we choose as the new invariant

$$p^* \; \equiv \; p \wedge x = t_k \; \equiv \; 1 \leq k \leq N \wedge sum = s_k \wedge x = t_k$$

and *repeat* the development process. We reuse the bound function $t = N - k$ and add the initialization $x := a[0]$. This yields the following proof outline for total correctness:

$$\{N > 0\}$$
$$k := 1; \; sum := a[0]; \; x := a[0];$$
$$\{\textbf{inv} : p^*\}\{\textbf{bd} : t\}$$
while $k \neq N$ **do**
$$\quad \{p^* \wedge k \neq N\}$$
$$\quad S_1^*;$$
$$\quad \{p^*[k := k+1]\}$$
$$\quad k := k+1$$
$$\quad \{p^*\}$$
od
$$\{p^* \wedge k = N\}$$
$$\{q\},$$

where S_1^* remains to be developed. To this end, we compare again the pre- and postcondition of S_1^*. We have

$$p^* \wedge k \neq N \ \rightarrow \ 1 \leq k+1 \leq N \wedge sum = s_k \wedge x = t_k$$

and

$$p^*[k := k+1]$$
$$\leftrightarrow \ 1 \leq k+1 \leq N \wedge sum = s_{k+1} \wedge x = t_{k+1}$$
$$\leftrightarrow \quad \{\text{see } p[k := k+1] \text{ in Solution 1}\}$$
$$\quad 1 \leq k+1 \leq N \wedge sum = min(s_k, t_{k+1}) \wedge x = t_{k+1}$$
$$\leftrightarrow \ 1 \leq k+1 \leq N \wedge sum = min(s_k, x) \wedge x = t_{k+1}.$$

To bring this condition closer to the form of the precondition, we express t_{k+1} with the help of t_k:

$$t_{k+1}$$
$$= \quad \{\text{definition of } t_k\}$$
$$\quad min \ \{s_{i,k} \mid 0 \leq i < k+1\}$$
$$= \quad \{\text{associativity of } min\}$$
$$\quad min(min \ \{s_{i,k} \mid 0 \leq i < k\}, \ s_{k,k})$$
$$= \quad \{s_{i,k} = s_{i,k-1} + a[k]\}$$
$$\quad min(min \ \{s_{i,k-1} + a[k] \mid 0 \leq i < k\}, \ a[k])$$
$$= \quad \{\text{property of } min\}$$
$$\quad min(min \ \{s_{i,k-1} \mid 0 \leq i < k\} \ + \ a[k], \ a[k])$$
$$= \quad \{\text{definition of } t_k\}$$
$$\quad min(t_k + a[k], a[k]).$$

Thus

$$p^*[k := k+1]$$
$$\leftrightarrow \ 1 \leq k+1 \leq N \wedge sum = min(s_k, x) \wedge x = min(t_k + a[k], a[k]).$$

Using the assignment axiom, the composition rule and the rule of consequence, it is easy to check that the precondition

$$1 \leq k+1 \leq N \wedge sum = s_k \wedge x = t_k$$

gets transformed into the postcondition

$$1 \leq k+1 \leq N \wedge sum = min(s_k, x) \wedge x = min(t_k + a[k], a[k])$$

by the following sequence of assignments:

$$S_1^* \ \equiv \ x := min(x + a[k], a[k]); \ sum := min(sum, x).$$

Thus we have now developed the following program *MINSUM* together with its correctness proof:

$$MINSUM \equiv k := 1; \ sum := a[0]; \ x := a[0];$$
$$\textbf{while } k \neq N \textbf{ do}$$
$$x := min(x + a[k], a[k]);$$
$$sum := min(sum, x);$$
$$k := k + 1$$
$$\textbf{od}.$$

To compute its result *MINSUM* needs only a number of steps proportional to N. This is indeed optimal for the problem of the minimum-sum section because each element of the section $a[0 : N - 1]$ needs to be checked at least once.

3.12 Exercises

Let $\mathcal{N}$ stand for $\mathcal{M}$ or $\mathcal{M}_{tot}$.

3.1. Prove the Input/Output Lemma 3.3.

3.2. Prove the Change and Access Lemma 3.4.

3.3. Prove that

(i) $\mathcal{N}[\![\textbf{if } B \textbf{ then } S_1 \textbf{ else } S_2 \textbf{ fi}]\!] = \mathcal{N}[\![\textbf{if } \neg B \textbf{ then } S_2 \textbf{ else } S_1 \textbf{ fi}]\!]$,
(ii) $\mathcal{N}[\![\textbf{while } B \textbf{ do } S \textbf{ od}]\!] =$
    $\mathcal{N}[\![\textbf{if } B \textbf{ then } S; \textbf{ while } B \textbf{ do } S \textbf{ od else } skip \textbf{ fi}]\!]$.

3.4. Which of the following correctness formulas are true in the sense of partial correctness?

(i) $\{\textbf{true}\} \ x := 100 \ \{\textbf{true}\}$,
(ii) $\{\textbf{true}\} \ x := 100 \ \{x = 100\}$,
(iii) $\{x = 50\} \ x := 100 \ \{x = 50\}$,
(iv) $\{y = 50\} \ x := 100 \ \{y = 50\}$,
(v) $\{\textbf{true}\} \ x := 100 \ \{\textbf{false}\}$,
(vi) $\{\textbf{false}\} \ x := 100 \ \{x = 50\}$.

Give both an informal argument and a formal proof in the system PW. Which of the above correctness formulas are true in the sense of total correctness?

3.5. Consider the program

$$S \equiv z := x; \ x := y; \ y := z.$$

Prove the correctness formula

$$\{x = x_0 \wedge y = y_0\}\ S\ \{x = y_0 \wedge y = x_0\}$$

in the system PW. What is the intuitive meaning of this formula?

3.6. Prove the Soundness Theorem 3.6.

3.7. The following "forward" assignment axiom was proposed in Floyd [1967a] for the case of simple variables and in de Bakker [1980] for the case of subscripted variables:

$$\{p\}\ u := t\ \{\exists y : (p[u := y] \wedge u = t[u := y])\}.$$

(i) Prove its truth. Show that it can be proved in the proof system PW. Show that the assignment axiom can be proved from the above axiom using the consequence rule.
(ii) Show that in general the simple "assignment axiom"

$$\{\textbf{true}\}\ u := t\ \{u = t\}$$

is not true. Investigate under which conditions on u and t it becomes true.

3.8. Prove the correctness formula

$$\{\textbf{true}\}\ \textbf{while true do}\ x := x - 1\ \textbf{od}\ \{\textbf{false}\}$$

in the system PW. Examine where an attempt at proving the same formula in the system TW fails.

3.9. Consider the following program S computing the product of two natural numbers x and y:

$$
\begin{aligned}
S \equiv\ &prod := 0;\ count := y; \\
&\textbf{while}\ count > 0\ \textbf{do} \\
&\qquad prod := prod + x; \\
&\qquad count := count - 1 \\
&\textbf{od},
\end{aligned}
$$

where $x, y, prod, count$ are integer variables.

(i) Exhibit the computation of S starting in a proper state σ with $\sigma(x) = 4$ and $\sigma(y) = 3$.
(ii) Prove the correctness formula

$$\{x \geq 0 \wedge y \geq 0\}\ S\ \{prod = x \cdot y\}$$

in the system TW.
(iii) State and prove a correctness formula about S expressing that the execution of S does not change the values of the variables x and y.

(iv) Determine the weakest precondition $wp(S, \textbf{true})$.

3.10. *Fibonacci number* F_n is defined inductively as follows:

$$F_0 = 0,$$
$$F_1 = 1,$$
$$F_n = F_{n-1} + F_{n-2} \text{ for } n \geq 2.$$

Extend the assertion language by a function symbol *fib* of type **integer** $\rightarrow$ **integer** such that for $n \geq 0$ the expression $fib(n)$ denotes F_n.

(i) Prove the correctness formula

$$\{n \geq 0\}\ S\ \{x = fib(n)\},$$

where

$$
\begin{aligned}
S \equiv\ & x := 0;\ y := 1;\ count := n; \\
& \textbf{while}\ count > 0\ \textbf{do} \\
& \qquad h := y;\ y := x + y;\ x := h; \\
& \qquad count := count - 1 \\
& \textbf{od}
\end{aligned}
$$

and $x, y, n, h, count$ are all integer variables.

(ii) Let a be an array of type **integer** $\rightarrow$ **integer**. Construct a **while** program S' with $n \notin var(S')$ such that

$$\{n \geq 0\}\ S'\ \{\forall(0 \leq k \leq n) : a[k] = fib(k)\}$$

is true in the sense of total correctness. Prove this correctness formula in the system TW.

3.11. Recall that

$$\textbf{if } B \textbf{ then } S \textbf{ fi} \equiv \textbf{if } B \textbf{ then } S \textbf{ else } skip \textbf{ fi}.$$

Show that the following proof rule is sound for partial correctness:

$$\frac{\{p \wedge B\}\ S\ \{q\}, p \wedge \neg B \rightarrow q}{\{p\}\ \textbf{if } B \textbf{ then } S \textbf{ fi}\ \{q\}}$$

3.12. For **while** programs S and Boolean conditions B let the **repeat**-loop be defined as follows:

$$\textbf{repeat } S \textbf{ until } B\ \equiv\ S;\ \textbf{while } \neg B \textbf{ do } S \textbf{ od}.$$

(i) Give the transition axioms or rules specifying the operational semantics of the **repeat**-loop.

(ii) Show that the following proof rule is sound for partial correctness:

$$\frac{\{p\}\ S\ \{q\},\, q \wedge \neg B \to p}{\{p\}\ \textbf{repeat}\ S\ \textbf{until}\ B\ \{q \wedge B\}}.$$

Give a sound proof rule for total correctness of **repeat**-loops.
(iii) Prove that

$$\mathcal{N}[\![\textbf{repeat repeat}\ S\ \textbf{until}\ B_1\ \textbf{until}\ B_2]\!]$$
$$= \mathcal{N}[\![\textbf{repeat}\ S\ \textbf{until}\ B_1 \wedge B_2]\!].$$

3.13. Suppose that

$$< S, \sigma > \to^* < R, \tau >,$$

where $R \not\equiv E$. Prove that $R \equiv \textbf{at}(T, S)$ for a subprogram T of S.
Hint. Prove by induction on the length of computation that R is a sequential composition of subprograms of S.

3.14. Consider the program DIV of Example 3.4 and the assertion

$$q \equiv quo \cdot y + rem = x \wedge 0 \le rem < y.$$

Determine the preconditions $wlp(DIV, q)$ and $wp(DIV, q)$.

3.15. Prove the Weakest Liberal Precondition Lemma 3.5.
Hint. For (ii) use the Substitution Lemma 2.4.

3.16. Prove the Weakest Precondition Lemma 3.6.
Hint. For (ii) use the Substitution Lemma 2.4.

3.17. Prove the Soundness Theorem 3.7.

3.13 Bibliographic Remarks

In this chapter we studied only the simplest class of deterministic programs, namely **while** programs. This class is the kernel of imperative programming languages; in this book it serves as the starting point for investigating recursive, object-oriented, parallel and distributed programs.

The approach presented here is usually called *Hoare's logic*. It has been successfully extended, in literally hundreds of papers, to handle other programming constructs. The survey paper Apt [1981] should help as a guide to the history of the first ten years in this vast domain. The history of program verification is traced in Jones [1992].

A reader who is interested in a more detailed treatment of the subject is advised to read de Bakker [1980], Reynolds [1981], Tucker and Zucker [1988], and/or Nielson and Nielson [2007]. Besides Hoare's logic other approaches to the verification of **while** programs also have been developed, for example, one based on denotational semantics. An introduction to this approach can be found in Loeckx and Sieber [1987]. This book also provides further pointers to the early literature.

The assignment axiom for simple variables is due to Hoare [1969] and for subscripted variables due to de Bakker [1980]. Different axioms for assignment to subscripted variables are given in Hoare and Wirth [1973], Gries [1978] and Apt [1981]. The composition rule, loop rule and consequence rules are due to Hoare [1969]. The conditional rule is due to Lauer [1971] where also the first soundness proof of (an extension of) the proof system PW is given. The loop II rule is motivated by Dijkstra [1982, pages 217–219].

The parallel assignment and the failure statements are from Dijkstra [1975]. The failure statement is a special case of the alternative command there considered and which we shall study in Chapter 10.

The invariance axiom and conjunction rule are due to Gorelick [1975] and the invariance rule and the ∃-introduction rule are essentially due to Harel [1979].

Completeness of the proof system PW is a special case of a completeness result due to Cook [1978]. The completeness proof of the proof system TW is a modification of an analogous proof by Harel [1979]. In our approach only one fixed interpretation of the assertion language is considered. This is not the case in Cook [1978] and Harel [1979] where the completeness theorems refer to a class of interpretations.

Clarke showed in [1979] that for deterministic programs with a powerful ALGOL-like procedure mechanism it is impossible to obtain a complete Hoare-style proof system even if —different from this book— only logical structures with finite data domains are considered. For more details see Section 5.6.

In Zwiers [1989] the auxiliary rules presented in Section 3.8 are called *adaptation rules*. The reason for their name is that they allow us to adapt a given correctness formula about a program to other pre- and postconditions. Adaptation rules are independent of the syntactic structure of the programs. Hence they can be used to reason about identifiers ranging over programs. Such identifiers appear in the treatment of recursion and in the derivation of programs from specifications. The name "adaptation rule" goes back to Hoare [1971a].

The program $PART$ for partitioning an array in Section 3.9 represents the body of the procedure *Partition* inside the recursive program *Quicksort* invented by Hoare [1961a,1962] (see Chapter 5). Partial correctness of *Partition* is shown in Foley and Hoare [1971]. An informal proof of termination of *Partition* is given in Hoare [1971b] as part of the proof of the program *Find* by Hoare [1961b]. In Filliâtre [2007] this informal correctness proof is formalized and certified using the interactive theorem prover Coq. Filliâtre follows Hoare's proof as closely as possible though does not explain which proof rules are used. He points out that two assertions used in Hoare [1971b] are not invariants of the outer loop of *Partition* but hold only in certain parts of the loop. This explains why our correctness proof of *PART* is more complicated than the informal argument given in Hoare [1971b]. Also our bound functions used to show the termination property **T** are more elaborate than in Hoare [1971b] because the invariants should imply that they are non-negative. These bound functions are (modulo an offset of 1) exactly as in Filliâtre [2007].

The systematic development of correct programs was first described in the book by Dijkstra [1976]. The approach has been further explained in Gries [1981]. Both Dijkstra and Gries base their work on program development on a class of nondeterministic programs called *guarded commands* which are studied in Chapter 10.

4 Recursive Programs

W HILE PROGRAMS, DISCUSSED in the previous chapter, are of
course extremely limited. Focusing on them allowed us to introduce two basic topics which form the subject of this book: semantics and
program verification. We now proceed by gradually introducing more powerful programming concepts and extending our analysis to them.

Every realistic programming language offers some way of structuring the
programs. Historically, the first concept allowing us to do so was procedures.
To systematically study their verification we proceed in two steps. In this
chapter we introduce parameterless procedures and in the next chapter procedures with parameters. This allows us to focus first on recursion, an important and powerful concept. To deal with it we need to modify appropriately
the methods introduced in the previous chapter.

We start by defining in Section 4.1 the syntax of programs in the context of
a set of declarations of parameterless recursive procedures. We call such programs recursive programs. In Section 4.2 we extend the semantics introduced

Krzysztof R. Apt et al., *Verification of Sequential and Concurrent Programs*,
Texts in Computer Science, DOI: 10.1007/978-1-84882-745-5_4,
© Springer-Verlag London Limited 2009

in Section 3.2 to recursive programs. Thanks to our focus on operational semantics, such an extension turns out to be very simple.

Verification of recursive programs calls for a non-trivial extension of the approach introduced in Section 3.3. In Section 4.3 we deal with partial correctness and total correctness. In each case we introduce proof rules that refer in their premises to proofs. Then, as a case study, we consider in Section 4.5 the correctness of a binary search program.

4.1 Syntax

Given a set of *procedure identifiers*, with typical elements $P, P_1, \ldots$, we extend the syntax of **while** programs studied in Chapter 3 by the following clause:

$$S ::= P.$$

A procedure identifier used as a subprogram is called a *procedure call*. Procedures are defined by *declarations* of the form

$$P :: S.$$

In this context S is called the *procedure body*. *Recursion* refers here to the fact that the procedure body S of P can contain P as a subprogram. Such occurrences of P are called *recursive calls*. From now on we assume a given set of procedure declarations D such that each procedure that appears in D has a unique declaration in D. To keep notation simple we omit the "{ }" brackets when writing specific sets of declarations, so we write $P_1 :: S_1, \ldots, P_n :: S_n$ instead of $\{P_1 :: S_1, \ldots, P_n :: S_n\}$.

A *recursive program* consists of a *main statement* S built according to the syntax of this section and a given set D of (recursive) procedure declarations. All procedure calls in the main statement refer to procedures that are declared in D. If D is clear from the context we refer to the main statement as a recursive program.

Example 4.1. Using this syntax the declaration of the proverbial factorial program can be written as follows:

$$Fac :: \textbf{if } x = 0 \textbf{ then } y := 1 \textbf{ else } x := x - 1; \; Fac; \; x := x + 1; \; y := y \cdot x \textbf{ fi.}$$
$$(4.1)$$

A main statement in the context of this declaration is the procedure call Fac. □

4.2 Semantics

We define the semantics of recursive programs by extending the transition system for **while** programs by the following transition axiom:

(viii) $< P, \sigma > \; \rightarrow \; < S, \sigma >$, where $P :: S \in D$.

This axiom captures the meaning of a procedure call by means of a *copy rule*, according to which a procedure call is dynamically replaced by the corresponding procedure body.

The concepts introduced in Definition 3.1, in particular that of a computation, extend in an obvious way to the current setting.

Example 4.2. Assume the declaration (4.1) of the factorial program. Then we have the following computation of the main statement Fac, where σ is a proper state with $\sigma(x) = 2$:

$$< Fac, \sigma >$$
$$\rightarrow\ < \textbf{if } x = 0 \textbf{ then } y := 1 \textbf{ else } x := x - 1;\ Fac;$$
$$x := x + 1;\ y := y \cdot x \textbf{ fi}, \sigma >$$
$$\rightarrow\ < x := x - 1;\ Fac;\ x := x + 1;\ y := y \cdot x, \sigma >$$
$$\rightarrow\ < Fac;\ x := x + 1;\ y := y \cdot x, \sigma[x := 1] >$$
$$\rightarrow\ < \textbf{if } x = 0 \textbf{ then } y := 1 \textbf{ else } x := x - 1;\ Fac;\ x := x + 1;\ y := y \cdot x \textbf{ fi};$$
$$x := x + 1;\ y := y \cdot x, \sigma[x := 1] >$$
$$\rightarrow\ < x := x - 1;\ Fac;\ x := x + 1;\ y := y \cdot x;$$
$$x := x + 1;\ y := y \cdot x, \sigma[x := 1] >$$
$$\rightarrow\ < Fac;\ x := x + 1;\ y := y \cdot x;\ x := x + 1;\ y := y \cdot x, \sigma[x := 0] >$$
$$\rightarrow\ < \textbf{if } x = 0 \textbf{ then } y := 1 \textbf{ else } x := x - 1;\ Fac;\ x := x + 1;\ y := y \cdot x \textbf{ fi};$$
$$x := x + 1;\ y := y \cdot x;\ x := x + 1;\ y := y \cdot x, \sigma[x := 0] >$$
$$\rightarrow\ < y := 1;\ x := x + 1;\ y := y \cdot x;\ x := x + 1;\ y := y \cdot x, \sigma[x := 0] >$$
$$\rightarrow\ < x := x + 1;\ y := y \cdot x;\ x := x + 1;\ y := y \cdot x, \sigma[y, x := 1, 0] >$$
$$\rightarrow\ < y := y \cdot x;\ x := x + 1;\ y := y \cdot x, \sigma[y, x := 1, 1] >$$
$$\rightarrow\ < x := x + 1;\ y := y \cdot x, \sigma[y, x := 1, 1] >$$
$$\rightarrow\ < y := y \cdot x, \sigma[y := 1] >$$
$$\rightarrow\ < E, \sigma[y := 2] >$$

□

Definition 4.1. Recall that we assumed a given set of procedure declarations D. We now extend two input/output semantics originally introduced for **while** programs to recursive programs by using the transition relation $\rightarrow$ defined by the axioms and rules (i)–(viii):

(i) the *partial correctness semantics* defined by

$$\mathcal{M}[\![S]\!](\sigma) = \{\tau \mid < S, \sigma > \rightarrow^* < E, \tau >\},$$

(ii) the *total correctness semantics* defined by

$$\mathcal{M}_{tot}[\![S]\!](\sigma) = \mathcal{M}[\![S]\!](\sigma) \cup \{\bot \mid S \text{ can diverge from } \sigma\}.$$

□

Example 4.3. Assume the declaration (4.1) of the factorial procedure. Then the following hold for the main statement Fac:

- if $\sigma(x) \geq 0$ then

$$\mathcal{M}[\![Fac]\!](\sigma) = \mathcal{M}_{tot}[\![Fac]\!](\sigma) = \{\sigma[y := \sigma(x)!]\},$$

where for $n \geq 0$, the expression $n!$ denotes the factorial of n, i.e., $0! = 1$ and for $n > 0$, $n! = 1 \cdot \ldots \cdot n$,
- if $\sigma(x) < 0$ then

$$\mathcal{M}[\![Fac]\!](\sigma) = \emptyset \text{ and } \mathcal{M}_{tot}[\![Fac]\!](\sigma) = \{\bot\}.$$

$\square$

Properties of the Semantics

In the Input/Output Lemma 3.3(v) we expressed the semantics of loops in terms of a union of semantics of its finite syntactic approximations. An analogous observation holds for recursive programs. In this lemma we refer to different sets of procedure declarations. To avoid confusion we then write $D \mid S$ when we consider S in the context of the set D of procedure declarations.

Recall that Ω is a **while** program such that for all proper states σ, $\mathcal{M}[\![\Omega]\!](\sigma) = \emptyset$. Given a declaration $D = P_1 :: S_1, \ldots, P_n :: S_n$ and a recursive program S, we define the kth *syntactic approximation* S^k of S by induction on $k \geq 0$:

$$\begin{aligned} S^0 &= \Omega, \\ S^{k+1} &= S[S_1^k/P_1, \ldots, S_n^k/P_n], \end{aligned}$$

where $S[R_1/P_1, \ldots, R_n/P_n]$ is the result of a simultaneous replacement in S of each procedure identifier P_i by the statement R_i. Furthermore, let D^k abbreviate $P_1 :: S_1^k, \ldots, P_n :: S_n^k$ and let $\mathcal{N}$ stand for $\mathcal{M}$ or $\mathcal{M}_{tot}$. The following lemma collects the properties of $\mathcal{N}$ we need.

Lemma 4.1. (Input/Output)

(i) $\mathcal{N}[\![D^k \mid S]\!] = \mathcal{N}[\![S^{k+1}]\!]$.

(ii) $\mathcal{N}[\![D \mid S]\!] = \mathcal{N}[\![D \mid S[S_1/P_1, \ldots, S_n/P_n]]\!]$.

    In particular, $\mathcal{N}[\![D \mid P_i]\!] = \mathcal{N}[\![D \mid S_i]\!]$ *for* $i = 1, \ldots, n$.

(iii) $\mathcal{M}[\![D \mid S]\!] = \bigcup_{k=0}^{\infty} \mathcal{M}[\![S^k]\!]$.

Proof. See Exercise 4.3. $\square$

Note that each S^k is a **while** statement, that is a program without procedure calls.

4.3 Verification

Partial Correctness

Let S be the main statement of a recursive program in the context of a set D of procedure declarations. As in the case of **while** programs we say that the correctness formula $\{p\}\ S\ \{q\}$ is true in the sense of *partial correctness*, and write $\models \{p\}\ S\ \{q\}$, if

$$\mathcal{M}[\![S]\!]([\![p]\!]) \subseteq [\![q]\!].$$

Assuming $D = P_1 :: S_1, \ldots, P_n :: S_n$, in order to prove $\models \{p\}\ S\ \{q\}$ we first prove

$$A \vdash \{p\}\ S\ \{q\}$$

for some sequence

$$A \equiv \{p_1\}\ P_1\ \{q_1\}, \ldots, \{p_n\}\ P_n\ \{q_n\}$$

of assumptions. Then to *discharge* these assumptions we additionally prove that for all $i = 1, \ldots, n$

$$A \vdash \{p_i\}\ S_i\ \{q_i\}.$$

We summarize these two steps by the following proof rule:

RULE 8: RECURSION

$$\frac{\begin{array}{l} \{p_1\}\ P_1\ \{q_1\}, \ldots, \{p_n\}\ P_n\ \{q_n\} \vdash \{p\}\ S\ \{q\}, \\ \{p_1\}\ P_1\ \{q_1\}, \ldots, \{p_n\}\ P_n\ \{q_n\} \vdash \{p_i\}\ S_i\ \{q_i\},\ i \in \{1, \ldots, n\}, \end{array}}{\{p\}\ S\ \{q\}}$$

where $D = P_1 :: S_1, \ldots, P_n :: S_n$.

The intuition behind this rule is as follows. Say that a program S is (p, q)-*correct* if $\{p\}\ S\ \{q\}$ holds in the sense of partial correctness. The second premise of the rule states that we can establish for $i = 1, \ldots, n$ the (p_i, q_i)-correctness of the procedure bodies S_i from the *assumption* of the (p_i, q_i)-correctness of the procedure calls P_i, for $i = 1, \ldots, n$. Then we can prove the (p_i, q_i)-correctness of the procedure calls P_i unconditionally, and thanks to the first premise establish the (p, q)-correctness of the recursive program S.

We still have to clarify the meaning of the $\vdash$ provability relation that we use in the rule premises. In these proofs we allow the axioms and proof rules of the proof system PW, and appropriately modified auxiliary axioms and proof rules introduced in Section 3.8. This modification consists of the adjustment of the conditions for specific variables so that they now also refer to the assumed set of procedure declarations D. To this end, we first extend the definition of $change(S)$.

Recall that the set $change(S)$ consisted of all simple and array variables that can be modified by S. This suggests the following extension of $change(S)$ to recursive programs and sets of procedure declarations:

$$change(P :: S) = change(S),$$
$$change(\{P :: S\} \cup D) = change(P :: S) \cup change(D),$$
$$change(P) = \emptyset.$$

Then we modify the auxiliary axioms and proof rules by adding the restriction that specific variables do not occur in $change(D)$. For example, the invariance axiom A2 now reads

$$\{p\} \ S \ \{p\}$$

where $free(p) \cap (change(D) \cup change(S)) = \emptyset$.

To prove partial correctness of recursive programs we use the following proof system PR:

PROOF SYSTEM PR :
   This system consists of the group of axioms
   and rules 1–6, 8, and A2–A6.

Thus PR is obtained by extending the proof system PW by the recursion rule 8 and the auxiliary rules A2–A6 where we use the versions of auxiliary rules modified by $change(D)$ as explained above.

In the actual proof not all assumptions about procedure calls are needed, only those assumptions that do appear in the procedure body. In particular, when we deal only with one recursive procedure and use the procedure call as the considered recursive program, the recursion rule can be simplified to

$$\frac{\{p\} \ P \ \{q\} \vdash \{p\} \ S \ \{q\}}{\{p\} \ P \ \{q\}}$$

where $D = P :: S$.

Further, when the procedure P is not recursive, that is, its procedure body S does not contain any procedure calls, the above rule can be further simplified to

$$\frac{\{p\} \ S \ \{q\}}{\{p\} \ P \ \{q\}}$$

It is straightforward how to extend the concept of a proof outline to that of a proof outline from a set of assumptions being correctness formulas: we simply allow each assumption as an additional formation axiom. Now, the premises of the considered recursion rule and all subsequently introduced recursion rules consist of the correctness proofs. We present them as proof outlines from a set of assumptions. These assumptions are correctness formulas about the calls of the considered procedures.

We illustrate this proof presentation by returning to the factorial program.

Example 4.4. Assume the declaration (4.1) of the factorial program. We prove the correctness formula

$$\{z = x \wedge x \geq 0\} \; Fac \; \{z = x \wedge y = x!\}$$

in the proof system PR. The assertion $z = x$ is used both in the pre- and postcondition to prove that the call of Fac does not modify the value of x upon termination. (Without it the postcondition $y = x!$ could be trivially achieved by setting both x and y to 1.)

To this end, we introduce the assumption

$$\{z = x \wedge x \geq 0\} \; Fac \; \{z = x \wedge y = x!\}$$

and show that

$$\{z = x \wedge x \geq 0\} \; Fac \; \{z = x \wedge y = x!\} \vdash \{z = x \wedge x \geq 0\} \; S \; \{z = x \wedge y = x!\},$$

where

$$S \equiv \textbf{if } x = 0 \textbf{ then } y := 1 \textbf{ else } x := x - 1; \; Fac; \; x := x + 1; \; y := y \cdot x \textbf{ fi}$$

is the procedure body of Fac.

First we apply the substitution rule to the assumption and obtain

$$\{z - 1 = x \wedge x \geq 0\} \; Fac \; \{z - 1 = x \wedge y = x!\}.$$

The proof that uses this assumption can now be presented in the form of a proof outline that we give in Figure 4.1. The desired conclusion now follows by the simplified form of the recursion rule.   □

Total Correctness

We say that the correctness formula $\{p\} \; S \; \{q\}$ is true in the sense of *total correctness*, and write $\models_{tot} \{p\} \; S \; \{q\}$, if

$$\mathcal{M}_{tot}[\![S]\!]([\![p]\!]) \subseteq [\![q]\!].$$

$\{z = x \wedge x \geq 0\}$
if $x = 0$
then
$\qquad \{z = x \wedge x \geq 0 \wedge x = 0\}$
$\qquad \{z = x \wedge 1 = x!\}$
$\qquad y := 1$
$\qquad \{z = x \wedge y = x!\}$
else
$\qquad \{z = x \wedge x \geq 0 \wedge x \neq 0\}$
$\qquad \{z - 1 = x - 1 \wedge x - 1 \geq 0\}$
$\qquad x := x - 1;$
$\qquad \{z - 1 = x \wedge x \geq 0\}$
$\qquad Fac;$
$\qquad \{z - 1 = x \wedge y = x!\}$
$\qquad x := x + 1;$
$\qquad \{z - 1 = x - 1 \wedge y = (x - 1)!\}$
$\qquad \{z - 1 = x - 1 \wedge y \cdot x = x!\}$
$\qquad y := y \cdot x$
$\qquad \{z - 1 = x - 1 \wedge y = x!\}$
$\qquad \{z = x \wedge y = x!\}$
fi
$\{z = x \wedge y = x!\}$

Fig. 4.1 Proof outline showing partial correctness of the factorial procedure.

In this subsection the provability sign $\vdash$ refers to the proof system for total correctness that consists of the proof system TW extended by the appropriately modified auxiliary rules introduced in Section 3.8.

Let $D = P_1 :: S_1, \ldots, P_n :: S_n$. In order to prove $\models_{tot} \{P\} S \{q\}$ we first prove

$$A \vdash \{p\}S\{q\}$$

for some sequence

$$A \equiv \{p_1\} \, P_1 \, \{q_1\}, \ldots, \{p_n\} \, P_n \, \{q_n\}$$

of assumptions. In order to *discharge* these assumptions we additionally prove that for $i = 1, \ldots, n$

$$\{p_1 \wedge t < z\} \, P_1 \, \{q_1\}, \ldots, \{p_n \wedge t < z\} \, P_n \, \{q_n\} \vdash \{p_i \wedge t = z\} \, S_i \, \{q_i\}$$

and

$$p_i \rightarrow t \geq 0$$

hold. Here t is an integer expression and z a fresh integer variable which is treated in the proofs

$$\{p_1 \wedge t < z\} P_1 \{q_1\}, \ldots, \{p_n \wedge t < z\} P_n \{q_n\} \vdash \{p_i \wedge t = z\} S_i \{q_i\},$$

for $i = 1, \ldots, n$, as a *constant*, which means that in these proofs neither the $\exists$-introduction rule nor the substitution rule of Section 3.8 is applied to z. The expression t plays the role analogous to the bound function of a loop.

We summarize these steps as the following proof rule:

RULE 9: RECURSION II

$$\{p_1\} P_1 \{q_1\}, \ldots, \{p_n\} P_n \{q_n\} \vdash \{p\} S \{q\},$$
$$\{p_1 \wedge t < z\} P_1 \{q_1\}, \ldots, \{p_n \wedge t < z\} P_n \{q_n\} \vdash$$
$$\{p_i \wedge t = z\} S_i \{q_i\}, \ i \in \{1, \ldots, n\},$$
$$\underline{p_i \rightarrow t \geq 0, \ i \in \{1, \ldots, n\}}$$
$$\{p\} S \{q\}$$

where $D = P_1 :: S_1, \ldots, P_n :: S_n$ and z is an integer variable that does not occur in p_i, t, q_i and S_i for $i \in \{1, \ldots, n\}$ and is treated in the proofs as a constant, which means that in these proofs neither the $\exists$-introduction rule A5 nor the substitution rule A7 is applied to z.

The intuition behind this rule is as follows. Say that a program S is (p, q, t)-*correct* if $\{p\} S \{q\}$ holds in the sense of total correctness, with at most t procedure calls in each computation starting in a proper state satisfying p, where $t \geq 0$.

The second premise of the rule states that we can establish for $i = 1, \ldots, n$ the (p_i, q_i, t)-correctness of the procedure bodies S_i from the assumption of the (p_i, q_i, z)-correctness of the procedure calls P_i, for $i = 1, \ldots, n$, where $z < t$. Then, thanks to the last premise, we can prove unconditionally $\{p_i\} P_i \{q_i\}$ in the sense of total correctness, for $i = 1, \ldots, n$, and thanks to the first premise, $\{p\} S \{q\}$ in the sense of total correctness.

To prove *total* correctness of *recursive* programs we use the following proof system TR:

> ### PROOF SYSTEM TR :
> This system consists of the group of axioms
> and rules 1–4, 6, 7, 9, and A3–A6.

Thus TR is obtained by extending proof system TW by the recursion II rule (rule 9) and the auxiliary rules A3–A6.

Again, when we deal only with one recursive procedure and use the procedure call as the statement in the considered recursive program, this rule can be simplified to

$$\frac{\{p \wedge t < z\}\ P\ \{q\} \vdash \{p \wedge t = z\}\ S\ \{q\},}{\{p\}\ P\ \{q\}}$$
$$p \to t \geq 0$$

where $D = P :: S$ and z is treated in the proof as a constant.

Decomposition

As for **while** programs it is sometimes more convenient to decompose the proof of total correctness of a recursive program into two separate proofs, one of partial correctness and one of termination. Formally, this can be done using the decomposition rule A1 introduced in Section 3.3, but with the provability signs $\vdash_p$ and $\vdash_t$ referring to the proof systems PR and TR, respectively.

Example 4.5. We apply the decomposition rule A1 to the factorial program studied in Example 4.4. Assume the declaration (4.1) of the factorial program. To prove the correctness formula

$$\{z = x \wedge x \geq 0\}\ Fac\ \{z = x \wedge y = x!\} \tag{4.2}$$

in the sense of total correctness, we build upon the fact that we proved it already in the sense of partial correctness.

Therefore we only need to establish termination. To this end, it suffices to prove the correctness formula

$$\{x \geq 0\}\ Fac\ \{\textbf{true}\} \tag{4.3}$$

in the proof system TR. We choose

$$t \equiv x$$

as the bound function. The proof outline presented in Figure 4.2 then shows that

$$\{x \geq 0 \wedge x < z\}\ Fac\ \{\textbf{true}\} \vdash \{x \geq 0 \wedge x = z\}\ S\ \{\textbf{true}\}$$

holds. Applying now the simplified form of the recursion II rule we get (4.3). By the consequence rule, we obtain $\{z = x \wedge x \geq 0\}\ Fac\ \{\textbf{true}\}$, as required by the decomposition rule to establish (4.2). $\square$

$$\{x \geq 0 \land x = z\}$$
if $x = 0$
then
    $\{x \geq 0 \land x = z \land x = 0\}$
    $\{\textbf{true}\}$
    $y := 1$
    $\{\textbf{true}\}$
else
    $\{x \geq 0 \land x = z \land x \neq 0\}$
    $\{x - 1 \geq 0 \land x - 1 < z\}$
    $x := x - 1;$
    $\{x \geq 0 \land x < z\}$
    $Fac;$
    $\{\textbf{true}\}$
    $x := x + 1;$
    $\{\textbf{true}\}$
    $y := y \cdot x$
    $\{\textbf{true}\}$
fi
$\{\textbf{true}\}$

Fig. 4.2 Proof outline showing termination of the factorial procedure.

Discussion

Let us clarify now the restrictions used in the recursion II rule. The following example explains why the restrictions we imposed on the integer variable z are necessary.

Example 4.6. Consider the trivially non-terminating recursive procedure declared by

$$P :: P.$$

We first show that when we are allowed to existentially quantify the variable z, we can prove $\{x \geq 0\}\ P\ \{\textbf{true}\}$ in the sense of total correctness, which is obviously wrong. Indeed, take as the bound function t simply the integer variable x. Then

$$x \geq 0 \rightarrow t \geq 0.$$

Next we show

$$\{x \geq 0 \land x < z\}\ P\ \{\textbf{true}\} \vdash \{x \geq 0 \land x = z\}\ P\ \{\textbf{true}\}.$$

Using the $\exists$-introduction rule A5 of Section 3.8 we existentially quantify z and obtain from the assumption the correctness formula

$$\{\exists z : (x \geq 0 \wedge x < z)\} \; P \; \{\textbf{true}\}.$$

But the precondition $\exists z : (x \geq 0 \wedge x < z)$ is equivalent to $x \geq 0$, so by the consequence rule we derive

$$\{x \geq 0\} \; P \; \{\textbf{true}\}.$$

Using the consequence rule again we can strengthen the precondition and obtain

$$\{x \geq 0 \wedge x = z\} \; P \; \{\textbf{true}\}.$$

Now we apply the simplified form of the recursion II rule and obtain $\{x \geq 0\} \; P \; \{\textbf{true}\}$.

In a similar way we can show that we must not apply the substitution rule A7 of Section 3.8 to the variable z. Indeed, substituting in the above assumption $\{x \geq 0 \wedge x < z\} \; P \; \{\textbf{true}\}$ the variable z by $x + 1$ (note that the application condition $\{x, z\} \cap var(P) = \emptyset$ of the substitution rule is satisfied), we obtain

$$\{x \geq 0 \wedge x < x + 1\} \; P \; \{\textbf{true}\}.$$

Since $x \geq 0 \wedge x = z \rightarrow x \geq 0 \wedge x < x + 1$, we obtain by the consequence rule

$$\{x \geq 0 \wedge x = z\} \; P \; \{\textbf{true}\},$$

as above. $\qquad\qquad\qquad\qquad\qquad\qquad\qquad\qquad\qquad\qquad\qquad\qquad\qquad\quad\square$

Soundness

We now establish soundness of the recursion rule and as a consequence that of the proof system PR in the sense of partial correctness. Below we write

$$\{p_1\} \; P_1 \; \{q_1\}, \ldots, \{p_n\} \; P_n \; \{q_n\} \models \{p\} \; S \; \{q\}$$

when the following holds:

for *all* sets of procedure declarations D
if $\models \{p_i\} \; P_i \; \{q_i\}$, for $i = 1, \ldots, n$, then $\models \{p\} \; S \; \{q\}$.

We shall need the following strengthening of the Soundness Theorem 3.1(i). Recall that the provability sign $\vdash$ refers to the proof system PW extended by the appropriately modified auxiliary axioms and proof rules introduced in Section 3.8.

Theorem 4.1. (Soundness of Proofs from Assumptions)

$$\{p_1\} \; P_1 \; \{q_1\}, \ldots, \{p_n\} \; P_n \; \{q_n\} \vdash \{p\} \; S \; \{q\}$$

implies

$$\{p_1\}\ P_1\ \{q_1\},\ldots,\{p_n\}\ P_n\ \{q_n\} \models \{p\}\ S\ \{q\}.$$

Proof. See Exercise 4.5.   □

Theorem 4.2. (Soundness of the Recursion Rule)
Assume that $D = P_1 :: S_1, \ldots, P_n :: S_n$. *Suppose that*

$$\{p_1\}\ P_1\ \{q_1\},\ldots,\{p_n\}\ P_n\ \{q_n\} \vdash \{p\}\ S\ \{q\}$$

and for $i = 1,\ldots,n$

$$\{p_1\}\ P_1\ \{q_1\},\ldots,\{p_n\}\ P_n\ \{q_n\} \vdash \{p_i\}\ S_i\ \{q_i\}.$$

Then

$$\models \{p\}\ S\ \{q\}.$$

Proof. By the Soundness Theorem 4.1, we have

$$\{p_1\}\ P_1\ \{q_1\},\ldots,\{p_n\}\ P_n\ \{q_n\} \models \{p\}\ S\ \{q\} \tag{4.4}$$

and for $i = 1,\ldots,n$

$$\{p_1\}\ P_1\ \{q_1\},\ldots,\{p_n\}\ P_n\ \{q_n\} \models \{p_i\}\ S_i\ \{q_i\}. \tag{4.5}$$

We first show that

$$\models \{p_i\}\ P_i\ \{q_i\} \tag{4.6}$$

for $i = 1,\ldots,n$. In the proof, as in the Input/Output Lemma 4.1, we refer to different sets of procedure declarations and write $D \mid S$ when we mean S in the context of the set D of procedure declarations. By the Input/Output Lemma 4.1(i) and (iii) we have

$$\mathcal{M}[\![D \mid P_i]\!] = \bigcup_{k=0}^{\infty} \mathcal{M}[\![P_i^k]\!] = \mathcal{M}[\![P_i^0]\!] \cup \bigcup_{k=0}^{\infty} \mathcal{M}[\![D^k \mid P_i]\!] = \bigcup_{k=0}^{\infty} \mathcal{M}[\![D^k \mid P_i]\!],$$

so

$$\models \{p_i\}\ D \mid P_i\ \{q_i\} \text{ iff for all } k \geq 0 \text{ we have } \models \{p_i\}\ D^k \mid P_i\ \{q_i\}.$$

We now prove by induction on k that for all $k \geq 0$

$$\models \{p_i\}\ D^k \mid P_i\ \{q_i\},$$

for $i = 1,\ldots,n$.
Induction basis: $k = 0$. Since $S_i^0 = \Omega$, by definition $\models \{p_i\}\ D^0 \mid P_i\ \{q_i\}$ holds, for $i = 1,\ldots,n$.

Induction step: $k \to k + 1$. By the induction hypothesis, we have
$\models \{p_i\} D^k \mid P_i \{q_i\}$, for $i = 1, \ldots, n$. Fix some $i \in \{1, \ldots, n\}$. By (4.5),
we obtain $\models \{p_i\} D^k \mid S_i \{q_i\}$. By the Input/Output Lemma 4.1(i) and (ii),

$$\mathcal{M}[\![D^k \mid S_i]\!] = \mathcal{M}[\![S_i^{k+1}]\!] = \mathcal{M}[\![D^{k+1} \mid S_i^{k+1}]\!] = \mathcal{M}[\![D^{k+1} \mid P_i]\!],$$

hence $\models \{p_i\} D^{k+1} \mid P_i \{q_i\}$.

This proves (4.6) for $i = 1, \ldots, n$. Now (4.4) and (4.6) imply $\models \{p\} S \{q\}$
(where we refer to the set D of procedure declarations).   □

With this theorem we can state the following soundness result.

Corollary 4.1. (Soundness of PR) *The proof system PR is sound for partial correctness of recursive programs.*

Proof. The proof combines Theorem 4.2 with Theorem 3.1(i) on soundness of the proof system PW and Theorem 3.7(i),(ii) on soundness of the auxiliary rules.   □

Next, we establish soundness of the recursion II rule and as a consequence that of the proof system TR in the sense of total correctness. Below we write

$$\{p_1\} P_1 \{q_1\}, \ldots, \{p_n\} P_n \{q_n\} \models_{tot} \{p\} S \{q\}$$

when the following holds:

for *all* sets of procedure declarations D
if $\models_{tot} \{p_i\} P_i \{q_i\}$, for $i = 1, \ldots, n$ then $\models_{tot} \{p\} S \{q\}$.

As in the case of partial correctness we need a strengthening of the Soundness Theorem 3.1(ii). Recall that in this section the provability sign $\vdash$ refers to the proof system for total correctness that consists of the proof system TW extended by the auxiliary axioms and proof rules introduced in Section 3.8.

Theorem 4.3. (Soundness of Proofs from Assumptions)

$$\{p_1\} P_1 \{q_1\}, \ldots, \{p_n\} P_n \{q_n\} \vdash \{p\} S \{q\}$$

implies

$$\{p_1\} P_1 \{q_1\}, \ldots, \{p_n\} P_n \{q_n\} \models_{tot} \{p\} S \{q\}.$$

Proof. See Exercise 4.6.   □

Additionally, we shall need the following lemma that clarifies the reason for the qualification that the integer variable z is used as a constant.

Theorem 4.4. (Instantiation) *Suppose that the integer variable z does not appear in S and in the proof*

$$\{p_1\}\ P_1\ \{q_1\},\ldots,\{p_n\}\ P_n\ \{q_n\} \vdash \{p\}\ S\ \{q\}$$

it is treated as a constant, that is, neither the $\exists$-introduction rule nor the substitution rule of Section 3.8 is applied to z. Then for all integers m

$$\{p_1\theta\}\ P_1\ \{q_1\theta\},\ldots,\{p_n\theta\}\ P_n\ \{q_n\theta\} \models_{tot} \{p\theta\}\ S\ \{q\theta\},$$

where $\theta \equiv [z := m]$.

Proof. See Exercise 4.7.   □

Finally, we shall need the following observation.

Lemma 4.2. (Fresh Variable) *Suppose that z is an integer variable that does not appear in D, S or q. Then*

$$\models_{tot} \{\exists z \geq 0 : p\}\ S\ \{q\} \text{ iff for all } m \geq 0,\ \models_{tot} \{p[z := m]\}\ S\ \{q\}.$$

Proof. See Exercise 4.8.   □

Theorem 4.5. (Soundness of the Recursion II Rule)
Assume that $D = P_1 :: S_1,\ldots,P_n :: S_n$. Suppose that

$$\{p_1\}\ P_1\ \{q_1\},\ldots,\{p_n\}\ P_n\ \{q_n\} \vdash \{p\}\ S\ \{q\}$$

and for $i = 1,\ldots,n$

$$\{p_1 \wedge t < z\}\ P_1\ \{q_1\},\ldots,\{p_n \wedge t < z\}\ P_n\ \{q_n\} \vdash \{p_i \wedge t = z\}\ S_i\ \{q_i\}$$

and
$$p_i \rightarrow t \geq 0,$$

where the fresh integer variable z is treated in the proofs as a constant. Then

$$\models_{tot} \{p\}\ S\ \{q\}.$$

Proof. By the Soundness Theorem 4.3 we have

$$\{p_1\}\ P_1\ \{q_1\},\ldots,\{p_n\}\ P_n\ \{q_n\} \models_{tot} \{p\}\ S\ \{q\}. \tag{4.7}$$

Further, by the Instantiation Theorem 4.4, we deduce for $i = 1,\ldots,n$ from

$$\{p_1 \wedge t < z\}\ P_1\ \{q_1\},\ldots,\{p_n \wedge t < z\}\ P_n\ \{q_n\} \vdash \{p_i \wedge t = z\}\ S_i\ \{q_i\}$$

that for all $m \geq 0$

$$\{p_1 \wedge t < m\} \ P_1 \ \{q_1\}, \ldots, \{p_n \wedge t < m\} \ P_n \ \{q_n\} \vdash \{p_i \wedge t = m\} \ S_i \ \{q_i\}.$$

Hence by the Soundness Theorem 4.3, for $i = 1, \ldots, n$ and $m \geq 0$

$$\{p_1 \wedge t < m\} \ P_1 \ \{q_1\}, \ldots, \{p_n \wedge t < m\} \ P_n \ \{q_n\} \models_{tot} \{p_i \wedge t = m\} \ S_i \ \{q_i\}. \tag{4.8}$$

We now show

$$\models_{tot} \{p_i\} \ P_i \ \{q_i\} \tag{4.9}$$

for $i = 1, \ldots, n$.

To this end, we exploit the fact that the integer variable z appears neither in p_i nor in t. Therefore the assertions p_i and $\exists z : (p_i \wedge t < z)$ are equivalent. Moreover, since $p_i \rightarrow t \geq 0$, we have

$$\exists z : (p_i \wedge t < z) \rightarrow \exists z \geq 0 : (p_i \wedge t < z).$$

So it suffices to show

$$\models_{tot} \{\exists z \geq 0 : (p_i \wedge t < z)\} \ P_i \ \{q_i\}$$

for $i = 1, \ldots, n$. Now, by the Fresh Variable Lemma 4.2 it suffices to prove that for all $m \geq 0$

$$\models_{tot} \{p_i \wedge t < m\} \ P_i \ \{q_i\}.$$

for $i = 1, \ldots, n$. We proceed by induction on m.

Induction basis: $m = 0$. By assumption, $p_i \rightarrow t \geq 0$ holds for $i = 1, \ldots, n$, so $(p_i \wedge t < 0) \rightarrow$ **false**. Hence the claim holds as $\models_{tot} \{$**false**$\} \ P_i \ \{q_i\}$.

Induction step: $m \rightarrow m + 1$. By the induction hypothesis, we have

$$\models_{tot} \{p_i \wedge t < m\} \ P_i \ \{q_i\},$$

for $i = 1, \ldots, n$.

By (4.8), we obtain $\models_{tot} \{p_i \wedge t = m\} \ S_i \ \{q_i\}$ for $i = 1, \ldots, n$, so by the Input/Output Lemma 4.1(ii) we have $\models_{tot} \{p_i \wedge t = m\} \ P_i \ \{q_i\}$ for $i = 1, \ldots, n$. But $t < m + 1$ is equivalent to $t < m \vee t = m$, so we obtain $\models_{tot} \{p_i \wedge t < m + 1\} \ P_i \ \{q_i\}$, for $i = 1, \ldots, n$.

This proves (4.9) for $i = 1, \ldots, n$. Now (4.7) and (4.9) imply $\models_{tot} \{p\} \ S \ \{q\}$. $\square$

With this theorem we can state the following soundness result.

Corollary 4.2. (Soundness of TR) *The proof system TR is sound for total correctness of recursive programs.*

Proof. The proof combines Theorem 4.5 with Theorem 3.1(ii) on soundness of the proof system *TW* and Theorem 3.7(iii) on soundness of the auxiliary rules.   □

4.4 Case Study: Binary Search

Consider a section $a[first : last]$ (so $first \leq last$) of an integer array a that is sorted in increasing order. Given a variable *val*, we want to find out whether its value occurs in the section $a[first : last]$, and if yes, to produce the index *mid* such that $a[mid] = val$. Since $a[first : last]$ is sorted, this can be done by means of the recursive binary search procedure shown in Figure 4.3. (An iterative version of this program is introduced in Exercise 4.10.)

$$BinSearch :: mid := (first + last) \ div \ 2;$$
$$\textbf{if } first \neq last$$
$$\textbf{then if } a[mid] < val$$
$$\textbf{then } first := mid + 1; \ BinSearch$$
$$\textbf{else if } a[mid] > val$$
$$\textbf{then } last := mid; \ BinSearch$$
$$\textbf{fi}$$
$$\textbf{fi}$$
$$\textbf{fi}$$

Fig. 4.3 The program *BinSearch*.

We now prove correctness of this procedure. To refer in the postcondition to the initial values of the variables *first* and *last*, we introduce variables f and l. Further, to specify that the array section $a[first : last]$ is sorted, we use the assertion $sorted(a[first : last])$ defined by

$$sorted(a[first : last]) \equiv \forall x, y : (first \leq x \leq y \leq last \rightarrow a[x] \leq a[y]).$$

Correctness of the *BinSearch* procedure is then expressed by the correctness formula

$$\{p\}BinSearch\{q\},$$

where

$$p \equiv f = first \wedge l = last \wedge first \leq last \wedge sorted(a[first : last]),$$

$$q \equiv f \leq mid \leq l \wedge (a[mid] = val \leftrightarrow \exists x \in [f : l] : a[x] = val).$$

The postcondition q thus states that mid is an index in the section $a[f : l]$ and $a[mid] = val$ exactly when the value of the variable val appears in the section $a[f : l]$.

Partial Correctness

In order to prove the partial correctness it suffices to show

$$\{p\}BinSearch\{q\} \vdash \{p\}S\{q\},$$

where $\vdash$ refers to a sound proof system for partial correctness and S denotes the body of $BinSearch$, and apply the simplified form of the recursion rule of Section 4.3.

To deal with the recursive calls of $BinSearch$ we adapt the assumption $\{p\}$ $BinSearch$ $\{q\}$ using the substitution rule and the invariance rule introduced in Section 3.8, to derive the correctness formulas

$$\{p[f := (f + l) \ div \ 2 + 1] \wedge r_1\} \ BinSearch \ \{q[f := (f + l) \ div \ 2 + 1] \wedge r_1\}$$

and

$$\{p[l := (f + l) \ div \ 2] \wedge r_2\} \ BinSearch \ \{q[l := (f + l) \ div \ 2] \wedge r_2\},$$

where

$$r_1 \equiv sorted(a[f : l]) \wedge a[(f + l) \ div \ 2] < val,$$

$$r_2 \equiv sorted(a[f : l]) \wedge val < a[(f + l) \ div \ 2].$$

Then, as in the case of the factorial program, we present the proof from these two assumptions in the form of a proof outline that we give in Figure 4.4.

Since we use the **if** B **then** S **fi** statement twice in the procedure body, we need to justify the appropriate two applications of the rule for this statement, introduced in Exercise 3.11. To this end, we need to check the following two implications:

$$(p \wedge mid = (first + last) \ div \ 2 \wedge first = last) \rightarrow q$$

and

$$(p \wedge mid = (first + last) \ div \ 2 \wedge first \neq last \wedge a[mid] = val) \rightarrow q,$$

that correspond to the implicit **else** branches. The first implication holds, since

$$(p \wedge mid = (first + last) \ div \ 2 \wedge first = last)$$
$$\rightarrow mid = f = l$$
$$\rightarrow a[mid] = val \leftrightarrow \exists x \in [f : l] : a[x] = val,$$

$\{p\}$
$mid := (first + last) \ div \ 2;$
$\{p \wedge mid = (first + last) \ div \ 2\}$
if $first \neq last$
then
   $\{p \wedge mid = (first + last) \ div \ 2 \wedge first \neq last\}$
   if $a[mid] < val$
   then
     $\{p \wedge mid = (first + last) \ div \ 2 \wedge first \neq last \wedge a[mid] < val\}$
     $\{(p[f := (f + l) \ div \ 2 + 1] \wedge r_1)[first := mid + 1]\}$
     $first := mid + 1;$
     $\{p[f := (f + l) \ div \ 2 + 1] \wedge r_1\}$
     $BinSearch$
     $\{q[f := (f + l) \ div \ 2 + 1] \wedge r_1\}$
     $\{q\}$
   else
     $\{p \wedge mid = (first + last) \ div \ 2 \wedge first \neq last \wedge a[mid] \geq val\}$
     if $a[mid] > val$
     then
       $\{p \wedge mid = (first + last) \ div \ 2 \wedge first \neq last \wedge a[mid] > val\}$
       $\{(p[l := (f + l) \ div \ 2] \wedge r_2)[last := mid]\}$
       $last := mid;$
       $\{p[l := (f + l) \ div \ 2] \wedge r_2\}$
       $BinSearch$
       $\{q[l := (f + l) \ div \ 2] \wedge r_2\}$
       $\{q\}$
     fi
     $\{q\}$
   fi
   $\{q\}$
fi
$\{q\}$

Fig. 4.4 Proof outline showing partial correctness of the *BinSearch* procedure.

while the second implication holds, since

$$first \leq last \wedge mid = (first + last) \ div \ 2 \rightarrow first \leq mid \leq last.$$

It remains to clarify two applications of the consequence rules. To deal with the one used in the **then** branch of the **if-then-else** statement note the following implication that allows us to limit the search to a smaller array section:

$$(sorted(a[f:l]) \land f \le m < l \land a[m] < val) \rightarrow$$
$$(\exists x \in [m+1:l] : a[x] = val \leftrightarrow \exists x \in [f:l] : a[x] = val). \qquad (4.10)$$

Next, note that

$$first < last \rightarrow (first + last) \; div \; 2 + 1 \le last,$$

so

$$p \land first \ne last \rightarrow p[f := (f+l) \; div \; 2+1][first := (f+l) \; div \; 2+1].$$

This explains the following sequence of implications:

$$p \land mid = (first + last) \; div \; 2 \land first \ne last \land a[mid] < val$$
$$\rightarrow \quad p[f := (f+l) \; div \; 2+1][first := (f+l) \; div \; 2+1]$$
$$\land \; mid = (f+l) \; div \; 2 \land r_1$$
$$\rightarrow p[f := (f+l) \; div \; 2+1][first := mid+1] \land r_1$$
$$\rightarrow (p[f := (f+l) \; div \; 2+1] \land r_1)[first := mid+1].$$

Finally, observe that by (4.10) with $m = (f+l) \; div \; 2$ we get by the definition of q and r_1

$$q[f := (f+l) \; div \; 2+1] \land r_1 \rightarrow q.$$

This justifies the first application of the consequence rule. We leave the justification of the second application as Exercise 4.9. This completes the proof of partial correctness.

Total Correctness

To deal with total correctness we use the proof methodology discussed in the previous section. We have $p \rightarrow first \le last$, so it suffices to prove $\{first \le last\} \; BinSearch \; \{\mathbf{true}\}$ in the sense of total correctness using the simplified form of the recursion II rule.

We use

$$t \equiv last - first$$

as the bound function. Then $first \le last \rightarrow t \ge 0$ holds, so it suffices to prove

$$\{first \le last \land t < z\} \; BinSearch \; \{\mathbf{true}\} \vdash \{first \le last \land t = z\} \; S \; \{\mathbf{true}\}.$$

We present the proof in the form of a proof outline that we give in Figure 4.5. The two applications of the consequence rule used in it are justified by the following sequences of implications:

$\{first \le last \wedge last - first = z\}$
$mid := (first + last) \ div \ 2;$
$\{first \le last \wedge last - first = z \wedge mid = (first + last) \ div \ 2\}$
if $first \ne last$
then
   $\{first < last \wedge last - first = z \wedge mid = (first + last) \ div \ 2\}$
   if $a[mid] < val$
   then
      $\{first < last \wedge last - first = z \wedge mid = (first + last) \ div \ 2\}$
      $\{(first \le last \wedge last - first < z)[first := mid + 1]\}$
      $first := mid + 1;$
      $\{first \le last \wedge last - first < z\}$
      BinSearch
      $\{\mathbf{true}\}$
   else
      $\{first < last \wedge last - first = z \wedge mid = (first + last) \ div \ 2\}$
      if $a[mid] > val$
      then
         $\{first < last \wedge last - first = z \wedge mid = (first + last) \ div \ 2\}$
         $\{(first \le last \wedge last - first < z)[last := mid]\}$
         $last := mid;$
         $\{first \le last \wedge last - first < z\}$
         BinSearch
         $\{\mathbf{true}\}$
      fi
      $\{\mathbf{true}\}$
   fi
   $\{\mathbf{true}\}$
fi
$\{\mathbf{true}\}$

Fig. 4.5 Proof outline showing termination of the *BinSearch* procedure.

$$first < last \wedge last - first = z \wedge mid = (first + last) \ div \ 2$$
$$\rightarrow \ first \le mid < last \wedge last - first = z$$
$$\rightarrow \ mid + 1 \le last \wedge last - (mid + 1) < z$$

and

$$first < last \wedge last - first = z \wedge mid = (first + last) \ div \ 2$$
$$\rightarrow \ first \le mid < last \wedge last - first = z$$
$$\rightarrow \ first \le mid \wedge mid - first < z.$$

Further, the Boolean expressions $a[mid] < val$ and $a[mid] > val$ are irrelevant for the proof, so drop them from the assertions of the proof outline. (Formally, this step is justified by the last two formation rules for proof outlines.)

This concludes the proof of termination.

4.5 Exercises

4.1. Using recursive procedures we can model the **while** B **do** S **od** loop as follows:

$$P :: \textbf{if } B \textbf{ then } S; \ P \textbf{ fi}.$$

Assume the above declaration.

(i) Prove that $\mathcal{M}[\![\textbf{while } B \textbf{ do } S \textbf{ od}]\!] = \mathcal{M}[\![P]\!]$.
(ii) Prove that $\mathcal{M}_{tot}[\![\textbf{while } B \textbf{ do } S \textbf{ od}]\!] = \mathcal{M}_{tot}[\![P]\!]$.

4.2. Let $D = P_1 :: S_1, \ldots, P_n :: S_n$. Prove that $P_i^{\,0} = \Omega$ and $P_i^{\,k+1} = S_i^k$ for $k \geq 0$.

4.3. Prove the Input/Output Lemma 4.1.

4.4. Intuitively, for a given set of procedure declarations a procedure is *nonrecursive* if it does not call itself, possibly through a chain of calls of other procedures. Formalize this definition.

Hint. Introduce the notion of a *call graph* in which the nodes are procedure identifiers and in which a directed arc connects two nodes P and Q if the body of P contains a call of Q.

4.5. Prove the Soundness Theorem 4.1.

4.6. Prove the Soundness Theorem 4.3.

4.7. Prove the Instantiation Theorem 4.4.

4.8. Prove the Fresh Variable Lemma 4.2.

4.9. Consider the *BinSearch* program studied in Section 4.5. Complete the proof of partial correctness discussed there by justifying the application of the consequence rule used in the proof outline of the **else** branch.

4.10. Consider the following iterative version of the *BinSearch* program studied in Section 4.5:

$$
\begin{aligned}
BinSearch \equiv \ & mid := (first + last) \ div \ 2; \\
& \textbf{while } first \neq last \wedge a[mid] \neq val \textbf{ do} \\
& \quad \textbf{if } a[mid] < val
\end{aligned}
$$

>   **then** $first := mid + 1$
>   **else** $last := mid$
>   **fi**;
> $mid := (first + last)\ div\ 2$
>   **od**

Prove partial and total correctness of this program w.r.t. the pre- and post-conditions used in Section 4.5.

4.11. Allow the failure statements in the main statements and procedure bodies. Add to the proof systems PR and TR the corresponding failure rules from Section 3.7 and prove the counterparts of the Soundness Corollary 4.1 and Soundness Corollary 4.2.

4.6 Bibliographic Remarks

Procedures (with parameters) were initially introduced in the programming language FORTRAN. However, recursion was not allowed. Recursive procedures were first introduced in ALGOL 60. Their semantics was defined by the so-called copy rule. For the case of parameterless procedures this rule says that at runtime a procedure call is treated like the procedure body inserted at the place of call, see, e.g., Grau, Hill, and Langmaack [1967].

Historically, reasoning about recursive programs focused initially on recursive program schemes and recursively defined functions, see, e.g., Loeckx and Sieber [1987]. The recursion rule is modelled after the so-called Scott induction rule that appeared first in the unpublished manuscript Scott and de Bakker [1969].

Example 4.4 is taken from Apt [1981]. It is also shown there that the considered proof system for partial correctness is incomplete if in the subsidiary proofs used in the premises of the recursion rule only the axioms and proof rules of the PW proof system are used. This clarifies why in Example 4.4 and in Section 4.5 we used in these subsidiary proofs the substitution and invariance rules. Completeness of the resulting proof system for partial correctness is established in Apt [1981]. Recursion II rule is taken from America and de Boer [1990], where also the completeness of the proof system TR for total correctness is established.

5 Recursive Programs with Parameters

N OW THAT WE understand the semantics and verification of recursive procedures without parameters, we extend our study to the case of recursive procedures with parameters. The presentation follows the one of the last chapter. In Section 5.1 we introduce the syntax of recursive procedures with parameters. We deal here with the most common parameter mechanism, namely call-by-value. To properly capture its meaning we need to introduce a block statement that allows us to distinguish between local and global variables.

In Section 5.2 we introduce the operational semantics that appropriately modifies the semantics of recursive procedures from the last chapter. The block statement is used to define the meaning of procedure calls. Then, in Section 5.3 we focus on program verification. The approach is a modification of the approach from the previous chapter, where the additional difficulty consists of a satisfactory treatment of parameters. Finally, as a case study, we consider in Section 5.5 the correctness of the *Quicksort* program.

Krzysztof R. Apt et al., *Verification of Sequential and Concurrent Programs*,
Texts in Computer Science, DOI: 10.1007/978-1-84882-745-5_5,
© Springer-Verlag London Limited 2009

5.1 Syntax

When considering recursive procedures with parameters we need to distinguish between local and global variables. To this end, we consider an extension of the syntax of **while** programs studied in Chapter 3 in which a *block statement* is allowed. It is introduced by the following clause:

$$S ::= \textbf{begin local } \bar{x} := \bar{t}; \ S_1 \textbf{ end}.$$

Informally, a block statement introduces a non-empty sequence of local variables, all of which are explicitly initialized by means of a parallel assignment, and provides an explicit scope for these local variables. The precise explanation of a scope is more complicated because the block statements can be nested.

Assuming $\bar{x} = x_1, \ldots, x_k$ and $\bar{t} = t_1, \ldots, t_k$, each occurrence of a local variable x_i within the statement S_1 *and not* within another block statement that is a subprogram of S_1 refers to the same variable. Each such variable x_i is initialized to the expression t_i by means of the parallel assignment $\bar{x} := \bar{t}$. Further, given a statement S' such that **begin local** $\bar{x} := \bar{t}; \ S_1$ **end** is a subprogram of S', all occurrences of x_i in S' outside this block statement refer to some other variable(s). Therefore we define

$$change(\textbf{begin local } \bar{x} := \bar{t}; \ S_1 \textbf{ end}) = change(S_1) \setminus \{\bar{x}\}.$$

Additionally, the procedure calls with parameters are introduced by the following clause:

$$S ::= P(t_1, \ldots, t_n).$$

Here P is a procedure identifier and $t_1, \ldots, t_n$ are expressions called *actual parameters*. To ensure that our analysis generalizes that of the previous chapter we assume that $n \geq 0$. When $n = 0$ the procedure P has no actual parameters and we are within the framework of the previous chapter. The statement $P(t_1, \ldots, t_n)$ is called a *procedure call*.

Procedures are now defined by *declarations* of the form

$$P(u_1, \ldots, u_n) :: S.$$

Here $u_1, \ldots, u_n$ are distinct simple variables, called *formal parameters* of the procedure P, and S is the *body* of the procedure P. From now on, as in the previous chapter, we assume a given set of procedure declarations D such that each procedure that appears in D has a unique declaration in D.

A *recursive program* consists of a *main statement* S built according to the syntax of this section and a given set D of such procedure declarations. We assume as in the previous chapter that all procedures whose calls appear in the main statement are declared in D. Additionally, we assume now that the procedure calls are *well-typed*, which means that the numbers of formal and actual parameters agree and that for each parameter position the types of the corresponding actual and formal parameters coincide. If D is clear from the context we refer to the main statement as a recursive program.

Given a recursive program, we call a variable x_i *local* if it appears within a statement S such that **begin local** $\bar{x} := \bar{t}$; S **end** with $\bar{x} = x_1, \ldots, x_k$ is a substatement of the main statement or of one of its procedure bodies, and *global* otherwise. To avoid possible name clashes between local and global variables of a program we simply assume that these sets of variables are disjoint. So given the procedure declaration

$$P :: \textbf{if } x = 1 \textbf{ then } b := \textbf{true else } b := \textbf{false fi}$$

the main statement

$$S \equiv \textbf{begin local } x := 1; \ P \textbf{ end}$$

is not allowed. If it were, the semantics we are about to introduce would allow us to conclude that $\{x = 0\}$ S $\{b\}$ holds. However, the customary semantics of the programs in the presence of procedures prescribes that in this case $\{x = 0\}$ S $\{\neg b\}$ should hold, as the meaning of a program should not depend on the choice of the names of its local variables. (This is a consequence of the so-called *static scope* of the variables that we assume here.)

This problem is trivially solved by just renaming the 'offensive' local variables to avoid name clashes, so by considering here the program **begin local** $y := 1$; P **end** instead. In what follows, when considering a recursive program S in the context of a set of procedure declarations D we always implicitly assume that the above syntactic restriction is satisfied.

Note that the above definition of programs puts no restrictions on the actual parameters in procedure calls; in particular they can be formal parameters or global variables. Let us look at an example.

Example 5.1. Using recursive programs with parameters, the factorial procedure from Example 4.1 can be rewritten as follows:

$$Fac(u) :: \textbf{if } u = 0 \textbf{ then } y := 1 \textbf{ else } Fac(u - 1); \ y := y \cdot u \textbf{ fi.} \qquad (5.1)$$

Here u is a formal parameter, $u - 1$ is an actual parameter, while y is a global variable. $\qquad \square$

The above version of the factorial procedure does not use any local variables. The procedure below does.

Example 5.2. Consider the following procedure Ct, standing for 'Countdown':

$$Ct(u) :: \textbf{begin local } v := u - 1; \textbf{ if } v \neq 0 \textbf{ then } Ct(v) \textbf{ fi end.} \qquad (5.2)$$

Here v is a local variable and is also used as an actual parameter. This procedure has no global variables.   □

So far we did not clarify why the block statement is needed when considering procedures with parameters. Also, we did not discuss the initialization of local variables. We shall consider these matters after having provided semantics to the considered class of programs.

5.2 Semantics

In order to define the semantics of the considered programs we extend the transition system of the previous chapter to take care of the block statement and of the procedure calls in the presence of parameters. The transition axiom for the block statement, given below, ensures that

- the local variables are initialized as prescribed by the parallel assignment,
- upon termination, the global variables whose names coincide with the local variables are restored to their initial values, held at the beginning of the block statement.

(ix) $< \textbf{begin local } \bar{x} := \bar{t}; \ S \textbf{ end}, \sigma > \ \to \ < \bar{x} := \bar{t}; \ S; \ \bar{x} := \sigma(\bar{x}), \sigma >.$

From now on, to ensure a uniform presentation for the procedures with and without parameters we identify the statement $\textbf{begin local } \bar{u} := \bar{t}; \ S \textbf{ end}$, when $\bar{u}$ is the empty sequence, with S. We then add the following transition axiom that deals with the procedure calls with parameters:

(x) $< P(\bar{t}), \sigma > \ \to \ < \textbf{begin local } \bar{u} := \bar{t}; \ S \textbf{ end}, \sigma >,$

where $P(\bar{u}) :: S \in D$.

So when the procedure P has no parameters, this transition axiom reduces to the transition axiom (viii).

In this axiom the formal parameters are *simultaneously* instantiated to the actual parameters and subsequently the procedure body is executed. In general, it is crucial that the passing of the values of the actual parameters to the formal ones takes place by means of a parallel assignment and not by a sequence of assignments. For example, given a procedure $P(u_1, u_2) :: S$ and the call $P(u_1 + 1, u_1)$, the parallel assignment $u_1, u_2 := u_1 + 1, u_1$ assigns a different value to the formal parameter u_2 than the sequence
$u_1 := u_1 + 1; \ u_2 := u_1.$

The block statement is needed to limit the scope of the formal parameters so that they are not accessible after termination of the procedure call. Also it ensures that the values of the formal parameters are not changed by a procedure call: note that, thanks to the semantics of a block statement, upon termination of a procedure call the formal parameters are restored to their initial values.

This transition axiom clarifies that we consider here the *call-by-value* parameter mechanism, that is, the values of the actual parameters are assigned to the formal parameters.

The following example illustrates the uses of the new transition axioms.

Example 5.3. Assume the declaration (5.1) of the *Fac* procedure. Then we have the following computation of the main statement $Fac(x)$, where σ is a proper state with $\sigma(x) = 2$:

$$< Fac(x), \sigma >$$
$\rightarrow\ <$ **begin local** $u := x;$
$\qquad\qquad$ **if** $u = 0$ **then** $y := 1$ **else** $Fac(u - 1);\ y := y \cdot u$ **fi end**, $\sigma >$
$\rightarrow\ < u := x;$ **if** $u = 0$ **then** $y := 1$ **else** $Fac(u - 1);\ y := y \cdot u$ **fi**;
$\qquad\qquad u := \sigma(u), \sigma >$
$\rightarrow\ <$ **if** $u = 0$ **then** $y := 1$ **else** $Fac(u - 1);\ y := y \cdot u$ **fi**;
$\qquad\qquad u := \sigma(u), \sigma[u := 2] >$
$\rightarrow\ < Fac(u - 1);\ y := y \cdot u;\ u := \sigma(u), \sigma[u := 2] >$
$\rightarrow\ <$ **begin local** $u := u - 1;$
$\qquad\qquad$ **if** $u = 0$ **then** $y := 1$ **else** $Fac(u - 1);\ y := y \cdot u$ **fi end**;
$\qquad\qquad y := y \cdot u;\ u := \sigma(u), \sigma[u := 2] >$
$\rightarrow\ < u := u - 1;$ **if** $u = 0$ **then** $y := 1$ **else** $Fac(u - 1);\ y := y \cdot u$ **fi**;
$\qquad\qquad u := 2;\ y := y \cdot u;\ u := \sigma(u), \sigma[u := 2] >$
$\rightarrow\ <$ **if** $u = 0$ **then** $y := 1$ **else** $Fac(u - 1);\ y := y \cdot u$ **fi**;
$\qquad\qquad u := 2;\ y := y \cdot u;\ u := \sigma(u), \sigma[u := 1] >$
$\rightarrow\ < Fac(u - 1);\ y := y \cdot u;\ u := 2;\ y := y \cdot u;\ u := \sigma(u), \sigma[u := 1] >$
$\rightarrow\ <$ **begin local** $u := u - 1;$
$\qquad\qquad$ **if** $u = 0$ **then** $y := 1$ **else** $Fac(u - 1);\ y := y \cdot u$ **fi end**;
$\qquad\qquad y := y \cdot u;\ u := 2;\ y := y \cdot u;\ u := \sigma(u), \sigma[u := 1] >$
$\rightarrow\ < u := u - 1;$ **if** $u = 0$ **then** $y := 1$ **else** $Fac(u - 1);\ y := y \cdot u$ **fi**;
$\qquad\qquad u := 1;\ y := y \cdot u;\ u := 2;\ y := y \cdot u;\ u := \sigma(u), \sigma[u := 1] >$
$\rightarrow\ <$ **if** $u = 0$ **then** $y := 1$ **else** $Fac(u - 1);\ y := y \cdot u$ **fi**; $u := 1;$
$\qquad\qquad y := y \cdot u;\ u := 2;\ y := y \cdot u;\ u := \sigma(u), \sigma[u := 0] >$
$\rightarrow\ < y := 1;\ u := 1;\ y := y \cdot u;\ u := 2;\ y := y \cdot u;\ u := \sigma(u), \sigma[u := 0] >$
$\rightarrow\ < u := 1;\ y := y \cdot u;\ u := 2;\ y := y \cdot u;\ u := \sigma(u), \sigma[u, y := 0, 1] >$
$\rightarrow\ < y := y \cdot u;\ u := 2;\ y := y \cdot u;\ u := \sigma(u), \sigma[u, y := 1, 1] >$
$\rightarrow\ < u := 2;\ y := y \cdot u;\ u := \sigma(u), \sigma[u, y := 1, 1] >$
$\rightarrow\ < y := y \cdot u;\ u := \sigma(u), \sigma[u, y := 2, 1] >$
$\rightarrow\ < u := \sigma(u), \sigma[u, y := 2, 2] >$
$\rightarrow\ < E, \sigma[y := 2] >$

$\square$

So in the above example during the computation of the procedure call $Fac(x)$ block statements of the form **begin local** $u := u - 1; S$ **end** are in-

troduced. The assignments $u := u - 1$ result from the calls $Fac(u - 1)$ and
are used to instantiate the formal parameter u to the value of the actual
parameter $u - 1$ that refers to a global variable u.

In general, block statements of the form **begin local** $\bar{x} := \bar{t}$; S **end**, in
which some variables from $\bar{x}$ appear in $\bar{t}$, arise in computations of the recursive
programs in which for some procedures some formal parameters appear in
an actual parameter. Such block statements also arise in reasoning about
procedure calls.

Exercise 5.1 shows that once we stipulate that actual parameters do not
contain formal parameters, such block statements cannot arise in the computations. We do not impose this restriction on our programs since this leads
to a limited class of recursive programs. For example, the factorial procedure
defined above does not satisfy this restriction.

The partial and total correctness semantics are defined exactly as in the
case of the recursive programs considered in the previous chapter.

Example 5.4. Assume the declaration (5.1) of the factorial procedure. Then
the following holds for the main statement $Fac(x)$:

- if $\sigma(x) \geq 0$ then

$$\mathcal{M}[\![Fac(x)]\!](\sigma) = \mathcal{M}_{tot}[\![Fac(x)]\!](\sigma) = \{\sigma[y := \sigma(x)!]\},$$

- if $\sigma(x) < 0$ then

$$\mathcal{M}[\![Fac(x)]\!](\sigma) = \emptyset \text{ and } \mathcal{M}_{tot}[\![Fac(x)]\!](\sigma) = \{\bot\}.$$

$\square$

Note that the introduced semantics treats properly the case when an actual
parameter of a procedure call contains a global variable of the procedure body.
To illustrate this point consider the call $Fac(y)$ in a state with $\sigma(y) = 3$.
Then, as in Example 5.3, we can calculate that the computation starting in
$< Fac(y), \sigma >$ terminates in a final state τ with $\tau(y) = 6$. So the final value
of y is the factorial of the value of the actual parameter, as desired.

Finally, we should point out some particular characteristics of our semantics of block statements in the case when in **begin local** $\bar{x} := \bar{t}$; S **end** a
variable from $\bar{x}$ appears in $\bar{t}$. For example, upon termination of the program

begin local $x := x + 1$; $y := x$ **end**; **begin local** $x := x + 1$; $z := x$ **end**

the assertion $y = z$ holds. The intuition here is that in each initialization
$x := x + 1$ the second occurrence of x refers to a *different* variable than the
first ocurrence of x, namely to the same variable *outside* the block statement.
Therefore $y = z$ holds upon termination. This corresponds with the semantics
of the procedure calls given by the transition axiom (x) when the actual
parameters contain formal parameters. Then this transition axiom generates

a block statement the initialization statement of which refers on the left-hand side to the formal parameters and on the right-hand side to the actual parameters of the procedure call.

As in the previous chapter we now consider syntactic approximations of the recursive programs and express their semantics in terms of these approximations. The following lemma is a counterpart of the Input/Output Lemma 4.1. As in the previous chapter, we write here $D \mid S$ when we consider the program S in the context of the set D of procedure declarations. The complication now is that in the case of procedure calls variable clashes can arise. We deal with them in the same way as in the definition of the transition axiom for the procedure call.

Given $D = P_1(\bar{u}_1) :: S_1, \ldots, P_n(\bar{u}_n) :: S_n$ and a recursive program S, we define the *kth syntactic approximation* S^k of S by induction on $k \geq 0$:

$$
\begin{aligned}
S^0 &= \Omega, \\
S^{k+1} &= S[S_1^k/P_1, \ldots, S_n^k/P_n],
\end{aligned}
$$

where $S[R_1/P_1, \ldots, R_n/P_n]$ is the result of a simultaneous replacement in S of each procedure identifier P_i by the statement R_i. For procedure calls this replacement is defined by

$$
P_i(\bar{t})[R_1/P_1, \ldots, R_n/P_n] \equiv R_i(\bar{t}) \equiv \textbf{begin local } \bar{u}_i := \bar{t};\ R_i \textbf{ end}.
$$

Furthermore, let D^k abbreviate $D = P_1(\bar{u}_1) :: S_1^k, \ldots, P_n(\bar{u}_n) :: S_n^k$ and let $\mathcal{N}$ stand for $\mathcal{M}$ or $\mathcal{M}_{tot}$. The following lemma collects the properties of $\mathcal{N}$ we need.

Lemma 5.1. (Input/Output)

(i) $\mathcal{N}[\![D^k \mid S]\!] = \mathcal{N}[\![S^{k+1}]\!]$.

(ii) $\mathcal{N}[\![D \mid S]\!] = \mathcal{N}[\![D \mid S[S_1/P_1, \ldots, S_n/P_n]]\!]$.

In particular, $\mathcal{N}[\![D \mid P_i(\bar{t})]\!] = \mathcal{N}[\![D \mid \textbf{begin local } \bar{u}_i := \bar{t};\ S_i \textbf{ end}]\!]$ for $i = 1, \ldots, n$.

(iii) $\mathcal{M}[\![D \mid S]\!] = \bigcup_{k=0}^{\infty} \mathcal{M}[\![S^k]\!]$.

Proof. See Exercise 5.2.   □

Note that, as in Chapter 4, each S^k is a statement without procedure calls.

5.3 Verification

The notions of partial and total correctness of the recursive programs with parameters are defined as in Chapter 4. First, we introduce the following rule that deals with the block statement:

RULE 10: BLOCK

$$\frac{\{p\}\ \bar{x} := \bar{t};\ S\ \{q\}}{\{p\}\ \textbf{begin local}\ \bar{x} := \bar{t};\ S\ \textbf{end}\ \{q\}}$$

where $\{\bar{x}\} \cap free(q) = \emptyset$.

Example 5.5. Let us return to the program

begin local $x := x + 1;\ y := x$ **end**; **begin local** $x := x + 1;\ z := x$ **end**.

Denote it by S. We prove $\{\textbf{true}\}\ S\ \{y = z\}$. It is straightforward to derive

$$\{x + 1 = u\}\ x := x + 1;\ y := x\ \{y = u\}.$$

By the above block rule, we then obtain

$$\{x + 1 = u\}\ \textbf{begin local}\ x := x + 1;\ y := x\ \textbf{end}\ \{y = u\}.$$

Applying next the invariance rule with $x + 1 = u$ and (a trivial instance of) the consequence rule we derive

$$\{x + 1 = u\}\ \textbf{begin local}\ x := x + 1;\ y := x\ \textbf{end}\ \{y = u \wedge x + 1 = u\}.$$
$$(5.3)$$

Similarly, we can derive

$$\{x + 1 = u\}\ \textbf{begin local}\ x := x + 1;\ z := x\ \textbf{end}\ \{z = u\}.$$

Applying to this latter correctness formula the invariance rule with $y = u$ and the consequence rule we obtain

$$\{y = u \wedge x + 1 = u\}\ \textbf{begin local}\ x := x + 1;\ z := x\ \textbf{end}\ \{y = z\}.\quad (5.4)$$

By the composition rule applied to (5.3) and (5.4), we obtain

$$\{x + 1 = u\}\ S\ \{y = z\},$$

from which the desired result follows by an application of the $\exists$-introduction rule (to eliminate the variable u in the precondition), followed by a trivial application of the consequence rule. $\square$

Partial Correctness: Non-recursive Procedures

Consider now partial correctness of recursive programs. The main issue is how to deal with the parameters of procedure calls. Therefore, to focus on this issue we discuss the parameters of non-recursive procedures first. The following *copy rule* shows how to prove correctness of non-recursive method calls:

$$\frac{\{p\} \textbf{ begin local } \bar{u} := \bar{t};\ S \textbf{ end } \{q\}}{\{p\}\ P(\bar{t})\ \{q\}}$$

where $P(\bar{u}) :: S \in D$.

Example 5.6. Let D contain the following declaration

$$add(x) :: sum := sum + x.$$

It is straightforward, using the above block rule, to derive

$$\{sum = z\} \textbf{ begin local } x := 1; sum := sum + x \textbf{ end } \{sum = z + 1\}$$

and, similarly,

$$\{sum = z + 1\} \textbf{ begin local } x := 2; sum := sum + x \textbf{ end } \{sum = z + 3\}.$$

By applying the above copy rule we then derive

$$\{sum = z\}\ add(1)\ \{sum = z + 1\}$$

and

$$\{sum = z + 1\}\ add(2)\ \{sum = z + 3\}.$$

We conclude

$$\{sum = z\}\ add(1);\ add(2)\ \{sum = z + 3\}$$

using the composition rule.   □

In many cases, however, we can also prove procedure calls correct by *instantiating generic* procedure calls, instead of proving for each specific call its corresponding block statement correct. By a generic call of a procedure P we mean a call of the form $P(\bar{x})$, where $\bar{x}$ is a sequence of fresh *variables* which represent the actual parameters. Instantiation of such calls is then taken care of by the following auxiliary proof rule that refers to the set of procedure declarations D:

RULE 11: INSTANTIATION

$$\frac{\{p\}\ P(\bar{x})\ \{q\}}{\{p[\bar{x} := \bar{t}]\}\ P(\bar{t})\ \{q[\bar{x} := \bar{t}]\}}$$

where $var(\bar{x}) \cap var(D) = var(\bar{t}) \cap change(D) = \emptyset$. The set $change(D)$ denotes all the global variables that can be modified by the body of some procedure declared by D.

Example 5.7. Let again D contain the following declaration

$$add(x) :: sum := sum + x.$$

In order to prove

$$\{sum = z\} \; add(1); \; add(2) \; \{sum = z + 3\}$$

we now introduce the following correctness formula

$$\{sum = z\} \; add(y) \; \{sum = z + y\}$$

of a generic call $add(y)$. We can derive this correctness formula from

$$\{sum = z\} \; \textbf{begin local } x := y; sum := sum + x \; \textbf{end} \; \{sum = z + y\}$$

by an application of the above copy rule. By the instantiation rule, we then obtain

$$\{sum = z\} \; add(1) \; \{sum = z + 1\} \text{ and } \{sum = z\} \; add(2) \; \{sum = z + 2\},$$

instantiating y by 1 and 2, respectively, in the above correctness formula of the generic call $add(y)$. An application of the substitution rule, replacing z in $\{sum = z\} \; add(2) \; \{sum = z + 2\}$ by $z + 1$, followed by an application of the consequence rule, then gives us

$$\{sum = z + 1\} \; add(2) \; \{sum = z + 3\}.$$

We conclude

$$\{sum = z\} \; add(1); add(2) \; \{sum = z + 3\}$$

using the composition rule.   □

Suppose now that we established $\{p\} \; S \; \{q\}$ in the sense of partial correctness for a **while** program S and that S is the body of a procedure P, i.e., that $P(\bar{u}) :: S$ is a given procedure declaration. Can we conclude then $\{p\} \; P(\bar{u}) \; \{q\}$? The answer is of course, 'no'. Take for example $S \equiv u := 1$. Then $\{u = 0\} \; S \; \{u = 1\}$ holds, but the correctness formula $\{u = 0\} \; P(\bar{u}) \; \{u = 1\}$ is not true. In fact, by the semantics of the procedure calls, $\{u = 0\} \; P(\bar{u}) \; \{u = 0\}$ is true. However, we cannot derive this formula by an application of the copy rule because the proof rule for block statements does not allow the local variable u to occur (free) in the postcondition. The following observation identifies the condition under which the above conclusion does hold.

Lemma 5.2. (Transfer) *Consider a* **while** *program S and a procedure P declared by $P(\bar{u}) :: S$. Suppose that $\vdash \{p\}\ S\ \{q\}$ and $var(\bar{u}) \cap change(S) = \emptyset$. Then*

$$\{p\}\ P(\bar{u})\ \{q\}$$

can be proved in the proof system PRP.

Proof. Let $\bar{x}$ be a sequence of simple variables of the same length as $\bar{u}$ such that $var(\bar{x}) \cap var(p, S, q) = \emptyset$. By the parallel assignment axiom 2',

$$\{p[\bar{u} := \bar{x}]\}\ \bar{u} := \bar{x}\ \{p \wedge \bar{u} = \bar{x}\}.$$

Further, by the assumption about $\bar{u}$ and the invariance rule,

$$\{p \wedge \bar{u} = \bar{x}\}\ S\ \{q \wedge \bar{u} = \bar{x}\},$$

so by the composition rule,

$$\{p[\bar{u} := \bar{x}]\}\ \bar{u} := \bar{x};\ S\ \{q \wedge \bar{u} = \bar{x}\}.$$

But $q \wedge \bar{u} = \bar{x} \rightarrow q[\bar{u} := \bar{x}]$, so by the consequence rule,

$$\{p[\bar{u} := \bar{x}]\}\ \bar{u} := \bar{x};\ S\ \{q[\bar{u} := \bar{x}]\}.$$

Further $var(\bar{u}) \cap free(q[\bar{u} = \bar{x}]) = \emptyset$, so by the block rule 10,

$$\{p[\bar{u} := \bar{x}]\}\ \textbf{begin local}\ \bar{u} := \bar{x};\ S\ \textbf{end}\ \{q[\bar{u} := \bar{x}]\}.$$

Hence by the above copy rule,

$$\{p[\bar{u} := \bar{x}]\}\ P(\bar{x})\ \{q[\bar{u} := \bar{x}]\}.$$

Now note that $var(\bar{x}) \cap var(p, q) = \emptyset$ implies both $p[\bar{u} := \bar{x}][\bar{x} := \bar{u}] \equiv p$ and $q[\bar{u} := \bar{x}][\bar{x} := \bar{u}] \equiv q$. Moreover, by the assumption $var(\bar{u}) \cap change(S) = \emptyset$, so by the instantiation rule 11 $\{p\}\ P(\bar{u})\ \{q\}$. $\qquad\qquad\square$

It should be noted that the use of the instantiation rule is restricted. It cannot be used to reason about a call $P(\bar{t})$, where some variables appearing in $\bar{t}$ are changed by the body of P itself.

Example 5.8. Let again D contain the declaration

$$add(x) :: sum := sum + x.$$

We cannot obtain the correctness formula

$$\{sum = z\}\ add(sum)\ \{sum = z + z\}$$

by instantiating some assumption about a generic call $add(y)$ because sum is changed by the body of add. □

Partial Correctness: Recursive Procedures

When we deal only with one recursive procedure and use the procedure call as the considered recursive program, the above copy rule needs to be modified to

$$\frac{\{p\}\ P(\bar{t})\ \{q\} \vdash \{p\}\ \textbf{begin local}\ \bar{u} := \bar{t};\ S\ \textbf{end}\ \{q\}}{\{p\}\ P(\bar{t})\ \{q\}}$$

where $D = P(\bar{u}) :: S$.

The provability relation $\vdash$ here refers to the axioms and proof rules of the proof system PW extended with the block rule 10, and appropriately modified auxiliary axioms and proof rules introduced in Section 3.8. This modification consists of a reference to the extended set $change(S)$, as defined in Section 4.3. Note that the presence of procedure calls with parameters does not affect the definition of $change(S)$.

In the case of a program consisting of mutually recursive procedure declarations we have the following generalization of the above rule.

RULE 12: RECURSION III

$$\frac{\begin{array}{l}\{p_1\}\ P_1(\bar{t}_1)\ \{q_1\},\ldots,\{p_n\}\ P_n(\bar{t}_n)\ \{q_n\} \vdash \{p\}\ S\ \{q\},\\ \{p_1\}\ P_1(\bar{t}_1)\ \{q_1\},\ldots,\{p_n\}\ P_n(\bar{t}_n)\ \{q_n\} \vdash \\ \quad \{p_i\}\ \textbf{begin local}\ \bar{u}_i := \bar{t}_i;\ S_i\ \textbf{end}\ \{q_i\},\ i \in \{1,\ldots,n\}\end{array}}{\{p\}\ S\ \{q\}}$$

where $P_i(\bar{u}_1) :: S_i \in D$ for $i \in \{1,\ldots,n\}$.

Note that this rule allows us to introduce an *arbitrary* set of assumptions about specific calls of procedures declared by D. In particular, we do not exclude that $P_i \equiv P_j$ for $i \neq j$.

To deal with recursion in general we modify appropriately the approach of Chapter 4. As in Section 4.3, we modify the auxiliary axioms and proof rules introduced in Section 3.8 so that the conditions for specific variables refer to the extended set $change(S)$.

To prove partial correctness of recursive programs with parameters we use then the following proof system PRP :

PROOF SYSTEM PRP :
This system consists of the group of axioms
and rules 1–6, 10–12, and A2–A6.

Thus $\underset{.}{PRP}$ is obtained by extending the proof system PW by the block rule 10, the instantiation rule 11, the recursion rule 12, and the auxiliary rules A2–A6.

Next, we prove a generic invariance property of arbitrary procedure calls. This property states that the values of the actual parameters remain unaffected by a procedure call when none of its variables can be changed within the set of procedure declarations D.

Lemma 5.3. (Procedure Call) *Suppose that* $\{\bar{z}\} \cap (var(D) \cup var(\bar{t})) = \emptyset$ *and* $var(\bar{t}) \cap change(D) = \emptyset$. *Then*

$$\{\bar{z} = \bar{t}\}\ P(\bar{t})\ \{\bar{z} = \bar{t}\}$$

can be proved in the proof system PRP.

Proof. First note that for each procedure declaration $P_i(\bar{u}) :: S_i$ from D the correctness formula

$$\{\bar{z} = \bar{x}\}\ \textbf{begin local}\ \bar{u}_i := \bar{x}_i;\ S_i\ \textbf{end}\ \{\bar{z} = \bar{x}\},$$

where $var(\bar{x}) \cap var(D) = \emptyset$, holds by the adopted modification of the invariance axiom. This yields by the recursion III rule (no assumptions are needed here)

$$\{\bar{z} = \bar{x}\}\ P(\bar{x})\ \{\bar{z} = \bar{x}\},$$

from which the conclusion follows by the instantiation axiom. $\qquad\square$

We now use the above observation to reason about a specific recursive program.

Example 5.9. Assume the declaration (5.1) of the factorial procedure. We first prove the correctness formula

$$\{x \geq 0\}\ Fac(x)\ \{y = x!\} \tag{5.5}$$

in the proof system PRP. To this end, we introduce the assumption

$$\{x \geq 0\}\ Fac(x)\ \{y = x!\}$$

and show that

$$\{x \geq 0\}\ Fac(x)\ \{y = x!\} \vdash \{x \geq 0\}\ \textbf{begin local}\ u := x;\ S\ \textbf{end}\ \{y = x!\},$$

where

$$S \equiv \textbf{if}\ u = 0\ \textbf{then}\ y := 1\ \textbf{else}\ Fac(u-1);\ y := y \cdot u\ \textbf{fi}$$

is the procedure body of *Fac*.

Note that $\{x, u\} \cap change(S) = \emptyset$, so we can apply the instantiation rule to the assumption to obtain

$$\{u - 1 \geq 0\} \; Fac(u - 1) \; \{y = (u - 1)!\}$$

and then apply the invariance rule to obtain

$$\{x = u \wedge u - 1 \geq 0\} \; Fac(u - 1) \; \{x = u \wedge y = (u - 1)!\}.$$

It is clear how to extend the notion of a proof outline to programs that include procedure calls with parameters and the block statement. So we present the desired proof in the form of a proof outline, given in Figure 5.1. It uses the last correctness formula as an assumption. Note that the block rule can be applied here since $u \notin free(y = x!)$. The desired conclusion (5.5) now follows by the simplified form of the recursion III rule.

$\{x \geq 0\}$
begin local
$\{x \geq 0\}$
$u := x$
$\{x = u \wedge u \geq 0\}$
if $u = 0$
then
       $\{x = u \wedge u \geq 0 \wedge u = 0\}$
       $\{x = u \wedge 1 = u!\}$
       $y := 1$
       $\{x = u \wedge y = u!\}$
else
       $\{x = u \wedge u \geq 0 \wedge u \neq 0\}$
       $\{x = u \wedge u - 1 \geq 0\}$
       $Fac(u - 1);$
       $\{x = u \wedge y = (u - 1)!\}$
       $\{x = u \wedge y \cdot u = u!\}$
       $y := y \cdot u$
       $\{x = u \wedge y = u!\}$
fi
$\{x = u \wedge y = u!\}$
$\{y = x!\}$
end
$\{y = x!\}$

Fig. 5.1 Proof outline showing partial correctness of the factorial procedure.

Additionally, by the generic property established in the Procedure Call Lemma 5.3, we have

$$\{z = x\}\ Fac(x)\ \{z = x\}, \tag{5.6}$$

that is, the call $Fac(x)$ does not modify x. Combining the two correctness formulas by the conjunction rule we obtain

$$\{z = x \wedge x \geq 0\}\ Fac(x)\ \{z = x \wedge y = x!\},$$

which specifies that $Fac(x)$ indeed computes in the variable y the factorial of the original value of x. $\qquad\qquad\square$

Modularity

In the example above we combined two correctness formulas derived independently. In some situations it is helpful to reason about procedure calls in a modular way, by first deriving one correctness formula and then using it in a proof of another correctness formula. The following modification of the above simplified version of the recursion III rule illustrates this principle, where we limit ourselves to a two-stage proof and one procedure:

RULE 12′: MODULARITY

$$\{p_0\}\ P(\bar{t})\ \{q_0\} \vdash \{p_0\}\ \textbf{begin local}\ \bar{u} := \bar{t};\ S\ \textbf{end}\ \{q_0\},$$
$$\frac{\{p_0\}\ P(\bar{t})\ \{q_0\}, \{p\}\ P(\bar{s})\ \{q\} \vdash \{p\}\ \textbf{begin local}\ \bar{u} := \bar{s};\ S\ \textbf{end}\ \{q\}}{\{p\}\ P(\bar{s})\ \{q\}}$$

where $D = P(\bar{u}) :: S$.

So first we derive an auxiliary property, $\{p_0\}\ P(\bar{t})\ \{q_0\}$ that we subsequently use in the proof of the 'main' property, $\{p\}\ P(\bar{s})\ \{q\}$. In general, more procedures may be used and an arbitrary 'chain' of auxiliary properties may be constructed. We shall illustrate this approach in the case study considered at the end of this chapter.

Total Correctness

Total correctness of recursive programs is dealt with analogously as in the case of parameterless procedures. The corresponding proof rule is an appropriate modification of recursion III rule. The provability sign $\vdash$ refers now to the proof system TW extended by the auxiliary rules, modified as explained earlier in this section, and the block and instantiation rules. It has the following form:

RULE 13: RECURSION IV

$$\frac{\begin{array}{c} \{p_1\} \ P_1(\bar{e}_1) \ \{q_1\}, \ldots, \{p_n\} \ P_n(\bar{e}_n) \ \{q_n\} \vdash \{p\} \ S \ \{q\}, \\ \{p_1 \wedge t < z\} \ P_1(\bar{e}_1) \ \{q_1\}, \ldots, \{p_n \wedge t < z\} \ P_n(\bar{e}_n) \ \{q_n\} \vdash \\ \{p_i \wedge t = z\} \ \textbf{begin local } \bar{u}_i := \bar{e}_i; \ S_i \ \textbf{end} \ \{q_i\}, \ i \in \{1, \ldots, n\} \end{array}}{\{p\} \ S \ \{q\}}$$

where $P_i(\bar{u}_i) :: S_i \in D$, for $i \in \{1, \ldots, n\}$, and z is an integer variable that does not occur in p_i, t, q_i and S_i for $i \in \{1, \ldots, n\}$ and is treated in the proofs as a constant, which means that in these proofs neither the $\exists$-introduction rule A5 nor the substitution rule A7 is applied to z. In these proofs we allow the axioms and proof rules of the proof system TW extended with the block rule, the instantiation rule and appropriately modified auxiliary axioms and proof rules introduced in Section 3.8. This modification consists of the reference to the extended set $change(S)$, as defined in Section 4.3.

To prove total correctness of recursive programs with parameters we use the following proof system TRP :

> PROOF SYSTEM TRP :
> This system consists of the group of axioms
> and rules 1–4, 6, 7, 10, 11, 13, and A3–A6.

Thus TRP is obtained by extending the proof system TW by the block rule 10, the instantiation rule 11, the recursion rule 13, and the auxiliary rules A3–A6.

As before, in the case of one recursive procedure this rule can be simplified to

$$\frac{\begin{array}{c} \{p \wedge t < z\} \ P(\bar{e}) \ \{q\} \vdash \{p \wedge t = z\} \ \textbf{begin local } \bar{u} := \bar{e}; \ S \ \textbf{end} \ \{q\}, \\ p \rightarrow t \geq 0 \end{array}}{\{p\} \ P(\bar{e}) \ \{q\}}$$

where $D = P(\bar{u}) :: S$ and z is an integer variable that does not occur in p, t, q and S and is treated in the proof as a constant.

Example 5.10. To illustrate the use of the simplified rule for total correctness we return to Example 5.9. We proved there the correctness formula

$$\{x \geq 0\} \ Fac(x) \ \{y = x!\}$$

in the sense of partial correctness, assuming the declaration (5.1) of the factorial procedure.

To prove termination it suffices to establish the correctness formula

$$\{x \geq 0\}\ Fac(x)\ \{\textbf{true}\}.$$

We choose

$$t \equiv x$$

as the bound function. Then $x \geq 0 \to t \geq 0$. Assume now

$$\{x \geq 0 \wedge x < z\}\ Fac(x)\ \{\textbf{true}\}.$$

We have $u \notin change(D)$, so by the instantiation rule

$$\{u - 1 \geq 0 \wedge u - 1 < z\}\ Fac(u - 1)\ \{\textbf{true}\}.$$

We use this correctness formula in the proof outline presented in Figure 5.2 that establishes that

$$\{x \geq 0 \wedge x < z\}\ Fac(x)\ \{\textbf{true}\}$$
$$\vdash \{x \geq 0 \wedge x = z\}\ \textbf{begin local}\ u := x;\ S\ \textbf{end}\ \{\textbf{true}\}.$$

Applying now the simplified form of the recursion IV rule we get the desired conclusion.   □

Soundness

We now prove the soundness of the proof system PRP for partial correctness of recursive programs with parameters. The establish soundness of the block rule we need the following lemma.

Lemma 5.4. (Block) *For all proper states σ and τ,*

$$\tau \in \mathcal{M}[\![\textbf{begin local}\ \bar{x} := \bar{t};\ S\ \textbf{end}]\!](\sigma)$$

implies that for some sequence of values $\bar{d}$

$$\tau[\bar{x} := \bar{d}] \in \mathcal{M}[\![\bar{x} := \bar{t};\ S]\!](\sigma).$$

Proof. See Exercise 5.3.   □

Theorem 5.1. (Soundness of the Block Rule) *Suppose that*

$$\models \{p\}\ \bar{x} := \bar{t};\ S\ \{q\},$$

$$\{x \geq 0 \land x = z\}$$
begin local
$$\{x \geq 0 \land x = z\}$$
$u := x$
$$\{u \geq 0 \land u = z\}$$
if $u = 0$
then
$\quad\quad\{u \geq 0 \land u = z \land u = 0\}$
$\quad\quad\{\mathbf{true}\}$
$\quad\quad y := 1$
$\quad\quad\{\mathbf{true}\}$
else
$\quad\quad\{u \geq 0 \land u = z \land u \neq 0\}$
$\quad\quad\{u - 1 \geq 0 \land u - 1 < z\}$
$\quad\quad Fac(u - 1);$
$\quad\quad\{\mathbf{true}\}$
$\quad\quad y := y \cdot u$
$\quad\quad\{\mathbf{true}\}$
fi
$\{\mathbf{true}\}$
end
$\{\mathbf{true}\}$

Fig. 5.2 Proof outline showing termination of the factorial procedure.

where $\{\bar{x}\} \cap free(q) = \emptyset$. *Then*

$$\models \{p\} \text{ begin local } \bar{x} := \bar{t}; \ S \text{ end } \{q\}.$$

Proof. Suppose that $\sigma \models p$ and $\tau \in \mathcal{M}[\![\text{begin local } \bar{x} := \bar{t}; \ S \text{ end}]\!](\sigma)$. Then by the Block Lemma 5.4 for some sequence of values $\bar{d}$

$$\tau[\bar{x} := \bar{d}] \in \mathcal{M}[\![\bar{x} := \bar{t}; \ S]\!](\sigma).$$

So by the assumption $\tau[\bar{x} := \bar{d}] \models q$. But $\{\bar{x}\} \cap free(q) = \emptyset$, hence $\tau \models q$. $\square$

To deal with the instantiation rule we shall need the following observation analogous to the Change and Access Lemma 3.4.

Lemma 5.5. (Change and Access) *Assume that*

$$D = P_1(\bar{u}_1) :: S_1, \ldots, P_n(\bar{u}_n) :: S_n.$$

For all proper states σ and τ, $i = 1, \ldots, n$ and sequences of expressions $\bar{t}$ such that $var(\bar{t}) \cap change(D) = \emptyset$,

$$\tau \in \mathcal{M}[\![P_i(\bar{t})]\!](\sigma)$$

implies

$$\tau[\bar{x} := \sigma(\bar{t})] \in \mathcal{M}[\![P_i(\bar{x})]\!](\sigma[\bar{x} := \sigma(\bar{t})]),$$

whenever $var(\bar{x}) \cap var(D) = \emptyset$.

Proof. See Exercise 5.4. □

Theorem 5.2. (Soundness of the Instantiation Rule)
Assume that $D = P_1(\bar{u}_1) :: S_1, \dots, P_n(\bar{u}_n) :: S_n$ *and suppose that*

$$\models \{p\}\ P_i(\bar{x})\ \{q\},$$

where $var(\bar{x}) \cap var(D) = \emptyset$. *Then*

$$\models \{p[\bar{x} := \bar{t}]\}\ P_i(\bar{t})\ \{q[\bar{x} := \bar{t}]\}$$

for all sequences of expressions $\bar{t}$ *such that* $var(\bar{t}) \cap change(D) = \emptyset$.

Proof. Suppose that $\sigma \models p[\bar{x} := \bar{t}]$ and $\tau \in \mathcal{M}[\![P_i(\bar{t})]\!](\sigma)$. By the Simultaneous Substitution Lemma 2.5, $\sigma[\bar{x} := \sigma(\bar{t})] \models p$, and by the Change and Access Lemma 5.5,

$$\tau[\bar{x} := \sigma(\bar{t})] \in \mathcal{M}[\![P_i(\bar{x})]\!](\sigma[\bar{x} := \sigma(\bar{t})]).$$

Hence by the assumption about the generic procedure call $P_i(\bar{x})$ we have $\tau[\bar{x} := \sigma(\bar{t})] \models q$, so, again by the Simultaneous Substitution Lemma 2.5, $\tau \models q[\bar{x} := \bar{t}]$. □

Finally, we deal with the recursion III rule. Recall that the provability sign $\vdash$ refers to the proof system PW augmented with the (modified as explained earlier in this section) auxiliary axioms and rules and the block and instantiation rules, in the implicit context of the set of procedure declarations D.

We shall need a counterpart of the Soundness Lemma 4.1, in which we use this implicit context D, as well. We write here

$$\{p_1\}\ P_1(\bar{t}_1)\ \{q_1\}, \dots, \{p_n\}\ P_n(\bar{t}_n)\ \{q_n\} \models \{p\}\ S\ \{q\}$$

when the following holds:

for *all* sets of procedure declarations D' such that $var(D') \subseteq var(D)$
if $\models \{p_i\}\ D'\mid P_i(\bar{t}_i)\ \{q_i\}$, for $i \in \{1, \dots, n\}$, then $\models \{p\}\ D'\mid S\ \{q\}$,

where, as in the Input/Output Lemma 5.1, $D'\mid S$ means that we evaluate S in the context of the set D' of the procedure declarations.

Theorem 5.3. (Soundness of Proof from Assumptions)
We have that

$$\{p_1\}\ P_1(\bar{t}_1)\ \{q_1\}, \ldots, \{p_n\}\ P_n(\bar{t}_n)\ \{q_n\} \vdash \{p\}\ S\ \{q\}$$

implies

$$\{p_1\}\ P_1(\bar{t}_1)\ \{q_1\}, \ldots, \{p_n\}\ P_n(\bar{t}_n)\ \{q_n\} \models \{p\}\ S\ \{q\}.$$

Proof. See Exercise 5.5.   □

Theorem 5.4. (Soundness of the Recursion III Rule)
Assume that $P_i(\bar{u}_i) :: S_i \in D$ *for* $i \in \{1, \ldots, n\}$. *Suppose that*

$$\{p_1\}\ P_1(\bar{t}_1)\ \{q_1\}, \ldots, \{p_n\}\ P_n(\bar{t}_1)\ \{q_n\} \vdash \{p\}\ S\ \{q\},$$

and for $i \in \{1, \ldots, n\}$

$$\{p_1\}\ P_1(\bar{t}_1)\ \{q_1\}, \ldots, \{p_n\}\ P_n(\bar{t}_n)\ \{q_n\} \vdash$$
$$\{p_i\}\ \textbf{begin local}\ \bar{u}_i := \bar{t}_i;\ S_i\ \textbf{end}\ \{q_i\}.$$

Then

$$\models \{p\}\ S\ \{q\}.$$

Proof. We proceed as in the proof of the Soundness Theorem 4.2. By the Soundness Theorem 5.3

$$\{p_1\}\ P_1(\bar{t}_1)\ \{q_1\}, \ldots, \{p_n\}\ P_n(\bar{t}_n)\ \{q_n\} \models \{p\}\ S\ \{q\} \tag{5.7}$$

and for $i \in \{1, \ldots, n\}$

$$\{p_1\}\ P_1(\bar{t}_1)\ \{q_1\}, \ldots, \{p_n\}\ P_n(\bar{t}_n)\ \{q_n\}$$
$$\models \{p_i\}\ \textbf{begin local}\ \bar{u}_i := \bar{t}_i;\ S_i\ \textbf{end}\ \{q_i\}. \tag{5.8}$$

We first show

$$\models \{p_i\}\ P_i(\bar{t}_i)\ \{q_i\} \tag{5.9}$$

for $i \in \{1, \ldots, n\}$.

In the proof write $D' \mid S$ when we mean S in the context of the set D' of procedure declarations. By the Input/Output Lemma 5.1(i) and (iii) we have

$$\mathcal{M}[\![D \mid P_i(\bar{t}_i)]\!]$$
$$= \bigcup_{k=0}^{\infty} \mathcal{M}[\![P_i(\bar{t}_i)^k]\!]$$
$$= \mathcal{M}[\![P_i(\bar{t}_i)^0]\!] \cup \bigcup_{k=0}^{\infty} \mathcal{M}[\![D^k \mid P_i(\bar{t}_i)]\!]$$
$$= \bigcup_{k=0}^{\infty} \mathcal{M}[\![D^k \mid P_i(\bar{t}_i)]\!],$$

so

$\models \{p_i\}\ D \mid P_i(\bar{t}_i)\ \{q_i\}$ iff for all $k \geq 0$ we have $\models \{p_i\}\ D^k \mid P_i(\bar{t}_i)\ \{q_i\}$.

We now prove by induction on k that for all $k \geq 0$

$$\models \{p_i\}\ D^k \mid P_i(\bar{t}_i)\ \{q_i\},$$

for $i \in \{1, \ldots, n\}$.

Induction basis. Since $S_i^0 = \Omega$, by definition $\models \{p_i\}\ D^0 \mid P_i(\bar{t}_i)\ \{q_i\}$, for $i \in \{1, \ldots, n\}$.

Induction step. By the induction hypothesis we have

$$\models \{p_i\}\ D^k \mid P_i(\bar{t}_i)\ \{q_i\},$$

for $i \in \{1, \ldots, n\}$. Fix $i \in \{1, \ldots, n\}$. Since $var(D^k) \subseteq var(D)$, by (5.8) we obtain

$$\models \{p_i\}\ D^k \mid \textbf{begin local}\ \bar{u}_i := \bar{t}_i;\ S_i\ \textbf{end}\ \{q_i\}.$$

Next, by the Input/Output Lemma 5.1(i) and (ii)

$$\begin{aligned}
&\mathcal{M}[\![D^k \mid \textbf{begin local}\ \bar{u}_i := \bar{t}_i;\ S_i\ \textbf{end}]\!] \\
&= \mathcal{M}[\![(\textbf{begin local}\ \bar{u}_i := \bar{t}_i;\ S_i\ \textbf{end})^{k+1}]\!] \\
&= \mathcal{M}[\![D^{k+1} \mid (\textbf{begin local}\ \bar{u}_i := \bar{t}_i;\ S_i\ \textbf{end})^{k+1}]\!] \\
&= \mathcal{M}[\![D^{k+1} \mid P_i(\bar{t}_i)]\!],
\end{aligned}$$

hence $\models \{p_i\}\ D^{k+1} \mid P_i(\bar{t}_i)\ \{q_i\}$.

This proves (5.9) for $i \in \{1, \ldots, n\}$. Now (5.7) and (5.9) imply $\models \{p\}\ S\ \{q\}$ (where we refer to the set D of procedure declarations). $\quad\Box$

With this theorem we can state the following soundness result.

Corollary 5.1. (Soundness of PRP) *The proof system PRP is sound for partial correctness of recursive programs with parameters.*

Proof. The proof combines Theorems 5.1, 5.2 and 5.4 with Theorem 3.1(i) on soundness of the proof system PW and Theorem 3.7(i),(ii) on soundness of the auxiliary rules. $\quad\Box$

Next, we establish soundness of the proof system TRP for total correctness of recursive programs with parameters. We proceed in an analogous way as in the case of the parameterless procedures.

Theorem 5.5. (Soundness of TRP) *The proof system TRP is sound for total correctness of recursive programs with parameters.*

Proof. See Exercise 5.7.   □

5.4 Case Study: *Quicksort*

In this section we establish correctness of the classical *Quicksort* sorting procedure, originally introduced in Hoare[1962]. For a given array a of type
integer $\to$ **integer** and integers x and y this algorithm sorts the section
$a[x:y]$ consisting of all elements $a[i]$ with $x \leq i \leq y$. Sorting is accomplished
'in situ', i.e., the elements of the initial (unsorted) array section are permuted
to achieve the sorting property. We consider here the following version of
Quicksort close to the one studied in Foley and Hoare [1971]. It consists of a
recursive procedure $Quicksort(m,n)$, where the formal parameters m,n and
the local variables v,w are all of type **integer**:

$$
\begin{aligned}
&Quicksort(m,n) :: \\
&\quad \textbf{if } m < n \\
&\quad \textbf{then } Partition(m,n); \\
&\qquad\quad \textbf{begin} \\
&\qquad\qquad \textbf{local } v,w := ri, le; \\
&\qquad\qquad Quicksort(m,v); \\
&\qquad\qquad Quicksort(w,n) \\
&\qquad\quad \textbf{end} \\
&\quad \textbf{fi}
\end{aligned}
$$

Quicksort calls a non-recursive procedure $Partition(m,n)$ which partitions
the array a suitably, using global variables ri, le, pi of type **integer** standing
for *pivot*, *left*, and *right* elements:

$$
\begin{aligned}
&Partition(m,n) :: \\
&\quad pi := a[m]; \\
&\quad le, ri := m, n; \\
&\quad \textbf{while } le \leq ri \textbf{ do} \\
&\qquad \textbf{while } a[le] < pi \textbf{ do } le := le + 1 \textbf{ od}; \\
&\qquad \textbf{while } pi < a[ri] \textbf{ do } ri := ri - 1 \textbf{ od}; \\
&\qquad \textbf{if } le \leq ri \textbf{ then} \\
&\qquad\quad swap(a[le], a[ri]); \\
&\qquad\quad le, ri := le + 1, ri - 1 \\
&\qquad \textbf{fi} \\
&\quad \textbf{od}
\end{aligned}
$$

Here, as in Section 3.9, for two given simple or subscripted variables u and v
the program $swap(u,v)$ is used to *swap* the values of u and v. So we stipulate
that the following correctness formula

$$\{x = u \land y = v\} \; swap(u,v) \; \{x = v \land y = u\}$$

holds in the sense of partial and total correctness, where x and y are fresh variables.

In the following D denotes the set of the above two procedure declarations and S_Q the body of the procedure $Quicksort(m, n)$.

Formal Problem Specification

Correctness of *Quicksort* amounts to proving that upon termination of the procedure call $Quicksort(m, n)$ the array section $a[m : n]$ is sorted and is a permutation of the input section. To write the desired correctness formula we introduce some notation. First, recall from Section 4.5 the assertion

$$sorted(a[first : last]) \equiv \forall x, y : (first \le x \le y \le last \to a[x] \le a[y])$$

stating that the integer array section $a[first : last]$ is sorted. To express the permutation property we use an auxiliary array a_0 in the section $a_0[x : y]$ of which we record the initial values of $a[x : y]$. Recall from Section 3.9 the abbreviations

$$bij(\beta, x, y) \equiv \beta \text{ is a bijection on } N \wedge \forall i \notin [x : y] : \beta(i) = i$$

stating that β is a bijection on N which is the identity outside the interval $[x : y]$ and

$$perm(a, a_0, [x : y]) \equiv \exists \beta : (bij(\beta, x, y) \wedge \forall i : a[i] = a_0[\beta(i)])$$

specifying that the array section $a[x : y]$ is a permutation of the array section $a_0[x : y]$ and that a and a_0 are the same elsewhere.

We can now express the correctness of *Quicksort* by means of the following correctness formula:

Q1 $\{a = a_0\}\ Quicksort(x, y)\ \{perm(a, a_0, [x : y]) \wedge sorted(a[x : y])\}.$

To prove correctness of *Quicksort* in the sense of partial correctness we proceed in stages and follow the modular approach explained in Section 5.3. In other words, we establish some auxiliary correctness formulas first, using among others the recursion III rule. Then we use them as premises in order to derive other correctness formulas, also using the recursion III rule.

Properties of Partition

In the proofs we shall use a number of properties of the *Partition* procedure. This procedure is non-recursive, so to verify them it suffices to prove the corresponding properties of the procedure body using the proof systems PW and TW.

More precisely, we assume the following properties of *Partition* in the sense of partial correctness:

P1 {**true**} *Partition*(m,n) $\{ri \leq n \wedge m \leq le\}$,

P2 $\{x' \leq m \wedge n \leq y' \wedge \ perm(a, a_0, [x' : y'])\}$
Partition(m,n)
$\{x' \leq m \wedge n \leq y' \wedge \ perm(a, a_0, [x' : y'])\}$,

P3 {**true**}
Partition(m,n)
$\{ \ le > ri \wedge$
$(\forall i \in [m : ri] : \ a[i] \leq pi) \wedge$
$(\forall i \in [ri + 1 : le - 1] : \ a[i] = pi) \wedge$
$(\forall i \in [le : n] : \ pi \leq a[i])\}$,

and the following property in the sense of total correctness:

PT4 $\{m < n\}$ *Partition*(m,n) $\{m < le \wedge ri < n\}$.

Property **P1** states the bounds for ri and le. We remark that $le \leq n$ and $m \leq ri$ need not hold upon termination. Property **P2** implies that the call *Partition*(n, k) permutes the array section $a[m : n]$ and leaves other elements of a intact, but actually is a stronger statement involving an interval $[x' : y']$ that includes $[m : n]$, so that we can carry out the reasoning about the recursive calls of *Quicksort*. Finally, property **P3** captures the main effect of the call *Partition*(n, k): the elements of the section $a[m : n]$ are rearranged into three parts, those smaller than pi (namely $a[m : ri]$), those equal to pi (namely $a[ri + 1 : le - 1]$), and those larger than pi (namely $a[le : n]$). Property **PT4** is needed in the termination proof of the *Quicksort* procedure: it implies that the subsections $a[m : ri]$ and $a[le : n]$ are strictly smaller than the section $a[m : n]$.

The correctness formulas **P1**–**P3** and **PT4** for the procedure call *Partition*(m,n) immediately follow from the properties **P1**–**P4** and **T** of the **while** program *PART* studied in Section 3.9 (see Exercise 5.8).

Auxiliary Proof: Permutation Property

In the remainder of this section we use the following abbreviation:

$$J \equiv m = x \wedge n = y.$$

We first extend the permutation property **P2** to the procedure *Quicksort*:

> **Q2** $\{perm(a, a_0, [x' : y']) \wedge x' \leq x \wedge y \leq y'\}$
>
> $Quicksort(x, y)$
>
> $\{perm(a, a_0, [x' : y'])\}$

Until further notice the provability symbol $\vdash$ refers to the proof system PW augmented with the the block rule, the instantiation rule and the auxiliary rules A3–A7.

The appropriate claim needed for the application of the recursion III rule is:

Claim 1.

> **P1, P2, Q2** $\vdash \{perm(a, a_0, [x' : y']) \wedge x' \leq x < y \leq y'\}$
>   **begin local** $m, n := x, y;\ S_Q$ **end**
> $\{perm(a, a_0, [x' : y'])\}.$

Proof. In Figure 5.3 a proof outline is given that uses as assumptions the correctness formulas **P1**, **P2**, and **Q2**. More specifically, the used correctness formula about the call of *Partition* is derived from **P1** and **P2** by the conjunction rule. In turn, the correctness formulas about the recursive calls of *Quicksort* are derived from **Q2** by an application of the instantiation rule and the invariance rule. This concludes the proof of Claim 1. □

We can now derive **Q2** by the recursion rule. In summary, we have proved

$$\textbf{P1, P2} \vdash \textbf{Q2}.$$

Auxiliary Proof: Sorting Property

We can now verify that the call $Quicksort(x, y)$ sorts the array section $a[x : y]$, so

Q3 $\{\textbf{true}\}\ Quicksort(x, y)\ \{sorted(a[x : y])\}.$

The appropriate claim needed for the application of the recursion III rule is:

$\{perm(a, a_0, [x' : y']) \land x' \leq x \land y \leq y'\}$
begin local
$\{perm(a, a_0, [x' : y']) \land x' \leq x \land y \leq y'\}$
$m, n := x, y;$
$\{perm(a, a_0, [x' : y']) \land x' \leq x \land y \leq y' \land J\}$
$\{perm(a, a_0, [x' : y']) \land x' \leq m \land n \leq y'\}$
if $m < n$ **then**
$\quad\{perm(a, a_0, [x' : y']) \land x' \leq m \land n \leq y'\}$
$\quad Partition(m, n);$
$\quad\{perm(a, a_0, [x' : y']) \land x' \leq m \land n \leq y' \land ri \leq n \land m \leq le\}$
$\quad$**begin local**
$\quad\{perm(a, a_0, [x' : y']) \land x' \leq m \land n \leq y' \land ri \leq n \land m \leq le\}$
$\quad v, w := ri, le;$
$\quad\{perm(a, a_0, [x' : y']) \land x' \leq m \land n \leq y' \land v \leq n \land m \leq w\}$
$\quad\{perm(a, a_0, [x' : y']) \land x' \leq m \land v \leq y' \land x' \leq w \land n \leq y'\}$
$\quad Quicksort(m, v);$
$\quad\{perm(a, a_0, [x' : y']) \land x' \leq w \land n \leq y'\}$
$\quad Quicksort(w, n)$
$\quad\{perm(a, a_0, [x' : y'])\}$
$\quad$**end**
$\quad\{perm(a, a_0, [x' : y'])\}$
fi
$\{perm(a, a_0, [x' : y'])\}$
end
$\{perm(a, a_0, [x' : y'])\}$

Fig. 5.3 Proof outline showing permutation property **Q2**.

Claim 2.

$\quad$ **P3**, **Q2**, **Q3** ⊢ {**true**}
$\quad\quad\quad$ **begin local** $m, n := x, y;$ S_Q **end**
$\quad\quad\quad$ {$sorted(a[x : y])$}.

Proof. In Figure 5.4 a proof outline is given that uses as assumptions the correctness formulas **P3**, **Q2**, and **Q3**. In the following we justify the correctness formulas about *Partition* and the recursive calls of *Quicksort* used in this proof outline. In the postcondition of *Partition* we use the following abbreviation:

$$K \equiv v < w \land$$
$$(\forall i \in [m : v] : a[i] \leq pi) \land$$
$$(\forall i \in [v + 1 : w - 1] : a[i] = pi) \land$$
$$(\forall i \in [w : n] : pi \leq a[i]).$$

```
{true}
begin local
{true}
m, n := x, y;
{J}
if m <'n then
    {J ∧ m < n}
    Partition(m, n);
    {J ∧ K[v, w := ri, le]}
    begin local
    {J ∧ K[v, w := ri, le]}
    v, w := ri, le;
    {J ∧ K}
    Quicksort(m, v);
    {sorted(a[m : v]) ∧ J ∧ K}
    Quicksort(w, n)
    {sorted(a[m : v] ∧ sorted(a[w : n] ∧ J ∧ K}
    {sorted(a[x : v] ∧ sorted(a[w : y] ∧ K[m, n := x, y]}
    {sorted(a[x : y])}
    end
    {sorted(a[x : y])}
fi
{sorted(a[x : y])}
end
{sorted(a[x : y])}
```

Fig. 5.4 Proof outline showing sorting property **Q3**.

Observe that the correctness formula

$$\{J\} \; Partition(m, n) \; \{J \wedge K[v, w := ri, le]\}$$

is derived from **P3** by the invariance rule. Next we verify the correctness formulas

$$\{J \wedge K\} \; Quicksort(m, v) \; \{sorted(a[m : v]) \wedge J \wedge K\}, \tag{5.10}$$

and

$$\begin{aligned} &\{sorted(a[m : v]) \wedge J \wedge K\} \\ &Quicksort(w, n) \\ &\{sorted(a[m : v] \wedge sorted(a[w : n] \wedge J \wedge K\}. \end{aligned} \tag{5.11}$$

about the recursive calls of *Quicksort*.

Proof of (5.10). By applying the instantiation rule to **Q3**, we obtain

A1   {**true**} *Quicksort*(m, v) {*sorted*$(a[m : v])$}.

Moreover, by the invariance axiom, we have

A2 $\{J\}$ *Quicksort*(m, v) $\{J\}$.

By applying the instantiation rule to **Q2**, we then obtain

$$\{perm(a, a_0, [x' : y']) \wedge x' \leq m \wedge v \leq y'\}$$
$$Quicksort(m, v)$$
$$\{perm(a, a_0, [x' : y'])\}.$$

Applying next the substitution rule with the substitution $[x', y' := m, v]$ yields

$$\{perm(a, a_0, [m : v]) \wedge m \leq m \wedge v \leq v\}$$
$$Quicksort(m, v)$$
$$\{perm(a, a_0, [m : v])\}.$$

So by a trivial application of the consequence rule, we obtain

$$\{a = a_0\} \; Quicksort(m, v) \; \{perm(a, a_0, [m : v])\}.$$

We then obtain by an application of the invariance rule

$$\{a = a_0 \wedge K[a := a_0]\} \; Quicksort(m, v) \; \{perm(a, a_0, [m : v]) \wedge K[a := a_0]\}.$$

Note now the following implications:

$$K \to \exists a_0 : (a = a_0 \wedge K[a := a_0]),$$
$$perm(a, a_0, [m : v]) \wedge K[a := a_0] \to K.$$

So we conclude

A3 $\{K\}$ *Quicksort*(m, v) $\{K\}$

by the $\exists$-introduction rule and the consequence rule. Combining the correctness formulas **A1**–**A3** by the conjunction rule we get (5.10).

Proof of (5.11). In a similar way as above, we can prove the correctness formula

$$\{a = a_0\} \; Quicksort(w, n) \; \{perm(a, a_0, [w : n])\}.$$

By an application of the invariance rule we obtain

$$\{a = a_0 \wedge sorted(a_0[m : v]) \wedge v < w\}$$
$$Quicksort(w, n)$$
$$\{perm(a, a_0, [w : n]) \wedge sorted(a_0[m : v]) \wedge v < w\}.$$

Note now the following implications:

$v < w \wedge sorted(a[m : v]) \rightarrow \exists a_0 : (a = a_0 \wedge sorted(a_0[m : v]) \wedge v < w),$

$(perm(a, a_0, [w : n]) \wedge sorted(a_0[m : v]) \wedge v < w) \rightarrow sorted(a[m : v]).$

So we conclude

B0 $\{v < w \wedge sorted(a[m : v])\}$ $Quicksort(w, n)$ $\{sorted(a[m : v])\}$

by the $\exists$-introduction rule and the consequence rule. Further, by applying the instantiation rule to **Q3** we obtain

B1 $\{\textbf{true}\}$ $Quicksort(w, n)$ $\{sorted(a[w : n])\}$.

Next, by the invariance axiom we obtain

B2 $\{J\}$ $Quicksort(w, m)$ $\{J\}$.

Further, using the implications

$$K \rightarrow \exists a_0 : (a = a_0 \wedge K[a := a_0]),$$
$$perm(a, a_0, [w : n]) \wedge K[a := a_0] \rightarrow K,$$

we can derive from **Q2**, in a similar manner as in the proof of **A3**,

B3 $\{K\}$ $Quicksort(w, n)$ $\{K\}$.

Note that **B1**–**B3** correspond to the properties **A1**–**A3** of the procedure call $Quicksort(m, v)$. Combining the correctness formulas **B0**–**B3** by the conjunction rule and observing that $K \rightarrow v < w$ holds, we get (5.11).

The final application of the consequence rule in the proof outline given in Figure 5.4 is justified by the following crucial implication:

$$sorted(a[x : v]) \wedge sorted(a[w : y]) \wedge K[m, n := x, y] \rightarrow$$
$$sorted(a[x : y]).$$

Also note that $J \wedge m \geq n \rightarrow sorted(a[x : y])$, so the implicit **else** branch is properly taken care of. This concludes the proof of Claim 2. □

We can now derive **Q3** by the recursion rule. In summary, we have proved

$$\textbf{P3, Q2} \vdash \textbf{Q3}.$$

The proof of partial correctness of *Quicksort* is now immediate: it suffices to combine **Q2** and **Q3** by the conjunction rule. Then after applying the substitution rule with the substitution $[x', y' := x, y]$ and the consequence rule we obtain **Q1**, or more precisely

$$\textbf{P1, P2, P3} \vdash \textbf{Q1}.$$

Total Correctness

To prove termination, by the decomposition rule discussed in Section 3.3 it suffices to establish

Q4   {**true**} $Quicksort(x, y)$ {**true**}

in the sense of total correctness. In the proof we rely on the property **PT4** of *Partition*:

$$\{m < n\}\ Partition(m, n)\ \{m < le \wedge ri < n\}.$$

The provability symbol $\vdash$ refers below to the proof system TW augmented with the block rule, the instantiation rule and the auxiliary rules A3–A7. For the termination proof of the recursive procedure call $Quicksort(x, y)$ we use

$$t \equiv \max(y - x, 0)$$

as the bound function. Since $t \geq 0$ holds, the appropriate claim needed for the application of the recursion IV rule is:

Claim 3.

> **PT4**, $\{t < z\}\ Quicksort(x, y)\ \{$**true**$\} \vdash$
> $\{t = z\}$ **begin local** $m, n := x, y;\ S_Q$ **end** {**true**}.

Proof.   In Figure 5.5 a proof outline for total correctness is given that uses as assumptions the correctness formulas **PT4** and $\{t < z\}\ Quicksort(x, y)\ \{$**true**$\}$. In the following we justify the correctness formulas about *Partition* and the recursive calls of *Quicksort* used in this proof outline. Since $m, n, z \notin change(D)$, we deduce from **PT4** using the invariance rule the correctness formula

$$\begin{aligned}&\{n - m = z \wedge m < n\}\\&Partition(m, n) \hspace{4cm} (5.12)\\&\{n - m = z \wedge m < n \wedge ri - m < n - m \wedge n - le < n - m\}.\end{aligned}$$

Consider now the assumption

$$\{t < z\}\ Quicksort(x, y)\ \{\textbf{true}\}.$$

Since $n, w, z \notin change(D)$, the instantiation rule and the invariance rule yield

$$\begin{aligned}&\{\max(v - m, 0) < z \wedge \max(n - w, 0) < z\}\\&Quicksort(m, v)\\&\{\max(n - w, 0) < z\}\end{aligned}$$

and

$$\{\max(n - w, 0) < z\}\ Quicksort(w, n)\ \{\textbf{true}\}.$$

$\{t = z\}$
begin local
$\{\max(y - x, 0) = z\}$
$m, n := x, y;$
$\{\max(n - m, 0) = z\}$
if $n < k$ **then**
$\qquad \{\max(n - m, 0) = z \wedge m < n\}$
$\qquad \{n - m = z \wedge m < n\}$
$\qquad Partition(m, n);$
$\qquad \{n - m = z \wedge m < n \wedge ri - m < n - m \wedge n - le < n - m\}$
$\qquad$ **begin local**
$\qquad \{n - m = z \wedge m < n \wedge ri - m < n - m \wedge n - le < n - m\}$
$\qquad v, w := ri, le;$
$\qquad \{n - m = z \wedge m < n \wedge v - m < n - m \wedge n - w < n - m\}$
$\qquad \{\max(v - m, 0) < z \wedge \max(n - w, 0) < z\}$
$\qquad Quicksort(m, v);$
$\qquad \{\max(n - w, 0) < z\}$
$\qquad Quicksort(w, n)$
$\qquad \{\textbf{true}\}$
$\qquad$ **end**
$\qquad \{\textbf{true}\}$
fi
$\{\textbf{true}\}$
end
$\{\textbf{true}\}$

Fig. 5.5 Proof outline establishing termination of the *Quicksort* procedure.

The application of the consequence rule preceding the first recursive call of *Quicksort* is justified by the following two implications:

$$(n - m = z \wedge m < n \wedge v - m < n - m) \rightarrow \max(v - m, 0) < z,$$
$$(n - m = z \wedge m < n \wedge n - w < n - m) \rightarrow \max(n - w, 0) < z.$$

This completes the proof of Claim 3. □

Applying now the simplified version of the recursion IV rule we derive **Q4**. In summary, we have proved

$$\textbf{PT4} \vdash \textbf{Q4}.$$

5.5 Exercises

5.1. Call a recursive program *proper* when its sets of local and global variables are disjoint, and *safe* when for all procedures no formal parameter appears in an actual parameter and for all its block statements **begin local** $\bar{x} := \bar{t}$; S **end** we have $var(\bar{x}) \cap var(\bar{t}) = \emptyset$.

Suppose that

$$< S, \sigma > \;\to^* \; < R, \tau >,$$

where σ is a proper state. Prove the following two properties of recursive programs.

(i) If S is proper, then so is R.
(ii) If S is safe, then so is R.

5.2. Prove the Input/Output Lemma 5.1.

5.3. Prove the Block Lemma 5.4.

5.4. Prove the Change and Access Lemma 5.5.

5.5. Prove the Soundness Theorem 5.4.

5.6. This exercise considers the modularity rule 12′ introduced in Section 5.3.

(i) Prove that this rule is a *derived rule*, in the sense that every proof of partial correctness that uses it can be converted into a proof that uses the recursion III rule instead. Conclude that this proof rule is sound in the sense of partial correctness.
(ii) Suggest an analogous modularity proof rule for total correctness.

5.7. Prove the Soundness Theorem 5.5 for the proof system *TRP*.

5.8. Consider the *Partition* procedure defined in Section 5.5. Prove the correctness formulas **P1–P3** and **PT4** for the procedure call $Partition(m, n)$ using the properties **P1–P4** and **T** of the **while** program *PART* from Section 3.9 and the Transfer Lemma 5.2.

5.9. Allow the failure statements in the main statements and procedure bodies. Add to the proof systems *PRP* and *TRP* the corresponding failure rules from Section 3.7 and prove the counterparts of the Soundness Corollary 5.1 and Soundness Theorem 5.5.

5.6 Bibliographic Remarks

The usual treatment of parameter mechanisms involves appropriate renaming of local variables to avoid variable clashes, see, e.g., Apt [1981]. The semantics and proof theory of the call-by-value parameter mechanism adopted here avoids any renaming and seems to be new. Recursion IV rule is a modification of the corresponding rule from America and de Boer [1990].

For other parameter mechanisms like call-by-name (as in ALGOL) or call-by-reference (as in Pascal) a renaming of local variables in procedure bodies is unavoidable to maintain the *static scope* of variables. In Olderog [1981] a proof system for programs with procedures having call-by-name parameters is presented, where local variables are renamed whenever the block of a procedure body is entered. This mimics the *copy rule* of ALGOL 60, see, e.g., Grau, Hill, and Langmaack [1967].

Clarke investigated programs with a powerful ALGOL-like procedure mechanism where recursive procedures can take *procedures as parameters*; in Clarke [1979] he showed that for such programs it is impossible to obtain a complete Hoare-style proof system even if —different from this book— only logical structures with finite data domains are considered. Clarke's article initiated an intense research on the question of whether complete Hoare-style proof systems could be obtained for programs with a restricted ALGOL-like procedure mechanism. For program classes with complete proof systems see, for example, Olderog [1981,1983a,1984] and Damm and Josko [1983]. An interesting survey over these results on completeness of Hoare's logic can be found in Clarke [1985].

The algorithm *Quicksort* is due to Hoare[1961a,1962]. The first proof of partial correctness of *Quicksort* is given in Foley and Hoare [1971]. That proof establishes the permutation and the sorting property simultaneously, in contrast to our modular approach. For dealing with recursive procedures, Foley and Hoare [1971] use proof rules corresponding to our rules for blocks, instantiation, and recursion III rule for the case of one recursive procedure. They also use a so-called *adaptation rule* of Hoare [1971a] that allows one to adapt a given correctness formula about a program to other pre- and postconditions. In our approach we use several auxiliary rules which together have the same effect as the adaptation rule. The expressive power of the adaptation rule has been analyzed in Olderog [1983b]. No proof rule for the termination of recursive procedures is proposed in Foley and Hoare [1971], only an informal argument is given why *Quicksort* terminates. In Kaldewaij [1990] a correctness proof of a non-recursive version of *Quicksort* is given.

6 Object-Oriented Programs

I
N THIS CHAPTER we study the verification of object-oriented programs. We focus on the following main characteristics of objects:

- objects possess (and *encapsulate*) their own local variables,
- objects interact via *method* calls,
- objects can be dynamically *created*.

In contrast to the formal parameters of procedures and the local variables of block statements which only exist *temporarily*, the local variables of an object exist *permanently*. To emphasize the difference between these temporary variables and the local variables of an object, the latter are called *instance* variables. The local state of an object is a mapping that assigns values to its instance variables. Each object represents its local state by a *pointer* to

Krzysztof R. Apt et al., *Verification of Sequential and Concurrent Programs*,
Texts in Computer Science, DOI: 10.1007/978-1-84882-745-5_6,
© Springer-Verlag London Limited 2009

it. *Encapsulation* means that the instance variables of an object cannot be directly accessed by other objects; they can be accessed only via method calls of the object.

A method call invokes a procedure which is executed by the called object. The execution of a method call thus involves a temporary *transfer* of control from the local state of the caller object to that of the called object (also referred to by *callee*). Upon termination of the method call the control returns to the local state of the caller. The method calls are the *only way* to transfer control from one object to another.

We start in Section 6.1 by defining the syntax of the object-oriented programming language. We first restrict the language to simple method calls which do not involve parameters. In Section 6.2 we introduce the corresponding operational semantics. This requires an appropriate extension of the concept of a state to properly deal with objects and instance variables.

In Section 6.3 we introduce the syntax and semantics of the assertion language. Expressions of the programming language only refer to the local state of the executing object. We call them *local expressions*. In order to express global properties we introduce in the assertion language a new kind of expression which allow us to *navigate* through the local object states. We call them *global expressions*.

Next, in Section 6.4, we introduce a new assignment axiom for the instance variables. The rules for partial and total correctness of recursive procedure calls with parameters (as described in Chapter 5) are naturally extended to method calls. In Section 6.5 we discuss the extension to method calls with parameters. In Section 6.6 we introduce a transformation of object-oriented programs into recursive programs and use it to prove soundness of the proof systems introduced for reasoning about object-oriented programs.

Next, in Section 6.7 we introduce a new assignment axiom for object creation. Finally, in Section 6.8 we prove as a case study the correctness of an object-oriented program that implements a search for zero in a *linked list* of integers, and in Section 6.9 the correctness of an object-oriented program that inserts a new object in a linked list.

6.1 Syntax

We first describe the syntax of the expressions of the considered programming language and then define the syntax of method calls, method definitions and object-oriented programs.

Local Expressions

The set of expressions used here extends the set of expressions introduced in Section 2.2. We call them *local expressions* to stress that they refer to local properties of objects. We begin by introducing a new basic type **object** which denotes the set of objects. A local expression (e.g, a variable) of type **object** denotes an object. Simple variables of type **object** and array variables with value type **object** are called *object* variables. As a specific case, we distinguish the simple object variable **this** which at each state denotes the currently executing object.

Recall from Section 2.2 that we denote the set of all simple and array variables by Var. We now introduce a new set $IVar$ of instance variables (so $Var \cap IVar = \emptyset$). An *instance variable* is a simple variable or an array variable. Thus we now have two kinds of variables: the up till now considered *normal* variables (Var), which are shared, and instance variables $(IVar)$, which are owned by objects. Each object has its own local state which assigns values to the instance variables. We stipulate that **this** is a normal variable, that is, **this** $\in Var$.

The only operation of a higher type which involves the basic type **object** (as argument type or as value type) is the equality $=_{\textbf{object}}$ (abbreviated by $=$). Further, as before we abbreviate $\neg(s = t)$ by $s \neq t$. Finally, the constant **null** of type **object** represents the *void reference*, a special construct which does not have a local state.

Example 6.1. Given an array variable $a \in Var \cup IVar$ of type **integer** $\rightarrow$ **object**,

- $a[0]$ is a local expression of type **object**,
- **this** $= a[0]$ and **this** $\neq$ **null** are local Boolean expressions.

□

Summarizing, the set of expressions defined in Section 2.2 is extended by the introduction of the basic type **object**, the constant **null** of type **object**, and the set $IVar$ of (simple and array) instance variables. Local object expressions, i.e., expressions of type **object**, can only be compared for equality. A variable is either a normal variable (in Var) or an instance variable (in $IVar$). Simple variables (in $Var \cup IVar$) can now be of type **object**. Also the argument and the value types of array variables (in $Var \cup IVar$) can be of type **object**. Finally, we have the distinguished normal object variable **this**.

Statements and Programs

We extend the definition of statements given in Section 3.1 with block statements, as introduced in Section 5.1, and *method calls* which are described by the following clause:

$$S ::= s.m.$$

The local object expression s in the method call $s.m$ denotes the *called object*. The identifier m denotes a method which is a special kind of procedure.

The methods are defined as parameterless procedures, by means of a definition

$$m :: S.$$

Here S is the *method body*. Because the statements now include method calls, we allow for recursive (albeit parameterless) methods. The instance variables appearing in the body S of a method definition are owned by the executing object which is denoted by the variable **this**. To ensure correct use of the variable **this**, we only consider statements in which **this** is read-only, that is, we disallow assignments to the variable **this**. Further, to ensure that instance variables are permanent, we require that in each block statement **begin local** $\bar{u} := \bar{t}; S$ **end** we have $var(\bar{u}) \subseteq Var \setminus \{\textbf{this}\}$, that is, instance variables are not used as local variables. However, when describing the semantics of method calls, we do use 'auxiliary' block statements in which the variable **this** *is* used as a local variable (see the discussion in Example 6.2), so in particular, it is initialized (and hence modified).

Apart from denoting the callee of a method call, local object expressions, as already indicated in Example 6.1, can appear in local Boolean expressions. Further, we allow for assignments to object variables. In particular, the assignment $u := \textbf{null}$ is used to assign to the object variable u the void reference, which is useful in programs concerned with dynamic data structures (such as lists), see Example 6.5. In turn, the assignment $u := v$ for the object variables u and v causes u and v to point to the same object. Particularly useful is the assignment of the form $x := \textbf{this}$ that causes x to point to the currently executing object. An example will be given below.

We now denote by D a set of method definitions. Object-oriented programs consist of a main statement S and a given set D of method definitions such that each method used has a unique declaration in D and each method call refers to a method declared in D. Finally, we assume that the name clashes between local variables and global variables are resolved in the same way as in Chapter 5, so by assuming that no local variable of S occurs in D.

From now on we assume a given set D of method definitions.

Example 6.2. Suppose that the set D contains the method definition

$$getx :: return := x,$$

where $return \in Var$ and $x \in IVar$. Then the method call

$$y.getx,$$

where $y \in Var \cup IVar$ is an object variable, assigns the value of the instance variable x of the called object denoted by y to the normal variable $return$. The execution of this method call by the current object, denoted by **this**, transfers control from the local state of the current object to that of the called object y. Semantically, this control transfer is described by the (implicit) assignment

$$\textbf{this} := y,$$

which sets the current executing object to the one denoted by y. After the execution of the method body control is transferred back to the calling object which is denoted by the previous value of **this**. Summarizing, the execution of a method call $y.getx$ can be described by the block statement

$$\textbf{begin local } \textbf{this} := y; \ return := x \textbf{ end}.$$

Because of the assignment **this** $:= y$, the instance variable x is owned within this block statement by the called object y. Note that upon termination the local variable **this** is indeed reset to its previous value (which denotes the calling object).

Consider now the main statement

$$y.getx; \ z := return.$$

Using the method call $y.getx$ it assigns to the instance variable z of the current object the value of the instance variable x of the object denoted by y, using the variable $return$.

The names of the instance variables can coincide. In case $x \equiv z$, the above main statement copies the value of the instance variable x owned by y to the instance variable x of the current object, denoted by **this**.   □

Example 6.3. Given an instance integer variable $count$ we define the methods inc and $reset$ as follows:

$$inc :: count := count + 1,$$
$$reset :: count := 0.$$

Assume now normal integer variables i, j and n, normal object variables up and $down$ and a normal array variable a of type **integer** $\rightarrow$ **integer**. The main statement

$$i := 0;$$
$$up.reset;$$
$$down.reset;$$
while $i \leq n$
do if $a[i] > j$
    then *up.inc*
    else if $a[i] < k$ **then** *down.inc* **fi**
    fi;
    $i := i + 1$
od

computes the number of integers greater than j and the number of integers smaller than k, stored in $a[0 : n]$, using two normal object variables *up* and *down*. Since *count* is an instance variable, the call *up.inc* of the method *inc* of *up* does not affect the value of *count* of the object *down* (and vice versa), assuming $up \neq down$, i.e., when *up* and *down* refer to *distinct* objects. □

The above example illustrates one of the main features of instance variables. Even though there is here only one variable *count*, during the program execution two instances (hence the terminology of an 'instance variable') of this variable are created and maintained: *up.count* and *down.count*. When the control is within the *up* object (that is, *up* is the currently executing object), then *up.count* is used, and when the control is within the *down* object, then *down.count* is used.

The next two examples illustrate the important role played by the instance object variables. They allow us to construct dynamic data structures, like lists.

Example 6.4. We represent a (non-circular) *linked list* using the instance object variable *next* that links the objects of the list, and the constant **null** that allows us to identify the last element of the list. We assume that each object stores a value, kept in an instance integer variable *val*. Additionally, we use the normal object variable *first* to denote (point to) the first object in the list, see for example Figure 6.1.

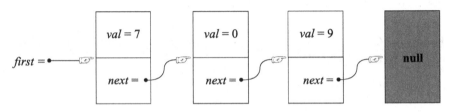

Fig. 6.1 A list.

We want to compute the sum of the instance variables *val*. To this end, we additionally use the normal integer variable *sum*, normal object variable *current* that (points to) denotes the current object, and two methods, *add* and *move*, defined as follows:

$$add :: sum := sum + val,$$
$$move :: current := next.$$

The first one updates the variable *sum*, while the second one allows us to progress to the next object in the list.

The following main statement then computes the desired sum:

$$sum := 0;$$
$$current := first;$$
while $current \neq$ **null do** $current.add;$ $current.move$ **od**.

$\square$

In this example the method call *current.move* is used to 'advance' the variable *current* to point to the next element of the list. Note that this effect of advancing the variable *current* cannot be achieved by using the assignment *current* := *next* instead. Indeed, the repeated executions of the assignment *current* := *next* can modify the variable *current* only once.

The next example presents a program that uses a recursive method.

Example 6.5. Consider again a non-circular linked list built using an instance object variable *next* and the constant **null**, representing the last element, such as the one depicted in Figure 6.1. Then, given an integer instance variable *val* and a normal object variable *return*, the following recursive method

$find ::$ **if** $val = 0$
  then $return :=$ **this**
  else if $next \neq$ **null**
    then $next.find$
    else $return :=$ **null**
    fi
  fi

returns upon termination of the call **this**.$find$ an object that stores zero. More precisely, if such an object exists, then upon termination the variable *return* points to the first object in the list that stores zero and otherwise the void reference (represented by the constant **null**) is returned. $\square$

This program is a typical example of recursion over dynamic data structures represented by objects. The recursive call of the method $find$ of the object denoted by the instance variable *next* involves a transfer of the control from the local state of the calling object **this** to the local state of the next object in the list. Since the variable *next* is an instance variable, which version of it is being referred to and which value it has depends on which object is currently executing.

More specifically, in the example list depicted in Figure 6.1 the call of the method *find* on the first object, i.e., one that stores the value 7, searches for the first object whose *val* variable equals zero. If such an object is found, it is returned using the object variable **this**. Note that the outer **else** branch leads to the call *next.find* of the *find* method of the object to which the variable *next* of the current object refers. So in the case of the list depicted in Figure 6.1 if the current object is the one that stores the value 7, then the method call *next.find* is the call of the *find* method of the object that stores the value 0. This call is conditional: if *next* equals **null**, then the search terminates and the void reference is returned, through the variable *return*. We shall return to this program in Section 6.8, where we shall prove its correctness.

Given a set D of method definitions, the set *change*(S), originally defined in Chapter 4 for the case of normal variables, now also includes the instance variables that can be modified by S. For example, for the main statement S in Example 6.3, we have *count* $\in$ *change*(S), given the declarations of the methods *inc* and *reset*. Note that *count* is owned by different objects and that the main statement changes the instance variable *count* of the object variables *up* and *down*.

6.2 Semantics

In this section we define the semantics of the introduced object-oriented programs. We first define the semantics of local expressions. This semantics requires an extension of the definition of state. Subsequently we introduce a revised definition of an update of a state and provide the transition axioms concerned with the newly introduced programming constructs.

Semantics of Local Expressions

The main difficulty in defining the semantics of local expressions is of course how to deal properly with the instance variables. As already mentioned above, each instance variable has a different version ('instance') in each object. Conceptually, when defining the semantics of an instance variable u we view it as a variable of the form **this**.u, where **this** represents the current object. So, given a proper state σ and a simple instance variable x we first determine the current object o, which is $\sigma(\textbf{this})$. Then we determine the *local state* of this object, which is $\sigma(o)$, or $\sigma(\sigma(\textbf{this}))$, and subsequently apply this local state to the considered instance variable x. This means that given a proper state

σ the value assigned to the instance variable x is $\sigma(o)(x)$, or, written out in full, $\sigma(\sigma(\mathbf{this}))(x)$. This two-step procedure is at the heart of the definition given below.

Let an infinite set $\mathcal{D}_{\mathbf{object}}$ of object identities be given. We introduce a value $\mathbf{null} \in \mathcal{D}_{\mathbf{object}}$. So in each proper state a variable of type $\mathbf{object}$ equals some object of $\mathcal{D}_{\mathbf{object}}$, which can be the $\mathbf{null}$ object. A proper state σ now additionally assigns to each object $o \in \mathcal{D}_{\mathbf{object}}$ its local state $\sigma(o)$. In turn, a local state $\sigma(o)$ of an object o assigns a value of appropriate type to each instance variable.

So the value of an instance variable $x \in IVar$ of an object $o \in \mathcal{D}_{\mathbf{object}}$ is given by $\sigma(o)(x)$ and, as before, the value of $x \in Var$ is given by $\sigma(x)$.

Note that the local state of the current object $\sigma(\mathbf{this})$ is given by $\sigma(\sigma(\mathbf{this}))$. Further, note that in particular, if an instance variable x is of type $\mathbf{Object}$, then for each object $o \in \mathcal{D}_{\mathbf{object}}$, $\sigma(o)(x)$ is either $\mathbf{null}$ or an object $o' \in \mathcal{D}_{\mathbf{object}}$, whose local state is $\sigma(o')$, i.e., $\sigma(\sigma(o)(x))$. This application of σ can of course be nested, to get local states of the form $\sigma(\sigma(\sigma(o)(x)))$, etc. Note that a state σ also assigns a local state $\sigma(\mathbf{null})$ to the $\mathbf{null}$ object. However, as we will see below this local state will never be accessed by an object-oriented program.

Formally, we extend the semantics of expressions $\mathcal{S}[\![s]\!](\sigma)$, given in Section 2.3, by the following clauses:

- if $s \equiv \mathbf{null}$ then

$$\mathcal{S}[\![s]\!](\sigma) = \mathbf{null}.$$

So the meaning of the void reference (i.e., the constant $\mathbf{null}$) is the $\mathbf{null}$ object,

- if $s \equiv x$ for some simple instance variable x then

$$\mathcal{S}[\![s]\!](\sigma) = \sigma(o)(x),$$

where $o = \sigma(\mathbf{this})$,

- if $s \equiv a[s_1, \ldots, s_n]$ for some instance array variable a then

$$\mathcal{S}[\![s]\!](\sigma) = \sigma(o)(a)(\mathcal{S}[\![s_1]\!](\sigma), \ldots, \mathcal{S}[\![s_n]\!](\sigma)),$$

where $o = \sigma(\mathbf{this})$.

We abbreviate $\mathcal{S}[\![s]\!](\sigma)$ by $\sigma(s)$. So for a simple instance variable

$$\sigma(x) = \sigma(\sigma(\mathbf{this}))(x). \tag{6.1}$$

Updates of States

Next, we proceed with the revision of the definition of a state update for the
case of instance variables. Here, the intuition we provided when explaining
the semantics of instance variables, is of help. Consider a proper state σ,
a simple instance variable x and a value d belonging to the type of x. To
perform the corresponding update of σ on x we first identify the current
object o, which is $\sigma(\textbf{this})$ and its local state, which is $\sigma(o)$, or $\sigma(\sigma(\textbf{this}))$,
that we denote by τ. Then we perform the appropriate update on the state
τ. So the desired update of σ is achieved by modifying τ to $\tau[x := d]$.

In general, let u be a (possibly subscripted) instance variable of type T
and τ a local state. We define for $d \in \mathcal{D}_T$

$$\tau[u := d]$$

analogously to the definition of state update given in Section 2.3.

Furthermore, we define for an object $o \in \mathcal{D}_{\textbf{object}}$ and local state τ, the
state update $\sigma[o := \tau]$ by

$$\sigma[o := \tau](o') = \begin{cases} \tau & \text{if } o = o' \\ \sigma(o') & \text{otherwise.} \end{cases}$$

We are now in a position to define the state update $\sigma[u := d]$ for a (possibly
subscripted) instance variable u of type T and $d \in \mathcal{D}_T$, as follows:

$$\sigma[u := d] = \sigma[o := \tau[u := d]],$$

where $o = \sigma(\textbf{this})$ and $\tau = \sigma(o)$. Note that the state update $\sigma[o := \tau[u := d]]$
assigns to the current object o the update $\tau[u := d]$ of its local state τ. In
its fully expanded form we get the following difficult to parse definition of a
state update:

$$\sigma[u := d] = \sigma[\sigma(\textbf{this}) := \sigma(\sigma(\textbf{this}))[u := d]].$$

Example 6.6. Let x be an integer instance variable, $o = \sigma(\textbf{this})$, and $\tau = \sigma(o)$. Then

$$\sigma[x := 1](x)$$
$$= \quad \{(6.1) \text{ with } \sigma \text{ replaced by } \sigma[x := 1]\}$$
$$\sigma[x := 1](\sigma[x := 1](\textbf{this}))(x)$$
$$= \quad \{\text{by the definition of state update, } \sigma[x := 1](\textbf{this}) = \sigma(\textbf{this}) = o\}$$
$$\sigma[x := 1](o)(x)$$

$=$ {definition of state update $\sigma[x := 1]$}

$\sigma[o := \tau[x := 1]](o)(x)$

$=$ {definition of state update $\sigma[o := \tau[x := 1]]$}

$\tau[x := 1](x)$

$=$ {definition of state update $\tau[x := 1]$}

1.

□

Semantics of Statements and Programs

To define the semantics of considered programs we introduce three transition axioms that deal with the assignment to (possibly subscripted) instance variables and with the method calls. The first axiom uses the state update defined above.

(xi) $< u := t, \sigma > \rightarrow < E, \sigma[u := \sigma(t)] >$,

(xii) $< s.m, \sigma > \rightarrow <$ **begin local this** $:= s;\ S$ **end**, $\sigma >$
   where $\sigma(s) \neq$ **null** and $m :: S \in D$,

(xiii) $< s.m, \sigma > \rightarrow < E, \textbf{fail} >$ where $\sigma(s) = $ **null**.

So thanks to the extended definition of a state update, the first transition axiom models the meaning of an assignment to an instance variable in exactly the same way as the meaning of the assignment to a normal variable.

The second transition axiom shows that we reduce the semantics of method calls to procedure calls with parameters by treating the variable **this** as a formal parameter and the called object as the corresponding actual parameter. The third transition axiom shows the difference between the method calls and procedure calls: if in the considered state σ the called object s equals the void reference (it equals **null**), then the method call yields a failure.

We could equally well dispense with the use of the block statement in the transition axiom (xii) by applying to the right configuration the transition axiom (ix) for the block statement. The resulting transition axiom would then take the form

$$< s.m, \sigma > \rightarrow < \textbf{this} := s; S; \textbf{this} := \sigma(\textbf{this}), \sigma >,$$

where $\sigma(s) \neq$ **null** and $m(\bar{u}) :: S \in D$. Then the variable **this** would remain a global variable throughout the computation.

We did not do this for a number of reasons:

- the proposed axiom captures explicitly the 'transitory' change of the value of the variable **this**,
- in the new recursion rule that deals with the method calls we do need the block statement anyway,
- later we shall need the block statement anyway, to define the meaning of the calls of methods with parameters.

Example 6.7. Given the method *getx* defined in Example 6.2 and an object variable y, we obtain the following computation:

$$< y.getx, \sigma >$$
$$\rightarrow \quad < \textbf{begin local this} := y; \; return := x \; \textbf{end}, \sigma >$$
$$\rightarrow \quad < \textbf{this} := y; \; return := x; \; \textbf{this} := \sigma(\textbf{this}), \sigma >$$
$$\rightarrow \quad < return := x; \; \textbf{this} := \sigma(\textbf{this}), \sigma[\textbf{this} := \sigma(y)] >$$
$$\rightarrow \quad \{\text{see simplification 1 below}\}$$
$$< \textbf{this} := \sigma(\textbf{this}), \sigma[\textbf{this} := \sigma(y)][return := \sigma(\sigma(y))(x)] >$$
$$\rightarrow \quad \{\text{see simplication 2 below}\}$$
$$< E, \sigma[return := \sigma(\sigma(y))(x)] > .$$

In the last two transitions we performed the following simplifications in configurations on the right-hand side.

Re: 1.

$$\sigma[\textbf{this} := \sigma(y)](x)$$
$$= \quad \{(6.1) \text{ with } \sigma \text{ replaced by } \sigma[\textbf{this} := \sigma(y)]\}$$
$$\sigma[\textbf{this} := \sigma(y)](\sigma[\textbf{this} := \sigma(y)](\textbf{this}))(x)$$
$$= \quad \{\text{by the definition state update, } \sigma[\textbf{this} := \sigma(y)](\textbf{this}) = \sigma(y)\}$$
$$\sigma[\textbf{this} := \sigma(y)](\sigma(y))(x)$$
$$= \quad \{\text{by the definition state update, } \sigma[\textbf{this} := \sigma(y)](\sigma(y)) = \sigma(\sigma(y))\}$$
$$\sigma(\sigma(y))(x)$$

Re: 2.

$$\sigma[\textbf{this} := \sigma(y)][return := \sigma(\sigma(y))(x)][\textbf{this} := \sigma(\textbf{this})]$$
$$= \quad \{\text{since } return \not\equiv \textbf{this}\}$$
$$\sigma[return := \sigma(\sigma(y))(x)][\textbf{this} := \sigma(y)][\textbf{this} := \sigma(\textbf{this})]$$
$$= \quad \{\text{the last update overrides the second update}$$
$$\quad \text{by the value } \textbf{this} \text{ has in } \sigma\}$$
$$\sigma[return := \sigma(\sigma(y))(x)]$$

This completes the calculation of the computation.   □

Lemma 6.1. (Absence of Blocking) *For every S that can arise during an execution of an object-oriented program, if $S \not\equiv E$ then for any proper state σ, such that $\sigma(\textbf{this}) \neq \textbf{null}$, there exists a configuration $< S_1, \tau >$ such that*

$$< S, \sigma > \; \rightarrow \; < S_1, \tau >,$$

where $\tau(\textbf{this}) \neq \textbf{null}$.

Proof. If $S \not\equiv E$ then any configuration $< S, \sigma >$ has a successor in the transition relation $\rightarrow$. To prove the preservation of the assumed property of the state it suffices to consider the execution of the $\textbf{this} := s$ assignment. Each such assignment arises only within the context of the block statement in the transition axiom (xii) and is activated in a state σ such that $\sigma(s) \neq \textbf{null}$. This yields a state τ such that $\tau(\textbf{this}) \neq \textbf{null}$. $\square$

When considering verification of object-oriented programs we shall only consider computations that start in a proper state σ such that $\sigma(\textbf{this}) \neq \textbf{null}$, i.e., in a state in which the current object differs from the void reference. The Absence of Blocking Lemma 6.1 implies that such computations never lead to a proper state in which this inequality is violated.

The partial correctness semantics is defined exactly as in the case of the recursive programs with parameters considered in Chapter 5. (Recall that we assumed a given set D of method declarations.)

The total correctness semantics additionally records failures. So, as in the case of the failure admitting programs from Section 3.7, we have for a proper state σ

$$\mathcal{M}_{tot}[\![S]\!](\sigma) = \quad \mathcal{M}[\![S]\!](\sigma)$$
$$\cup \; \{\bot \mid S \text{ can diverge from } \sigma\}$$
$$\cup \; \{\textbf{fail} \mid S \text{ can fail from } \sigma\}.$$

Example 6.8. Let us return to Example 6.2. On the account of Example 6.7 the following holds for the object variable y:

- if $\sigma(y) \neq \textbf{null}$ then

$$\mathcal{M}[\![y.getx]\!](\sigma) = \mathcal{M}_{tot}[\![y.getx]\!](\sigma) = \{\sigma[return := \sigma(\sigma(y))(x)]\},$$

- if $\sigma(y) = \textbf{null}$ then

$$\mathcal{M}[\![y.getx]\!](\sigma) = \emptyset \text{ and } \mathcal{M}_{tot}[\![y.getx]\!](\sigma) = \{\textbf{fail}\}.$$

$\square$

6.3 Assertions

Local expressions of the programming language only refer to the local state of the executing object and do not allow us to distinguish between different versions of the instance variables. In the assertions we need to be more explicit. So we introduce the set of *global expressions* which extends the set of local expressions introduced in Subsection 6.1 by the following additional clauses:

- if s is a global expression of type **object** and x is an instance variable of a basic type T then $s.x$ is a global expression of type T,
- if s is a global expression of type **object**, $s_1, \ldots, s_n$ are global expressions of type $T_1, \ldots, T_n$, and a is an array instance variable of type $T_1 \times \ldots \times T_1 \to T$ then $s.a[s_1, \ldots, s_n]$ is a global expression of type T.

In particular, every local expression is also a global expression.

Example 6.9. Consider a normal integer variable i, a normal variable x of type **object**, a normal array variable of type **integer** $\to$ **object**, and an instance variable *next* of type **object**.

Using them and the normal **this** variable (that is of type **object**) we can generate the following global expressions:

- *next*, *next.next*, etc.,
- **this**.*next*, **this**.*next.next*, etc.,
- *x.next*, *x.next.next*, etc.,
- *a*[*i*].*next*,

all of type **object**. In contrast, *next*.**this** and *next.x* are not global expressions, since neither **this** nor x are instance variables.   □

We call a global expression of the form $s.u$ a *navigation expression* since it allows one to *navigate* through the local states of the objects. For example, the global expression *next.next* refers to the object that can be reached by 'moving' to the object denoted by the value of *next* of the current object **this** and evaluate the value of its variable *next*.

We define the semantics of global expressions as follows:

- for a simple instance variable x of type T,

$$\mathcal{S}[\![s.x]\!](\sigma) = \sigma(o)(x),$$

where $\mathcal{S}[\![s]\!](\sigma) = o$,
- for an instance array variable a with value type T

$$\mathcal{S}[\![s.a[s_1, \ldots, s_n]]\!](\sigma) = \sigma(o)(a)(\mathcal{S}[\![s_1]\!](\sigma), \ldots, \mathcal{S}[\![s_n]\!](\sigma)),$$

where $\mathcal{S}[\![s]\!](\sigma) = o$.

We abbreviate $\mathcal{S}[\![t]\!](\sigma)$ by $\sigma(t)$.

So for a (simple or subscripted) instance variable u the semantics of u and **this**.u coincide, that is, for all proper states σ we have $\sigma(u) = \sigma(\textbf{this}.u)$. In other words, we can view an instance variable u as an abbreviation for the global expression **this**.u.

Note that this semantics also provides meaning to global expressions of the form **null**.u. However, such expressions are meaningless when specifying correctness of programs because the local state of the **null** object can never be reached in computations starting in a proper state σ such that $\sigma(\textbf{this}) \neq \textbf{null}$ (see the Absence of Blocking Lemma 6.1).

Example 6.10. If x is an object variable and σ a proper state such that $\sigma(x) \neq \textbf{null}$, then for all simple instance variables y

$$\sigma(x.y) = \sigma(\sigma(x))(y).$$

$\square$

Assertions are constructed from global Boolean expressions as in Section 2.5. This means that only normal variables can be quantified.

Substitution

The substitution operation $[u := t]$ was defined in Section 2.7 only for the normal variables u and for the expressions and assertions as defined there. We now extend the definition to the case of instance variables u and global expressions and assertions constructed from them.

Let u be a (simple or subscripted) instance variable and s and t global expressions. In general, the substitution $[u := t]$ replaces every possible alias $e.u$ of u by t. In addition to the possible aliases of subscripted variables, we now also have to consider the possibility that the global expression $e[u := t]$ denotes the current object **this**. This explains the use of conditional expressions below.

Here are the main cases of the definition substitution operation $s[u := t]$:

- if $s \equiv x \in Var$ then
$$x[u := t] \equiv x$$

- if $s \equiv e.u$ and u is a simple instance variable then

$$s[u := t] \equiv \textbf{if } e' = \textbf{this then } t \textbf{ else } e'.u \textbf{ fi}$$

where $e' \equiv e[u := t]$,
- if $s \equiv e.a[s_1, \ldots, s_n]$ and $u \equiv a[t_1, \ldots, t_n]$ then

$$s[u := t] \equiv \textbf{if } e' = \textbf{this} \wedge \bigwedge_{i=1}^{n} s_i' = t_i \textbf{ then } t \textbf{ else } e'.a[s_1', \ldots, s_n'] \textbf{ fi}$$

where $e' \equiv e[u := t]$ and $s_i' \equiv s_i[u := t]$ for $i \in \{1, \ldots, n\}$.

The following example should clarify this definition.

Example 6.11. Suppose that $s \equiv \textbf{this}.u$. Then

$$\textbf{this}.u[u := t]$$
$$\equiv \textbf{if this}[u := t] = \textbf{this then } t \textbf{ else } \ldots \textbf{ fi}$$
$$\equiv \textbf{if this} = \textbf{this then } t \textbf{ else } \ldots \textbf{ fi}.$$

So $\textbf{this}.u[u := t]$ and t are equal, i.e., for all proper states σ we have $\sigma(\textbf{this}.u[u := t]) = \sigma(t)$.

Next, suppose that $s \equiv \textbf{this}.a[x]$, where x is a simple variable. Then

$$\textbf{this}.a[x][a[x] := t]$$
$$\equiv \textbf{if this}[a[x] := t] = \textbf{this} \wedge x[a[x] := t] = x \textbf{ then } t \textbf{ else } \ldots \textbf{ fi}$$
$$\equiv \textbf{if this} = \textbf{this} \wedge x = x \textbf{ then } t \textbf{ else } \ldots \textbf{ fi}.$$

So $\textbf{this}.a[x][a[x] := t]$ and t are equal.

Finally, for a simple instance variable u and a normal object variable x we have

$$x.u[u := t]$$
$$\equiv \textbf{if } x[u := t] = \textbf{this then } t \textbf{ else } x[u := t].u \textbf{ fi}$$
$$\equiv \textbf{if } x = \textbf{this then } t \textbf{ else } x.u \textbf{ fi}.$$

$\square$

The substitution operation is then extended to assertions in the same way as in Section 2.5 and the semantics of assertions is defined as in Section 2.6. We have the following counterpart of the Substitution Lemma 2.4.

Lemma 6.2. (Substitution of Instance Variables) *For all global expressions s and t, all assertions p, all simple or subscripted instance variables u of the same type as t and all proper states σ,*

(i) $\sigma(s[u := t]) = \sigma[u := \sigma(t)](s)$,
(ii) $\sigma \models p[u := t]$ iff $\sigma[u := \sigma(t)] \models p$.

Proof. See Exercise 6.3. $\square$

6.4 Verification

We now study partial and total correctness of object-oriented programs. To this end, we provide a new definition of a meaning of an assertion, now defined by

$[\![p]\!] = \{\sigma \mid \sigma \text{ is a proper state such that } \sigma(\textbf{this}) \neq \textbf{null and } \sigma \models p\},$

and say that an assertion p is *is true*, or *holds*, if

$[\![p]\!] = \{\sigma \mid \sigma \text{ is a proper state such that } \sigma(\textbf{this}) \neq \textbf{null}\}.$

This new definition ensures that when studying program correctness we limit ourselves to meaningful computations of object-oriented programs.

The correctness notions are then defined in the familiar way using the semantics $\mathcal{M}$ and $\mathcal{M}_{tot}$. In particular, total correctness is defined by:

$$\models_{tot} \{p\} \, S \, \{q\} \text{ if } \mathcal{M}_{tot}[\![S]\!]([\![p]\!]) \subseteq [\![q]\!].$$

Since by definition **fail**, $\perp \notin [\![q]\!]$ holds, as in the case of the failure admitting programs from Section 3.7, $\models_{tot} \{p\} \, S \, \{q\}$ implies that S neither fails nor diverges when started in a proper state σ satisfying p and such that $\sigma(\textbf{this}) \neq \textbf{null}$.

Partial Correctness

We begin, as usual, with partial correctness. We have the following axiom for assignments to (possibly subscripted) instance variables.

AXIOM 14: ASSIGNMENT TO INSTANCE VARIABLES

$$\{p[u := t]\} \, u := t \, \{p\}$$

where u is a (possibly subscripted) instance variable.

So this axiom uses the new substitution operation defined in the section above.

To adjust the correctness formulas that deal with generic method calls to specific objects we modify the instantiation rule 11 of Section 5.3 as follows. We refer here to the given set D of method declarations.

RULE 15: INSTANTIATION II

$$\frac{\{p\} \, y.m \, \{q\}}{\{p[y := s]\} \, s.m \, \{q[y := s]\}}$$

where $y \notin var(D)$ and $var(s) \cap change(D) = \emptyset$.

The recursion III rule for partial correctness of recursive procedure calls with parameters that we introduced in Chapter 5 can be readily modified to deal with the method calls. To this end, it suffices to treat the variable **this** as a formal parameter of every method definition and the callee of a method call as the corresponding actual parameter. This yields the following proof rule that deals with partial correctness of recursive methods. Below the provability symbol $\vdash$ refers to the proof system PW augmented with the assignment axiom 14, the block rule, the instantiation II rule and the auxiliary axioms and rules A2–A7.

RULE 16: RECURSION V

$$\frac{\begin{array}{l} \{p_1\}\ s_1.m_1\ \{q_1\},\ldots,\{p_n\}\ s_n.m_n\ \{q_n\} \vdash \{p\}\ S\ \{q\}, \\ \{p_1\}\ s_1.m_1\ \{q_1\},\ldots,\{p_n\}\ s_n.m_n\ \{q_n\} \vdash \\ \qquad \{p_i\}\ \textbf{begin local this} := s_i;\ S_i\ \textbf{end}\ \{q_i\},\ i \in \{1,\ldots,n\} \end{array}}{\{p\}\ S\ \{q\}}$$

where $m_i :: S_i \in D$, for $i \in \{1,\ldots,n\}$.

To prove *partial* correctness of *object*-oriented programs we use the following proof system PO:

> PROOF SYSTEM PO :
> This system consists of the group of axioms
> and rules 1–6, 10, 14–16, and A2–A7.

We assume here and in the other proof systems presented in this chapter that the substitution rule A7 and the $\exists$-introduction rule A5 refer to the normal variables, i.e., we cannot substitute or eliminate instance variables.

Thus PO is obtained by extending the proof system PW by the block rule, the assignment to instance variables axiom, the instantiation II rule, the recursion V rule, and the auxiliary axioms and rules A2–A7.

When we deal only with one, non-recursive method and use the method call as the considered program, the recursion V rule can be simplified to

$$\frac{\{p\}\ \textbf{begin local this} := s;\ S\ \textbf{end}\ \{q\}}{\{p\}\ s.m\ \{q\}}$$

where $D = m :: S$.

We now illustrate the above proof system by two examples in which we use this simplified version of the recursion V rule.

Example 6.12. Given the method definition

$$inc :: count := count + 1$$

where *count* is an instance integer variable, we prove the following invariance property

$$\{\textbf{this} \neq other \wedge \textbf{this}.count = z\}\ other.inc\ \{\textbf{this}.count = z\},$$

where $z \in Var$. To this end, we first prove

$$\{u \neq other \wedge u.count = z\}$$
$$\textbf{begin local this} := other; \; count := count + 1 \; \textbf{end} \qquad (6.2)$$
$$\{u.count = z\},$$

where $u \in Var$ is a fresh variable.

By the assignment axiom for normal variables, we have

$$\{\textbf{if } u = other \textbf{ then } count + 1 \textbf{ else } u.count \textbf{ fi} = z\}$$
$$\textbf{this} := other$$
$$\{\textbf{if } u = \textbf{this then } count + 1 \textbf{ else } u.count \textbf{ fi} = z\}.$$

Further, by the assignment axiom for instance variables we have

$$\{(u.count = z)[count := count + 1]\} \; count := count + 1 \; \{u.count = z\}.$$

Since $u[count := count + 1] \equiv u$, we have

$$(u.count = z)[count := count + 1]$$
$$\equiv \textbf{if } u = \textbf{this then } count + 1 \textbf{ else } u.count \textbf{ fi} = z.$$

Clearly,

$$u \neq other \wedge u.count = z \rightarrow \textbf{if } u = other \textbf{ then } count + 1 \textbf{ else } u.count \textbf{ fi} = z.$$

So we obtain the above correctness formula (6.2) by an application of the composition rule, the consequence rule and, finally, the block rule.

We can now apply the recursion V rule. This way we establish

$$\{u \neq other \wedge u.count = z\} \; other.inc \; \{u.count = z\}.$$

Finally, using the substitution rule A7 with the substitution $u := \textbf{this}$ we obtain the desired correctness formula. □

Example 6.13. Given an arbitrary method m (so in particular for the above method inc), we now wish to prove the correctness formula

$$\{other = \textbf{null}\} \; other.m \; \{\textbf{false}\}$$

in the sense of partial correctness. To this end, it suffices to prove

$$\{other = \textbf{null}\}$$
$$\textbf{begin local this} := other; \; S \; \textbf{end} \qquad (6.3)$$
$$\{\textbf{false}\}$$

where m is defined by $m :: S$, and apply the recursion V rule.

Now, by the assignment axiom for normal variables we have

$$\{other = \textbf{null}\} \textbf{ this} := other \ \{\textbf{this} = \textbf{null}\}.$$

But by the new definition of truth of assertions we have $[\![\textbf{this} = \textbf{null}]\!] = \emptyset$, i.e.,

$$\textbf{this} = \textbf{null} \rightarrow \textbf{false}$$

holds. By the consequence rule we therefore obtain

$$\{other = \textbf{null}\} \textbf{ this} := other \ \{\textbf{false}\}.$$

Further, by the invariance axiom A2 we have

$$\{\textbf{false}\} \ S \ \{\textbf{false}\},$$

so by the composition rule and the block rule we obtain (6.3).

Note that by the substitution rule A7 and the consequence rule this implies the correctness formula

$$\{\textbf{true}\} \ \textbf{null}.m \ \{\textbf{false}\}$$

in the sense of partial correctness.   □

Total Correctness

We next introduce the proof system for total correctness. Below, the provability symbol $\vdash$ refers to the proof system TW augmented with the assignment axiom 14, the block rule, the instantiation II rule and the auxiliary rules A3–A7.

In order to prove absence of failures due to calls of a method on **null**, we proceed as in the failure II rule of Section 3.7 and add similar conditions to premises of the recursion rule. For proving absence of divergence we proceed in an analogous way as in Chapter 5 in the case of procedures with parameters. This results in the following rule.

RULE 17: RECURSION VI

$$\{p_1\} \ s_1.m_1 \ \{q_1\}, \ldots, \{p_n\} \ s_n.m_n \ \{q_n\} \vdash \{p\} \ S \ \{q\},$$
$$\{p_1 \wedge t < z\} \ s_1.m_1 \ \{q_1\}, \ldots, \{p_n \wedge t < z\} \ s_n.m_n \ \{q_n\} \vdash$$
$$\quad \{p_i \wedge t = z\} \ \textbf{begin local this} := s_i; \ S_i \ \textbf{end} \ \{q_i\}, \ i \in \{1, \ldots, n\},$$
$$p_i \rightarrow s_i \neq \textbf{null}, \ i \in \{1, \ldots, n\}$$

$$\overline{\{p\} \ S \ \{q\}}$$

where $m_i :: S_i \in D$, for $i \in \{1, \ldots, n\}$, and z is an integer variable that does not occur in p_i, t, q_i and S_i for $i \in \{1, \ldots, n\}$ and is treated in the proofs as a constant.

To prove total correctness of object-oriented programs we use then the following proof system TO :

> PROOF SYSTEM TO :
> > This system consists of the group of axioms
> > and rules 1–4, 6, 7, 10, 14, 15, 17, and A3–A7.

Thus TO is obtained by extending proof system TW by the block rule, the assignment to instance variables axiom, instantiation II rule, the recursion VI rule, and the auxiliary rules A3–A6.

Example 6.14. Given the method *inc* defined as in Example 6.12, so by

$$inc :: count := count + 1,$$

we now prove the correctness formula

$$\{\textbf{this} \neq other \wedge other \neq \textbf{null} \wedge \textbf{this}.count = z\} \; other.inc \; \{\textbf{this}.count = z\}$$

in the sense of total correctness. We already proved in Example 6.12

> $\{u \neq other \wedge u.count = z\}$
> **begin local this** $:= other;$ $count := count + 1$ **end**
> $\{u.count = z\},$

and the proof is equally valid in the sense of total correctness. So by the consequence rule we obtain

> $\{u \neq other \wedge other \neq \textbf{null} \wedge u.count = z\}$
> **begin local this** $:= other;$ $count := count + 1$ **end**
> $\{u.count = z\}.$

Because of the form of the precondition we can use the recursion VI rule to derive

$$\{u \neq other \wedge other \neq \textbf{null} \wedge u.count = z\} \; other.inc \; \{u.count = z\},$$

from which the desired correctness formula follows by the substitution rule A7.   □

6.5 Adding Parameters

We now extend the syntax of the object-oriented programs by allowing parametrized method calls. To this end, we introduce the following rule:

$$S ::= s.m(t_1, \ldots, t_n),$$

where, as before, s is the local object expression and m is a method, and $t_1, \ldots, t_n$, are the actual parameters of a basic type. A method is now defined by means of a definition

$$m(u_1, \ldots, u_n) :: S,$$

where the formal parameters $u_1, \ldots, u_n \in Var$ are of a basic type. We assume that $n \geq 0$, so that we generalize the case studied so far.

As before, a program consists of a main statement and a set D of method definitions, where we stipulate the same restrictions concerning the use of method calls and of the object variable **this** as in the case of parameterless methods.

Further, we assume the same restriction as in Chapter 5 in order to avoid name clashes between local variables and global variables.

Example 6.15. Consider an instance variable x and the method $setx$ defined by

$$setx(u) :: x := u.$$

Then the main statement

$$y.setx(t)$$

sets the value of the instance variable x of the object y to the value of the local expression t.   □

Example 6.16. Consider an instance object variable $next$ and the method definition

$$setnext(u) :: next := u.$$

Then the main statement

$$x.setnext(next); \ next := x$$

inserts in this list the object denoted by the object variable x between the current object denoted by **this** and the next one, denoted by $next$, see Figures 6.2 and 6.3.   □

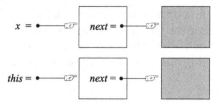

Fig. 6.2 A linked list before the object insertion.

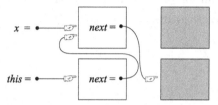

Fig. 6.3 A linked list after the object insertion.

Semantics

The semantics of a method call with parameters is described by the following counterparts of the transitions axioms (xii) and (xiii):

(xiv) $< s.m(\bar{t}), \sigma > \rightarrow < \textbf{begin local this}, \bar{u} := s, \bar{t};\ S\ \textbf{end}, \sigma >$
   where $\sigma(s) \neq \textbf{null}$ and $m(\bar{u}) :: S \in D$,

(xv) $< s.m(\bar{t}), \sigma > \rightarrow < E, \textbf{fail} >$ where $\sigma(s) = \textbf{null}$.

Example 6.17. Consider the definition of the method *setnext* of Example 6.16. Assuming that x is a normal variable, $\sigma(\textbf{this}) = o$ and $\sigma(x) = o'$, we have the following sequence of transitions:

$$< x.setnext(next), \sigma >$$
$$\rightarrow\ < \textbf{begin local this}, u := x, next;\ next := u\ \textbf{end}, \sigma >$$
$$\rightarrow\ < \textbf{this}, u := x, next;\ next := u;\ \textbf{this}, u := \sigma(\textbf{this}), \sigma(u), \sigma >$$
$$\rightarrow\ < next := u;\ \textbf{this}, u := \sigma(\textbf{this}), \sigma(u), \sigma' >$$
$$\rightarrow\ < \textbf{this}, u := \sigma(\textbf{this}), \sigma(u), \sigma'[next := \sigma(o)(next)] >$$
$$\rightarrow\ < E, \sigma[o' := \tau[next := \sigma(o)(next)]] >,$$

where σ' denotes the state

$$\sigma[\textbf{this}, u := o', \sigma(o)(next)]$$

and $\tau = \sigma(o')$. The first transition expands the method call into the corresponding block statement which is entered by the second transition. The third transition then initializes the local variables **this** and u which results in the state σ'. The assignment $next := u$ is executed next. Note that

$$\sigma'[next := \sigma'(u)]$$
$$= \quad \{\text{by the definition of } \sigma'\}$$
$$\sigma'[next := \sigma(o)(next)]$$
$$= \quad \{\text{by the definition of state update, } \sigma'(\textbf{this}) = o' \text{ and } \sigma'(o') = \tau \}$$
$$\sigma'[o' := \tau[next := \sigma(o)(next)]].$$

$\square$

Partial Correctness

The proof rules introduced in the previous section are extended to method calls with parameters, analogously to the way we extended in Chapter 5 the proof rules for recursive procedures to recursive procedures with parameters.

More specifically, the adjustment of the generic method calls is taken care of by the following proof rule that refers to the set D of the assumed method declarations:

RULE 18: INSTANTIATION III

$$\frac{\{p\}\; y.m(\bar{x})\; \{q\}}{\{p[y, \bar{x} := s, \bar{t}]\}\; s.m(\bar{t})\; \{q[y, \bar{x} := s, \bar{t}]\}}$$

where $y, \bar{x}$ is a sequence of simple variables in Var which do not appear in D and $var(s, \bar{t}) \cap change(D) = \emptyset$.

Next, the following proof rule is a modification of the recursion III rule for procedures with parameters to methods with parameters. The provability symbol $\vdash$ refers here to the proof system PW augmented with the assignment axiom 14, the block rule, the instantiation III rule and the auxiliary axioms and rules A2–A7.

RULE 19: RECURSION VII

$$\{p_1\}\; s_1.m_1(\bar{t}_1)\; \{q_1\}, \ldots, \{p_n\}\; s_n.m_n(\bar{t}_n)\; \{q_n\} \vdash \{p\}\; S\; \{q\},$$
$$\{p_1\}\; s_1.m_1(\bar{t}_1)\; \{q_1\}, \ldots, \{p_n\}\; s_n.m_n(\bar{t}_n)\; \{q_n\} \vdash$$
$$\underline{\{p_i\}\; \textbf{begin local this}, \bar{u}_i := s_i, \bar{t}_i;\; S_i\; \textbf{end}\; \{q_i\},\; i \in \{1, \ldots, n\}}$$
$$\{p\}\; S\; \{q\}$$

where $m_i(\bar{u}_i) :: S_i \in D$ for $i \in \{1, \ldots, n\}$.

To prove partial correctness of object-oriented programs with parameters we use the following proof system POP :

> PROOF SYSTEM POP :
> This system consists of the group of axioms
> and rules 1–6, 10, 14, 18, 19, and A2–A7.

Thus POP is obtained by extending the proof system PW by the block rule, the assignment to instance variables axiom, the instantiation III rule, the recursion VII rule, and the auxiliary axioms and rules A2–A7.

Example 6.18. Consider, as in Example 6.15, an instance variable x and the method $setx$ defined by $setx(u) :: x := u$. We prove the correctness formula

$$\{\textbf{true}\}\ y.setx(z)\ \{y.x = z\}$$

in the sense of partial correctness. By the recursion VII rule, it suffices to derive the correctness formula

$$\{\textbf{true}\}\ \textbf{begin local this}, u := y, z;\ x := u\ \textbf{end}\ \{y.x = z\}.$$

To prove the last correctness formula we first use the assignment axiom for instance variables to derive

$$\{(y.x = z)[x := u]\}\ x := u\ \{y.x = z\},$$

where by the definition of substitution

$$(y.x = z)[x := u] \equiv \textbf{if}\ y = \textbf{this then}\ u\ \textbf{else}\ y.x\ \textbf{fi} = z.$$

Finally, by the assignment axiom for normal variables we have

> $\{\textbf{if}\ y = y\ \textbf{then}\ z\ \textbf{else}\ y.x\ \textbf{fi} = z\}$
> $\textbf{this}, u := y, z$
> $\{\textbf{if}\ y = \textbf{this then}\ u\ \textbf{else}\ y.x\ \textbf{fi} = z\}.$

By the composition and the consequence rule we obtain

$$\{\textbf{true}\}\ \textbf{this}, u := y, z;\ x := u\ \{y.x = z\}.$$

An application of the block rule concludes the proof.

Note that even though the assignment to the variable **this** does not appear in the considered program, it is crucial in establishing the program correctness. □

Total Correctness

We conclude the discussion by introducing the following proof rule for total correctness of method calls with parameters. The provability symbol $\vdash$ refers here to the proof system TW augmented with the assignment axiom 14, the block rule, the instantiation III rule and the auxiliary rules A3–A7.

RULE 20: RECURSION VIII

$$\begin{array}{c} \{p_1\}\ s_1.m_1(\bar{e}_1)\ \{q_1\}, \ldots, \{p_n\}\ s_n.m_n(\bar{e}_n)\ \{q_n\} \vdash \{p\}\ S\ \{q\}, \\ \{p_1 \wedge t < z\}\ s_1.m_1(\bar{e}_1)\ \{q_1\}, \ldots, \{p_n \wedge t < z\}\ s_n.m_n(\bar{e}_n)\ \{q_n\} \vdash \\ \{p_i \wedge t = z\}\ \textbf{begin local this}, \bar{u}_i := s_i, \bar{e}_i;\ S_i\ \textbf{end}\ \{q_i\},\ i \in \{1,\ldots,n\} \\ p_i \rightarrow s_i \neq \textbf{null},\ i \in \{1,\ldots,n\} \\ \hline \{p\}\ S\ \{q\} \end{array}$$

where $m_i(\bar{u}_i) :: S_i \in D$, for $i \in \{1, \ldots, n\}$, and z is an integer variable that does not occur in p_i, t, q_i and S_i for $i \in \{1, \ldots, n\}$ and is treated in the proofs as a constant.

To prove *total* correctness of *o*bject-oriented programs with *p*arameters we use the following proof system TOP :

> PROOF SYSTEM TOP :
> This system consists of the group of axioms
> and rules 1–4, 6, 7, 10, 14, 18, 20, and A3–A7.

Thus TOP is obtained by extending the proof system TW by the block rule, the assignment to instance variables axiom, the instantiation III rule, the recursion VIII rule, and the auxiliary rules A3–A7.

Example 6.19. Given the method *setx* defined as in Example 6.15 we now prove the correctness formula

$$\{y \neq \textbf{null}\}\ y.setx(z)\ \{y.x = z\}$$

in the sense of total correctness.

We already proved in Example 6.18

$$\{\textbf{true}\}\ \textbf{begin local this}, u := y, z;\ x := u\ \textbf{end}\ \{y.x = z\}$$

and the proof is equally valid in the sense of total correctness. So by the consequence rule we obtain

$$\{y \neq \textbf{null}\}\ \textbf{begin local this}, u := y, z;\ x := u\ \textbf{end}\ \{y.x = z\}.$$

Because of the form of the precondition we can now derive the desired correctness formula using the recursion VIII rule. □

6.6 Transformation of Object-Oriented Programs

The proof rules for reasoning about the correctness of object-oriented programs (with parameters) are derived from the corresponding proof rules for recursive programs of Chapter 5. In this section we define the underlying transformation of object-oriented programs (with parameters) into recursive programs augmented by the failure statement from Section 3.7. This statement is needed to take care of the method calls on the void reference. We prove then that this transformation preserves both partial and total correctness and use this fact to prove soundness of the introduced proof systems.

First we transform instance variables into normal *array* variables. For example, an instance variable x of a basic type T is transformed into a normal array variable x of type

$$\textbf{object} \rightarrow T.$$

The normal array variable x stores for each object the value of its instance variable x. Similarly, an instance array variable a of type $T_1 \times \ldots \times T_n \rightarrow T$ is transformed into a normal array variable a of type

$$\textbf{object} \times T_1 \times \ldots \times T_n \rightarrow T.$$

Then for every state σ we denote by $\Theta(\sigma)$ the corresponding 'normal' state (as defined in Section 2.3) which represents the instance variables as (additional) normal variables. We have

- $\Theta(\sigma)(x) = \sigma(x)$, for every normal variable x,
- $\Theta(\sigma)(x)(o) = \sigma(o)(x)$, for every object $o \in \mathcal{D}_{\textbf{object}}$ and normal array variable x of type $\textbf{object} \rightarrow T$ being the translation of an instance variable x of a basic type T,
- $\Theta(\sigma)(a)(o, d_1, \ldots, d_n) = \sigma(o)(a)(d_1, \ldots, d_n)$, for every object $o \in \mathcal{D}_{\textbf{object}}$ and normal array variable a of type $\textbf{object} \times T_1 \times \ldots \times T_n \rightarrow T$ being the translation of an instance array variable a of type $T_1 \times \ldots \times T_n \rightarrow T$, and $d_i \in \mathcal{D}_{T_i}$, for $i \in \{1, \ldots, n\}$.

Next we define for every local expression s of the object-oriented programming language the normal expression $\Theta(s)$ by induction on the structure of s. We have the following basic cases.

- $\Theta(x) \equiv x$, for every normal variable x,
- $\Theta(x) \equiv x[\textbf{this}]$, for every instance variable x of a basic type,
- $\Theta(a[s_1, \ldots, s_n]) \equiv a[\textbf{this}, \Theta(s_1), \ldots, \Theta(s_n)]$, for every instance array variable a.

The following lemma clarifies the outcome of this transformation.

Lemma 6.3. (Translation) *For all proper states* σ

(i) for all local expressions s

$$\mathcal{S}[\![s]\!](\sigma) = \mathcal{S}[\![\Theta(s)]\!](\Theta(\sigma)),$$

where $\mathcal{S}[\![\Theta(s)]\!](\Theta(\sigma))$ *refers to the semantics of expressions defined in Section 2.3,*

(ii) for all (possibly subscripted) instance variables u and values d of the same type as u

$$\sigma[u := d] = \Theta(\sigma)[\Theta(u) := d].$$

Proof. The proof proceeds by a straightforward induction on the structure of s and case analysis of u, see Exercise 6.9. ☐

Next, we extend Θ to statements of the considered object-oriented language, by induction on the structure of the statements.

- $\Theta(u := s) \equiv \Theta(u) := \Theta(s)$,
- $\Theta(s.m(s_1, \ldots, s_n)) \equiv$ **if** $\Theta(s) \neq$ **null** $\rightarrow$ $m(\Theta(s), \Theta(s_1), \ldots, \Theta(s_n))$ **fi**,
- $\Theta(S_1;\ S_2) \equiv \Theta(S_1);\ \Theta(S_2)$,
- $\Theta($**if** B **then** S_1 **else** S_2 **fi**$) \equiv$ **if** $\Theta(B)$ **then** $\Theta(S_1)$ **else** $\Theta(S_2)$ **fi**,
- $\Theta($**while** B **do** S **od**$) \equiv$ **while** $\Theta(B)$ **do** $\Theta(S)$ **od**,
- $\Theta($**begin local** $\bar{u} := \bar{t}; S$ **end**$) \equiv$ **begin local** $\bar{u} := \Theta(\bar{t})$ **end**,
  where $\Theta(\bar{t})$ denotes the result of applying to the expressions of $\bar{t}$.

So the translation of a method call transforms the called object s into an additional actual parameter of a call of the procedure m. Additionally a check for a failure is made. Consequently, we transform every method definition

$$m(u_1, \ldots, u_n) :: S$$

into a procedure declaration

$$m(\textbf{this}, u_1, \ldots, u_n) :: \Theta(S),$$

which transforms the distinguished normal variable **this** into an additional formal parameter of the procedure m. This way the set D of method definitions is transformed into the set

$$\Theta(D) = \{m(\textbf{this}, u_1, \ldots, u_n) :: \Theta(S) \mid m(u_1, \ldots, u_n) :: S \in D\}$$

of the corresponding procedure declarations.

We establish the correspondence between an object-oriented program S and its transformation $\Theta(S)$ using an alternative semantics of the recursive programs augmented by the failure statement. This way we obtain a precise match between S and $\Theta(S)$. This alternative semantics is defined using a new transition relation $\Rightarrow$ for configurations involving recursive programs augmented by the failure statement, defined as follows:

1. $\dfrac{< S, \sigma > \; \rightarrow \; < S', \tau >}{< S, \sigma > \Rightarrow < S', \tau >}$ where S is not a failure statement,

2. $\dfrac{< S, \sigma > \Rightarrow < S', \tau >}{< \mathbf{if}\ b \rightarrow S\ \mathbf{fi}, \sigma > \Rightarrow < S', \tau >}$ where $\sigma \models b$,

3. $< \mathbf{if}\ b \rightarrow S\ \mathbf{fi}, \sigma > \Rightarrow < E, \mathbf{fail} >$ where $\sigma \models \neg b$.

So in the transition relation $\Rightarrow$ a successful transition of a failure statement consists of a transition of its main body, i.e., the successful evaluation of the Boolean guard itself does not give rise to a transition.

Example 6.20. Let $\sigma(x) = 2$ and $\sigma(z) = 4$. We have

$$< \mathbf{if}\ x \neq 0 \rightarrow y := z\ div\ x\ \mathbf{fi}, \sigma > \Rightarrow < E, \sigma[y := 2] >,$$

whereas
$$< \mathbf{if}\ x \neq 0 \rightarrow y := z\ div\ x\ \mathbf{fi}, \sigma >$$
$$\rightarrow \; < y := z\ div\ x, \sigma >$$
$$\rightarrow \; < E, \sigma[y := 2] > .$$

$\square$

We have the following correspondence between the two semantics.

Lemma 6.4. (Correspondence) *For all recursive programs S augmented by the failure statement and proper states σ*

$$< S, \sigma > \rightarrow^* < S', \tau > \text{ iff } < S, \sigma > \Rightarrow^* < S', \tau >,$$

where τ is either a proper state or **fail**.

Proof. The proof proceeds by induction on the number of transitions, see Exercise 6.10. $\square$

Further, we have the following correspondence between an object-oriented program S and its transformation $\Theta(S)$.

Lemma 6.5. (Transformation) *For all object-oriented programs S and proper states σ*

$$< S, \sigma > \rightarrow < S', \tau > \text{ iff } < \Theta(S), \sigma > \Rightarrow < \Theta(S'), \tau >,$$

where τ is either a proper state or **fail**.

214 6 *Object-Oriented Programs*

Proof. The proof proceeds by induction on the structure of S, see Exercise 6.11. □

The following theorem then states the correctness of the transformation Θ.

Theorem 6.1. (Correctness of Θ) *For all object-oriented programs S (with a set of method declarations D) and proper states σ*

(i) $\mathcal{M}[\![S]\!](\sigma) = \mathcal{M}[\![S]\!](\Theta(\sigma))$,
(ii) $\mathcal{M}_{tot}[\![S]\!](\sigma) = \mathcal{M}_{tot}[\![\Theta(S)]\!](\Theta(\sigma))$,

where the given set D of method declarations is transformed into $\Theta(D)$.

Proof. The proof combines the Correspondence Lemma 6.4 and the Transformation Lemma 6.5, see Exercise 6.12. □

Soundness

Given the above transformation, soundness of the proof systems for partial and total correctness of object-oriented programs can be reduced to soundness of the corresponding proof systems for recursive programs augmented by the failure statement. For this reduction we also have to transform expressions of the assertion language. For every global expression e we define $\Theta(e)$ by induction on the structure of e, assuming the above transformation of instance variables. We have the following main case of navigation expressions:

$$\Theta(e.x) = x[\Theta(e)].$$

The transformation $\Theta(e)$ is extended to a transformation $\Theta(p)$ of assertions by a straightforward induction on the structure of p. Correctness of this transformation of assertions is stated in the following lemma. For the assertions introduced in this chapter we use a more restrictive meaning, so only an implication holds here.

Lemma 6.6. (Assertion) *For all assertions p and proper states σ*

$$\text{if } \sigma \in [\![p]\!] \text{ then } \Theta(\sigma) \in [\![\Theta(p)]\!].$$

Proof. The proof proceeds by induction on the structure of p, see Exercise 6.13. □

Corollary 6.1. (Translation I) *For all correctness formulas $\{p\}\, S\, \{q\}$, where S is an object-oriented program,*

$$if \models \{\Theta(p)\} \; \Theta(S) \; \{\Theta(q)\} \; then \models \{p\} \; S \; \{q\},$$

and

$$if \models_{tot} \{\Theta(p)\} \; \Theta(S) \; \{\Theta(q)\} \; then \models_{tot} \{p\} \; S \; \{q\}.$$

Proof. It follows directly by the Assertion Lemma 6.6 and the Correctness Theorem 6.1. □

Finally, we show that a correctness proof of an object-oriented program can be translated to a correctness proof of the corresponding recursive program. We need the following lemmas which state that (partial and total) correctness proofs of a method call from a given set of assumptions can be translated to correctness proofs of the corresponding procedure call from the corresponding set of assumptions. For a given set of assumptions A about method calls, we define the set of assumptions $\Theta(A)$ about the corresponding procedure calls by

$$\{\Theta(p)\} \; m(\Theta(s), \Theta(\bar{t})) \; \{\Theta(q)\} \in \Theta(A) \; \text{iff} \; \{p\} \; s.m(\bar{t}) \; \{q\} \in A.$$

Lemma 6.7. (Translation of Partial Correctness Proofs of Method Calls) *Let A be a given set of assumptions about method calls. If*

$$A \vdash \{p\} \; s.m(\bar{t}) \; \{q\},$$

then

$$\Theta(A) \vdash \{\Theta(p)\} \; m(\Theta(s), \Theta(\bar{t})) \; \{\Theta(q)\},$$

where the proofs consist of the applications of the consequence rule, the instantiation III rule, and the auxiliary axioms and rules A2–A7.

Proof. The proof proceeds by induction on the length of the derivation, see Exercise 6.14. □

Lemma 6.8. (Translation of Total Correctness Proofs of Method Calls) *Let A be a given set of assumptions about method calls such that for $\{p'\} \; S \; \{q'\} \in A$ we have $p' \rightarrow s \neq \textbf{null}$. If*

$$A \vdash \{p\} \; s.m(\bar{t}) \; \{q\}$$

then

$$\Theta(A) \vdash \{\Theta(p)\} \; m(\Theta(s), \Theta(\bar{t})) \; \{\Theta(q)\},$$

and

$$\Theta(p) \rightarrow \Theta(s) \neq \textbf{null},$$

where the proofs consist of the applications of the consequence rule, the instantiation III rule, and the auxiliary rules A3–A7.

Proof. The proof proceeds by induction on the length of the derivation, see Exercise 6.15. □

Next, we generalize the above lemmas about method calls to statements.

Lemma 6.9. (Translation Correctness Proofs Statements) *Let A a be set of assumptions about method calls and* $\{p\}\ S\ \{q\}$ *a correctness formula of an object-oriented statement S such that*

$$A \vdash \{p\}\ S\ \{q\},$$

where $\vdash$ *either refers to the proof system PW or the proof system TW, both extended with the block rule, the assignment axiom for instance variables, and the instantiation rule III. In case of a total correctness proof we additionally assume that* $p' \rightarrow s \neq \textbf{null}$, *for* $\{p'\}\ S\ \{q'\} \in A$. *Then*

$$\Theta(A) \vdash \{\Theta(p)\}\ \Theta(S)\ \{\Theta(q)\}.$$

Proof. The proof proceeds by induction on the structure of S. We treat the main case of a method call and for the remaining cases we refer to Exercise 6.16. Let $S \equiv s.m(\bar{t})$. We distinguish the following cases:

Partial correctness. By the Translation Lemma 6.7 we obtain

$$\Theta(A) \vdash \{\Theta(p)\}\ m(\Theta(s), \Theta(\bar{t}))\ \{\Theta(q)\},$$

from which by the consequence rule we derive

$$\Theta(A) \vdash \{\Theta(p) \wedge \Theta(s) \neq \textbf{null}\}\ m(\Theta(s), \Theta(\bar{t}))\ \{\Theta(q)\}.$$

We conclude by the failure rule from Section 3.7

$$\Theta(A) \vdash \{\Theta(p)\}\ \textbf{if}\ \Theta(s) \neq \textbf{null} \rightarrow m(\Theta(s), \Theta(\bar{t}))\ \textbf{fi}\ \{\Theta(q)\}.$$

Total correctness. By the Translation Lemma 6.8 we obtain

$$\Theta(A) \vdash \{\Theta(p)\}\ m(\Theta(s), \Theta(\bar{t}))\ \{\Theta(q)\}$$

and

$$\Theta(p) \rightarrow \Theta(s) \neq \textbf{null}.$$

By the failure rule II from Section 3.7 we conclude

$$\Theta(A) \vdash \{\Theta(p)\}\ \textbf{if}\ \Theta(s) \neq \textbf{null} \rightarrow m(\Theta(s), \Theta(\bar{t}))\ \textbf{fi}\ \{\Theta(q)\}.$$

$\square$

Finally, we have arrived at the following conclusion.

Corollary 6.2. (Translation II) *For all correctness formulas* $\{p\}\ S\ \{q\}$, *where S is an object-oriented program,*

(i) if $\{p\}\ S\ \{q\}$ is derivable in the proof system POP, then
$\{\Theta(p)\}\ \Theta(S)\ \{\Theta(q)\}$ is derivable from PRP,

(ii) if $\{p\}\ S\ \{q\}$ is derivable in the proof system TOP,
then $\{\Theta(p)\}\ \Theta(S)\ \{\Theta(q)\}$ is derivable from TRP.

Proof. The proof proceeds by an induction on the length of the derivation. The case of an application of the recursion rules VII and VIII is dealt with by the Translation Lemma 6.9, see Exercise 6.17. □

We can now establish soundness of the considered proof systems.

Theorem 6.2. (Soundness of POP and TOP)

(i) *The proof system POP is sound for partial correctness of object-oriented programs with parameters.*

(ii) *The proof system TOP is sound for total correctness of object-oriented programs with parameters.*

Proof. By the Translation Corollaries 6.1 and 6.2, Soundness Corollary 5.1 and Soundness Theorem 5.5. □

6.7 Object Creation

In this section we introduce and discuss the dynamic creation of objects. We extend the set of object-oriented programs with the following statement:

$$S :: u := \textbf{new},$$

where u is an object variable and **new** is a keyword that may not be used as part of local expressions in the programming language. Informally, the execution of this statement consists of creating a *new* object and assigning its identity to the variable u.

Example 6.21. Given the method definition

$$setnext(u) :: next := u,$$

which sets the instance object variable *next*, the following method inserts a *new* element in a list of objects linked by their instance variable *next*:

```
insert :: begin local
         z := next;
         next := new;
         next.setnext(z)
         end.
```

More specifically, a call **this**.*insert* inserts a new element between the object **this** and the next object in the list denoted by the instance variable *next* (of the current object **this**). The local variable z is used to store the old value of the instance variable *next*. After the assignment of a new object to this variable, the method call *next.setnext*(z) sets the instance variable *next* of the newly created object to the value of z.   □

Throughout this section we restrict ourselves to *pure* object-oriented programs in which a local object expression s can only be compared for equality (like in $s = t$) or appear as an argument of a conditional construct (like in **if** B **then** s **else** t **fi**). By definition, in local expressions we do not allow

- arrays with arguments of type **object**,
- any constant of type **object** different from **null**,
- any constant *op* of a higher type different from equality which involves **object** as an argument or value type.

We call local expressions obeying these restrictions *pure*.

Example 6.22. We disallow local expressions $a[s_1, \ldots, s_i, \ldots, s_n]$, where s_i is an object expression. We *do* allow for arrays with value type **object**, e.g., arrays of type **integer** $\rightarrow$ **object**. As another example, we disallow in local expressions constants like the identity function *id* on objects.   □

Semantics

In order to model the dynamic creation of objects we introduce an instance Boolean variable *created* which indicates for each object whether it has been created. We do not allow this instance variable to occur in programs. It is only used to define the semantics of programs. In order to allow for unbounded object creation we require that $\mathcal{D}_{\textbf{object}}$ is an infinite set, whereas in every state σ the set of created objects, i.e., those objects $o \in \mathcal{D}_{\textbf{object}}$ for which $\sigma(o)(\textit{created}) = \textbf{true}$, is finite.

We extend the *state update* by $\sigma[u := \textbf{new}]$ which describes an assignment involving as a *side-effect* the creation of a new object and its default initialization. To describe this default initialization of instance variables of newly created objects, we introduce an element $\textit{init}_T \in \mathcal{D}_T$ for every basic type T. We define $\textit{init}_{\textbf{object}} = \textbf{null}$ and $\textit{init}_{\textbf{Boolean}} = \textbf{true}$. Further, let *init* denote the local (object) state such that

- if $v \in \textit{IVar}$ is of a basic type T then

$$init(v) = init_T,$$

- if the value type of an array variable $a \in IVar$ is T and $d_i \in \mathcal{D}_{T_i}$ for $i \in \{1, \ldots, n\}$ then

$$init(a)(d_1, \ldots, d_n) = init_T.$$

To generate new objects we introduce a function ν such that for every (proper) state σ the object $\nu(\sigma)$ does not exist in σ. Formally, we have for every (proper) state σ

$$\nu(\sigma) \in \mathcal{D}_{\mathbf{object}} \text{ and } \sigma(\nu(\sigma))(created) = \mathbf{false}.$$

The state update $\sigma[u := \mathbf{new}]$ is then defined by

$$\sigma[o := init][u := o],$$

where $o = \nu(\sigma)$.

The *operational semantics* of an object creation statement is described by the following rule:

(xvi) $< u := \mathbf{new}, \sigma > \rightarrow < E, \sigma[u := \mathbf{new}] >,$

where u is a (possibly subscripted) object variable.

Example 6.23. For a (proper) state σ let O defined by

$$O = \{o \in \mathcal{D}_{\mathbf{object}} \mid \sigma(o)(created) = \mathbf{true}\}$$

denote the (finite) set of created objects in σ. Consider $o = \nu(\sigma)$. Thus $\sigma(o)(created) = \mathbf{false}$ and $o \notin O$. Given the instance object variable $next$ we have the following transition:

$$< next := \mathbf{new}, \sigma > \ \rightarrow \ < E, \tau > \text{ where } \tau = \sigma[o := init][next := o] > .$$

Then $\tau(next) = \tau(\tau(\mathbf{this}))(next) = o$, $\tau(o)(created) = \mathbf{true}$ and $\tau(o)(next) = \mathbf{null}$. The set of created objects in τ is given by $O \cup \{o\}$. □

Assertions

In the programming language we can only refer to objects that exist; objects that have not been created cannot be referred to and thus do not play a role. We want to reason about programs at the same level of abstraction. Therefore, we do not allow the instance Boolean variable *created* to occur in assertions. Further, we restrict the semantics of assertions (as defined in Section 6.3) to states which are *consistent*. By definition, these are states in which **this** and **null** refer to created objects and all (possibly subscripted) normal object variables and all (possibly subscripted) instance object variables of created objects also refer to created objects.

Example 6.24. Let σ be a consistent (proper) state. We have that $\sigma(\textbf{null})(created) = \textbf{true}$ and $\sigma(\sigma(\textbf{this}))(created) = \textbf{true}$. For every normal object variable x with $\sigma(x) = o$ we have $\sigma(o)(created) = \textbf{true}$. Further, for every instance object variable y we have that $\sigma(\sigma(y))(created) = \textbf{true}$. Note that $\sigma(y) = \sigma(\sigma(\textbf{this}))(y)$. In general, for every global object expression s we have $\sigma(\sigma(s))(created) = \textbf{true}$. That is, in σ we can only refer to created objects. □

In order to reason about object creation we wish to define a *substitution operation* $[x := \textbf{new}]$, where $x \in Var$ is a simple object variable, such that

$$\sigma \models p[x := \textbf{new}] \text{ iff } \sigma[x := \textbf{new}] \models p$$

holds for all assertions p and all states σ. However, we cannot simply replace x in p by the keyword **new** because it is *not* an expression of the assertion language. Also, the newly created object does not exist in σ and thus cannot be referred to in σ, the state prior to its creation. To obtain a simple definition of $p[x := \textbf{new}]$ by induction on p, we restrict ourselves here to assertions p in which object expressions can only be compared for equality or dereferenced, and object expressions do not appear as an argument of any other construct (including the conditional construct).

Formally, a global expression in which object expressions s can only be compared for equality (like in $s = t$) or dereferenced (like in $s.x$) is called *pure*. By definition, in pure global expressions we disallow

- arrays with arguments of type **object**,
- any constant of type **object** different from **null**,
- any constant op of a higher type different from equality which involves **object** as an argument or value type,
- conditional object expressions.

Note that in contrast to pure local expressions, in pure global expressions we also disallow object expressions as arguments of a conditional construct, like in **if** B **then** x **else** y **fi** where x and y are object variables. On the other hand, in pure global expressions we can dereference object expressions, like in $s.x$ where s is an object expression.

An *assertion* is called *pure* if it is built up from pure global expressions by Boolean connectives and quantification, but not over object variables or array variables with value type **object**. Such quantification requires a more sophisticated analysis as the following example shows.

Example 6.25. Consider the assertion

$$p \equiv \forall x : \exists n : a[n] = x,$$

where a is a normal array variable of type **integer** $\rightarrow$ **object**, $n \in Var$ is an integer variable, and $x \in Var$ is a simple object variable. Note that p is not pure. Since we restrict the semantics of assertions to consistent states, the universal quantifier $\forall x$ and the elements of the array a range over created objects. Thus p states that the array a stores all created objects (and only those). As a consequence p is affected by an object creation statement $u :=$ **new**. More specifically, we do *not* have

$$\{p\} \ u := \textbf{new} \ \{p\},$$

so the invariance axiom does not hold any more. In fact,

$$\{p\} \ u := \textbf{new} \ \{\forall n : a[n] \neq u\}$$

holds.   □

First, we define the substitution operation for expressions. The formal definition of $s[x := \textbf{new}]$, where $s \not\equiv x$ is a pure global expression and $x \in Var$ is a simple object variable, proceeds by induction on the structure of s. We have the following main cases:

- if $s \equiv x.u$ and the (possibly subscripted) instance variable u is of type T then
$$x.u[x := \textbf{new}] \equiv init_T,$$

- if $s \equiv s_1.u$ for $s_1 \not\equiv x$ then
$$s[x := \textbf{new}] \equiv s_1[x := \textbf{new}].u[x := \textbf{new}],$$

- if $s \equiv (s_1 = s_2)$ for $s_1 \not\equiv x$ and $s_2 \not\equiv x$ then
$$s[x := \textbf{new}] \equiv (s_1[x := \textbf{new}] = s_2[x := \textbf{new}]),$$

- if $s \equiv (x = t)$ (or $s \equiv (t = x)$) for $t \not\equiv x$ then
$$s[x := \textbf{new}] \equiv \textbf{false},$$

- if $s \equiv (x = x)$ then
$$s[x := \textbf{new}] \equiv \textbf{true}.$$

The other cases are standard.

Example 6.26. Let $s \equiv$ **if** B **then** s_1 **else** s_2 **fi** be a pure global expression and $x \in Var$ be a simple object variable. Then

$$s[x := \textbf{new}] \equiv \textbf{if } B[x := \textbf{new}] \textbf{ then } s_1[x := \textbf{new}] \textbf{ else } s_2[x := \textbf{new}] \textbf{ fi}.$$

Note that this is well-defined: since s cannot be an object expression we have that $s_1 \not\equiv x$ and $s_2 \not\equiv x$. Similarly, if $s \equiv a[s_1, \ldots, s_n]$ is a pure global expression then

$$s[x := \textbf{new}] \equiv a[s_1[x := \textbf{new}], \ldots, s_n[x := \textbf{new}]].$$

Note that $s_i \not\equiv x$ because s_i cannot be an object expression, for $i \in \{1, \ldots, n\}$.

Next we calculate

$$(x = \textbf{this})[x := \textbf{new}] \equiv \textbf{false},$$

$$(a[s] = x)[x := \textbf{new}] \equiv \textbf{false},$$

and

$$(x.y = \textbf{this})[x := \textbf{new}]$$
$$\equiv (x.y)[x := \textbf{new}] = \textbf{this}[x := \textbf{new}]$$
$$\equiv init_T = \textbf{this},$$

where the instance variable y is of type T. $\square$

To prove correctness of the substitution operation $[x := \textbf{new}]$ for object creation we need the following lemma which states that no pure global expression other than x can refer to the newly created object.

Lemma 6.10. *Let $s \not\equiv x$ be a pure global object expression and $x \in Var$ be a simple object variable. Further, let σ be a consistent proper state. Then*

$$\sigma[x := \textbf{new}](s) \neq \sigma[x := \textbf{new}](x).$$

Proof. The proof proceeds by induction on the structure of s (see Exercise 6.18). $\square$

The following example shows that in the above lemma the restriction to pure global expressions and to consistent (proper) states is necessary.

Example 6.27. Let x be a normal object variable. Then we have for global expressions s of the form

- $s \equiv id(x)$, where the constant id is interpreted as the identity function on objects, and
- $s \equiv \textbf{if true then } x \textbf{ else } y \textbf{ fi}$, where y is also a normal object variable,

that $\sigma[x := \textbf{new}](s) = \sigma[x := \textbf{new}](x)$.

Next, consider a normal object variable $y \not\equiv x$ and a state σ such that $\sigma(y) = \nu(\sigma)$. Then $\sigma(\sigma(y))(created) = \textbf{false}$ by the definition of the function ν. So σ is not a consistent state. We calculate that $\sigma[x := \textbf{new}](y) = \sigma(y) = \sigma[x := \textbf{new}](x)$. $\square$

We extend the substitution operation to pure assertions along the lines of Section 2.7. We have the following substitution lemma.

Lemma 6.11. (Substitution for Object Creation) *For all pure global expressions s, all pure assertions p, all simple object variables x and all consistent proper states σ,*

(i) $\sigma(s[x := \mathbf{new}]) = \sigma[x := \mathbf{new}](s)$,
(ii) $\sigma \models p[x := \mathbf{new}]$ iff $\sigma[x := \mathbf{new}] \models p$.

Proof. The proof proceeds by induction on the complexity of s and p, using Lemma 6.10 for the base case of Boolean expressions (see Exercise 6.19). □

The following lemma shows that the restriction concerning conditional expressions in pure assertions does not affect the expressiveness of the assertion language because conditional expressions can always be removed. The restriction only simplified the definition of substitution operator $[x := \mathbf{new}]$.

Lemma 6.12. (Conditional Expressions) *For every assertion p there exists a logically equivalent assertion which does not contain conditional expressions.*

Proof. See Exercise 6.20.   □

The following example gives an idea of the proof.

Example 6.28. A Boolean conditional expression **if** B **then** s **else** t **fi** can be eliminated using the following logical equivalence:

$$\mathbf{if}\ B\ \mathbf{then}\ s\ \mathbf{else}\ t\ \mathbf{fi} \leftrightarrow (B \wedge s) \vee (\neg B \wedge t).$$

A conditional expression **if** B **then** s **else** t **fi** in the context of an equality or a dereferencing operator can be moved outside as follows:

- (**if** B **then** s **else** t **fi** $= t'$) $=$ **if** B **then** $s = t'$ **else** $t = t'$ **fi**,
- **if** B **then** s **else** t **fi**.$y =$ **if** B **then** $s.y$ **else** $t.y$ **fi**.

In general, we have the equality

$$op(t_1, \ldots, \mathbf{if}\ B\ \mathbf{then}\ s\ \mathbf{else}\ t\ \mathbf{fi}, \ldots, t_n)$$
$$= \mathbf{if}\ B\ \mathbf{then}\ op(t_1, \ldots, s, \ldots, t_n)\ \mathbf{else}\ op(t_1, \ldots, t, \ldots, t_n)\ \mathbf{fi}$$

for every constant op of a higher type.   □

Verification

The correctness notions for object-oriented programs with object creation are defined in the familiar way using the semantics $\mathcal{M}$ and $\mathcal{M}_{tot}$ (note that the partial correctness and the total correctness semantics of an object creation statement coincide). To ensure that when studying program correctness we limit ourselves to meaningful computations of object-oriented programs, we provide the following new definition of the meaning of an assertion:

$$[\![p]\!] = \{\, \sigma \mid \sigma \text{ is a consistent proper state such that}$$
$$\sigma(\textbf{this}) \neq \textbf{null} \text{ and } \sigma \models p \,\},$$

and say that an assertion p is *is true*, or *holds*, if

$$[\![p]\!] = \{\sigma \mid \sigma \text{ is a consistent proper state such that } \sigma(\textbf{this}) \neq \textbf{null}\}.$$

We have the following axiom and rule for object creation.

AXIOM 21: OBJECT CREATION

$$\{p[x := \textbf{new}]\}\ x := \textbf{new}\ \{p\},$$

where $x \in Var$ is a simple object variable and p is a pure assertion.

RULE 22: OBJECT CREATION

$$\frac{p' \rightarrow p[u := x]}{\{p'[x := \textbf{new}]\}\ u := \textbf{new}\ \{p\}}$$

where u is a subscripted normal object variable or a (possibly subscripted) instance object variable, $x \in Var$ is a fresh simple object variable which does not occur in p, and p' is a pure assertion.

The substitution $[u := x]$ replaces every possible alias of u by x. Note that this rule models the object creation $u := \textbf{new}$ by the statement

$$x := \textbf{new}; u := x,$$

and as such allows for the application of the substitution $[x := \textbf{new}]$ defined above.

Example 6.29. Consider the object creation statement

$$next := \textbf{new}$$

for the object instance variable $next$ and the postcondition

$$p \ \equiv\ y.next = next.$$

We wish to prove

$$\{y = \textbf{this}\}\ next := \textbf{new}\ \{p\}.$$

First, we calculate for a fresh variable $x \in Var$:

$$p[next := x] \equiv \text{if } y = \text{this then } x \text{ else } y.next \text{ fi} = x.$$

Consider now

$$p' \equiv \text{if } y = \text{this then } x = x \text{ else } y.next = x \text{ fi}.$$

Observe that $p' \rightarrow p[next := x]$. Next, we calculate

$p'[x := \text{new}]$
$\equiv \text{if } (y = \text{this})[x := \text{new}]$
   $\text{then}(x = x)[x := \text{new}] \text{ else } (y.next = x)[x := \text{new}] \text{ fi}$
$\equiv \text{if } y = \text{this then true else false fi},$

which is logically equivalent to $y = \text{this}$. By the object creation rule and the consequence rule, we thus derive

$$\{y = \text{this}\} \ next := \text{new} \ \{p\},$$

as desired. □

To prove partial correctness of object-oriented programs with object creation we use the following proof system POC :

> PROOF SYSTEM POC :
>   This system consists of the group of axioms
>   and rules 1–6, 10, 14, 18, 19, 21, 22 and A2–A7.

Thus POC is obtained by extending the proof system POP by the axiom and rule for object creation.

To prove total correctness of object-oriented programs with object creation we use the following proof system TOC:

> PROOF SYSTEM TOC :
>   This system consists of the group of axioms
>   and rules 1–4, 6, 7, 10, 14, 18, 20–22 and A3–A7.

Thus TOC is obtained by extending the proof system TOP by the axiom and rule for object creation.

Soundness

We have the following soundness theorem for object creation.

Theorem 6.3. (Soundness of POC and TOC)

(i) *The proof system POC is sound for partial correctness of object-oriented programs with object creation.*

(ii) *The proof system TOC is sound for total correctness of object-oriented programs with object creation.*

Proof. Axiom 21 is true and rule 22 is sound, see Exercise 6.21.   □

6.8 Case Study: Zero Search in Linked List

We now return to the method $find$ defined in Example 6.5:

$$find :: \textbf{if } val = 0$$
$$\textbf{then } return := \textbf{this}$$
$$\textbf{else if } next \neq \textbf{null}$$
$$\textbf{then } next.find$$
$$\textbf{else } return := \textbf{null}$$
$$\textbf{fi}$$
$$\textbf{fi}$$

where val is an instance integer variable, $next$ is an instance object variable, and $return$ is a normal object variable used to store the result of the method.

In order to reason about this method we introduce a normal array variable a of type **integer** $\rightarrow$ **object** such that the section $a[k : n]$ stores a linked list of objects, as expressed by

$$\forall i \in [k : n - 1] : a[i].next = a[i + 1].$$

Partial Correctness

We first prove that upon termination the call **this**.$find$ returns in the variable $return$ the *first* object which can be reached from **this** that stores zero, if there exists such an object and otherwise $return = $ **null**. To this end, we introduce the assertion p defined by

$$p \equiv y = a[k] \land a[n] = return \, \land$$
$$\forall i \in [k : n - 1] : (a[i] \neq \textbf{null} \land a[i].val \neq 0 \land a[i].next = a[i + 1]),$$

where y is a normal object variable and k and n are normal integer variables. The variable y is used as a generic representation of the caller of the method $find$. The assertion p states that the section $a[k : n]$ stores a linked list of objects which starts with the object y, ends with $return$, and all its objects, except possibly the last one, are different from **null** and do not store zero.

We prove

$$\{\textbf{true}\} \ \textbf{this}.find \ \{q[y := \textbf{this}]\},$$

where q is defined by

$$q \equiv (return = \textbf{null} \lor return.val = 0) \land \exists \ a : \exists \ k : \exists \ n \geq k : p.$$

The postcondition q thus states that the returned object is **null** or stores zero and that for some array section $a[k : n]$ the above assertion p holds.

We establish a more general correctness formula, namely

$$\{\textbf{true}\} \ y.find \ \{q\}.$$

from which the desired formula follows by the instantiation II rule.

By the recursion V rule it suffices to prove

$$\{\textbf{true}\} \ y.find \ \{q\} \vdash \{\textbf{true}\} \ \textbf{begin local this} := y; \ S \ \textbf{end} \ \{q\},$$

where S denotes the body of the method $find$ and $\vdash$ refers to the proof system POP with the recursion VII rule omitted.

We present the proof in the form of a proof outline that we give in Figure 6.4.

To justify this proof outline it suffices to establish the following three claims.

Claim 1. $\{\textbf{this} = y \land val = 0\} \ return := \textbf{this} \ \{q\}$.

Proof. We show

$$(\textbf{this} = y \land val = 0) \rightarrow q[return := \textbf{this}],$$

from which the claim follows by the assignment axiom for normal variables and the consequence rule.

First, since val is an instance variable, we have

$$val = 0 \rightarrow \textbf{this}.val = 0,$$

which takes care of the first conjunct of $q[return := \textbf{this}]$.

Next, to satisfy the second conjunct of $q[return := \textbf{this}]$ under the assumption $\textbf{this} = y$, it suffices to take array a such that $a[k] = y$ and $n = k$. Indeed, we then have both $y = a[k]$ and $a[n] = \textbf{this}$ and the third conjunct of $p[return := \textbf{this}]$ vacuously holds since we then have $k > n - 1$. □

Claim 2.
$\{\textbf{true}\} \ y.find \ \{q\} \vdash \{\textbf{this} = y \land val \neq 0 \land next \neq \textbf{null}\} \ next.find \ \{q\}$.

{**true**}
begin local
{**true**}
this := y;
{**this** = y}
if $val = 0$
then
       {**this** = $y \wedge val = 0$}
       $return :=$ **this**
       {q}
else
       {**this** = $y \wedge val \neq 0$}
       if $next \neq$ **null**
       then
              {**this** = $y \wedge val \neq 0 \wedge next \neq$ **null**}
              $next.find$
              {q}
       else
               {**this** = $y \wedge val \neq 0 \wedge next =$ **null**}
               $return :=$ **null**
               {q}
       fi
       {q}
fi
{q}
end
{q}

Fig. 6.4 Proof outline showing partial correctness of the *find* method.

Proof. We first apply the instantiation II rule to the assumption and obtain

$$\{\textbf{true}\}\ next.find\ \{q[y := next]\}.$$

Next, applying the invariance rule we obtain

{**this** = $y \wedge val \neq 0 \wedge next \neq$ **null**}
$next.find$
{$q[y := next] \wedge$ **this** = $y \wedge val \neq 0 \wedge next \neq$ **null**}.

Now, observe that

$$(q[y := next] \wedge \textbf{this} = y \wedge val \neq 0 \wedge next \neq \textbf{null}) \rightarrow q.$$

Indeed, the first conjunct of $q[y := next]$ and q are identical. Further, assuming $q[y := next] \wedge \mathbf{this} = y \wedge val \neq 0 \wedge next \neq \mathbf{null}$ we first take the array section $a[k : n]$ which ensures the truth of the second conjunct of $q[y := next]$. Then the array section $a[k-1 : n]$ with $a[k-1] = y$ ensures the truth of the second conjunct of $q[y := next]$. Indeed, we then have $a[k-1] \neq \mathbf{null} \wedge a[k-1].val \neq 0 \wedge a[k-1].next = a[k]$, as by the definition of the meaning of an assertion both $\mathbf{this} \neq \mathbf{null}$ and $val = \mathbf{this}.val \wedge next = \mathbf{this}.next$.

We now obtain the desired conclusion by an application of the consequence rule. □

Claim 3. $\{\mathbf{this} = y \wedge val \neq 0 \wedge next = \mathbf{null}\}$ $return := \mathbf{null}$ $\{q\}$.

Proof. We show

$$(\mathbf{this} = y \wedge val \neq 0 \wedge next = \mathbf{null}) \rightarrow q[return := \mathbf{null}],$$

from which the claim follows by the assignment axiom and the consequence rule.

The first conjunct of $q[return := \mathbf{null}]$ holds since it contains $\mathbf{null} = \mathbf{null}$ as a disjunct. Next, to satisfy the second conjunct of $q[return := \mathbf{null}]$ under the assumption $\mathbf{this} = y \wedge val \neq 0 \wedge next = \mathbf{null}$, it suffices to take array a such that $a[k] = y$ and $n = k + 1$. Indeed, we then have both $y = a[k]$ and $a[n] = \mathbf{null}$. Moreover, the third conjunct of $p[return := \mathbf{this}]$ holds since we then have $a[k] \neq \mathbf{null} \wedge a[k].val \neq 0 \wedge a[k].next = a[k + 1]$, as by the definition of the meaning of an assertion $\mathbf{this} \neq \mathbf{null}$. □

Total Correctness

In order for $\mathbf{this}.find$ to terminate we require that the chain of objects starting from $\mathbf{this}$ and linked by $next$ ends with $\mathbf{null}$ or contains an object that stores zero.

To express this we first introduce the following assertion p:

$$p \equiv k \leq n \wedge (a[n] = \mathbf{null} \vee a[n].val = 0) \wedge$$
$$\forall i \in [k : n - 1] : (a[i] \neq \mathbf{null} \wedge a[i].next = a[i + 1]),$$

which states that the section $a[k : n]$ stores a linked list of objects that ends with $\mathbf{null}$ or with an object that stores zero. Let r be defined by

$$r \equiv y = a[k] \wedge y \neq \mathbf{null} \wedge p.$$

We now prove

$$\{\exists a : \exists k : \exists n \geq k : r[y := \mathbf{this}]\} \ \mathbf{this}.find \ \{\mathbf{true}\}$$

in the sense of total correctness.

As the bound function we choose

$$t \equiv n - k.$$

As in the proof of partial correctness we use the normal object variable y as a generic representation of the caller of the method $find$.

We now show

$$\{r \wedge t < z\} \ y.find \ \{\textbf{true}\} \vdash$$
$$\{r \wedge t = z\} \ \textbf{begin local this} := y; \ S \ \textbf{end} \ \{\textbf{true}\} \tag{6.4}$$

where, as above, S denotes the body of the method $find$ and where $\vdash$ refers to the proof system TOP with the recursion VIII rule omitted.

To this end, we again present the proof in the form of a proof outline that we give in Figure 6.5.

We only need to justify the correctness formula involving the method call $next.find$. To this end, we first apply the instantiation II rule to the assumption and replace y by $next$:

$$\{r[y := next] \wedge n - k < z\} \ next.find \ \{\textbf{true}\}.$$

Next, we apply the substitution rule and replace k by $k + 1$:

$$\{r[k, y := k + 1, next] \wedge n - (k + 1) < z\} \ next.find \ \{\textbf{true}\}.$$

Now note that

$$(r \wedge \textbf{this} = y \wedge t = z \wedge val \neq 0 \wedge next \neq \textbf{null})$$
$$\rightarrow (r[k, y := k + 1, next] \wedge n - (k + 1) < z).$$

Indeed, we have by the definition of r

$$r \wedge \textbf{this} = y \wedge val \neq 0$$
$$\rightarrow (a[n] = \textbf{null} \vee a[n].val = 0) \wedge \textbf{this} = a[k] \wedge val \neq 0 \wedge k \leq n$$
$$\rightarrow (a[n] = \textbf{null} \vee a[n].val = 0) \wedge a[k] \neq \textbf{null} \wedge a[k].val \neq 0 \wedge k \leq n$$
$$\rightarrow k < n,$$

where the second implication holds since

$$\textbf{this} \neq \textbf{null} \wedge val = \textbf{this}.val.$$

Hence

$\{r \wedge t = z\}$
begin local
$\{r \wedge t = z\}$
this $:= y;$
$\{r \wedge \mathbf{this} = y \wedge t = z\}$
if $val = 0$
then

  $\{\mathbf{true}\}$
  $return := \mathbf{this}$
  $\{\mathbf{true}\}$

else

  $\{r \wedge \mathbf{this} = y \wedge t = z \wedge val \neq 0\}$
  if $next \neq \mathbf{null}$
  then

    $\{r \wedge \mathbf{this} = y \wedge t = z \wedge val \neq 0 \wedge next \neq \mathbf{null}\}$
    $\{r[k, y := k + 1, next] \wedge n - (k + 1) < z\}$
    $next.find$
    $\{\mathbf{true}\}$

  else

    $\{\mathbf{true}\}$
    $return := \mathbf{null}$
    $\{\mathbf{true}\}$

  fi
  $\{\mathbf{true}\}$

fi
$\{\mathbf{true}\}$
end
$\{\mathbf{true}\}$

Fig. 6.5 Proof outline showing termination of the $find$ method.

$(r \wedge \mathbf{this} = y \wedge t = z \wedge val \neq 0 \wedge next \neq \mathbf{null})$
$\rightarrow (\mathbf{this} = a[k] \wedge k < n \wedge next \neq \mathbf{null} \wedge p)$
$\rightarrow (\mathbf{this} = a[k] \wedge a[k].next = a[k + 1] \wedge next \neq \mathbf{null} \wedge p[k := k + 1])$
$\rightarrow (next = a[k + 1] \wedge next \neq \mathbf{null} \wedge p[k := k + 1])$
$\rightarrow r[k, y := k + 1, next],$

where we make use of the fact that $next = \mathbf{this}.next$.
 Moreover

$$t = z \rightarrow n - (k + 1) < z.$$

This completes the justification of the proof outline. By the recursion VI rule we now derive from (6.4) and the fact that $r \rightarrow y \neq \mathbf{null}$ the correctness formula

$$\{r\}\ y.find\ \{\textbf{true}\}.$$

By the instantiation II rule we now obtain

$$\{r[y := \textbf{this}]\}\ \textbf{this}.find\ \{\textbf{true}\},$$

from which the desired correctness formula follows by the elimination rule.

6.9 Case Study: Insertion into a Linked List

We now return to the *insert* method defined in Example 6.21:

$$insert :: \textbf{begin local}$$
$$z := next;$$
$$next := \textbf{new};$$
$$next.setnext(z)$$
$$\textbf{end}$$

where the method *setnext* is defined by

$$setnext(u) :: next := u.$$

In order to express the correctness of the *insert* method we introduce as in the previous case study an array variable $a \in Var$ of type $\textbf{integer} \to \textbf{object}$ to store the list of objects linked by their instance variable *next*. Further, we introduce the simple object variable $y \in Var$ to represent a generic caller and the integer variable $k \in Var$ to denote the position of the insertion.

As a precondition we use the assertion

$$p \equiv y = a[k] \wedge k \geq 0 \wedge \forall n \geq 0 : a[n].next = a[n+1],$$

which states that y appears at the kth position and that the objects stored in a are linked by the value of their instance variable *next*. Note that we also require for $a[n] = \textbf{null}$ that $a[n].next = a[n+1]$. By putting $\textbf{null}.next = \textbf{null}$ this requirement can easily be met.

Insertion of a new object at position k is described by the postcondition

$$q \equiv q_0 \wedge q_1 \wedge q_2,$$

where

- $q_0 \equiv \forall n \geq 0 : \textbf{if}\ a[n] \neq a[k]\ \textbf{then}\ a[n].next = a[n+1]\ \textbf{fi}$,
- $q_1 \equiv \forall n \geq 0 : a[n] \neq a[k].next$,
- $q_2 \equiv a[k].next.next = a[k+1]$.

The assertion q_0 states that the chain of objects is 'broken' at the kth position. The assertion q_1 states that the instance variable *next* of the object at position k points to a new object. Finally, the assertion q_2 states that the instance variable *next* of this new object refers to the object at position $k+1$.

We prove

$$\{p\}\ y.insert\ \{q\}$$

in the sense of partial correctness. By the simplified version of the recursion V rule, it suffices to prove

$$\{p\}\ \textbf{begin local}\ \ this := y;\ S\ \textbf{end}\ \{q\},$$

where S denotes the body of the method *insert*. For this it suffices, by the recursion VII rule, to prove for suitable assertions p' and q'

$$\{p'\}\ next.setnext(z)\ \{q'\} \vdash \{p\}\ \textbf{begin local}\ \ this := y;\ S\ \textbf{end}\ \{q\} \quad (6.5)$$

and

$$\{p'\}\ \textbf{begin local}\ \ this, u := next, z;\ next := u\ \textbf{end}\ \{q'\}, \quad (6.6)$$

where $\vdash$ refers to the proof system POC with the recursion VII rule omitted.

We prove (6.5) and (6.6) in the form of proof outlines given below in Figures 6.6 and 6.7, respectively.

In these proofs we use

$$p' \equiv q_0 \wedge q_1 \wedge k \geq 0 \wedge \textbf{this} = a[k] \wedge z = a[k+1]$$

and

$$q' \equiv q.$$

For the justification of these proof outlines we introduce the abbreviation $t(l, v)$ defined by

$$t(l, v) \equiv (a[l].next)[next := v]$$
$$\equiv \textbf{if}\ a[l] = \textbf{this then}\ v\ \textbf{else}\ a[l].next\ \textbf{fi},$$

where $l \in Var$ ranges over simple integer variables and $v \in Var$ ranges over simple object variables.

To justify the proof outline in Figure 6.6 it suffices to establish the following four claims.

Claim 1. $\{p\}\ \textbf{this} := y\ \{p \wedge \textbf{this} = y\}$.

Proof. By the assignment axiom for normal variables we have

$$\{p \wedge y = y\}\ \textbf{this} := y\ \{p \wedge \textbf{this} = y\}.$$

So we obtain the desired result by a trivial application of the consequence rule. $\square$

Claim 2. $\{p \wedge \textbf{this} = y\}\ z := next\ \{p \wedge \textbf{this} = y \wedge z = next\}$.

$\{p\}$
begin local
$\{p\}$
this $:= y;$
$\{p \wedge \mathbf{this} = y\}$
begin local
$\{p \wedge \mathbf{this} = y\}$
$z := next;$
$\{p \wedge \mathbf{this} = y \wedge z = next\}$
$\{p \wedge k \geq 0 \wedge \mathbf{this} = a[k] \wedge z = a[k+1]\}$
$next := \mathbf{new};$
$\{q_0 \wedge q_1 \wedge k \geq 0 \wedge \mathbf{this} = a[k] \wedge z = a[k+1]\}$
$next.setnext(z)$
$\{q\}$
end
$\{q\}$
end
$\{q\}$

Fig. 6.6 Proof outline showing partial correctness of the *insert* method.

Proof. This claim also follows by an application of the assignment axiom for normal variables and a trivial application of the consequence rule. $\square$

Claim 3. $(p \wedge \mathbf{this} = y \wedge z = next) \rightarrow (k \geq 0 \wedge \mathbf{this} = a[k] \wedge z = a[k+1]).$

Proof. It suffices to observe that

- $(p \wedge \mathbf{this} = y) \rightarrow \mathbf{this} = a[k],$
- $(\mathbf{this} = a[k] \wedge z = next) \rightarrow z = a[k].next,$
- $p \rightarrow a[k].next = a[k+1].$

For the second implication recall that $z = next$ stands for $z = \mathbf{this}.next$. $\square$

Claim 4. $\{p \wedge k \geq 0 \wedge \mathbf{this} = a[k] \wedge z = a[k+1]\}$
$\qquad next := \mathbf{new}$
$\qquad \{q_0 \wedge q_1 \wedge k \geq 0 \wedge \mathbf{this} = a[k] \wedge z = a[k+1]\}.$

Proof. First, we introduce a fresh simple object variable $x \in Var$ and calculate

$$q_0[next := x] \equiv \forall n \geq 0 : \mathbf{if}\ a[n] \neq a[k]\ \mathbf{then}\ t(n, x) = a[n+1]\ \mathbf{fi},$$

where $t(n, x) \equiv \mathbf{if}\ a[n] = \mathbf{this}\ \mathbf{then}\ x\ \mathbf{else}\ a[n].next\ \mathbf{fi}$. We observe that $\mathbf{this} = a[k] \wedge a[n] \neq a[k]$ implies $a[n] \neq \mathbf{this}$ and that $a[n] \neq \mathbf{this}$ implies $t(n, x) = a[n].next$. Replacing $t(n, x)$ in $q_0[next := x]$ by $a[n].next$ we obtain q_0 itself. So we have that

$$\textbf{this} = a[k] \wedge q_0 \rightarrow q_0[next := x].$$

Since x does not occur in $\textbf{this} = a[k] \wedge q_0$, we have

$$\textbf{this} = a[k] \wedge q_0 \equiv (\textbf{this} = a[k] \wedge q_0)[x := \textbf{new}]$$

and derive by the object creation rule

$$\{\textbf{this} = a[k] \wedge q_0\}\; next := \textbf{new}\; \{q_0\}.$$

Since $p \rightarrow q_0$, we derive by the consequence rule that

$$\{p \wedge \textbf{this} = a[k]\}\; next := \textbf{new}\; \{q_0\}. \tag{6.7}$$

Next, we calculate

$$q_1[next := x] \equiv \forall n \geq 0 : a[n] \neq t(k, x),$$

where $t(k, x) \equiv \textbf{if}\; a[k] = \textbf{this}\; \textbf{then}\; x\; \textbf{else}\; a[k].next\; \textbf{fi}$. Since

$$a[n] \neq t(k, x) \leftrightarrow \textbf{if}\; a[k] = \textbf{this}\; \textbf{then}\; a[n] \neq x\; \textbf{else}\; a[n] \neq a[k].next\; \textbf{fi}$$

it follows that

$$\forall n \geq 0 : \textbf{if}\; a[k] = \textbf{this}\; \textbf{then}\; a[n] \neq x\; \textbf{else}\; a[n] \neq a[k].next\; \textbf{fi}$$
$$\rightarrow q_1[next := x].$$

Now we calculate

$$\textbf{if}\; a[k] = \textbf{this}\; \textbf{then}\; a[n] \neq x\; \textbf{else}\; a[n] \neq a[k].next\; \textbf{fi}[x := \textbf{new}]$$
$$\equiv \textbf{if}\; (a[k] = \textbf{this})[x := \textbf{new}]$$
$$\quad \textbf{then}\; (a[n] \neq x)[x := \textbf{new}]$$
$$\quad \textbf{else}\; (a[n] \neq a[k].next)[x := \textbf{new}]$$
$$\quad \textbf{fi}$$
$$\equiv \textbf{if}\; a[k] = \textbf{this}\; \textbf{then}\; \neg false\; \textbf{else}\; a[n] \neq a[k].next\; \textbf{fi}.$$

So

$$(\forall n \geq 0 : \textbf{if}\; a[k] = \textbf{this}\; \textbf{then}\; a[n] \neq x\; \textbf{else}\; a[n] \neq a[k].next\; \textbf{fi})[x := \textbf{new}]$$
$$\equiv \forall n \geq 0 : \textbf{if}\; a[k] = \textbf{this}\; \textbf{then}\; \neg false\; \textbf{else}\; a[n] \neq a[k].next\; \textbf{fi}.$$

Further, we have

$$\textbf{this} = a[k] \rightarrow \forall n \geq 0 : \textbf{if}\; a[k] = \textbf{this}\; \textbf{then}\; \neg false\; \textbf{else}\; a[n] \neq a[k].next\; \textbf{fi}.$$

So by the object creation rule and the consequence rule, we derive

$$\{\mathbf{this} = a[k]\}\ next := new\ \{q_1\}. \tag{6.8}$$

By an application of the conjunction rule to the correctness formulas (6.7) and (6.8), we therefore obtain

$$\{p \wedge \mathbf{this} = a[k]\}\ next := \mathbf{new}\ \{q_0 \wedge q_1\}.$$

An application of the invariance rule then gives us the desired result.   □

$\{q_0 \wedge q_1 \wedge k \geq 0 \wedge \mathbf{this} = a[k] \wedge z = a[k+1]\}$
begin local
$\{q_0 \wedge q_1 \wedge k \geq 0 \wedge \mathbf{this} = a[k] \wedge z = a[k+1]\}$
$\mathbf{this}, u := next, z;$
$\{q_0 \wedge q_1 \wedge k \geq 0 \wedge \mathbf{this} = a[k].next \wedge u = a[k+1]\}$
$next := u$
$\{q\}$
end
$\{q\}$

Fig. 6.7 Proof outline showing partial correctness of the *setnext* method.

To justify the proof outline in Figure 6.7 it suffices to establish the following two claims.

Claim 5. $\{q_0 \wedge q_1 \wedge k \geq 0 \wedge \mathbf{this} = a[k] \wedge z = a[k+1]\}$
    $\mathbf{this}, u := next, z$
    $\{q_0 \wedge q_1 \wedge k \geq 0 \wedge \mathbf{this} = a[k].next \wedge u = a[k+1]\}.$

Proof. By the assignment axiom for normal variables and the consequence rule, it suffices to observe that $\mathbf{this} = a[k] \rightarrow next = a[k].next$.   □

Claim 6. $\{q_0 \wedge q_1 \wedge k \geq 0 \wedge \mathbf{this} = a[k].next \wedge u = a[k+1]\}$
    $next := u$
    $\{q\}.$

Proof. First, we calculate

$$q_0[next := u] \equiv \forall n \geq 0 : \mathbf{if}\ a[n] \neq a[k]\ \mathbf{then}\ t(n, u) = a[n+1]\ \mathbf{fi},$$

where $t(n, u) \equiv \mathbf{if}\ a[n] = \mathbf{this}\ \mathbf{then}\ u\ \mathbf{else}\ a[n].next\ \mathbf{fi}$. Next we observe that $q_1 \wedge \mathbf{this} = a[k].next \wedge n \geq 0$ implies $a[n] \neq \mathbf{this}$ and $a[n] \neq \mathbf{this}$ implies $t(n, u) = a[n].next$. Replacing $t(n, u)$ in $q_0[next := u]$ by $a[n].next$ we obtain q_0 itself. From this we conclude

$$(q_0 \wedge q_1 \wedge \mathbf{this} = a[k].next) \rightarrow q_0[next := u].$$

By the assignment axiom for instance variables and the consequence rule, we therefore derive the correctness formula

$$\{q_0 \wedge q_1 \wedge \textbf{this} = a[k].next\} \ next := u \ \{q_0\}. \tag{6.9}$$

Next, we calculate

$$q_1[next := u] \equiv \forall n \geq 0 : a[n] \neq t(k, u),$$

where $t(k, u) \equiv \textbf{if } a[k] = \textbf{this then } u \textbf{ else } a[k].next \textbf{ fi}$. Note that $q_1 \wedge k \geq 0 \wedge \textbf{this} = a[k].next$ implies $a[k] \neq \textbf{this}$ and $a[k] \neq \textbf{this}$ implies $t(k, u) = a[k].next$. Replacing $t(k, u)$ in $q_1[next := u]$ by $a[k].next$ we obtain q_1 itself. From this we conclude

$$(q_1 \wedge k \geq 0 \wedge \textbf{this} = a[k].next) \to q_1[next := u].$$

By the assignment axiom for instance variables and the consequence rule, we thus derive the correctness formula

$$\{q_1 \wedge k \geq 0 \wedge \textbf{this} = a[k].next\} \ next := u \ \{q_1\}. \tag{6.10}$$

Finally, we calculate

$$q_2[next := u] \equiv \textbf{if this} = t(k, u) \textbf{ then } u \textbf{ else } t(k, u).next \textbf{ fi} = a[k + 1].$$

As already inferred above, we have that $q_1 \wedge k \geq 0 \wedge \textbf{this} = a[k].next$ implies $t(k, u) = a[k].next$. Replacing $t(k, u)$ in $q_2[next := u]$ by $a[k].next$ we obtain the assertion

$$\textbf{if this} = a[k].next \textbf{ then } u \textbf{ else } a[k].next.next \textbf{ fi} = a[k + 1]$$

which is clearly implied by $\textbf{this} = a[k].next \wedge u = a[k + 1]$. From this we conclude

$$(q_1 \wedge k \geq 0 \wedge \textbf{this} = a[k].next \wedge u = a[k + 1]) \to q_2[next := u].$$

By the assignment axiom for instance variables and the consequence rule, we thus derive the correctness formula

$$\{q_1 \wedge k \geq 0 \wedge \textbf{this} = a[k].next \wedge u = a[k + 1]\} \ next := u \ \{q_2\}. \tag{6.11}$$

Applying the conjunction rule to the correctness formulas (6.9), (6.10) and (6.11) finally gives us the desired result. □

6.10 Exercises

6.1. Compute

(i) $\sigma[a[0] := 1](y.a[x])$ where $y, x \in Var$ and $a \in IVar$,
(ii) $\sigma[x := \sigma(\mathbf{this})][y := 0](x.y)$ where $x \in Var$ and $y \in IVar$,
(iii) $\sigma[\sigma(\mathbf{this}) := \tau[x := 0]](x)$, where $x \in IVar$,
(iv) $\sigma(y.next.next)$.

6.2. Compute

(i) $(z.x)[x := 0]$,
(ii) $(z.a[y])[a[0] := 1]$,
(iii) $(\mathbf{this}.next.next)[next := y]$.

6.3. Prove the Substitution Lemma 6.2.

6.4. Given an instance variable x and the method $getx$ to get its value defined by

$$getx :: r := x,$$

where r is a normal variable, prove

$$\{\mathbf{true}\} \; y.getx \; \{r = y.x\}.$$

6.5. Given the method definition

$$inc :: count := count + 1,$$

where $count$ is an instance integer variable, prove

$$\{up.count = z\} \; up.inc \; \{up.count = z + 1\},$$

where z is a normal variable.

6.6. Let $next$ be an instance object variable and r be a normal object variable. The following method returns the value of $next$:

$$getnext :: r := next.$$

Prove

$$\{next.next = z\}next.getnext; \; next := r\{next = z\},$$

where z is a normal object variable.

6.7. We define the method $insert$ by

$$insert(u) :: u.setnext(next); next := u,$$

where $next$ is an instance object variable, u is a normal object variable and $setnext$ is defined by

$$setnext(u) :: next := u.$$

Prove

$$\{z = next\} \text{ } \textbf{this}.insert(x) \text{ } \{next = x \wedge x.next = z\},$$

where x and z are normal object variables.

6.8. To compute the sum of the instance integer variables val we used in Example 6.4 a normal integer variable sum, a normal object variable $current$ that points to the current object, and two methods, add and $move$, defined as follows:

$$add :: sum := sum + val,$$
$$move :: current := next.$$

Then the following main statement S computes the desired sum:

$S \equiv sum := 0;$
$\quad\quad current := first;$
$\quad\quad \textbf{while } current \neq \textbf{null do } current.add; \text{ } current.move \textbf{ od}.$

Let a be a normal array variable of type $\textbf{integer} \rightarrow \textbf{object}$ and the assertions p and q be defined by

$$p \equiv a[0] = first \wedge a[n] = \textbf{null} \wedge \forall i \in [0 : n-1] : a[i] \neq \textbf{null} \wedge a[i].next = a[i+1]$$

and

$$q \equiv sum = \sum_{i=0}^{n-1} a[i].$$

Prove $\{p\} \text{ } S \text{ } \{q\}$ in the sense of both partial and total correctness.

6.9. Prove the Translation Lemma 6.3.

6.10. Prove the Correspondence Lemma 6.4.

6.11. Prove the Transformation Lemma 6.5.

6.12. Prove the Correctness Theorem 6.1.

6.13. Prove the Assertion Lemma 6.6.

6.14. Prove the Translation Lemma 6.7.

6.15. Prove the Translation Lemma 6.8.

6.16. Prove the Translation of Correctness Proofs of Statements Lemma 6.9.

6.17. Prove the Translation Corollary 6.2.

6.18. Prove Lemma 6.10.

6.19. Prove the Substitution for Object Creation Lemma 6.11.

6.20. Prove the Conditional Expressions Lemma 6.12.

6.21. Prove Theorem 6.3.

6.22. Given the normal array variable a of type **integer** $\rightarrow$ **object** and the normal integer variable n, let the assertion p be defined by

$$p \equiv \forall i \in [0 : n] : \forall j \in [0 : n] : \textbf{if } i \neq j \textbf{ then } a[i] \neq a[j] \textbf{ fi}.$$

Prove

$$\{p\}\ n := n + 1; a[n] := \textbf{new}\ \{p\}.$$

6.11 Bibliographic Remarks

Dahl and Nygaard [1966] introduced in the 1960s the first object-oriented programming language called Simula. The language Smalltalk introduced in the 1970s strictly defines all the basic computational concepts in terms of objects and method calls. Currently, one of the most popular object-oriented languages is Java.

The proof theory for recursive method calls presented here is based on de Boer [1991b]. Pierik and de Boer [2005] describe an extension to the typical object-oriented features of *inheritance* and *subtyping*. There is a large literature on assertional proof methods for object-oriented languages, notably for Java. For example, Jacobs [2004] discusses a weakest pre-condition calculus for Java programs with JML annotations. The Java Modeling Language (JML) can be used to specify Java classes and interfaces by adding annotations to Java source files. An overview of its tools and applications is discussed in Burdy et al. [2005]. In Huisman and Jacobs [2000] a Hoare logic for Java with abnormal termination caused by failures is described.

Object-oriented programs in general give rise to dynamically evolving *pointer* structures as they occur in programming languages like Pascal. There is a large literature on logics dealing in different ways with the problem of *aliasing*. One of the early approaches to reasoning about linked data structures is described in Morris [1982]. A more recent approach is that of *separation logic* described in Reynolds [2002]. Abadi and Leino [2003] introduce a Hoare logic for object-oriented programs based on a global store model which provides an explicit treatment of aliasing and object creation in the assertion language. Banerjee and Naumann [2005] further discuss restrictions on aliasing to ensure encapsulation of classes in an object-oriented programming language with pointers and subtyping.

Recent work on assertional methods for object-oriented programming languages by Barnett et al. [2005] focuses on *object invariants* and a corresponding methodology for *modular* verification. Müller, Poetzsch-Heffter and

Leavens [2006] also introduce a class of invariants which support modular reasoning about complex object structures.

There exist a number of tools based on theorem provers which assist in (semi-)automated correctness proofs of object-oriented programs. In particular, Flanagan et al. [2002] describe ECS/Java (Extended Static Checker for Java) which supports the (semi-)automated verification of annotated Java programs. The KeY Approach of Beckert, Hähnle and Schmitt [2007] to the verification of object-oriented software is based on *dynamic logic*.

Part III
Parallel Programs

7 Disjoint Parallel Programs

A S WE HAVE seen in Chapter 1, concurrent programs can be quite difficult to understand in detail. That is why we introduce and study them in several stages. In this part of the book we study parallel programs, and in this chapter we investigate disjoint parallelism, the simplest form of parallelism. Disjointness means here that the component programs have only reading access to common variables.

Many phenomena of parallel programs can already be explained in this setting. In Chapter 8 we study parallelism with shared variables and in Chapter 9 we add synchronization to shared variable parallelism. Disjoint parallelism provides a good preparation for studying these extensions. Disjoint parallelism is also a good starting point for studying distributed programs in Chapter 11.

Under what conditions can parallel execution be reduced to a sequential execution? In other words, is there any simple syntactic criterion that guarantees that all computations of a parallel program are equivalent to the

Krzysztof R. Apt et al., *Verification of Sequential and Concurrent Programs*,
Texts in Computer Science, DOI: 10.1007/978-1-84882-745-5_7,
© Springer-Verlag London Limited 2009

sequential execution of its components? Such questions led Hoare to an introduction of the concept of disjoint parallelism (Hoare [1972,1975]). In this chapter we present an in-depth study of this concept.

After introducing the syntax of disjoint parallel programs (Section 7.1) we define their semantics (Section 7.2). We then prove that all computations of a disjoint parallel program starting in the same initial state produce the same output (the Determinism Lemma).

In Section 7.3 we study the proof theory of disjoint parallel programs. The proof rule for disjoint parallelism simply takes the conjunction of pre- and postconditions of the component programs. Additionally, we need a proof rule dealing with the so-called auxiliary variables; these are variables used to express properties about the program execution that cannot be expressed solely in terms of program variables.

As a case study we prove in Section 7.4 the correctness of a disjoint parallel program *FIND* that searches for a positive element in an integer array.

7.1 Syntax

Two **while** programs S_1 and S_2 are called *disjoint* if neither of them can change the variables accessed by the other one; that is, if

$$change(S_1) \cap var(S_2) = \emptyset$$

and

$$var(S_1) \cap change(S_2) = \emptyset.$$

Recall from Chapter 3 that for an arbitrary program S, $change(S)$ is the set of simple and array variables of S that can be modified by it; that is, to which a value is assigned within S by means of an assignment. Note that disjoint programs are allowed to read the same variables.

Example 7.1. The programs $x := z$ and $y := z$ are disjoint because $change(x := z) = \{x\}$, $var(y := z) = \{y, z\}$ and $var(x := z) = \{x, z\}$, $change(y := z) = \{y\}$.

On the other hand, the programs $x := z$ and $y := x$ are not disjoint because $x \in change(x := z) \cap var(y := x)$, and the programs $a[1] := z$ and $y := a[2]$ are not disjoint because $a \in change(a[1] := z) \cap var(y := a[2])$. $\quad\square$

Disjoint parallel programs are generated by the same clauses as those defining **while** programs in Chapter 3 together with the following clause for *disjoint parallel composition*:

$$S ::= [S_1 \| \ldots \| S_n],$$

where for $n > 1$, $S_1, \ldots, S_n$ are pairwise disjoint **while** programs, called the (*sequential*) *components* of S. Thus we do not allow nested parallelism, but we allow parallelism to occur within sequential composition, conditional statements and **while** loops.

It is useful to extend the notion of disjointness to expressions and assertions. An expression t and a program S are called *disjoint* if S cannot change the variables of t; that is, if

$$change(S) \cap var(t) = \emptyset.$$

Similarly, an assertion p and a program S are called *disjoint* if S cannot change the variables of p; that is, if

$$change(S) \cap var(p) = \emptyset.$$

7.2 Semantics

We now define semantics of disjoint parallel programs in terms of transitions. Intuitively, a disjoint parallel program $[S_1\|\ldots\|S_n]$ performs a transition if one of its components performs a transition. This form of modeling concurrency is called *interleaving*. Formally, we expand the transition system for **while** programs by the following transition rule

(xvii)
$$\frac{< S_i, \sigma > \; \rightarrow \; < T_i, \tau >}{< [S_1\|\ldots\|S_i\|\ldots\|S_n], \sigma > \; \rightarrow \; < [S_1\|\ldots\|T_i\|\ldots\|S_n], \tau >}$$

where $i \in \{1, \ldots, n\}$.

Computations of disjoint parallel programs are defined like those of sequential programs. For example,

$$< [x := 1 \| y := 2 \| z := 3], \sigma >$$
$$\rightarrow \; < [E \| y := 2 \| z := 3], \sigma[x := 1] >$$
$$\rightarrow \; < [E \| E \| z := 3], \sigma[x := 1][y := 2] >$$
$$\rightarrow \; < [E \| E \| E], \sigma[x := 1][y := 2][z := 3] >$$

is a computation of $[x := 1 \| y := 2 \| z := 3]$ starting in σ.

Recall that the empty program E denotes termination. For example, $[E \| y := 2 \| z := 3]$ denotes a parallel program where the first component has terminated. We wish to express the idea that a disjoint parallel program $S \equiv [S_1\|\ldots\|S_n]$ terminates if and only if all its components $S_1, \ldots, S_n$ terminate. To this end we identify

$$[E\|\ldots\|E] \equiv E.$$

This identification allows us to maintain the definition of a terminating computation given in Definition 3.1. For example, the final configuration in the above computation is the terminating configuration

$$< E, \sigma[x := 1][y := 2][z := 3] > .$$

By inspection of the above transition rules, we obtain

Lemma 7.1. (Absence of Blocking) *Every configuration $< S, \sigma >$ with $S \not\equiv E$ and a proper state σ has a successor configuration in the transition relation $\rightarrow$.*

Thus when started in a state σ a disjoint parallel program $S \equiv [S_1\|\ldots\|S_n]$ terminates or diverges. Therefore we introduce two types of input/output semantics for disjoint programs in just the same way as for **while** programs.

Definition 7.1. For a disjoint parallel program S and a proper state σ

(i) the *partial correctness semantics* is a mapping

$$\mathcal{M}[\![S]\!] : \Sigma \to \mathcal{P}(\Sigma)$$

with

$$\mathcal{M}[\![S]\!](\sigma) = \{\tau \mid <S, \sigma> \to^* <E, \tau>\}$$

(ii) and the *total correctness semantics* is a mapping

$$\mathcal{M}_{tot}[\![S]\!] : \Sigma \to \mathcal{P}(\Sigma \cup \{\bot\})$$

with

$$\mathcal{M}_{tot}[\![S]\!](\sigma) = \mathcal{M}[\![S]\!](\sigma) \cup \{\bot \mid S \text{ can diverge from } \sigma\}.$$

Recall that $\bot$ is the error state standing for divergence.   □

Determinism

Unlike **while** programs, disjoint parallel programs can generate more than
one computation starting in a given initial state. Thus determinism in the
sense of the Determinism Lemma 3.1 does not hold. However, we can prove
that all computations of a disjoint parallel program starting in the same
initial state produce the same output. Thus a weaker form of determinism
holds here, in that for every disjoint parallel program S and proper state
σ, $\mathcal{M}_{tot}[\![S]\!](\sigma)$ has exactly one element, either a proper state or the error
state $\bot$. This turns out to be a simple corollary to some results concerning
properties of abstract *reduction systems*.

Definition 7.2. A *reduction system* is a pair $(A, \to)$ where A is a set and
$\to$ is a binary relation on A; that is, $\to\, \subseteq A \times A$. If $a \to b$ holds, we say
that a can be *replaced* by b. Let $\to^*$ denote the transitive reflexive closure
of $\to$.

   We say that $\to$ satisfies the *diamond property* if for all $a, b, c \in A$ with
$b \neq c$

implies that for some $d \in A$

$\rightarrow$ is called *confluent* if for all $a, b, c \in A$

implies that for some $d \in A$

$$
\begin{array}{ccc}
b & & c \\
* \searrow & & \swarrow * \\
& d. &
\end{array}
$$

$\square$

The following lemma due to Newman [1942] is of importance to us.

Lemma 7.2. (Confluence) *For all reduction systems* $(A, \rightarrow)$ *the following holds: if a relation* $\rightarrow$ *satisfies the diamond property then it is confluent.*

Proof. Suppose that $\rightarrow$ satisfies the diamond property. Let $\rightarrow^n$ stand for the n-fold composition of $\rightarrow$. A straightforward proof by induction on $n \geq 0$ shows that $a \rightarrow b$ and $a \rightarrow^n c$ implies that for some $i \leq n$ and some $d \in A$, $b \rightarrow^i d$ and $c \rightarrow^\epsilon d$. Here $c \rightarrow^\epsilon d$ iff $c \rightarrow d$ or $c = d$. Thus $a \rightarrow b$ and $a \rightarrow^* c$ implies that for some $d \in A$, $b \rightarrow^* d$ and $c \rightarrow^* d$.

This implies by induction on $n \geq 0$ that if $a \rightarrow^* b$ and $a \rightarrow^n c$ then for some $d \in A$ we have $b \rightarrow^* d$ and $c \rightarrow^* d$. This proves confluence. $\square$

To deal with infinite sequences, we need the following lemma.

Lemma 7.3. (Infinity) *Consider a reduction system* $(A, \rightarrow)$ *where* $\rightarrow$ *satisfies the diamond property and elements* $a, b, c \in A$ *with* $a \rightarrow b$, $a \rightarrow c$ *and* $b \neq c$. *If there exists an infinite sequence* $a \rightarrow b \rightarrow \ldots$ *passing through* b *then there exists also an infinite sequence* $a \rightarrow c \rightarrow \ldots$ *passing through* c.

Proof. Consider an infinite sequence $a_0 \rightarrow a_1 \rightarrow \ldots$ where $a_0 = a$ and $a_1 = b$.

Case 1. For some $i \geq 0$, $c \rightarrow^* a_i$.
   Then $a \rightarrow c \rightarrow^* a_i \rightarrow \ldots$ is the desired sequence.

Case 2. For no $i \geq 0$, $c \rightarrow^* a_i$.
   We construct by induction on i an infinite sequence $c_0 \rightarrow c_1 \rightarrow \ldots$ such that $c_0 = c$ and for all $i \geq 0$ $a_i \rightarrow c_i$. c_0 is already correctly defined. For $i = 1$ note that $a_0 \rightarrow a_1$, $a_0 \rightarrow c_0$ and $a_1 \neq c_0$. Thus by the diamond property there exists a c_1 such that $a_1 \rightarrow c_1$ and $c_0 \rightarrow c_1$.
   Consider now the induction step. We have $a_i \rightarrow a_{i+1}$ and $a_i \rightarrow c_i$ for some $i > 0$. Also, since $c \rightarrow^* c_i$, by the assumption $c_i \neq a_{i+1}$. Again by the diamond property for some c_{i+1}, $a_{i+1} \rightarrow c_{i+1}$ and $c_i \rightarrow c_{i+1}$. $\square$

Definition 7.3. Let $(A, \to)$ be a reduction system and $a \in A$. An element $b \in A$ is $\to$-maximal if there is no c with $b \to c$. We define now

$$yield(a) = \quad \{b \mid a \to^* b \text{ and } b \text{ is } \to\text{-maximal}\}$$
$$\cup \ \{\bot \mid \text{ there exists an infinite sequence } a \to a_1 \to \ldots\}$$

$\square$

Lemma 7.4. (Yield) *Let $(A, \to)$ be a reduction system where $\to$ satisfies the diamond property. Then for every a, $yield(a)$ has exactly one element.*

Proof. Suppose that for some $\to$-maximal b and c, $a \to^* b$ and $a \to^* c$. By Confluence Lemma 7.2, there is some $d \in A$ with $b \to^* d$ and $c \to^* d$. By the $\to$-maximality of b and c, both $b = d$ and $c = d$; thus $b = c$.

Thus the set $\{b \mid a \to^* b, b \text{ is } \to\text{-maximal}\}$ has at most one element. Suppose it is empty. Then $yield(a) = \{\bot\}$.

Suppose now that it has exactly one element, say b. Assume by contradiction that there exists an infinite sequence $a \to a_1 \to \ldots$. Consider a sequence $b_0 \to b_1 \to \ldots \to b_k$ where $b_0 = a$ and $b_k = b$. Then $k > 0$. Let $b_0 \to \ldots \to b_\ell$ be the longest prefix of $b_0 \to \ldots \to b_k$ which is an initial fragment of an infinite sequence $a \to c_1 \to c_2 \to \ldots$. Then ℓ is well defined, $b_\ell = c_\ell$ and $\ell < k$, since b_k is $\to$-maximal. Thus $b_\ell \to b_{\ell+1}$ and $b_\ell \to c_{\ell+1}$. By the definition of ℓ, $b_{\ell+1} \neq c_{\ell+1}$. By the Infinity Lemma 7.3 there exists an infinite sequence $b_\ell \to b_{\ell+1} \to \ldots$. This contradicts the choice of ℓ. $\square$

To apply the Yield Lemma 7.4 to the case of disjoint parallel programs, we need the following lemma.

Lemma 7.5. (Diamond) *Let S be a disjoint parallel program and σ a proper state. Whenever*

$$< S, \sigma >$$
$$\swarrow \qquad \searrow$$
$$< S_1, \sigma_1 > \neq < S_2, \sigma_2 >,$$

then for some configuration $< T, \tau >$

$$< S_1, \sigma_1 > \qquad < S_2, \sigma_2 >$$
$$\searrow \qquad \swarrow$$
$$< T, \tau >.$$

Proof. By the Determinism Lemma 3.1 and the interleaving transition rule (viii), the program S is of the form $[T_1\|\ldots\|T_n]$ where $T_1, \ldots, T_n$ are pairwise disjoint **while** programs, and S_1 and S_2 result from S by transitions of two of these **while** programs, some T_i and T_j, with $i \neq j$. More precisely, for some **while** programs T_i' and T_j'

$$S_1 = [T_1\|\ldots\|T_i'\|\ldots\|T_n],$$
$$S_2 = [T_1\|\ldots\|T_j'\|\ldots\|T_n],$$
$$<T_i,\sigma> \;\rightarrow\; <T_i',\sigma_1>,$$
$$<T_j,\sigma> \;\rightarrow\; <T_j',\sigma_2>.$$

Define T and τ as follows:

$$T = [T_1'\|\ldots\|T_n'],$$

where for $k \in \{1,\ldots,n\}$ with $k \neq i$ and $k \neq j$

$$T_k' = T_k$$

and for any variable u

$$\tau(u) = \begin{cases} \sigma_1(u) \text{ if} & u \in change(T_i), \\ \sigma_2(u) \text{ if} & u \in change(T_j), \\ \sigma(u) \;\; \text{otherwise.} \end{cases}$$

By disjointness of T_i and T_j, the state τ is well defined. Using the Change and Access Lemma 3.4 it is easy to check that both $<S_1,\sigma_1> \;\rightarrow\; <T,\tau>$ and $<S_2,\sigma_2> \;\rightarrow\; <T,\tau>$. $\Box$

As an immediate corollary we obtain the desired result.

Lemma 7.6. (Determinism) *For every disjoint parallel program S and proper state σ, $\mathcal{M}_{tot}[\![S]\!](\sigma)$ has exactly one element.*

Proof. By Lemmata 7.4 and 7.5 and observing that for every proper state σ, $\mathcal{M}_{tot}[\![S]\!](\sigma) = yield(<S,\sigma>)$. $\Box$

Sequentialization

The Determinism Lemma helps us provide a quick proof that disjoint parallelism reduces to sequential composition. In Section 7.3 this reduction enables us to state a first, very simple proof rule for disjoint parallelism. To relate the computations of sequential and parallel programs, we use the following general notion of equivalence.

Definition 7.4. Two computations are *input/output equivalent*, or simply *i/o equivalent*, if they start in the same state and are either both infinite or both finite and then yield the same final state. In later chapters we also consider error states such as **fail** or Δ among the final states. $\Box$

Lemma 7.7. (Sequentialization) *Let $S_1, \ldots, S_n$ be pairwise disjoint* **while** *programs. Then*

$$\mathcal{M}[\![[S_1 \| \ldots \| S_n]]\!] = \mathcal{M}[\![S_1; \ldots; S_n]\!],$$

and

$$\mathcal{M}_{tot}[\![[S_1 \| \ldots \| S_n]]\!] = \mathcal{M}_{tot}[\![S_1; \ldots; S_n]\!].$$

Proof. We call a computation of $[S_1 \| \ldots \| S_n]$ *sequentialized* if the components $S_1, \ldots, S_n$ are activated in a sequential order: first execute exclusively S_1, then, in case of termination of S_1, execute exclusively S_2, and so forth.

We claim that every computation of $S_1; \ldots; S_n$ is i/o equivalent to a sequentialized computation of $[S_1 \| \ldots \| S_n]$.

This claim follows immediately from the observation that the computations of $S_1; \ldots; S_n$ are in a one-to-one correspondence with the sequentialized computations of $[S_1 \| \ldots \| S_n]$. Indeed, by replacing in a computation of $S_1; \ldots; S_n$ each configuration of the form

$$< T;\ S_{k+1};\ \ldots;\ S_n, \tau >$$

by

$$< [E \| \ldots \| E \| T \| S_{k+1} \| \ldots \| S_n], \tau >$$

we obtain a sequentialized computation of $[S_1 \| \ldots \| S_n]$. Conversely, in a sequentialized computation of $[S_1 \| \ldots \| S_n]$ each configuration is of the latter form, so by applying to such a computation the above replacement operation in the reverse direction, we obtain a computation of $S_1; \ldots; S_n$.

This claim implies that for every state σ

$$\mathcal{M}_{tot}[\![S_1;\ \ldots;\ S_n]\!](\sigma) \subseteq \mathcal{M}_{tot}[\![[S_1 \| \ldots \| S_n]]\!](\sigma).$$

By the Determinism Lemmata 3.1 and 7.6, both sides of the above inclusion have exactly one element. Thus in fact equality holds. This also implies

$$\mathcal{M}[\![S_1;\ \ldots;\ S_n]\!](\sigma) = \mathcal{M}[\![[S_1 \| \ldots \| S_n]]\!](\sigma)$$

and completes the proof of the lemma.   □

7.3 Verification

Partial and total correctness of disjoint parallel programs $S \equiv [S_1 \| \ldots \| S_n]$ are defined as for **while** programs. Thus for partial correctness we have

$$\models \{p\}\ S\ \{q\} \text{ iff } \mathcal{M}[\![S]\!]([\![p]\!]) \subseteq [\![q]\!]$$

and for total correctness

$$\models_{tot} \{p\}\ S\ \{q\} \text{ iff } \mathcal{M}_{tot}[\![S]\!]([\![p]\!]) \subseteq [\![q]\!].$$

Parallel Composition

The Sequentialization Lemma 7.7 suggests the following proof rule for disjoint parallel programs.

RULE 23: SEQUENTIALIZATION

$$\frac{\{p\}\ S_1;\ \ldots;\ S_n\ \{q\}}{\{p\}\ [S_1\|\ldots\|S_n]\ \{q\}}$$

By the Sequentialization Lemma 7.7 this rule is sound for both partial and total correctness. Thus when added to the previous proof systems PW or TW for partial or total correctness of **while** programs, it yields a sound proof system for partial or total correctness of disjoint parallel programs. For a very simple application let us look at the following example.

Example 7.2. We wish to show

$$\models_{tot} \{x = y\}\ [x := x + 1 \| y := y + 1]\ \{x = y\};$$

that is, if x and y have identical values initially, the same is true upon termination of the parallel program. By the sequentialization rule it suffices to show

$$\models_{tot} \{x = y\}\ x := x + 1;\ y := y + 1\ \{x = y\},$$

which is an easy exercise in the proof system TW of Chapter 3.   □

Though simple, the sequentialization rule has an important methodological drawback. Proving its premise amounts —by the composition rule— to proving

$$\{p\}\ S_1\ \{r_1\}, \ldots, \{r_{i-1}\}\ S_i\ \{r_i\}, \ldots, \{r_{n-1}\}\ S_n\ \{q\}$$

for appropriate assertions $r_1, \ldots, r_{n-1}$. Thus the pre- and post-assertions of different components of $[S_1\|\ldots\|S_n]$ must fit exactly. This does not reflect the idea of disjoint parallelism that $S_1, \ldots, S_n$ are independent programs.

What we would like is a proof rule where the input/output specification of $[S_1\|\ldots\|S_n]$ is simply the *conjunction* of the input/output specifications of its components $S_1, \ldots, S_n$. This aim is achieved by the following proof rule for disjoint parallel programs proposed in Hoare [1972].

RULE 24: DISJOINT PARALLELISM

$$\frac{\{p_i\}\ S_i\ \{q_i\}, i \in \{1, \ldots, n\}}{\{\bigwedge_{i=1}^{n}\ p_i\}\ [S_1\|\ldots\|S_n]\ \{\bigwedge_{i=1}^{n}\ q_i\}}$$

where $free(p_i, q_i) \cap change(S_j) = \emptyset$ for $i \neq j$.

The premises of this rule are to be proven in the proof systems PW or TW for **while** programs. Depending on whether we choose PW or TW, the conclusion of the rule holds in the sense of partial or total correctness, respectively.

This proof rule links parallel composition of programs with logical conjunction of the corresponding pre- and postconditions and also sets the basic pattern for the more complicated proof rules needed to deal with shared variables and synchronization in Chapters 8 and 9. In the present case of disjoint parallel programs the proof rule allows us to reason *compositionally* about the input/output behavior of disjoint parallel programs: once we know the pre- and postconditions of the component programs we can deduce that the logical conjunction of these conditions yields the pre- and postcondition of the parallel program.

Requiring disjointness of the pre- and postconditions and the component programs in the disjoint parallelism rule is necessary.

Without it we could, for example, derive from the true formulas

$$\{y = 1\}\ x := 0\ \{y = 1\} \text{ and } \{\textbf{true}\}\ y := 0\ \{\textbf{true}\}$$

the conclusion

$$\{y = 1\}\ [x := 0\|y := 0]\ \{y = 1\},$$

which is of course wrong.

However, due to this restriction the disjoint parallelism rule is weaker than the sequentialization rule. For example, one can show that the correctness formula

$$\{x = y\}\ [x := x + 1\|y := y + 1]\ \{x = y\}$$

of Example 7.2 cannot be proved using the disjoint parallelism rule (see Exercise 7.9). Intuitively, we cannot express in a single assertion p_i or q_i any relationship between variables changed in different components, such as the relationship $x = y$. But let us see in more detail where a possible proof breaks down.

Clearly, we can use a fresh variable z to prove

$$\{x = z\}\ x := x + 1\ \{x = z + 1\}$$

and

$$\{y = z\}\ y := y + 1\ \{y = z + 1\}.$$

Thus by the disjoint parallelism rule we obtain

$$\{x = z \wedge y = z\}\ [x := x + 1 \| y := y + 1]\ \{x = z + 1 \wedge y = z + 1\}.$$

Now the consequence rule yields

$$\{x = z \wedge y = z\}\ [x := x + 1 \| y := y + 1]\ \{x = y\}.$$

But we cannot simply replace the preassertion $x = z \wedge y = z$ by $x = y$ because the implication

$$x = y \rightarrow x = z \wedge y = z$$

does not hold. On the other hand, we have

$$\{x = y\}\ z := x\ \{x = z \wedge y = z\};$$

so by the composition rule

$$\{x = y\}\ z := x;\ [x := x + 1 \| y := y + 1]\ \{x = y\}. \tag{7.1}$$

To complete the proof we would like to drop the assignment $z := x$. But how might we justify this step?

Auxiliary Variables

What is needed here is a new proof rule allowing us to delete assignments to so-called auxiliary variables.

The general approach thus consists of extending the program by the assignments to auxiliary variables, proving the correctness of the extended program and then deleting the added assignments. Auxiliary variables should neither influence the control flow nor the data flow of the program, but only record some additional information about the program execution. The following definition identifies sets of auxiliary variables in an extended program.

Definition 7.5. Let A be a set of simple variables in a program S. We call A a *set of auxiliary variables* of S if each variable from A occurs in S only in assignments of the form $z := t$ with $z \in A$.   □

Since auxiliary variables do not appear in Boolean expressions, they cannot influence the control flow in S, and since they are not used in assignments to variables outside of A, auxiliary variables cannot influence the data flow in S. As an example, consider the program

$$S \equiv z := x;\ [x := x + 1 \| y := y + 1].$$

Then
$$\emptyset, \{y\}, \{z\}, \{x, z\}, \{y, z\}, \{x, y, z\}$$

are all sets of auxiliary variables of S.

Now we can state the announced proof rule which was first introduced in Owicki and Gries [1976a].

RULE 25: AUXILIARY VARIABLES

$$\frac{\{p\} \; S \; \{q\}}{\{p\} \; S_0 \; \{q\}}$$

where for some set of auxiliary variables A of S with $free(q) \cap A = \emptyset$, the program S_0 results from S by deleting all assignments to variables in A.

This deletion process can result in incomplete programs. For example, taking $A = \{y\}$ and

$$S \equiv z := x; \; [x := x + 1 \| y := y + 1],$$

the literal deletion of the assignment $y := y + 1$ would yield

$$z := x; \; [x := x + 1\| \; \bullet \;]$$

with a "hole" $\bullet$ in the second component. By convention, we fill in such "holes" by *skip*. Thus in the above example we obtain

$$S' \equiv z := x; \; [x := x + 1 \| skip].$$

Like the disjoint parallelism rule, the auxiliary variables rule is appropriate for both partial and total correctness.

Example 7.3. As an application of the auxiliary variables rule we can now complete the proof of our running example. We have already proved the correctness formula (7.1); that is,

$$\{x = y\} \; z := x; \; [x := x + 1 \| y := y + 1] \; \{x = y\}$$

with the rule of disjoint parallelism. Using the auxiliary variables rule we can delete the assignment to z and obtain

$$\{x = y\} \; [x := x + 1 \| y := y + 1] \; \{x = y\},$$

the desired correctness formula.

In this proof the auxiliary variable z served to link the values of the program variables x and y. In general, auxiliary variables serve to record additional information about the course of computation in a program that is not directly expressible in terms of the program variables. This additional information then makes possible the correctness proof. In the next chapter we explain, in the setting of general parallelism, how auxiliary variables can be introduced in a systematic way.   □

Summarizing, for proofs of *partial* correctness of disjoint parallel programs we use the following proof system *PP*.

> PROOF SYSTEM *PP* :
> This system consists of the group of axioms
> and rules 1–6, 24, 25 and A2–A6.

For proofs of *total* correctness of disjoint parallel programs we use the following proof system *TP*.

> PROOF SYSTEM *TP* :
> This system consists of the group of axioms
> and rules 1–5, 7, 24, 25 and A3–A6.

Proof outlines for partial and total correctness of parallel programs are generated in a straightforward manner by the formation axioms and rules given for **while** programs together with the following formation rule:

(ix)

$$\{p_i\}\ S_i^*\ \{q_i\}, i \in \{1,\ldots,n\}$$

$$\overline{\{\bigwedge_{i=1}^n p_i\}\ [\{p_1\}\ S_1^*\ \{q_1\}\|\ldots\|\{p_n\}\ S_n^*\ \{q_n\}]\ \{\bigwedge_{i=1}^n q_i\}}.$$

Whether some variables are used as auxiliary variables is not visible from proof outlines; it has to be stated separately.

Example 7.4. The following proof outline records the proof of the correctness formula (7.1) in the proof systems *PP* and *TP*:

$$\{x = y\}$$
$$z := x;$$
$$\{x = z \wedge y = z\}$$
$$[\ \{x = z\}\ x := x + 1\ \{x = z + 1\}$$
$$\|\ \{y = z\}\ y := y + 1\ \{y = z + 1\}]$$
$$\{x = z + 1 \wedge y = z + 1\}$$
$$\{x = y\}.$$

Here z is just a normal program variable. If one wants to use it as an auxiliary variable, the corresponding application of Rule 17 has to be stated separately as in Example 7.3.   □

Soundness

We finish this section by proving soundness of the systems *PP* and *TP*. To this end we prove soundness of the new proof rules 24 and 25.

Lemma 7.8. (Disjoint Parallelism) *The disjoint parallelism rule (rule 24) is sound for partial and total correctness of disjoint parallel programs.*

Proof. Suppose the premises of the disjoint parallelism rule are true in the sense of partial correctness for some p_is, q_is and S_is, $i \in \{1, \ldots, n\}$ such that $free(p_i, q_i) \cap change(S_j) = \emptyset$ for $i \neq j$.

By the truth of the invariance axiom (Axiom A2 —see Theorem 3.7)

$$\models \{p_i\} \, S_j \, \{p_i\} \tag{7.2}$$

and

$$\models \{q_i\} \, S_j \, \{q_i\} \tag{7.3}$$

for $i, j \in \{1, \ldots, n\}$ such that $i \neq j$. By the soundness of the conjunction rule (Rule A4 —see Theorem 3.7), (7.2), (7.3) and the assumed truth of the premises of the disjoint parallelism rule,

$$\models \{\bigwedge_{i=1}^{n} p_i\} \, S_1 \, \{q_1 \wedge \bigwedge_{i=2}^{n} p_i\},$$
$$\models \{q_1 \wedge \bigwedge_{i=2}^{n} p_i\} \, S_2 \, \{q_1 \wedge q_2 \wedge \bigwedge_{i=3}^{n} p_i\},$$
$$\ldots$$
$$\models \{\bigwedge_{i=1}^{n-1} q_i \wedge p_n\} \, S_n \, \{\bigwedge_{i=1}^{n} q_i\}.$$

By the soundness of the composition rule

$$\models \{\bigwedge_{i=1}^{n} p_i\} \, S_1; \, \ldots; \, S_n \, \{\bigwedge_{i=1}^{n} q_i\};$$

so by the soundness of the sequentialization rule 23

$$\models \{\bigwedge_{i=1}^{n} p_i\} \, [S_1 \| \ldots \| S_n] \, \{\bigwedge_{i=1}^{n} q_i\}.$$

An analogous proof using the invariance rule A6 instead of the invariance axiom takes care of total correctness. $\square$

To prove soundness of the rule of auxiliary variables, we use the following lemma which allows us to insert *skip* statements into any disjoint parallel program without changing its semantics.

Lemma 7.9. (Stuttering) *Consider a disjoint parallel program S. Let S^* result from S by replacing an occurrence of a substatement T in S by "skip; T" or "T; skip". Then*

$$\mathcal{M}[\![S]\!] = \mathcal{M}[\![S^*]\!]$$

and

$$\mathcal{M}_{tot}[\![S]\!] = \mathcal{M}_{tot}[\![S^*]\!].$$

Proof. See Exercise 7.4.   □

The name of this lemma is motivated by the fact that after inserting some *skip* statement into a disjoint parallel program we obtain a program in whose computations certain states are repeated.

Lemma 7.10. (Auxiliary Variables) *The auxiliary variables rule (rule 25) is sound for partial and total correctness of disjoint parallel programs.*

Proof. Let A be a set of simple variables and S a disjoint parallel program. If $A \cap var(S)$ is a set of auxiliary variables of S, then we say that A *agrees with* S. We then denote the program obtained from S by deleting from it all the assignments to the variables of A by S_A, and the program obtained from S by replacing by *skip* all the assignments to the variables of A by $S[A := skip]$.

Suppose now that A agrees with S. Then the Boolean expressions within S and the assignments within S to the variables outside A do not contain any variables from A. Thus, if

$$< S[A := skip], \sigma > \; \rightarrow \; < S_1', \sigma_1' > \; \rightarrow \ldots \rightarrow \; < S_i', \sigma_i' > \; \rightarrow \ldots \quad (7.4)$$

is a computation of $S[A := skip]$ starting in σ, then the corresponding computation of S starting in σ

$$< S, \sigma > \; \rightarrow \; < S_1, \sigma_1 > \; \rightarrow \ldots \rightarrow \; < S_i, \sigma_i > \; \rightarrow \ldots \quad (7.5)$$

is such that for all i

$$A \text{ agrees with } S_i, \; S_i' \equiv S_i[A := skip], \; \sigma_i'[Var - A] = \sigma_i[Var - A]. \quad (7.6)$$

Conversely, if (7.5) is a computation of S starting in σ, then the corresponding computation of $S[A := skip]$ starting in σ is of the form (7.4) where (7.6) holds.

Thus, using the **mod** notation introduced in Section 2.3,

$$\mathcal{M}[\![S]\!](\sigma) = \mathcal{M}[\![S[A := skip]]\!](\sigma) \textbf{ mod } A$$

and

$$\mathcal{M}_{tot}[\![S]\!](\sigma) = \mathcal{M}_{tot}[\![S[A := skip]]\!](\sigma) \textbf{ mod } A.$$

Note that $S[A := skip]$ can be obtained from S_A by inserting some *skip* statements. Thus, by the Stuttering Lemma 7.9,

$$\mathcal{M}[\![S_A]\!](\sigma) = \mathcal{M}[\![S[A := skip]]\!](\sigma)$$

and

$$\mathcal{M}_{tot}[\![S_A]\!](\sigma) = \mathcal{M}_{tot}[\![S[A := skip]]\!](\sigma).$$

Consequently,

$$\mathcal{M}[\![S]\!](\sigma) = \mathcal{M}[\![S_A]\!](\sigma) \bmod A \qquad (7.7)$$

and

$$\mathcal{M}_{tot}[\![S]\!](\sigma) = \mathcal{M}_{tot}[\![S_A]\!](\sigma) \bmod A. \qquad (7.8)$$

By (7.7) for any assertion p

$$\mathcal{M}[\![S]\!]([\![p]\!]) = \mathcal{M}[\![S_A]\!]([\![p]\!]) \bmod A.$$

Thus, by Lemma 2.3(ii), for any assertion q such that $free(q) \cap A = \emptyset$

$$\mathcal{M}[\![S]\!]([\![p]\!]) \subseteq [\![q]\!] \text{ iff } \mathcal{M}[\![S_A]\!]([\![p]\!]) \subseteq [\![q]\!].$$

This proves the soundness of the auxiliary variables rule for partial correctness. The case of total correctness is handled analogously using (7.8) instead of (7.7). □

Corollary 7.1. (Soundness of PP and TP)

(i) *The proof system PP is sound for partial correctness of disjoint parallel programs.*

(ii) *The proof system TP is sound for total correctness of disjoint parallel programs.*

Proof. The proofs of truth and soundness of the other axioms and proof rules of *PP* and *TP* remain valid for disjoint parallel programs. These proofs rely on the Input/Output Lemma 3.3 and the Change and Access Lemma 3.4, which also hold for disjoint parallel programs (see Exercises 7.1 and 7.2). □

7.4 Case Study: Find Positive Element

We study here a problem treated in Owicki and Gries [1976a]. Consider an integer array a and a constant $N \geq 1$. The task is to write a program *FIND* that finds the smallest index $k \in \{1, \ldots, N\}$ with

$$a[k] > 0$$

if such an element of a exists; otherwise the dummy value $k = N + 1$ should be returned.

Formally, the program *FIND* should satisfy the input/output specification

{**true**}
FIND   (7.9)
$\{1 \leq k \leq N + 1 \wedge \forall (1 \leq l < k) : a[l] \leq 0 \wedge (k \leq N \rightarrow a[k] > 0)\}$

in the sense of total correctness. Clearly, we require $a \notin change(FIND)$.

To speed up the computation, *FIND* is split into two components which are executed in parallel: the first component S_1 searches for an odd index k and the second component S_2 for an even one. The component S_1 uses a variable i for the (odd) index currently being checked and a variable *oddtop* to mark the end of the search:

$$S_1 \equiv \textbf{while } i < oddtop \textbf{ do}$$
$$\textbf{if } a[i] > 0 \textbf{ then } oddtop := i$$
$$\textbf{else } i := i + 2 \textbf{ fi}$$
$$\textbf{od}.$$

The component S_2 uses variables j and *eventop* for analogous purposes:

$$S_2 \equiv \textbf{while } j < eventop \textbf{ do}$$
$$\textbf{if } a[j] > 0 \textbf{ then } eventop := j$$
$$\textbf{else } j := j + 2 \textbf{ fi}$$
$$\textbf{od}.$$

The parallel program *FIND* is then given by

$$FIND \equiv i := 1; \; j := 2; \; oddtop := N + 1; \; eventop := N + 1;$$
$$[S_1 \| S_2];$$
$$k := min(oddtop, eventop).$$

This is a version of the program *FINDPOS* studied in Owicki and Gries [1976a] where the loop conditions have been simplified to achieve disjoint parallelism. The original, more efficient, program *FINDPOS* is discussed in Section 8.6.

To prove that *FIND* satisfies its input/output specification (7.9), we first deal with its components. The first component S_1 searching for an odd index stores its result in the variable *oddtop*. Thus it should satisfy

$$\{i = 1 \wedge oddtop = N + 1\} \; S_1 \; \{q_1\} \tag{7.10}$$

in the sense of total correctness where q_1 is the following adaptation of the postcondition of (7.9):

$$q_1 \equiv \quad 1 \leq oddtop \leq N + 1$$
$$\wedge \; \forall l : (odd(l) \wedge 1 \leq l < oddtop \rightarrow a[l] \leq 0)$$
$$\wedge \; (oddtop \leq N \rightarrow a[oddtop] > 0).$$

Similarly, the second component S_2 should satisfy

$$\{j = 2 \wedge eventop = N + 1\} \; S_2 \; \{q_2\}, \tag{7.11}$$

where

$$q_2 \equiv \quad 2 \leq eventop \leq N + 1$$
$$\wedge \ \forall l : (even(l) \wedge 1 \leq l < eventop \rightarrow a[l] \leq 0)$$
$$\wedge \ (eventop \leq N \rightarrow a[eventop] > 0).$$

The notation $odd(l)$ and $even(l)$ expresses that l is odd or even, respectively.

We prove (7.10) and (7.11) using the proof system TW for total correctness of **while** programs. We start with (7.10). As usual, the main task is to find an appropriate invariant p_1 and a bound function t_1 for the loop in S_1.

As a loop invariant p_1 we choose a slight generalization of the postcondition q_1 which takes into account the loop variable i of S_1:

$$p_1 \equiv \quad 1 \leq oddtop \leq N + 1 \wedge odd(i) \wedge 1 \leq i \leq oddtop + 1$$
$$\wedge \ \forall l : (odd(l) \wedge 1 \leq l < i \rightarrow a[l] \leq 0)$$
$$\wedge \ (oddtop \leq N \rightarrow a[oddtop] > 0).$$

As a bound function t_1, we choose

$$t_1 \equiv oddtop + 1 - i.$$

Note that the invariant p_1 ensures that $t_1 \geq 0$ holds.

We verify our choices by exhibiting a proof outline for the total correctness of S_1:

```
{inv : p₁}{bd : t₁}
while i < oddtop do
      {p₁ ∧ i < oddtop}
      if a[i] > 0  then {p₁ ∧ i < oddtop ∧ a[i] > 0}
                        {    1 ≤ i ≤ N + 1 ∧ odd(i) ∧ 1 ≤ i ≤ i + 1
                         ∧ ∀l : (odd(l) ∧ 1 ≤ l < i → a[l] ≤ 0)
                         ∧ (i ≤ N → a[i] > 0)}
                        oddtop := i
                        {p₁}
               else {p₁ ∧ i < oddtop ∧ a[i] ≤ 0}
                        {    1 ≤ oddtop ≤ N + 1 ∧ odd(i + 2)
                         ∧ 1 ≤ i + 2 ≤ oddtop + 1
                         ∧ ∀l : (odd(l) ∧ 1 ≤ l < i + 2 → a[l] ≤ 0)
                         ∧ (oddtop ≤ N → a[oddtop] > 0)}
                        i := i + 2
                        {p₁}
      fi
      {p₁}
od
{p₁ ∧ oddtop ≤ i}
{q₁}.
```

It is easy to see that in this outline all pairs of subsequent assertions form valid implications as required by the consequence rule. Also, the bound function t_1 decreases with each iteration through the loop.

For the second component S_2 we choose of course a similar invariant p_2 and bound function t_2:

$$p_2 \equiv \quad 2 \le eventop \le N+1 \wedge even(j) \wedge j \le eventop+1$$
$$\wedge \; \forall l : (even(l) \wedge 1 \le l < j \rightarrow a[l] \le 0)$$
$$\wedge \; (eventop \le N \rightarrow a[eventop] > 0),$$

and

$$t_2 \equiv eventop + 1 - j.$$

The verification of (7.11) with p_2 and t_2 is symmetric to (7.10) and is omitted.

We can now apply the rule of disjoint parallelism to (7.10) and (7.11) because the corresponding disjointness conditions are satisfied. We obtain

$$\{p_1 \wedge p_2\} \tag{7.12}$$
$$[S_1 \| S_2]$$
$$\{q_1 \wedge q_2\}.$$

To complete the correctness proof, we look at the following proof outlines

$$\{\mathbf{true}\} \tag{7.13}$$
$$i := 1; \; j := 2; \; oddtop := N+1; \; eventop := N+1;$$
$$\{p_1 \wedge p_2\}$$

and

$$\{q_1 \wedge q_2\} \tag{7.14}$$
$$\{ \quad 1 \le min(oddtop, eventop) \le N+1$$
$$\wedge \; \forall(1 \le l < min(oddtop, eventop)) : a[l] \le 0$$
$$\wedge \; (min(oddtop, eventop) \le N \rightarrow a[min(oddtop, eventop)] > 0)\}$$
$$k := min(oddtop, eventop)$$
$$\{1 \le k \le N+1 \; \wedge \; \forall(1 \le l < k) : a[l] \le 0 \; \wedge \; (k \le N \rightarrow a[k] > 0)\}.$$

Applying the composition rule to (7.12), (7.13) and (7.14) yields the desired formula (7.9) about *FIND*.

7.5 Exercises

7.1. Prove the Input/Output Lemma 3.3 for disjoint parallel programs.

7.2. Prove the Change and Access Lemma 3.4 for disjoint parallel programs.

7.3. Let x and y be two distinct integer variables and let s and t be integer expressions containing some free variables. State a condition on s and t such that

$$\mathcal{M}[\![x := s; \; y := t]\!] = \mathcal{M}[\![y := t; \; x := s]\!]$$

holds.

7.4. Prove the Stuttering Lemma 7.9.

7.5. Consider a computation ξ of a disjoint parallel program $S \equiv [S_1 \| \ldots \| S_n]$. Every program occurring in a configuration of ξ is the parallel composition of n components. To distinguish among the transitions of different components, we attach labels to the transition arrow $\rightarrow$ and write

$$< U, \sigma > \xrightarrow{i} < V, \tau >$$

if $i \in \{1, \ldots, n\}$ and $< U, \sigma > \rightarrow < V, \tau >$ is a transition in ξ caused by the activation of the ith component of U. Thus the labeled arrows $\xrightarrow{i}$ are relations between configurations which are included in the overall transition relation $\rightarrow$.

Recall from Section 2.1 that for arbitrary binary relations $\rightarrow_1$ and $\rightarrow_2$ the *relational composition* $\rightarrow_1 \circ \rightarrow_2$ is defined as follows:

$$a \rightarrow_1 \circ \rightarrow_2 b \text{ if for some } c, a \rightarrow_1 c \text{ and } c \rightarrow_2 b.$$

We say that $\rightarrow_1$ and $\rightarrow_2$ *commute* if

$$\rightarrow_1 \circ \rightarrow_2 = \rightarrow_2 \circ \rightarrow_1.$$

Prove that for $i, j \in \{1, \ldots, n\}$ the transition relations $\xrightarrow{i}$ and $\xrightarrow{j}$ commute. *Hint.* Use the Change and Access Lemma 3.4.

7.6. Prove that

$$\mathcal{M}_{tot}[\![[S_1 \| \ldots \| S_n]]\!] = \mathcal{M}_{tot}[\![S_1; \; \ldots; \; S_n]\!]$$

using Exercise 7.5.

7.7. Call a program S *determinate* if for all proper states σ, $\mathcal{M}_{tot}[\![S]\!](\sigma)$ is a singleton.

Prove that if S_1, S_2 are determinate and B is a Boolean expression, then

(i) $S_1; \; S_2$ is determinate,
(ii) **if** B **then** S_1 **else** S_2 **fi** is determinate,
(iii) **while** B **do** S_1 **od** is determinate.

7.8. Provide an alternative proof of the Determinism Lemma 7.6 using Exercises 7.6 and 7.7.

7.9. Show that the correctness formula

$$\{x = y\} \; [x := x + 1 \| y := y + 1] \; \{x = y\}$$

cannot be proved in the proof systems PW +rule 24 and TW +rule 24.

7.10. Prove the correctness formula

$$\{x = y\}\ [x := x + 1 \| y := y + 1]\ \{x = y\}$$

in the proof system PW +rule A5 +rule 24.

7.6 Bibliographic Remarks

The symbol $\|$ denoting parallel composition is due to Hoare [1972]. The interleaving semantics presented here is a widely used approach to modeling parallelism. Alternatives are the semantics of *maximal parallelism* of Salwicki and Müldner [1981] and semantics based on *partial orders* among the configurations in computations —see, for example, Best [1996] and Fokkinga, Poel and Zwiers [1993].

Abstract reduction systems as used in Section 7.2 are extensively covered in Terese [2003]. The sequentialization rule (rule 23) and the disjoint parallelism rule (rule 24) were first discussed in Hoare [1975], although on the basis of an informal semantics only. The proof of the Sequentialization Lemma 7.7 is based on the fact that transitions of disjoint programs commute, see Exercises 7.5 and 7.6. Semantic commutativity of syntactically nondisjoint statements was studied by Best and Lengauer [1989].

The need for auxiliary variables in correctness proofs was first realized by Clint [1973]. A critique of auxiliary variables ranging over an unbounded domain of values can be found in Clarke [1980]. The name of the Stuttering Lemma is motivated by the considerations of Lamport [1983].

The program *FIND* studied in Section 7.4 is a disjoint parallelism version of the program *FINDPOS* due to Rosen [1974]. Its correctness proof is a variation of the corresponding proof of *FINDPOS* in Owicki and Gries [1976a].

8 Parallel Programs with Shared Variables

D ISJOINT PARALLELISM IS a rather restricted form of concurrency. In applications, concurrently operating components often share resources, such as a common database, a line printer or a data bus. Sharing is necessary when resources are too costly to have one copy for each component, as in the case of a large database. Sharing is also useful to establish communication between different components, as in the case of a data bus. This form of concurrency can be modeled by means of parallel programs with *shared variables*, variables that can be changed and read by several components.

Design and verification of parallel programs with shared variables are much more demanding than those of disjoint parallel programs. The reason is that the individual components of such a parallel program can *interfere* with each

Krzysztof R. Apt et al., *Verification of Sequential and Concurrent Programs*,
Texts in Computer Science, DOI: 10.1007/978-1-84882-745-5_8,
© Springer-Verlag London Limited 2009

other by changing the shared variables. To restrict the points of interference, we consider so-called *atomic regions* whose execution cannot be interrupted by other components.

After illustrating the problems with shared variables in Section 8.1 we introduce the syntax of this class of programs in Section 8.2. In Section 8.3 we define the semantics of these programs.

Next, we study the verification of parallel programs with shared variables. We follow here the approach of Owicki and Gries [1976a]. In Section 8.4 we deal with partial correctness. The proof rule for parallelism with shared variables includes a test of interference freedom of proof outlines for the component programs. Intuitively, interference freedom means that none of the proof outlines invalidates the (intermediate) assertions in any other proof outline.

In Section 8.5 we deal with total correctness. To prove termination of parallel programs with shared variables, we have to strengthen the notion of a proof outline for the total correctness of a component program and extend the test of interference freedom appropriately.

As a case study we prove in Section 8.6 the correctness of a more efficient version of the program *FIND* of Chapter 7 which uses shared variables.

In Section 8.7 we consider two program transformations that allow us to introduce in parallel programs more points of interference without changing the correctness properties. We demonstrate the use of these transformations in Section 8.8, where we prove as a case study partial correctness of the zero search program *ZERO*-3 from Chapter 1.

8.1 Access to Shared Variables

The input/output behavior of a disjoint parallel program can be determined by looking only at the input/output behavior of its components. This is no longer the case when shared variables are allowed. Here the program executions have to be considered.

Example 8.1. Consider the two component programs

$$S_1 \equiv x := x + 2 \text{ and } S_1' \equiv x := x + 1; \ x := x + 1.$$

In isolation both programs exhibit the same input/output behavior, since they increase the value of the variable x by 2. However, when executed in parallel with the component

$$S_2 \equiv x := 0,$$

S_1 and S_1' behave differently. Indeed, upon termination of

$$[S_1 \| S_2]$$

the value of x can be either 0 or 2 depending on whether S_1 or S_2 is executed first. On the other hand, upon termination of

$$[S_1' \| S_2]$$

the value of x can be 0, 1 or 2. The new value 1 is obtained when S_2 is executed between the two assignments of S_1'. □

The informal explanation of these difficulties clarifies that the input/output (i/o) behavior of a parallel program with shared variables critically depends on the way its components access the shared variables during its computation. Therefore any attempt at understanding parallelism with shared variables begins with the understanding of the access to shared variables. The explanation involves the notion of an atomic action.

In this context, by an *action A* we mean a statement or a Boolean expression. An action A within a component S_i of a parallel program $S \equiv [S_1 \| \ldots \| S_n]$ with shared variables is called *indivisible* or *atomic* if during its execution the other components S_j $(j \neq i)$ may not change the variables of A. Thus during the execution of A only A itself may change the variables in $var(A)$. Computer hardware guarantees that certain actions are atomic.

The computation of each component S_i can be thought of as a sequence of executions of atomic actions: at each instance of time each component is ready to execute one of its atomic actions. The components proceed *asynchronously*; that is, there is no assumption made about the relative speed at which different components execute their atomic actions.

The executions of atomic actions within two different components of a parallel program with shared variables may overlap provided these actions do not change each other's variables. But because of this restriction, their possibly overlapping execution can be modeled by executing them sequentially, in any order. This explains why asynchronous computations are modeled here by *interleaving*.

There still remains the question of what size of atomic actions can be assumed. We discuss this point in Sections 8.2 and 8.3.

8.2 Syntax

Formally, shared variables are introduced by dropping the disjointness requirement for parallel composition. Atomic regions may appear inside a parallel composition. Syntactically, these are statements enclosed in angle brackets $\langle$ and $\rangle$.

Thus we first define *component programs* as programs generated by the same clauses as those defining **while** programs in Chapter 3 together with the following clause for atomic regions:

$$S ::= \langle S_0 \rangle,$$

where S_0 is loop-free and does not contain further atomic regions.

Parallel programs with shared variables (or simply *parallel programs*) are generated by the same clauses as those defining **while** programs together with the following clause for parallel composition:

$$S ::= [S_1 \| \ldots \| S_n],$$

where $S_1, \ldots, S_n$ are component programs $(n > 1)$. Again, we do not allow nested parallelism, but we allow parallelism within sequential composition, conditional statements and **while** loops.

Intuitively, an execution of $[S_1 \| \ldots \| S_n]$ is obtained by interleaving the atomic, that is, noninterruptible, steps in the executions of the components $S_1, \ldots, S_n$. By definition,

- Boolean expressions,
- assignments and *skip*, and
- atomic regions

are all evaluated or executed as atomic steps. The reason why an atomic region is required to be loop-free, is so its execution is then guaranteed to terminate; thus atomic steps are certain to terminate. An interleaved execution of $[S_1 \| \ldots \| S_n]$ terminates if and only if the individual execution of each component terminates.

For convenience, we identify

$$\langle A \rangle \equiv A$$

if A is an *atomic statement*, that is, an assignment or *skip*. By a *normal* subprogram of a program S we mean a subprogram of S not occurring within any atomic region of S. For example, the assignment $x := 0$, the atomic region $\langle x := x + 2;\ z := 1 \rangle$ and the program $x := 0;\ \langle x := x + 2;\ z := 1 \rangle$ are the only normal subprograms of $x := 0;\ \langle x := x + 2;\ z := 1 \rangle$.

As usual, we assume that all considered programs are syntactically correct. Thus when discussing an atomic region $\langle S \rangle$ it is assumed that S is loop-free.

8.3 Semantics

The semantics of parallel programs is defined in the same way as that of disjoint parallel programs, by using transition axioms and rules (i)–(vii) introduced in Section 3.2 together with transition rule (xvii) introduced in Section 7.2. So, as in Chapter 7, parallelism is modeled here by means of interleaving. To complete the definition we still need to define the semantics of atomic regions. This is achieved by the following transition rule

$$(\text{xviii}) \quad \frac{< S, \sigma > \to^* < E, \tau >}{< \langle S \rangle, \sigma > \to < E, \tau >}.$$

This rule formalizes the intuitive meaning of atomic regions by reducing each terminating computation of the "body" S of an atomic region $\langle S \rangle$ to a one-step computation of the atomic region. This reduction prevents interference of other components in a computation of $\langle S \rangle$ within the context of a parallel composition.

As in Section 7.2 the following obvious lemma holds.

Lemma 8.1. (Absence of Blocking) *Every configuration $< S, \sigma >$ with $S \not\equiv E$ and a proper state σ has a successor configuration in the transition relation $\to$.*

This leads us, as in Section 7.2, to two semantics of parallel programs, partial correctness semantics $\mathcal{M}$ and total correctness semantics $\mathcal{M}_{tot}$, defined as before.

In the informal Section 8.1 we have already indicated that parallel programs with shared variables can exhibit nondeterminism. Here we state this fact more precisely.

Lemma 8.2. (Bounded Nondeterminism) *Let S be a parallel program and σ a proper state. Then $\mathcal{M}_{tot}[\![S]\!](\sigma)$ is either finite or it contains $\bot$.*

This lemma stands in sharp contrast to the Determinism Lemma 7.6 for disjoint parallelism. The proof combines a simple observation on the transition relation $\rightarrow$ with a fundamental result about trees due to König [1927] (see also Knuth [1968,page 381]).

Lemma 8.3. (Finiteness) *For every parallel program S and proper state σ, the configuration $< S, \sigma >$ has only finitely many successors in the relation $\rightarrow$.*

Proof. The lemma follows immediately from the shape of the transition axioms and rules (i) – (xviii) defining the transition relation.   □

Lemma 8.4. (König's Lemma) *Any finitely branching tree is either finite or it has an infinite path.*

Proof. Consider an infinite, but finitely branching tree T. We construct an infinite path in T, that is, an infinite sequence

$$\xi : N_0 \ N_1 \ N_2 \ \ldots$$

of nodes so that, for each $i \geq 0$, N_{i+1} is a child of N_i. We construct ξ by induction on i so that every N_i is the root of an infinite subtree of T.

Induction basis : $i = 0$. As node N_0 we take the root of T.

Induction step : $i \longrightarrow i + 1$. By induction hypothesis, N_i is the root of an infinite subtree of T. Since T is finitely branching, there are only finitely many children $M_1, \ldots, M_n$ of N_i. Thus at least one of these children, say M_j, is a root of an infinite subtree of T. Then we choose M_j as node N_{i+1}. This completes the inductive definition of ξ.   □

We now turn to the

Proof of Lemma 8.2. By Lemma 8.3, the set of computation sequences of S starting in σ can be represented as a *finitely branching* computation tree. By König's Lemma 8.4, this tree is either finite or it contains an infinite path. Clearly, finiteness of the computation tree implies finiteness of $\mathcal{M}_{tot}[\![S]\!](\sigma)$, and by definition an infinite path in the tree means that S can diverge from σ, thus yielding $\perp \in \mathcal{M}_{tot}[\![S]\!](\sigma)$.   □

Atomicity

According to the given transition rules, our semantics of parallelism assumes that Boolean expressions, assignments, *skip* and atomic regions are evaluated or executed as atomic actions. But is this assumption guaranteed by conventional computer hardware? The answer is no. Usually, we may assume only that the hardware guarantees the atomicity of a *single critical reference*, that is, an exclusive read or write access to a single shared variable, either a simple one or a subscripted one.

For illustration, consider the program

$$S \equiv [x := y \| y := x].$$

Under the single reference assumption, executing the assignment $x := y$ requires two atomic variable accesses: first y is read and then x is changed (to the value of y). Symmetrically, the same holds for $y := x$. Thus executing S in a state with $x = 1$ and $y = 2$ can result in the following three final states:

(i) $x = y = 2$,
(ii) $x = y = 1$,
(iii) $x = 2$ and $y = 1$.

Note that (iii) is obtained if both x and y are first read and then changed. This result is impossible in our semantics of parallelism where the whole assignment is treated as one atomic action.

Thus, in general, our semantics of parallelism does not model the reality of conventional hardware. Fortunately, this is not such a severe shortcoming as it might seem at first sight. The reason is that by using additional variables every component program can be transformed into an equivalent one where each atomic action contains exactly one shared variable access. For example, the program S above can be transformed into

$$S' \equiv [AC_1 := y; \ x := AC_1 \| AC_2 := x; \ y := AC_2].$$

The additional variables AC_i represent local accumulators as used in conventional computers to execute assignments. Now our operational semantics of S' mirrors exactly its execution on a conventional computer. Indeed, for S', the final states (i)–(iii) above are all possible.

Summarizing, in our semantics of parallelism the grain of atomicity was chosen to yield a simple definition. This definition is not realistic, but for programs all of whose atomic actions contain at most one shared variable access, this definition models exactly their execution on conventional computer hardware. Moreover, in correctness proofs of parallel programs it is most convenient not to be confined to the grain of atomicity as provided by real computers, but to work with *virtual atomicity*, freely defined by atomic regions $\langle S_0 \rangle$. Generally speaking, we can observe the following dichotomy:

• The smaller the grain of atomicity the more realistic the program.
• The larger the grain of atomicity the easier the correctness proof of the program.

Further elaboration of this observation can be found at the end of Section 8.4 and in Sections 8.7 and 8.8.

8.4 Verification: Partial Correctness

Component Programs

Partial correctness of component programs is proved by using the rules of the
system PW for the partial correctness of **while** programs plus the following
rule dealing with atomic regions:

RULE 26: ATOMIC REGION

$$\frac{\{p\}\ S\ \{q\}}{\{p\}\ \langle S \rangle\ \{q\}}$$

This rule is sound for partial (and total) correctness of component programs
because atomicity has no influence on the input/output behavior of individual
component programs.

Proof outlines for partial correctness of component programs are generated
by the formation rules (i)–(vii) given for **while** programs plus the following
one.

(x)

$$\frac{\{p\}\ S^*\ \{q\}}{\{p\}\ \langle S^* \rangle\ \{q\}}$$

where as usual S^* stands for an annotated version of S.

A proof outline $\{p\}\ S^*\ \{q\}$ for partial correctness is called *standard* if
within S^* every *normal* subprogram T is preceded by exactly one assertion,
called $pre(T)$, and there are no further assertions within S^*. In particular,
there are no assertions within atomic regions. The reason for this omission is
because the underlying semantics of parallel programs with shared variables
causes atomic regions to be executed as indivisible actions. This is explained
more fully when we discuss the notion of interference freedom.

For **while** programs the connection between standard proof outlines and
computations is stated in the Strong Soundness Theorem 3.3. We need here
an analogous result. To this end we use the notation $\mathbf{at}(T, S)$ introduced in
Definition 3.7, but with the understanding that T is a normal subprogram of
a component program S. Note that no additional clause dealing with atomic
regions is needed in this definition.

Lemma 8.5. (Strong Soundness for Component Programs) *Consider
a component program S with a standard proof outline $\{p\}\ S^*\ \{q\}$ for partial
correctness. Suppose*

$$< S, \sigma > \ \to^* \ < R, \tau >$$

*holds for a proper state σ satisfying p, a program R and a proper state τ.
Then*

- *either $R \equiv \mathbf{at}(T, S)$ for some normal subprogram T of S and $\tau \models pre(T)$*
- *or $R \equiv E$ and $\tau \models q$.*

Proof. Removing all brackets $\langle$ and $\rangle$ from S and the proof outline $\{p\}\ S^*\ \{q\}$ yields a **while** program S_1 with a proof outline $\{p\}\ S_1^*\ \{q\}$ for partial correctness. Inserting appropriate assertions in front of the subprograms of S_1 that are nonnormal subprograms of S yields a standard proof outline $\{p\}\ S_1^{**}\ \{q\}$ for partial correctness. By transition rule (xiv) defining the semantics of atomic regions, for any program R

$$< S, \sigma > \to^* < R, \tau > \quad \text{iff} \quad < S_1, \sigma > \to^* < R_1, \tau >,$$

where R_1 is obtained from R by removing from it all brackets $\langle$ and $\rangle$. The claim now follows by the Strong Soundness Theorem 3.3.   □

This shows that the introduction of atomic regions leads to a straightforward extension of the proof theory from **while** programs to component programs.

No Compositionality of Input/Output Behavior

Much more complicated is the treatment of parallel composition. As already shown in Example 8.1, the input/output behavior of a parallel program cannot be determined solely from the input/output behavior of its components. Let us make this observation more precise by examining correctness formulas for the programs of Example 8.1.

In isolation the component programs $x := x + 2$ and $x := x + 1;\ x := x + 1$ exhibit the same input/output behavior. Indeed, for all assertions p and q we have

$$\models \{p\}\ x := x + 2\ \{q\} \quad \text{iff} \quad \models \{p\}\ x := x + 1;\ x := x + 1\ \{q\}.$$

However, the parallel composition with $x := 0$ leads to a different input/output behavior. On the one hand,

$$\models \{\mathbf{true}\}\ [x := x + 2 \| x := 0]\ \{x = 0 \lor x = 2\}$$

holds but

$$\not\models \{\mathbf{true}\}\ [x := x + 1;\ x := x + 1 \| x := 0]\ \{x = 0 \lor x = 2\}$$

since here the final value of x might also be 1.

We can summarize this observation as follows: the input/output behavior of parallel programs with shared variables is *not compositional*; that is, there is no proof rule that takes input/output specifications $\{p_i\}\ S_i\ \{q_i\}$ of component programs S_i as premises and yields the input/output specification $\{\bigwedge_{i=1}^{n} p_i\}$ $[S_1\|\ldots\|S_n]$ $\{\bigwedge_{i=1}^{n} q_i\}$ for the parallel program as a conclusion under some nontrivial conditions. Recall that this is possible for disjoint parallel programs —see the sequentialization rule 23.

For parallel programs $[S_1\|\ldots\|S_n]$ with shared variables we have to investigate *how* the input/output behavior is affected by each action in the computations of the component programs S_i.

Parallel Composition: Interference Freedom

To reason about parallel programs with shared variables we follow the approach of Owicki and Gries [1976a] and consider proof outlines instead of correctness formulas. By the Strong Soundness for Component Programs Lemma 8.5, the intermediate assertions of proof outlines provide information about the course of the computation: whenever the control of a component program in a given computation reaches a control point annotated by an assertion, this assertion is true.

Unfortunately, this strong soundness property of proof outlines no longer holds when the component programs are executed in parallel. Indeed, consider the proof outlines

$$\{x = 0\}\; x := x + 2\; \{x = 2\}$$

and

$$\{x = 0\}\; x := 0\; \{\textbf{true}\}$$

and a computation of the parallel program $[x := x + 2 \| x := 0]$ starting in a state satisfying $x = 0$. Then the postcondition $x = 2$ does not necessarily hold after $x := x + 2$ has terminated because the assignment $x := 0$ could have reset the variable x to 0.

The reason is that the above proof outlines do not take into account a possible interaction, or as we say, *interference*, among components. This brings us to the following important notion of *interference freedom* due to Owicki and Gries [1976a].

Definition 8.1. (Interference Freedom: Partial Correctness)

(i) Let S be a component program. Consider a standard proof outline $\{p\}\; S^*\; \{q\}$ for partial correctness and a statement R with the precondition $pre(R)$. We say that R *does not interfere with* $\{p\}\; S^*\; \{q\}$ if

- for all assertions r in $\{p\}\; S^*\; \{q\}$ the correctness formula

$$\{r \wedge pre(R)\}\; R\; \{r\}$$

holds in the sense of partial correctness.

(ii) Let $[S_1\|\dots\|S_n]$ be a parallel program. Standard proof outlines $\{p_i\}\ S_i^*\ \{q_i\}$, $i \in \{1,\dots,n\}$, for partial correctness are called *interference free* if no normal assignment or atomic region of a program S_i interferes with the proof outline $\{p_j\}\ S_j^*\ \{q_j\}$ of another program S_j where $i \neq j$. □

Thus interference freedom means that the execution of atomic steps of one component program never falsifies the assertions used in the proof outline of any other component program.

With these preparations we can state the following conjunction rule for general parallel composition.

RULE 27: PARALLELISM WITH SHARED VARIABLES

The standard proof outlines $\{p_i\}\ S_i^*\ \{q_i\}$, $i \in \{1,\dots,n\}$, are interference free

$$\{\bigwedge_{i=1}^{n} p_i\}\ [S_1\|\dots\|S_n]\ \{\bigwedge_{i=1}^{n} q_i\}$$

Note that the conclusion in this rule is the same as that in the disjoint parallelism rule 24. However, its premises are now much more complicated. Instead of simply checking the correctness formulas $\{p_i\}\ S_i\ \{q_i\}$ for disjointness, their *proofs* as recorded in the standard proof outlines $\{p_i\}\ S_i^*\ \{q_i\}$ must be tested for interference freedom. The restriction to *standard* proof outlines reduces the amount of testing to a minimal number of assertions.

The test of interference freedom makes correctness proofs for parallel programs more difficult than for sequential programs. For example, in the case of two component programs of length ℓ_1 and ℓ_2, proving interference freedom requires proving $\ell_1 \times \ell_2$ additional correctness formulas. In practice, however, most of these formulas are trivially satisfied because they check an assignment or atomic region R against an assertion that is disjoint from R.

Example 8.2. As a first application of the parallelism with shared variables rule let us prove partial correctness of the parallel programs considered in Section 8.1.

(i) First we consider the program $[x := x + 2 \| x := 0]$. The standard proof outlines

$$\{x = 0\}\ x := x + 2\ \{x = 2\}$$

and

$$\{\textbf{true}\}\ x := 0\ \{x = 0\}$$

are obviously correct, but they are not interference free. For instance, the assertion $x = 0$ is not preserved under the execution of $x := x + 2$. Similarly, $x = 2$ is not preserved under the execution of $x := 0$.

However, by weakening the postconditions, we obtain standard proof outlines

$$\{x = 0\}\ x := x + 2\ \{x = 0 \lor x = 2\}$$

and

$$\{\textbf{true}\}\ x := 0\ \{x = 0 \lor x = 2\}$$

which are interference free. For example, the assignment $x := x + 2$ of the first proof outline does not interfere with the postcondition of the second proof outline because

$$\{x = 0 \land (x = 0 \lor x = 2)\}\ x := x + 2\ \{x = 0 \lor x = 2\}$$

holds. Thus the parallelism with shared variables rule yields

$$\{x = 0\}\ [x := x + 2 \| x := 0]\ \{x = 0 \lor x = 2\}.$$

(ii) Next we study the program $[x := x + 1;\ x := x + 1 \| x := 0]$. Consider the following proof outlines:

$$\{x = 0\}$$
$$x := x + 1;$$
$$\{x = 0 \lor x = 1\}$$
$$x := x + 1$$
$$\{\textbf{true}\}$$

and

$$\{\textbf{true}\}\ x := 0\ \{x = 0 \lor x = 1 \lor x = 2\}.$$

To establish their interference freedom seven interference freedom checks need to be made. All of them obviously hold. This yields by the parallelism with shared variables rule

$$\{x = 0\}\ [x := x + 1;\ x := x + 1 \| x := 0]\ \{x = 0 \lor x = 1 \lor x = 2\}.$$

(iii) Finally, we treat the first component in the parallel program from the previous example as an atomic region. Then the proof outlines

$$\{x = 0\}\ \langle x := x + 1;\ x := x + 1 \rangle\ \{\textbf{true}\}$$

and

$$\{\textbf{true}\}\ x := 0\ \{x = 0 \lor x = 2\}$$

are clearly interference free. This proves by the parallelism with shared variables rule the correctness formula

$$\{x = 0\}\ [\langle x := x + 1;\ x := x + 1 \rangle \| x := 0]\ \{x = 0 \lor x = 2\}.$$

Thus when executed in parallel with $x := 0$, the atomic region $\langle x := x + 1;\ x := x + 1 \rangle$ behaves exactly like the single assignment $x := x + 2$.   □

Auxiliary Variables Needed

However, once a slightly stronger claim about the program from Example 8.2(i) is considered, the parallelism with shared variables rule 27 becomes too weak to reason about partial correctness.

Lemma 8.6. (Incompleteness) *The correctness formula*

$$\{\mathbf{true}\}\ [x := x + 2 \| x := 0]\ \{x = 0 \lor x = 2\} \tag{8.1}$$

is not a theorem in the proof system PW + rule 27.

Proof. Suppose by contradiction that this correctness formula can be proved in the system *PW* + rule 27. Then, for some interference free proof outlines

$$\{p_1\}\ x := x + 2\ \{q_1\},$$

and

$$\{p_2\}\ x := 0\ \{q_2\},$$

the implications

$$\mathbf{true} \to p_1 \land p_2 \tag{8.2}$$

and

$$q_1 \land q_2 \to x = 0 \lor x = 2 \tag{8.3}$$

hold. Then by (8.2) both p_1 and p_2 are true.

Thus $\{\mathbf{true}\}\ x := x + 2\ \{q_1\}$ holds, so by the Soundness Theorem 3.1 the assertion $q_1[x := x + 2]$ is true. Since x ranges over all integers,

$$q_1 \tag{8.4}$$

itself is true. Also, $\{\mathbf{true}\}\ x := 0\ \{q_2\}$ implies by the Soundness Theorem 3.1

$$q_2[x := 0]. \tag{8.5}$$

Moreover, by interference freedom $\{\mathbf{true} \land q_2\}\ x := x + 2\ \{q_2\}$ which gives

$$q_2 \to q_2[x := x + 2]. \tag{8.6}$$

By induction (8.5) and (8.6) imply

$$\forall x : (x \geq 0 \land even(x) \to q_2). \tag{8.7}$$

Now by (8.3) and (8.4) we obtain from (8.7)

$$\forall x : (x \geq 0 \land even(x) \to x = 0 \lor x = 2)$$

which gives a contradiction. □

Summarizing, in any interference free proof outline of the above form, the postcondition q_2 of $x := 0$ would hold for every even $x \geq 0$, whereas it should hold only for $x = 0$ or $x = 2$. The reason for this mismatch is that we cannot express in terms of the variable x the fact that the first component $x := x + 2$ should still be executed.

What is needed here is the rule of auxiliary variables (rule 25) introduced in Chapter 7.

Example 8.3. We now prove the correctness formula (8.1) using additionally the rule of auxiliary variables. The proof makes use of an auxiliary Boolean variable "*done*" indicating whether the assignment $x := x + 2$ has been executed. This leads us to consider the correctness formula

$$
\begin{aligned}
&\{\mathbf{true}\} \\
&done := \mathbf{false}; \hspace{5cm} (8.8) \\
&[\langle x := x + 2; \ done := \mathbf{true}\rangle \| x := 0] \\
&\{x = 0 \lor x = 2\}.
\end{aligned}
$$

Since $\{done\}$ is indeed a set of auxiliary variables of the extended program, the rule of auxiliary variables allows us to deduce (8.1) whenever (8.8) has been proved.

To prove (8.8), we consider the following standard proof outlines for the components of the parallel composition:

$$\{\neg done\}\ \langle x := x + 2;\ done := \mathbf{true}\rangle\ \{\mathbf{true}\} \hspace{2cm} (8.9)$$

and

$$\{\mathbf{true}\}\ x := 0\ \{(x = 0 \lor x = 2) \land (\neg done \rightarrow x = 0)\}. \hspace{1cm} (8.10)$$

Note that the atomic region rule 26 is used in the proof of (8.9).

It is straightforward to check that (8.9) and (8.10) are interference free. To this purpose four correctness formulas need to be verified. For example, the proof that the atomic region in (8.9) does not interfere with the postcondition of (8.10) is as follows:

$$
\begin{aligned}
&\{(x = 0 \lor x = 2) \land (\neg done \rightarrow x = 0) \land \neg done\} \\
&\{x = 0\} \\
&\langle x := x + 2;\ done := \mathbf{true}\rangle \\
&\{x = 2 \land done\} \\
&\{(x = 0 \lor x = 2) \land (\neg done \rightarrow x = 0)\}.
\end{aligned}
$$

The remaining three cases are in fact trivial. The parallelism with shared variables rule 27 applied to (8.9) and (8.10) and the consequence rule now yield

$$
\begin{aligned}
&\{\neg done\} \\
&[\langle x := x + 2;\ done := \mathbf{true}\rangle \| x := 0] \hspace{3cm} (8.11) \\
&\{x = 0 \lor x = 2\}.
\end{aligned}
$$

On the other hand, the correctness formula

$$\{\textbf{true}\}\ done := \textbf{false}\ \{\neg done\} \tag{8.12}$$

obviously holds. Thus, applying the composition rule to (8.11) and (8.12) yields (8.8) as desired. □

The above correctness proof is more complicated than expected. In particular, the introduction of the auxiliary variable *done* required some insight into the execution of the given program. The use of *done* brings up two questions: how do we find appropriate auxiliary variables? Is there perhaps a systematic way of introducing them? The answer is affirmative. Following the lines of Lamport [1977], one can show that it is sufficient to introduce a separate *program counter* for each component of a parallel program. A program counter is an auxiliary variable that has a different value in front of every substatement in a component. It thus mirrors exactly the control flow in the component. In most applications, however, only partial information about the control flow is sufficient. This can be represented by a few suitable auxiliary variables such as the variable *done* above.

It is interesting to note that the atomicity of $\langle x := x + 2;\ done := \textbf{true}\rangle$ is decisive for the correctness proof in Example 8.3. If the sequence of the two assignments were interruptable, we would have to consider the proof outlines

$$\{\neg done\}\ x := x + 2;\ \{\neg done\}\ done := \textbf{true}\ \{\textbf{true}\}$$

and

$$\{\textbf{true}\}\ x := 0\ \{(x = 0 \lor x = 2) \land (\neg done \to x = 0)\}$$

which are not interference free. For example, the assignment $x := x + 2$ interferes with the postcondition of $x := 0$. The introduction of the atomic region $\langle x := x + 2;\ done := \textbf{true}\rangle$ is a typical example of *virtual atomicity* mentioned in Section 8.3: this atomic region is not a part of the original program; it appears only in its correctness proof.

Summarizing, to prove partial correctness of parallel programs with shared variables, we use the following proof system *PSV*:

PROOF SYSTEM *PSV* :
This system consists of the group of axioms
and rules 1–6, 25–27 and A2–A6.

Soundness

We now prove soundness of PSV for partial correctness. Since we have already noted the soundness of the atomic region rule 26, we concentrate here on the soundness proofs of the auxiliary variables rule 25 and the parallelism with shared variables rule 27.

Lemma 8.7. (Auxiliary Variables) *The rule of auxiliary variables (rule 25) is sound for partial (and total) correctness of parallel programs.*

Proof. The proof of Lemma 7.10 stating soundness of rule 25 for disjoint parallel programs does not depend on the assumption of disjoint parallelism. See also Exercise 8.3.   □

To prove the soundness of the parallelism with shared variables rule 27 for partial correctness we first show a stronger property: considering simultaneously the interference free standard proof outlines $\{p_1\}\, S_1^*\, \{q_1\}$, $...,\{p_n\}\, S_n^*\, \{q_n\}$ yields a valid annotation for the parallel program $[S_1\|...\|S_n]$. More precisely, in a computation of $[S_1\|...\|S_n]$ starting in a state satisfying $\bigwedge_{i=1}^{n} p_i$, whenever the control in a component S_i reaches a point annotated by an assertion, this assertion is true. This is the strong soundness property for parallel programs.

Lemma 8.8. (Strong Soundness for Parallel Programs) *Let $\{p_i\}\, S_i^*\, \{q_i\}$, $i \in \{1,\ldots,n\}$, be interference free standard proof outlines for partial correctness for component programs S_i. Suppose that*

$$< [S_1\|...\|S_n], \sigma > \;\to^*\; < [R_1\|...\|R_n], \tau >$$

for some state σ satisfying $\bigwedge_{i=1}^{n} p_i$, some component programs R_i with $i \in \{1,\ldots,n\}$ and some state τ. Then for $j \in \{1,\ldots,n\}$

- *if $R_j \equiv \mathbf{at}(T, S_j)$ for a normal subprogram T of S_j, then $\tau \models pre(T)$;*
- *if $R_j \equiv E$ then $\tau \models q_j$.*

In particular, whenever

$$< [S_1\|...\|S_n], \sigma > \;\to^*\; < E, \tau >$$

then $\tau \models \bigwedge_{i=1}^{n} q_i$.

Proof. Fix $j \in \{1,\ldots,n\}$. It is easy to show that either $R_j \equiv \mathbf{at}(T, S_j)$ for a normal subprogram T of S_j or $R_j \equiv E$ (see Exercise 8.4). In the first case let r stand for $pre(T)$ and in the second case let r stand for q_j. We need to show $\tau \models r$.

The proof is by induction on the length ℓ of the transition sequence

$$< [S_1\|...\|S_n], \sigma > \;\to^*\; < [R_1\|...\|R_n], \tau > .$$

Induction basis : $\ell = 0$. Then $p_j \to r$ and $\sigma = \tau$; thus $\sigma \models p_j$ and hence $\tau \models r$.

Induction step : $\ell \longrightarrow \ell + 1$. Then for some R'_k and τ'

$$< [S_1\|\ldots\|S_n], \sigma > \;\to^*\; < [R_1\|\ldots\|R'_k\|\ldots\|R_n], \tau' >$$
$$\to\; < [R_1\|\ldots\|R_k\|\ldots\|R_n], \tau >;$$

that is, the last step in the transition sequence was performed by the kth component. Thus

$$< R'_k, \tau' > \;\to\; < R_k, \tau > .$$

Two cases naturally arise.

Case 1 $j = k$.

Then an argument analogous to the one given in the proof of the Strong Soundness Theorem 3.3 and the Strong Soundness for Component Programs Lemma 8.5 shows that $\tau \models r$.

Case 2 $j \neq k$.

By the induction hypothesis $\tau' \models r$. If the last step in the computation consists of an evaluation of a Boolean expression, then $\tau \doteq \tau'$ and consequently $\tau \models r$.

Otherwise the last step in the computation consists of an execution of an assignment A or an atomic region A. Thus

$$< A, \tau' > \;\to\; < E, \tau > .$$

By the induction hypothesis, $\tau' \models pre(A)$. Thus $\tau' \models r \wedge pre(A)$. By interference freedom and the Soundness Theorem 3.1,

$$\models \{r \wedge pre(A)\} \; A \; \{r\}.$$

Thus $\tau \models r$.   □

Corollary 8.1. (Parallelism with Shared Variables) *The parallelism with shared variables rule 27 is sound for partial correctness of parallel programs.*

Corollary 8.2. (Soundness of PSV) *The proof system PSV is sound for partial correctness of parallel programs.*

Proof. Follows by the same argument as the one given in the proof of the Soundness Corollary 7.1.   □

8.5 Verification: Total Correctness

Component Programs

Total correctness of component programs can be proved by using the proof system TW for the total correctness of **while** programs together with the atomic region rule 26 for atomic regions introduced in Section 8.4. This rule is clearly sound for total correctness.

However, somewhat unexpectedly, this approach leads to a definition of proof outlines for total correctness that is too weak for our purposes. To ensure that, as a next step, total correctness of parallel programs can be proved by using interference free proof outlines for total correctness of the component programs, we must strengthen the premises of the formation rule (viii) of Chapter 3 defining the proof outlines for total correctness of a **while** loop:

$$\frac{\begin{array}{l} \{p \wedge B\}\ S^*\ \{p\}, \\ \{p \wedge B \wedge t = z\}\ S^{**}\ \{t < z\}, \\ p \rightarrow t \geq 0 \end{array}}{\{\textbf{inv} : p\}\{\textbf{bd} : t\}\ \textbf{while}\ B\ \textbf{do}\ \{p \wedge B\}\ S^*\ \{p\}\ \textbf{od}\ \{p \wedge \neg B\}}$$

where t is an integer expression and z is an integer variable not occurring in p, t, B or S^{**}. We clarify this point at the end of this section.

In the premises of this rule we separated proofs outlines involving S^* and S^{**} for the facts that the assertion p is kept invariant and that the bound function t decreases, but only the proof S^* for the invariant p is recorded in the proof outline of the **while** loop. In the context of parallel programs it is possible that components interfere with the termination proofs of other components. To eliminate this danger we now strengthen the definition of a proof outline for total correctness and require that in proof outlines of loops **while** B **do** S **od** the bound function t is such that

(i) all normal assignments and atomic regions inside S decrease t or leave it unchanged,
(ii) on each syntactically possible path through S at least one normal assignment or atomic region decreases t.

By a *path* we mean here a possibly empty finite sequence of normal assignments and atomic regions. Intuitively, for a sequential component program S, $path(S)$ stands for the set of all syntactically possible paths through the component program S, where each path is identified with the sequence of normal assignments and atomic regions lying on it. This intuition is not completely correct because for **while**-loops we assume that they immediately terminate.

The idea is that if the bound function t is to decrease along every syntactically possible path while never being increased, then it suffices to assume that every **while** loop is exited immediately. Indeed, if along such "shorter" paths the decrease of the bound function t is guaranteed, then it is also guaranteed along the "longer" paths that do take into account the loop bodies.

The formal definition of $path(S)$ is as follows.

Definition 8.2. For a sequential component S, we define the set $path(S)$ by induction on S:

- $path(skip) = \{\varepsilon\}$,
- $path(u := t) = \{u := t\}$,
- $path(\langle S \rangle) = \{\langle S \rangle\}$,
- $path(S_1; \ S_2) = path(S_1) \ ; \ path(S_2)$,
- $path(\textbf{if } B \textbf{ then } S_1 \textbf{ else } S_2 \textbf{ fi}) = path(S_1) \cup path(S_2)$,
- $path(\textbf{while } B \textbf{ do } S \textbf{ od}) = \{\varepsilon\}$. □

In the above definition ε denotes the empty sequence and sequential composition $\pi_1; \ \pi_2$ of paths π_1 and π_2 is lifted to sets Π_1, Π_2 of paths by putting

$$\Pi_1; \ \Pi_2 = \{\pi_1; \ \pi_2 \mid \pi_1 \in \Pi_1 \text{ and } \pi_2 \in \Pi_2\}.$$

For any path π we have $\pi; \ \varepsilon = \varepsilon; \ \pi = \pi$.

We can now formulate the revised definition of a proof outline.

Definition 8.3. (Proof Outline: Total Correctness) Proof outlines and standard proof outlines for the total correctness of component programs are generated by the same formation axioms and rules as those used for defining (standard) proof outlines for the partial correctness of component programs. The only exception is the formation rule (v) dealing with **while** loops which is replaced by the following formation rule.

(xi)

> (1) $\{p \wedge B\} \ S^* \ \{p\}$ is standard,
> (2) $\{pre(R) \wedge t = z\} \ R \ \{t \leq z\}$ for every normal
>   assignment and atomic region R within S,
> (3) for each path $\pi \in path(S)$ there exists
>   a normal assignment or atomic region R in π
>   such that
> $\{pre(R) \wedge t = z\} \ R \ \{t < z\}$,
> (4) $p \rightarrow t \geq 0$
>
> ―――――――――――――――――――――――――――――――――――――
> $\{\textbf{inv} : p\}\{\textbf{bd} : t\} \textbf{ while } B \textbf{ do } \{p \wedge B\} \ S^* \ \{p\} \textbf{ od } \{p \wedge \neg B\}$

where t is an integer expression and z is an integer variable not occurring in p, t, B or S^*, and where $pre(R)$ stands for the assertion preceding R in the standard proof outline $\{p \wedge B\} \ S^* \ \{p\}$ for total correctness. □

Note that in premise (1) formation rule (xi) expects a standard proof outline for total correctness but in its conclusion it produces a "non-standard"
proof outline for the **while** loop. To obtain a standard proof outline in the
conclusion, it suffices to remove from it the assertions $p \land B$ and p surround-
ing S^*.

Convention In this and the next chapter we always refer to proof outlines
that satisfy the stronger conditions of Definition 8.3.   □

Parallel Composition: Interference Freedom

The total correctness of a parallel program is proved by considering interference free standard proof outlines for the total correctness of its component
programs. In the definition of interference freedom both the assertions and
the bound functions appearing in the proof outlines must now be tested. This
is done as follows.

Definition 8.4. (Interference Freedom: Total Correctness)

(1) Let S be a component program. Consider a standard proof outline
$\{p\}\ S^*\ \{q\}$ for total correctness and a statement A with the precondition $pre(A)$. We say that A *does not interfere* with $\{p\}\ S^*\ \{q\}$ if the
following two conditions are satisfied:

(i) for all assertions r in $\{p\}\ S^*\ \{q\}$ the correctness formula

$$\{r \land pre(A)\}\ A\ \{r\}$$

holds in the sense of total correctness,
(ii) for all bound functions t in $\{p\}\ S^*\ \{q\}$ the correctness formula

$$\{pre(A) \land t = z\}\ A\ \{t \leq z\}$$

holds in the sense of total correctness, where z is an integer variable
not occurring in A, t or $pre(A)$.

(2) Let $[S_1\|\ldots\|S_n]$ be a parallel program. Standard proof outlines
$\{p_i\}\ S_i^*\ \{q_i\}$, $i \in \{1,\ldots,n\}$, for total correctness are called *interference
free* if no normal assignment or atomic region A of a component program
S_i interferes with the proof outline $\{p_j\}\ S_j^*\ \{q_j\}$ of another component
program S_j where $i \neq j$.   □

Thus interference freedom for total correctness means that the execution
of atomic steps of one component program neither falsifies the assertions

(condition (i)) nor increases the bound functions (condition (ii)) used in the proof outline of any other component program.

Note that the correctness formulas of condition (ii) have the same form as the ones considered in the second premise of formation rule (xi) for proof outlines for total correctness of **while** loops. In particular, the value of bound functions may drop during the execution of other components.

As in the case of partial correctness, normal assignments and atomic regions need not be checked for interference freedom against assertions and bound functions from which they are disjoint.

By referring to this extended notion of interference freedom, we may reuse the parallelism with shared variables rule 27 for proving total correctness of parallel programs. Altogether we now use the following proof system *TSV* for *total* correctness of parallel programs with *shared* variables.

> PROOF SYSTEM *TSV* :
> This system consists of the group of axioms
> and rules 1–5, 7, 25–27 and A3–A6.

Example 8.4. As a first application of this proof system let us prove that the program

$$S \equiv [\textbf{while } x > 2 \textbf{ do } x := x - 2 \textbf{ od} \| x := x - 1]$$

satisfies the correctness formula

$$\{x > 0 \land even(x)\} \ S \ \{x = 1\}$$

in the sense of total correctness. We use the following standard proof outlines for the components of S:

> $\{\textbf{inv} : x > 0\}\{\textbf{bd} : x\}$
> **while** $x > 2$ **do**
> $\quad \{x > 2\}$
> $\quad x := x - 2$
> **od**
> $\{x = 1 \lor x = 2\}$

and

$$\{even(x)\} \ x := x - 1 \ \{odd(x)\}.$$

Here $even(x)$ and $odd(x)$ express that x is an even or odd integer value, respectively. These proof outlines satisfy the requirements of Definition 8.4: the only syntactic path in the loop body consists of the assignment $x := x - 2$, and the bound function $t \equiv x$ gets decreased by executing this assignment.

Interference freedom of the proof outlines is easily shown. For example,

$$\{x > 2 \land even(x)\} \ x := x - 1 \ \{x > 2\},$$

holds because of $x > 2 \wedge even(x) \rightarrow x > 3$. Thus the parallelism with shared variables rule 27 used now for total correctness is applicable and yields the desired correctness result.   □

Soundness

Finally, we prove soundness of the system *TSV* for total correctness. To this end we first establish the following lemma.

Lemma 8.9. (Termination) *Let* $\{p_i\}$ S_i^* $\{q_i\}$, $i \in \{1, \ldots, n\}$, *be interference free standard proof outlines for total correctness for component programs* S_i. *Then*

$$\perp \notin \mathcal{M}_{tot}[\![S_1\|\ldots\|S_n]\!]([\![\bigwedge_{i=1}^{n} p_i]\!]).$$ (8.13)

Proof. Suppose that the converse holds. Consider an infinite computation ξ of $[S_1\|\ldots\|S_n]$ starting in a state σ satisfying $\bigwedge_{i=1}^{n} p_i$. For some loop **while** B **do** S **od** within a component S_i infinitely many configurations in ξ are of the form

$$< [T_1\|\ldots\|T_n], \tau >$$ (8.14)

such that $T_i \equiv \mathbf{at}(\mathbf{while}\ B\ \mathbf{do}\ S\ \mathbf{od}, S_i)$ and the ith component is activated in the transition step from the configuration (8.14) to its successor configuration in ξ.

Let p be the invariant and t the bound function associated with this loop. By the Strong Soundness for Parallel Programs Lemma 8.8, for each configuration of the form (8.14) we have $\tau \models p$ because $p \equiv pre(\mathbf{while}\ B\ \mathbf{do}\ S\ \mathbf{od})$. But $p \rightarrow t \geq 0$ holds by virtue of the definition of the proof outline for total correctness of component programs (Definition 8.3), so for each configuration of the form (8.14)

$$\tau(t) \geq 0.$$ (8.15)

Consider now two consecutive configurations in ξ of the form (8.14), say $< R_1, \tau_1 >$ and $< R_2, \tau_2 >$. In the segment η of ξ starting at $< R_1, \tau_1 >$ and ending with $< R_2, \tau_2 >$ a single iteration of the loop **while** B **do** S **od** took place. Let $\pi \in path(S)$ be the path through S, in the sense of Definition 8.2, which was taken in this iteration.

Let A be a normal assignment or an atomic region executed within the segment η, say in the state σ_1, and let σ_2 be the resulting state. Thus

$$< A, \sigma_1 > \rightarrow < E, \sigma_2 >.$$

By Lemma 8.8, $\sigma_1 \models pre(A)$. Suppose that A is a subprogram of S_j where $i \neq j$. Then by the definition of interference freedom (Definition 8.4(1)(ii)), we have $\{pre(A) \wedge t = z\}\ A\ \{t < z\}$ and thus $\sigma_2(t) \leq \sigma_1(t)$.

Suppose that A is a subprogram of S_i. Then A belongs to π. Thus by the definition of the proof outline for total correctness of loops $\{pre(A) \wedge t = z\} \; A \; \{t \le z\}$ and thus $\sigma_2(t) \le \sigma_1(t)$. Moreover, for some A belonging to the path π we actually have $\{pre(A) \wedge t = z\} \; A \; \{t < z\}$ and thus $\sigma_2(t) < \sigma_1(t)$.

This shows that the value of t during the execution of the segment η decreases; that is,

$$\tau_2(t) < \tau_1(t). \tag{8.16}$$

Since this is true for any two consecutive configurations of the form (16) in the infinite computation ξ, the statements (8.15) and (8.16) yield a contradiction. This proves (8.13). □

Corollary 8.3. (Parallelism with Shared Variables) *The parallelism with shared variables rule 27 is sound for total correctness of parallel programs.*

Proof. Consider interference free standard proof outlines for total correctness for component programs of a parallel program. Then the Termination Lemma 8.9 applies. By removing from each of these proof outlines all annotations referring to the bound functions, we obtain interference free standard proof outlines for partial correctness. The desired conclusion now follows from the Parallelism with Shared Variables Corollary 8.1. □

Corollary 8.4. (Soundness of TSV) *The proof system TSV is sound for total correctness of parallel programs.*

Proof. Follows by the same argument as the one given in the proof of the Soundness Corollary 7.1. □

Discussion

It is useful to see why we could not retain in this section the original formation rule (formation rule (viii)) defining proof outlines for total correctness for a **while** loop.

Consider the following parallel program

$$S \equiv [S_1 \| S_2],$$

where

$$S_1 \equiv \textbf{while } x > 0 \textbf{ do}$$
$$y := 0;$$
$$\textbf{if } y = 0 \textbf{ then } x := 0$$
$$\textbf{else } y := 0 \textbf{ fi}$$
$$\textbf{od}$$

and

$$S_2 \equiv \textbf{while } x > 0 \textbf{ do}$$
$$y := 1;$$
$$\textbf{if } y = 1 \textbf{ then } x := 0$$
$$\textbf{else } y := 1 \textbf{ fi}$$
$$\textbf{od}.$$

Individually, the **while** programs S_1 and S_2 satisfy the proof outlines for total correctness in which all assertions, including the loop invariants, equal **true** and the bound functions are in both cases $max(x, 0)$.

Indeed, in the case of S_1 we have

$$\{x > 0 \wedge max(x, 0) = z\}$$
$$\{z > 0\}$$
$$y := 0;$$
$$\textbf{if } y = 0 \textbf{ then } x := 0 \textbf{ else } y := 0 \textbf{ fi}$$
$$\{x = 0 \wedge z > 0\}$$
$$\{max(x, 0) < z\}$$

and analogously for the case of S_2.

Suppose now for a moment that we adopt the above proof outlines as proof outlines for total correctness of the component programs S_1 and S_2. Since

$$\{max(x, 0) = z\} \; x := 0 \; \{max(x, 0) \le z\}$$

holds, we conclude that these proof outlines are interference free in the sense of Definition 8.4. By the parallelism with shared variables rule 27 we then obtain the correctness formula

$$\{\textbf{true}\} \; S \; \{\textbf{true}\}$$

in the sense of total correctness.

However, it is easy to see that the parallel program S can diverge. Indeed, consider the following initial fragment of a computation of S starting in a state σ in which x is positive:

$$< [S_1\|S_2], \sigma >$$
$$\xrightarrow{1} < [y := 0; \ \textbf{if} \ldots \textbf{fi}; \ S_1\|S_2], \sigma >$$
$$\xrightarrow{2} < [y := 0; \ \textbf{if} \ldots \textbf{fi}; \ S_1\|y := 1; \ \textbf{if} \ldots \textbf{fi}; \ S_2], \sigma >$$
$$\xrightarrow{1} < [\textbf{if} \ldots \textbf{fi}; \ S_1\|y := 1; \ \textbf{if} \ldots \textbf{fi}; \ S_2], \sigma[y := 0] >$$
$$\xrightarrow{2} < [\textbf{if} \ldots \textbf{fi}; \ S_1\|\textbf{if} \ldots \textbf{fi}; \ S_2], \sigma[y := 1] >$$
$$\xrightarrow{1} < [y := 0; \ S_1\|\textbf{if} \ldots \textbf{fi}; \ S_2], \sigma[y := 1] >$$
$$\xrightarrow{1} < [S_1\|\textbf{if} \ldots \textbf{fi}; \ S_2], \sigma[y := 0] >$$
$$\xrightarrow{2} < [S_1\|y := 1; \ S_2], \sigma[y := 0] >$$
$$\xrightarrow{2} < [S_1\|S_2], \sigma[y := 1] > .$$

To enhance readability in each step we annotated the transition relation $\rightarrow$ with the index of the activated component. Iterating the above scheduling of the component programs we obtain an infinite computation of S.

Thus with proof outlines for total correctness in the sense of Definition 3.8, the parallelism with shared variables rule 27 would become unsound. This explains why we revised the definition of proof outlines for total correctness. It is easy to see why with the new definition of proof outlines for total correctness we can no longer justify the proof outlines suggested above. Indeed, along the path $y := 0; \ y := 0$ of the first loop body the proposed bound function $max(x,0)$ does not decrease. This path cannot be taken if S_1 is executed in isolation but it can be taken due to interference with S_2 as the above example shows.

Unfortunately, the stronger premises in the new formation rule (xi) for total correctness proof outlines of **while** loops given in Definition 8.3 reduce its applicability. For example, we have seen that the component program S_1 terminates when considered in isolation. This can be easily proved using the loop II rule (rule 7) but we cannot record this proof as a proof outline for total correctness in the sense of Definition 8.3 because on the path $y := 0$ the variable x is not decreased.

However, as we are going to see, many parallel programs can be successfully handled in the way proposed here.

8.6 Case Study: Find Positive Element More Quickly

In Section 7.4, we studied the problem of finding a positive element in an array a : **integer** $\rightarrow$ **integer**. As solution we presented a disjoint parallel program *FIND*. Here we consider an improved program *FINDPOS* for the same problem. Thus it should satisfy the correctness formula

{**true**}
FINDPOS   (8.17)
$\{1 \le k \le N + 1 \wedge \forall (0 < l < k) : a[l] \le 0 \wedge (k \le N \rightarrow a[k] > 0)\}$

in the sense of total correctness, where $a \notin change(FINDPOS)$. Just as in *FIND*, the program *FINDPOS* consists of two components S_1 and S_2 activated in parallel. S_1 searches for an odd index k of a positive element and S_2 searches for an even one.

What is new is that now S_1 should stop searching once S_2 has found a positive element and vice versa for S_2. Thus some communication should take place between S_1 and S_2. This is achieved by making *oddtop* and *eventop* shared variables of S_1 and S_2 by refining the loop conditions of S_1 and S_2 into

$$i < min\{oddtop, eventop\} \text{ and } j < min\{oddtop, eventop\},$$

respectively. Thus the program *FINDPOS* is of the form

$$FINDPOS \equiv i := 1; \ j := 2; \ oddtop := N + 1; \ eventop := N + 1;$$
$$[S_1 \| S_2];$$
$$k := min(oddtop, eventop),$$

where

$$S_1 \equiv \textbf{while } i < min(oddtop, eventop) \textbf{ do}$$
$$\textbf{if } a[i] > 0 \textbf{ then } oddtop := i$$
$$\textbf{else } i := i + 2 \textbf{ fi}$$
$$\textbf{od}$$

and

$$S_2 \equiv \textbf{while } j < min(oddtop, eventop) \textbf{ do}$$
$$\textbf{if } a[j] > 0 \textbf{ then } eventop := j$$
$$\textbf{else } j := j + 2 \textbf{ fi}$$
$$\textbf{od}.$$

This program is studied in Owicki and Gries [1976a].

To prove (8.17) in the system *TSV*, we first construct appropriate proof outlines for S_1 and S_2. Let p_1, p_2 and t_1, t_2 be the invariants and bound functions introduced in Section 7.4; that is,

$$p_1 \equiv \quad 1 \leq oddtop \leq N + 1 \wedge odd(i) \wedge 1 \leq i \leq oddtop + 1$$
$$\wedge \ \forall l : (odd(l) \wedge 1 \leq l < i \rightarrow a[l] \leq 0)$$
$$\wedge \ (oddtop \leq N \rightarrow a[oddtop] > 0),$$

$$t_1 \equiv oddtop + 1 - i,$$

$$p_2 \equiv \quad 2 \leq eventop \leq N + 1 \wedge even(j) \wedge j \leq eventop + 1$$
$$\wedge \ \forall l : (even(l) \wedge 1 \leq l < j \rightarrow a[l] \leq 0)$$
$$\wedge \ (eventop \leq N \rightarrow a[eventop] > 0),$$

$$t_2 \equiv eventop + 1 - j.$$

Then we consider the following standard proof outlines for total correctness. For S_1

$\{\mathbf{inv} : p_1\}\{\mathbf{bd} : t_1\}$
while $i < min(oddtop, eventop)$ **do**
    $\{p_1 \land i < oddtop\}$
    if $a[i] > 0$ **then** $\{p_1 \land i < oddtop \land a[i] > 0\}$
               $oddtop := i$
            else $\{p_1 \land i < oddtop \land a[i] \leq 0\}$
               $i := i + 2$
  fi
od
$\{p_1 \land i \geq min(oddtop, eventop)\}$

and there is a symmetric standard proof outline for S_2. Except for the new postconditions which are the consequences of the new loop conditions, all other assertions are taken from the corresponding proof outlines in Section 7.4. Note that the invariants and the bound functions satisfy the new conditions formulated in Definition 8.3.

To apply the parallelism with shared variables rule 27 for the parallel composition of S_1 and S_2, we must show interference freedom of the two proof outlines. This amounts to checking 24 correctness formulas! Fortunately, 22 of them are trivially satisfied because the variable changed by the assignment does not appear in the assertion or bound function under consideration. The only nontrivial cases deal with the interference freedom of the postcondition of S_1 with the assignment to the variable *eventop* in S_2 and, symmetrically, of the postcondition of S_2 with the assignment to the variable *oddtop* in S_1.

We deal with the postcondition of S_1,

$$p_1 \land i \geq min(oddtop, eventop),$$

and the assignment *eventop* $:= j$. Since $pre(eventop := j)$ implies $j < eventop$, we have the following proof of interference freedom:

    $\{p_1 \land i \geq min(oddtop, eventop) \land pre(eventop := j)\}$
    $\{p_1 \land i \geq min(oddtop, eventop) \land j < eventop\}$
    $\{p_1 \land i \geq min(oddtop, j)\}$
    $eventop := j$
    $\{p_1 \land i \geq min(oddtop, eventop)\}.$

An analogous argument takes care of the postcondition of S_2. This finishes the overall proof of interference freedom of the two proof outlines.

An application of the parallelism with shared variables rule 27 now yields

$\{p_1 \land p_2\}$
$[S_1 \| S_2]$
$\{p_1 \land p_2 \land i \geq min(oddtop, eventop) \land j \geq min(oddtop, eventop)\}.$

By the assignment axiom and the consequence rule,

{**true**}
$i := 1; \ j := 2; \ oddtop := N + 1; \ eventop := N + 1;$
$[S_1 \| S_2]$
$\{ \quad min(oddtop, eventop) \leq N + 1$
$\quad \wedge \quad \forall (0 < l < min(oddtop, eventop)) : a[l] \leq 0$
$\quad \wedge \quad (min(oddtop, eventop) \leq N \rightarrow a[min(oddtop, eventop)] > 0)\}.$

Hence the final assignment $k := min(oddtop, eventop)$ in *FINDPOS* establishes the desired postcondition of (8.17).

8.7 Allowing More Points of Interference

The fewer points of interference there are, the simpler the correctness proofs of parallel programs become. On the other hand, the more points of interference parallel programs have, the more realistic they are. In this section we present two program transformations that allow us to introduce more points of interference without changing the program semantics. The first transformation achieves this by reducing the size of atomic regions.

Theorem 8.1. (Atomicity) *Consider a parallel program of the form $S \equiv S_0; \ [S_1 \| \dots \| S_n]$ where S_0 is a **while** program. Let T result from S by replacing in one of its components, say S_i with $i > 0$, either*

- *an atomic region $\langle R_1; \ R_2 \rangle$ where one of the R_ls is disjoint from all components S_j with $j \neq i$ by*

$$\langle R_1 \rangle; \ \langle R_2 \rangle$$

or

- *an atomic region $\langle$ **if** B **then** R_1 **else** R_2 **fi** $\rangle$ where B is disjoint from all components S_j with $j \neq i$ by*

$$\textbf{if } B \textbf{ then } \langle R_1 \rangle \textbf{ else } \langle R_2 \rangle \textbf{ fi}.$$

Then the semantics of S and T agree; that is,

$$\mathcal{M}[\![S]\!] = \mathcal{M}[\![T]\!] \ and \ \mathcal{M}_{tot}[\![S]\!] = \mathcal{M}_{tot}[\![T]\!].$$

Proof. We treat the case when S has no initialization part S_0 and when T results from S by splitting $\langle R_1; \ R_2 \rangle$ into $\langle R_1 \rangle; \ \langle R_2 \rangle$. We proceed in five steps.

Step 1 We first define *good* and *almost good* (fragments of) computations for the program T. By an R_k-transition, $k \in \{1, 2\}$, we mean a transition occurring in a computation of T which is of the form

$$< [U_1\|\ldots\|\langle R_k\rangle;\ U_i\|\ldots\|U_n], \sigma > \ \rightarrow\ < [U_1\|\ldots\|U_i\|\ldots\|U_n], \tau > .$$

We call a fragment ξ of a computation of T *good* if in ξ each R_1-transition is immediately followed by the corresponding R_2-transition, and we call ξ *almost good* if in ξ each R_1-transition is eventually followed by the corresponding R_2-transition.

Observe that every finite computation of T is almost good.

Step 2 To compare the computations of S and T, we use the i/o equivalence introduced in Definition 7.4. We prove the following two claims.

- Every computation of S is i/o equivalent to a good computation of T,
- every good computation of T is i/o equivalent to a computation of S.

First consider a computation ξ of S. Every program occurring in a configuration of ξ is a parallel composition of n components. For such a program U let the program $split(U)$ result from U by replacing in the ith component of U every occurrence of $\langle R_1;\ R_2\rangle$ by $\langle R_1\rangle;\ \langle R_2\rangle$. For example, $split(S) \equiv T$. We construct an i/o equivalent good computation of T from ξ by replacing

- every transition of the form

$$< [U_1\|\ldots\|\langle R_1;\ R_2\rangle;\ U_i\|\ldots\|U_n], \sigma >$$
$$\rightarrow\ < [U_1\|\ldots\|U_i\|\ldots\|U_n], \tau >$$

with two consecutive transitions

$$< split([U_1\|\ldots\|\langle R_1;\ R_2\rangle;\ U_i\|\ldots\|U_n]), \sigma >$$
$$\rightarrow\ < split([U_1\|\ldots\|\langle R_2\rangle;\ U_i\|\ldots\|U_n]), \sigma_1 >$$
$$\rightarrow\ < split([U_1\|\ldots\|U_i\|\ldots\|U_n]), \tau >,$$

where the intermediate state σ_1 is defined by

$$< \langle R_1\rangle, \sigma > \ \rightarrow\ < E, \sigma_1 >,$$

- every other transition

$$< U, \sigma > \ \rightarrow\ < V, \tau >$$

with

$$< split(U), \sigma > \ \rightarrow\ < split(V), \tau > .$$

Now consider a good computation η of T. By applying the above replacement operations in the reverse direction we construct from η an i/o equivalent computation of S.

Step 3 For the comparison of computations of T we use i/o equivalence, but to reason about it we also introduce a more discriminating variant that we call "permutation equivalence".

First consider an arbitrary computation ξ of T. Every program occurring in a configuration of ξ is the parallel composition of n components. To distinguish between different kinds of transitions in ξ, we attach labels to the transition arrow $\rightarrow$. We write

$$< U, \sigma > \overset{R_k}{\rightarrow} < V, \tau >$$

if $k \in \{1, 2\}$ and $< U, \sigma > \rightarrow < V, \tau >$ is an R_k-transition of the i-th component of U,

$$< U, \sigma > \overset{i}{\rightarrow} < V, \tau >$$

if $< U, \sigma > \rightarrow < V, \tau >$ is any other transition caused by the activation of the ith component of U, and

$$< U, \sigma > \overset{j}{\rightarrow} < V, \tau >$$

if $j \neq i$ and $< U, \sigma > \rightarrow < V, \tau >$ is a transition caused by the activation of the jth component of U.

Hence, a unique label is associated with each transition arrow in a computation of T. This enables us to define the following.

Two computations η and ξ of T are *permutation equivalent* if

- η and ξ start in the same state,
- for all states σ, η terminates in σ iff ξ terminates in σ,
- the possibly infinite sequence of labels attached to the transition arrows in η and ξ are permutations of each other.

Clearly, permutation equivalence of computations of T implies their i/o equivalence.

Step 4 We prove now that every computation of T is i/o equivalent to a good computation of T. To this end, we establish two simpler claims.

Claim 1 Every computation of T is i/o equivalent to an almost good computation of T.

Proof of Claim 1. Consider a computation ξ of T that is not almost good. Then by the observation stated at the end of Step 1, ξ is infinite. More precisely, there exists a suffix ξ_1 of ξ that starts in a configuration $< U, \sigma >$ with an R_1-transition and then continues with infinitely many transitions not involving the ith component, say,

$$\xi_1 : < U, \sigma > \overset{R_1}{\rightarrow} < U_0, \sigma_0 > \overset{j_1}{\rightarrow} < U_1, \sigma_1 > \overset{j_2}{\rightarrow} \dots,$$

where $j_k \neq i$ for $k \geq 1$. Using the Change and Access Lemma 3.4 we conclude the following: if R_1 is disjoint from S_j with $j \neq i$, then there is also an infinite transition sequence of the form

$$\xi_2 :< U, \sigma > \xrightarrow{j_1} < V_1, \tau_1 > \xrightarrow{j_2} \ldots,$$

and if R_2 is disjoint from S_j with $j \neq i$, then there is also an infinite transition sequence of the form

$$\xi_3 :< U, \sigma > \xrightarrow{R_1} < U_0, \sigma_0 > \xrightarrow{R_2} < V_0, \tau_0 > \xrightarrow{j_1} < V_1, \tau_1 > \xrightarrow{j_2} \ldots .$$

We say that ξ_2 is obtained from ξ_1 by *deletion* of the initial R_1-transition and ξ_3 is obtained from ξ_1 by *insertion* of an R_2-transition. Replacing the suffix ξ_1 of ξ by ξ_2 or ξ_3 yields an almost good computation of T which is i/o equivalent to ξ.

Claim 2 Every almost good computation of T is permutation equivalent to a good computation of T.

Proof of Claim 2. Using the Change and Access Lemma 3.4 we establish the following: if R_k with $k \in \{1, 2\}$ is disjoint from S_j with $j \neq i$, then the relations $\xrightarrow{R_k}$ and $\xrightarrow{j}$ *commute*, or

$$\xrightarrow{R_k} \circ \xrightarrow{j} = \xrightarrow{j} \circ \xrightarrow{R_k},$$

where $\circ$ denotes relational composition (see Section 2.1). Repeated application of this commutativity allows us to permute the transitions of every almost good fragment ξ_1 of a computation of T of the form

$$\xi_1 :< U, \sigma > \xrightarrow{R_1} \circ \xrightarrow{j_1} \circ \ldots \circ \xrightarrow{j_m} \circ \xrightarrow{R_2} < V, \tau >$$

with $j_k \neq i$ for $k \in \{1, \ldots, m\}$ into a good order, that is, into

$$\xi_2 :< U, \sigma > \xrightarrow{j_1} \circ \ldots \circ \xrightarrow{j_m} \circ \xrightarrow{R_1} \circ \xrightarrow{R_2} < V, \tau >$$

or

$$\xi_3 :< U, \sigma > \xrightarrow{R_1} \circ \xrightarrow{R_2} \circ \xrightarrow{j_1} \circ \ldots \circ \xrightarrow{j_m} < V, \tau >$$

depending on whether R_1 or R_2 is disjoint from S_j with $j \neq i$.

Consider now an almost good computation ξ of T. We construct from ξ a permutation equivalent good computation ξ^* of T by successively replacing every almost good fragment of ξ of the form ξ_1 by a good fragment of the form ξ_2 or ξ_3.

Claims 1 and 2 together imply the claim of Step 4.

Step 5 By combining the results of Steps 3 and 5, we get the claim of the theorem for the case when S has no initialization part S_0 and T results from S by splitting $\langle R_1; R_2 \rangle$ into $\langle R_1 \rangle; \langle R_2 \rangle$. The cases when S has an initialization part S_0 and where T results from S by splitting the atomic region $\langle$**if** B **then** R_1 **else** R_2 **fi**$\rangle$ are left as Exercise 8.11.   □

Corollary 8.5. (Atomicity) *Under the assumptions of the Atomicity Theorem, for all assertions p and q*

$$\models \{p\}\ S\ \{q\}\ \textit{iff}\ \models \{p\}\ T\ \{q\}$$

and analogously for $\models_{tot}$.

The second transformation moves initializations of a parallel program inside one of its components.

Theorem 8.2. (Initialization) *Consider a parallel program of the form*

$$S \equiv S_0;\ R_0;\ [S_1\|\ldots\|S_n],$$

where S_0 and R_0 are **while** *programs. Suppose that for some $i \in \{1,\ldots,n\}$ the initialization part R_0 is disjoint from all component programs S_j with $j \neq i$. Then the program*

$$T \equiv S_0;\ [S_1\|\ldots\|R_0;\ S_i\|\ldots\|S_n]$$

has the same semantics as S; that is,

$$\mathcal{M}[\![S]\!] = \mathcal{M}[\![T]\!]\ \textit{and}\ \mathcal{M}_{tot}[\![S]\!] = \mathcal{M}_{tot}[\![T]\!].$$

Proof. The proof can be structured similarly to the one of the Atomicity Theorem and is left as Exercise 8.12.   □

Corollary 8.6. (Initialization) *Under the assumptions of the Initialization Theorem, for all assertions p and q*

$$\models \{p\}\ S\ \{q\}\ \textit{iff}\ \models \{p\}\ T\ \{q\}$$

and analogously for $\models_{tot}$.

The program S considered in the Atomicity Corollary 8.5 and Initialization Corollary 8.6 admits fewer points for possible interference among its components and thus fewer computations than the corresponding program T. Therefore S is easier to prove correct. Thus in correctness proofs we apply the program transformations for atomicity and initialization "backwards"; that is, programs of the form T are replaced by programs of the form S and then verified. Examples show that this approach often avoids the need for auxiliary variables in the sense of rule 25.

We could have reformulated the Corollaries 8.5 and 8.6 also as proof rules and integrated them in the proof systems *PSV* and *TSV* introduced in Sections 8.4 and 8.5. However, we prefer to keep them separate to stress their status as additional program transformations.

8.8 Case Study: Parallel Zero Search

Let us consider Solution 3 to the zero search problem given in Section 1.1, that is, the parallel program

$$ZERO\text{-}3 \equiv found := \textbf{false}; \; [S_1 \| S_2]$$

with

$$S_1 \equiv x := 0;$$
$$\quad \textbf{while } \neg found \textbf{ do}$$
$$\qquad x := x + 1;$$
$$\qquad \textbf{if } f(x) = 0 \textbf{ then } found := \textbf{true fi}$$
$$\quad \textbf{od}$$

and

$$S_2 \equiv y := 1;$$
$$\quad \textbf{while } \neg found \textbf{ do}$$
$$\qquad y := y - 1;$$
$$\qquad \textbf{if } f(y) = 0 \textbf{ then } found := \textbf{true fi}$$
$$\quad \textbf{od}.$$

We wish to prove the partial correctness of this solution, that is, that in case of termination $ZERO\text{-}3$ has indeed found a zero of the function f in one of its variables x or y:

$$\models \{\textbf{true}\} \; ZERO\text{-}3 \; \{f(x) = 0 \vee f(y) = 0\}. \qquad (8.18)$$

Termination cannot be proved here; it holds only under the assumption of *fairness* (see Chapter 1).

We proceed in two steps.

Step 1. Simplifying the program

We first use the Atomicity Corollary 8.5 and Initialization Corollary 8.6 and reduce the original problem (8.18) to the following claim

$$\models \{\exists u : f(u) = 0\} \; T \; \{f(x) = 0 \vee f(y) = 0\}, \qquad (8.19)$$

where

$$T \equiv found := \textbf{false}; \; x := 0; \; y := 1;$$
$$\quad [T_1 \| T_2]$$

with

$$T_1 \equiv \textbf{while } \neg found \textbf{ do}$$
$$\langle \; x := x + 1;$$
$$\textbf{if } f(x) = 0 \textbf{ then } found := \textbf{true fi}\rangle$$
$$\textbf{od}$$

and

$$T_2 \equiv \textbf{while } \neg found \textbf{ do}$$
$$\langle \; y := y - 1;$$
$$\textbf{if } f(y) = 0 \textbf{ then } found := \textbf{true fi}\rangle.$$
$$\textbf{od}.$$

Both corollaries are applicable here by virtue of the fact that x does not appear in S_2 and y does not appear in S_1. Recall that by assumption, assignments and the *skip* statement are considered to be atomic regions.

Step 2. Proving partial correctness

We prove (8.19) in the proof system *PSV* for partial correctness of parallel programs with shared variables introduced in Section 8.4. To this end, we need to construct interference free standard proof outlines for partial correctness of the sequential components T_1 and T_2 of T.

For T_1 we use the invariant

$$\begin{aligned} p_1 \equiv \quad & x \geq 0 & (8.20)\\ \wedge \;\; & (found \rightarrow (x > 0 \wedge f(x) = 0) \vee (y \leq 0 \wedge f(y) = 0)) & (8.21)\\ \wedge \;\; & (\neg found \wedge x > 0 \rightarrow f(x) \neq 0) & (8.22) \end{aligned}$$

to construct the standard proof outline

$$\{\textbf{inv} : p_1\}$$
$$\textbf{while } \neg found \textbf{ do}$$
$$\{x \geq 0 \;\wedge\; (found \rightarrow y \leq 0 \wedge f(y) = 0) \qquad\qquad (8.23)$$
$$\wedge \; (x > 0 \rightarrow f(x) \neq 0)\}$$
$$\langle \; x := x + 1;$$
$$\textbf{if } f(x) = 0 \textbf{ then } found := \textbf{true fi}\rangle$$
$$\textbf{od}$$
$$\{p_1 \wedge found\}.$$

Similarly, for T_2 we use the invariant

$$\begin{aligned} p_2 \equiv \quad & y \leq 1 & (8.24)\\ \wedge \;\; & (found \rightarrow (x > 0 \wedge f(x) = 0) \vee (y \leq 0 \wedge f(y) = 0)) & (8.25)\\ \wedge \;\; & (\neg found \wedge y \leq 0 \rightarrow f(y) \neq 0) & (8.26) \end{aligned}$$

to construct the standard proof outline

$\{\mathbf{inv}: p_2\}$
while $\neg found$ **do**
$\qquad \{y \le 1 \ \wedge \ (found \rightarrow x > 0 \wedge f(x) = 0)$
$\qquad\qquad \wedge \ (y \le 0 \rightarrow f(y) \neq 0)\}$
$\qquad \langle \ y := y - 1;$
$\qquad\qquad \mathbf{if} \ f(y) = 0 \ \mathbf{then} \ found := \mathbf{true} \ \mathbf{fi}\rangle$
od
$\{p_2 \wedge found\}.$

The intuition behind the invariants p_1 and p_2 is as follows. Conjuncts (8.20) and (8.24) state the range of values that the variables x and y may assume during the execution of the loops T_1 and T_2.

Thanks to the initialization of x with 0 and y with 1 in T, the condition $x > 0$ expresses the fact that the loop T_1 has been traversed at least once, and the condition $y \le 0$ similarly expresses the fact that the loop T_2 has been traversed at least once. Thus the conjuncts (8.21) and (8.25) in the invariants p_1 and p_2 state that if the variable $found$ is true, then the loop T_1 has been traversed at least once and a zero x of f has been found, or that the loop T_2 has been traversed at least once and a zero y of f has been found.

The conjunct (8.22) in p_1 states that if the variable $found$ is false and the loop T_1 has been traversed at least once, then x is not a zero of f. The conjunct (8.26) in p_2 has an analogous meaning.

Let us discuss now the proof outlines. In the first proof outline the most complicated assertion is (8.23). Note that

$$p_1 \wedge \neg found \rightarrow (8.23)$$

as required by the definition of a proof outline. (We cannot use, instead of (8.23), the assertion $p_1 \wedge \neg found$ because the latter assertion does not pass the interference freedom test with respect to the loop body in T_2.)

Given (8.23) as a precondition, the loop body in T_1 establishes the invariant p_1 as a postcondition, as required. Notice that the conjunct

$$found \rightarrow y \le 0 \wedge f(y) = 0$$

in the precondition (8.23) is necessary to establish the conjunct (8.21) in the invariant p_1. Indeed, without this conjunct in (8.23), the loop body in T_1 would fail to establish (8.21) since initially

$$found \wedge x > 0 \wedge f(x) = 0 \wedge f(x+1) \neq 0 \wedge y \le 0 \wedge f(y) \neq 0$$

might hold.

Next we deal with the interference freedom of the above proof outlines. In total six correctness formulas must be proved. The three for each component are pairwise symmetric.

The most interesting case is the interference freedom of the assertion (8.23) in the proof outline for T_1 with the loop body in T_2. It is proved by the following proof outline:

$$\{ \quad x \geq 0 \wedge (found \rightarrow y \leq 0 \wedge f(y) = 0) \wedge (x > 0 \rightarrow f(x) \neq 0)$$
$$\wedge \quad y \leq 1 \wedge (found \rightarrow x > 0 \wedge f(x) = 0) \wedge (y \leq 0 \rightarrow f(y) \neq 0)\}$$
$$\{x \geq 0 \wedge y \leq 1 \wedge \neg found \wedge (x > 0 \rightarrow f(x) \neq 0)\}$$
$$\langle \; y := y - 1;$$
$$\textbf{if } f(y) = 0 \textbf{ then } found := \textbf{true fi}\rangle$$
$$\{x \geq 0 \wedge (found \rightarrow y \leq 0 \wedge f(y) = 0) \wedge (x > 0 \rightarrow f(x) \neq 0)\}.$$

Note that the first assertion in the above proof outline indeed implies $\neg found$:

$$(found \rightarrow (x > 0 \wedge f(x) = 0)) \wedge (x > 0 \rightarrow f(x) \neq 0)$$

implies

$$found \rightarrow (f(x) \neq 0 \wedge f(x) = 0)$$

implies

$$\neg found.$$

This information is recorded in the second assertion of the proof outline and used to establish the last assertion.

The remaining cases in the interference freedom proof are straightforward and left to the reader.

We now apply the parallelism with shared variables rule 27 and get

$$\{p_1 \wedge p_2\} \; [T_1 \| T_2] \; \{p_1 \wedge p_2 \wedge found\}.$$

Since for the initialization part of T the correctness formula

$$\{\textbf{true}\} \; found := \textbf{false}; x := 0 : y := 1 \; \{p_1 \wedge p_2\}$$

holds, a straightforward application of the rule for sequential composition and the consequence rule yields the desired partial correctness result (8.18).

Of course, we could have avoided applying the program transformations in Step 1 and proved the correctness formula (8.18) directly in the proof system *PSV*. But this would lead to a more complicated proof because *ZERO*-3 contains more interference points than T and thus requires a more complex test of interference freedom. In fact, we need auxiliary variables in the sense of rule 25 to deal with the initialization $x := 0$ and $y := 1$ within the parallel composition in *ZERO*-3 (see Exercise 8.8). This shows that the Atomicity Theorem 8.1 and the Initialization Theorem 8.2 simplify the task of proving parallel programs correct.

8.9 Exercises

8.1. Prove the Input/Output Lemma 3.3 for parallel programs.

8.2. Prove the Change and Access Lemma 3.4 for parallel programs.

8.3. Prove the Stuttering Lemma 7.9 for parallel programs.

8.4. Suppose that

$$< [S_1\|\dots\|S_n], \sigma > \;\rightarrow^* \; < [R_1\|\dots\|R_n], \tau > .$$

Prove that for $j \in \{1, \dots, n\}$ either $R_j \equiv E$ or $R_j \equiv \mathbf{at}(T, S_j)$ for a normal subprogram T of S_j.
Hint. See Exercise 3.13.

8.5.

(i) Prove the correctness formula

$$\{x = 0\}\ [x := x + 1 \| x := x + 2]\ \{x = 3\}$$

in the proof system PW + rule 27.
(ii) By contrast, show that the correctness formula

$$\{x = 0\}\ [x := x + 1 \| x := x + 1]\ \{x = 2\}$$

is not a theorem in the proof system PW + rule 27.
(iii) Explain the difference between (i) and (ii), and prove the correctness formula of (ii) in the proof system PSV.

8.6. Prove the correctness formula

$$\{\mathbf{true}\}\ [x := x + 2;\ x := x + 2 \| x := 0]\ \{x = 0 \lor x = 2 \lor x = 4\}$$

in the proof system PSV.

8.7. Show that the rule of disjoint parallelism (rule 24) is not sound for parallel programs.
Hint. Consider the component programs $x := 0$ and $x := 1;\ y := x$.

8.8. Consider the parallel program *ZERO-3* from the Case Study 8.8. Prove the correctness formula

$$\{\exists u : f(u) = 0\}\ ZERO\text{-}3\ \{f(x) = 0 \lor f(y) = 0\}$$

in the proof system PSV.
Hint. Introduce two Boolean auxiliary variables $init_1$ and $init_2$ to record whether the initializations $x := 0$ and $y := 1$ of the component programs S_1 and S_2 of *ZERO-3* have been executed. Thus instead of S_1 consider

$$S_1' \equiv \langle x := 0;\ init_1 := \textbf{true} \rangle;$$
$$\textbf{while}\ \neg found\ \textbf{do}$$
$$x := x + 1;$$
$$\textbf{if}\ f(x) = 0\ \textbf{then}\ found := \textbf{true}\ \textbf{fi}$$
$$\textbf{od}$$

and analogously with S_2. Use

$$
\begin{aligned}
p_1 \equiv\quad & init_1 \wedge x \geq 0 \\
& \wedge\ (found \rightarrow \quad (x > 0 \wedge f(x) = 0) \\
& \qquad\qquad\qquad \vee\ (init_2 \wedge y \leq 0 \wedge f(y) = 0)) \\
& \wedge\ (\neg found \wedge x > 0 \rightarrow f(x) \neq 0)
\end{aligned}
$$

as a loop invariant in S_1' and a symmetric loop invariant in S_2' to prove

$$\{\neg found \wedge \neg init_1 \wedge \neg init_2\}\ [S_1' \| S_2']\ \{f(x) = 0 \vee f(y) = 0\}.$$

Finally, apply the rule of auxiliary variables (rule 25).

8.9. Consider the parallel program *ZERO-2* from Solution 2 in Section 1.1.

(i) Prove the correctness formula

$$\{\textbf{true}\}\ ZERO\text{-}2\ \{f(x) = 0 \vee f(y) = 0\}$$

in the proof system *PSV*.
Hint. Introduce a Boolean auxiliary variable to indicate which of the components of *ZERO-2* last updated the variable *found*.
(ii) Show that the above correctness formula is false in the sense of total correctness by describing an infinite computation of *ZERO-2*.

8.10. The parallel programs considered in Case Studies 7.4 and 8.6 both begin with the initialization part

$$i := 1;\ j := 2;\ oddtop := N + 1;\ eventop := N + 1.$$

Investigate which of these assignments can be moved inside the parallel composition without invalidating the correctness formulas (8.15) in Section 7.4 and (8.17) in Section 8.6.
Hint. Apply the Initialization Theorem 8.2 or show that the correctness formulas (8.15) in Section 7.4 and (8.17) in Section 8.6 are invalidated.

8.11. Prove the Atomicity Theorem 8.1 for the cases when S has an initialization part and when T is obtained from S by splitting the atomic region $\langle \textbf{if}\ B\ \textbf{then}\ R_1\ \textbf{else}\ R_2\ \textbf{fi} \rangle$.

8.12. Prove the Initialization Theorem 8.2.

8.13. Prove the Sequentialization Lemma 7.7 using the Stuttering Lemma 7.9 and the Initialization Theorem 8.2.

8.14. Consider component programs $S_1, \ldots, S_n$ and $T_1, \ldots, T_n$ such that S_i is disjoint from T_j whenever $i \neq j$. Prove that the parallel programs

$$S \equiv [S_1 \| \ldots \| S_n]; [T_1 \| \ldots \| T_n]$$

and

$$T \equiv [S_1; \; T_1 \| \ldots \| S_n; \; T_n]$$

have the same semantics under $\mathcal{M}$, $\mathcal{M}_{tot}$ and $\mathcal{M}_{fair}$. In the terminology of Elrad and Francez [1982] the subprograms $[S_1 \| \ldots \| S_n]$ and $[T_1 \| \ldots \| T_n]$ of S are called *layers* of the parallel program T.

8.10 Bibliographic Remarks

As already mentioned, the approach to partial correctness and total correctness followed here is due to Owicki and Gries [1976a] and is known as the "Owicki/Gries method." A similar proof technique was introduced independently in Lamport [1977]. The presentation given here differs in the way total correctness is handled. Our presentation follows Apt, de Boer and Olderog [1990], in which the stronger formation rule for proof outlines for total correctness of **while** loops (formation rule (viii) given in Definition 8.3) was introduced.

The Owicki/Gries method has been criticized because of its missing compositionality as shown by the global test of interference freedom. This motivated research on compositional semantics and proof methods for parallel programs —see, for example, Brookes [1993] and de Boer [1994].

Atomic regions were considered by many authors, in particular Lipton [1975], Lamport [1977] and Owicki [1978]. The Atomicity Theorem 8.1 and the Initialization Theorem 8.2 presented in Section 8.7 are inspired by the considerations of Lipton [1975].

A systematic derivation of a parallel program for zero search is presented by Knapp [1992]. The derivation is carried out in the framework of UNITY.

The transformation of a layered program into a fully parallel program presented in Exercise 8.14 is called the law of *Communication Closed Layers* in Janssen, Poel and Zwiers [1991] and Fokkinga, Poel and Zwiers [1993] and is the core of a method for developing parallel programs.

9 Parallel Programs with Synchronization

F OR MANY APPLICATIONS the classes of parallel programs considered so far are not sufficient. We need parallel programs whose components can *synchronize* with each other. That is, components must be able to suspend their execution and *wait* or get *blocked* until the execution of the other components has changed the shared variables in such a way that a certain condition is fulfilled. To formulate such waiting conditions we extend the program syntax of Section 9.1 by a synchronization construct, the **await** statement introduced in Owicki and Gries [1976a].

This construct permits a very flexible way of programming, but at the same time opens the door for subtle programming errors where the program execution ends in a *deadlock*. This is a situation where some components of a parallel program did not terminate and all nonterminated components

Krzysztof R. Apt et al., *Verification of Sequential and Concurrent Programs*,
Texts in Computer Science, DOI: 10.1007/978-1-84882-745-5_9,
© Springer-Verlag London Limited 2009

are blocked because they wait eternally for a certain condition to become satisfied. The formal definition is given in Section 9.2 on semantics.

In this chapter we present a method of Owicki and Gries [1976a] for proving *deadlock freedom*. For a clear treatment of this verification method we introduce in Section 9.3 besides the usual notions of partial and total correctness an intermediate property called *weak total correctness* which guarantees termination but not yet deadlock freedom.

As a first case study we prove in Section 9.4 the correctness of a typical synchronization problem: the *consumer/producer problem*. In Section 9.5 we consider another classical synchronization problem: the *mutual exclusion problem*. We prove correctness of two solutions to this problem, one formulated in the language without synchronization and another one in the full language of parallel programs with synchronization.

In Section 9.6 we restate two program transformations of Section 8.7 in the new setting where synchronization is allowed. These transformations are used in the case study in Section 9.7 where we prove correctness of the *zero search* program *ZERO*-6 from Chapter 1.

9.1 Syntax

A *component program* is now a program generated by the same clauses as those defining **while** programs in Chapter 3 together with the following clause for **await** statements:

$$S ::= \textbf{await } B \textbf{ then } S_0 \textbf{ end},$$

where S_0 is loop free and does not contain any **await** statements.

Thanks to this syntactic restriction no divergence or deadlock can occur during the execution of S_0, which significantly simplifies our analysis.

Parallel programs with synchronization (or simply *parallel programs*) are then generated by the same clauses as those defining **while** programs, together with the usual clause for parallel composition:

$$S ::= [S_1 \| \ldots \| S_n],$$

where $S_1, \ldots, S_n$ are component programs $(n > 1)$. Thus, as before, we do not allow nested parallelism, but we do allow parallelism within sequential composition, conditional statements and **while** loops. Note that **await** statements may appear only within the context of parallel composition.

Throughout this chapter the notions of a component program and a parallel program always refer to the above definition.

To explain the meaning of **await** statements, let us imagine an interleaved execution of a parallel program where one component is about to execute a statement **await** B **then** S **end**. If B evaluates to true, then S is executed as an atomic region whose activation cannot be interrupted by the other components. If B evaluates to false, the component gets *blocked* and the other components take over the execution. If during their execution B becomes true, the blocked component can resume its execution. Otherwise, it remains blocked forever.

Thus **await** statements model *conditional atomic regions*. If $B \equiv \textbf{true}$, we obtain the same effect as with an unconditional atomic region of Chapter 8. Hence we identify

$$\textbf{await true then } S \textbf{ end} \equiv \langle S \rangle.$$

As an abbreviation we also introduce

$$\textbf{wait } B \equiv \textbf{await } B \textbf{ then } skip \textbf{ end}.$$

For the extended syntax of this chapter, a subprogram of a program S is called *normal* if it does not occur within an **await** statement of S.

9.2 Semantics

The transition system for parallel programs with synchronization consists of the axioms and rules (i)–(vii) introduced in Section 3.2, the interleaving rule xvii introduced in Section 7.2 and the following transition rule:

(xix)
$$\frac{< S, \sigma > \rightarrow^* < E, \tau >}{< \textbf{await } B \textbf{ then } S \textbf{ end}, \sigma > \rightarrow < E, \tau >}$$

where $\sigma \models B$.

This transition rule formalizes the intuitive meaning of conditional atomic regions. If B evaluates to true, the statement **await** B **then** S **end** is executed like an atomic region $\langle S \rangle$, with each terminating computation of S reducing to an uninterruptible one-step computation of **await** B **then** S **end**.

If B evaluates to false, the rule does not allow us to derive any transition for **await** B **then** S **end**. In that case transitions of other components can be executed. A deadlock arises if the program has not yet terminated, but all nonterminated components are blocked. Formally, this amounts to saying that no transition is possible.

Definition 9.1. Consider a parallel program S, a proper state σ and an assertion p.

(i) A configuration $< S, \sigma >$ is called *deadlock* if $S \not\equiv E$ and there is no successor configuration of $< S, \sigma >$ in the transition relation $\rightarrow$.

(ii) The program S *can deadlock from* σ if there exists a computation of S starting in σ and ending in a deadlock.

(iii) The program S is *deadlock free (relative to p)* if there is no state σ (satisfying p) from which S can deadlock.   □

Thus, for parallel programs with synchronization, there is no analogue to the Absence of Blocking Lemma 8.1. Consequently, when started in a proper state σ, a parallel program S can now terminate, diverge or deadlock. Depending on which of these outcomes is recorded, we distinguish three variants of semantics:

- partial correctness semantics:

$$\mathcal{M}[\![S]\!](\sigma) = \{\tau \mid < S, \sigma > \rightarrow^* < E, \tau >\},$$

- weak total correctness semantics:

$$\mathcal{M}_{wtot}[\![S]\!](\sigma) = \mathcal{M}[\![S]\!](\sigma) \cup \{\bot \mid S \text{ can diverge from } \sigma\},$$

- total correctness semantics:

$$\mathcal{M}_{tot}[\![S]\!](\sigma) = \mathcal{M}_{wtot}[\![S]\!](\sigma) \cup \{\Delta \mid S \text{ can deadlock from } \sigma\}.$$

As mentioned in Section 2.6, Δ is one of the special states, in addition to $\bot$ and **fail**, which can appear in the semantics of a program but which will never satisfy an assertion. The new intermediate semantics $\mathcal{M}_{wtot}$ is not interesting in itself, but it is useful when justifying proof rules for total correctness.

9.3 Verification

Each of the above three variants of semantics induces in the standard way a corresponding notion of program correctness. For example, weak total correctness is defined as follows:

$$\models_{wtot} \{p\} \, S \, \{q\} \text{ iff } \mathcal{M}_{wtot}[\![S]\!]([\![p]\!]) \subseteq [\![q]\!].$$

First we deal with partial correctness.

Partial Correctness

For component programs, we use the proof rules of the system PW for **while** programs plus the following proof rule given in Owicki and Gries [1976a]:

RULE 28: SYNCHRONIZATION

$$\frac{\{p \wedge B\} \, S \, \{q\}}{\{p\} \text{ await } B \text{ then } S \text{ end } \{q\}}$$

The soundness of the synchronization rule is an immediate consequence of the transition rule (xix) defining the semantics of **await** statements. Note that with $B \equiv \textbf{true}$ we get the atomic region rule 26 as a special case.

Proof outlines for partial correctness of component programs are generated by the same formation rules as those used for **while** programs together with the following one:

(xii)

$$\frac{\{p \wedge B\} \, S^* \, \{q\}}{\{p\} \text{ await } B \text{ then } \{p \wedge B\} \, S^* \, \{q\} \text{ end } \{q\}}$$

where S^* stands for an annotated version of S.

The definition of a *standard* proof outline is stated as in the previous chapter, but it refers now to the extended notion of a normal subprogram given in Section 9.1. Thus there are no assertions within **await** statements.

The connection between standard proof outlines and computations of component programs can be stated analogously to the Strong Soundness for Component Programs Lemma 8.5 and the Strong Soundness Theorem 3.3. We use the notation $\mathbf{at}(T, S)$ introduced in Definition 3.7 but with the understanding that T is a normal subprogram of a component program S. Note that no additional clause dealing with **await** statements is needed in this definition.

Lemma 9.1. (Strong Soundness for Component Programs) *Consider a component program S with a standard proof outline $\{p\}\, S^*\, \{q\}$ for partial correctness. Suppose that*

$$< S, \sigma > \to^* < R, \tau >$$

for a proper state σ satisfying p, a program R and a proper state τ. Then

- *either $R \equiv \mathbf{at}(T, S)$ for some normal subprogram T of S and $\tau \models pre(T)$*
- *or $R \equiv E$ and $\tau \models q$.*

Proof. See Exercise 9.5.   □

Interference freedom refers now to **await** statements instead of atomic regions. Thus standard proof outlines $\{p_i\}\, S_i^*\, \{q_i\}$, $i \in \{1, \ldots, n\}$, for partial correctness are called *interference free* if no normal assignment or **await** statement of a component program S_i interferes (in the sense of the previous chapter) with the proof outline of another component program S_j, $i \neq j$.

For parallel composition we use the parallelism with shared variables rule 27 from the previous chapter but refer to the above notions of a standard proof outline and interference freedom.

Summarizing, we use the following proof system *PSY* for partial correctness of *parallel programs with synchronization*:

> PROOF SYSTEM *PSY* :
> This system consists of the group of axioms
> and rules 1–6, 25, 27, 28 and A2–A6.

Example 9.1. We wish to prove the correctness formula

$$\{x = 0\}\ [\mathbf{await}\ x = 1\ \mathbf{then}\ skip\ \mathbf{end}\|x := 1]\ \{x = 1\}$$

in the proof system *PSY*. For its components we consider the following proof outlines for partial correctness:

$$\{x = 0 \lor x = 1\}\ \mathbf{await}\ x = 1\ \mathbf{then}\ skip\ \mathbf{end}\ \{x = 1\}$$

and
$$\{x = 0\}\ x := 1\ \{x = 1\}.$$

Interference freedom of the assertions in the first proof outline under the execution of the assignment $x := 1$ is easy to check. In detail let us test the assertions of the second proof outline. For the precondition $x = 0$ we have

$$\{x = 0 \wedge (x = 0 \vee x = 1)\}\ \textbf{await}\ x = 1\ \textbf{then}\ skip\ \textbf{end}\ \{x = 0\}$$

because by the synchronization rule 28 it suffices to show

$$\{x = 0 \wedge (x = 0 \vee x = 1) \wedge x = 1\}\ skip\ \{x = 0\},$$

which holds trivially since its precondition is equivalent to **false**.
For the postcondition $x = 1$ we have

$$\{x = 1 \wedge (x = 0 \vee x = 1)\}\ \textbf{await}\ x = 1\ \textbf{then}\ skip\ \textbf{end}\ \{x = 1\},$$

because by the synchronization rule 28 it suffices to show

$$\{x = 1 \wedge (x = 0 \vee x = 1) \wedge x = 1\}\ skip\ \{x = 1\},$$

which is obviously true. Thus the parallelism with shared variables rule 27 is applicable and yields the desired result.   □

Weak Total Correctness

The notion of a weak total correctness combines partial correctness with divergence freedom. It is introduced only for component programs, and used as a stepping stone towards total correctness of parallel programs. By definition, a correctness formula $\{p\}\ S\ \{q\}$ is true in the sense of weak total correctness if

$$\mathcal{M}_{wtot}[\![S]\!]([\![p]\!]) \subseteq [\![q]\!]$$

holds. Since $\perp \notin [\![q]\!]$, every execution of S starting in a state satisfying p is finite and thus either terminates in a state satisfying q or gets blocked.

Proving weak total correctness of component programs is simple. We use the proof rules of the system TW for **while** programs and the synchronization rule 28 when dealing with **await** statements. Note that the synchronization rule is sound for weak total correctness but not for total correctness because the execution of **await** B **then** S **end** does not terminate when started in a state satisfying $\neg B$. Instead it gets blocked. This blocking can only be resolved with the help of other components executed in parallel.

To prove total correctness of parallel programs with **await** statements we need to consider interference free proof outlines for weak total correctness of component programs. To define the proof outlines we proceed as in the case of total correctness in Chapter 8 (see Definitions 8.2 and 8.3 and the convention that follows the latter definition).

First we must ensure that **await** statements decrease or leave unchanged the bound functions of **while** loops. To this end, we adapt Definition 8.2 of the set $path(S)$ for a component program S by replacing the clause $path(\langle S \rangle) = \{\langle S \rangle\}$ with

- $path($**await** B **then** S **end**$) = \{$**await** B **then** S **end**$\}$.

With this change, (standard) proof outlines for weak total correctness of component programs are defined by the same rules as those used for (standard) proof outlines for total correctness in Definition 8.3 together with rule (xii) dealing with **await** statements.

Standard proof outlines $\{p_i\}\ S_i^*\ \{q_i\}$, $i \in \{1, \ldots, n\}$, for weak total correctness are called *interference free* if no normal assignment or **await** statement of a component program S_i interferes with the proof outline of another component program S_j, $i \neq j$.

Total Correctness

Proving total correctness is now more complicated than in Chapter 8 because in the presence of **await** statements program termination not only requires divergence freedom (absence of infinite computations), but also deadlock freedom (absence of infinite blocking). Deadlock freedom is a *global* property that can be proved only by examining all components of a parallel program together. Thus none of the components of a terminating program need to terminate when considered in isolation; each of them may get blocked (see Example 9.2 below).

To prove total correctness of a parallel program, we first prove weak total correctness of its components, and then establish deadlock freedom.

To prove deadlock freedom of a parallel program, we examine interference free standard proof outlines for weak total correctness of its component programs and use the following method of Owicki and Gries [1976a]:

1. Enumerate all *potential* deadlock situations.
2. Show that none of them can actually occur.

This method is sound because in the proof of the Deadlock Freedom Lemma 9.5 below we show that every deadlock in the sense of Definition 9.1 is also a potential deadlock.

Definition 9.2. Consider a parallel program $S \equiv [S_1 \| \ldots \| S_n]$.

  (i) A tuple $(R_1, \ldots, R_n)$ of statements is called a *potential deadlock of S* if the following two conditions hold:

- For every $i \in \{1, \ldots, n\}$, R_i is either an **await** statement in the component S_i or the symbol E which stands for the empty statement and represents termination of S_i,
- for some $i \in \{1, \ldots, n\}$, R_i is an **await** statement in S_i.

(ii) Given interference free standard proof outlines $\{p_i\}\, S_i^*\, \{q_i\}$ for weak total correctness, $i \in \{1, \ldots, n\}$, we associate with every potential deadlock of S a corresponding tuple $(r_1, \ldots, r_n)$ of assertions by put-ting for $i \in \{1, \ldots, n\}$:

- $r_i \equiv pre(R_i) \wedge \neg B$ if $R_i \equiv$ **await** B **then** S **end**,
- $r_i \equiv q_i$ if $R_i \equiv E$.   □

If we can show $\neg \bigwedge_{i=1}^{n} r_i$ for every such tuple $(r_1, \ldots, r_n)$ of assertions, none of the potential deadlocks can actually arise. This is how deadlock freedom is established in the second premise of the following proof rule for total correctness of parallel programs.

RULE 29: PARALLELISM WITH DEADLOCK FREEDOM

(1) The standard proof outlines $\{p_i\}\, S_i^*\, \{q_i\}, i \in \{1, \ldots, n\}$
    for weak total correctness are interference free,
(2) For every potential deadlock $(R_1, \ldots, R_n)$ of
    $[S_1 \| \ldots \| S_n]$ the corresponding tuple of
    assertions $(r_1, \ldots, r_n)$ satisfies $\neg \bigwedge_{i=1}^{n} r_i$.

$$\{\textstyle\bigwedge_{i=1}^{n} p_i\}\ [S_1 \| \ldots \| S_n]\ \{\textstyle\bigwedge_{i=1}^{n} q_i\}$$

To prove *total* correctness of parallel programs with *synchronization*, we use the following proof system TSY:

> PROOF SYSTEM TSY:
> This system consists of the group of axioms
> and rules 1–5, 7, 25, 28, 29 and A2–A6.

Proof outlines for parallel programs with synchronization are defined in a straightforward manner (cf. Chapter 7).

The following example illustrates the use of rule 29 and demonstrates that for the components of parallel programs we cannot prove in isolation more than weak total correctness.

Example 9.2. We now wish to prove the correctness formula

$$\{x = 0\}\ [\textbf{await}\ x = 1\ \textbf{then}\ skip\ \textbf{end} \| x := 1]\ \{x = 1\} \qquad (9.1)$$

of Example 9.1 in the proof system TSY. For the component programs we use the following interference free standard proof outlines for weak total correctness:

$$\{x = 0 \vee x = 1\} \textbf{ await } x = 1 \textbf{ then } skip \textbf{ end } \{x = 1\} \qquad (9.2)$$

and

$$\{x = 0\}\ x := 1\ \{x = 1\}.$$

Formula (9.2) is proved using the synchronization rule 28; it is true only in the sense of weak total correctness because the execution of the **await** statement gets blocked when started in a state satisfying $x = 0$.

Deadlock freedom is proved as follows. The only potential deadlock is

$$(\textbf{await } x = 1 \textbf{ then } skip \textbf{ end}, E). \qquad (9.3)$$

The corresponding pair of assertions is

$$((x = 0 \vee x = 1) \wedge x \neq 1, x = 1),$$

the conjunction of which is clearly false. This shows that deadlock cannot arise. Rule 29 is now applicable and yields (9.1) as desired. □

Soundness

We now prove the soundness of *PSY*. Since we noted already the soundness of the synchronization rule 28, we concentrate here on the soundness proofs of the auxiliary variables rule 25 and the parallelism with shared variables rule 27.

Lemma 9.2. (Auxiliary Variables) *The auxiliary variables rule 25 is sound for partial (and total) correctness of parallel programs with synchronization.*

Proof. See Exercise 9.6. □

To prove the soundness of the parallelism with shared variables rule 27 for partial correctness of parallel programs with synchronization, we proceed as in the case of parallel programs with shared variables in Chapter 8. Namely, we first prove the following lemma analogous to the Strong Soundness for Parallel Programs Lemma 8.8.

Lemma 9.3. (Strong Soundness for Parallel Programs with Synchronization) *Let $\{p_i\}\ S_i^*\ \{q_i\}$, $i \in \{1, \ldots, n\}$, be interference free standard proof outlines for partial correctness for component programs S_i. Suppose that*

$$< [S_1 \| \ldots \| S_n], \sigma > \rightarrow^* < [R_1 \| \ldots \| R_n], \tau >$$

for some state σ satisfying $\bigwedge_{i=1}^{n} p_i$, some component programs R_i with $i \in \{1, \ldots, n\}$ and some state τ. Then for $j \in \{1, \ldots, n\}$

- *if $R_j \equiv \mathbf{at}(T, S_j)$ for a normal subprogram T of S_j, then $\tau \models pre(T)$,*
- *if $R_j \equiv E$, then $\tau \models q_j$.*

Proof. Fix $j \in \{1, \ldots, n\}$. It is easy to show that either $R_j \equiv \mathbf{at}(T, S_j)$ for a normal subprogram T of S_j or $R_j \equiv E$ (see Exercise 9.4). In the first case let r stand for $pre(T)$ and in the second case let r stand for q_j. We need to show $\tau \models r$.

The proof is by induction on the length of the transition sequence considered in the formulation of the lemma, and proceeds analogously to the proof of the Strong Soundness for Parallel Programs Lemma 8.8. We need only to consider one more case in the induction step: the last transition of the considered transition sequence is due to a step

$$< R'_k, \tau' > \; \rightarrow \; < R_k, \tau > \tag{9.4}$$

of the kth component executing an **await** statement, say **await** B **then** S **end**. Then

$$R'_k \equiv \mathbf{at}(\mathbf{await}\ B\ \mathbf{then}\ S\ \mathbf{end}, S_k).$$

By the induction hypothesis $\tau' \models pre(\mathbf{await}\ B\ \mathbf{then}\ S\ \mathbf{end})$. Also by the semantics of **await** statements $\tau' \models B$. Two cases now arise.

Case 1 $j = k$.

By the definition of a proof outline, in particular formation rule (xii) for the **await** statements, there exist assertions p and q and an annotated version S^* of S such that the following three properties hold:

$$pre(\mathbf{await}\ B\ \mathbf{then}\ S\ \mathbf{end}) \rightarrow p, \tag{9.5}$$

$$\{p \wedge B\}\ S^*\ \{q\} \text{ is a proof outline for partial correctness}, \tag{9.6}$$

$$q \rightarrow r. \tag{9.7}$$

Here r is the assertion associated with R_j and defined in the proof of the Strong Soundness for Parallel Programs Lemma 8.8, so $r \equiv pre(T)$ if $R_j \equiv \mathbf{at}(T, S_j)$ for a normal subprogram T of S_j and $r \equiv q_j$ if $R_j \equiv E$.

Since $\tau' \models pre(\mathbf{await}\ B\ \mathbf{then}\ S\ \mathbf{end}) \wedge B$, by (9.5)

$$\tau' \models p \wedge B. \tag{9.8}$$

By (9.4)

$$< \mathbf{await}\ B\ \mathbf{then}\ S\ \mathbf{end}, \tau' > \; \rightarrow \; < E, \tau >,$$

so by the definition of semantics

$$< S', \tau' > \; \rightarrow^* \; < E, \tau > . \tag{9.9}$$

Now by (9.6), (9.8) and (9.9), and by virtue of the Strong Soundness Theorem 3.3 we get $\tau \models q$. By (9.7) we conclude $\tau \models r$.

Case 2 $j \neq k$.

The argument is the same as in the proof of the Strong Soundness for Parallel Programs Lemma 8.8.   □

Corollary 9.1. (Parallelism) *The parallelism with shared variables rule 27 is sound for partial correctness of parallel programs with synchronization.*

Corollary 9.2. (Soundness of PSY) *The proof system PSY is sound for partial correctness of parallel programs with synchronization.*

Proof. We use the same argument as in the proof of the Soundness Corollary 7.1.   □

Next, we prove soundness of the proof system *TSY* for total correctness of parallel programs with synchronization. We concentrate here on the soundness proof of the new parallelism rule 29. To this end we establish the following two lemmata. The first one is an analogue of Termination Lemma 8.9.

Lemma 9.4. (Divergence Freedom) *Let* $\{p_i\}\, S_i^*\, \{q_i\}$, $i \in \{1,\dots,n\}$, *be interference free standard proof outlines for weak total correctness for component programs* S_i. *Then*

$$\bot \notin \mathcal{M}_{tot}[\![S_1\|\dots\|S_n]\!](\,[\![\textstyle\bigwedge_{i=1}^n\, p_i]\!]).$$

Proof. The proof is analogous to the proof of the Termination Lemma 8.9. It relies now on the definition of proof outlines for weak total correctness and the Strong Soundness for Component Programs Lemma 9.1 instead of Definition 8.3 and the Strong Soundness for Parallel Programs Lemma 8.8.

Lemma 9.5. (Deadlock Freedom) *Let* $\{p_i\}\, S_i^*\, \{q_i\}$, $i \in \{1,\dots,n\}$, *be interference free standard proof outlines for partial correctness for component programs* S_i. *Suppose that for every potential deadlock* $(R_1,\dots,R_n)$ *of* $[S_1\|\dots\|S_n]$ *the corresponding tuple of assertions* $(r_1,\dots,r_n)$ *satisfies* $\neg\bigwedge_{i=1}^n\, r_i$. *Then*

$$\Delta \notin \mathcal{M}_{tot}[\![S_1\|\dots\|S_n]\!](\,[\![\textstyle\bigwedge_{i=1}^n\, p_i]\!]).$$

Proof. Suppose that the converse holds. Then for some states σ and τ and component programs $T_1,\dots,T_n$

$$< [S_1\|\dots\|S_n],\sigma > \;\rightarrow^*\; < [T_1\|\dots\|T_n],\tau >, \qquad (9.10)$$

where $< [T_1\|\dots\|T_n],\tau >$ is a deadlock.

By the definition of deadlock,

(i) for every $i \in \{1, \ldots, n\}$ either

$$T_i \equiv \mathbf{at}(R_i, S_i) \tag{9.11}$$

for some **await** statement R_i in the component program S_i, or

$$T_i \equiv E, \tag{9.12}$$

(ii) for some $i \in \{1, \ldots, n\}$ case (9.11) holds.

By collecting the **await** statements R_i satisfying (9.11) and by defining $R_i \equiv E$ in case of (9.12), we obtain a potential deadlock $(R_1, \ldots, R_n)$ of $[S_1 \| \ldots \| S_n]$. Consider now the corresponding tuple of assertions $(r_1, \ldots, r_n)$ and fix some $i \in \{1, \ldots, n\}$.

If $R_i \equiv \mathbf{await}\ B\ \mathbf{then}\ S\ \mathbf{end}$ for some B and S, then $r_i \equiv pre(R_i) \wedge \neg B$. By the Strong Soundness for Component Programs Lemma 9.1, (9.10) and (9.11) we have $\tau \models pre(R_i)$. Moreover, since $< [T_1 \| \ldots \| T_n], \tau >$ is a deadlock, $\tau \models \neg B$ also. Thus $\tau \models r_i$.

If $R_i \equiv E$, then $r_i \equiv q_i$. By the Strong Soundness for Component Programs Lemma 9.1, (9.10) and (9.11) we have $\tau \models r_i$, as well.

Thus $\tau \models \bigwedge_{i=1}^{n} r_i$; so $\neg \bigwedge_{i=1}^{n} r_i$ is not true. This is a contradiction. $\square$

Corollary 9.3. (Parallelism) *Rule 29 is sound for total correctness of parallel programs with synchronization.*

Proof. Consider interference free standard proof outlines for weak total correctness for component programs. Then Lemma 9.4 applies. By removing from each of these proof outlines all annotations referring to the bound functions, we obtain interference free proof outlines for partial correctness. The claim now follows from the Parallelism Corollary 9.1 and the Deadlock Freedom Lemma 9.5. $\square$

Corollary 9.4. (Soundness of TSY) *The proof system TSY is sound for total correctness of parallel programs with synchronization.*

Proof. We use the same argument as that in the proof of the Soundness Corollary 7.1. $\square$

9.4 Case Study: Producer/Consumer Problem

A recurring task in the area of parallel programming is the coordination of producers and consumers. A producer generates a stream of $M \geq 1$ values for a consumer. We assume that the producer and consumer work in parallel and proceed at a variable but roughly equal pace.

The problem is to coordinate their work so that all values produced arrive at the consumer and in the order of production. Moreover, the producer should not have to wait with the production of a new value if the consumer is momentarily slow with its consumption. Conversely, the consumer should not have to wait if the producer is momentarily slow with its production.

The general idea of solving this producer/consumer problem is to interpose a buffer between producer and consumer. Thus the producer adds values to the buffer and the consumer removes values from the buffer. This way small variations in the pace of producers are not noticeable to the consumer and vice versa. However, since in reality the storage capacity of a buffer is limited, say to $N \geq 1$ values, we must synchronize producer and consumer in such a way that the producer never attempts to add a value into the full buffer and that the consumer never attempts to remove a value from the empty buffer.

Following Owicki and Gries [1976a], we express the producer/consumer problem as a parallel program PC with shared variables and **await** statements. The producer and consumer are modeled as two components $PROD$ and $CONS$ of a parallel program. Production of a value is modeled as reading an integer value from a finite section

$$a[0 : M - 1]$$

of an array a of type **integer** $\rightarrow$ **integer** and consumption of a value as writing an integer value into a corresponding section

$$b[0 : M - 1]$$

of an array b of type **integer** $\rightarrow$ **integer**. The buffer is modeled as a section

$$buffer[0 : N - 1]$$

of a shared array $buffer$ of type **integer** $\rightarrow$ **integer**. M and N are integer constants $M, N \geq 1$. For a correct access of the buffer the components $PROD$ and $CONS$ share an integer variable in counting the number of values added to the buffer and an integer variable out counting the number of values removed from the buffer. Thus at each moment the buffer contains $in - out$ values; it is full if $in - out = N$ and it is empty if $in - out = 0$. Adding and removing values to and from the buffer is performed in a cyclic order

$$buffer[0], \ldots, buffer[N - 1], buffer[0], \ldots, buffer[N - 1], buffer[0], \ldots .$$

Thus the expressions $in \bmod N$ and $out \bmod N$ determine the subscript of the buffer element where the next value is to be added or removed. This explains why we start numbering the buffer elements from 0 onwards.

With these preparations we can express the producer/consumer problem by the following parallel program:

$$PC \equiv in := 0; \; out := 0; \; i := 0; \; j := 0; \; [PROD\|CONS],$$

where

$$PROD \equiv \textbf{while } i < M \textbf{ do}$$
$$x := a[i];$$
$$ADD(x);$$
$$i := i + 1$$
$$\textbf{od}$$

and

$$CONS \equiv \textbf{while } j < M \textbf{ do}$$
$$REM(y);$$
$$b[j] := y;$$
$$j := j + 1$$
$$\textbf{od}.$$

Here i, j, x, y are integer variables and $ADD(x)$ and $REM(y)$ abbreviate the following synchronized statements for adding and removing values from the shared buffer:

$$ADD(x) \equiv \textbf{wait } in - out < N;$$
$$buffer[in \bmod N] := x;$$
$$in := in + 1$$

and

$$REM(y) \equiv \textbf{wait } in - out > 0;$$
$$y := buffer[out \bmod N];$$
$$out := out + 1.$$

Recall that for a Boolean expression B the statement **wait** B abbreviates **await** B **then** *skip* **end**.

We claim the following total correctness property:

$$\models_{tot} \{\textbf{true}\} \; PC \; \{\forall k : (0 \le k < M \rightarrow a[k] = b[k])\}, \qquad (9.13)$$

stating that the program PC is deadlock free and terminates with all values from $a[0 : M - 1]$ copied in that order into $b[0 : M - 1]$. The verification of (9.13) follows closely the presentation in Owicki and Gries [1976a].

First consider the component program $PROD$. As a loop invariant we take

$$
\begin{aligned}
p_1 \equiv \quad & \forall k : (out \le k < in \rightarrow a[k] = buffer[k \bmod N]) & (9.14)\\
& \wedge \;\; 0 \le in - out \le N & (9.15)\\
& \wedge \;\; 0 \le i \le M & (9.16)\\
& \wedge \;\; i = in & (9.17)
\end{aligned}
$$

and as a bound function
$$t_1 \equiv M - i.$$

Further, we introduce the following abbreviation for the conjunction of some of the lines in p_1:
$$I \equiv (9.14) \wedge (9.15)$$

and
$$I_1 \equiv (9.14) \wedge (9.15) \wedge (9.16).$$

As a standard proof outline we consider

$\{\mathbf{inv} : p_1\}\{\mathbf{bd} : t_1\}$
while $i < M$ **do**
$\quad \{p_1 \wedge i < M\}$
$\quad x := a[i];$
$\quad \{p_1 \wedge i < M \wedge x = a[i]\}$
$\quad \mathbf{wait}\ in - out < N;$
$\quad \{p_1 \wedge i < M \wedge x = a[i] \wedge in - out < N\}$
$\quad buffer[in \bmod N] := x;$
$\quad \{p_1 \wedge i < M \wedge a[i] = buffer[in \bmod N] \wedge in - out < N\} \qquad (9.18)$
$\quad in := in + 1;$
$\quad \{I_1 \wedge i + 1 = in \wedge i < M\} \qquad\qquad\qquad\qquad\qquad (9.19)$
$\quad i := i + 1$
od
$\{p_1 \wedge i = M\}.$

Clearly, this is indeed a proof outline for weak total correctness of $PROD$. In particular, note that (9.18) implies

$$\forall k : (out \le k < in + 1 \to a[k] = buffer[k \bmod N]),$$

which justifies the conjunct (9.14) of the postcondition (9.19) of the assignment $in := in + 1$. Note also that the bound function t_1 clearly satisfies the conditions required by the definition of proof outline.

Now consider the component program $CONS$. As a loop invariant we take

$$
\begin{aligned}
p_2 \equiv \quad & I & (9.20) \\
& \wedge \quad \forall k : (0 \le k < j \to a[k] = b[k]) & (9.21) \\
& \wedge \quad 0 \le j \le M & (9.22) \\
& \wedge \quad j = out, & (9.23)
\end{aligned}
$$

letting the I-part of p_1 reappear here, and as a bound function we take

$$t_2 \equiv M - j.$$

Let us abbreviate
$$I_2 \equiv (9.20) \wedge (9.21) \wedge (9.22),$$

and consider the following standard proof outline:

$\{\mathbf{inv} : p_2\}\{\mathbf{bd} : t_2\}$
$\mathbf{while}\ j < M\ \mathbf{do}$
$\quad \{p_2 \wedge j < M\}$
$\quad \mathbf{wait}\ in - out > 0;$
$\quad \{p_2 \wedge j < M \wedge in - out > 0\}$
$\quad y := buffer[out\ mod\ N];$
$\quad \{p_2 \wedge j < M \wedge in - out > 0 \wedge y = a[j]\}$ \hfill (9.24)
$\quad out := out + 1;$
$\quad \{I_2 \wedge j + 1 = out \wedge j < M \wedge y = a[j]\}$
$\quad b[j] := y;$
$\quad \{I_2 \wedge j + 1 = out \wedge j < M \wedge a[j] = b[j]\}$
$\quad j := j + 1$
$\mathbf{od}$
$\{p_2 \wedge j = M\}.$

Clearly, this is a correct proof outline for weak total correctness. In particular, the conjunct $y = a[j]$ in the assertion (9.24) is obtained by noting that $y = buffer[out\ mod\ N]$ is a postcondition for the assignment $y := buffer[out\ mod\ N]$ and by calculating

$$
\begin{aligned}
&buffer[out\ mod\ N] \\
=\ & \{(14) \wedge in - out > 0\} \\
&a[out] \\
=\ & \{(23)\} \\
&a[j].
\end{aligned}
$$

Also the bound function t_2 satisfies the conditions required by the definition of proof outline.

Let us now turn to the test of interference freedom of the two proof outlines. Naive calculations suggest that 80 correctness formulas must be checked! However, most of these checks can be dealt with by a single argument, that the I-part of p_1 and p_2 is kept invariant in both proof outlines. In other words, all assignments T in the proof outlines for $PROD$ and $CONS$ satisfy

$$\{I \wedge pre(T)\}\ T\ \{I\}.$$

It thus remains to check the assertions outside the I-part against possible interference. Consider first the proof outline for $PROD$. Examine all conjuncts occurring in the assertions used in this proof outline. Among them, apart from I, only the conjunct $in - out < N$ contains a variable that is changed in the component $CONS$. But this change is done only by the assignment $out := out + 1$. Obviously, we have here interference freedom:

$$\{in - out < N\}\ out := out + 1\ \{in - out < N\}.$$

Now consider the proof outline for $CONS$. Examine all conjuncts occurring in the assertions used in this proof outline. Among them, apart from I, only the conjunct $in - out > 0$ contains a variable that is changed in the component $PROD$. But this change is done only by the assignment $in := in + 1$. Obviously, we again have interference freedom:

$$\{in - out > 0\} \; in := in + 1 \; \{in - out > 0\}.$$

Next, we show deadlock freedom. The potential deadlocks are

$$(\textbf{wait } in - out < N, \textbf{wait } in - out > 0),$$
$$(\textbf{wait } in - out < N, E),$$
$$(E, \textbf{wait } in - out > 0),$$

and logical consequences of the corresponding pairs of assertions from the above proof outlines are

$$(in - out \geq N, in - out \leq 0),$$
$$(in < M \wedge in - out \geq N, out = M),$$
$$(in = M, out < M \wedge in - out \leq 0).$$

Since $N \geq 1$, the conjunction of the corresponding two assertions is false in all three cases. This proves deadlock freedom.

We can now apply rule 29 for the parallel composition of $PROD$ and $CONS$ and obtain

$$\{p_1 \wedge p_2\} \; [PROD \| CONS] \; \{p_1 \wedge p_2 \wedge in = M \wedge j = M\}.$$

Since
$$\{\textbf{true}\} \; in := 0; \; out := 0; \; i := 0; \; j := 0 \; \{p_1 \wedge p_2\}$$

and

$$p_1 \wedge p_2 \wedge i = M \wedge j = M \rightarrow \forall k : (0 \leq k < M \rightarrow a[k] = b[k]),$$

we obtain the desired correctness formula (9.13) about PC by straightforward applications of the composition rule and the consequence rule.

9.5 Case Study: The Mutual Exclusion Problem

Problem Formulation

Another classical problem in parallel programming is mutual exclusion, first investigated in Dijkstra [1968]. Consider n processes, $n \geq 2$, running indefinitely that share a resource, say a printer. The *mutual exclusion problem* is

the task of synchronizing these processes in such a way that the following
two conditions are satisfied:

(i) *mutual exclusion*:
   at any point of time at most one process uses the resource,
(ii) *absence of blocking*:
   the imposed synchronization discipline does not prevent the processes
   from running indefinitely,
(iii) *individual accessibility*:
   if a process is trying to acquire the resource, eventually it will succeed.

Conditions (i) and (ii) are instances of a *safety property* whereas condition
(iii) is an instance of a *liveness property*. Intuitively, a safety property is a
condition that holds in every state in the computations of a program whereas
a liveness property is a condition that for all computations is eventually
satisfied. A formulation of condition (iii) in our proof theoretic framework is
possible but awkward (see Olderog and Apt [1988]). Therefore its treatment
is omitted in this book.

An appropriate framework for the treatment of liveness properties is *tem-poral logic* (see Manna and Pnueli [1991,1995]). To this end, however, tem-poral logic uses a more complex assertion language and more complex proof
principles.

To formalize conditions (i) and (ii) we assume that each process S_i is an
eternal loop of the following form:

$$S_i \equiv \textbf{while true do}$$
$$NC_i;$$
$$ACQ_i;$$
$$CS_i;$$
$$REL_i$$
$$\textbf{od},$$

where NC_i (abbreviation for *noncritical section*) denotes a part of the pro-gram in which process S_i does not use the resource, ACQ_i (abbreviation for
acquire protocol) denotes the part of the program that process S_i executes
to acquire the resource, CS_i (abbreviation for *critical section*) denotes a loop
free part of the program in which process S_i uses the resource and REL_i (ab-breviation for *release protocol*) denotes the part of the program that process
S_i executes to release the resource. Additionally we assume that

$$(var(NC_i) \cup var(CS_i)) \cap (var(ACQ_j) \cup var(REL_j)) = \emptyset$$

for $i, j \in \{1, \ldots, n\}$ such that $i \neq j$; that is, the acquire and release protocols
use fresh variables. We also assume that no **await** statements are used inside
the sections NC_i and CS_i.

Then we consider a parallel program

$$S \equiv INIT;\ [S_1\|\ldots\|S_n],$$

where $INIT$ is a loop free **while** program in which the variables used in the acquire and release protocols are initialized.

Assume first that S is a parallel program without synchronization, that is, a program in the language studied in Chapter 8. Then we can formalize conditions (i) and (ii) as follows:

(a) mutual exclusion:
no configuration in a computation of S is of the form

$$< [R_1\|\ldots\|R_n], \sigma >,$$

where for some $i, j \in \{1, \ldots, n\}$, $i \neq j$

$$R_i \equiv \mathbf{at}(CS_i, S_i),$$

$$R_j \equiv \mathbf{at}(CS_j, S_j);$$

(b) absence of blocking:
no computation of S ends in a deadlock.

Note that in the case where S is a parallel program without synchronization, condition (ii) is actually automatically satisfied, and in the case where S is a parallel program with synchronization it indeed reduces to (b) due to the syntactic form of S.

A trivial solution to the mutual exclusion problem would be to turn the critical section CS_i into an atomic region:

$$
\begin{aligned}
S_i \equiv\ &\textbf{while true do}\\
&\quad NC_i;\\
&\quad \langle CS_i \rangle\\
&\textbf{od}.
\end{aligned}
$$

Here we have chosen $ACQ_i \equiv$ "$\langle$" and $REL_i \equiv$ "$\rangle$". Of course, this choice guarantees mutual exclusion because in a computation of S the ith component of S can never be of the form $R_i \equiv \mathbf{at}(CS_i, S_i)$.

However, we are interested here in more realistic solutions in which ACQ_i and REL_i are implemented by more primitive programming constructs.

Verification

Conditions (a) and (b) refer to semantics. To verify them we propose proof theoretic conditions that imply them. These conditions can then be established by means of an axiomatic reasoning.

To reason about the mutual exclusion condition (a) we use the following lemma.

Lemma 9.6. (Mutual Exclusion) *Suppose that for some assertions p_i with $i \in \{1, \ldots, n\}$, $\{$**true**$\}$ $INIT$ $\{\bigwedge_{i=1}^{n} p_i\}$ holds and $\{p_i\}$ S_i^* $\{$**false**$\}$ for $i \in \{1, \ldots, n\}$ are interference free standard proof outlines for partial correctness of the component programs S_i such that*

$$\neg(pre(CS_i) \wedge pre(CS_j))$$

holds for $i \in \{1, \ldots, n\}, i \neq j$. Then the mutual exclusion condition (a) is satisfied for the parallel program S.

Proof. This is an immediate consequence of the Strong Soundness Lemma 9.3. □

To reason about the absence of blocking condition (b) we use the Deadlock Freedom Lemma 9.5. Also, we use auxiliary variables. The following lemma allows us to do so.

Lemma 9.7. (Auxiliary Variables) *Suppose that S' is a parallel program with or without synchronization, A is a set of auxiliary variables of S' and S is obtained from S' by deleting all assignments to the variables in A.*

(i) If S' satisfies the mutual exclusion condition (a), then so does S.
(ii) If S' is deadlock free relative to some assertion p, then so is S.

Proof. See Exercise 9.7. □

A Busy Wait Solution

First, let us consider the case of parallel programs without synchronization. When the acquire protocol for each process S_i for $i \in \{1, \ldots, n\}$ is of the form

$$ACQ_i \equiv T_i; \textbf{ while } \neg B_i \textbf{ do } skip \textbf{ od},$$

where T_i is loop free, we call such a solution to the mutual exclusion problem a *busy wait solution* and the loop **while** $\neg B_i$ **do** *skip* **od** a *busy wait loop*.

We consider here the following simple busy wait solution to the mutual exclusion problem for two processes due to Peterson [1981]. Let

$$MUTEX\text{-}B \equiv flag_1 := \textbf{false}; \ flag_2 := \textbf{false}; \ [S_1 \| S_2],$$

where

$S_1 \equiv$ **while true do**
    NC_1;
    $flag_1 :=$ **true**; $turn := 1$;
    while $\neg(flag_2 \rightarrow turn = 2)$ **do** *skip* **od**;
    CS_1;
    $flag_1 :=$ **false**
od

and

$S_2 \equiv$ **while true do**
    NC_2;
    $flag_2 :=$ **true**; $turn := 2$;
    while $\neg(flag_1 \rightarrow turn = 1)$ **do** *skip* **od**;
    CS_2;
    $flag_2 :=$ **false**
od.

Intuitively, the Boolean variable $flag_i$ indicates whether the component S_i intends to enter its critical section, $i \in \{1, 2\}$. The variable $turn$ is used to resolve simultaneity conflicts: in case both components S_1 and S_2 intend to enter their critical sections, the component that set the variable $turn$ first is delayed in a busy wait loop until the other component alters the value of $turn$. (Note that $\neg(flag_i \rightarrow turn = i)$ is equivalent to $flag_i \wedge turn \neq i$ for $i \in \{1, 2\}$).

To prove correctness of this solution we introduce two auxiliary variables, $after_1$ and $after_2$, that serve to indicate whether in the acquire protocol of S_i ($i \in \{1, 2\}$) the control is after the assignment $turn := i$. Thus we consider now the following extended program

$$MUTEX\text{-}B' \equiv flag_1 :=\text{ \bf false};\ flag_2 :=\text{ \bf false};\ [S_1' \| S_2'],$$

where

$S_1' \equiv$ **while true do**
    NC_1;
    $\langle flag_1 :=$ **true**; $after_1 :=$ **false**$\rangle$;
    $\langle turn := 1;\ after_1 :=$ **true**$\rangle$;
    while $\neg(flag_2 \rightarrow turn = 2)$ **do** *skip* **od**;
    CS_1;
    $flag_1 :=$ **false**
od

and

$S_2' \equiv$ **while true do**
    NC_2;
    $\langle flag_2 :=$ **true**; $after_2 :=$ **false**$\rangle$;

$\langle turn := 2;\ after_2 := \textbf{true} \rangle;$
while $\neg(flag_1 \to turn = 1)$ **do** *skip* **od**;
$CS_2;$
$flag_2 := \textbf{false}$
od.

With the help of the Mutual Exclusion Lemma 9.6 we prove now the mutual exclusion condition (a) for the extended program $MUTEX\text{-}B'$. To this end we consider the following standard proof outlines for partial correctness of the component programs S_1' and S_2' where we treat the parts NC_i and CS_i as *skip* statements and use the abbreviation

$$I \equiv turn = 1 \lor turn = 2.$$

$\{\textbf{inv} : \neg flag_1\}$
while true do
$\quad \{\neg flag_1\}$
$\quad NC_1;$
$\quad \{\neg flag_1\}$
$\quad \langle flag_1 := \textbf{true};\ after_1 := \textbf{false} \rangle;$
$\quad \{flag_1 \land \neg after_1\}$
$\quad \langle turn := 1;\ after_1 := \textbf{true} \rangle;$
$\quad \{\textbf{inv} : flag_1 \land after_1 \land I\}$
$\quad \textbf{while } \neg(flag_2 \to turn = 2) \textbf{ do}$
$\quad\quad \{flag_1 \land after_1 \land I\}$
$\quad\quad skip$
$\quad \textbf{od}$
$\quad \{flag_1 \land after_1 \land (flag_2 \land after_2 \to turn = 2)\}$
$\quad CS_1;$
$\quad \{flag_1\}$
$\quad flag_1 := \textbf{false}$
od
$\{\textbf{false}\}$

and

$\{\textbf{inv} : \neg flag_2\}$
while true do
$\quad \{\neg flag_2\}$
$\quad NC_2;$
$\quad \{\neg flag_2\}$
$\quad \langle flag_2 := \textbf{true};\ after_2 := \textbf{false} \rangle;$
$\quad \{flag_2 \land \neg after_2\}$
$\quad \langle turn := 2;\ after_2 := \textbf{true} \rangle;$
$\quad \{\textbf{inv} : flag_2 \land after_2 \land I\}$
$\quad \textbf{while } \neg(flag_1 \to turn = 1) \textbf{ do}$
$\quad\quad \{flag_2 \land after_2 \land I\}$

$$skip$$
$$\textbf{od}$$
$$\{flag_2 \wedge after_2 \wedge (flag_1 \wedge after_1 \to turn = 1)\}$$
$$CS_2;$$
$$\{flag_2\}$$
$$flag_2 := \textbf{false}$$
$$\textbf{od}$$
$$\{\textbf{false}\}.$$

First, let us check that these are indeed proof outlines for partial correctness of S_1' and S_2'. The only interesting parts are the busy wait loops. For the busy wait loop in S_1'

$$\{\textbf{inv} : flag_1 \wedge after_1 \wedge I\}$$
$$\textbf{while } \neg(flag_2 \to turn = 2) \textbf{ do}$$
$$\quad \{flag_1 \wedge after_1 \wedge I\}$$
$$\quad skip$$
$$\textbf{od}$$
$$\{flag_1 \wedge after_1 \wedge I \wedge (flag_2 \to turn = 2)\}$$

is a correct proof outline and so is

$$\{\textbf{inv} : flag_1 \wedge after_1 \wedge I\}$$
$$\textbf{while } \neg(flag_2 \to turn = 2) \textbf{ do}$$
$$\quad \{flag_1 \wedge after_1 \wedge I\}$$
$$\quad skip$$
$$\textbf{od}$$
$$\{flag_1 \wedge after_1 \wedge (flag_2 \wedge after_2 \to turn = 2)\},$$

because $I \wedge (flag_2 \to turn = 2)$ trivially implies the conjunct

$$flag_2 \wedge after_2 \to turn = 2.$$

A similar argument can be used for the busy wait loop in S_2'.

Next we show interference freedom of the above proof outlines. In the proof outline for S_1' only the assertion

$$pre(CS_1) \equiv flag_1 \wedge after_1 \wedge (flag_2 \wedge after_2 \to turn = 2)$$

can be invalidated by a statement from S_2' because all other assertions contain only variables that are local to S_1' or the obviously interference-free conjunct I. The only normal assignments or **await** statements of S_2' that can invalidate it are $\langle flag_2 := \textbf{true}; \ after_2 := \textbf{false}\rangle$ and $\langle turn := 2; \ after_2 := \textbf{true}\rangle$. Clearly both

$$\{pre(CS_1)\} \ \langle flag_2 := \textbf{true}; \ after_2 := \textbf{false}\rangle \ \{pre(CS_1)\}$$

and

$$\{pre(CS_1)\} \; \langle turn := 2; \; after_2 := \textbf{true} \rangle \; \{pre(CS_1)\}$$

hold. Thus no normal assignment or **await** statement of S_2' interferes with
the proof outline for S_1'. By symmetry the same holds with S_1' and S_2' interchanged. This shows that the above proof outlines for S_1' and S_2' are interference free.

By the implication

$$pre(CS_1) \wedge pre(CS_2) \rightarrow turn = 1 \wedge turn = 2,$$

we have

$$\neg(pre(CS_1) \wedge pre(CS_2)).$$

Thus the Mutual Exclusion Lemma 9.6 yields the mutual exclusion condition
(a) for the extended parallel program $MUTEX\text{-}B'$ and the Auxiliary Variables
Lemma 9.7 (i) for the original program $MUTEX\text{-}B$.

A Solution Using Semaphores

In this subsection we consider a solution to the mutual exclusion problem for
n processes due to Dijkstra [1968]. It uses the concept of a semaphore as a
synchronization primitive. A *semaphore* is a shared integer variable, say *sem*,
on which only the following operations are allowed:

- initialization: $sem := k$ where $k \geq 0$,
- P–operation: $P(sem) \equiv \textbf{await} \; sem > 0 \; \textbf{then} \; sem := sem - 1 \; \textbf{end}$,
- V–operation: $V(sem) \equiv sem := sem + 1$.

The letters P and V originate from the Dutch verbs "passeren" (to pass)
and "vrijgeven" (to free).

A *binary semaphore* is a semaphore that can take only two values: 0 and
1. To model a binary semaphore it is convenient to use a Boolean variable,
say *out*, and redefine the semaphore operations as follows:

- initialization: $out := \textbf{true}$,
- P–operation: $P(out) \equiv \textbf{await} \; out \; \textbf{then} \; out := \textbf{false} \; \textbf{end}$,
- V–operation: $V(out) \equiv out := \textbf{true}$.

The solution to the mutual exclusion problem using binary semaphores
has the following simple form:

$$MUTEX\text{-}S \equiv out := \textbf{true}; \; [S_1 \| \ldots \| S_n]$$

where for $i \in \{1, \ldots, n\}$

$$S_i \equiv \textbf{while true do}$$
$$NC_i;$$
$$P(out);$$
$$CS_i;$$
$$V(out)$$
$$\textbf{od}.$$

Intuitively, the binary semaphore *out* indicates whether all processes are out of their critical sections.

To prove correctness of this solution, we have to prove the properties (a) and (b). To this end, we introduce an auxiliary variable *who* that indicates which component, if any, is inside the critical section. Thus we consider now the following extended program

$$MUTEX\text{-}S' \equiv out := \textbf{true}; \ who := 0; \ [S_1'\|\ldots\|S_n'],$$

where for $i \in \{1, \ldots, n\}$

$$S_i' \equiv \textbf{while true do}$$
$$NC_i;$$
$$\textbf{await } out \textbf{ then } out := \textbf{false}; \ who := i \textbf{ end};$$
$$CS_i;$$
$$\langle out := \textbf{true}; \ who := 0 \rangle$$
$$\textbf{od}.$$

Note that the binary *P*- and *V*-operations have been extended to atomic actions embracing assignment to the auxiliary variable *who*.

For the component programs S_i' for $i \in \{1, \ldots, n\}$ we use the assertion

$$I \equiv (\bigvee_{j=0}^{n} who = j) \wedge (who = 0 \leftrightarrow out)$$

in the following standard proof outlines for partial correctness:

$$\{\textbf{inv} : who \neq i \wedge I\}$$
$$\textbf{while true do}$$
$$\{who \neq i \wedge I\}$$
$$NC_i;$$
$$\{who \neq i \wedge I\}$$
$$\textbf{await } out \textbf{ then } out := \textbf{false}; \ who := i \textbf{ end};$$
$$\{\neg out \wedge who = i\}$$
$$CS_i;$$
$$\{\neg out \wedge who = i\}$$
$$\langle out := \textbf{true}; \ who := 0 \rangle$$
$$\textbf{od}$$
$$\{\textbf{false}\}.$$

Considered in isolation these are correct proof outlines. We now prove their interference freedom. First we consider the assertion $who \neq i \wedge I$ occurring three times in the proof outline of S'_i. This assertion is kept invariant under both the extended P-operation

$$\textbf{await } out \textbf{ then } out := \textbf{false}; \ who := i \textbf{ end}$$

and the V-operation

$$\langle out := \textbf{true}; \ who := 0 \rangle$$

from any S'_j with $i \neq j$. Next we consider the assertion $\neg out \wedge who = i$ occurring twice in S'_i. To show that this assertion is kept invariant under the extended P-operation, we consider the body of this **await** statement. We have

$$\{\neg out \wedge who = i \wedge out\}$$
$$\{\textbf{false}\}$$
$$out := \textbf{false}; \ who := j$$
$$\{\textbf{false}\}$$
$$\{\neg out \wedge who = i\};$$

so by the synchronization rule 28

$$\{\neg out \wedge who = i \wedge \textbf{true}\}$$
$$\textbf{await } out \textbf{ then } out := \textbf{false}; \ who := j \textbf{ end}$$
$$\{\neg out \wedge who = i\}.$$

For the extended V-operation $\langle out := \textbf{true}; \ who := 0 \rangle$ from S'_j with $i \neq j$ the atomic region rule 26 (as a special case of the synchronization rule 28) yields

$$\{\neg out \wedge who = i \wedge \neg out \wedge who = j\}$$
$$\{\textbf{false}\}$$
$$out := \textbf{true}; \ who := 0$$
$$\{\textbf{false}\}$$
$$\{\neg out \wedge who = i\}.$$

This finishes the proof of interference freedom.

To prove the mutual exclusion condition (a) note that for $i, j \in \{1, \ldots, n\}$ such that $i \neq j$

$$pre(CS_i) \wedge pre(CS_j) \rightarrow who = i \wedge who = j;$$

so

$$\neg(pre(CS_i) \wedge pre(CS_j))$$

holds. It suffices now to apply the Mutual Exclusion Lemma 9.6 and the Auxiliary Variables Lemma 9.7(i).

Finally, we prove the absence of blocking condition (b), thus showing that
MUTEX-S is deadlock free. To this end, we investigate the potential deadlocks of *MUTEX-S'* and the corresponding tuple of assertions $(r_1, \ldots, r_n)$.
We need to show that $\neg \bigwedge_{i=1}^{n} r_i$ holds. Because of the form of the postconditions of S_i'' for $i \in \{1, \ldots, n\}$ it suffices to consider the case where each r_i is
associated with the precondition of the **await** statement of S_i', that is, where
for $i \in \{1, \ldots, n\}$

$$r_i \equiv who \neq i \wedge I \wedge \neg out.$$

By the form of I,

$$(\bigwedge_{i=1}^{n} r_i) \rightarrow who = 0 \wedge (who = 0 \leftrightarrow out) \wedge \neg out,$$

so

$$\neg \bigwedge_{i=1}^{n} r_i$$

indeed holds. By virtue of the Deadlock Freedom Lemma 9.5 this proves
deadlock freedom of *MUTEX-S'* and the deadlock freedom of *MUTEX-S*
now follows by the Auxiliary Variables Lemma 9.7(ii).

9.6 Allowing More Points of Interference

As in Chapter 8 we can apply program transformations to parallel programs
with synchronization. These transformations are the same as in Section 8.7
and as before can be used in two ways. First, they allow us to derive from a
parallel program another parallel program with more points of interference.
Second, they can be used to simplify a correctness proof of a parallel program
by applying them in a reverse direction. In the next section we illustrate the
second use of them.

Theorem 9.1. (Atomicity) *Consider a parallel program with synchroniza-
tion of the form $S \equiv S_0; [S_1 \| \ldots \| S_n]$ where S_0 is a **while** program. Let T
result from S by replacing in one of its components, say S_i with $i > 0$, either*

- *an atomic region $\langle R_1;\ R_2 \rangle$ where one of the R_ls is disjoint from all components S_j with $j \neq i$ by*

$$\langle R_1 \rangle;\ \langle R_2 \rangle$$

or

- *an atomic region $\langle$**if** B **then** R_1 **else** R_2 **fi**$\rangle$ where B is disjoint from all
  components S_j with $j \neq i$ by*

$$\textbf{if } B \textbf{ then } \langle R_1 \rangle \textbf{ else } \langle R_2 \rangle \textbf{ fi.}$$

Then the semantics of S and T agree; that is,

$$\mathcal{M}[\![S]\!] = \mathcal{M}[\![T]\!] \text{ and } \mathcal{M}_{tot}[\![S]\!] = \mathcal{M}_{tot}[\![T]\!].$$

Proof. See Exercise 9.9.   □

Corollary 9.5. (Atomicity) *Under the assumptions of the Atomicity Theorem 9.1, for all assertions p and q*

$$\models \{p\} \ S \ \{q\} \ iff \ \models \{p\} \ T \ \{q\}$$

and analogously for $\models_{tot}$.

Theorem 9.2. (Initialization) *Consider a parallel program with synchronization of the form*

$$S \equiv S_0; \ R_0; \ [S_1\|\ldots\|S_n],$$

where S_0 *and* R_0 *are* **while** *programs. Suppose that for some* $i \in \{1, \ldots, n\}$ *the initialization part* R_0 *is disjoint from all component programs* S_j *with* $j \neq i$. *Then the program*

$$T \equiv S_0; \ [S_1\|\ldots\|R_0; \ S_i\|\ldots\|S_n]$$

has the same semantics as S; that is,

$$\mathcal{M}[\![S]\!] = \mathcal{M}[\![T]\!] \text{ and } \mathcal{M}_{tot}[\![S]\!] = \mathcal{M}_{tot}[\![T]\!].$$

Proof. See Exercise 9.10.   □

Corollary 9.6. (Initialization) *Under the assumptions of the Initialization Theorem 9.2, for all assertions p and q*

$$\models \{p\} \ S \ \{q\} \ iff \ \models \{p\} \ T \ \{q\}$$

and analogously for $\models_{tot}$.

9.7 Case Study: Synchronized Zero Search

We wish to prove the correctness of Solution 6 to the zero search problem given in Section 1.1. That is, we wish to prove that due to the incorporated synchronization constructs the parallel program

$$ZERO\text{-}6 \equiv turn := 1; found := \textbf{false}; [S_1\|S_2]$$

with

$$S_1 \equiv x := 0;$$
$$\quad \textbf{while } \neg found \textbf{ do}$$
$$\qquad \textbf{wait } turn = 1;$$
$$\qquad turn := 2;$$
$$\qquad x := x + 1;$$
$$\qquad \textbf{if } f(x) = 0 \textbf{ then } found := \textbf{true fi}$$
$$\quad \textbf{od};$$
$$\quad turn := 2$$

and

$$S_2 \equiv y := 1;$$
$$\quad \textbf{while } \neg found \textbf{ do}$$
$$\qquad \textbf{wait } turn = 2;$$
$$\qquad turn := 1;$$
$$\qquad y := y - 1;$$
$$\qquad \textbf{if } f(y) = 0 \textbf{ then } found := \textbf{true fi}$$
$$\quad \textbf{od};$$
$$\quad turn := 1$$

finds a zero of the function f provided such a zero exists:

$$\models_{tot} \{\exists u : f(u) = 0\} \ ZERO\text{-}6 \ \{f(x) = 0 \lor f(y) = 0\}. \qquad (9.25)$$

As in the Case Study of Section 8.8 we proceed in four steps.

Step 1. Simplifying the Program

We apply the Atomicity Corollary 9.5 and Initialization Corollary 9.6 to reduce the original problem (9.25) to the following claim

$$\models_{tot} \{\exists u : f(u) = 0\} \ T \ \{f(x) = 0 \lor f(y) = 0\}, \qquad (9.26)$$

where

$$T \equiv turn := 1; \ found := \textbf{false};$$
$$\quad x := 0; \ y := 1;$$
$$\quad [T_1 \| T_2]$$

with

$$T_1 \equiv \textbf{while } \neg found \textbf{ do}$$
$$\qquad \textbf{wait } turn = 1;$$
$$\qquad turn := 2;$$
$$\qquad \langle \ x := x + 1;$$
$$\qquad \textbf{if } f(x) = 0 \textbf{ then } found := \textbf{true fi} \rangle$$

$$\textbf{od};$$
$$turn := 2$$

and

$$
\begin{aligned}
T_2 \equiv\ &\textbf{while } \neg found \textbf{ do} \\
&\quad \textbf{wait } turn = 2; \\
&\quad turn := 1; \\
&\quad \langle\ y := y - 1; \\
&\qquad \textbf{if } f(y) = 0 \textbf{ then } found := \textbf{true fi} \rangle \\
&\textbf{od}; \\
&turn := 1.
\end{aligned}
$$

Both corollaries are applicable here because x does not appear in S_2 and y does not appear in S_1.

Step 2. Decomposing Total Correctness

To prove (9.26) we use the fact that total correctness can be decomposed into termination and partial correctness. More precisely we use the following observation.

Lemma 9.8. (Decomposition) *For all programs R and all assertions p and q*

$$\models_{tot} \{p\}\ R\ \{q\} \textit{ iff } \models_{tot} \{p\}\ R\ \{\textbf{true}\} \textit{ and } \models \{p\}\ R\ \{q\}.$$

Proof. By the definition of total and partial correctness. $\qquad\qquad\square$

Thus to prove (9.26) it suffices to prove

$$\models_{tot} \{\exists u : f(u) = 0\}\ T\ \{\textbf{true}\} \tag{9.27}$$

and

$$\models \{\exists u : f(u) = 0\}\ T\ \{f(x) = 0 \lor f(y) = 0\}. \tag{9.28}$$

Step 3. Proving Termination

We prove (9.27) in the proof system TSY for total correctness introduced in Section 9.3. To prove deadlock freedom we need two Boolean auxiliary variables $after_1$ and $after_2$ to indicate whether the execution of the component programs T_1 and T_2 is just after one of the assignments to the variable $turn$. Thus instead of T we consider the augmented program

$$U \equiv turn := 1; \; found := \textbf{false};$$
$$x := 0; \; y := 1;$$
$$after_1 := \textbf{false}; \; after_2 := \textbf{false};$$
$$[U_1 \| U_2]$$

with

$$U_1 \equiv \textbf{while } \neg found \textbf{ do}$$
$$\textbf{wait } turn = 1;$$
$$\langle turn := 2; \; after_1 := \textbf{true}\rangle;$$
$$\langle \; x := x + 1;$$
$$\textbf{if } f(x) = 0 \textbf{ then } found := \textbf{true fi};$$
$$after_1 := \textbf{false}\rangle$$
$$\textbf{od};$$
$$\langle turn := 2; \; after_1 := \textbf{true}\rangle$$

and

$$U_2 \equiv \textbf{while } \neg found \textbf{ do}$$
$$\textbf{wait } turn = 2;$$
$$\langle turn := 1; \; after_2 := \textbf{true}\rangle;$$
$$\langle \; y := y - 1;$$
$$\textbf{if } f(y) = 0 \textbf{ then } found := \textbf{true fi};$$
$$after_2 := \textbf{false}\rangle$$
$$\textbf{od};$$
$$\langle turn := 1; \; after_2 := \textbf{true}\rangle.$$

The rule of auxiliary variables (rule 25) is sound for total correctness of parallel programs with synchronization (see the Auxiliary Variables Lemma 9.2); so to prove (9.27) it suffices to prove

$$\models_{tot} \{\exists u : f(u) = 0\} \; U \; \{\textbf{true}\}. \tag{9.29}$$

To prove (9.29) we first deal with the case of a *positive* zero u of f:

$$\models_{tot} \{f(u) = 0 \land u > 0\} \; U \; \{\textbf{true}\}. \tag{9.30}$$

In this case the component U_1 of U is responsible for finding the zero. This observation is made precise in the proof outlines for weak total correctness of the component programs U_1 and U_2. For U_1 we take as a loop invariant

$$p_1 \equiv \quad f(u) = 0 \land u > 0 \land x \le u \tag{9.31}$$
$$\land \quad (turn = 1 \lor turn = 2) \tag{9.32}$$
$$\land \quad (\neg found \rightarrow x < u) \tag{9.33}$$
$$\land \quad \neg after_1 \tag{9.34}$$

and as a bound function

$$t_1 \equiv u - x.$$

Let us abbreviate the first two lines in p_1:

$$I_1 \equiv (9.31) \wedge (9.32).$$

Then we consider the following standard proof outline for U_1:

> $\{\mathbf{inv} : p_1\}\{\mathbf{bd} : t_1\}$
> $\mathbf{while}\ \neg found\ \mathbf{do}$
> $\{I_1 \wedge (found \wedge after_2 \rightarrow turn = 1)$ (9.35)
> $\wedge\ x < u \wedge \neg after_1$ $\}$
> $\mathbf{wait}\ turn = 1;$
> $\{I_1 \wedge x < u \wedge \neg after_1\}$
> $\langle turn := 2;\ after_1 := \mathbf{true}\rangle$
> $\{I_1 \wedge x < u \wedge after_1\}$
> $\langle\ x := x + 1;$
> $\mathbf{if}\ f(x) = 0\ \mathbf{then}\ found := \mathbf{true}\ \mathbf{fi};$
> $after_1 := \mathbf{false}\rangle$
> $\mathbf{od};$
> $\{found \wedge (turn = 1 \vee turn = 2) \wedge \neg after_1\}$
> $\langle turn := 2;\ after_1 := \mathbf{true}\rangle$
> $\{found \wedge after_1\}.$

It is easy to check that this is indeed a proof outline for weak total correctness of U_1. In particular, note that $p_1 \wedge \neg found$ trivially implies the conjunct

$$found \wedge after_2 \rightarrow turn = 1 \qquad (9.36)$$

in assertion (9.35). This conjunct is crucial for showing deadlock freedom below. Note also that the bound function t_1 clearly satisfies the conditions required by the definition of proof outline.

Now consider the component program U_2. As a loop invariant we simply take

$$
\begin{aligned}
p_2 \equiv\ &x \leq u & (9.37)\\
&\wedge\ (turn = 1 \vee turn = 2) & (9.32)\\
&\wedge\ \neg after_2, & (9.38)
\end{aligned}
$$

but as a bound function we need to take

$$t_2 \equiv turn + int(\neg after_1) + u - x.$$

For U_2 considered in isolation, the variable $turn$ would suffice as a bound function, but when U_2 is considered in parallel with U_1 the remaining summands of t_2 are needed to achieve interference freedom. Let us abbreviate

$$I_2 \equiv (9.37) \wedge (9.32)$$

and consider the following standard proof outline for U_2:

$\{\textbf{inv}: p_2\}\{\textbf{bd}: t_2\}$
while $\neg found$ **do**
    $\{I_2 \wedge (found \wedge after_1 \rightarrow turn = 2) \wedge \neg after_2\}$
    wait $turn = 2$;
    $\{I_2 \wedge \neg after_2\}$
    $\langle turn := 1;\ after_2 := \textbf{true}\rangle$
    $\{I_2 \wedge after_2\}$
    $\langle\ y := y - 1;$
       if $f(y) = 0$ **then** $found := \textbf{true}$ **fi**;
       $after_2 := \textbf{false}\rangle$
od;
$\{found\}$
$\langle turn := 1;\ after_2 := \textbf{true}\rangle$
$\{found \wedge after_2\}.$

Clearly, this is indeed a proof outline for weak total correctness of U_2. In particular, note that the bound function t_2 satisfies

$$p_2 \rightarrow t_2 \geq 0$$

and that it is decreased along every syntactically possible path through the loop in U_2 because the variable $turn$ drops from 2 to 1.

Let us now check the two proof outlines for interference freedom. In total we have to check 64 correctness formulas. However, a careful inspection of the proof outlines shows that only a few parts of the assertions and bound functions of each proof outline contain variables that can be modified by the other component. For the proof outline of U_1 there are the conjuncts

$$turn = 1 \vee turn = 2, \tag{9.32}$$
$$\neg found \rightarrow x < u, \tag{9.33}$$
$$found \wedge after_2 \rightarrow turn = 1. \tag{9.36}$$

Conjunct (9.32) is obviously preserved under the execution of the statements in U_2. Conjunct (9.33) is preserved because the only way U_2 can modify the variable $found$ is by changing its value from **false** to **true**. With $found$ evaluating to true, conjunct (9.33) is trivially satisfied. Finally, conjunct (9.36) is preserved because, by the proof outline of U_2, whenever the variable $after_2$ is set to **true**, the variable $turn$ is simultaneously set to 1.

For the proof outline of U_2, only the conjuncts

$$turn = 1 \vee turn = 2, \tag{9.32}$$
$$found \wedge after_1 \rightarrow turn = 2 \tag{9.39}$$

and the bound function

$$t_2 \equiv turn + int(\neg after_1) + u - x$$

contain variables that can be modified by U_1. Conjuncts (9.32) and (9.39) are dealt with analogously to the conjuncts (9.32) and (9.36) from the proof outline of U_1. Thus it remains to show that none of the atomic regions in U_1 can increase the value of t_2. This amounts to checking the following two correctness formulas:

$$\{(turn = 1 \lor turn = 2) \land \neg after_1 \land t_2 = z\}$$
$$\langle turn := 2; \; after_1 := \textbf{true}\rangle$$
$$\{t_2 \leq z\}$$

and

$$\{after_1 \land t_2 = z\}$$
$$\langle \; x := x + 1;$$
$$\quad \textbf{if } f(x) = 0 \textbf{ then } found := \textbf{true fi};$$
$$\quad after_1 := \textbf{false}\rangle$$
$$\{t_2 \leq z\}.$$

Both correctness formulas are clearly true. This completes the proof of interference freedom.

Next, we show deadlock freedom. The potential deadlocks are

$$(\textbf{wait } turn = 1, \textbf{wait } turn = 2),$$
$$(\textbf{wait } turn = 1, E),$$
$$(E, \textbf{wait } turn = 2),$$

and logical consequences of the corresponding pairs of assertions from the above proof outlines are

$$((turn = 1 \lor turn = 2) \land turn \neq 1, turn \neq 2),$$
$$((found \land after_2 \rightarrow turn = 1) \land turn \neq 1, found \land after_2),$$
$$(found \land after_1, (found \land after_1 \rightarrow turn = 2) \land turn \neq 2).$$

Obviously, the conjunction of the corresponding two assertions is false in all three cases. This proves deadlock freedom.

Thus we can apply rule 29 for the parallel composition of U_1 and U_2 and obtain

$$\{p_1 \land p_2\} \; [U_1 \| U_2] \; \{found \land after_1 \land after_2\}.$$

Since

$$\{f(u) = 0 \land u > 0\}$$
$$turn := 1; \; found := \textbf{false};$$
$$x := 0; \; y := 1;$$
$$after_1 := \textbf{false}; \; after_2 := \textbf{false};$$
$$\{p_1 \land p_2\}$$

and

$$found \land after_1 \land after_2 \rightarrow \textbf{true},$$

we obtain the statement (9.30) about U by virtue of the soundness of the composition rule and of the consequence rule.

For the case in which f has a zero $u \le 0$ we must prove

$$\models_{tot} \{f(u) = 0 \wedge u \le 0\} \ U \ \{\textbf{true}\}. \tag{9.40}$$

Instead of the component U_1, now the component U_2 of U is responsible for finding a zero. Hence the proof of (9.40) in the system TSY is entirely symmetric to that of (9.30) and is therefore omitted.

Finally, we combine the results (9.30) and (9.40). By the soundness of the disjunction rule (rule A3) and of the consequence rule, we obtain

$$\models_{tot} \{f(u) = 0\} \ U \ \{\textbf{true}\}.$$

Final application of the $\exists$-introduction rule (rule A5) yields the desired termination result (9.29) for U.

Step 4. Proving Partial Correctness

Finally, we prove (9.28) in the proof system PSY for partial correctness introduced in Section 9.3. We have isolated this step because we can reuse here the argument given in Step 4 of the Case Study of Section 8.8. Indeed, to construct interference free proof outlines for partial correctness of the component programs T_1 and T_2 of T, we reuse the invariants p_1 and p_2 given there:

$$
\begin{aligned}
p_1 \equiv \quad & x \ge 0 \\
& \wedge \ (found \to (x > 0 \wedge f(x) = 0) \vee (y \le 0 \wedge f(y) = 0)) \\
& \wedge \ (\neg found \wedge x > 0 \to f(x) \ne 0)
\end{aligned}
$$

and

$$
\begin{aligned}
p_2 \equiv \quad & y \le 1 \\
& \wedge \ (found \to (x > 0 \wedge f(x) = 0) \vee (y \le 0 \wedge f(y) = 0)) \\
& \wedge \ (\neg found \wedge y \le 0 \to f(y) \ne 0).
\end{aligned}
$$

The intuition behind these invariants was explained in Step 4 of Section 8.8. For convenience let us introduce names for two other assertions appearing in the proof outlines of Section 8.8:

$$
\begin{aligned}
r_1 \equiv x \ge 0 \ & \wedge \ (found \to y \le 0 \wedge f(y) = 0) \\
& \wedge \ (x > 0 \to f(x) \ne 0)
\end{aligned}
$$

and

$$
\begin{aligned}
r_2 \equiv y \le 1 \ & \wedge \ (found \to x > 0 \wedge f(x) = 0) \\
& \wedge \ (y \le 0 \to f(y) \ne 0).
\end{aligned}
$$

From Section 8.8 we now "lift" the standard proof outlines to the present programs T_1 and T_2. Since the variable $turn$ does not occur in the assertions used in the proof outlines in Section 8.8, any statement accessing $turn$ preserves these assertions.

Thus for T_1 we consider now the standard proof outline

> $\{\textbf{inv} : p_1\}$
> $\textbf{while } \neg found \textbf{ do}$
> $\quad \{r_1\}$
> $\quad \textbf{wait } turn = 1;$
> $\quad \{r_1\}$
> $\quad turn := 2;$
> $\quad \{r_1\}$
> $\quad \langle\ x := x + 1;$
> $\quad\quad \textbf{if } f(x) = 0 \textbf{ then } found := \textbf{true fi}\rangle$
> $\textbf{od};$
> $\{p_1 \wedge found\}$
> $turn := 2$
> $\{p_1 \wedge found\}$

and similarly for T_2 the standard proof outline

> $\{\textbf{inv} : p_2\}$
> $\textbf{while } \neg found \textbf{ do}$
> $\quad \{r_2\}$
> $\quad \textbf{wait } turn = 2;$
> $\quad \{r_2\}$
> $\quad turn := 1;$
> $\quad \{r_2\}$
> $\quad \langle\ y := y - 1;$
> $\quad\quad \textbf{if } f(y) = 0 \textbf{ then } found := \textbf{true fi}\rangle$
> $\textbf{od};$
> $\{p_2 \wedge found\}$
> $turn := 1$
> $\{p_2 \wedge found\}.$

From Section 8.8 we can also lift the test of interference freedom to the present proof outlines. Indeed, consider any of the correctness formulas to be checked for this test. Either it has already been checked in Section 8.8, for example,

> $\{r_1 \wedge r_2\}$
> $\langle\ y := y - 1;$
> $\quad \textbf{if } f(y) = 0 \textbf{ then } found := \textbf{true fi}\rangle$
> $\{r_1\},$

or it trivially holds because only the variable $turn$, which does not occur in any of the assertions, is modified.

Thus we can apply rule 27 to the parallel composition of T_1 and T_2 and obtain

$$\{p_1 \wedge p_2\}\ [T_1 \| T_2]\ \{p_1 \wedge p_2 \wedge found\}.$$

From this correctness formula proving the desired partial correctness result (9.28) is straightforward.

This concludes the proof of (9.25).

9.8 Exercises

9.1. Prove the Input/Output Lemma 3.3 for parallel programs with synchronization.

9.2. Prove the Change and Access Lemma 3.4 for parallel programs with synchronization.

9.3. Prove the Stuttering Lemma 7.9 for parallel programs with synchronization.

9.4. Suppose that

$$< [S_1 \| \ldots \| S_n], \sigma > \rightarrow^* < [R_1 \| \ldots \| R_n], \tau > .$$

Prove that for $j \in \{1, \ldots, n\}$ either $R_j \equiv E$ or $R_j \equiv \mathbf{at}(T, S_j)$ for a normal subprogram T of S_j.
Hint. See Exercise 3.13.

9.5. Prove the Strong Soundness for Component Programs Lemma 9.1.
Hint. See the proof of the Strong Soundness for Component Programs Lemma 8.5.

9.6. Prove the Auxiliary Variables Lemma 9.2.
Hint. Use Exercise 9.3.

9.7. Prove the Auxiliary Variables Lemma 9.7.
Hint. See the proof of the Auxiliary Variables Lemma 7.10.

9.8. Consider the following solution to the producer/consumer problem in which the synchronization is achieved by means of semaphores:

$$PC' \equiv full := 0;\ empty := N;\ i := 0;\ j := 0;\ [PROD' \| CONS'],$$

where

$$PROD' \equiv \mathbf{while}\ i < M\ \mathbf{do}$$
$$x := a[i];$$
$$P(empty);$$

$$buffer[i \bmod N] := x;$$
$$V(full);$$
$$i := i + 1$$
     od

and

$$CONS' \equiv \textbf{while } j < M \textbf{ do}$$
$$P(full);$$
$$y := buffer[j \bmod N];$$
$$V(empty);$$
$$b[j] := y;$$
$$j := j + 1$$
     od.

Prove that

$$\models_{tot} \{\textbf{true}\}\ PC'\ \{\forall k : (0 \le k < M \to a[k] = b[k])\}.$$

9.9. Prove the Atomicity Theorem 9.1.
Hint. Modify the proof of the Atomicity Theorem 8.1.

9.10. Prove the Initialization Theorem 9.2.

9.11. Consider the programs *ZERO*-5 and *ZERO*-6 of Section 1.1. Show that the total correctness of *ZERO*-6 as proven in Case Study 9.7 implies total correctness of *ZERO*-5.

9.9 Bibliographic Remarks

As already mentioned, this chapter owes much to Owicki and Gries [1976a]: the idea of modeling synchronization by **await** statements, the approach to proving deadlock freedom and the solution to the producer/consumer problem presented in Section 9.4 are from this source. The intermediate notion of weak total correctness is new, introduced here for a clean formulation of the proof rule for parallelism with deadlock freedom. Schneider and Andrews [1986] provide an introduction to the verification of parallel programs using the method of Owicki and Gries.

Nipkow and Nieto [1999] formalized the method of Owicki and Gries in the interactive theorem prover Isabelle/HOL introduced by Nipkow, Paulson and Wenzel [2002], which is based on higher-order logic. More precisely, they formalize syntax, semantics, and proof rules for partial correctness of parallel programs as discussed in this chapter (essentially the proof system *PSY*). They proved soundness of the proof rules and verified a number of examples including the producer/consumer case study in Isabelle/HOL, using the tactics of that theorem prover.

Balser [2006] formalized parallel programs with synchronization and their verification on the basis of dynamic logic in the KIV system, see Balser et al. [2000]. His approach combines symbolic execution of the operational semantics of the programs with induction.

The **await** statement is a more flexible and structured synchronization construct than the classical semaphore introduced in Dijkstra [1968]. However, the price is its inefficiency when implemented directly —during its execution by one component of a parallel program all other components need to be suspended.

In Hoare [1972] a more efficient synchronization construct called *conditional critical region* is introduced. In Owicki and Gries [1976b] a proof theory to verify parallel programs using conditional regions is proposed.

Several other solutions to the producer/consumer problem and the mutual exclusion problem are analyzed in Ben-Ari [1990]. More solutions to the mutual exclusion problem are discussed in Raynal [1986].

The Atomicity and the Initialization Theorems stated in Section 9.6 are —as are their counterparts in Chapter 8— inspired by Lipton [1975].

Part IV
Nondeterministic and Distributed Programs

10 *Nondeterministic Programs*

I N THE PREVIOUS chapters we have seen that parallel programs introduce nondeterminism: from a given initial state several computations resulting in different final states may be possible. This nondeterminism is implicit; that is, there is no explicit programming construct for expressing it.

In this chapter we introduce a class of programs that enable an explicit description of nondeterminism. This is the class of Dijkstra's [1975,1976] *guarded commands*; it represents a simple extension of **while** programs considered in Chapter 3. Dijkstra's guarded commands are also a preparation for the study of distributed programs in Chapter 11.

In Section 10.1 we introduce the syntax and in Section 10.2 the semantics of the nondeterministic programs. In Section 10.3 we discuss the advantages of this language. As we are going to see, nondeterministic program constructs have the advantage that they allow us to avoid a too detailed description or *overspecification* of the intended computations.

Krzysztof R. Apt et al., *Verification of Sequential and Concurrent Programs*,
Texts in Computer Science, DOI: 10.1007/978-1-84882-745-5_10,
© Springer-Verlag London Limited 2009

Verification of nondeterministic programs is considered in Section 10.4; the proof rules are a simple modification of the corresponding rules for **while** programs introduced in Chapter 3. In Section 10.5 we return to an approach originated by Dijkstra [1976], and first explained in Section 3.10, allowing us to develop programs together with their correctness proofs. We extend this approach to nondeterministic programs and illustrate it by the case study of a *welfare crook* program.

Finally, in Section 10.6 we study transformation of parallel programs into nondeterministic programs.

10.1 Syntax

We expand the grammar for **while** programs by adding for each $n \geq 1$ the following production rules:

- **if** *command* or *alternative command*

$$S ::= \textbf{if } B_1 \rightarrow S_1 \square \ldots \square B_n \rightarrow S_n \textbf{ fi},$$

- **do** *command* or *repetitive command*

$$S ::= \textbf{do } B_1 \rightarrow S_1 \square \ldots \square B_n \rightarrow S_n \textbf{ od}.$$

These new commands are also written as

$$\textbf{if } \square_{i=1}^{n} B_i \rightarrow S_i \textbf{ fi} \text{ and } \textbf{do } \square_{i=1}^{n} B_i \rightarrow S_i \textbf{ od},$$

respectively. A Boolean expression B_i within S is called a *guard* and a command S_i within S is said to be *guarded* by B_i. Therefore the construct $B_i \rightarrow S_i$ is called a *guarded command*.

The symbol $\square$ represents a nondeterministic choice between guarded commands $B_i \rightarrow S_i$. More precisely, in the context of an alternative command

$$\textbf{if } B_1 \rightarrow S_1 \square \ldots \square B_n \rightarrow S_n \textbf{ fi}$$

a guarded command $B_i \rightarrow S_i$ can be chosen only if its guard B_i evaluates to true; then S_i remains to be executed. If more than one guard B_i evaluates to true *any* of the corresponding statements S_i may be executed next. There is no rule saying which statement should be selected. If all guards evaluate to false, the alternative command will signal a failure. So the alternative command is a generalization of the failure statement that we considered in Section 3.7.

The selection of guarded commands in the context of a repetitive command

$$\textbf{do } B_1 \rightarrow S_1 \square \ldots \square B_n \rightarrow S_n \textbf{ od}$$

is performed in a similar way. The difference is that after termination of a selected statement S_i the whole command is repeated starting with a new evaluation of the guards B_i. Moreover, contrary to the alternative command, the repetitive command properly terminates when all guards evaluate to false.

We call the programs generated by this grammar *nondeterministic programs*.

10.2 Semantics

Again we wish to support this intuitive explanation of meaning of nondeterministic programs by a precise operational semantics. First, we expand the transition system for **while** programs by the following transition axioms, where σ is a proper state:

(xx) $< \textbf{if } \square_{i=1}^n \ B_i \rightarrow S_i \ \textbf{fi}, \sigma > \ \rightarrow \ < S_i, \sigma >$
 where $\sigma \models B_i$ and $i \in \{1, \dots, n\}$,

(xxi) $< \textbf{if } \square_{i=1}^n \ B_i \rightarrow S_i \ \textbf{fi}, \sigma > \ \rightarrow \ < E, \textbf{fail} >$ where $\sigma \models \bigwedge_{i=1}^n \ \neg B_i$,

(xxii) $< \textbf{do } \square_{i=1}^n \ B_i \rightarrow S_i \ \textbf{od}, \sigma > \ \rightarrow \ < S_i; \ \textbf{do } \square_{i=1}^n \ B_i \rightarrow S_i \ \textbf{od}, \sigma >$
 where $\sigma \models B_i$ and $i \in \{1, \dots, n\}$,

(xxiii)$< \textbf{do } \square_{i=1}^n \ B_i \rightarrow S_i \ \textbf{od}, \sigma > \ \rightarrow \ < E, \sigma >$ where $\sigma \models \bigwedge_{i=1}^n \ \neg B_i$.

Here **fail** is an exceptional state, originally considered in Section 3.7 in the context of the semantics of the failure statement, that represents a runtime detectable failure or abortion. For a nondeterministic program S a transition

$$< S, \sigma > \ \rightarrow \ < R, \tau >$$

is possible if and only if it is deducible in the extended transition system. Note that as in in Section 3.7 configurations of the form $< S, \textbf{fail} >$ have no successor in the transition relation $\rightarrow$.

As before, the semantics $\mathcal{M}[\![S]\!]$ of nondeterministic programs S is based on the transition relation $\rightarrow$, but it now maps proper initial states into sets possibly containing *several* final states. So, as in the case of the failure admitting programs considered in Section 3.7 we consider the following two semantics, where σ is a proper state:

• partial correctness semantics:

$$\mathcal{M}[\![S]\!](\sigma) = \{\tau \mid < S, \sigma > \ \rightarrow^* \ < E, \tau >\},$$

• total correctness semantics:

$$\mathcal{M}_{tot}[\![S]\!](\sigma) = \quad \mathcal{M}[\![S]\!](\sigma)$$
$$\cup \ \{\bot \mid S \text{ can diverge from } \sigma\}$$
$$\cup \ \{\textbf{fail} \mid S \text{ can fail from } \sigma\}.$$

Properties of Semantics

However, we now admit nondeterminism. So, in contrast to Section 3.7, both the partial correctness semantics $\mathcal{M}[\![S]\!](\sigma)$ and the total correctness semantics $\mathcal{M}_{tot}[\![S]\!](\sigma)$ can yield more than one outcome. But, as with the parallel programs of Chapters 8 and 9, the nondeterminism is bounded for the class of nondeterministic programs studied in this chapter.

Lemma 10.1. (Bounded Nondeterminism) *Let S be a nondeterministic program and σ a proper state. Then $\mathcal{M}_{tot}[\![S]\!](\sigma)$ is either finite or it contains $\perp$.*

Proof. For nondeterministic programs S each configuration $< S, \sigma >$ has only finitely many successors in the transition relation $\rightarrow$, so we can apply again König's Lemma 8.4.   □

Note that the conventional conditionals and loops can be modeled by alternative and repetitive commands.

Lemma 10.2. (Correspondence)

(i) $\mathcal{M}_{tot}[\![\text{if } B \text{ then } S_1 \text{ else } S_2 \text{ fi}]\!] = \mathcal{M}_{tot}[\![\text{if } B \rightarrow S_1 \square \neg B \rightarrow S_2 \text{ fi}]\!]$,
(ii) $\mathcal{M}_{tot}[\![\text{while } B \text{ do } S \text{ od}]\!] = \mathcal{M}_{tot}[\![\text{do } B \rightarrow S \text{ od}]\!]$.   □

Therefore, we shall identify from now on:

$$\text{if } B \text{ then } S_1 \text{ else } S_2 \text{ fi} \equiv \text{if } B \rightarrow S_1 \square \neg B \rightarrow S_2 \text{ fi}$$

and

$$\text{while } B \text{ do } S \text{ od} \equiv \text{do } B \rightarrow S \text{ od}.$$

As in Chapter 3 we can express the semantics of loops by the semantics of their syntactic approximations. Let Ω be a nondeterministic program such that $\mathcal{M}[\![\Omega]\!](\sigma) = \emptyset$ holds for all proper states σ. We define by induction on $k \geq 0$ the *kth syntactic approximation* of a loop **do** $\square_{i=1}^{n} B_i \rightarrow S_i$ **od** as follows:

$$(\text{do } \square_{i=1}^{n} B_i \rightarrow S_i \text{ od})^0 \quad = \Omega,$$
$$(\text{do } \square_{i=1}^{n} B_i \rightarrow S_i \text{ od})^{k+1} = \text{if } \square_{i=1}^{n} B_i \rightarrow S_i; (\text{do } \square_{i=1}^{n} B_i \rightarrow S_i \text{ od})^k$$
$$\square \bigwedge_{i=1}^{n} \neg B_i \rightarrow skip$$
$$\text{fi}.$$

The above **if** command has $n + 1$ guarded commands where the last one models the case of termination.

Let $\mathcal{N}$ stand for $\mathcal{M}$ or $\mathcal{M}_{tot}$. We extend $\mathcal{N}$ to deal with the error states $\perp$ and **fail** by

$$\mathcal{M}[\![S]\!](\perp) = \mathcal{M}[\![S]\!](\text{fail}) = \emptyset$$

and

$$\mathcal{M}_{tot}[\![S]\!](\bot) = \{\bot\} \text{ and } \mathcal{M}_{tot}[\![S]\!](\mathbf{fail}) = \{\mathbf{fail}\}$$

and to deal with sets $X \subseteq \Sigma \cup \{\bot\} \cup \{\mathbf{fail}\}$ by

$$\mathcal{N}[\![S]\!](X) = \bigcup_{\sigma \in X} \mathcal{N}[\![S]\!](\sigma).$$

The following lemmata are counterparts of the Input/Output Lemma 3.3 and the Change and Access Lemma 3.4, now formulated for nondeterministic programs.

Lemma 10.3. (Input/Output)

(i) $\mathcal{N}[\![S]\!]$ is monotonic; that is, $X \subseteq Y \subseteq \Sigma \cup \{\bot\}$ implies $\mathcal{N}[\![S]\!](X) \subseteq \mathcal{N}[\![S]\!](Y)$.

(ii) $\mathcal{N}[\![S_1;\ S_2]\!](X) = \mathcal{N}[\![S_2]\!](\mathcal{N}[\![S_1]\!](X))$.

(iii) $\mathcal{N}[\![(S_1;\ S_2);\ S_3]\!](X) = \mathcal{N}[\![S_1;\ (S_2;\ S_3)]\!](X)$.

(iv) $\mathcal{M}[\![\mathbf{if}\ \Box_{i=1}^{n}\ B_i \to S_i\ \mathbf{fi}]\!](X) = \cup_{i=1}^{n} \mathcal{M}[\![S_i]\!](X \cap [\![B_i]\!])$.

(v) if $X \subseteq \cup_{i=1}^{n} [\![B_i]\!]$ then

$$\mathcal{M}_{tot}[\![\mathbf{if}\ \Box_{i=1}^{n}\ B_i \to S_i\ \mathbf{fi}]\!](X) = \cup_{i=1}^{n} \mathcal{M}_{tot}[\![S_i]\!](X \cap [\![B_i]\!]).$$

(vi) $\mathcal{M}[\![\mathbf{do}\ \Box_{i=1}^{n}\ B_i \to S_i\ \mathbf{od}]\!] = \cup_{k=0}^{\infty} \mathcal{M}[\![(\mathbf{do}\ \Box_{i=1}^{n}\ B_i \to S_i\ \mathbf{od})^k]\!]$.

Proof. See Exercise 10.1.   □

Lemma 10.4. (Change and Access)

(i) For all proper states σ and τ, $\tau \in \mathcal{N}[\![S]\!](\sigma)$ implies

$$\tau[Var - change(S)] = \sigma[Var - change(S)].$$

(ii) For all proper states σ and τ, $\sigma[var(S)] = \tau[var(S)]$ implies

$$\mathcal{N}[\![S]\!](\sigma) = \mathcal{N}[\![S]\!](\tau) \ \mathbf{mod}\ Var - var(S).$$

Proof. See Exercise 10.2.   □

10.3 Why Are Nondeterministic Programs Useful?

Let us discuss the main arguments in favor of Dijkstra's language for nondeterministic programs.

Symmetry

Dijkstra's "guarded commands" allow us to present Boolean tests in a symmetric manner. This often enhances the clarity of programs.

As an example consider the **while** program that describes the well-known algorithm for finding the *greatest common divisor* (*gcd*) of two natural numbers, initially stored in the variables x and y:

> **while** $x \neq y$ **do**
>   **if** $x > y$ **then** $x := x - y$ **else** $y := y - x$ **fi**
> **od**.

Using the repetitive command the same algorithm can be written in a more readable and symmetric way:

$$GCD \equiv \textbf{do}\ x > y \rightarrow x := x - y\ \square\ x < y \rightarrow y := y - x\ \textbf{od}.$$

Note that both programs terminate with the *gcd* stored in the variables x and y.

Nondeterminism

Nondeterministic programs allow us to express nondeterminism through the use of nonexclusive guards. Surprisingly often, it is both clumsy and unnecessary to specify a sequential algorithm in a deterministic way —the remaining choices can be resolved in an arbitrary way and need not concern the programmer. As a simple example, consider the problem of computing the maximum of two numbers. Using the conditional statement this can be written as

> **if** $x \geq y$ **then** $max := x$ **else** $max := y$ **fi**

So we broke the tie $x = y$ in 'favour' of the variable x. Using the alternative command the the maximum can be computed in a more natural, symmetric, way that involves nondeterminism:

> **if** $x \geq y \rightarrow max := x\ \square\ y \geq x \rightarrow max := y$**fi**.

Next, the following nondeterministic program computes the largest powers of 2 and 3 that divide a given integer x:

> $twop := 0;\ threep := 0;$
> **do** 2 *divides* $x \rightarrow x := x$ *div* 2; $twop := twop + 1$
> $\square$ 3 *divides* $x \rightarrow x := x$ *div* 3; $threep := threep + 1$
> **od**.

If 6 divides x, both guards can be chosen. In fact, it does not matter which one will be chosen —the final values of the variables *twop* and *threep* will always be the same.

These examples are perhaps somewhat contrived. A more interesting non-deterministic program is presented in Section 10.5.

Failures

Recall that an alternative command fails rather than terminates if none of the guards evaluates to true. We presented already in Section 3.7 a number of natural examples concerning the failure statement that showed the usefulness of failures.

Modeling Concurrency

Nondeterminism arises naturally in the context of parallel programs. For example, upon termination of the program

$$S \equiv [x := 0 \| x := 1 \| x := 2]$$

the variable x may have one of the values 1, 2 or 3. Which one depends on the order in which the three assignments are executed.

We can use nondeterministic programs to model this behavior. For example, S can be modeled by the following program:

$$
\begin{aligned}
T \;\equiv\; & turn_1 := \textbf{true};\; turn_2 := \textbf{true};\; turn_3 := \textbf{true}; \\
& \textbf{do } turn_1 \rightarrow x := 0;\; turn_1 := \textbf{false} \\
& \square \quad turn_2 \rightarrow x := 1;\; turn_2 := \textbf{false} \\
& \square \quad turn_3 \rightarrow x := 2;\; turn_3 := \textbf{false} \\
& \textbf{od}.
\end{aligned}
$$

The variables $turn_1, turn_2$ und $turn_3$ are used to model the control flow of the parallel program S. Of course, the input/output behavior of S could have been modeled by a much simpler program without such extra variables, for example, by

$$\textbf{if true} \rightarrow x := 0 \;\square\; \textbf{true} \rightarrow x := 1 \;\square\; \textbf{true} \rightarrow x := 2 \;\textbf{fi}.$$

The point is that the transition from S to T can be easily generalized to a transformation of arbitrary parallel programs into nondeterministic ones. (see Section 10.6).

10.4 Verification

We now study partial and total correctness of nondeterministic programs.

Partial Correctness

We first present a proof system *PN* for partial correctness of nondeterministic programs. *PN* includes axioms 1 and 2 and rules 3 and 6 introduced for *PW*, the system for partial correctness of **while** programs. But rules 4 and 5 of *PW* are now replaced by:

RULE 30: ALTERNATIVE COMMAND

$$\frac{\{p \wedge B_i\}\ S_i\ \{q\}, i \in \{1, \ldots, n\}}{\{p\}\ \mathbf{if}\ \square_{i=1}^n\ B_i \to S_i\ \mathbf{fi}\ \{q\}}$$

RULE 31: REPETITIVE COMMAND

$$\frac{\{p \wedge B_i\}\ S_i\ \{p\}, i \in \{1, \ldots, n\}}{\{p\}\ \mathbf{do}\ \square_{i=1}^n\ B_i \to S_i\ \mathbf{od}\ \{p \wedge \bigwedge_{i=1}^n \neg B_i\}}$$

Additionally, as explained in Section 3.8, *PN* includes the group of axioms and rules A2–A6. Summarizing, we use the following proof system.

> PROOF SYSTEM *PN* :
> This system consists of the group of axioms
> and rules 1, 2, 3, 6, 30, 31 and A2–A6.

Total Correctness

To lift *PN* to a system for total correctness, we have to show absence of failures and absence of divergence. Since failures arise only if none of the guards in an alternative command evaluates to true, their absence is proved by adding a new premise in the rule for alternative commands. Thus we consider

RULE 32: ALTERNATIVE COMMAND II

$$p \to \bigvee_{i=1}^{n} B_i,$$
$$\{p \wedge B_i\}\, S_i\, \{q\}, i \in \{1, \ldots, n\}$$
$$\{p\}\ \text{if } \square_{i=1}^{n} B_i \to S_i \text{ fi } \{q\}$$

As for **while** loops, absence of divergence is proved by adding to the repetitive command rule 31 premises dealing with the bound function. Thus we consider

RULE 33: REPETITIVE COMMAND II

$$\{p \wedge B_i\}\, S_i\, \{p\}, i \in \{1, \ldots, n\},$$
$$\{p \wedge B_i \wedge t = z\}\, S_i\, \{t < z\}, i \in \{1, \ldots, n\},$$
$$p \to t \geq 0$$
$$\{p\}\ \text{do } \square_{i=1}^{n} B_i \to S_i \text{ od } \{p \wedge \bigwedge_{i=1}^{n} \neg B_i\}$$

where t is an integer expression and z is an integer variable not occurring in p, t, B_i or S_i for $i \in \{1, \ldots, n\}$.

Summarizing, we consider the following proof system *TN* for total correctness of nondeterministic programs.

PROOF SYSTEM *TN* :
This system consists of the group of axioms and rules 1, 2, 3, 6, 32, 33 and A3–A6.

Again we present correctness proofs in the form of proof outlines. The definition of proof outlines for nondeterministic programs is analogous to that for **while** programs. Thus, in the definition of a proof outline for *total correctness*, the formation rules about alternative and repetitive commands are as follows.

Let S^* and S^{**} stand for the program S annotated with assertions and integer expressions. Then

(xiii)

$$p \to \bigvee_{i=1}^{n} B_i,$$
$$\{p \wedge B_i\}\, S_i^*\, \{q\}, i \in \{1, \ldots, n\}$$
$$\{p\}\ \text{if } \square_{i=1}^{n} B_i \to \{p \wedge B_i\}\, S_i^*\, \{q\} \text{ fi } \{q\}$$

(xiv)

$$\{p \wedge B_i\} \ S_i^* \ \{p\}, i \in \{1, \dots, n\},$$
$$\{p \wedge B_i \wedge t = z\} \ S_i^{**} \ \{t < z\}, i \in \{1, \dots, n\},$$
$$p \to t \geq 0$$

$$\{\mathbf{inv} : p\}\{\mathbf{bd} : t\} \ \mathbf{do} \ \square_{i=1}^n \ B_i \to \{p \wedge B_i\} \ S_i^* \ \{p\} \ \mathbf{od} \ \{p \wedge \bigwedge_{i=1}^n \neg B_i\}$$

where t is an integer expression and z is an integer variable not occurring in p, t, B_i or S_i for $i \in \{1, \dots, n\}$.

In proof outlines for *partial correctness* we drop in (xiii) the first premise and in (xiv) the premises mentioning the bound function t and $\{\mathbf{bd} : t\}$ in the conclusion.

Example 10.1. The following is a proof outline for total correctness of the program GCD mentioned in the beginning of Section 10.3:

$$\{x = x_0 \wedge y = y_0 \wedge x_0 > 0 \wedge y_0 > 0\}$$
$$\{\mathbf{inv} : p\}\{\mathbf{bd} : t\}$$
$$\mathbf{do} \ x > y \to \ \{p \wedge x > y\}$$
$$\qquad\qquad x := x - y$$
$$\square \ \ x < y \to \ \{p \wedge x < y\}$$
$$\qquad\qquad x := y - x$$
$$\mathbf{od}$$
$$\{p \wedge \neg(x > y) \wedge \neg(x < y)\}$$
$$\{x = y \wedge y = gcd(x_0, y_0)\}.$$

The binary function symbol gcd is to be interpreted as the "greatest common divisor of." The fresh variables x_0 and y_0 used in the pre- and postconditions represent the initial values of x and y. As an invariant we use here

$$p \equiv gcd(x, y) = gcd(x_0, y_0) \wedge x > 0 \wedge y > 0$$

and as a bound function $t \equiv x + y$. $\qquad\qquad\qquad\qquad\qquad\qquad \square$

Soundness

Let us investigate now the soundness of the proof systems PN and TN for nondeterministic programs. With the definitions as in Chapter 3 we have:

Theorem 10.1. (Soundness of PN and TN)

(i) The proof system PN is sound for partial correctness of nondeterministic programs.

(ii) The proof system TN is sound for total correctness of nondeterministic programs.

Proof. It is enough to show that all proof rules are sound under the corresponding notions of correctness. We leave the details to the reader as all cases are similar to those considered in the proof of the Soundness of PW and TW Theorem 3.1 (see Exercise 10.6). □

As before, proof outlines $\{p\}\ S^*\ \{q\}$ for partial correctness enjoy the following property: whenever the control of S in a given computation started in a state satisfying p reaches a point annotated by an assertion, this assertion is true. This intuitive property can be expressed as a Strong Soundness Theorem about PN analogous to the Strong Soundness Theorem 3.3, but we refrain here from repeating the details.

10.5 Case Study: The Welfare Crook Problem

In this section we generalize the approach of Section 3.10 to the systematic program development to the case of nondeterministic programs. Suppose we want to find a nondeterministic program R of the form

$$R \equiv T;\ \mathbf{do}\ \square_{i=1}^{n}\ B_i \to S_i\ \mathbf{od}$$

that satisfies, for a given precondition r and postcondition q, the correctness formula

$$\{r\}\ R\ \{q\}. \tag{10.1}$$

As before, we postulate that for some variables in r and q, say $x_1, \ldots, x_n$,

$$x_1, \ldots, x_n \notin change(R).$$

To prove (10.1), it suffices to find a loop invariant p and a bound function t satisfying the following five conditions:

1. p is initially established; that is, $\{r\}\ T\ \{p\}$ holds;
2. p is a loop invariant; that is, $\{p \wedge B_i\}\ S_i\ \{p\}$ for $i \in \{1, \ldots, n\}$ holds;
3. upon loop termination q is true; that is, $p \wedge \bigwedge_{i=1}^{n} \neg B_i \to q$;
4. p implies $t \geq 0$; that is, $p \to t \geq 0$;
5. t is decreased with each iteration; that is, $\{p \wedge B_i \wedge t = z\}\ S_i\ \{t < z\}$ for $i \in \{1, \ldots, n\}$ holds, where z is a fresh variable.

As before, we represent the conditions 1–5 as a proof outline for total correctness:

$$\{r\}$$
$$T;$$
$$\{\mathbf{inv}:p\}\{\mathbf{bd}:t\}$$
$$\mathbf{do}\ \square_{i=1}^{n}\ B_i \rightarrow \{p \wedge B_i\}\ S_i^*\ \mathbf{od}$$
$$\{p \wedge \bigwedge_{i=1}^{n} \neg B_i\}$$
$$\{q\}.$$

The next step consists of finding an invariant by generalizing the postcondition.

We illustrate the development of a nondeterministic program that follows these steps by solving the following problem due to W. Feijen. We follow here the exposition of Gries [1981]. Given are three magnetic tapes, each containing a list of different names in alphabetical order. The first contains the names of people working at IBM Yorktown Heights, the second the names of students at Columbia University and the third the names of people on welfare in New York City. Practically speaking, all three lists are endless, so no upper bounds are given. It is known that at least one person is on all three lists. The problem is to develop a program $CROOK$ to locate the alphabetically first such person.

Slightly more abstractly, we consider three *ordered arrays* a, b, c of type **integer** $\rightarrow$ **integer**, that is, such that $i < j$ implies $a[i] < a[j]$, and similarly for b and c. We suppose that there exist values $iv \geq 0, jv \geq 0$ and $kv \geq 0$ such that

$$a[iv] = b[jv] = c[kv]$$

holds, and moreover we suppose that the triple (iv, jv, kv) is the smallest one in the lexicographic ordering among those satisfying this condition. The values iv, jv and kv can be used in the assertions but *not* in the program. We are supposed to develop a program that computes them.

Thus our precondition r is a list of the assumed facts —that a, b, c are ordered together with the formal definition of iv, jv and kv. We omit the formal definition. The postcondition is

$$q \equiv i = iv \wedge j = jv \wedge k = kv,$$

where i, j, k are integer variables of the still to be constructed program $CROOK$. Additionally we require $a, b, c, iv, jv, kv \notin change(CROOK)$.

Assuming that the search starts from the beginning of the lists, we are brought to the following invariant by placing appropriate bounds on i, j and k:

$$p \equiv 0 \leq i \leq iv \wedge 0 \leq j \leq jv \wedge 0 \leq k \leq kv \wedge r.$$

A natural choice for the bound function is

$$t \equiv (iv - i) + (jv - j) + (kv - k).$$

The invariant is easily established by

$$i := 0; \ j := 0; \ k := 0.$$

The simplest ways to decrease the bound functions are the assignments $i :=$ $i + 1, j := j + 1$ and $k := k + 1$. In general, it is necessary to increment all three variables, so we arrive at the following incomplete proof outline:

$$\{r\}$$
$$i := 0; \ j := 0; \ k := 0;$$
$$\{\textbf{inv} : p\}\{\textbf{bd} : t\}$$
$$\textbf{do } B_1 \rightarrow \{p \wedge B_1\} \ i := i + 1$$
$$\square \quad B_2 \rightarrow \{p \wedge B_2\} \ j := j + 1$$
$$\square \quad B_3 \rightarrow \{p \wedge B_3\} \ k := k + 1$$
$$\textbf{od}$$
$$\{p \wedge \neg B_1 \wedge \neg B_2 \wedge \neg B_3\}$$
$$\{q\},$$

where B_1, B_2 and B_3 are still to be found. Of course the simplest choice for B_1, B_2 and B_3 are, respectively, $i \neq iv, j \neq jv$ and $k \neq kv$ but the values iv, jv and kv cannot be used in the program. On the other hand, $p \wedge i \neq iv$ is equivalent to $p \wedge i < iv$ which means by the definition of iv, jv and kv that $a[i]$ is not the crook. Now, assuming p, the last statement is guaranteed if $a[i] < b[j]$. Indeed, a, b and c are ordered, so $p \wedge a[i] < b[j]$ implies $a[i] < b[jv] = a[iv]$ which implies $i < iv$.

We can thus choose $a[i] < b[j]$ for the guard B_1. In a similar fashion we can choose the other two guards which yield the following proof outline:

$$\{r\}$$
$$i := 0; \ j := 0; \ k = 0;$$
$$\{\textbf{inv} : p\}\{\textbf{bd} : t\}$$
$$\textbf{do } a[i] < b[j] \rightarrow \quad \{p \wedge a[i] < b[j]\}$$
$$\{p \wedge i < iv\}$$
$$i := i + 1$$
$$\square \quad b[j] < c[k] \rightarrow \quad \{p \wedge b[j] < c[k]\}$$
$$\{p \wedge j < jv\}$$
$$j := j + 1$$
$$\square \quad c[k] < a[i] \rightarrow \quad \{p \wedge c[k] < a[i]\}$$
$$\{p \wedge k < kv\}$$
$$k := k + 1$$
$$\textbf{od}$$
$$\{p \wedge \neg(a[i] < b[j]) \wedge \neg(b[j] < c[k]) \wedge \neg(c[k] < a[i])\}$$
$$\{q\}.$$

Summarizing, we developed the following desired program:

$$CROOK \equiv i := 0; \ j := 0; \ k := 0;$$
$$\textbf{do } a[i] < b[j] \rightarrow i := i + 1$$
$$\square \ \ b[j] < c[k] \rightarrow j := j + 1$$
$$\square \ \ c[k] < a[i] \rightarrow k := k + 1$$
$$\textbf{od}.$$

In developing this program the crucial step consisted of the choice of the guards B_1, B_2 and B_3. Accidentally, the choice made turned out to be sufficient to ensure that upon loop termination the postcondition q holds.

10.6 Transformation of Parallel Programs

Let us return now to the issue of modeling parallel programs by means of nondeterministic programs, originally mentioned in Section 10.3.

Reasoning about parallel programs with shared variables is considerably more complicated than reasoning about sequential programs:

- the input/output behavior is not *compositional*, that is, cannot be solely determined by the input/output behavior of their components,
- correctness proofs require a complicated test of interference freedom.

The question arises whether we cannot avoid these difficulties by decomposing the task of verifying parallel programs into two steps:

(1) transformation of the considered parallel programs in nondeterministic sequential ones,
(2) verification of the resulting nondeterministic programs using the proof systems of this chapter.

For disjoint parallelism this can be done very easily. Recall from the Sequentialization Lemma 7.7 that every disjoint parallel program $S \equiv [S_1 \| \ldots \| S_n]$ is equivalent to the **while** program $T \equiv S_1; \ \ldots; \ S_n$.

For parallel programs with shared variables things are more difficult. First, since these programs exhibit nondeterminism, such a transformation yields nondeterministic programs. Second, to simulate all the possible interleavings of the atomic actions, this transformation requires additional variables acting as program counters. More precisely, the transformation of a parallel program

$$S \equiv [S_1 \| \ldots \| S_n]$$

in the syntax of Chapter 9 into a nondeterministic program $T(S)$ introduces a fresh integer variable pc_i for each component S_i. This variable models a *program counter* for S_i which during its execution always points to that atomic action of S_i which is to be executed next. To define the values of the program counters, the component programs $S_1, \ldots, S_n$ are labeled in a preparatory step.

In general, a component program R is transformed into a labeled program $\hat{R}$ by inserting in R pairwise distinct natural numbers k as labels of the form "k :" at the following positions outside of any atomic region and any **await** statement:

- in front of each *skip* statement,
- in front of each assignment $u := t$,
- in front of each **if** symbol,
- in front of each **while** symbol,
- in front of each atomic region $\langle S_0 \rangle$,
- in front of each **await** symbol.

For a labeled program $\hat{R}$ let $first(\hat{R})$ denote the first label in $\hat{R}$ and $last(\hat{R})$ the last label in $\hat{R}$. For each labeled component program $\hat{S}_i$ of S we require that the labels are chosen as consecutive natural numbers starting at 0. Thus the labels in $\hat{S}_i$ are

$$first(\hat{S}_i) = 0, 1, 2, 3, \ldots, last(\hat{S}_i).$$

For checking termination we define

$$term_i = last(\hat{S}_i) + 1.$$

Now we transform S into $T(S)$ by referring to the labeled component programs $\hat{S}_1, \ldots, \hat{S}_n$:

$$
\begin{aligned}
T(S) \equiv\ & pc_1 := 0;\ \ldots\ pc_n := 0; \\
& \textbf{do}\ T_1(\hat{S}_1)(term_1) \\
& \square\ \ T_2(\hat{S}_2)(term_2) \\
& \quad \cdots\cdots\cdots\cdots\cdots \\
& \square\ \ T_n(\hat{S}_n)(term_n) \\
& \textbf{od}; \\
& \textbf{if}\ TERM \rightarrow skip\ \textbf{fi}.
\end{aligned}
$$

Here $pc_1, \ldots, pc_n$ are integer variables that do not occur in S and that model the program counters of the components S_i. The Boolean expression

$$TERM \equiv \bigwedge_{i=1}^{n} pc_i = term_i$$

represents the termination condition for the labeled components $\hat{S}_1, \ldots, \hat{S}_n$.

Each component transformation $T_i(\hat{S}_i)(term_i)$ translates into one or more guarded commands, separated by the $\square$ symbol. We define these component transformations

$$T_i(\hat{R})(c)$$

by induction on the structure of the labeled component program $\hat{R}$, taking an additional label $c \in N$ as a parameter modeling the continuation value that the program counter pc_i assumes upon termination of $\hat{R}$:

- $T_i(k : skip)(c) \equiv pc_i = k \to pc_i := c$,

- $T_i(k : u := t)(c) \equiv pc_i = k \to u := t;\ pc_i := c$,

- $T_i(\hat{R}_1; \hat{R}_2)(c) \equiv$
  $\quad T_i(\hat{R}_1)(first(\hat{R}_2))$
  $\quad \square\ T_i(\hat{R}_2)(c)$,

- $T_i(k : \textbf{if } B \textbf{ then } \hat{R}_1 \textbf{ else } \hat{R}_2 \textbf{ fi})(c) \equiv$
  $\quad pc_i = k \wedge B \to pc_i := first(\hat{R}_1)$
  $\quad \square\ pc_i = k \wedge \neg B \to pc_i := first(\hat{R}_2)$
  $\quad \square\ T_i(\hat{R}_1)(c)$
  $\quad \square\ T_i(\hat{R}_2)(c)$,

- $T_i(k : \textbf{while } B \textbf{ do } \hat{R} \textbf{ od})(c) \equiv$
  $\quad pc_i = k \wedge B \to pc_i := first(\hat{R})$
  $\quad \square\ pc_i = k \wedge \neg B \to pc_i := c$
  $\quad \square\ T_i(\hat{R})(k)$,

- $T_i(k : \langle S_0 \rangle)(c) \equiv pc_i = k \to S_0;\ pc_i := c$,

- $T_i(k : \textbf{await } B \textbf{ then } S_0 \textbf{ end})(c) \equiv pc_i = k \wedge B \to S_0;\ pc_i := c$.

To see this transformation in action let us look at an example.

Example 10.2. Consider the parallel composition $S \equiv [S_1 \| S_2]$ in the program *FINDPOS* of Case Study 8.6. The corresponding labeled components are

$$\hat{S}_1 \equiv 0: \textbf{while } i < min(oddtop, eventop) \textbf{ do}$$
$$\qquad 1: \textbf{if } a[i] > 0 \ \textbf{ then } 2: oddtop := i \ \textbf{ else } 3: i := i + 2 \textbf{ fi}$$
$$\quad \textbf{od}$$

and

$$\hat{S}_2 \equiv 0: \textbf{while } j < min(oddtop, eventop) \textbf{ do}$$
$$\qquad 1: \textbf{if } a[j] > 0 \ \textbf{ then } 2: eventop := j \ \textbf{ else } 3: j := j + 2 \textbf{ fi}$$
$$\quad \textbf{od}.$$

Since each component program uses the labels 1, 2, 3, the termination values are $term_1 = term_2 = 4$. Therefore S is transformed into

$$T(S) \equiv pc_1 := 0;\ pc_2 := 0;$$
$$\qquad \textbf{do } T_1(\hat{S}_1)(4)$$
$$\qquad \square\ T_2(\hat{S}_2)(4)$$
$$\qquad \textbf{od};$$
$$\qquad \textbf{if } pc_1 = 4 \wedge pc_2 = 4 \to skip \textbf{ fi},$$

where for the first component we calculate

$$T_1(\hat{S}_1)(4) \equiv pc_1 = 0 \wedge i < min(oddtop, eventop) \rightarrow pc_1 := 1$$
$$\square \; pc_1 = 0 \wedge \neg(i < min(oddtop, eventop)) \rightarrow pc_1 := 4$$
$$\square \; T_1(1 : \mathbf{if} \ldots \mathbf{fi})(0),$$

$$T_1(1 : \mathbf{if} \ldots \mathbf{fi})(0) \equiv pc_1 = 1 \wedge a[i] > 0 \rightarrow pc_1 := 2$$
$$\square \; pc_1 = 1 \wedge \neg(a[i] > 0) \rightarrow pc_1 := 3$$
$$\square \; T_1(2 : oddtop := i)(0)$$
$$\square \; T_1(3 : i := i + 2)(0),$$

$$T_1(2 : oddtop := i)(0) \equiv pc_1 = 2 \rightarrow oddtop := i; \; pc_1 := 0,$$

$$T_1(3 : i := i + 2)(0) \equiv pc_1 = 3 \rightarrow i := i + 2; \; pc_1 := 0.$$

Altogether we obtain the following nondeterministic program:

$$T(S) \equiv pc_1 := 0; \; pc_2 := 0;$$
$$\mathbf{do} \; pc_1 = 0 \wedge i < min(oddtop, eventop) \rightarrow pc_1 := 1$$
$$\square \; pc_1 = 0 \wedge \neg(i < min(oddtop, eventop)) \rightarrow pc_1 := 4$$
$$\square \; pc_1 = 1 \wedge a[i] > 0 \rightarrow pc_1 := 2$$
$$\square \; pc_1 = 1 \wedge \neg(a[i] > 0) \rightarrow pc_1 := 3$$
$$\square \; pc_1 = 2 \rightarrow oddtop := i; \; pc_1 := 0$$
$$\square \; pc_1 = 3 \rightarrow i := i + 2; \; pc_1 := 0$$
$$\square \; pc_2 = 0 \wedge j < min(oddtop, eventop) \rightarrow pc_2 := 1$$
$$\square \; pc_2 = 0 \wedge \neg(j < min(oddtop, eventop)) \rightarrow pc_2 := 4$$
$$\square \; pc_2 = 1 \wedge a[j] > 0 \rightarrow pc_2 := 2$$
$$\square \; pc_2 = 1 \wedge \neg(a[j] > 0) \rightarrow pc_2 := 3$$
$$\square \; pc_2 = 2 \rightarrow eventop := j; \; pc_2 := 0$$
$$\square \; pc_2 = 3 \rightarrow j := j + 2; \; pc_2 := 0$$
$$\mathbf{od};$$
$$\mathbf{if} \; pc_1 = 4 \wedge pc_2 = 4 \rightarrow skip \; \mathbf{fi}$$

Note that upon termination of the **do** loop the assertion $pc_1 = 4 \wedge pc_2 = 4$ holds, so the final **if** statement has no effect here. □

For parallel programs S with shared variables, one can prove that S and $T(S)$ are equivalent modulo the program counter variables. In other words, using the **mod** notation of Section 2.3, we have for every proper state σ:

$$\mathcal{M}_{tot}[\![S]\!](\sigma) = \mathcal{M}_{tot}[\![T(S)]\!](\sigma) \; \mathbf{mod} \; \{pc_1, \ldots, pc_n\}.$$

For parallel programs with synchronization the relationship between S and $T(S)$ is more complex because deadlocks of S are transformed into failures of $T(S)$ (see Exercise 10.9). As an illustration let us look at the following artificial parallel program with an atomic region and an **await** statement.

Example 10.3. Consider the parallel program $S \equiv [S_1 \| S_2 \| S_3]$ with the following labeled components:

$\hat{S}_1 \equiv 0 : \textbf{if } x = 0 \textbf{ then } 1 : x := x + 1; 2 : x := x + 2 \textbf{ else } 3 : x := x - 1 \textbf{ fi},$
$\hat{S}_2 \equiv 0 : \textbf{while } y < 10 \textbf{ do } 1 : \langle y := y + 1; z := z - 1 \rangle \textbf{ od},$
$\hat{S}_3 \equiv 0 : \textbf{await } z \neq y \textbf{ then } done := true \textbf{ end}.$

Note that $term_1 = 4$, $term_2 = 2$, and $term_3 = 1$. Thus S is transformed into the following nondeterministic program:

$$T(S) \equiv pc_1 := 0;\ pc_2 := 0;\ pc_3 := 0;$$
$$\textbf{do } T_1(\hat{S}_1)(4)$$
$$\square\ T_2(\hat{S}_2)(2)$$
$$\square\ T_3(\hat{S}_3)(1)$$
$$\textbf{od};$$
$$\textbf{if } pc_1 = 4 \wedge pc_2 = 2 \wedge pc_3 = 1 \rightarrow skip \textbf{ fi}$$

where we calculate for the component transformations:

$$T_1(\hat{S}_1)(4) \equiv pc_1 = 0 \wedge x = 0 \rightarrow pc_1 := 1$$
$$\square\ pc_1 = 0 \wedge \neg(x = 0) \rightarrow pc_1 := 3$$
$$\square\ pc_1 = 1 \rightarrow x := x + 1;\ pc_1 := 2$$
$$\square\ pc_1 = 2 \rightarrow x := x + 2;\ pc_1 := 4$$
$$\square\ pc_1 = 3 \rightarrow x := x - 1;\ pc_1 := 4,$$

$$T_2(\hat{S}_2)(2) \equiv pc_2 = 0 \wedge y < 10 \rightarrow pc_2 := 1$$
$$\square\ pc_2 = 0 \wedge \neg(y < 10) \rightarrow pc_2 := 2$$
$$\square\ pc_2 = 1 \rightarrow y := y + 1;\ z := z - 1;\ pc_1 := 0,$$

$$T_3(\hat{S}_3)(1) \equiv pc_3 = 0 \wedge z \neq y \rightarrow done := true;\ pc_3 := 1.$$

Altogether we obtain

$$T(S) \equiv pc_1 := 0;\ pc_2 := 0;\ pc_3 := 0;$$
$$\textbf{do } pc_1 = 0 \wedge x = 0 \rightarrow pc_1 := 1$$
$$\square\ pc_1 = 0 \wedge \neg(x = 0) \rightarrow pc_1 := 3$$
$$\square\ pc_1 = 1 \rightarrow x := x + 1;\ pc_1 := 2$$
$$\square\ pc_1 = 2 \rightarrow x := x + 2;\ pc_1 := 4$$
$$\square\ pc_1 = 3 \rightarrow x := x - 1;\ pc_1 := 4$$
$$\square\ pc_2 = 0 \wedge y < 10 \rightarrow pc_2 := 1$$
$$\square\ pc_2 = 0 \wedge \neg(y < 10) \rightarrow pc_2 := 2$$
$$\square\ pc_2 = 1 \rightarrow y := y + 1;\ z := z - 1;\ pc_1 := 0$$
$$\square\ pc_3 = 0 \wedge z \neq y \rightarrow done := true;\ pc_3 := 1$$
$$\textbf{od};$$
$$\textbf{if } pc_1 = 4 \wedge pc_2 = 2 \wedge pc_3 = 1 \rightarrow skip \textbf{ fi}.$$

Consider now a state σ satisfying $z = y = 10$. Then S can deadlock from σ. So $\Delta \in \mathcal{M}_{tot}[\![S]\!](\sigma)$. By contrast, the do loop in $T(S)$ terminates in a state satisfying $pc_1 = 4 \wedge pc_2 = 2 \wedge pv_3 = 0$. However, the final if statement in $T(S)$ converts this "premature" termination into a failure. So $\textbf{fail} \in \mathcal{M}_{tot}[\![T(S)]\!](\sigma)$. $\qquad\square$

These examples reveal one severe drawback of the transformation: the structure of the original parallel program gets lost. Instead, we are faced with a nondeterministic program on the level of an assembly language where each atomic action is explicitly listed. Therefore we do not pursue this approach any further.

In the next chapter we are going to see, however, that for distributed programs a corresponding transformation into nondeterministic programs does preserve the program structure without introducing auxiliary variables and is thus very well suited as a basis for verification.

10.7 Exercises

10.1. Prove the Input/Output Lemma 10.3.

10.2. Prove the Change and Access Lemma 10.4.

10.3. Let π be a permutation of the indices $\{1, \ldots, n\}$. Prove that for $\mathcal{N} = \mathcal{M}$ and $\mathcal{N} = \mathcal{M}_{tot}$:

(i) $\mathcal{N}[\![\mathbf{if}\ \square_{i=1}^{n}\ B_i \to S_i\ \mathbf{fi}]\!] = \mathcal{N}[\![\mathbf{if}\ \square_{i=1}^{n}\ B_{\pi(i)} \to S_{\pi(i)}\ \mathbf{fi}]\!]$,

(ii) $\mathcal{N}[\![\mathbf{do}\ \square_{i=1}^{n}\ B_i \to S_i\ \mathbf{od}]\!] = \mathcal{N}[\![\mathbf{do}\ \square_{i=1}^{n}\ B_{\pi(i)} \to S_{\pi(i)}\ \mathbf{od}]\!]$.

10.4. Prove that for $\mathcal{N} = \mathcal{M}$ and $\mathcal{N} = \mathcal{M}_{tot}$:

(i)

$$
\begin{aligned}
&\mathcal{N}[\![\mathbf{do}\ \square_{i=1}^{n}\ B_i \to S_i\ \mathbf{od}]\!] \\
&= \mathcal{N}[\![\ \mathbf{if}\ \square_{i=1}^{n}\ B_i \to S_i;\ \mathbf{do}\ \square_{i=1}^{n}\ B_i \to S_i\ \mathbf{od} \\
&\qquad \square \bigwedge_{i=1}^{n}\ \neg B_i \to skip \\
&\quad \mathbf{fi}]\!],
\end{aligned}
$$

(ii)

$$
\begin{aligned}
&\mathcal{N}[\![\mathbf{do}\ \square_{i=1}^{n}\ B_i \to S_i\ \mathbf{od}]\!] \\
&= \mathcal{N}[\![\mathbf{do}\ \bigvee_{i=1}^{n}\ B_i \to \mathbf{if}\ \square_{i=1}^{n}\ B_i \to S_i\ \mathbf{fi}\ \mathbf{od}]\!].
\end{aligned}
$$

10.5. Which of the following correctness formulas are true in the sense of total correctness?

(i) $\{\mathbf{true}\}\ \mathbf{if}\ x > 0 \to x := 0 \square x < 0 \to x := 0\ \mathbf{fi}\ \{x = 0\}$,

(ii) $\{\mathbf{true}\}\ \mathbf{if}\ x > 0 \to x := 1 \square x < 0 \to x := 1\ \mathbf{fi}\ \{x = 1\}$,

(iii)

$$
\begin{aligned}
&\{\mathbf{true}\} \\
&\mathbf{if}\ x > 0 \to x := 0 \\
&\square\ x = 0 \to skip \\
&\square\ x < 0 \to x := 0 \\
&\mathbf{fi} \\
&\{x = 0\},
\end{aligned}
$$

(iv)

> {**true**}
> **if** $x > 0 \rightarrow x := 1$
> $\square\, x = 0 \rightarrow skip$
> $\square\, x < 0 \rightarrow x := 1$
> **fi**
> {$x = 1$},

(v) {**true**} **if** $x > 0$ **then** $x := 0$ **else** $x := 0$ **fi** {$x = 0$},
(vi) {**true**} **if** $x > 0$ **then** $x := 1$ **else** $x := 1$ **fi** {$x = 1$}.

Give both an informal argument and a formal proof in the systems TN or TW.

10.6. Prove the Soundness of PN and TN Theorem 10.1.
Hint. Follow the pattern of the proof of the Soundness of PW and TW Theorem 3.1 and use Lemma 10.3.

10.7. Develop systematically a program that checks if x appears in an array section $a[0 : n - 1]$.

10.8. Transform the parallel program $MUTEX\text{-}S$ of Section 9.5, which ensures mutual exclusion with the help of semaphores, into a nondeterministic program using the transformation of Section 10.6.

10.9. Prove that for every parallel program $S \equiv [S_1\|\ldots\|S_n]$ with shared variables there exists a nondeterministic program $T(S)$ and a set of variables $\{pc_1, \ldots, pc_n\}$ not appearing in S such that for all proper states σ

$$\mathcal{M}_{tot}[\![S]\!](\sigma) = \mathcal{M}_{tot}[\![T(S)]\!](\sigma) \bmod \{pc_1, \ldots, pc_n\}.$$

Which semantic relationship can be established for the case of parallel programs with synchronization?
Hint. See the discussion at the end of Section 10.6.

10.10. Define the weakest liberal precondition and the weakest precondition of a nondeterministic program by analogy with **while** programs (see Definition 3.10). Assume the analogue of the Definability Theorem 3.4 for nondeterministic programs. Prove that

(i) $wlp(S_1;\ S_2, q) \leftrightarrow wlp(S_1, wlp(S_2, q))$,

(ii) $wlp(\textbf{if } \square_{i=1}^{n} B_i \rightarrow S_i \textbf{ fi}, q) \leftrightarrow \bigwedge_{i=1}^{n}(B_i \rightarrow wlp(S_i, q))$,

(iii)

$$wlp(\textbf{do } \square_{i=1}^{n} B_i \rightarrow S_i \textbf{ od}, q) \wedge B_i$$
$$\rightarrow wlp(S_i, wlp(\textbf{do } \square_{i=1}^{n} B_i \rightarrow S_i \textbf{ od}, q)) \qquad \text{for } i \in \{1, \ldots, n\},$$

(iv) $wlp(\textbf{do } \square_{i=1}^{n} B_i \rightarrow S_i \textbf{ od}, q) \wedge \bigwedge_{i=1}^{n} \neg B_i \rightarrow q$,

(v) $\models \{p\}\ S\ \{q\}$ iff $p \to wlp(S, q)$.

Prove that the above statements (i), (iii) and (iv) hold when wlp is replaced by wp. Also prove that

(vi) $\models_{tot} \{p\}\ S\ \{q\}$ iff $p \to wp(S, q)$,

(vii) $wp(\mathbf{if}\ \square_{i=1}^{n}\ B_i \to S_i\ \mathbf{fi}, q) \leftrightarrow (\bigvee_{i=1}^{n} B_i) \wedge \bigwedge_{i=1}^{n}(B_i \to wp(S_i, q))$.

10.11.

   (i) Prove that the proof system PN is complete for partial correctness of nondeterministic programs.
   (ii) Suppose that the set of all integer expressions is expressive in the sense of Definition 3.13. Prove that the proof system TN is complete for total correctness of nondeterministic programs.

Hint. Modify the proof of the Completeness Theorem 3.5 and use Exercise 10.10.

10.8 Bibliographic Remarks

We have studied here a number of issues concerning a special type of nondeterministic programs introduced in Dijkstra [1975]. Their correctness and various semantics are discussed in de Bakker [1980] and Apt [1984].

Their systematic development was originated in Dijkstra [1976] and was popularized and further explained in Gries [1981]. In the 1980s the journal *Science of Computer Programming* carried a regular problem section on this matter edited by M. Rem. The program for the *welfare crook* developed in Section 10.5 is due to W. Feijen. The presentation chosen here is due to Gries [1981].

The first treatment of nondeterminism in the framework of program verification is due to Lauer [1971], where a proof rule for the **or** construct (the meaning of S_1 **or** S_2 is to execute either S_1 or S_2) is introduced. This approach to nondeterminism is extensively discussed in de Bakker [1980] where further references can be found.

The idea of linking parallel programs to nondeterministic programs goes back to the work of Ashcroft and Manna [1971] and Flon and Suzuki [1978, 1981]. This approach reappears in the book on UNITY by Chandy and Misra [1988], and in the work on *action systems* by Back [1989] and Back and von Wright [2008]. UNITY programs and action systems are particularly simple nondeterministic programs consisting of an initialization part and a single **do** loop containing only atomic actions. This is exactly the class of nondeterministic programs into which we have transformed parallel programs in Section 10.6.

The main emphasis of the work of Chandy and Misra and of Back lies in the systematic development of parallel programs on the basis of equivalent non-deterministic ones. The systematic development of parallel implementations starting from sequential programs of a particular simple form (i.e., nested **for** loops) is pursued by Lengauer [1993].

Related to the approach of action systems are the system specification method TLA (Temporal Logic of Actions) by Lamport [1994,2003] and the abstract machines in the B-method by Abrial [1996]. The latter method has recently been extended to Event-B (see, for example, Abrial and Hallerstede [2007] and Abrial [2009]). Also here the basic form of the specifications consists of an initialization part and a single **do** loop containing only atomic actions.

11 *Distributed Programs*

M ANY REAL SYSTEMS consist of a number of physically distributed components that work independently using their private storage, but also communicate from time to time by explicit message passing. Such systems are called *distributed systems*.

Distributed programs are abstract descriptions of distributed systems. A distributed program consists of a collection of processes that work concurrently and communicate by explicit message passing. Each process can access a set of variables which are disjoint from the variables that can be changed by any other process.

There are two ways of organizing message passing. We consider here *synchronous communication* where the sender of a message can deliver it only when the receiver is ready to accept it at the same moment. An example is communication by telephone. Synchronous communication is also called *handshake* communication or *rendezvous*. Another possibility is *asynchronous*

Krzysztof R. Apt et al., *Verification of Sequential and Concurrent Programs*,
Texts in Computer Science, DOI: 10.1007/978-1-84882-745-5_11,
© Springer-Verlag London Limited 2009

communication where the sender can always deliver its message. This stipulates an implicit buffer where messages are kept until the receiver collects them. Communication by mail is an example. Asynchronous communication can be modeled by synchronous communication if the buffer is introduced as an explicit component of the distributed system.

As a syntax for distributed programs we introduce in Section 11.1 a subset of the language CSP (Communicating Sequential Processes) due to Hoare [1978,1985]. This variant of CSP extends Dijkstra's guarded command language (studied in Chapter 10) and disjoint parallel composition (studied in Chapter 7) by adding input/output commands for synchronous communication. From the more recent version of CSP from Hoare [1985] we use two concepts here: communication channels instead of process names and output guards in the alternatives of repetitive commands. Hoare's CSP is also the kernel of the programming language OCCAM (see INMOS [1984]) used for distributed transputer systems.

In Section 11.2 we define the semantics of distributed programs by formalizing the effect of a synchronous communication. In particular, synchronous communication may lead to *deadlock*, a situation where some processes of a distributed program wait indefinitely for further communication with other processes.

Distributed programs can be transformed in a direct way into nondeterministic programs, without the use of control variables. This transformation is studied in detail in Section 11.3. It is the key for a simple proof theory for distributed programs which is presented in Section 11.4. As in Chapter 9, we proceed in three steps and consider first partial correctness, then weak total correctness which ignores deadlocks, and finally total correctness. As a case study we prove in Section 11.5 the correctness of a data transmission problem.

11.1 Syntax

Distributed programs consist of a parallel composition of sequential processes. So we introduce first the notion of a process.

Sequential Processes

A (*sequential*) *process* is a statement of the form

$$S \equiv S_0; \; \mathbf{do} \; \square_{j=1}^m \, g_j \to S_j \; \mathbf{od},$$

where $m \geq 0$ and $S_0, \ldots, S_m$ are nondeterministic programs as defined in Chapter 10. S_0 is the *initialization part* of S and

$$\mathbf{do} \; \square_{j=1}^m \, g_j \to S_j \; \mathbf{od}$$

is the *main loop* of S. Note that there may be further **do** loops inside S. By convention, when $m = 0$ we identify the main loop with the statement *skip*. Then S consists only of the nondeterministic program S_0. Thus any nondeterministic program is a process. Also, when the initialization part equals *skip*, we drop the subprogram S_0 from a process.

The $g_1, \ldots, g_m$ are *generalized guards* of the form

$$g \equiv B; \alpha$$

where B is a Boolean expression and α an *input/output command* or *i/o command* for short, to be explained in a moment. If $B \equiv \mathbf{true}$, we abbreviate

$$\mathbf{true}; \alpha \equiv \alpha.$$

The main loop terminates when all Boolean expressions within its generalized guards evaluate to false.

Input/output commands refer to *communication channels* or *channels* for short. Intuitively, such channels represent connections between the processes along which values can be transmitted. For simplicity we assume the following:

- channels are *undirected*; that is, they can be used to transmit values in both directions;
- channels are *untyped*; that is, they can be used to transmit values of different types.

An *input command* is of the form $c?u$ and an *output command* is of the form $c!t$ where c is a communication channel, u is a simple or subscripted variable and t is an expression.

An input command $c?u$ expresses the request to receive a value along the channel c. Upon reception this value is assigned to the variable u. An output command $c!t$ expresses the request to send the value of the expression t along channel c. Each of these requests is delayed until the other request is present. Then *both* requests are performed together or *synchronously*. In particular, an output command cannot be executed independently. The joint execution of two i/o commands $c?u$ and $c!t$ is called a *communication* of the value of t along channel c to the variable u.

While values of different types can be communicated along the same channel, each individual communication requires two i/o commands of a matching type. This is made precise in the following definition.

Definition 11.1. We say that two i/o commands *match* when they refer to the same channel, say c, one of them is an input command, say $c?u$, and the other an output command, say $c!t$, such that the types of u and t agree. We say that two generalized guards *match* if their i/o commands match.   □

Two generalized guards contained in two different processes can be passed jointly when they match and their Boolean parts evaluate to true. Then the communication between the i/o commands takes place. The effect of a communication between two matching i/o commands $\alpha_1 \equiv c?u$ and $\alpha_2 \equiv c!t$ is the assignment $u := t$. Formally, for two such commands we define

$$Eff(\alpha_1, \alpha_2) \equiv Eff(\alpha_2, \alpha_1) \equiv u := t.$$

For a process S let $change(S)$ denote the set of all simple or array variables that appear in S on the left-hand side of an assignment or in an input command, let $var(S)$ denote the set of all simple or array variables appearing in S, and finally let $channel(S)$ denote the set of channel names that appear in S. Processes S_1 and S_2 are called *disjoint* if the following condition holds:

$$change(S_1) \cap var(S_2) = var(S_1) \cap change(S_2) = \emptyset.$$

We say that a channel c *connects* two processes S_i and S_j if

$$c \in channel(S_i) \cap channel(S_j).$$

Distributed Programs

Now, *distributed programs* are generated by the following clause for parallel composition:

$$S ::= [S_1 \| \ldots \| S_n],$$

where for $n \geq 1$ and sequential processes $S_1, \ldots, S_n$ the following two conditions are satisfied:

(i) *Disjointness*: the processes $S_1, \ldots, S_n$ are pairwise disjoint.
(ii) *Point-to-Point Connection*: for all i, j, k such that $1 \le i < j < k \le n$

$$channel(S_i) \cap channel(S_j) \cap channel(S_k) = \emptyset$$

holds.

Condition (ii) states that in a distributed program each communication channel connects at most two processes. Note that as in previous chapters we disallow nested parallelism.

A distributed program $[S_1 \| \ldots \| S_n]$ terminates when all of its processes S_i terminate. This means that distributed programs may fail to terminate because of divergence of a process or an abortion arising in one of the processes. However, they may also fail to terminate because of a deadlock. A *deadlock* arises here when not all processes have terminated, none of them has ended in a failure and yet none of them can proceed. This will happen when all nonterminated processes are in front of their main loops but no pair of their generalized guards matches.

We now illustrate the notions introduced in this section by two examples. To this end, we assume a new basic type **character** which stands for symbols from the ASCII character set. We consider sequences of such characters represented as finite sections of arrays of type **integer** $\to$ **character**.

Example 11.1. We now wish to write a program

$$SR \equiv [SENDER \| RECEIVER],$$

where the process *SENDER* sends to the process *RECEIVER* a sequence of M ($M \ge 1$) characters along a channel *link*. We assume that initially this sequence is stored in the section $a[0 : M - 1]$ of an array a of type **integer** $\to$ **character** in the process *SENDER*. Upon termination of SR we want this sequence to be stored in the section $b[0 : M - 1]$ of an array b of type **integer** $\to$ **character** in the process *RECEIVER*, see Figure 11.1.

The sequential processes of SR can be defined as follows:

$$SENDER \equiv i := 0; \ \textbf{do} \ i \ne M; link!a[i] \to i := i + 1 \ \textbf{od},$$

$$RECEIVER \equiv j := 0; \ \textbf{do} \ j \ne M; link?b[j] \to j := j + 1 \ \textbf{od}.$$

The processes first execute independently of each other their initialization parts $i := 0$ and $j := 0$. Then the first communication along the channel *link* occurs with the effect of $b[0] := a[0]$. Subsequently both processes independently increment their local variables i and j. Then the next communication along the channel *link* occurs with the effect of $b[1] := a[1]$. This character-by-character transmission from a into b proceeds until the processes *SENDER* and *RECEIVER* have both executed their main loops M times. Then $i = j = M$ holds and SR terminates with the result that the

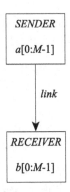

Fig. 11.1 Sending characters along a channel.

character sequence in $a[0 : M - 1]$ has been completely transmitted into $b[0 : M - 1]$. Note that in the program SR the sequence of communications between $SENDER$ and $RECEIVER$ is uniquely determined. □

Example 11.2. We now wish to transmit and process a sequence of characters. To this end, we consider a distributed program

$$TRANS \equiv [SENDER \| FILTER \| RECEIVER].$$

The intention now is that the process $FILTER$ pass all the characters from $SENDER$ to $RECEIVER$ with the exception that it delete from the sequence all blank characters, see Figure 11.2.

As before, the sequence of characters is initially stored in the section $a[0 : M - 1]$ of an array a of type **integer** $\rightarrow$ **character** in the process $SENDER$. The process $FILTER$ has an array b of the same type serving as an intermediate store for processing the character sequence and the process $RECEIVER$ has an array c of the same type to store the result of the filtering process. For coordinating its activities the process $FILTER$ uses two integer variables in and out pointing to elements in the array b.

The processes of $TRANS$ are defined as follows:

$$
\begin{aligned}
SENDER \equiv \quad & i := 0;\ \textbf{do}\ i \neq M;\ input!a[i] \rightarrow i := i + 1\ \textbf{od}, \\[4pt]
FILTER \equiv \quad & in := 0;\ out := 0;\ x := \text{`\ '}; \\
& \textbf{do}\ x \neq \text{`*'};\ input?x \rightarrow \\
& \qquad\qquad \textbf{if}\ x = \text{`\ '} \rightarrow skip \\
& \qquad\qquad \square\ x \neq \text{`\ '} \rightarrow b[in] := x; \\
& \qquad\qquad\qquad\qquad\qquad in := in + 1 \\
& \qquad\qquad \textbf{fi} \\
& \quad\ \square\ out \neq in;\ output!b[out] \rightarrow out := out + 1 \\
& \textbf{od},
\end{aligned}
$$

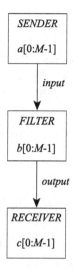

Fig. 11.2 A transmission problem.

$$RECEIVER \equiv j := 0; \ y := \text{' '};$$
$$\textbf{do } y \neq \text{'*'}; output?y \to c[j] := y; j := j + 1 \textbf{ od.}$$

The process *FILTER* can communicate with both other processes. Along channel *input* it is ready to receive characters from process *SENDER* until '*' has been received. Along channel *output* it is ready to transmit all nonblank characters to the process *RECEIVER*. If the Boolean parts $x \neq$ '*' and *out* $\neq$ *in* of the generalized guards are both true, the choice whether to receive a new character along channel *input* or to transmit a processed character along channel *output* is *nondeterministic*. Thus the distributed program *TRANS* can pursue computations with different communication sequences among its processes.

What about termination? The process *SENDER* terminates once it has sent all its M characters to the *FILTER*. The process *FILTER* terminates when it has received the character '*' *and* it has transmitted to *RECEIVER* all nonblank characters it has received. Finally, the process *RECEIVER* terminates once it has received from *FILTER* the character '*'. Thus *TRANS* terminates if *SENDER* sends as the last of its M characters the '*'.

If *SENDER* did not send any '*', a deadlock would arise when the processes *FILTER* and *RECEIVER* waited in vain for some further input. A deadlock would also arise if *SENDER* sent the '*' too early, that is, before M characters have been sent, because then *FILTER* would not accept any further characters from the *SENDER*. □

11.2 Semantics

We now provide a precise operational semantics of distributed programs by formalizing the above informal remarks. The following transition axiom formalizes the termination of a main loop within a process:

(xxiv) $< \mathbf{do}\ \square_{j=1}^{m}\ g_j \rightarrow S_j\ \mathbf{od}, \sigma > \ \rightarrow\ < E, \sigma >$
      where for $j \in \{1, \ldots, m\}$ $g_j \equiv B_j; \alpha_j$ and $\sigma \models \bigwedge_{j=1}^{m} \neg B_j$.

Next, we consider the effect of a communication. We allow the following transition axiom:

(xxv) $< [S_1\|\ldots\|S_n], \sigma > \ \rightarrow\ < [S_1'\|\ldots\|S_n'], \tau >$
      where for some $k, \ell \in \{1, \ldots, n\}$, $k \neq \ell$

$$S_k \equiv \mathbf{do}\ \square_{j=1}^{m_1}\ g_j \rightarrow R_j\ \mathbf{od},$$
$$S_\ell \equiv \mathbf{do}\ \square_{j=1}^{m_2}\ h_j \rightarrow T_j\ \mathbf{od},$$

for some $j_1 \in \{1, \ldots, m_1\}$ and $j_2 \in \{1, \ldots, m_2\}$ the generalized guards $g_{j_1} \equiv B_1; \alpha_1$ and $h_{j_2} \equiv B_2; \alpha_2$ match, and

(1) $\sigma \models B_1 \wedge B_2$,
(2) $\mathcal{M}[\![Eff(\alpha_1, \alpha_2)]\!](\sigma) = \{\tau\}$,
(3) $S_i' \equiv S_i$ for $i \neq k, \ell$,
(4) $S_k' \equiv R_{j_1};\ S_k$,
(5) $S_\ell' \equiv T_{j_2};\ S_\ell$.

Let us clarify the meaning of this transition by discussing its conditions. The form of the processes S_k and S_ℓ indicates that each of them is about to execute its main loop. The generalized guards g_{j_1} and h_{j_2} match, so syntactically a communication between S_k and S_ℓ can take place.

Condition (1) states the semantic condition for this communication: the Boolean parts of g_{j_1} and h_{j_2} hold in the initial state σ. This enables g_{j_1} and h_{j_2} to pass jointly. The new state τ is obtained by executing the assignment statement representing the effect of the communication —see (2). This communication involves only processes S_k and S_ℓ; hence (3). Finally, processes S_k and S_ℓ enter the respective branches of their main loops; hence (4) and (5).

The above transition axiom explains how main loops are executed. It involves exactly two processes but is represented as a transition of a parallel composition of n processes. Other transitions of a parallel composition of processes are generated as in Chapter 7, by adopting the interleaving rule (xvii) from Section 7.2. The meaning of distributed programs is thus defined by expanding the transition system for nondeterministic programs by transition rule (xvii) and the above transition axioms (xxiv) and (xxv).

For distributed programs S we distinguish three variants of input/output semantics:

- partial correctness semantics:

$$\mathcal{M}[\![S]\!](\sigma) = \{\tau \mid < S, \sigma > \rightarrow^* < E, \tau >\},$$

- weak total correctness semantics:

$$\mathcal{M}_{wtot}[\![S]\!](\sigma) = \mathcal{M}[\![S]\!](\sigma) \cup \{\perp \mid S \text{ can diverge from } \tau\}$$
$$\cup \{\mathbf{fail} \mid S \text{ can fail from } \tau\},$$

- total correctness semantics:

$$\mathcal{M}_{tot}[\![S]\!](\sigma) = \mathcal{M}_{wtot}[\![S]\!](\sigma) \cup \{\Delta \mid S \text{ can deadlock from } \sigma\}.$$

Here we consider a proper state σ and three kinds of special states: $\perp$ representing divergence, **fail** representing failure and Δ representing deadlock. Divergence, failure and deadlock are defined as in Chapters 3, 10 and 9, respectively. So, divergence arises when there is an infinite computation

$$< S, \sigma > \rightarrow \ldots$$

—it is possible due to the presence of the repetitive commands. Failure arises when there exists a computation of the form

$$< S, \sigma > \rightarrow \ldots \rightarrow < S_1, \mathbf{fail} >$$

—it is possible due to the presence of the alternative commands. A deadlock takes place when there exists a computation of the form

$$< S, \sigma > \rightarrow \ldots \rightarrow < R, \tau >,$$

with $R \not\equiv E$, such that the configuration of $< R, \tau >$ has no successor. This is possible due to the presence of i/o commands.

Only the total correctness semantics takes all of these possibilities into account. As in Chapter 9, weak total correctness results from total correctness by ignoring deadlock. Note, however, that due to the presence of alternative statements in the language of this chapter, weak total correctness now also records failures. The semantics of weak total correctness is not interesting in itself but helps us to modularize proofs of total correctness.

We conclude this section by proving the bounded nondeterminism of distributed programs.

Lemma 11.1. (Bounded Nondeterminism) *Let S be a distributed program and σ a proper state. Then $\mathcal{M}_{tot}[\![S]\!](\sigma)$ is either finite or it contains $\perp$.*

Proof. For distributed programs S every configuration $< S, \sigma >$ has only finitely many successors in the transition relation $\rightarrow$, so the same argument as in the proof of the Bounded Nondeterminism Lemma 8.2 based on the König's Lemma 8.4 is applicable.   □

11.3 Transformation into Nondeterministic Programs

The meaning of distributed programs can be better understood through a transformation into nondeterministic programs. In contrast to the transformation of parallel programs into nondeterministic programs described in Section 10.6 we do not need here any additional control variables. This is due to the simple form of the distributed programs considered here, where i/o commands appear only in the main loop. In the next section we use this transformation as a basis for the verification of distributed programs.

Throughout this section we consider a distributed program

$$S \equiv [S_1 \| \ldots \| S_n],$$

where each process S_i for $i \in \{1, \ldots, n\}$ is of the form

$$S_i \equiv S_{i,0}; \ \mathbf{do} \ \square_{j=1}^{m_i} B_{i,j}; \alpha_{i,j} \rightarrow S_{i,j} \ \mathbf{od}.$$

As abbreviation we introduce

$$\Gamma = \{(i, j, k, \ell) \mid \alpha_{i,j} \text{ and } \alpha_{k,\ell} \text{ match and } i < k\}.$$

We transform S into the following nondeterministic program $T(S)$:

$$
\begin{aligned}
T(S) \equiv \ & S_{1,0}; \ \ldots; \ S_{n,0}; \\
& \mathbf{do} \ \square_{(i,j,k,\ell) \in \Gamma} \ B_{i,j} \wedge B_{k,\ell} \rightarrow \ Eff(\alpha_{i,j}, \alpha_{k,\ell}); \\
& \hspace{6.5cm} S_{i,j}; \ S_{k,\ell} \\
& \mathbf{od},
\end{aligned}
$$

where the use of elements of Γ to "sum" all guards in the loop should be clear. In particular, when $\Gamma = \emptyset$ we drop this loop from $T(S)$.

Semantic Relationship Between S and $T(S)$

The semantics of S and $T(S)$ are not identical because the termination behavior is different. Indeed, upon termination of S the assertion

$$TERM \equiv \bigwedge_{i=1}^{n} \bigwedge_{j=1}^{m_i} \neg B_{i,j}$$

holds. On the other hand, upon termination of $T(S)$ the assertion

$$BLOCK \equiv \bigwedge_{(i,j,k,\ell) \in \Gamma} \neg (B_{i,j} \wedge B_{k,\ell})$$

holds. Clearly

$$TERM \rightarrow BLOCK$$

but not the other way round. States that satisfy $BLOCK \wedge \neg TERM$ are deadlock states of S.

The semantics of the programs S and $T(S)$ are related in a simple way by means of the following theorem that is crucial for our considerations.

Theorem 11.1. (Sequentialization) *For all proper states σ*

(i) $\mathcal{M}[\![S]\!](\sigma) = \mathcal{M}[\![T(S)]\!](\sigma) \cap [\![TERM]\!]$,

(ii) $\{\bot, \mathbf{fail}\} \cap \mathcal{M}_{wtot}[\![S]\!](\sigma) = \emptyset$ *iff* $\{\bot, \mathbf{fail}\} \cap \mathcal{M}_{tot}[\![T(S)]\!](\sigma) = \emptyset$,

(iii) $\Delta \notin \mathcal{M}_{tot}[\![S]\!](\sigma)$ *iff* $\mathcal{M}[\![T(S)]\!](\sigma) \subseteq [\![TERM]\!]$.

The Sequentialization Theorem relates a distributed program to a nondeterministic program. In contrast to previous theorems concerning correctness of program transformations (Sequentialization Lemma 7.7, Atomicity Theorem 8.1 and Initialization Theorem 8.2) we do not obtain here a precise match between the semantics of S and the transformed program $T(S)$.

One of the reasons is that the termination conditions for S and $T(S)$ are different. As noted above, upon termination of S, the condition $TERM$ holds, whereas upon termination of $T(S)$ only a weaker condition $BLOCK$ holds. This explains why the condition $TERM$ appears in (i).

Next, the sequentialization of the executions of the subprograms $S_{i,j}$ can "trade" a failure for divergence, or vice versa. A trivial example for this is a program S of the form

$$S \equiv [S_{1,0}; skip \parallel S_{2,0}; skip].$$

Then $T(S)$ is of the form

$$T(S) \equiv S_{1,0}; S_{2,0}; skip.$$

Suppose now that $S_{1,0}$ yields $\bot$ and $S_{2,0}$ yields $\mathbf{fail}$. Then S can fail whereas $T(S)$ diverges. If on the other hand $S_{1,0}$ yields $\mathbf{fail}$ and $S_{2,0}$ yields $\bot$, then S can diverge, whereas $T(S)$ fails. This explains why in (ii) we have to deal with $\mathbf{fail}$ and $\bot$ together.

Finally, deadlocks do not arise when executing nondeterministic programs. Deadlocks of S are transformed into terminal configurations of $T(S)$ in whose state the condition *TERM* does not hold. A simple example for this is the program

$$S \equiv [\textbf{do } c!1 \rightarrow skip \textbf{ od} \parallel skip].$$

Then $T(S) \equiv skip$ because the set Γ of matching guards is empty. Thus S ends in a deadlock whereas $T(S)$ terminates in a state satisfying $\neg TERM$. The contraposition of this observation is stated in (iii).

To prove the above theorem we introduce some auxiliary notions and prove some of their properties.

In a transition of a computation of S either one or two processes are activated, depending on whether transition rule (xvii) or axiom (xxiv) is used, or transition axiom (xxv) applies. When one process is activated in a transition, then we attach to $\rightarrow$ its index and when two processes are activated, say S_i and S_j with $i < j$, then we attach to $\rightarrow$ the pair (i, j).

If a transition $C \xrightarrow{i} D$ is obtained by applying transition rule (xvii), then we say that the process S_i *executes a private action in* $C \xrightarrow{i} D$, and if it is obtained by applying transition axiom (xxiv), then we say that the process S_i *exits its main loop in* $C \xrightarrow{i} D$. Alternatively, we can say that the transition $C \xrightarrow{i} D$ consists of a *private action of S_i* or of the *main loop exit of S_i*. Finally, if $C \xrightarrow{(i,j)} D$, then we say that each of the processes S_i and S_j *takes part in a communication in* $C \xrightarrow{(i,j)} D$.

Fix now some $A, B \in \{1, \ldots, n\} \cup \{(i, j) \mid i, j \in \{1, \ldots, n\} \text{ and } i < j\}$. We say that the relations $\xrightarrow{A}$ and $\xrightarrow{B}$ *commute*, if for all configurations C, D where D is not a failure,

$$C \xrightarrow{A} \circ \xrightarrow{B} D \text{ iff } C \xrightarrow{B} \circ \xrightarrow{A} D,$$

where $\circ$ denotes relational composition as defined in Section 2.1.

The following two simple lemmata are of importance to us.

Lemma 11.2. (Commutativity)

(i) *For $i, j \in \{1, \ldots, n\}$ the relations $\xrightarrow{i}$ and $\xrightarrow{j}$ commute.*

(ii) *For distinct $i, j, k \in \{1, \ldots, n\}$ with $i < j$, the relations $\xrightarrow{(i,j)}$ and $\xrightarrow{k}$ commute.*

Proof. See Exercise 11.2. $\square$

Lemma 11.3. (Failure) *Consider configurations C, F where F is a failure and distinct $i, j, B \in \{1, \ldots, n\}$. Suppose that $A = i$ or $A = (i, j)$ with $i < j$. Then*

$$C \xrightarrow{A} \circ \xrightarrow{B} F \text{ implies } C \xrightarrow{B} F'$$

for some failure F'.

Proof. *See Exercise 11.2.*

Proof of the Sequentialization Theorem 11.1

We follow the approach of the Atomicity Theorem 8.1.

Step 1 We first introduce the notion of a good computation of the distributed program S. We call a computation of S *good* if the components $S_1, \ldots, S_n$ of S are activated in the following order:

(i) first execute the subprograms $S_{1,0}, \ldots, S_{n,0}$ of $S_1, \ldots, S_n$, respectively, in that order, for as long as possible;
(ii) in case no failure or divergence arises,

- pick up a pair of matching generalized guards $g_{i,j}$ and $g_{k,\ell}$ whose Boolean parts evaluate to true, contained, respectively, in processes S_i and S_k with $i < k$;
- perform the communication, and
- execute the subprograms $S_{i,j}$ and $S_{k,\ell}$ of S_i and S_k, respectively, in that order, for as long as possible;

(iii) repeat step (ii) for as long as possible;
(iv) in case no failure or divergence arises, exit the main loop wherever possible, in the order determined by the processes' indices.

A transition sequence is *good* if it is a prefix of a good computation.

Step 2 We now define a notion of equivalence between the computations of S and $T(S)$. Let η be a computation of S and ξ a computation of $T(S)$.
We say that η and ξ are *1-equivalent* if

(i) η and ξ start in the same state,
(ii) for all states σ such that $\sigma \models \mathit{TERM}$, η terminates in σ iff ξ terminates in σ,
(iii) for all states σ such that $\sigma \models \neg \mathit{TERM}$, η ends in a deadlock with state σ iff ξ terminates in σ,
(iv) η ends in a failure iff ξ ends in a failure,
(v) η is infinite iff ξ is infinite.

We prove the following two claims.

- Every computation of $T(S)$ is 1-equivalent to a good computation of S;
- every good computation of S is 1-equivalent to a computation of $T(S)$.

Consider a computation ξ of $T(S)$ starting in a state σ. We construct a 1-equivalent good computation η of S which proceeds through the same sequence of states as ξ (disregarding their repetitions) by analyzing the successive transitions of ξ. Let $< S', \sigma >$ be a configuration occurring in ξ. Then S' is of one of the following forms:

1. $R;\ S''$ where R is a substatement of the process S_i,
2. $\mathbf{do}\ \Box_{(i,j,k,\ell) \in \Gamma}\ B_{i,j} \wedge B_{k,\ell} \to Eff(\alpha_{i,j}, \alpha_{k,\ell});\ S_{i,j};\ S_{k,\ell}\ \mathbf{od}$,
3. $Eff(\alpha_{i,j}, \alpha_{k,\ell});\ S''$ for some i, j, k, ℓ and S'',
4. E.

The initial configuration of η is $< S, \sigma >$. Let $< R', \sigma' >$ be the last constructed configuration of η and let $< S', \sigma' > \ \to\ < T, \sigma'' >$ be the currently analyzed transition of ξ.

(a) If S' is of the form 1, then we obtain the next configuration of η by activating in $< R', \sigma' >$ the process S_i so that it executes the action performed in $< S', \sigma' > \ \to\ < T, \sigma'' >$, by using transition rule (xvii) introduced in Section 7.2.
(b) If S' is of the form 2 and T is of the form 3, then we obtain the next configuration of η by activating in $< R', \sigma' >$ processes S_i and S_k so that they take part in a communication between $\alpha_{i,j}$ and $\alpha_{k,l}$, by using transition axiom (xxv) introduced in the previous section. Let the resulting state be τ. In this case the next configuration of ξ is $< T, \sigma'' > \ \to\ < S'', \tau >$ and we skip its analysis.
(c) If S' is of the form 2 and T is of the form 4, then we obtain the next k configurations of η, where $k \in \{0, \dots, n\}$, by activating in the order determined by their indices those processes S_i for which $\sigma \models \bigwedge_{j=1}^{m_i} \neg B_{i,j}$ holds (k denotes the total number of such processes). All these processes exit their main loops; so for each of them we use transition axiom (xxiv) introduced in the previous section.

We first prove that a sequence so constructed is indeed a computation of S. To this end we need to check that adjacent configurations form legal transitions. Case (a) is clear. For case (b) it suffices to note that the transition $< S', \sigma' > \ \to\ < T, \sigma'' >$ in ξ could take place only when $\sigma' \models B_{i,j} \wedge B_{k,\ell}$; thus condition 1 for using transition axiom (xxv) is satisfied.

Finally, case (c) arises when the transition $< S', \sigma' > \ \to\ < T, \sigma'' >$ consists of the main loop exit within $T(S)$. By assumption, ξ properly terminates. By construction, for each activated process S_i the corresponding condition for using transition axiom (xxiv) is satisfied.

In the above construction the case when S' is of the form 3 does not arise because in case (b) we skipped the analysis of one transition.

Thus η is a computation of S and by construction it is a good one.

To see that ξ and η are 1-equivalent, notice that conditions (i), (iv) and (v) are already satisfied. Moreover, if in case (c) $\sigma \models TERM$ holds, then $j = n$ so all processes $S_1, \dots, S_n$ exit their main loops and η terminates. Also, if in case (c) $\sigma \models \neg TERM$ holds, then η ends in a deadlock. Thus conditions (ii) and (iii) are also satisfied.

We have thus established the first of the two claims formulated at the beginning of this step. The second claim follows by noticing that the above construction in fact establishes a 1-1 correspondence between all computations of $T(S)$ and all good computations of S.

Step 3 We define a notion of equivalence between the computations of S. Let η and ξ be computations of S.

We say that η and ξ are *2-equivalent* if

   (i) η and ξ start in the same state,
  (ii) for all states σ, η terminates in σ iff ξ terminates in σ,
 (iii) η ends in a failure or is infinite iff ξ ends in a failure or is infinite,
 (iv) for all states σ, η ends in a deadlock with state σ iff ξ ends in a deadlock with state σ.

For example, if η and ξ start in the same state, η ends in a failure and ξ is infinite, then η and ξ are 2-equivalent.

Step 4 We prove that every computation of S is 2-equivalent to a good computation of S.

First, we define a number of auxiliary concepts concerning computations of S. Let ξ be a computation of S and let C be a configuration in ξ. Denote by $\xi[C]$ the prefix of ξ ending in C.

We say that a process S_i is *passive after C in ξ* if it is not activated in ξ after C. Note that S_i is passive after C in ξ iff

- for a subprogram R of S_i, in every configuration of ξ after C, the ith process is of the form $\mathbf{at}(R, S_i)$.

We say that a process S_i is *abandoned in ξ* if for some configuration C in ξ

- S_i is passive after C in ξ,
- i is the least index in $\{1, \ldots, n\}$ such that a private action of S_i can be executed in C.

Let $C(S_i)$ be the first such configuration in ξ. Note that $C(S_i)$ is not the last configuration of ξ.

Consider two processes S_i and S_j that are abandoned in ξ. We say that S_i is *abandoned before S_j in ξ* if $C(S_i)$ occurs in ξ before $C(S_j)$.

We now define an operation on computations of S. Let ξ be such a computation and assume that S_i is a process that is abandoned in ξ. A computation η of S is obtained by *inserting a step* of S_i in ξ as follows. Denote $C(S_i)$ by C. Suppose that $C \xrightarrow{i} D$ for some D.

If D is a failure, then η is defined as $\xi[C]$ followed by the transition $C \xrightarrow{i} D$.

Otherwise, let ξ' be the suffix of ξ starting at the first configuration of ξ after C. Perform the following two steps:

- In all configurations of ξ', change the ith process to the ith process of D,
- in all states of ξ' change the values of the variables in $change(S_i)$ to their values in the state of D.

Let γ be the resulting computation. η is now defined as $\xi[C]$ followed by $C \xrightarrow{i} D$ followed by γ.

It is easy to see that due to disjointness of the processes, η is indeed a computation of S that starts in the same state as ξ (see Exercise 11.3).

We call a computation of S *almost good* if no process S_i is abandoned in it. To establish the claim formulated at the beginning of this step we prove two simpler claims.

Claim 1 Every computation ξ of S is 2-equivalent to an almost good computation of S.

Proof of Claim 1. Suppose ξ is a terminating computation or ends in a deadlock. Then no process is abandoned in it, so it is almost good.

Suppose ξ is a computation that ends in a failure or is infinite. Assume ξ is not almost good. Let $P_1, \ldots, P_k \in \{S_1, \ldots, S_n\}$, where $k \geq 1$, be the list of all processes abandoned in ξ, ordered in such a way that each P_j is abandoned in ξ before P_{j+1}.

Repeat for as long as possible the following steps, where initially $\gamma = \xi$ and $j = 1$:

(i) insert in γ for as long as possible a step of P_j consisting of a *private action*,

(ii) rename γ to the resulting computation and increment j.

Suppose that for any γ and j step (i) does not insert any failure in γ and terminates. Then after executing steps (i) and (ii) j times, $P_{j+1}, \ldots, P_k$ is the list of all processes abandoned in the resulting computation. Thus after k repetitions of steps (i) and (ii) the resulting computation γ is almost good and either ends in a failure or is infinite.

Otherwise for some j step (i) inserts a failure in γ or does not terminate. Then the resulting computation is also almost good and either ends in a failure or is infinite.

In both cases by definition the resulting computation is 2-equivalent to ξ.

□

Claim 2 Every almost good computation ξ of S is 2-equivalent to a good computation of S.

Proof of Claim 2. We distinguish three cases.

Case 1 ξ is properly terminating or ends in a deadlock.

Then repeatedly using the Commutativity Lemma 11.2 we can transform ξ to a 2-equivalent good computation (see Exercise 11.4).

Case 2 ξ ends in a failure.

Then repeatedly using the Commutativity Lemma 11.2 and the Failing Lemma 11.3 we can transform ξ to a 2-equivalent failing computation (see Exercise 11.4).

Case 3 ξ is infinite.

Suppose that ξ starts in a state σ. We first construct a series $\xi_1, \xi_2, \ldots$ of good transition sequences starting in $< S, \sigma >$ such that for every $k > 0$

- ξ_{k+1} extends ξ_k,
- ξ_{k+1} can be extended to an infinite almost good computation of S.

We proceed by induction. Define ξ_1 to be $< S, \sigma >$.

Suppose that ξ_k has been defined ($k > 0$) and let γ be an extension of ξ_k to an infinite almost good computation of S.

Let C be the last configuration of ξ_k. Suppose that there exists a transition $C \xrightarrow{i} D$ in which the process S_i executes a private action. Choose the least such i. Let $F \xrightarrow{A} G$ with $A = i$ be the first transition in γ after C in which the process S_i is activated. Such a transition exists, since in γ no process is abandoned.

If such a transition $C \xrightarrow{i} D$ does not exist, then in C only the main loops' exits or communications can be performed. Let $F \xrightarrow{A} G$ with $A = (i, j)$ be the first transition in γ after C in which a communication is performed. Such a transition exists since γ is infinite.

By repeatedly applying the Commutativity Lemma 11.2, we obtain an infinite almost good computation with a transition $C \xrightarrow{A} D'$. Define now ξ_{k+1} as ξ_k followed by $C \xrightarrow{A} D'$.

Now using the series $\xi_1, \xi_2, \ldots$, we can construct an infinite good computation of S starting in σ by defining its kth configuration to be the kth configuration of ξ_k. $\qquad\square$

Claims 1 and 2 imply the claim formulated at the beginning of this step because 2-equivalence is an equivalence relation.

Step 5 Combining the claims of Steps 2 and 4 we obtain by virtue of the introduced notions of 1- and 2-equivalence the proof of the claims (i)–(iii) of the theorem. $\qquad\square$

11.4 Verification

The three variants of semantics of distributed programs yield in the by now standard way three notions of program correctness: partial correctness, weak total correctness and total correctness.

For the verification of these correctness properties we follow Apt [1986] and introduce particularly simple proof rules which we obtain from the Sequentialization Theorem 11.1. Throughout this section we adopt the notation of the previous section. In particular, S stands for a distributed program of the form $[S_1 \| \ldots \| S_n]$ where each process S_i for $i \in \{1, \ldots, n\}$ is of the form

$$S_i \equiv S_{i,0}; \ \textbf{do} \ \square_{j=1}^{m_i} \ B_{i,j}; \alpha_{i,j} \to S_{i,j} \ \textbf{od}.$$

Partial Correctness

Consider first partial correctness. We augment the proof system *PN* for partial correctness of nondeterministic programs by the following rule:

RULE 34: DISTRIBUTED PROGRAMS

$$
\frac{
\begin{array}{l}
\{p\} \ S_{1,0}; \ \ldots; \ S_{n,0} \ \{I\}, \\
\{I \wedge B_{i,j} \wedge B_{k,\ell}\} \ Eff(\alpha_{i,j}, \alpha_{k,\ell}); \ S_{i,j}; \ S_{k,\ell} \ \{I\} \\
\quad \text{for all } (i, j, k, \ell) \in \Gamma
\end{array}
}{
\{p\} \ S \ \{I \wedge TERM\}
}
$$

We call an assertion I that satisfies the premises of the above rule a *global invariant relative to* p. Also, we refer to a statement of the form $Eff(\alpha_{i,j}, \alpha_{k,\ell}); \ S_{i,j}; \ S_{k,\ell}$ as a *joint transition (within S)* and to $B_{i,j} \wedge B_{k,\ell}$ as the *Boolean condition* of this transition. An execution of a joint transition corresponds to a joint execution of a pair of branches of the main loops with matching generalized guards.

Informally the above rule can be phrased as follows. If I is established upon execution of all the $S_{i,0}$ sections and is preserved by each joint transition started in a state satisfying its Boolean condition, then I holds upon termination. This formulation explains why we call I a global invariant. The word "global" relates to the fact that we reason here about all processes simultaneously and consequently adopt a "global" view.

When proving that an assertion is a global invariant we usually argue informally, but with arguments that can easily be formalized in the underlying proof system *PN*.

Weak Total Correctness

Here we consider weak total correctness, which combines partial correctness with absence of failures and divergence freedom. Consequently, we augment the proof system *TN* for total correctness of nondeterministic programs by the following strengthening of the distributed programs rule 34:

RULE 35: DISTRIBUTED PROGRAMS II

(1) $\{p\}\ S_{1,0};\ \ldots;\ S_{n,0}\ \{I\}$,

(2) $\{I \wedge B_{i,j} \wedge B_{k,\ell}\}\ Eff(\alpha_{i,j}, \alpha_{k,\ell});\ S_{i,j};\ S_{k,\ell}\ \{I\}$
    for all $(i, j, k, \ell) \in \Gamma$,

(3) $\{I \wedge B_{i,j} \wedge B_{k,\ell} \wedge t = z\}\ Eff(\alpha_{i,j}, \alpha_{k,\ell});\ S_{i,j};\ S_{k,\ell}\ \{t < z\}$
    for all $(i, j, k, \ell) \in \Gamma$,

(4) $I \to t \geq 0$

$$\{p\}\ S\ \{I \wedge \textit{TERM}\}$$

where t is an integer expression and z is an integer variable not appearing in p, t, I or S.

Total Correctness

Finally, consider total correctness. We must take care of deadlock freedom. We now augment the proof system *TN* for total correctness of nondeterministic programs by a strengthened version of the distributed programs II rule 35. It has the following form:

RULE 36: DISTRIBUTED PROGRAMS III

(1) $\{p\}\ S_{1,0};\ \ldots;\ S_{n,0}\ \{I\}$,

(2) $\{I \wedge B_{i,j} \wedge B_{k,\ell}\}\ Eff(\alpha_{i,j}, \alpha_{k,\ell});\ S_{i,j};\ S_{k,\ell}\ \{I\}$
    for all $(i, j, k, \ell) \in \Gamma$,

(3) $\{I \wedge B_{i,j} \wedge B_{k,\ell} \wedge t = z\}\ Eff(\alpha_{i,j}, \alpha_{k,\ell});\ S_{i,j};\ S_{k,\ell}\ \{t < z\}$
    for all $(i, j, k, \ell) \in \Gamma$,

(4) $I \to t \geq 0$,

(5) $I \wedge \textit{BLOCK} \to \textit{TERM}$

$$\{p\}\ S\ \{I \wedge \textit{TERM}\}$$

where t is an integer expression and z is an integer variable not appearing in p, t, I or S.

The new premise (5) allows us to deduce additionally that S is deadlock free relative to p, and consequently to infer the conclusion in the sense of total correctness.

Proof Systems

Also, we use the following auxiliary rules which allow us to present the proofs in a more convenient way.

RULE A8:

$$\frac{I_1 \text{ and } I_2 \text{ are global invariant relative to } p}{I_1 \wedge I_2 \text{ is a global invariant relative to } p}$$

RULE A9:

$$\frac{\begin{array}{l} I \text{ is a global invariant relative to } p, \\ \{p\} \ S \ \{q\} \end{array}}{\{p\} \ S \ \{I \wedge q\}}$$

We use rule A8 in the proofs of partial correctness and rule A9 in the proofs of partial, weak total and total correctness. Note that rule A8 has several conclusions; so it is actually a convenient shorthand for a number of closely related rules.

We thus use three proof systems: a proof system PDP for partial correctness of distributed programs, a proof system WDP for weak total correctness of distributed programs and a proof system TDP for total correctness of distributed programs. These systems consist of the following axioms and proof rules.

PROOF SYSTEM PDP :
This system consists of the proof system PN augmented by the group of axioms and rules 34, A8 and A9.

PROOF SYSTEM WDP :
This system consists of the proof system TN augmented by the group of axioms and rules 35 and A9.

PROOF SYSTEM TDP :
This system consists of the proof system TN augmented by the group of axioms and rules 36 and A9.

Example 11.3. As a first application of the above proof systems we prove the correctness of the program SR from Example 11.1. More precisely, we prove

$$\{M \geq 1\} \; SR \; \{a[0 : M - 1] = b[0 : M - 1]\}$$

in the sense of total correctness. As a global invariant relative to $M \geq 1$ we choose

$$I \equiv a[0 : i - 1] = b[0 : j - 1] \wedge 0 \leq i \leq M,$$

where $a[0 : j - 1] = b[0 : j - 1]$ is an abbreviation for the assertion

$$\forall (0 \leq k < j) : a[k] = b[k] \wedge i = j.$$

As a termination function we choose $t \equiv M - i$.

In the program SR there is only one joint transition to consider, namely,

$$b[j] := a[i]; i := i + 1; j := j + 1$$

with the Boolean condition $i \neq M \wedge j \neq M$. Thus the premises of the distributed programs III rule 36 amount to the following:

(1) $\{M \geq 1\}\; i := 0; j := 0 \; \{I\}$,
(2) $\{I \wedge i \neq M \wedge j \neq M\} \; b[j] := a[i]; \; i := i + 1; \; j := j + 1 \; \{I\}$,
(3) $\{I \wedge i \neq M \wedge j \neq M \wedge t = z\}$
    $\quad b[j] := a[i]; \; i := i + 1; \; j := j + 1$
    $\quad \{t < z\}$,
(4) $I \rightarrow t \geq 0$,
(5) $(I \wedge \neg(i \neq M \wedge j \neq M)) \rightarrow i = M \wedge j = M$.

All these premises can be easily verified. Thus the distributed programs III rule 36 together with the rule of consequence yields the desired correctness result. □

Soundness

To establish soundness of the above three proof systems we establish first soundness of the corresponding three proof rules for distributed programs.

Theorem 11.2. (Distributed Programs I) *The distributed programs rule 34 is sound for partial correctness.*

Proof. Assume that all premises of rule 34 are true in the sense of partial correctness. By the soundness for partial correctness of the composition rule (rule 3) and of the rule of repetitive command (rule 31) we conclude

$$\models \{p\} \; T(S) \; \{I \wedge BLOCK\}. \tag{11.1}$$

Now

$$\mathcal{M}[\![S]\!]([\![p]\!])$$
$$= \quad \{\text{Sequentialization Theorem 11.1(i)}\}$$
$$\mathcal{M}[\![T(S)]\!]([\![p]\!]) \cap [\![\textit{TERM}]\!]$$
$$\subseteq \quad \{(11.1)\}$$
$$[\![I \wedge \textit{BLOCK}]\!] \cap [\![\textit{TERM}]\!]$$
$$\subseteq \quad \{[\![I \wedge \textit{BLOCK}]\!] \subseteq [\![I]\!]\}$$
$$[\![I \wedge \textit{TERM}]\!];$$

that is,

$$\models \{p\}\ S\ \{I \wedge \textit{TERM}\}.$$

This concludes the proof.   □

Theorem 11.3. (Distributed Programs II) *The distributed programs II rule 35 is sound for weak total correctness.*

Proof. The proof is similar to that of the Distributed Programs I Theorem 11.2. Assume that all premises of rule 35 are true in the sense of total correctness. By an argument analogous to the one presented in the proof of Distributed Programs I Theorem 11.2 we obtain

$$\models_{tot} \{p\}\ T(S)\ \{I \wedge \textit{BLOCK}\}. \tag{11.2}$$

Also, since the premises of the distributed programs II rule 35 include all premises of the distributed programs rule 34 and total correctness implies partial correctness, we have by Distributed Programs I Theorem 11.2

$$\models \{p\}\ S\ \{I \wedge \textit{TERM}\}. \tag{11.3}$$

Suppose now that $\sigma \models p$. Then by (11.2) $\{\perp, \textbf{fail}\} \mathrm{i} \mathcal{M}_{tot}[\![T(S)]\!](\sigma) = \emptyset$; so by the Sequentialization Theorem 11.1 (ii) $\{\perp, \textbf{fail}\} \cap \mathcal{M}_{wtot}[\![S]\!](\sigma) = \emptyset$. This in conjunction with (11.3) establishes

$$\models_{wtot} \{p\}\ S\ \{I \wedge \textit{TERM}\},$$

which concludes the proof.   □

Finally, the soundness of the distributed programs III rule 36 is an immediate consequence of the following lemma. Here, as in Chapter 9, a program S is *deadlock free relative to p* if S cannot deadlock from any state σ for which $\sigma \models p$.

Lemma 11.4. (Deadlock Freedom) *Assume that I is a global invariant relative to p; that is, I satisfies premises (1) and (2) above in the sense*

of partial correctness, and assume that premise (5) holds as well; that is,
$I \wedge BLOCK \rightarrow TERM$. *Then S is deadlock free relative to p.*

Proof. As in the proof of the Distributed Programs I Theorem 11.2

$$\models \{p\}\, T(S)\, \{I \wedge BLOCK\};$$

so by the assumption and the soundness of the consequence rule

$$\models \{p\}\, T(S)\, \{TERM\}.$$

Thus,

$$\mathcal{M}[\![T(S)]\!](\sigma) \subseteq [\![TERM]\!]$$

for all σ such that $\sigma \models p$. Now by Sequentialization Theorem 11.1(iii) we get
the desired conclusion.   □

We can now establish the desired result.

Theorem 11.4. (Distributed Programs III) *The distributed programs III
rule 36 is sound for total correctness.*

Proof. By the Distributed Programs II Theorem 11.3 and the Deadlock
Freedom Lemma 11.4.   □

The following theorem summarizes the above results.

Theorem 11.5. (Soundness of PDP, WDP and TDP)

(i) *The proof system PDP is sound for partial correctness of distributed
    programs.*
(ii) *The proof system WDP is sound for weak total correctness of distributed
    programs.*
(iii) *The proof system TDP is sound for total correctness of distributed pro-
    grams.*

Proof. See Exercise 11.6.   □

A key to the proper understanding of the proof systems *PDP*, *WDP* and
TDP studied in this chapter is the Sequentialization Theorem 11.1 relating a
distributed program S to its transformed nondeterministic version $T(S)$. This
connection allows us to prove the correctness of S by studying the correctness
of $T(S)$ instead, and the distributed program rules 34, 35 and 36 do just this
—their premises refer to the subprograms of $T(S)$ and not S.

As we saw in Section 10.6, the same approach could be used when dealing
with parallel programs. However, there such a transformation of a parallel
program into a nondeterministic program necessitates in general a use of

auxiliary variables. This adds to the complexity of the proofs and makes the approach clumsy and artificial. Here, thanks to the special form of the programs, the transformation turns out to be very simple and no auxiliary variables are needed. We can summarize this discussion by conceding that the proof method presented here exploits the particular form of the programs studied.

11.5 Case Study: A Transmission Problem

We now wish to prove correctness of the distributed program

$$TRANS \equiv [SENDER \| FILTER \| RECEIVER]$$

solving the transmission problem of Example 11.2. Recall that the process *SENDER* is to transmit to the process *RECEIVER* through the process *FILTER* a sequence of M characters represented as a section $a[0 : M]$ of an array a of type **integer** $\rightarrow$ **character**. We have $M \geq 1$ and $a \notin change(TRANS)$. For the transmission there is a channel *input* between *SENDER* and *FILTER* and a channel *output* between *FILTER* and *RECEIVER*.

The task of *FILTER* is to delete all blanks ' ' in the transmitted sequence. A special character '*' is used to mark the end of the sequence; that is, we have $a[M-1] = $ "*". *FILTER* uses an array b of the same type as the array a as an intermediate store. Upon termination of *TRANS* the result of the transmission should be stored in the process *RECEIVER* in an array c of the same type as the array a.

The program *TRANS* is a typical example of a transmission problem where the process *FILTER* acts as an intermediary process between the processes *SENDER* and *RECEIVER*.

We first formalize the correctness property we wish to prove about it. As a precondition we choose

$$p \equiv M \geq 1 \wedge a[M-1] = \text{`*'} \wedge \forall (0 \leq i < M-1) : a[i] \neq \text{`*'}.$$

To formulate the postcondition we need a function

$$delete : \textbf{character}^* \rightarrow \textbf{character}^*,$$

where **character*** denotes the set of all strings over the alphabet **character**. This mapping is defined inductively as follows:

- $delete(\varepsilon) = \varepsilon$,
- $delete(w.\text{` '}) = delete(w)$,
- $delete(w.a) = delete(w).a$ \qquad if $a \neq \text{` '}$.

Here ε denotes the empty string, w stands for an arbitary string over **character** and a for an arbitrary symbol from **character**. The postcondition can now be formulated as

$$q \equiv c[0 : j - 1] = delete(a[0 : M - 1]).$$

Our aim in this case study is to show

$$\models_{tot} \{p\} \; TRANS \; \{q\}. \tag{11.4}$$

We proceed in four steps.

Step 1. Decomposing Total Correctness

We use the fact that a proof of total correctness of a distributed program can be decomposed into proofs of

- partial correctness,
- absence of failures and of divergence,
- deadlock freedom.

Step 2. Proving Partial Correctness

We first prove (11.4) in the sense of partial correctness; that is, we show

$$\models \{p\} \; TRANS \; \{q\}.$$

To this end we first need an appropriate global invariant I of $TRANS$ relative to p. We put

$$
\begin{aligned}
I \equiv \quad & b[0 : in - 1] = delete(a[0 : i - 1]) \\
\wedge \quad & b[0 : out - 1] = c[0 : j - 1] \\
\wedge \quad & out \leq in.
\end{aligned}
$$

Here in and out are the integer variables used in the process $FILTER$ to point at elements of the array b. We now check that I indeed satisfies the premises of the distributed programs rule 34. Recall that these premises refer to the transformed nondeterministic version $T(TRANS)$ of the program $TRANS$:

$$
\begin{aligned}
T(TRANS) \equiv \; & i := 0; \; in := 0; \; out := 0; \\
& x := \text{` '}; \; j := 0; \; y := \text{` '}; \\
& \textbf{do } i \neq M \;\wedge\; x \neq \text{`*'} \rightarrow \; x := a[i]; \; i := i + 1; \\
& \qquad\qquad\qquad\qquad \textbf{if } x = \text{` '} \rightarrow \; skip \\
& \qquad\qquad\qquad\qquad \square \; x \neq \text{` '} \rightarrow \; b[in] := x;
\end{aligned}
$$

$$in := in + 1$$
$$\textbf{fi}$$
$$\square \; out \neq in \wedge y \neq \text{`*'} \rightarrow \; y := b[out]; \; out := out + 1;$$
$$c[j] := y; j := j + 1$$
$$\textbf{od}.$$

(a) First we consider the initialization part. Clearly, we have

$$\{p\}$$
$$i := 0; \; in := 0; \; out := 0;$$
$$x := \text{` '}; \; j := 0; \; y := \text{` '}$$
$$\{I\}$$

as by convention $a[0 : -1], b[0 : -1]$ and $c[0 : -1]$ denote empty strings.

(b) Next we show that every communication along the channel *input* involving
the matching i/o commands *input!a[i]* and *input?x* preserves the invariant I.
The corresponding premise of the distributed programs rule 34 refers to the
first part of the **do** loop in $T(TRANS)$:

$$\{I \wedge i \neq M \wedge x \neq \text{`*'}\}$$
$$x := a[i]; \; i := i + 1;$$
$$\textbf{if } x = \text{` '} \rightarrow \; skip$$
$$\square \; x \neq \text{` '} \rightarrow \; b[in] := x;$$
$$in := in + 1$$
$$\textbf{fi}$$
$$\{I\}.$$

We begin with the first conjunct of I; that is, $b[0 : in-1] = delete(a[0 : i-1])$.
By the definition of the mapping *delete* the correctness formulas

$$\{b[0 : in - 1] = delete(a[0 : i - 1])\}$$
$$x := a[i]; \; i := i + 1;$$
$$\{b[0 : in - 1] = delete(a[0 : i - 2]) \wedge a[i - 1] = x\}$$

and

$$\{b[0 : in - 1] = delete(a[0 : i - 2]) \wedge a[i - 1] = x \wedge x = \text{` '}\}$$
$$skip$$
$$\{b[0 : in - 1] = delete(a[0 : i - 1])\}$$

and

$$\{b[0 : in - 1] = delete(a[0 : i - 2]) \wedge a[i - 1] = x \wedge x \neq \text{` '}\}$$
$$b[in] := x; \; in := in + 1$$
$$\{b[0 : in - 1] = delete(a[0 : i - 1])\}$$

hold. Thus the alternative command rule and the composition rule yield

$$\{b[0 : in - 1] = delete(a[0 : i - 1])\}$$
$$x := a[i]; \; i := i + 1;$$

if $x = `\ ' \rightarrow skip$
$\square \ x \neq `\ ' \rightarrow \ b[in] := x;$
$\qquad\qquad\qquad in := in + 1$
fi
$\{b[0 : in - 1] = delete(a[0 : i - 1])\}.$

Now we consider the last two conjuncts of I; that is,

$$b[0 : out - 1] = c[0 : j - 1] \wedge out \leq in.$$

Since this assertion is disjoint from the program part considered here (the assignment $b[in] := x$ does not modify the section $b[0 : out - 1]$), we can apply the invariance rule A6 to deduce that I is preserved altogether.

(c) Next we show that also every communication along the channel *output* involving the matching i/o commands *output*!$b[out]$ and *output*?y preserves the invariant I. The corresponding premise of the distributed programs rule 34 refers to the second part of the **do** loop in $T(TRANS)$:

$\{I \wedge out \neq in \wedge y \neq `*'\}$
$y := b[out]; \ out := out + 1;$
$c[j] := y; \ j := j + 1$
$\{I\}.$

First we consider the last two conjuncts of I. We have

$\{b[0 : out - 1] = c[0 : j - 1] \wedge out \leq in \wedge out \neq in\}$
$y := b[out]; \ out := out + 1;$
$c[j] := y; \ j := j + 1$
$\{b[0 : out - 1] = c[0 : j - 1] \wedge out \leq in\}.$

Since the first conjunct of I is disjoint from the above program part, the invariance rule rule A6 yields that the invariant I is preserved altogether.

Thus we have shown that I is indeed a global invariant relative to p. Applying the distributed programs rule 34 we now get

$$\models \{p\} \ TRANS \ \{I \wedge TERM\},$$

where

$$TERM \ \equiv \ i = M \wedge x = `*' \wedge out = in \wedge y = `*'.$$

By the consequence rule, the correctness formula (11.4) holds in the sense of partial correctness.

Step 3. Proving Absence of Failures and of Divergence

We now prove (11.4) in the sense of weak total correctness; that is,

$$\models_{wtot} \{p\}\ TRANS\ \{q\}.$$

Since in *TRANS* the only alternative command consists of a complete case distinction, no failure can occur. Thus it remains to show the absence of divergence. To this end we use the following bound function:

$$t \equiv 2 \cdot (M - i) + in - out.$$

Here $M - i$ is the number of characters that remain to be transmitted and $in - out$ is the number of characters buffered in the process *FILTER*. The factor 2 for $M - i$ guarantees that the value of t decreases if a communication along the channel *input* with $i := i + 1; in := in + 1$ as part of the joint transition occurs. A communication along the channel *output* executes $out := out + 1$ without modifying i and in and thus it obviously decrements t.

However, to apply the distributed programs rule 35 we need to use an invariant which guarantees that t remains nonnegative. The invariant I of Step 2 is not sufficient for this purpose since the values of M and i are not related. Let us consider

$$I_1 \equiv i \le M \wedge out \le in.$$

It is straightforward to prove that I_1 is a global invariant relative to p with $I_1 \to t \ge 0$. Thus rule 35 is applicable and yields

$$\models_{wtot} \{p\}\ TRANS\ \{I_1 \wedge TERM\}.$$

Applying rule A9 to this result and the previous invariant I we now get

$$\models_{wtot} \{p\}\ TRANS\ \{I \wedge I_1 \wedge TERM\},$$

which implies (11.4) in the sense of weak total correctness.

Step 4. Proving Deadlock Freedom

Finally, we prove deadlock freedom. By the Deadlock Freedom Lemma 11.4, it suffices to find a global invariant I' relative to p for which

$$I' \wedge BLOCK \to TERM \tag{11.5}$$

holds. For the program *TRANS* we have

$$BLOCK \equiv (i = M \vee x = `*') \wedge (out = in \vee y = `*')$$

and, as noted before,

$$TERM \equiv i = M \wedge x = \text{`*'} \wedge out = in \wedge y = \text{`*'}.$$

We exhibit I' "in stages" by first introducing global invariants I_2, I_3 and I_4 relative to p with

$$I_2 \rightarrow (i = M \leftrightarrow x = \text{`*'}), \tag{11.6}$$

$$I_3 \wedge i = M \wedge x = \text{`*'} \wedge out = in \rightarrow y = \text{`*'}, \tag{11.7}$$

$$I_4 \wedge i = M \wedge x = \text{`*'} \wedge y = \text{`*'} \rightarrow out = in. \tag{11.8}$$

Then we put

$$I' \equiv I_2 \wedge I_3 \wedge I_4.$$

By rule A8 I' is also a global invariant relative to p. Note that each of the equalities used in (11.6), (11.7) and (11.8) is a conjunct of $TERM$; (11.6), (11.7) and (11.8) express certain implications between these conjuncts which guarantee that I' indeed satisfies (11.5).

It remains to determine I_2, I_3 and I_4. We put

$$I_2 \equiv p \wedge (i > 0 \vee x = \text{`*'} \rightarrow x = a[i - 1]).$$

I_2 relates variables of the processes $SENDER$ and $FILTER$. It is easy to check that I_2 is indeed a global invariant relative to p. Note that (11.6) holds.

Next, we consider

$$I_3 \equiv I \wedge p \wedge (j > 0 \rightarrow y = c[j - 1]).$$

The last conjunct of I_3 states a simple property of the variables of the process $RECEIVER$. Again I_3 is a global invariant relative to p. The following sequence of implications proves (11.7):

$$I_3 \wedge i = M \wedge x = \text{`*'} \wedge out = in$$
$$\rightarrow \quad \{\text{definition of } I\}$$
$$I_3 \wedge c[0 : j - 1] = delete(a[0 : M - 1])$$
$$\rightarrow \quad \{p \text{ implies } a[0 : M - 1] = \text{`*'}\}$$
$$I_3 \wedge c[j - 1] = \text{`*'} \wedge j > 0$$
$$\rightarrow \quad \{\text{definition of } I_3\}$$
$$y = \text{`*'}.$$

Finally, we put

$$I_4 \equiv I \wedge p \wedge (y = \text{`*'} \rightarrow c[j - 1] = \text{`*'}).$$

Here as well, the last conjunct describes a simple property of the variables of the process $RECEIVER$. It is easy to show that I_4 is a global invariant relative to p. We prove the property (11.8):

$$I_4 \wedge i = M \wedge x = \text{`*'} \wedge y = \text{`*'}$$

$\rightarrow \quad \{\text{definition of } I_4\}$

$$I_4 \wedge c[j-1] = \text{`*'}$$

$\rightarrow \quad \{\text{definition of } I \text{ and } p\}$

$$I_4 \wedge b[out-1] = a[M-1]$$

$\rightarrow \quad \{\text{there is only one `*' in } a[0:M-1],$

$\qquad \text{namely } a[M-1], \text{ so the first conjunct}$

$\qquad \text{of } I \text{ implies } b[in-1] = a[M-1]\}$

$$out = in.$$

We have thus proved (11.5), that is, the deadlock freedom of the program *TRANS*. Together with the result from Step 3 we have established the desired correctness formula (11.4) in the sense of total correctness.

11.6 Exercises

11.1. Let S be a distributed program. Prove that if $< S, \sigma > \rightarrow < S_1, \tau >$, then S_1 is also a distributed program.

11.2. Let $S \equiv [S_1 \| \ldots \| S_n]$ be a distributed program.

  (i) Prove the Commutativity Lemma 11.2.
  (ii) Prove that for distinct $i, j, k, \ell \in \{1, \ldots, n\}$ with $i < j$ and $k < \ell$, the relations $\xrightarrow{(i,j)}$ and $\xrightarrow{(k,\ell)}$ commute.
  (iii) Prove the Failure Lemma 11.3.

Hint. Use the Change and Access Lemma 10.4.

11.3. Consider Step 4 of the proof of the Sequentialization Theorem 11.1. Prove that the result of inserting a step of a process in a computation of S is indeed a computation of S.
Hint. Use the Change and Access Lemma 10.4.

11.4. Prove Claim 2 in the proof of the Sequentialization Theorem 11.1 when ξ is terminating or ends in a deadlock or ends in a failure.

11.5. Prove the Change and Access Lemma 3.4 for distributed programs and the partial correctness, weak total correctness and total correctness semantics.
Hint. Use the Sequentialization Theorem 11.1.

11.6. Prove the Soundness of PDP, WDP and TDP Theorem 11.5.

11.7. Given a section $a[1 : n]$ of an array a of type **integer** $\rightarrow$ **integer** the process $CENTER$ should compute in an integer variable x the weighted sum $\sum_{i=1}^{n} w_i \cdot a[i]$. We assume that the weights w_i are stored in a distributed fashion in separate processes P_i, and that the multiplications are carried out by the processes P_i while the addition is carried out by the process $CENTER$.

Thus $CENTER$ has to communicate in an appropriate way with these processes P_i. We stipulate that for this purpose communication channels $link_i$ are available and consider the following distributed program:

$$WSUM \equiv [CENTER \parallel P_1 \parallel \ldots \parallel P_n],$$

where

$$
\begin{aligned}
CENTER \equiv \quad & x := 0;\ to[1] := \textbf{true};\ \ldots\ ;\ to[n] := \textbf{true}; \\
& from[1] := \textbf{true};\ \ldots\ ;\ from[n] := \textbf{true}; \\
& \textbf{do}\ to[1]; link!a[1] \rightarrow to[1] := \textbf{false}; \\
& \quad\ \text{......................................} \\
& \quad to[n]; link!a[n] \rightarrow to[n] := \textbf{false}; \\
& \quad from[1]; link?y \rightarrow x := x + y;\ from[1] := \textbf{false}; \\
& \quad\ \text{......................................} \\
& \quad from[n]; link?y \rightarrow x := x + y;\ from[n] := \textbf{false}; \\
& \textbf{od}
\end{aligned}
$$

and

$$
\begin{aligned}
P_i \equiv \quad & rec_i := \textbf{false};\ sent_i := \textbf{false}; \\
& \textbf{do}\ \neg rec_i; link?z_i \rightarrow rec_i := \textbf{true} \\
& \quad rec_i \wedge \neg sent_i; link!w_i \cdot z_i \rightarrow sent_i := \textbf{true} \\
& \textbf{od}
\end{aligned}
$$

for $i \in \{1, ..., n\}$. The process $CENTER$ uses Boolean control variables $to[i]$ and $from[i]$ of two arrays to and $from$ of type **integer** $\rightarrow$ **Boolean**. Additionally, each process P_i uses two Boolean control variables rec_i und $sent_i$.

Prove the total correctness of $WSUM$:

$$\models_{tot} \{\textbf{true}\}\ WSUM\ \{x = \textstyle\sum_{i=1}^{n} w_i \cdot a[i]\}.$$

11.8. Let X_0 and Y_0 be two disjoint, nonempty finite sets of integers. We consider the following problem of *set partition* due to Dijkstra [1977] (see also Apt, Francez and de Roever [1980]): the union $X_0 \cup Y_0$ should be partitioned in two sets X and Y such that X has the same number of elements as X_0, Y has the same number of elements as Y_0 and all elements of X are smaller than those of Y.

To solve this problem we consider a distributed program $SETPART$ consisting of two processes $SMALL$ and BIG which manipulate local variables X and Y for finite sets of integers and communicate with each other along channels big and $small$:

$$SETPART \equiv [SMALL \parallel BIG].$$

Initially, the sets X_0 and Y_0 are stored in X and Y. Then the process *SMALL* repeatedly sends the maximum of the set stored in X along the channnel *big* to the process *BIG*. This process sends back the minimum of the updated set Y along the channel *small* to the process *SMALL*. This exchange of values terminates as soon as the process *SMALL* gets back the maximum just sent to *BIG*.

Altogether the processes of *SETPART* are defined as follows:

$$
\begin{aligned}
SMALL \;\equiv\; & more := \textbf{true};\; send := \textbf{true}; \\
& mx := max(X); \\
& \textbf{do } more \wedge send;\, big\,!\,mx \rightarrow send := \textbf{false} \\
& \square \quad more \wedge \neg send;\, small\,?\,x \rightarrow \\
& \qquad \textbf{if } mx = x \rightarrow more := \textbf{false} \\
& \qquad \square\; mx \neq x \rightarrow\; X := X - \{mx\} \cup \{x\}; \\
& \qquad\qquad\qquad\qquad mx := max(X); \\
& \qquad\qquad\qquad\qquad send := \textbf{true} \\
& \qquad \textbf{fi} \\
& \textbf{od},
\end{aligned}
$$

$$
\begin{aligned}
BIG \;\equiv\; & go := \textbf{true}; \\
& \textbf{do } go;\, big\,?\,y \rightarrow\; Y := Y \cup \{y\}; \\
& \qquad\qquad\qquad\qquad mn := min(Y); \\
& \qquad\qquad\qquad\qquad Y := Y - \{mn\} \\
& \square\quad go;\, small\,!\,mn \rightarrow go := (mn \neq y) \\
& \textbf{od}.
\end{aligned}
$$

The Boolean variables *more, send* and *go* are used to coordinate the behavior of *SMALL* and *BIG*. In particular, thanks to the variable *send* the processes *SMALL* and *BIG* communicate in an alternating fashion along the channels *big* and *small*. The integer variables mx, x, mn, y are used to store values from the sets X and Y.

Prove the total correctness of the program *SETPART* for the precondition

$$
p \equiv X \cap Y = \emptyset \wedge X \neq \emptyset \wedge Y \neq \emptyset \wedge X = X_0 \wedge Y = Y_0
$$

and the postcondition

$$
\begin{aligned}
q \equiv\; & X \cup Y = X_0 \cup Y_0 \\
& \wedge\; card\, X = card\, X_0 \wedge card\, Y = card\, Y_0 \\
& \wedge\; max(X) < min(Y).
\end{aligned}
$$

Recall from Section 2.1 that for a finite set A, *card* A denotes the number of its elements.

11.9. Extend the syntax of distributed programs by allowing the clauses defining nondeterministic programs in Chapter 10 in addition to the clause for parallel composition. Call the resulting programs *general distributed programs*.

(i) Extend the definition of semantics to general distributed programs.
(ii) Let $R \equiv S_0; \ [S_1\|\ldots\|R_0; \ S_i\|\ldots\|S_n]$ be a general distributed program where R_0 and S_0 are nondeterministic programs. Consider the general distributed program $T \equiv S_0; \ R_0; \ [S_1\|\ldots\|S_i\|\ldots\|S_n]$. Prove that

$$\mathcal{M}[\![R]\!] = \mathcal{M}[\![T]\!].$$

What can be stated for $\mathcal{M}_{wtot}$ and $\mathcal{M}_{tot}$?

Hint. Use the Sequentialization Theorem 11.1 and the Input/Output Lemma 10.3.

11.7 Bibliographic Remarks

We have studied here distributed programs that can be defined in a simple subset of CSP of Hoare [1978]. This subset was introduced in Apt [1986]. In the original definition of CSP i/o commands can appear at every position where assignments are allowed. On the other hand, process names were used instead of channel names in i/o commands, and output commands were not allowed as guards of alternative and repetitive commands. A modern version of CSP without these restrictions is presented in Hoare [1985]. This book takes up concepts from process algebra as in CCS (Calculus for Communicating Systems) of Milner [1980,1989]. The most complete presentation of this modern CSP can be found in Roscoe [1998].

A first semantics of CSP programs can be found in Francez et al. [1979]. Simplified definitions are given in Francez, Lehmann and Pnueli [1984] and in Brookes, Hoare and Roscoe [1984]. The operational semantics presented here is based on Plotkin [1982].

Proof systems for the verification of CSP programs were first introduced in Apt, Francez, and de Roever [1980], and in Levin and Gries [1981]. These proof systems represent an analogue of the Owicki/Gries method described in Chapter 8: first proof outlines are established for the sequential processes of a distributed program and then their compatibility is checked using a so-called *cooperation test*. This test is a counterpart of the test of interference freedom for parallel programs. The proof systems of Apt, Francez, and de Roever and of Levin and Gries are explained in Francez [1992]. An overview of various proof systems for CSP is given in Hooman and de Roever [1986].

The approach to verification of distributed programs presented in this chapter is due to Apt [1986]. The basic idea is to avoid the complex cooperation test by considering only a subset of CSP programs. In Apt, Bougé and Clermont [1987], and in Zöbel [1988] it has been shown that each CSP program can indeed be transformed into a program in this subset called its *normal form*. The price of this transformation is that it introduces additional control variables into the normal form program in the same way as program counter variables were introduced to transform parallel programs into nondeterministic ones in Section 10.6.

For CSP programs that manipulate a finite state space, behavioral properties can be verified automatically using the so-called FDR *model checker*, a commercially available tool, see Roscoe [1994] and Formal Systems (Europe) Ltd. [2003]. For general CSP programs the compositional verification techniques of Zwiers [1989] can be used. See also de Roever et al. [2001].

Research on CSP led to the design of the programming language OCCAM, see INMOS [1984], for distributed transputer systems. A systematic development of OCCAM programs from specifications has been studied as part of the European basic research project ProCoS (Provably Correct Systems), see Bowen et al. [1996] for an overview and the papers by Schenke [1999], Schenke and Olderog [1999], and Olderog and Rössig [1993] for more details.

CSP has been combined with specification methods for data (and time) to integrated specification formalisms for reactive (and real-time) systems. Examples of such combinations are CSP-OZ by Fischer [1997], Circus by Woodcock and Cavalcanti [2002], and, for the case of real-time, TCOZ by Mahony and Dong [1998] and CSP-OZ-DC by Hoenicke and Olderog [2002] and Hoenicke [2006]. For applications of CSP-OZ see the papers by Fischer and Wehrheim [1999], Möller et al. [2008], and Basin et al. [2007]. For automatic verification of CSP-OZ-DC specifications against real-time properties we refer to Meyer et al. [2008].

12 *Fairness*

A S WE HAVE seen in the zero search example of Chapter 1, fairness is an important hypothesis in the study of parallel programs. Fairness models the idea of "true parallelism," where every component of a parallel program progresses with unknown, but positive speed. In other words, every component eventually executes its next enabled atomic instruction.

Semantically, fairness can be viewed as an attempt at reducing the amount of nondeterminism in the computations of programs. Therefore fairness can be studied in any setting where nondeterminism arises. In this chapter we study fairness in the simplest possible setting of this book, the class of nondeterministic programs studied in Chapter 10.

Since parallel and distributed programs can be transformed into nondeterministic ones (see Sections 10.6 and 11.3), the techniques presented here

Krzysztof R. Apt et al., *Verification of Sequential and Concurrent Programs*,
Texts in Computer Science, DOI: 10.1007/978-1-84882-745-5_12,
© Springer-Verlag London Limited 2009

can in principle be applied to the study of fairness for concurrent programs. However, a more direct approach is possible that does not involve any program transformations. The precise presentation is beyond the scope of this edition of the book.

In Section 12.1 we provide a rigorous definition of fairness. The assumption of fairness leads to so-called unbounded nondeterminism; this makes reasoning about fairness difficult. In Section 12.2 we outline an approach to overcome this difficulty by reducing fair nondeterminism to usual nondeterminism by means of a program transformation.

To cope with the unbounded nondeterminism induced by fairness, this transformation uses an additional programming construct: the random assignment. In Section 12.4 semantics and verification of nondeterministic programs in presence of random assignment are discussed. In Section 12.5 random assignments are used to construct an abstract scheduler *FAIR* that exactly generates all fair computations. We also show that two widely used schedulers, the round robin scheduler and a scheduler based on queues, are specific instances of *FAIR*.

In Section 12.6 we define the program transformation announced in Section 12.2 by embedding the scheduler *FAIR* into a given nondeterministic program. In Section 12.7 this transformation is used to develop a proof rule dealing with fairness.

We demonstrate the use of this proof rule in two case studies. In Section 12.8 we apply this proof rule in a case study that deals with a nondeterministic version of the zero search program of Chapter 1, and in Section 12.9 we prove correctness of a nondeterministic program for the asynchronous computation of fixed points. In both cases the assumption of fairness is crucial in the termination proof.

12.1 The Concept of Fairness

To illustrate the concept of fairness in the setting of nondeterministic programs, consider the program

$$PU1 \equiv signal := \textbf{false};$$
$$\textbf{do } \neg signal \rightarrow \text{``print next line''}$$
$$\square \quad \neg signal \rightarrow signal := \textbf{true}$$
$$\textbf{od}.$$

The letters P and U in the program name $PU1$ stand for *printer* and *user*; the first guarded command is meant to represent a printer that continuously outputs a line from a file until the user, here represented by the second guarded command, signals that it should terminate. But does the printer actually receive the termination signal? Well, assuming that the user's assignment $signal := \textbf{true}$ is eventually executed the program $PU1$ terminates.

However, the semantics of nondeterministic programs as defined in Chapter 10 does not guarantee this. Indeed, it permits infinite computations that continuously select the first guarded command. To enforce termination one has to assume fairness.

Often two variants of fairness are distinguished. *Weak fairness* requires that every guarded command of a **do** loop, which is from some moment on continuously enabled, is activated infinitely often. Under this assumption a computation of $PU1$ cannot forever activate its first component (the printer) because the second command (the user) is continuously enabled. Thus the assignment $signal := \textbf{true}$ of $PU1$ is eventually executed. This leads to termination of $PU1$.

$PU1$ is a particularly simple program because the guards of its **do** loop are identical. Thus, as soon as this guard becomes false, the loop is certain to terminate. Loops with different guards can exhibit more complicated computations. Consider, for example, the following variant of our printer-user program:

$$PU2 \equiv signal := \textbf{false};\ full\text{-}page := \textbf{false};\ \ell := 0;$$
$$\textbf{do } \neg signal \rightarrow \text{``print next line''};$$
$$\ell := (\ell + 1) \textbf{ mod } 30;$$
$$full\text{-}page := \ell = 0$$
$$\square \quad \neg signal \wedge full\text{-}page \rightarrow signal := \textbf{true}$$
$$\textbf{od}.$$

Again, the printer, represented by the first command, continuously outputs a line from a file until the user, represented by the second command, signals that it should terminate. But the user will issue the termination signal only if the printer has completed its current page. We assume that each page consists of 30 lines, which are counted modulo 30 in the integer variable ℓ.

What about termination of $PU2$? Since the guard "*full-page*" of the second command is never continuously enabled, the assumption of weak fairness does not rule out an infinite computation where only the first command is activated. Under what assumption does *PU2* terminate, then? This question brings us to the notion of *strong fairness*; it requires that every guarded command that is enabled infinitely often is also activated infinitely often.

Under this assumption, a computation of *PU2* cannot forever activate its first command because the guard "*full-page*" of the second command is then infinitely often enabled. Thus the assignment *signal* := **true** is eventually executed, causing termination of *PU2*.

In this book, we understand by *fairness* the notion of strong fairness. We investigate fairness only for the class of nondeterministic programs that we call *one-level* nondeterministic programs. These are programs of the form

$$S_0; \ \textbf{do} \ B_1 \rightarrow S_1 \square \ldots \square B_n \rightarrow S_n \ \textbf{od},$$

where $S_0, S_1, \ldots, S_n$ are **while** programs.

Selections and Runs

Let us now be more precise about fairness. Since it can be expressed exclusively in terms of enabled and activated components, we abstract from all other details in computations and introduce the notions of selection and run. This simplifies the definition and subsequent analysis of fairness, both here and later for parallel programs.

A *selection (of n components)* is a pair

$$(E, i)$$

consisting of a nonempty set $E \subseteq \{1, \ldots, n\}$ of enabled components and an activated component $i \in E$. A *run (of n components)* is a finite or infinite sequence

$$(E_0, i_0) \ldots (E_j, i_j) \ldots$$

of selections.

A run is called *fair* if it satisfies the following condition:

$$\forall (1 \leq i \leq n) : (\overset{\infty}{\exists} j \in \mathbb{N} : i \in E_j \rightarrow \overset{\infty}{\exists} j \in \mathbb{N} : i = i_j).$$

The quantifier $\overset{\infty}{\exists}$ stands for "there exist infinitely many," and $\mathbb{N}$ denotes the set $\{0, 1, 2, 3, \ldots\}$. Thus, in a fair run, every component i which is enabled infinitely often, is also activated infinitely often. In particular, every finite run is fair.

Next, we link runs to the computations of one-level nondeterministic programs

$$S \equiv S_0; \ \textbf{do} \ B_1 \rightarrow S_1 \square \ldots \square B_n \rightarrow S_n \ \textbf{od}$$

defined above. A transition

$$< T_j, \sigma_j > \ \rightarrow \ < T_{j+1}, \sigma_{j+1} >$$

in a computation of S is called a *loop transition* if

$$T_j \equiv \mathbf{do}\ B_1 \rightarrow S_1 \square \ldots \square B_n \rightarrow S_n\ \mathbf{od}\ \text{and}\ \sigma_j \models \bigvee_{i=1}^{n} B_i.$$

The *selection* (E_j, i_j) *of a loop transition* is given by

$$E_j = \{i \in \{1, \ldots, n\} \mid \sigma_j \models B_i)\}$$

and

$$T_{j+1} \equiv S_{i_j};\ T_j,$$

meaning that E_j is the set of indices i of enabled guards B_i and i_j is the index of the command activated in the transition. Note that $E_j \neq \emptyset$.

The *run of a computation* of S

$$\xi :< S, \sigma >=< T_0, \sigma_0 > \ \rightarrow \ldots \rightarrow \ < T_j, \sigma_j > \ \rightarrow \ldots$$

is defined as the run

$$(E_{j_0}, i_{j_0}) \ldots (E_{j_k}, i_{j_k}) \ldots$$

recording all selections of loop transitions in ξ. Here $j_0 < \ldots < j_k < \ldots$ is the subsequence of indices $j \geq 0$ picking up all loop transitions

$$< T_{j_k}, \sigma_{j_k} > \ \rightarrow \ < T_{j_k+1}, \sigma_{j_k+1} >$$

in ξ. Thus computations that do not pass through any loop transition yield the empty run. A *run of a program* S is the run of one of its computations.

A *computation* is *fair* if its run is fair. Thus for fairness only loop transitions are relevant; transitions inside the deterministic parts $S_0, S_1, \ldots, S_n$ of S do not matter. Note that every finite computation is fair.

Example 12.1. To practice with this definition, let us look at the program *PU1* again. A computation of *PU1* that exclusively activates the first component (the printer) yields the run

$$(\{1, 2\}, 1)(\{1, 2\}, 1) \ldots (\{1, 2\}, 1) \ldots .$$

Since the index 2 (representing the second component) is never activated, the run and hence the computation is not fair. Every fair computation of *PU1* is finite, yielding a run of the form

$$(\{1, 2\}, 1) \ldots (\{1, 2\}, 1)(\{1, 2\}, 2).$$

□

Fair Nondeterminism Semantics

The *fair nondeterminism semantics* of one-level nondeterministic programs
S is defined as follows where σ is a proper state:

$$\mathcal{M}_{fair}[\![S]\!](\sigma) = \quad \{\tau \mid < S, \sigma > \rightarrow^* < E, \tau >\}$$
$$\cup \ \{\perp \mid S \text{ can diverge from } \sigma \text{ in a fair computation}\}$$
$$\cup \ \{\mathbf{fail} \mid S \text{ can fail from } \sigma\}.$$

We see that $\mathcal{M}_{fair}[\![S]\!]$ is like $\mathcal{M}_{tot}[\![S]\!]$ except that only fair computations are
considered. Notice that this affects only the diverging computations yielding
$\perp$.

How does this restriction to fair computations affect the results of programs? The answer is given in the following example.

Example 12.2. Consider a slight variation of the program *PU1*, namely

$$PU3 \ \equiv \ signal := \mathbf{false}; \ count := 0;$$
$$\mathbf{do} \ \neg signal \rightarrow \ \text{``print next line''};$$
$$count := count + 1$$
$$\square \ \ \neg signal \rightarrow \ signal := \mathbf{true}$$
$$\mathbf{od}.$$

The variable *count* counts the number of lines printed. Let σ be a state
with $\sigma(count) = 0$ and $\sigma(signal) = \mathbf{true}$. For $i \geq 0$ let σ_i be as σ but with
$\sigma_i(count) = i$. Ignoring the possible effect of the command "print next line",
we obtain

$$\mathcal{M}_{tot}[\![PU3]\!](\sigma) = \{\sigma_i \mid i \geq 0\} \cup \{\perp\}$$

but

$$\mathcal{M}_{fair}[\![PU3]\!](\sigma) = \{\sigma_i \mid i \geq 0\}.$$

We see that under the assumption of fairness *PU3* always terminates ($\perp$ is
not present) but still there are infinitely many final states possible: σ_i with
$i \geq 0$. This phenomenon differs from the bounded nondeterminism proved for
$\mathcal{M}_{tot}$ in the Bounded Nondeterminism Lemma 10.1; it is called *unbounded
nondeterminism*.   □

12.2 Transformational Semantics

Fair nondeterminism was introduced by restricting the set of allowed computations. This provides a clear definition but no insight on how to reason about or prove correctness of programs that assume fairness.

We wish to provide such an insight by applying the *principle of transformational semantics*:

> Reduce the new concept (here fair nondeterminism semantics) to known concepts (here total correctness semantics) with the help of program transformations.

In other words, we are looking for a transformation T_{fair} which transforms each one-level nondeterministic program S into another nondeterministic program $T_{fair}(S)$ satisfying the semantic equation

$$\mathcal{M}_{fair}[\![S]\!] = \mathcal{M}_{tot}[\![T_{fair}(S)]\!]. \tag{12.1}$$

The benefits of T_{fair} are twofold. First, it provides us with information on how to implement fairness. Second, T_{fair} serves as a stepping stone for developing a proof system for fair nondeterminism. We start with the following conclusion of (12.1):

$$\models_{fair} \{p\}\ S\ \{q\} \text{ iff } \models_{tot} \{p\}\ T_{fair}(S)\ \{q\}, \tag{12.2}$$

which states that a program S is correct in the sense of fair total correctness (explained in Section 12.7) if and only if its transformed version $T_{fair}(S)$ is correct in the sense of usual total correctness. Corollary (12.2) suggests using the transformation T_{fair} itself as a proof rule in a system for fair nondeterminism. This is a valid approach, but we can do slightly better here: by informally "absorbing" the parts added to S by T_{fair} into the pre- and postconditions p and q we obtain a system for proving

$$\models_{fair} \{p\}\ S\ \{q\}$$

directly without reference to T_{fair}. So, T_{fair} is used only to motivate and justify the new proof rules.

The subsequent sections explain this transformational semantics approach in detail.

12.3 Well-Founded Structures

We begin by introducing well-founded structures. The reason is that to prove termination of programs involving unbounded nondeterminism (see Example 12.2), we need bound functions that take values in more general structures than integers.

Definition 12.1. Let $(P, <)$ be an *irreflexive partial order*, that is, let P be a set and $<$ an irreflexive transitive relation on P. We say that $<$ is *well-founded on a subset* $W \subseteq P$ if there is no infinite descending chain

$$\ldots < w_2 < w_1 < w_0$$

of elements $w_i \in W$. The pair $(W, <)$ is then called a *well-founded structure*. If $w < w'$ for some $w, w' \in W$ we say that w is *less than* w' or w' is *greater than* w. $\Box$

Of course, the natural numbers form a well-founded structure $(\mathbb{N}, <)$ under the usual relation $<$. But also the extension $(\mathbb{N} \cup \{\omega\}, <)$, with ω denoting an "unbounded value" satisfying

$$n < \omega$$

for all $n \in \mathbb{N}$, is well-founded. We mention two important construction principles for building new well-founded structures from existing ones.

Let $(W_1, <_1)$ and $(W_1, <_2)$ be two well-founded structures. Then the structure $(W_1 \times W_2, <_{com})$ with $<_{com}$ denoting the *componentwise* order on $W_1 \times W_2$ defined by

$$(m_1, m_2) <_{com} (n_1, n_2) \text{ iff } m_1 <_1 n_1 \text{ or } m_2 <_2 n_2$$

is well-founded, and the structure $(W_1 \times W_2, <_{lex})$ with $<_{lex}$ denoting the *lexicographic* order on $W_1 \times W_2$ defined by

$$(m_1, m_2) <_{lex} (n_1, n_2) \text{ iff } (m_1 <_1 n_1) \text{ or } (m_1 = n_1 \text{ and } m_2 <_2 n_2)$$

is also well-founded.

Similarly, given well-founded structures $(W_1, <_1), \ldots, (W_n, <_n)$, we can define the componentwise and the lexicographic orders on the products $W_1 \times \ldots \times W_n$ ($n > 1$). These also are well-founded.

12.4 Random Assignment

Note that we cannot expect the transformed program $T_{fair}(S)$ to be another nondeterministic program in the syntax of Section 10.1, because the semantics $\mathcal{M}_{tot}$ yields bounded nondeterminism (Bounded Nondeterminism Lemma 10.1) for these programs whereas $\mathcal{M}_{fair}$ yields unbounded nondeterminism (Example 12.2).

But we can find a transformation T_{fair} where the transformed program $T_{fair}(S)$ uses an *additional* language construct: the *random assignment*

$$x :=?.$$

It assigns an arbitrary nonnegative integer to the integer variable x. The random assignment is an explicit form of unbounded nondeterminism. In the transformation T_{fair} it will localize the unbounded nondeterminism implicitly induced by the assumption of fairness. Thus; random assignments will enable us to reason about programs under fairness assumptions. In this section we present a semantics and proof theory of random assignments as an extension of ordinary nondeterministic programs.

Semantics

The random assignment $x :=?$ terminates for any initial state σ, but there are infinitely many possibilities for the final state —one for each non-negative value that might be assigned to x. This idea is captured in the following transition axiom where σ is a proper state:

(xxvi) $< x :=?, \sigma > \ \rightarrow \ < E, \sigma[x := d] >$ for every natural number $d \geq 0$.

The semantics of nondeterministic programs with random assignments is defined just as in Section 10.2, but with the transition relation $\rightarrow$ referring to this additional transition axiom. In particular, we have

$$\mathcal{N}[\![x :=?]\!](\sigma) = \{\sigma[x := d] \mid d \geq 0\}$$

for a proper state σ and $\mathcal{N} = \mathcal{M}$ or $\mathcal{N} = \mathcal{M}_{tot}$.

Verification

The proof theory of random assignments in isolation is simple. We just need the following axiom.

AXIOM 37: RANDOM ASSIGNMENT

$$\{\forall x \geq 0 : p\} \ x :=? \ \{p\}$$

Thus, to establish an assertion p after the random assignment $x :=?$, p must hold before $x :=?$ for all possible values of x generated by this assignment; that is, for all integers $x \geq 0$. Thus, as with the assignment axiom 2 for ordinary assignments, this axiom formalizes backward reasoning about random assignments. By the above semantics, the random assignment axiom is sound for partial and total correctness.

But does it suffice when added to the previous proof systems for non-deterministic programs? For partial correctness the answer is "yes." Thus for proofs of *partial* correctness of *n*ondeterministic programs with *r*andom assignments we consider the following proof system *PNR*.

PROOF SYSTEM *PNR* :
This system consists of the proof system
PN augmented with axiom 37.

Proving termination, however, gets more complicated: the repetitive command II rule 33 of Section 10.4, using an integer-valued bound function t, is no longer sufficient. The reason is that in the presence of random assignments some repetitive commands always terminate but the actual number of repetitions does not depend on the initial state and is unbounded.

To illustrate this point, consider the program

$$S_\omega \equiv \mathbf{do}\ b \wedge x > 0\ \rightarrow x := x - 1$$
$$\square\quad b \wedge x < 0\ \rightarrow x := x + 1$$
$$\square\quad \neg b\qquad\ \ \rightarrow x :=?;\ b := \mathbf{true}$$
$$\mathbf{od}.$$

Activated in a state where b is true, this program terminates after $|x|$ repetitions. Thus $t = |x|$ is an appropriate bound function for showing

$$\{b\}\ S_\omega\ \{\mathbf{true}\}$$

with the rule of repetitive commands II.

S_ω also terminates when activated in a state σ where b is false, but we cannot predict the number of repetitions from σ. This number is known only after the random assignment $x :=?$ has been executed; then it is $|x|$ again. Thus any bound function t on the number of repetitions has to satisfy

$$t \geq |x|$$

for all $x \geq 0$. Clearly, this is impossible for any integer valued t. Consequently, the rule of repetitive commands II is not sufficient to show

$$\{\neg b\}\ S_\omega\ \{\mathbf{true}\}.$$

The following, more general proof rule for repetitive commands assumes a well-founded structure $(W, <)$ to be a part of the underlying semantic domain $\mathcal{D}$ (cf. Section 2.3). Variables ranging over W can appear only in assertions and not in programs. As before, program variables range only over the standard parts of the domain $\mathcal{D}$ like the integers or the Booleans.

RULE 38: REPETITIVE COMMAND III

$$\frac{\{p \wedge B_i\}\ S_i\ \{p\}, i \in \{1,\dots,n\},}{\{p\}\ \mathbf{do}\ \square_{i=1}^{n}\ B_i \rightarrow S_i\ \mathbf{od}\ \{p \wedge \bigwedge_{i=1}^{n}\ \neg B_i\}}$$

$$\{p \wedge B_i \wedge t = \alpha\}\ S_i\ \{t < \alpha\}, i \in \{1,\dots,n\},$$
$$p \rightarrow t \in W$$

where

(i) t is an expression which takes values in an irreflexive partial order $(P, <)$ that is well-founded on the subset $W \subseteq P$,

(ii) α is a simple variable ranging over P that does not occur in p, t, B_i or S_i for $i \in \{1, \dots, n\}$.

The expression t is the bound function of the repetitive command. Since it takes values in W that are decreased by every execution of a command S_i, the well-foundedness of $<$ on W guarantees the termination of the whole repetitive command $\mathbf{do}\ \square_{i=1}^{n}\ B_i \rightarrow S_i\ \mathbf{od}$. Note that with $P = \mathbb{Z}$, the set of integers, and $W = \mathbb{N}$, the set of natural numbers, the rule reduces to the previous repetitive command II rule 33. Often P itself is well-founded. Then we take $W = P$.

For proofs of total correctness of nondeterministic programs with random assignments we use the following proof system TNR.

PROOF SYSTEM TNR :
This system is obtained from the proof system TN
by adding axiom 37 and replacing rule 33 by rule 38.

Example 12.3. As a simple application of the system TNR let us prove the termination of the program S_ω considered above; that is,

$$\vdash_{TNR}\ \{\mathbf{true}\}\ S_\omega\ \{\mathbf{true}\}.$$

As a loop invariant we can simply take the assertion **true**. To find an appropriate bound function, we recall our informal analysis of S_ω. Activated in a state where b is true, S_ω terminates after $|x|$ repetitions. But activated in a state where b is false, we cannot predict the number of repetitions of S_ω. Only after executing the random assignment $x :=?$ in the first round of S_ω do we know the remaining number of repetitions.

This suggests using the well-founded structure

$$(\mathbb{N} \cup \{\omega\}, <)$$

discussed earlier. Recall that ω represents an unknown number which will become precise as soon as ω is decreased to some $\alpha < \omega$ that must be in $\mathbb{N}$. With this intuition the number of repetitions can be expressed by the bound function

$$t \equiv \textbf{if } b \textbf{ then } |x| \textbf{ else } \omega \textbf{ fi}.$$

Of course, we have to check whether the premises of the repetitive command
III rule 38 are really satisfied. We take here

$$P = W = \mathbb{N} \cup \{\omega\}$$

so that rule 38 is applied with both t and α ranging over $\mathbb{N} \cup \{\omega\}$. The
premises dealing with the loop invariant are trivially satisfied. Of the premises
dealing with the decrease of the bound function,

$$\vdash_{TNR} \{b \wedge x > 0 \wedge t = \alpha\} \; x := x - 1 \; \{t < \alpha\} \tag{12.3}$$

and

$$\vdash_{TNR} \{b \wedge x < 0 \wedge t = \alpha\} \; x := x + 1 \; \{t < \alpha\} \tag{12.4}$$

are easy to establish because t ranges over $\mathbb{N}$ when b evaluates to true.
   Slightly more involved is the derivation of

$$\vdash_{TNR} \{\neg b \wedge t = \alpha\} \; x :=?; \; b := \textbf{true} \; \{t < \alpha\}. \tag{12.5}$$

By the axiom of random assignment we have

$$\{\forall x \geq 0 : |x| < \alpha\} \; x :=? \; \{|x| < \alpha\}.$$

Since x is an integer variable, the quantifier $\forall x \geq 0$ ranges over all natural
numbers. Since on the other hand α ranges over $\mathbb{N} \cup \{\omega\}$ and by definition
$n < \omega$ for all $n \in \mathbb{N}$, the rule of consequence yields

$$\{\omega = \alpha\} \; x :=? \; \{|x| < \alpha\}.$$

Using the (ordinary) axiom of assignment and the rule of sequential composition, we have

$$\{\omega = \alpha\} \; x :=?; \; b := \textbf{true} \; \{b \wedge |x| < \alpha\}.$$

Thus, by the rule of consequence,

$$\{\neg b \wedge \omega = \alpha\} \; x :=?; \; b := \textbf{true} \; \{b \wedge |x| < \alpha\}.$$

Finally, using the definition of t in another application of the rule of consequence yields

$$\{\neg b \wedge t = \alpha\} \; x :=?; \; b := \textbf{true} \; \{t < \alpha\}.$$

Since we applied only proof rules of the system *TNR*, we have indeed established (12.5).
   Thus an application of the repetitive command III rule 38 yields the desired
termination result:

$$\vdash_{TNR} \{\textbf{true}\} \; S_\omega \; \{\textbf{true}\}.$$

As before, we can represent proofs by proof outlines. The above proof of total correctness is represented as follows:

$\{\textbf{inv} : \textbf{true}\}$
$\{\textbf{bd} : \textbf{if } b \textbf{ then } |x| \textbf{ else } \omega \textbf{ fi}\}$
$\textbf{do } b \wedge x > 0 \rightarrow \quad \{b \wedge x > 0\}$
$\qquad\qquad\qquad\qquad x := x - 1$
$\square \quad b \wedge x < 0 \rightarrow \quad \{b \wedge x < 0\}$
$\qquad\qquad\qquad\qquad x := x + 1$
$\square \quad \neg b \rightarrow \qquad\qquad \{\neg b\}$
$\qquad\qquad\qquad\qquad x :=?; \ b := \textbf{true}$
$\textbf{od}$
$\{\textbf{true}\}.$

This concludes the example.   □

The following theorem can be proved by a simple modification of the argument used to prove the Soundness of PW and TW Theorem 3.1.

Theorem 12.1. (Soundness of PNR and TNR)

(i) The proof system PNR is sound for partial correctness of nondeterministic programs with random assignments.
(ii) The proof system TNR is sound for total correctness of nondeterministic programs with random assignments.

Proof. See Exercise 12.3.   □

12.5 Schedulers

Using random assignments we wish to develop a transformation T_{fair} which reduces fair nondeterminism to ordinary nondeterminism. We divide this task into two subtasks:

- the development of a *scheduler* that enforces fairness in abstract runs,
- the *embedding* of the schedulers into nondeterministic programs.

In this section we deal with schedulers so that later, when considering parallel programs, we can reuse all results obtained here. In addition, schedulers are interesting in their own right because they explain how to implement fairness.

In general, a scheduler is an automaton that enforces a certain discipline on the computations of a nondeterministic or parallel program. To this end, the scheduler keeps in its local state sufficient information about the run of a computation, and engages in the following interaction with the program:

At certain moments during a computation, the program pre-sents the set E of currently enabled components to the scheduler (provided $E \neq \emptyset$). By consulting its local state, the scheduler returns to the program a nonempty subset I of E. The idea is that whatever component $i \in I$ is activated next, the resulting computation will still satisfy the intended discipline. So the program selects one component $i \in I$ for activation, and the scheduler updates its local state accordingly.

We call a pair (E, i), where $E \cup \{i\} \subseteq \{1, \dots, n\}$, a *selection (of n components)*. From a more abstract point of view, we may ignore the actual interaction between the program and scheduler and just record the result of this interaction, the selection (E, i) checked by the scheduler. Summarizing, we arrive at the following definition.

Definition 12.2. A *scheduler (for n components)* is given by

- a set of local *scheduler states* σ, which are disjoint from the program states,
- a subset of *initial* scheduler states, and
- a ternary *scheduling relation*
  $sch \subseteq$
  {scheduler states} $\times$ {selections of n components} $\times$ {scheduler states}
  which is *total* in the following sense:

$$\forall \sigma \forall E \neq \emptyset \; \exists i \in E \; \exists \sigma' : (\sigma, (E, i), \sigma') \in sch.$$

Thus for every scheduler state σ and every nonempty set E of enabled components there exists a component $i \in E$ such that the selection (E, i) of n components together with the updated local state σ' satisfies the scheduling relation.   □

Thus, given the local state σ of the scheduler,

$$I = \{i \mid \exists \sigma' : (\sigma, (E, i), \sigma') \in sch\}$$

is the subset returned by the scheduler to the program. Totality of the scheduling relation ensures that this set I is nonempty. Consequently a scheduler can never block the computation of a program but only influence its direction. Consider now a finite or infinite run

$$(E_0, i_0)(E_1, i_1) \dots (E_j, i_j) \dots$$

and a scheduler SCH. We wish to ensure that sufficiently many, but not necessarily all, selections (E_j, i_j) are checked by SCH. To this end, we take a so-called *check set*

$$C \subseteq \mathbb{N}$$

representing the positions of selections to be checked.

Definition 12.3.   (i) A run

$$(E_0, i_0)(E_1, i_1)...(E_j, i_j)...$$

can be checked by SCH at every position in C if there exists a finite or infinite sequence

$$\sigma_0 \sigma_1 ... \sigma_j, ...$$

of scheduler states, with σ_0 being an initial scheduler state, such that for all $j \geq 0$

$$(\sigma_j, (E_j, i_j), \sigma_{j+1}) \in sch \qquad \text{if } j \in C$$

and

$$\sigma_j = \sigma_{j+1} \qquad\qquad\qquad \text{otherwise.}$$

We say that a run *can be checked by SCH* if it can be checked by *SCH* at every position; that is, for the check set $C = \mathbb{N}$.
  (ii) A scheduler *SCH* for n components is called *fair* (for a certain subset of runs) if every run of n components which (is in this subset and) can be checked by *SCH* is fair.
 (iii) A fair scheduler *SCH* for n components is called *universal* if every fair run of n components can be checked by *SCH*. □

Thus for $j \in C$ the scheduling relation sch checks the selection (E_j, i_j) made in the run using and updating the current scheduler state; for $j \notin C$ there is no interaction with the scheduler and hence the current scheduler state remains unchanged (for technical convenience, however, this is treated as an identical step with $\sigma_j = \sigma_{j+1}$).
  For example, with $C = \{2n + 1 \mid n \in \mathbb{N}\}$ every second selection in a run is checked. This can be pictured as follows:

Run: $(E_0, i_0)\ (E_1, i_1)\ (E_2, i_2)\ (E_3, i_3)...$
                       $\downarrow\ \uparrow$ $\downarrow\ \uparrow$
Scheduler: $\sigma_0 = \sigma_1\ SCH\ \sigma_2 = \sigma_3\ SCH\ \sigma_4....$

Note that the definition of checking applies also in the case of finite runs H and infinite check sets C.

The Scheduler FAIR

Using the programming syntax of this section, we now present a specific scheduler *FAIR*. For n components it is defined as follows:

• The scheduler state is given by n integer variables $z_1, ..., z_n$,

- this state is initialized nondeterministically by the random assignments

$$INIT \equiv z_1 :=?; \ \ldots; \ z_n :=?,$$

- the scheduling relation $sch(\sigma, (E, i), \sigma')$ holds iff σ, E, i, σ' are as follows:

(i) σ is given by the current values of $z_1, \ldots, z_n$,

(ii) E and i satisfy the condition

$$SCH_i \equiv z_i = min \ \{z_k \mid k \in E\},$$

(iii) σ' is obtained from σ by executing

$$UPDATE_i \equiv z_i :=?;$$
$$\textbf{for all } j \in \{1, \ldots, n\} - \{i\} \textbf{ do}$$
$$\textbf{if } j \in E \textbf{ then } z_j := z_j - 1 \textbf{ fi}$$
$$\textbf{od},$$

where we use the abbreviation

$$\textbf{for all } j \in \{1, \ldots, n\} - \{i\} \textbf{ do } S_j \textbf{ od}$$
$$\equiv S_1; \ \ldots; \ S_{i-1}; \ S_{i+1}; \ \ldots; \ S_n.$$

The scheduling variables $z_1, \ldots, z_n$ represent *priorities* assigned to the n components. A component i has higher priority than a component j if $z_i < z_j$. Initially, the components are assigned arbitrary priorities. If during a run *FAIR* is presented with a set E of enabled components, it selects a component $i \in E$ that has maximal priority; that is, with

$$z_i = min \ \{z_k \mid k \in E\}.$$

For any nonempty set E and any values of $z_1, \ldots, z_n$ there exists some (but not necessarily unique) $i \in E$ with this property. Thus the scheduling relation *sch* of *FAIR* is total as required by Definition 12.2.

The update of the scheduling variables guarantees that the priorities of all enabled but not selected components j get increased. The priority of the selected component i, however, gets reset arbitrarily. The idea is that by gradually increasing the priority of enabled components j their activation cannot be refused forever. The following theorem makes this idea precise.

Theorem 12.2. (Fair Scheduling) *For n components FAIR is a universal fair scheduler. In other words, a run of n components is fair iff it can be checked by FAIR.*

Proof. "if": Consider a run

$$(E_0, i_0) \ldots (E_j, i_j) \ldots \tag{12.6}$$

that is checked at every position. Let

$$\sigma_0 \ldots \sigma_j \ldots$$

be a sequence of scheduler states of $FAIR$ satisfying $sch(\sigma_j, (E_j, i_j), \sigma_{j+1})$ for every $j \in \mathbb{N}$. We claim that (12.6) is fair.

Suppose the contrary. Then there exists some component $i \in \{1, \ldots, n\}$ which is infinitely often enabled, but from some moment $j_0 \geq 0$ on never activated. Formally,

$$(\overset{\infty}{\exists} j \in \mathbb{N} : i \in E_j) \wedge (\forall j \geq j_0 : i \neq i_j).$$

Since (12.6) is checked at every position, the variable z_i of $FAIR$, which gets decremented whenever the component i is enabled but not activated, becomes arbitrarily small, in particular, smaller than $-n$ in some state σ_j with $j \geq j_0$. But this is impossible because the assertion

$$INV \equiv \bigwedge_{k=1}^{n} card \; \{i \in \{1, \ldots, n\} \mid z_i \leq -k\} \leq n - k$$

holds in every scheduler state σ_j of $FAIR$. INV states, in particular, for $k = 1$ that at most $n - 1$ of the scheduling variables $z_1, \ldots, z_n$ of $FAIR$ can have values ≤ -1, and for $k = n$ that none of the scheduling variables can have values $\leq -n$.

We prove this invariant by induction on $j \geq 0$, the index of the state σ_j. In σ_0 we have $z_1, \ldots, z_n \geq 0$ so that INV is trivially satisfied. Assume now that INV holds in σ_j. We show that INV also holds in σ_{j+1}. Suppose INV is false in σ_{j+1}. Then there is some $k \in \{1, \ldots, n\}$ such that there are at least $n - k + 1$ indices i for which $z_i \leq -k$ holds in σ_{j+1}. Let I be the set of all these indices. Note that I is nonempty and $card \; I \geq n - k + 1$. By the definition of $FAIR$, $z_i \leq -k + 1$ holds for all $i \in I$ in σ_j. Thus $card \; I \leq n - k + 1$ by the induction hypothesis. So actually $card \; I = n - k + 1$ and

$$I = \{i \in \{1, \ldots, n\} \mid \sigma_j \models z_i \leq -k + 1\}.$$

Since $FAIR$ checks the run (12.6) at position j, we have $sch(\sigma_j, (E_j, i_j), \sigma_{j+1})$. By the definition of $FAIR$, the activated component i_j is in I. This is a contradiction because then $z_{i_j} \geq 0$ holds in σ_{j+1} due to the $UPDATE_{i_j}$ part of $FAIR$. Thus INV remains true in σ_{j+1}.

"only if": Conversely, let the run

$$(E_0, i_0) \ldots (E_j, i_j) \ldots \tag{12.7}$$

be fair. We show that (12.7) can be checked at every position by constructing a sequence

$$\sigma_0 \ldots \sigma_j \ldots$$

of scheduler states of *FAIR* satisfying $sch(\sigma_j, (E_j, i_j), \sigma_{j+1})$ for every $j \in \mathbb{N}$. The construction proceeds by assigning appropriate values to the sche-duling variables $z_1, \ldots, z_n$ of *FAIR*. For $i \in \{1, \ldots, n\}$ and $j \in \mathbb{N}$ we put

$$\sigma_j(z_i) = card\ \{\ell \mid j \leq \ell < m_{i,j} \wedge i \in E_\ell\},$$

where

$$m_{i,j} = min\ \{m \mid j \leq m \wedge (i_m = i \vee \forall n \geq m : i \notin E_n)\}.$$

Thus $\sigma_j(z_i)$ counts the number of times (ℓ) the ith component will be enabled ($i \in E_\ell$) before its next activation ($i_m = i$) or before its final "retirement" ($\forall n \geq m : i \notin E_n$). Note that the minimum $m_{i,j} \in \mathbb{N}$ exists because the run (12.7) is fair. In this construction the variables $z_1, \ldots, z_n$ have values ≥ 0 in every state σ_j and exactly one variable z_i with $i \in E_j$, has the value 0. This i is the index of the component activated next. It is easy to see that this construction of values $\sigma_j(z_i)$ is possible with the assignments in *FAIR*.   □

The universality of *FAIR* implies that every other fair scheduler can be obtained by implementing the nondeterministic choices in *FAIR*. Following Dijkstra [1976] and Park [1979], *implementing* nondeterminism means narrowing the set of nondeterministic choices. For example, a random assignment $z :=?$ can be implemented by any ordinary assignment $z := t$ where t evaluates to a nonnegative value.

The Scheduler *RORO*

The simplest scheduler is the *round robin scheduler RORO*. For n components it selects the enabled components clockwise in the cyclic ordering

$$1 \to 2 \to \ldots \to n \to 1,$$

thereby skipping over momentarily disabled components.

Is *RORO* a fair scheduler? The answer is "no." To see this, consider a run of three components 1, 2, 3 where 1 and 3 are always enabled but 2 is enabled only at every second position in the run. Then *RORO* schedules the enabled components as follows:

$$(\{1, 2, 3\}, 1)(\{1, 3\}, 3)(\{1, 2, 3\}, 1)(\{1, 3\}, 3)\ldots\ .$$

Thus, component 2 is never selected by *RORO*, even though it is enabled infinitely often. Hence, the run is unfair.

However, it is easy to see that *RORO* is a fair scheduler for monotonic runs.

Definition 12.4. A possibly infinite run

$$(E_0, i_0)(E_1, i_1)\ldots(E_j, i_j)\ldots$$

is called *monotonic* if

$$E_0 \supseteq E_1 \supseteq \ldots \supseteq E_j \supseteq \ldots. \qquad \Box$$

Obviously, the run considered above is not monotonic. Note that one-level nondeterministic programs

$$S \equiv S_0;\ \textbf{do}\ B \to S_1 \square \ldots \square B \to S_n\ \textbf{od}$$

with identical guards have only monotonic runs. Thus for these programs *RORO* can be used as a fair scheduler.

How can we obtain *RORO* from *FAIR*? Consider the following implementation of the random assignments in *FAIR* for n components:

$$INIT \equiv z_1 := 1;\ \ldots;\ z_n := n,$$
$$SCH_i \equiv z_i = min\ \{z_k \mid k \in E\},$$
$$UPDATE_i \equiv z_i := n;$$
$$\textbf{for all}\ j \in \{1, \ldots, n\} - \{i\}\ \textbf{do}$$
$$\textbf{if}\ j \in E\ \textbf{then}\ z_j := z_j - 1\ \textbf{fi}$$
$$\textbf{od}.$$

By the Fair Scheduling Theorem 12.2, this is a fair scheduler for arbitrary runs. When applied to a monotonic run, it always schedules the next enabled component in the cyclic ordering $1 \to 2 \to \ldots \to n \to 1$. Thus for monotonic runs the above is an implementation of the round robin scheduler *RORO*, systematically obtained from the general scheduler *FAIR*.

Clearly, this implementation of *RORO* is too expensive in terms of storage requirements. Since we only need to remember which component was selected as the last one, the variables $z_1, \ldots, z_n$ of *RORO* can be condensed into a single variable z ranging over $\{1, \ldots, n\}$ and pointing to the index of the last selected component. This idea leads to the following alternative implementation of *RORO*:

$$INIT \equiv z := 1,$$
$$SCH_i \equiv i = succ^m(z)\ \text{where}\ m = min\ \{k \mid succ^k(z) \in E\},$$
$$UPDATE_i \equiv succ^{m+1}(z).$$

Here $succ(\cdot)$ is the successor function in the cyclic ordering $1 \to 2 \to \ldots \to n \to 1$ and $succ^k(\cdot)$ is the kth iteration of this successor function.

This implementation uses only n scheduler states. It follows from a result of Fischer and Paterson [1983] that this number is optimal for fair schedulers for monotonic runs of n components.

The Scheduler QUEUE

As we have seen, for nonmonotonic runs fairness cannot be enforced by the inexpensive round robin scheduler. Fischer and Paterson [1983] have shown that any fair scheduler that is applicable for arbitrary runs of n components needs at least $n! = 1 \cdot 2 \cdot \ldots \cdot n$ scheduler states.

One way of organizing such a scheduler is by keeping the components in a queue. In each check the scheduler activates that enabled component which is earliest in the queue. This component is then placed at the end of the queue. Fairness is guaranteed since every enabled but not activated component advances one position in the queue. Let us call this scheduler *QUEUE*.

Consider once more a run of three components 1, 2, 3 where 1 and 3 are always enabled but 2 is enabled only at every second position in the run. Then *QUEUE* schedules the enabled components as follows:

Run: $(\{\,1,2,3\}, 1)(\{\,1,3\}, 3)(\{\,1,2,3\}, 2)(\{\,1,3\}, 1)$
         $\downarrow \quad \uparrow \quad \downarrow \quad \uparrow \quad \downarrow \quad \uparrow \quad \downarrow \quad \uparrow$
QUEUE: 1.2.3   2.3.1   2.1.3   1.3.2

Run: $(\{\,1,2,3\}, 3)(\{\,1,3\}, 1)(\{\,1,2,3\}, 2)(\{\,1,3\}, 3)$
         $\downarrow \quad \uparrow \quad \downarrow \quad \uparrow \quad \downarrow \quad \uparrow \quad \downarrow \quad \uparrow$
QUEUE: 3.2.1   2.1.3   2.3.1   3.1.2

Run: $(\{\,1,2,3\}, 1)$ $\ldots$
         $\downarrow \quad \uparrow$
QUEUE: 1.2.3 $\ldots$

Below each selection of the run we exhibit the value of the queue on which this selection is based. We see that the ninth selection $(\{1,2,3\},1)$ in the run is based on the same queue value 1.2.3 as the first selection $(\{1,2,3\},1)$. Thus every component gets activated infinitely often.

The effect of *QUEUE* can be modeled by implementing the random assignments of the general scheduler *FAIR* as follows:

$$INIT \equiv z_1 := 0; \ z_2 := n; \ \ldots; \ z_n := (n-1) \cdot n,$$
$$SCH_i \equiv z_i := min \ \{z_k \mid k \in E\},$$
$$UPDATE_i \equiv z_i := n + max \ \{z_1, \ldots, z_n\};$$

forall $j \in \{1, \ldots, n\} - \{i\}$ **do**

if $j \in E$ then $z_j := z_j - 1$ fi

od.

The idea is that in the $QUEUE$ component i comes before component j iff $z_i < z_j$ holds in the above implementation. Since $FAIR$ leaves the variables z_j of disabled components j unchanged and decrements those of enabled but not activated ones, some care had to be taken in the implementation of the random assignment of $FAIR$ in order to prevent any change of the order of components within the queue. More precisely, the order "component i before component j," represented by $z_i < z_j$ should be preserved as long as neither i nor j is activated. That is why initially and in every update we keep a difference of n between the new value of z_i and all previous values. This difference is sufficient because a component that is enabled n times is selected at least once.

12.6 Transformation

We can now present the transformation T_{fair} reducing fair nondeterminism to the usual nondeterminism in the sense of transformational semantics of Section 12.2:

$$\mathcal{M}_{fair}[\![S]\!] = \mathcal{M}_{tot}[\![T_{fair}(S)]\!].$$

Given a one-level nondeterministic program

$$S \equiv S_0; \ \mathbf{do} \ \square_{i=1}^{n} \ B_i \to S_i \ \mathbf{od},$$

the transformed program $T_{fair}(S)$ is obtained by embedding the scheduler $FAIR$ into S:

$$T_{fair}(S) \equiv S_0; \ INIT;$$
$$\mathbf{do} \ \square_{i=1}^{n} \ B_i \wedge SCH_i \to UPDATE_i; \ S_i \ \mathbf{od},$$

where we interpret E as the set of indices $k \in \{1, \ldots, n\}$ for which B_k holds:

$$E = \{k \mid 1 \le k \le n \wedge B_k\}.$$

We see that the interaction between the program S and the scheduler $FAIR$ takes place in the guards of the **do** loop in $T_{fair}(S)$. The guard of the ith component can be passed only if it is enabled and selected by $FAIR$; that is, when both B_i and SCH_i evaluate to true.

Expanding the abbreviations *INIT*, *SCH$_i$* and *UPDATE$_i$* from *FAIR* yields:

$$T_{fair}(S) \equiv S_0; \; z_1 :=?; \; \ldots; \; z_n :=?;$$

$$\textbf{do } \square_{i=1}^n \; B_i \wedge z_i = min \; \{z_k \mid 1 \leq k \leq n \wedge B_k\} \rightarrow$$

$$z_i :=?;$$

$$\textbf{for all } j \in \{1, \ldots, n\} - \{i\} \textbf{ do}$$

$$\textbf{if } B_j \textbf{ then } z_j := z_j - 1 \textbf{ fi}$$

$$\textbf{od};$$

$$S_i$$

$$\textbf{od}.$$

In case of identical guards $B_1 \equiv \ldots \equiv B_n$ the transformation simplifies to

$$T_{fair}(S) \equiv S_0; \; z_1 :=?; \; \ldots; \; z_n :=?;$$

$$\textbf{do } \square_{i=1}^n \; B_i \wedge z_i = min \; \{z_1, \ldots, z_n\} \rightarrow$$

$$z_i :=?;$$

$$\textbf{for all } j \in \{1, \ldots, n\} - \{i\} \textbf{ do}$$

$$z_j := z_j - 1$$

$$\textbf{od};$$

$$S_i$$

$$\textbf{od}.$$

In both cases we assume that the variables $z_1, \ldots, z_n$ do not occur in S.

Example 12.4. The printer-user program

$$PU1 \equiv signal := \textbf{false};$$

$$\textbf{do } \neg signal \rightarrow \text{"print next line"}$$

$$\square \quad \neg signal \rightarrow signal := \textbf{true}$$

$$\textbf{od}$$

discussed in Section 12.1 is transformed into

$$T_{fair}(PU1) \equiv signal := \textbf{false}; \; z_1 :=?; \; z_2 :=?;$$

$$\textbf{do } \neg signal \wedge z_1 \leq z_2 \rightarrow z_1 :=?; \; z_2 := z_2 - 1;$$

$$\text{"print next line"}$$

$$\square \quad \neg signal \wedge z_2 \leq z_1 \rightarrow z_2 :=?; \; z_1 := z_1 - 1;$$

$$signal := \textbf{true}$$

$$\textbf{od}.$$

Note that in $T_{fair}(PU1)$ it is impossible to activate exclusively the first component of the **do** loop because in every round through the loop the variable z_2 gets decremented. Thus eventually the conjunct

$$z_1 \leq z_2$$

of the first guard will be falsified, but then the second guard with the conjunct

$$z_2 \leq z_1$$

will be enabled. Thus the second component of the **do** loop is eventually activated. This leads to termination of $T_{fair}(PU1)$.

Thus for *PU1* the aim of our transformation T_{fair} is achieved: with the help of the scheduling variables z_1 and z_2, the transformed program $T_{fair}(PU1)$ generates exactly the fair computations of the original program *PU1*. □

But what is the semantic relationship between S and $T_{fair}(S)$ in general? Due to the presence of the scheduling variables $z_1, \ldots, z_n$ in $T_{fair}(S)$, the best we can prove is that the semantics $\mathcal{M}_{fair}[\![S]\!]$ and $\mathcal{M}_{tot}[\![T_{fair}(S)]\!]$ agree *modulo* $z_1, \ldots, z_n$; that is, the final states agree on all variables except $z_1, \ldots, z_n$. To express this we use the **mod** notation introduced in Section 2.3.

Theorem 12.3. (Embedding) *For every one-level nondeterministic program S and every proper state σ*

$$\mathcal{M}_{fair}[\![S]\!](\sigma) = \mathcal{M}_{tot}[\![T_{fair}(S)]\!](\sigma) \text{ mod } Z,$$

where Z is the set of scheduling variables z_i used in T_{fair}.

Proof. Let us call two computations *Z-equivalent* if they start in the same state and either both diverge or both terminate in states that agree modulo Z.

We prove the following two claims:

(i) every computation of $T_{fair}(S)$ is Z-equivalent to a fair computation of S,

(ii) every fair computation of S is Z-equivalent to a computation of $T_{fair}(S)$.

To this end, we relate the computations of $T_{fair}(S)$ and S more intimately. A computation ξ^* of $T_{fair}(S)$ is called an *extension* of a computation ξ of S to the variables of Z if ξ^* results from ξ by adding transitions dealing exclusively with the variables in Z and by assigning in each state of ξ^* appropriate values to the variables in Z. Conversely, a computation ξ of S is called a *restriction* of a computation ξ^* of $T_{fair}(S)$ to the variables in Z if all transitions referring to the variables in Z are deleted and the values of the variables in Z are reset in all states of ξ to the values in the first state of ξ^*.

Observe the following equivalences:

	ξ is a fair computation of S
iff	{definition of fairness}
	ξ is a computation of S with a fair run
iff	{Theorem 12.2}
	ξ is a computation of S with a run that can be checked by the scheduler *FAIR*.

By these equivalences and the construction of T_{fair}, we conclude now:

(i) If ξ is a fair computation of S, there exists an extension ξ^* of ξ to the variables in Z which is a computation of $T_{fair}(S)$.

(ii) If ξ^* is a computation of $T_{fair}(S)$, the restriction ξ of ξ^* to the variables in Z is a prefix of a fair computation of S. We say "prefix" because it is conceivable that ξ^* exits the loop in $T_{fair}(S)$ due to the additional condition SCH_i in the guards, whereas S could continue looping and thus yield a longer computation than ξ. Fortunately, these premature loop exits cannot happen because the scheduling relation of *FAIR* is *total* (cf. Definition 12.2). Thus if some guard B_i of S evaluates to true, one of the extended guards $B_i \wedge SCH_i$ of $T_{fair}(S)$ will also evaluate to true. Hence the above restriction ξ of ξ^* is really a fair computation of S.

Clearly, if ξ^* is an extension of ξ or ξ is a restriction of ξ^*, then ξ and ξ^* are Z-equivalent. Thus, (i') and (ii') imply (i) and (ii), establishing the claim of the theorem.   □

12.7 Verification

Total Correctness

The semantics $\mathcal{M}_{fair}$ induces the following notion of program correctness: a correctness formula $\{p\}\, S\, \{q\}$ is true in the sense of *fair total correctness*, abbreviated

$$\models_{fair} \{p\}\, S\, \{q\},$$

if

$$\mathcal{M}_{fair}[\![S]\!]([\![p]\!]) \subseteq [\![q]\!].$$

The transformation T_{fair} enables us to develop a proof system for fair total correctness. The starting point is the following corollary of the Embedding Theorem 12.3.

Corollary 12.1. (Fairness) *Let p and q be assertions that do not contain $z_1, \ldots, z_n$ as free variables and let S be a one-level nondeterministic program. Then*   □

$$\models_{fair} \{p\}\, S\, \{q\} \text{ iff } \models_{tot} \{p\}\, T_{fair}(S)\, \{q\}.$$

Thus, in order to prove fair total correctness of S, it suffices to prove total correctness of $T_{fair}(S)$. This suggests the proof rule

$$\frac{\{p\}\, T_{fair}(S)\, \{q\}}{\{p\}\, S\, \{q\}}$$

for fair total correctness. Its premise has to be established in the proof system *TNR* for total correctness of nondeterministic programs with random assignments introduced in Section 12.4.

But, in fact, we can do slightly better by "absorbing" the parts *INIT*, SCH_i and $UPDATE_i$ added to S by T_{fair} into the assertions p and q. This process of absorption yields a new proof rule for fair repetition which in its premise deals with the *original* one-level nondeterministic program S and which uses the scheduling variables $z_1, \ldots, z_n$ of $T_{fair}(S)$ only in the assertions. Thus T_{fair} allows us to derive and justify this new rule.

RULE 39: FAIR REPETITION

> (1) $\{p \wedge B_i\}\ S_i\ \{p\}, i \in \{1, \ldots, n\}$,
> (2) $\{p \wedge B_i \wedge \bar{z} \geq 0$
> $\qquad \wedge \exists z_i \geq 0 : t[z_j := \textbf{if } B_j \textbf{ then } z_j + 1 \textbf{ else } z_j \textbf{ fi}]_{j \neq i} = \alpha\}$
> $\qquad S_i$
> $\qquad \{t < \alpha\}, i \in \{1, \ldots, n\}$,
> (3) $p \wedge \bar{z} \geq 0 \rightarrow t \in W$
>
> ---
>
> (4) $\{p\}\ \textbf{do } \square_{i=1}^{n}\ B_i \rightarrow S_i\ \textbf{od}\ \{p \wedge \bigwedge_{i=1}^{n} \neg B_i\}$

where

(i) t is an expression which takes values in an irreflexive partial order $(P, <)$ that is well-founded on the subset $W \subseteq P$,

(ii) $z_1, \ldots, z_n$ are integer variables that do not occur in p, B_i or S_i, for $i \in \{1, \ldots, n\}$,

(iii) $t[z_j := \textbf{if } B_j \textbf{ then } z_j + 1 \textbf{ else } z_j \textbf{ fi}]_{j \neq i}$ denotes the expression that results from t by substituting for every occurrence of z_j in t the conditional expression $\textbf{if } B_j \textbf{ then } z_j + 1 \textbf{ else } z_j \textbf{ fi}$; here j ranges over the set $\{1, \ldots, n\} - \{i\}$,

(iv) $\bar{z} \geq 0$ abbreviates $z_1 \geq 0 \wedge \ldots \wedge z_n \geq 0$,

(v) α is a simple variable ranging over P and not occurring in p, t, B_i or S_i, for $i \in \{1, \ldots, n\}$.

For identical guards $B_1 \equiv \ldots \equiv B_n \equiv B$ this rule can be simplified. In particular, the substitution

$$t[z_j := \textbf{if } B_j \textbf{ then } z_j + 1 \textbf{ else } z_j \textbf{ fi}]_{j \neq i}$$

in premise (2) simplifies to

$$t[z_j := z_j + 1]_{j \neq i}$$

because for each j the condition $B_j \equiv B_i$ evaluates to true. This yields the following specialization of the fair repetition rule 39.

RULE 39': FAIR REPETITION (IDENTICAL GUARDS)

$(1')$ $\{p \wedge B\}\, S_i\, \{p\}, i \in \{1, \ldots, n\}$,

$(2')$ $\{p \wedge B \wedge \bar{z} \geq 0 \wedge \exists z_i \geq 0 : t[z_j := z_j + 1]_{j \neq i} = \alpha\}$
S_i
$\{t < \alpha\}, i \in \{1, \ldots, n\}$,

$(3')$ $p \wedge \bar{z} \geq 0 \to t \in W$

$(4')$ $\{p\}$ **do** $\square_{i=1}^{n}\, B \to S_i$ **od** $\{p \wedge \neg B\}$

where conditions analogous to (i)–(v) hold.

Except for the additional variables $z_1, \ldots, z_n$ the fair repetition rules 39 and 39' follow the pattern of the usual rule for total correctness of repetitive commands in the system *TNR* (rule 38). Premise (1) of rule 39 establishes partial correctness of the **do** loop by showing that p is a loop invariant. Premise (2) of rule 39 establishes that t is a bound function of the loop, but with the variables $z_1, \ldots, z_n$ as "helpful ingredients."

Let us explain this point for the simplified fair repetition rule 39'. The variables $z_1, \ldots, z_n$ may occur only in the expression t. In the precondition of $(2')$ the value $z_j + 1$ instead of z_j appears in t for all indices $j \neq i$. Among other things this precondition states that for some value of z_i

$$t[z_j := z_j + 1]_{j \neq i} = \alpha.$$

In the postcondition of $(2')$ we have to show that

$$t < \alpha.$$

Obviously, decrementing $z_j + 1$ to z_j is "helpful" for establishing that t has dropped below α. On the other hand, the value of z_i is not helpful for calculating the value of t because in the precondition of $(2')$ it is under the scope of an existential quantifier.

As we see in the subsequent soundness proof of the fair repetition rule 39, the precondition of premise (2) results from calculating the postcondition of the $UPDATE_i$ part in the transformation T_{fair}.

We prove *f*air total correctness of one-level *n*ondeterministic programs using the following proof system *FN*.

PROOF SYSTEM *FN* :
This system is obtained from the proof system *TN* by replacing rule 33 by rule 39.

Notice that the random assignment axiom 37 is not included in *FN*; this axiom is needed only to prove the soundness of the fair repetition rule 39.

Let us demonstrate the power of the system *FN*, in particular that of rule 39 (and 39′), by a few examples. In the more complicated examples we use *proof outlines for fair total correctness*. They are defined in the usual way, with reference to the premises of rule 39, when dealing with loop invariants p and bound functions t.

Example 12.5. Consider the printer-user program

$$PU1 \equiv signal := \textbf{false};$$
$$\textbf{do } \neg signal \rightarrow \text{ "print next line"}$$
$$\square \quad \neg signal \rightarrow signal := \textbf{true}$$
$$\textbf{od}$$

of Section 12.1. We wish to prove that *PU1* terminates under the assumption of fairness, that is,

$$\models_{fair} \{\textbf{true}\} \ PU1 \ \{\textbf{true}\}.$$

Since printing a line does not change the variable *signal*, we identify

$$\text{"print next line"} \ \equiv \ skip.$$

Using the new proof system *FN*, we first prove

$$\{\textbf{true}\}$$
$$\textbf{do } \neg signal \rightarrow skip$$
$$\square \quad \neg signal \rightarrow signal := \textbf{true} \qquad\qquad\qquad (12.8)$$
$$\textbf{od}$$
$$\{signal\}$$

with its fair repetition rule 39′ dealing with identical guards. Finding an appropriate loop invariant is trivial: we just take

$$p \equiv \textbf{true}.$$

More interesting is the choice of the bound function t. We take the conditional expression

$$t \equiv \textbf{if } \neg signal \textbf{ then } z_2 + 1 \textbf{ else } 0 \textbf{ fi}.$$

Here we use the scheduling variable z_2 associated with the second component of the **do** loop. Clearly, t ranges over the set Z of integers which, under the usual ordering $<$, is well-founded on the subset

$$W = \mathbb{N}$$

of natural numbers.

Intuitively, t counts the maximal number of rounds through the loop. If the signal is true, the loop terminates, hence no round will be performed. If the signal is false, $z_2 + 1$ rounds will be performed: the scheduling variable

z_2 counts how many rounds the second component of the loop has *neglected* and +1 counts the final round through the second component.

Formally, we check the premises (1')-(3') of the fair repetition rule 39'. Premises (1') and (3') are obviously satisfied. The interesting premise is (2') which deals with the decrease of the bound function.

(a) For the first component of the **do** loop we have to prove

$$\{ \quad \textbf{true} \wedge \neg signal \wedge z_1 \geq 0 \wedge z_2 \geq 0$$
$$\wedge \; \exists z_1 \geq 0 : \textbf{if } \neg signal \textbf{ then } z_2 + 2 \textbf{ else } 0 \textbf{ fi} = \alpha\}$$
$$skip \tag{12.9}$$
$$\{\textbf{if } \neg signal \textbf{ then } z_2 + 1 \textbf{ else } 0 \textbf{ fi} < \alpha\}$$

in the system *FN*. By the skip axiom 1 and the consequence rule 6, it suffices to show that the precondition implies the postcondition. This amounts to checking the implication

$$z_2 + 2 = \alpha \to z_2 + 1 < \alpha$$

which is clearly true.

Thus, when the first component is executed, the scheduling variable z_2 is responsible for the decrease of the bound function t.

(b) For the second component we have to prove

$$\{ \quad \textbf{true} \wedge \neg signal \wedge z_1 \geq 0 \wedge z_2 \geq 0$$
$$\wedge \; \exists z_2 \geq 0 : \textbf{if } \neg signal \textbf{ then } z_2 + 1 \textbf{ else } 0 \textbf{ fi} = \alpha\}$$
$$signal := \textbf{true} \tag{12.10}$$
$$\{\textbf{if } \neg signal \textbf{ then } z_2 + 1 \textbf{ else } 0 \textbf{ fi} < \alpha\}$$

in *FN*. By the assignment axiom 2 and the rule of consequence, it suffices to show

$$\exists z_2 \geq 0 : \; z_2 + 1 = \alpha \to 0 < \alpha.$$

Since $\exists z_2 \geq 0 : \; z_2 + 1 = \alpha$ is equivalent to $\alpha \geq 1$, this implication is true.

Thus, when the second component is executed, the program variable *signal* is responsible for the decrease of t.

By (12.9) and (12.10), premise (2') is proved in *FN*. Now an application of the fair repetition rule 39' yields (12.8). Finally, (12.8) implies

$$\models_{fair} \{\textbf{true}\} \; PU1 \; \{\textbf{true}\},$$

the desired termination result about *PU1*.   □

Example 12.6. More complicated is the analysis of the modified printer-user program

$$PU2 \equiv signal := \textbf{false}; \; \textit{full-page} := \textbf{false}; \; \ell := 0;$$
$$\left. \begin{array}{l} \textbf{do } \neg signal \rightarrow \text{``print next line''}; \\ \qquad \ell := (\ell + 1) \textbf{ mod } 30; \\ \qquad \textit{full-page} := \ell = 0 \end{array} \right\} \text{printer}$$
$$\left. \square \; \neg signal \wedge \textit{full-page} \rightarrow signal := \textbf{true} \right\} \text{user}$$
$$\qquad \textbf{od}$$

of Section 12.1. We wish to prove that under the assumption of fairness $PU2$ terminates in a state where the printer has received the signal of the user and completed its current page, that is,

$$\models_{fair} \{\textbf{true}\} \; PU2 \; \{signal \wedge \textit{full-page}\}.$$

A proof outline for fair total correctness in the system FN has the following structure:

$$\begin{array}{l}
\{\textbf{true}\} \\
signal := \textbf{false}; \\
\textit{full-page} := \textbf{false}; \\
\ell := 0; \\
\{\neg signal \wedge \neg \textit{full-page} \wedge \ell = 0\} \\
\{\textbf{inv} : p\}\{\textbf{bd} : t\} \\
\textbf{do } \neg signal \rightarrow \{p \wedge \neg signal\} \\
\qquad\qquad\quad skip; \\
\qquad\qquad\quad \ell := (\ell + 1) \textbf{ mod } 30; \\
\qquad\qquad\quad \textit{full-page} := \ell = 0 \\
\qquad\qquad\quad \{p\} \\
\square \quad \neg signal \wedge \textit{full-page} \rightarrow \{p \wedge \neg signal \wedge \textit{full-page}\} \\
\qquad\qquad\qquad\qquad\qquad\quad signal := \textbf{true} \\
\qquad\qquad\qquad\qquad\qquad\quad \{p\} \\
\textbf{od} \\
\{p \wedge signal \wedge (signal \vee \neg \textit{full-page})\} \\
\{signal \wedge \textit{full-page}\},
\end{array}$$

where we again identify

$$\text{``print next line''} \equiv skip.$$

The crucial task now is finding an appropriate loop invariant p and an appropriate bound function t that satisfy the premises of the fair repetition rule 39 and thus completing the proof outline.

As an invariant we take the assertion

$$p \equiv 0 \leq \ell \leq 29 \wedge signal \rightarrow \textit{full-page}.$$

The bounds for the variable ℓ appear because ℓ is incremented modulo 30. Since the implications

$$\neg signal \wedge \neg full\text{-}page \wedge \ell = 0 \rightarrow p$$

and

$$p \wedge signal \rightarrow signal \wedge full\text{-}page$$

are true, p fits into the proof outline as given outside the **do** loop. To check that p is kept invariant within the loop, we have to prove premise (1) of the fair repetition rule 39. This is easily done because the loop components consist only of assignment statements.

More difficult is the choice of a suitable bound function t. As in the previous example *PU1*, the second component *signal* := **true** is responsible for the (fair) termination of the loop. But because of the different guards in the loop, the bound function

$$t \equiv \textbf{if } \neg signal \textbf{ then } z_2 + 1 \textbf{ else } 0 \textbf{ fi}$$

used for *PU1* is not sufficient any more to establish premise (2) of the fair repetition rule 39.

Indeed, for the first component we should prove

$$
\begin{aligned}
&\{\quad p \wedge \neg signal \wedge z_1 \geq 0 \wedge z_2 \geq 0 \\
&\quad\ \wedge \textbf{ if } full\text{-}page \textbf{ then } z_2 + 2 \textbf{ else } z_2 + 1 \textbf{ fi} = \alpha\} \\
&skip; \\
&\left.\begin{array}{l} \ell := (\ell + 1) \textbf{ mod } 30; \\ full\text{-}page := \ell = 0 \end{array}\right\} \equiv S_1 \\
&\{z_2 + 1 < \alpha\},
\end{aligned}
$$

which is wrong if *full-page* is initially false. In this case, however, the execution of the command S_1 *approaches* a state where *full-page* is true. If ℓ drops from 29 to 0, S_1 sets *full-page* to true immediately. Otherwise S_1 increments ℓ by 1 so that ℓ gets closer to 29 with the subsequent drop to 0.

Thus we observe here a hierarchy of changes:

- a change of the variable ℓ indicates progress toward
- a change of the variable *full-page* which (by fairness) indicates prog-ress toward
- a selection of the second component that, by changing the variable signal, leads to termination of the loop.

Proving termination of a loop with such a hierarchy of changes is best done by a bound function t ranging over a product P of structures ordered lexicographically by $<_{lex}$ (cf. Section 12.4).

Here we take

$$P = \mathbb{Z} \times \mathbb{Z} \times \mathbb{Z},$$

which under $<_{lex}$ is well-founded on the subset

$$W = \mathbb{N} \times \mathbb{N} \times \mathbb{N},$$

and

$$t \equiv \textbf{if } \neg signal \textbf{ then } (z_2 + 1, int(\textit{full-page}), 29 - \ell)$$
$$\textbf{else } (0, 0, 0) \textbf{ fi},$$

where $int(\textbf{true}) = 1$ and $int(\textbf{false}) = 0$ (cf. Section 2.2). This definition of t reflects the intended hierarchy of changes: a change in the first component (variable z_2) weighs more than a change in the second component (variable *full-page*), which in turn weighs more than a change in the third component (variable ℓ).

Now we can prove premise (2) of the fair repetition rule 39. For the first loop component we have the following proof outline:

$$\{ \quad p \wedge \neg signal \wedge z_1 \geq 0 \wedge z_2 \geq 0 \qquad \qquad (12.11)$$
$$\wedge \textbf{ if } \textit{full-page} \textbf{ then } (z_2 + 2, 0, 29 - \ell)$$
$$\textbf{else } (z_2 + 1, 1, 29 - \ell) \textbf{ fi} = \alpha\}$$

$skip;$

$$\{\textbf{if } \ell < 29 \textbf{ then } (z_2 + 1, 1, 29 - \ell - 1) \qquad \qquad (12.12)$$
$$\textbf{else } (z_2 + 1, 0, 0) \textbf{ fi} <_{lex} \alpha\}$$

$\ell := (\ell + 1) \textbf{ mod } 30;$

$$\{(z_2 + 1, int(\neg(\ell = 0)), 29 - \ell) <_{lex} \alpha\} \qquad \qquad (12.13)$$

$\textit{full-page} := \ell = 0$

$$\{(z_2 + 1, int(\neg \textit{full-page}), 29 - \ell) <_{lex} \alpha\}. \qquad \qquad (12.14)$$

Obviously, the assertion (12.13) is obtained from (12.14) by performing the backward substitution of the assignment axiom. To obtain assertion (12.12) from (12.13) we recalled the definition of "modulo 30":

$$\ell := (\ell + 1) \textbf{ mod } 30$$

abbreviates

$$\ell := \ell + 1;$$
$$\textbf{if } \ell < 30 \textbf{ then } skip \textbf{ else } \ell := 0 \textbf{ fi},$$

and we applied the corresponding proof rules. Finally, by the skip axiom and the rule of consequence, the step from assertion (12.11) to assertion (12.12) is proved if we show the following implication:

$$\textbf{if } \textit{full-page} \textbf{ then } (z_2 + 2, 0, 29 - \ell)$$
$$\textbf{else } (z_2 + 1, 1, 29 - \ell) \textbf{ fi} = \alpha$$

$$\rightarrow$$

$$\textbf{if } \ell < 29 \textbf{ then } (z_2 + 1, 1, 29 - \ell - 1)$$
$$\textbf{else } (z_2 + 1, 0, 0) \textbf{ fi} <_{lex} \alpha.$$

We proceed by case analysis.

Case 1 *full-page* is true.

Then the implication is justified by looking at the first component of α : $z_2 + 1 < z_2 + 2$.

Case 2 *full-page* is false.

If $\ell = 29$, the implication is justified by the second component of α since $0 < 1$; if $\ell < 29$, it is justified by the third component of α since $29 - \ell - 1 < 29 - \ell$.

Compared with the first loop component dealing with the second loop component is simpler: the correctness formula

$$\begin{aligned} \{ \quad & p \wedge \neg signal \wedge \textit{full-page} \wedge z_1 \geq 0 \wedge z_2 \geq 0 \\ & \wedge \; \exists z_2 \geq 0 : (z_2 + 1, 0, 29 - \ell) = \alpha \} \\ & signal := \textbf{true} \\ & \{(0, 0, 0) <_{lex} \alpha \} \end{aligned}$$

is true because the first component of α is ≥ 1. This finishes the proof of premise (2) of the fair repetition rule 39.

Since premise (3) of rule 39 is obviously true, we have now a complete proof outline for fair total correctness for the program *PU2*. Hence,

$$\models_{fair} \{\textbf{true}\} \; PU2 \; \{signal \wedge \textit{full-page}\}$$

as desired. $\square$

Soundness

Finally, we prove soundness of the proof system FN. We concentrate here on the soundness proof of the fair repetition rule.

Theorem 12.4. (Soundness of the Fair Repetition Rule) *The fair repetition rule 39 is sound for fair total correctness; that is, if its premises (1)–(3) are true in the sense of total correctness, then its conclusion (12.2) is true in the sense of fair total correctness.*

Proof. Let $S \equiv \textbf{do} \; \square_{i=1}^{n} \; B_i \rightarrow S_i \; \textbf{od}$. By the Fairness Corollary 12.1,

$$\models_{fair} \{p\} \; S \; \{p \wedge \bigwedge_{i=1}^{n} \neg B_i\} \; \text{iff} \; \models_{tot} \{p\} \; T_{fair}(S) \; \{p \wedge \bigwedge_{i=1}^{n} \neg B_i\}.$$

Thus rule 39 is sound if the truth of its premises (1)–(3) implies the truth of

$$\{p\} \; T_{fair}(S) \; \{p \wedge \bigwedge_{i=1}^{n} \neg B_i\},$$

all in the sense of total correctness.

To show the latter, we establish three claims. In their proofs we repeatedly use the Soundness of PNR and TNR Theorem 12.1(ii), which states soundness of the proof system *TNR* for total correctness of nondeterministic programs with random assignments. Let *INIT*, SCH_i and $UPDATE_i$ be the parts added to S by T_{fair} and let *INV* be the standard invariant established for *FAIR* in the proof of the Fair Scheduling Theorem 12.2:

$$INV \equiv \bigwedge_{k=1}^{n} card\ \{i \in \{1,\ldots,n\} \mid z_i \leq -k\} \leq n - k.$$

The first claim establishes this invariant for the loop in $T_{fair}(S)$ by merging the invariants of *FAIR* and S.

Claim 1 For $i \in \{1,\ldots,n\}$

$$\models_{tot} \{p \wedge B_i\}\ S_i\ \{p\} \tag{12.15}$$

implies

$$\models_{tot} \{p \wedge INV \wedge B_i \wedge SCH_i\}\ UPDATE_i;\ S_i\ \{p \wedge INV\}. \tag{12.16}$$

Proof of Claim 1. Since S_i does not change $z_1,\ldots,z_n$, the free variables of *INV*, (12.15) implies by the soundness of the invariance rule A6

$$\models_{tot} \{p \wedge INV \wedge B_i\}\ S_i\ \{p \wedge INV\}. \tag{12.17}$$

By the proof of the Fair Scheduling Theorem 12.2, $UPDATE_i$ satisfies

$$\models_{tot} \{INV \wedge SCH_i\}\ UPDATE_i\ \{INV\}. \tag{12.18}$$

Since $UPDATE_i$ only changes the variables $z_1,\ldots,z_n$ and they are not free in p or B_i, (12.18) implies by the soundness of the invariance rule A6

$$\models_{tot} \{p \wedge INV \wedge B_i \wedge SCH_i\}\ UPDATE_i\ \{p \wedge INV \wedge B_i\}. \tag{12.19}$$

Now by the soundness of the composition rule, (12.19) and (12.17) imply (12.16). $\qquad\Box$

Define the expression t' by the following substitution performed on t:

$$t' \equiv t[z_i := z_i + n]_{i \in \{1,\ldots,n\}}.$$

This substitution represents a *shift by n* in the values of z_i. It allows us to consider t in the following claim only for values $z_i \geq 0$ whereas t' takes care of all the values that are possible for z_i due to the invariant *INV* of the scheduler *FAIR*, namely $z_i \geq -n$.

Claim 2 For $i \in \{1, \ldots, n\}$

$$\models_{tot} \{ \quad p \wedge B_i \wedge \bar{z} \geq 0$$
$$\wedge \; \exists z_i \geq 0 : t[z_j := \textbf{if } B_j \textbf{ then } z_j + 1 \textbf{ else } z_j \textbf{ fi}]_{j \neq i} = \alpha \}$$
$$S_i \qquad\qquad\qquad\qquad\qquad\qquad\qquad\qquad\qquad\qquad\qquad\qquad (12.20)$$
$$\{ t < \alpha \}$$

implies

$$\models_{tot} \{ p \wedge INV \wedge B_i \wedge SCH_i \wedge t' = \alpha \}$$
$$UPDATE_i; \; S_i \qquad\qquad\qquad\qquad\qquad\qquad\qquad\qquad (12.21)$$
$$\{ t' < \alpha \}.$$

Proof of Claim 2. Fix $i \in \{1, \ldots, n\}$. Since the variables $z_1, \ldots, z_n$ are not free in p, B_i or S_i, substituting for $j \in \{1, \ldots, n\}$ the expression $z_j + n$ for z_j in the pre- and postcondition of (12.20) yields:

$$\models_{tot} \{ \quad p \wedge B_i \wedge \bar{z} \geq -n$$
$$\wedge \; \exists z_i \geq -n : t'[z_j := \textbf{if } B_j \textbf{ then } z_j + 1 \textbf{ else } z_j \textbf{ fi}]_{j \neq i} = \alpha \}$$
$$S_i \qquad\qquad\qquad\qquad\qquad\qquad\qquad\qquad\qquad\qquad\qquad\qquad (12.22)$$
$$\{ t' < \alpha \}.$$

We use here the abbreviation

$$\bar{z} \geq -n \equiv z_1 \geq -n \wedge \ldots \wedge z_n \geq -n$$

and the definition of t'. This explains the change in the range of the existential quantifier over the bound variable z_i.

Next, by the truth of the axioms for ordinary and random assignments 2 and 37 and the soundness of the conditional rule 4 and the consequence rule 6 we get

$$\models_{tot} \{ z_i \geq -n \wedge t' = \alpha \}$$
$$UPDATE_i \qquad\qquad\qquad\qquad\qquad\qquad\qquad\qquad\qquad\qquad (12.23)$$
$$\{ \exists z_i \geq -n : t'[z_j := \textbf{if } B_j \textbf{ then } z_j + 1 \textbf{ else } z_j \textbf{ fi}]_{j \neq i} = \alpha \}.$$

INV implies $z_i \geq -n$, so combining (12.19), established in the proof of Claim 1, and (12.23) yields by the soundness of the conjunction rule A4 and of the consequence rule

$$\models_{tot} \{ p \wedge INV \wedge B_i \wedge SCH_i \wedge t' = \alpha \}$$
$$UPDATE_i \qquad\qquad\qquad\qquad\qquad\qquad\qquad\qquad\qquad\qquad (12.24)$$
$$\{ \quad p \wedge INV \wedge B_i$$
$$\wedge \; \exists z_i \geq -n : t'[z_j := \textbf{if } B_j \textbf{ then } z_j + 1 \textbf{ else } z_j \textbf{ fi}]_{j \neq i} = \alpha \}.$$

Since INV implies $\bar{z} \geq -n$, the postcondition of (12.24) implies

$$p \wedge B_i \wedge \bar{z} \geq -n$$
$$\wedge \; \exists z_i \geq -n : t'[z_j := \textbf{if } B_j \textbf{ then } z_j + 1 \textbf{ else } z_j \textbf{ fi}]_{j \neq i} = \alpha,$$

the precondition of (12.22). Thus, by the soundness of the consequence rule and the composition rule, (12.24) and (12.22) imply (12.21). $\qquad \square$

Claim 3

$$p \wedge \bar{z} \geq 0 \rightarrow t \in W \qquad (12.25)$$

implies

$$p \wedge INV \rightarrow t' \in W. \qquad (12.26)$$

Proof of Claim 3. By the definition of INV, the implication

$$p \wedge INV \rightarrow p \wedge \bar{z} + n \geq 0$$

holds, with $\bar{z} + n \geq 0$ abbreviating $z_1 + n \geq 0 \wedge \ldots \wedge z_n + n \geq 0$. Also, substituting everywhere in (12.25) the expression $z_i + n$ for $z_i, i \in \{1, \ldots, n\}$, yields:

$$p \wedge \bar{z} + n \geq 0 \rightarrow t[z_i := z_i + n]_{i \in \{1, \ldots, n\}} \in W.$$

Thus, by the definition of t', (12.26) follows. $\qquad \square$

We now return to the main proof. By Claims 1–3, the truth of the premises (1)–(3) of the fair repetition rule 39 implies the truth of the following (correctness) formulas (in the sense of total correctness):

$$\{p \wedge INV \wedge B_i \wedge SCH_i\} \ UPDATE_i; \ S_i \ \{p \wedge INV\},$$

$$\{p \wedge INV \wedge B_i \wedge SCH_i \wedge t = \alpha\} \ UPDATE_i; \ S_i \ \{t' < \alpha\}, i \in \{1, \ldots, n\},$$

$$p \wedge INV \rightarrow t' \in W.$$

Also $\{p\} \ INIT \ \{p \wedge INV\}$ is true, since $z_1, \ldots, z_n$ do not appear in p. The soundness of the composition rule and the repetitive command III rule 38 implies the truth of

$$\{p\} \ INIT; \ \mathbf{do} \ \square_{i=1}^n B_i \wedge SCH_i \rightarrow UPDATE_i; \ S_i \ \mathbf{od} \ \{p \wedge \bigwedge_{i=1}^n \neg B_i\},$$

that is, the truth of

$$\{p\} \ T_{fair}(S) \ \{p \wedge \bigwedge_{i=1}^n \neg B_i\},$$

all in the sense of total correctness. This concludes the proof of Theorem 12.4. $\qquad \square$

Corollary 12.2. (Soundness of FN) *The proof system FN is sound for fair total correctness of one-level nondeterministic programs.*

12.8 Case Study: Zero Search

In this section we study a nondeterministic solution to our introductory problem of zero search. Recall from Section 1.1 that given a function f from integers to integers the problem is to write a program that finds a zero of f provided such a zero exists.

Here we consider the nondeterministic program

$$ZERO\text{-}N \equiv found := \textbf{false};\ x := 0;\ y := 1;$$
$$\textbf{do}\ \neg found \to\ x := x + 1;$$
$$found := f(x) = 0$$
$$\square\ \ \neg found \to\ y := y - 1;$$
$$found := f(y) = 0$$
$$\textbf{od}.$$

ZERO-N searches for a zero of f with the help of two subprograms: one is searching for this zero by incrementing its test values ($x := x + 1$) and the other one by decrementing them ($y := y - 1$). The idea is that *ZERO-N* finds the desired zero by activating these subprograms in a nondeterministic, but fair order.

Summarizing, we wish to prove

$$\models_{fair} \{\exists u : f(u) = 0\}\ S\ \{f(x) = 0 \vee f(y) = 0\}.$$

The correctness proof takes place in the new proof system *FN* and is divided into three steps.

Step 1 We first show that *ZERO-N* works correctly if f has a *positive* zero u:

$$\models_{fair} \{f(u) = 0 \wedge u > 0\}\ ZERO\text{-}N\ \{f(x) = 0 \vee f(y) = 0\}. \tag{12.27}$$

A proof outline for fair total correctness has the following structure:

$$\{f(u) = 0 \wedge u > 0\}$$
$$found := \textbf{false};$$
$$x := 0;$$
$$y := 1;$$
$$\{f(u) = 0 \wedge u > 0 \wedge \neg found \wedge x = 0 \wedge y = 1\}$$
$$\{\textbf{inv} : p\}\{\textbf{bd} : t\}$$
$$\textbf{do}\ \neg found \to\ \{p \wedge \neg found\}$$
$$x := x + 1;$$
$$found := f(x) = 0$$
$$\{p\}$$
$$\square\ \ \neg found \to\ \{p \wedge \neg found\}$$
$$y := y - 1;$$
$$found := f(y) = 0$$

$$\{p\}$$

od
$$\{p \wedge found\}$$
$$\{f(x) = 0 \vee f(y) = 0\}.$$

It remains to find a loop invariant p and a bound function t that will complete this outline.

Since the variable u is left unchanged by the program *ZERO-N*, certainly

$$f(u) = 0 \wedge u > 0$$

is an invariant. But for the completion of the proof outline we need a stronger invariant relating u to the program variables x and *found*. We take as an overall invariant

$$p \equiv \quad f(u) = 0 \wedge u > 0 \wedge x \le u$$
$$\wedge \text{ if } found \text{ then } f(x) = 0 \vee f(y) = 0 \text{ else } x < u \text{ fi}.$$

Notice that the implications

$$f(u) = 0 \wedge u > 0 \wedge \neg found \wedge x = 0 \wedge y = 1 \rightarrow p$$

and

$$p \wedge found \rightarrow f(x) = 0 \vee f(y) = 0$$

are obviously true and thus confirm the proof outline as given outside the **do** loop.

To check the proof outline inside the loop, we need an appropriate bound function. We observe the following hierarchy of changes:

- by the assumption of fairness, executing the second loop component brings us closer to a switch to the first loop component,
- executing the first loop component brings us closer to the desired zero u by incrementing the test value x by 1.

Hence, we take as partial order the set

$$P = \mathbb{Z} \times \mathbb{Z},$$

ordered lexicographically by $<_{lex}$ and well-founded on the subset

$$W = \mathbb{N} \times \mathbb{N},$$

and as bound function

$$t \equiv (u - x, z_1).$$

In t the scheduling variable z_1 counts the number of executions of the second loop component before the next switch to the first one, and $u-x$, the distance between the current test value x and the zero u, counts the remaining number of executions of the first loop component.

We now show that our choices of p and t complete the overall proof outline as given inside the **do** loop. To this end, we have to prove in system *FN* the premises $(1')$–$(3')$ of the fair repetition rule $39'$.

We begin with premise $(1')$. For the first loop component we have the following proof outline:

$$\{p \wedge \neg found\}$$
$$\{f(u) = 0 \wedge u > 0 \wedge x < u\}$$
$$x := x + 1$$
$$\{f(u) = 0 \wedge u > 0 \wedge x \leq u\}$$
$$\{\quad f(u) = 0 \wedge u > 0 \wedge x \leq u$$
$$\wedge \ \textbf{if } f(x) = 0 \textbf{ then } f(x) = 0 \textbf{ else } x < u \textbf{ fi}\}$$
$$found := f(x) = 0$$
$$\{\quad f(u) = 0 \wedge u > 0 \wedge x \leq u$$
$$\wedge \ \textbf{if } found \textbf{ then } f(x) = 0 \textbf{ else } x < u \textbf{ fi}\}$$
$$\{p\}.$$

Clearly, all implications expressed by successive assertions in this proof outline are true. The assignments are dealt with by backward substitution of the assignment axiom.

This is also the case for the proof outline of the second loop component:

$$\{p \wedge \neg found\}$$
$$\{f(u) = 0 \wedge u > 0 \wedge x < u\}$$
$$y := y + 1$$
$$\{f(u) = 0 \wedge u > 0 \wedge x < u\}$$
$$\{f(u) = 0 \wedge u > 0 \wedge x < u \wedge f(y) = 0 \rightarrow f(y) = 0\}$$
$$found := f(y) = 0$$
$$\{f(u) = 0 \wedge u > 0 \wedge x < u \wedge found \rightarrow f(y) = 0\}$$
$$\{\quad f(u) = 0 \wedge u > 0 \wedge x \leq u$$
$$\wedge \ \textbf{if } found \textbf{ then } f(y) = 0 \textbf{ else } x < u \textbf{ fi}\}$$
$$\{p\}.$$

We now turn to premise $(2')$ of rule $39'$. For the first loop component we have the proof outline:

$$\{\quad \neg found \wedge f(u) = 0 \wedge u > 0 \wedge x < u$$
$$\wedge \ z_1 \geq 0 \wedge z_2 \geq 0 \wedge \exists z_1 \geq 0 : (u - x, z_1) = \alpha\}$$
$$\{\exists z_1 \geq 0 : (u - x, z_1) = \alpha\}$$
$$\{(u - x - 1, z_1) <_{lex} \alpha\}$$
$$x := x + 1;$$
$$\{(u - x, z_1) <_{lex} \alpha\}$$
$$found := f(x) = 0$$
$$\{(u - x, z_1) <_{lex} \alpha\}$$
$$\{t <_{lex} \alpha\}.$$

Thus the bound function t drops below α because the program variable x is incremented in the direction of the zero u.

For the second loop component we have the proof outline:

$$\{ \quad \neg found \land f(u) = 0 \land u > 0 \land x < u$$
$$\land \ z_1 \geq 0 \land z_2 \geq 0 \land (u - x, z_1 + 1) = \alpha \}$$
$$\{(u - x, z_1 + 1) = \alpha\}$$
$$\{(u - x, z_1) <_{lex} \alpha\}$$
$$y := y - 1;$$
$$found := f(y) = 0$$
$$\{(u - x, z_1) <_{lex} \alpha\}$$
$$\{t <_{lex} \alpha\}.$$

Notice that we can prove that the bound function t drops here below α only with the help of the scheduling variable z_1; the assignments to the program variables y and $found$ do not affect t at all.

Finally, premise $(3')$ of rule $39'$ follows from the implications

$$p \land \bar{z} \geq 0 \rightarrow x \leq u \land z_1 \geq 0$$

and

$$x \leq u \land z_1 \geq 0 \rightarrow t \in W.$$

This completes the proof of (12.27).

Step 2 Next we assume that f has a zero $u \leq 0$. The claim now is

$$\models_{fair} \{f(u) = 0 \land u \leq 0\} \ ZERO\text{-}N \ \{f(x) = 0 \lor f(y) = 0\}. \qquad (12.28)$$

Its proof is entirely symmetric to that of Step 1: instead of the first loop component now the second one is responsible for finding the zero.

In fact, as loop invariant we take

$$p \equiv \quad f(u) = 0 \land u \leq 0 \land u \leq y$$
$$\land \ \textbf{if } found \textbf{ then } f(x) = 0 \lor f(y) = 0 \textbf{ else } u < y \textbf{ fi}$$

and as bound function

$$t \equiv (y - u, z_2).$$

The well-founded structure is as before:

$$W = \mathbb{N} \times \mathbb{N}.$$

Step 3 We combine the results (12.27) and (12.28) of Step 1 and Step 2. Using the disjunction rule A3 and the rule of consequence, we obtain

$$\models_{fair} \{f(u) = 0\} \ ZERO\text{-}N \ \{f(x) = 0 \lor f(y) = 0\}.$$

A final application of the $\exists$-introduction rule A5 yields

$$\models_{fair} \{\exists u : f(u) = 0\} \ ZERO\text{-}N \ \{f(x) = 0 \lor f(y) = 0\},$$

the desired result about *ZERO-N.*

12.9 Case Study: Asynchronous Fixed Point Computation

In this section we verify a nondeterministic program for computing fixed points. The correctness of this program depends on the fairness assumption. For pedagogical reasons we first study an example where the main idea for the termination argument is exercised.

Example 12.7. Consider a program

$$S \equiv \textbf{do } B_1 \rightarrow S_1 \Box \ldots \Box B_n \rightarrow S_n \textbf{ od}$$

with the following property: the index set $\{1, \ldots, n\}$ is partitioned into sets K and L with $L \neq \emptyset$, such that executing any subprogram S_k with $k \in K$ does not change the program state, whereas executing any subprogram S_ℓ with $\ell \in L$ yields a new program state which is closer to a terminal state of S.

More specifically, we take

$$B \equiv x \neq 0, \ S_k \equiv skip \text{ for } k \in K \text{ and } S_\ell \equiv x := x - 1 \text{ for } \ell \in L,$$

where x is an integer variable. For any choice of K and L we wish to prove

$$\models_{fair} \{x \geq 0\} \ S \ \{x = 0\}$$

with the help of the fair repetition rule 39′ of system *FN*. As invariant we take

$$p \equiv x \geq 0.$$

This choice obviously satisfies premise (1) of rule 39′.

To find an appropriate bound function, let us first consider the case where $K = \{1, \ldots, n-1\}$ and $L = \{n\}$; that is, where

$$S \equiv \textbf{do } \underbrace{x \neq 0 \rightarrow skip \ \Box \ldots \Box \ x \neq 0 \rightarrow skip}_{n-1 \text{ times}} \ \Box \ x \neq 0 \rightarrow x := x - 1 \textbf{ od.}$$

As in Example 12.6, we observe a hierarchy of changes:

- executing one of the $n-1$ subprograms *skip*; the assumption of fairness implies that the subprogram $S_n \equiv x := x - 1$ cannot be neglected forever,
- executing S_n decrements x, thus bringing us closer to the termination of S.

Since the number of rounds through the loop during which S_n is neglected is counted by the scheduling variable z_n referring to S_n, we arrive at the bound function

$$t \equiv (x, z_n)$$

ranging over the well-founded structure $W = \mathbb{N} \times \mathbb{N}$ ordered lexicographically by $<_{lex}$.

Clearly, p and t satisfy premise (3) of rule 39'. By the simple form of the subprograms of S, checking premise (2) of rule 39' boils down to checking the following implications:

- for $S_k \equiv skip$ where $k \in \{1, \ldots, n-1\}$:

$$x > 0 \wedge z_n \geq 0 \wedge (x, z_n + 1) = \alpha \rightarrow (x, z_n) <_{lex} \alpha,$$

- for $S_n \equiv x := x - 1$:

$$x > 0 \wedge z_n \geq 0 \wedge \exists z_n \geq 0 : (x, z_n) = \alpha \rightarrow (x - 1, z_n) <_{lex} \alpha.$$

These implications are obviously true.

Thus the fair repetition rule 39' and the rule of consequence yield

$$\models_{fair} \{x \geq 0\}\ S\ \{x = 0\}$$

as claimed.

Let us now turn to the general case of sets K and L where it is not only subprogram S_n that is responsible for decrementing x, but *any* subprogram S_ℓ with $\ell \in L$ will do. Then the number of rounds neglecting any of these subprograms is given by $min\ \{z_\ell \mid \ell \in L\}$ with z_ℓ being the scheduling variable referring to S_ℓ. This leads to

$$t \equiv (x, min\ \{z_\ell \mid \ell \in L\})$$

as a suitable bound function for the general case. $\qquad \square$

Before we formulate the problem we wish to solve, we need to introduce some auxiliary notions first. A *partial order* is a pair $(A, \sqsubseteq)$ consisting of a set A and a reflexive, antisymmetric and transitive relation $\sqsubseteq$ on A.

Consider now a partial order $(A, \sqsubseteq)$. Let $a \in A$ and $X \subseteq A$. Then a is called the *least* element of X if $a \in X$ and $a \sqsubseteq x$ for all $x \in X$. The element a is called an *upper bound* of X if $x \sqsubseteq a$ for all $x \in X$. Note that upper bounds of X need not be elements of X. Let U be the set of all upper bounds of X. Then a is called the *least upper bound* of X if a is the least element of U.

A partial order $(A, \sqsubseteq)$ is called *complete* if A contains a least element and if for every ascending chain

$$a_0 \sqsubseteq a_1 \sqsubseteq a_2 \ldots$$

of elements from A the set

$$\{a_0,\, a_1,\, a_2, \ldots\}$$

has a least upper bound.

Now we turn to the problem of computing fixed points. Let $(L, \sqsubseteq)$ be a complete partial order. For $x, y \in L$ we write $x \sqsubset y$ if $x \sqsubseteq y$ and $x \neq y$. Let $\sqsupset$ denote the inverse of $\sqsubseteq$; so $x \sqsupset y$ if $y \sqsubset x$ holds. Assume that $(L, \sqsubseteq)$ has the *finite chain property*, that is, every ascending chain

$$x_1 \sqsubseteq x_2 \sqsubseteq x_3 \sqsubseteq \ldots$$

of elements $x_i \in L$ stabilizes. In other words, there is no infinite increasing chain

$$x_1 \sqsubset x_2 \sqsubset x_3 \sqsubset \ldots$$

in L, or equivalently, the inverse relation $\sqsupset$ is well-founded on L.

We consider here the n-fold Cartesian product L^n of L for some $n \geq 2$. The relation $\sqsubseteq$ is extended componentwise from L to L^n:

$$(x_1, \ldots, x_n) \sqsubseteq (y_1, \ldots, y_n) \text{ iff } \forall (1 \leq i \leq n) : x_i \sqsubseteq y_i.$$

We also extend the relation $\sqsubset$ and its inverse $\sqsupset$:

$$\begin{aligned}(x_1, \ldots, x_n) \sqsubset (y_1, \ldots, y_n) \text{ iff } \quad &(x_1, \ldots, x_n) \sqsubseteq (y_1, \ldots, y_n) \\ \text{and } &(x_1, \ldots, x_n) \neq (y_1, \ldots, y_n),\end{aligned}$$

$$(x_1, \ldots, x_n) \sqsupset (y_1, \ldots, y_n) \text{ iff } \quad (y_1, \ldots, y_n) \sqsubset (x_1, \ldots, x_n).$$

Then also the pair $(L^n, \sqsubseteq)$ is a complete partial order with the finite chain property. Let $\emptyset$ denote the least element in L^n.

Consider now a function

$$F : L^n \to L^n$$

which is *monotonic* under $\sqsubseteq$; that is, whenever $(x_1, \ldots, x_n) \sqsubseteq (y_1, \ldots, y_n)$ then $F(x_1, \ldots, x_n) \sqsubseteq F(y_1, \ldots, y_n)$.

By F_i we denote the ith component function

$$F_i : L^n \to L$$

of F. Thus we define F_i as follows:

$$F_i(x_1, \ldots, x_n) = y_i \text{ iff } F(x_1, \ldots, x_n) = (y_1, \ldots, y_n).$$

Since $\sqsubseteq$ is defined componentwise and F is monotonic, the functions F_i are also monotonic under $\sqsubseteq$.

By a general theorem due to Knaster and Tarski (see Tarski [1955]), F has a *least fixed point* $\mu F \in L^n$; that is,

$$F(\mu F) = \mu F$$

and

$$F(x_1,\ldots,x_n) = (x_1,\ldots,x_n) \text{ implies } \mu F \sqsubseteq (x_1,\ldots,x_n).$$

Usually μF is computed as follows. Starting with the least element $\emptyset$ in L^n the operator F is applied iteratively:

$$\emptyset \sqsubseteq F(\emptyset) \sqsubseteq F(F(\emptyset)) \sqsubseteq F(F(F(\emptyset))) \sqsubseteq \ldots .$$

By the finite chain property of L^n, this iteration process will surely stabilize by the least fixed point μF. Since an application of F requires a simultaneous update of all n components of its arguments, this method of computing μF is called a *synchronous* fixed point computation.

Following Cousot and Cousot [1977b] we are interested here in a more flexible method. We wish to compute μF *asynchronously* by employing n subprograms S_i, for $i \in \{1,\ldots,n\}$, where each of them is allowed to apply only the ith component function F_i. These subprograms are activated nondeterministically by the following program:

$$AFIX \equiv \textbf{do } B \to x_1 := F_1(\bar{x})\square\ldots\square B \to x_n := F_n(\bar{x}) \textbf{ od},$$

where $\bar{x} \equiv (x_1,\ldots,x_n)$ and $B \equiv \bar{x} \neq F(\bar{x})$. In general $AFIX$ will not compute μF, but the claim is that it will do so under the assumption of fairness:

$$\models_{fair} \{\bar{x} = \emptyset\} \ AFIX \ \{\bar{x} = \mu F\}. \tag{12.29}$$

This correctness result is a special case of a more general theorem proved in Cousot and Cousot [1977b].

We would like to prove (12.29) in the system FN. To this end, we proceed in two steps.

Step 1 We start with an informal analysis of $AFIX$. Consider a computation

$$\xi :< AFIX, \sigma >=< S_1, \sigma_1 > \to \ldots \to < S_j, \sigma_j > \to \ldots$$

of $AFIX$ and the abbreviations $\sigma_j(\bar{x}) = (\sigma_j(x_1),\ldots,\sigma_j(x_n))$ for $j \geq 1$ and

$$F_i[\bar{x}] = (x_1,\ldots,x_{i-1}, F_i(\bar{x}), x_{i+1},\ldots,x_n)$$

for $i \in \{1,\ldots,n\}$. Since $\sigma_1(\bar{x}) = \emptyset$ holds and the component functions F_i are monotonic, the assertion

$$\emptyset \sqsubseteq \bar{x} \sqsubseteq F_i[\bar{x}] \sqsubseteq \mu F \tag{12.30}$$

is true for $i \in \{1,\ldots,n\}$ in every state σ_j of ξ. Thus, by the least fixed point property, $\bar{x} = \mu F$ holds as soon as $AFIX$ has terminated with $\bar{x} = F(\bar{x})$.

But why does $AFIX$ terminate? Note that by (12.30) $AFIX$ produces an ascending chain

$$\sigma_1(\bar{x}) \sqsubseteq \ldots \sqsubseteq \sigma_j(\bar{x}) \sqsubseteq \ldots$$

of values in the variable $\bar{x}$. That there exists a state σ_j in which $\bar{x} = F(\bar{x})$ relies on the following two facts.

(i) By the finite chain property of L and hence L^n, the values $\sigma_j(\bar{x}) \in L^n$ cannot be increased infinitely often.

(ii) By the assumption of fairness, the values $\sigma_j(\bar{x})$ cannot be constant arbitrarily long without increasing.

(i) is clear, but (ii) needs a proof. Consider some nonterminal state σ_j in ξ (thus satisfying $B \equiv \bar{x} \neq F(\bar{x})$) for which either $\sigma_j(\bar{x}) = \sigma_1(\bar{x})$ (start) or $\sigma_{j-1}(\bar{x}) \sqsubset \sigma_j(\bar{x})$ (increase just happened) holds. Then we can find two index sets K and L, both depending on σ_j, which partition the subprograms $S_1, \ldots, S_n$ of *AFIX* into subsets $\{S_k \mid k \in K\}$ and $\{S_\ell \mid \ell \in L\}$ such that the S_k stabilize the values of $\bar{x}$, so for $k \in K$, $\bar{x} = F_k[\bar{x}]$ holds in σ_j, whereas the S_ℓ increase the values of $\bar{x}$, so for $\ell \in L$, $\bar{x} \sqsubset F_\ell[\bar{x}]$ holds in σ_j. Note that $L \neq \emptyset$ holds because σ_j is nonterminal.

Thus, as long as subprograms S_k with $k \in K$ are executed, the program *AFIX* generates states $\sigma_{j+1}, \sigma_{j+2}, \ldots$ satisfying

$$\sigma_j(\bar{x}) = \sigma_{j+1}(\bar{x}) = \sigma_{j+2}(\bar{x}) = \ldots .$$

But as soon as a subprogram S_ℓ with $\ell \in L$ is executed in some state σ_m with $j \leq m$, we get the desired next increase

$$\sigma_m(\bar{x}) \sqsubset \sigma_{m+1}(\bar{x})$$

after σ_j. Fairness guarantees that such an increase will indeed happen.

The situation is close to that investigated in Example 12.7, except for the following changes:

- instead of decrementing an integer variable x, here $\bar{x} = (x_1, \ldots, x_n)$ is increased in the ordering $\sqsubseteq$ on L^n,
- the number of possible increases of $\bar{x}$ is unknown but finite,
- the index sets K and L depend on the state σ_j.

Step 2 With this informal discussion in mind, we are now prepared for the formal correctness proof. The essential step is the application of the fair repetition rule 39'. A suitable invariant is

$$p \equiv \bigwedge_{i=1}^{n} (\emptyset \sqsubseteq \bar{x} \sqsubseteq F_i[\bar{x}] \sqsubseteq \mu F).$$

Clearly, p satisfies premise (1') of rule 39'.

By analogy to Example 12.7, we take as the well-founded structure the set

$$W = L^n \times \mathbb{N}$$

ordered lexicographically as follows:

$$(\bar{x}, u) <_{lex} (\bar{y}, v) \text{ iff } \bar{x} \sqsupset \bar{y} \text{ or } (\bar{x} = \bar{y} \text{ and } u < v),$$

with the inverse relation $\sqsupset$ in the first component because increasing $\bar{x}$ means getting closer to the desired fixed point, hence termination. The components $\bar{x}$ and u of pairs $(\bar{x}, u) \in L^n \times \mathbb{N}$ correspond to the facts (i) and (ii) about the termination of $AFIX$ explained in Step 1. Since L^n has the finite chain property, $<_{lex}$ is indeed well-founded on $L^n \times \mathbb{N}$. The bound function ranging over W is given by

$$t \equiv (\bar{x}, min \{z_\ell \mid 1 \le \ell \le n \wedge \bar{x} \sqsubset F_\ell[\bar{x}]\}).$$

Compared with Example 12.7, the condition $\ell \in L$ is replaced here by "$1 \le \ell \le n \wedge \bar{x} \sqsubset F_\ell[\bar{x}]$."

To establish premise $(2')$ of rule $39'$, we have to prove the correctness formula

$$\{p \wedge B \wedge \bar{z} \ge 0 \wedge \exists z_i \ge 0 : t[z_j := z_j + 1]_{j \ne i} = \alpha\}$$
$$x_i := F_i(\bar{x})$$
$$\{t <_{lex} \alpha\}$$

for $i \in \{1, \ldots, n\}$. By the assignment axiom, it suffices to prove the implication

$$p \wedge B \wedge \bar{z} \ge 0 \wedge \exists z_i \ge 0 : t[z_j := z_j + 1]_{j \ne i} = \alpha$$
$$\rightarrow t[x_i := F_i(\bar{x})] <_{lex} \alpha. \tag{12.31}$$

We distinguish two cases.

Case 1 $\bar{x} \sqsubset F_i[\bar{x}]$.

Then $t[x_i := F_i(\bar{x})] <_{lex} \alpha$ by the first component in the lexicographical order.

Case 2 $\bar{x} = F_i[\bar{x}]$.

Since $B \equiv \bar{x} \ne F(\bar{x})$ holds, there exist indices $\ell \in \{1, \ldots, n\}$ with $\bar{x} \sqsubset F_\ell[\bar{x}]$. Moreover, $\ell \ne i$ for all such indices because $\bar{x} = F_i[\bar{x}]$. Thus implication (12.31) is equivalent to

$$p \wedge B \wedge \bar{z} \ge 0 \wedge (\bar{x}, min \{z_\ell + 1 \mid 1 \le \ell \le n \wedge \bar{x} \sqsubset F_\ell(\bar{x})\}) = \alpha$$
$$\rightarrow (\bar{x}, min \{z_\ell \mid 1 \le \ell \le n \wedge \bar{x} \sqsubset F_\ell(\bar{x})\}) <_{lex} \alpha.$$

So $(\bar{x}, min \{z_\ell \mid \ldots\}) <_{lex} \alpha$ by the second component in the lexicographical order.

This proves (12.31) and hence premise $(2')$ of the fair repetition rule $39'$. Since premise $(3')$ of rule $39'$ is clearly satisfied, we have proved

$$\models_{fair} \{p\} \, AFIX \, \{p \wedge \neg B\}.$$

By the rule of consequence, we obtain the desired correctness result (12.29).

12.10 Exercises

12.1. Prove the Input/Output Lemma 10.3 for nondeterministic programs with random assignments.

12.2. Prove the Change and Access Lemma 10.4 for non- deterministic programs with random assignments.

12.3. Prove the Soundness of *PNR* and *TNR* Theorem 12.1.

12.4. The instruction $x :=? \leq y$ which sets x to a value smaller or equal to y was proposed in Floyd [1967b].

(i) Define the instruction's semantics.
(ii) Suggest an axiom for this instruction.
(iii) Prove that for some nondeterministic program S

$$\mathcal{M}_{tot}[\![x :=? \leq y]\!] = \mathcal{M}_{tot}[\![S]\!].$$

12.5. Prove that for no nondeterministic program S

$$\mathcal{M}_{tot}[\![x :=?]\!] = \mathcal{M}_{tot}[\![S]\!].$$

Hint. Use the Bounded Nondeterminism Lemma 10.1.

12.6. Formalize forward reasoning about random assignments by giving an alternative axiom of the form $\{p\}\ x :=?\ \{\ldots\}$.

12.7. Consider the program

$$S \equiv \textbf{do } x \geq 0 \to x := x - 1;\ y :=?$$
$$\quad \square \ \ y \geq 0 \to y := y - 1$$
$$\textbf{od},$$

where x and y are integer variables.

(i) Prove termination of S by proving the correctness formula

$$\{\textbf{true}\}\ S\ \{\textbf{true}\}$$

in the system TNR.
(ii) Explain why it is impossible to use an integer expression as a bound function in the termination proof of S.
    Hint. Show that for a given initial state σ with $\sigma(x) > 0$ it is impossible to predict the number of loop iterations in S.

12.8. Give for the printer-user program *PU1* considered in Example 12.4 a simplified transformed program $T^*_{fair}(PU1)$ which uses only one scheduling variable z, such that

$$\mathcal{M}_{fair}[\![PU1]\!] = \mathcal{M}_{tot}[\![T^*_{fair}(PU1)]\!] \textbf{ mod } \{z\}.$$

12.9. Consider the premises (2) and (2′) of the fair repetition rules 39 and 39′. Let z_1 and z_2 be integer variables. For which of the expressions $t \equiv z_1 + z_2$, $t \equiv (z_1, z_2)$ and $t \equiv (z_2, z_1)$ is the correctness formula

$$\{\exists z_1 \geq 0 : t[z_1 := z_1 + 1] = \alpha\} \; skip \; \{t < \alpha\}$$

true? Depending on the form of t, the symbol $<$ is interpreted as the usual ordering on $\mathbb{Z}$ or as the lexicographic ordering on $\mathbb{Z} \times \mathbb{Z}$.

12.10. Consider the one-level nondeterministic program

$$S \equiv \mathbf{do} \; x > 0 \to go := \mathbf{true}$$
$$\square \quad x > 0 \to \mathbf{if} \; go \; \mathbf{then} \; x := x - 1; \; go := \mathbf{false} \; \mathbf{fi}$$
$$\mathbf{od},$$

where x is an integer variable and go is a Boolean variable.

(i) Show that S can diverge from any state σ with $\sigma(x) > 0$.
(ii) Show that every fair computation of S is finite.
(iii) Exhibit the transformed program $T_{fair}(S)$.
(iv) Show that every computation of $T_{fair}(S)$ is fair.
(v) Prove the fair termination of S by proving the correctness formula

$$\{\mathbf{true}\} \; S \; \{\mathbf{true}\}$$

in the system *FN*.

12.11. Consider a run
$$(E_0, i_0) \ldots (E_j, i_j) \ldots$$

of n components. We call it *weakly fair* if it satisfies the following condition:

$$\forall (1 \leq i \leq n) : (\overset{\infty}{\forall} j \in \mathbb{N} : i \in E_j \to \overset{\infty}{\exists} j \in \mathbb{N} : i = i_j).$$

The quantifier $\overset{\infty}{\forall}$ is dual to $\overset{\infty}{\exists}$ and stands for "for all but finitely many."

(i) Define a *weakly fair nondeterminism semantics* $\mathcal{M}_{wfair}$ of one-level non-deterministic programs by analogy with $\mathcal{M}_{fair}$. Prove that for all one-level nondeterministic programs S and proper states σ

$$\mathcal{M}_{fair}[\![S]\!](\sigma) \subseteq \mathcal{M}_{wfair}[\![S]\!](\sigma).$$

(ii) Define a scheduler *WFAIR* as the scheduler *FAIR* but with

$$UPDATE_i \equiv z_i := ?;$$
$$\mathbf{for \; all} \; j \in \{1, \ldots, n\} - \{i\} \; \mathbf{do}$$
$$\mathbf{if} \; j \in E \; \mathbf{then} \; z_j := z_j - 1 \; \mathbf{else} \; z_j := ? \; \mathbf{fi}$$
$$\mathbf{od}.$$

Define the notions of a *weakly fair* scheduler and of a *universal* weakly fair scheduler by analogy with fair schedulers (see Definition 12.3). Prove that for n components *WFAIR* is a universal weakly fair scheduler.

Hint. Modify the proof of the *FAIR* Scheduling Theorem 12.2.

(iii) Define a transformation T_{wfair} by analogy with the transformation T_{fair}. Prove that for every one-level nondeterministic program S and every proper state σ

$$\mathcal{M}_{wfair}[\![S]\!](\sigma) = \mathcal{M}_{tot}[\![T_{wfair}(S)]\!](\sigma) \bmod Z,$$

where Z is the set of scheduling variables z_i used in T_{wfair}.

Hint. Modify the proof of the Embedding Theorem 12.3.

(iv) Define the notion of weakly fair total correctness by analogy with fair total correctness. Consider the following *weakly fair repetition rule:*

> (1) $\{p \wedge B_i\}\ S_i\ \{p\}, i \in \{1, \ldots, n\}$,
> (2) $\{p \wedge B_i \wedge \bar{z} \geq 0$
> $\qquad \wedge\ \exists z_i \geq 0 : \exists \bar{u} \geq 0 : t[\textbf{if } B_j \textbf{ then } z_j + 1 \textbf{ else } u_j \textbf{ fi}]_{j \neq i} = \alpha\}$
> $\qquad S_i$
> $\qquad \{t < \alpha\}, i \in \{1, \ldots, n\}$,
> (3) $p \wedge \bar{z} \geq 0 \rightarrow t \in W$

$$\{p\}\ \textbf{do } \square_{i=1}^n\ B_i \rightarrow S_i\ \textbf{od}\ \{p \wedge \bigwedge_{i=1}^n \neg B_i\}$$

where

- $u_1, \ldots, u_n$ are integer variables that do not occur in p, t, B_i or S_i, for $i \in \{1, \ldots, n\}$,
- $\exists \bar{u} \geq 0$ abbreviates $\exists u_1 \geq 0 : \ldots : \exists u_n \geq 0$,

and conditions (i)–(v) of the fair repetition rule 39 hold.

Prove that the weakly fair repetition rule is sound for weakly fair total correctness.

Hint. Modify the proof of the Soundness of the Fair Repetition Rule Theorem 12.4.

(v) Identify

$$\text{``print next line''} \equiv skip.$$

Prove

$$\{\textbf{true}\}\ PU1\ \{\textbf{true}\}$$

in the sense of weakly fair total correctness using the weakly fair repetition rule. The program *PU1* is defined in Section 12.1.

12.11 Bibliographic Remarks

Nondeterministic programs augmented by the random assignment are extensively studied in Apt and Plotkin [1986], where several related references can be found.

The verification method presented in this chapter is based on the transformational approach of Apt and Olderog [1983]. Different methods were proposed independently in Lehmann, Pnueli and Stavi [1981] and Grumberg, Francez, Makowsky and de Roever [1985].

In all these papers fairness was studied only for one-level nondeterministic programs. In Apt, Pnueli and Stavi [1984] the method of Apt and Olderog [1983] was generalized to arbitrary nondeterministic programs. Francez [1986] provides an extensive coverage of the subject including a presentation of these methods.

We discussed here two versions of fairness —strong and weak. Some other versions are discussed in Francez [1986]. More recently an alternative notion, called *finitary fairness*, was proposed by Alur and Henzinger [1994]. Finitary fairness requires that for every run of a system there is an unknown but fixed bound k such that no enabled transition is postponed more than k consecutive times.

Current work in this area has concentrated on the study of fairness for concurrent programs. Early references include Olderog and Apt [1988], where the transformational approach discussed here was extended to parallel programs and Back and Kurki-Suonio [1988] and Apt, Francez and Katz [1988], where fairness for distributed programs was studied. More recent references include Francez, Back and Kurki-Suonio [1992] and Joung [1996].

In Olderog and Podelski [2009] it is investigated whether the approach of explicit fair scheduling also works with *dynamic control*, i.e., when new processes may be created dynamically. It is shown that the schedulers defined in Olderog and Apt [1988] carry over to weak fairness but not to strong fairness.

The asynchronous fixpoint computation problem studied in Section 12.9 has numerous applications, for example in logic programming, see Lassez and Maher [1984], and in constraint programming, see van Emden [1997].

Appendix A *Semantics*

The following transition axioms and rules were used in this book to define semantics of the programming languages.

(i) $< skip, \sigma > \;\to\; < E, \sigma >$

(ii) $< u := t, \sigma > \;\to\; < E, \sigma[u := \sigma(t)] >$

    where $u \in Var$ is a simple variable or $u \equiv a[s_1, \ldots, s_n]$, for $a \in Var$.

(ii′) $< \bar{x} := \bar{t}, \sigma > \;\to\; < E, \sigma[\bar{x} := \sigma(\bar{t})] >$

(iii) $\dfrac{< S_1, \sigma > \;\to\; < S_2, \tau >}{< S_1;\; S, \sigma > \;\to\; < S_2;\; S, \tau >}$

(iv) $< \textbf{if } B \textbf{ then } S_1 \textbf{ else } S_2 \textbf{ fi}, \sigma > \;\to\; < S_1, \sigma >$ where $\sigma \models B$.

(v) $< \textbf{if } B \textbf{ then } S_1 \textbf{ else } S_2 \textbf{ fi}, \sigma > \;\to\; < S_2, \sigma >$ where $\sigma \models \neg B$.

(iv′) $< \textbf{if } B \to S \textbf{ fi}, \sigma > \;\to\; < S, \sigma >$ where $\sigma \models B$.

(v′) $< \textbf{if } B \to S \textbf{ fi}, \sigma > \;\to\; < E, \textbf{fail} >$ where $\sigma \models \neg B$.

(vi) $< \textbf{while } B \textbf{ do } S \textbf{ od}, \sigma > \;\to\; < S;\; \textbf{while } B \textbf{ do } S \textbf{ od}, \sigma >$
    where $\sigma \models B$.

(vii) $< \textbf{while } B \textbf{ do } S \textbf{ od}, \sigma > \;\to\; < E, \sigma >$ where $\sigma \models \neg B$.

(viii) $< P, \sigma > \;\to\; < S, \sigma >$, where $P :: S \in D$.

(ix) $< \textbf{begin local } \bar{x} := \bar{t};\; S \textbf{ end}, \sigma > \;\to\; < \bar{x} := \bar{t};\; S; \bar{x} := \sigma(\bar{x}), \sigma >$

(x) $< P(\bar{t}), \sigma > \;\to\; < \textbf{begin local } \bar{u} := \bar{t} \textbf{ end}, \sigma >$
    where $P(\bar{u}) :: S \in D$.

(xi) $< u := t, \sigma > \to < E, \sigma[u := \sigma(t)] >$
    where u is a (possibly subscripted) instance variable.

(xii) $< s.m, \sigma > \to < \textbf{begin local this} := s;\; S \textbf{ end}, \sigma >$
    where $\sigma(s) \neq \textbf{null}$ and $m :: S \in D$.

(xiii) $< s.m, \sigma > \rightarrow < E, \textbf{fail} >$ where $\sigma(s) = \textbf{null}$.

(xiv) $< s.m(\bar{t}), \sigma > \rightarrow < \textbf{begin local this}, \bar{u} := s, \bar{t}; S \textbf{ end}, \sigma >$

where $\sigma(s) \neq \textbf{null}$ and $m(\bar{u}) :: S \in D$.

(xv) $< s.m(\bar{t}), \sigma > \rightarrow < E, \textbf{fail} >$ where $\sigma(s) = \textbf{null}$.

(xvi) $< u := \textbf{new}, \sigma > \rightarrow < E, \sigma[u := \textbf{new}] >$,

where u is a (possibly subscripted) object variable.

(xvii) $$\frac{< S_i, \sigma > \ \rightarrow \ < T_i, \tau >}{< [S_1\|\ldots\|S_i\|\ldots\|S_n], \sigma > \ \rightarrow \ < [S_1\|\ldots\|T_i\|\ldots\|S_n], \tau >}$$
where $i \in \{1, \ldots, n\}$

(xviii) $$\frac{< S, \sigma > \ \rightarrow^* \ < E, \tau >}{< \langle S \rangle, \sigma > \ \rightarrow \ < E, \tau >}$$

(xix) $$\frac{< S, \sigma > \ \rightarrow^* \ < E, \tau >}{< \textbf{await } B \textbf{ then } S \textbf{ end}, \sigma > \ \rightarrow \ < E, \tau >} \text{ where } \sigma \models B.$$

(xx) $< \textbf{if } \square_{i=1}^n B_i \rightarrow S_i \textbf{ fi}, \sigma > \ \rightarrow \ < S_i, \sigma >$

where $\sigma \models B_i$ and $i \in \{1, \ldots, n\}$.

(xxi) $< \textbf{if } \square_{i=1}^n B_i \rightarrow S_i \textbf{ fi}, \sigma > \ \rightarrow \ < E, \textbf{fail} >$ where $\sigma \models \bigwedge_{i=1}^n \neg B_i$.

(xxii) $< \textbf{do } \square_{i=1}^n B_i \rightarrow S_i \textbf{ od}, \sigma > \ \rightarrow \ < S_i; \ \textbf{do } \square_{i=1}^n B_i \rightarrow S_i \textbf{ od}, \sigma >$

where $\sigma \models B_i$ and $i \in \{1, \ldots, n\}$.

(xxiii) $< \textbf{do } \square_{i=1}^n B_i \rightarrow S_i \textbf{ od}, \sigma > \ \rightarrow \ < E, \sigma >$ where $\sigma \models \bigwedge_{i=1}^n \neg B_i$.

(xxiv) $< \textbf{do } \square_{j=1}^m g_j \rightarrow S_j \textbf{ od}, \sigma > \ \rightarrow \ < E, \sigma >$

where for $j \in \{1, \ldots, m\}$ $g_j \equiv B_j; \alpha_j$ and $\sigma \models \bigwedge_{j=1}^m \neg B_j$.

(xxv) $< [S_1\|\ldots\|S_n], \sigma > \ \rightarrow \ < [S_1'\|\ldots\|S_n'], \tau >$

where for some $k, \ell \in \{1, \ldots, n\}, \ k \neq \ell$

$$S_k \equiv \textbf{do } \square_{j=1}^{m_1} g_j \rightarrow R_j \textbf{ od},$$

$$S_\ell \equiv \textbf{do } \square_{j=1}^{m_2} h_j \rightarrow T_j \textbf{ od},$$

for some $j_1 \in \{1, \ldots, m_1\}$ and $j_2 \in \{1, \ldots, m_2\}$ the generalized guards $g_{j_1} \equiv B_1; \alpha_1$ and $h_{j_2} \equiv B_2; \alpha_2$ match, and

(1) $\sigma \models B_1 \wedge B_2$,

(2) $\mathcal{M}[\![Eff(\alpha_1, \alpha_2)]\!](\sigma) = \{\tau\}$,

(3) $S_i' \equiv S_i$ for $i \neq k, \ell$,

(4) $S_k' \equiv R_{j_1}; S_k$,

(5) $S_\ell' \equiv T_{j_2}; S_\ell$.

(xxvi) $< x := ?, \sigma > \ \rightarrow \ < E, \sigma[x := d] >$ for every natural number d.

Appendix B *Axioms and Proof Rules*

The following axioms and proof rules were used in the proof systems studied in this book.

AXIOM 1: SKIP

$$\{p\}\ skip\ \{p\}$$

AXIOM 2: ASSIGNMENT

$$\{p[u := t]\}\ u := t\ \{p\}$$

where $u \in Var$ or $u \equiv a[s_1, \ldots, s_n]$, for $a \in Var$.

AXIOM 2': PARALLEL ASSIGNMENT

$$\{p[\bar{x} := \bar{t}]\}\ \bar{x} := \bar{t}\ \{p\}$$

RULE 3: COMPOSITION

$$\frac{\{p\}\ S_1\ \{r\}, \{r\}\ S_2\ \{q\}}{\{p\}\ S_1;\ S_2\ \{q\}}$$

RULE 4: CONDITIONAL

$$\frac{\{p \wedge B\}\ S_1\ \{q\}, \{p \wedge \neg B\}\ S_2\ \{q\}}{\{p\}\ \text{if } B \text{ then } S_1 \text{ else } S_2 \text{ fi } \{q\}}$$

RULE 4': FAILURE

$$\frac{\{p \wedge B\}\ S\ \{q\}}{\{p\}\ \text{if } B \to S \text{ fi } \{q\}}$$

RULE 4″: FAILURE II

$$\frac{p \to B, \{p\}\ S\ \{q\}}{\{p\}\ \text{if}\ B \to S\ \text{fi}\ \{q\}}$$

RULE 5: LOOP

$$\frac{\{p \wedge B\}\ S\ \{p\}}{\{p\}\ \text{while}\ B\ \text{do}\ S\ \text{od}\ \{p \wedge \neg B\}}$$

RULE 6: CONSEQUENCE

$$\frac{p \to p_1, \{p_1\}\ S\ \{q_1\}, q_1 \to q}{\{p\}\ S\ \{q\}}$$

RULE 7: LOOP II

$$\frac{\begin{array}{l}\{p \wedge B\}\ S\ \{p\}, \\ \{p \wedge B \wedge t = z\}\ S\ \{t < z\}, \\ p \to t \geq 0\end{array}}{\{p\}\ \text{while}\ B\ \text{do}\ S\ \text{od}\ \{p \wedge \neg B\}}$$

where t is an integer expression and z is an integer variable that does not appear in p, B, t or S.

RULE 8: RECURSION

$$\frac{\begin{array}{l}\{p_1\}\ P_1\ \{q_1\}, \dots, \{p_n\}\ P_n\ \{q_n\} \vdash \{p\}\ S\ \{q\}, \\ \{p_1\}\ P_1\ \{q_1\}, \dots, \{p_n\}\ P_n\ \{q_n\} \vdash \{p_i\}\ S_i\ \{q_i\}, i \in \{1, \dots, n\}\end{array}}{\{p\}\ S\ \{q\}}$$

where $D = P_1 :: S_1, \dots, P_n :: S_n$.

RULE 9: RECURSION II

$$\frac{\begin{array}{l}\{p_1\}\ P_1\ \{q_1\}, \dots, \{p_n\}\ P_n\ \{q_n\} \vdash \{p\}\ S\ \{q\}, \\ \{p_1 \wedge t < z\}\ P_1\ \{q_1\}, \dots, \{p_n \wedge t < z\}\ P_n\ \{q_n\} \vdash \\ \qquad \{p_i \wedge t = z\}\ S_i\ \{q_i\},\ i \in \{1, \dots, n\}, \\ p_i \to t \geq 0,\ i \in \{1, \dots, n\}\end{array}}{\{p\}\ S\ \{q\}}$$

where $D = P_1 :: S_1, \dots, P_n :: S_n$ and z is an integer variable that does not occur in p_i, t, q_i and S_i for $i \in \{1, \dots, n\}$ and is treated in the proofs as a constant.

RULE 10: BLOCK

$$\frac{\{p\}\ \bar{x} := \bar{t};\ S\ \{q\}}{\{p\}\ \textbf{begin local}\ \bar{x} := \bar{t};\ S\ \textbf{end}\ \{q\}}$$

where $\{\bar{x}\} \cap free(q) = \emptyset$.

RULE 11: INSTANTIATION

$$\frac{\{p\}\ P(\bar{x})\ \{q\}}{\{p[\bar{x} := \bar{t}]\}\ P(\bar{t})\ \{q[\bar{x} := \bar{t}]\}}$$

where $var(\bar{x}) \cap var(D) = var(\bar{t}) \cap change(D) = \emptyset$.

RULE 12: RECURSION III

$$\frac{\begin{array}{l}\{p_1\}\ P_1(\bar{t}_1)\ \{q_1\}, \ldots, \{p_n\}\ P_n(\bar{t}_n)\ \{q_n\} \vdash \{p\}\ S\ \{q\}, \\ \{p_1\}\ P_1(\bar{t}_1)\ \{q_1\}, \ldots, \{p_n\}\ P_n(\bar{t}_n)\ \{q_n\} \vdash \\ \qquad \{p_i\}\ \textbf{begin local}\ \bar{u}_i := \bar{t}_i;\ S_i\ \textbf{end}\ \{q_i\},\ i \in \{1, \ldots, n\}\end{array}}{\{p\}\ S\ \{q\}}$$

where $P_i(\bar{u}_i) :: S_i \in D$ for $i \in \{1, \ldots, n\}$.

RULE 12′: MODULARITY

$$\frac{\begin{array}{l}\{p_0\}\ P(\bar{x})\ \{q_0\} \vdash \{p_0\}\ \textbf{begin local}\ \bar{u} := \bar{x};\ S\ \textbf{end}\ \{q_0\}, \\ \{p_0\}\ P(\bar{x})\ \{q_0\}, \{p\}\ P(\bar{x})\ \{q\} \vdash \{p\}\ \textbf{begin local}\ \bar{u} := \bar{x};\ S\ \textbf{end}\ \{q\}\end{array}}{\{p\}\ P(\bar{x})\ \{q\}}$$

where $var(\bar{x}) \cap var(D) = \emptyset$ and $D = P(\bar{u}) :: S$.

RULE 13: RECURSION IV

$$\frac{\begin{array}{l}\{p_1\}\ P_1(\bar{e}_1)\ \{q_1\}, \ldots, \{p_n\}\ P_n(\bar{e}_n)\ \{q_n\} \vdash_{tot} \{p\}\ S\ \{q\}, \\ \{p_1 \wedge t < z\}\ P_1(\bar{e}_1)\ \{q_1\}, \ldots, \{p_n \wedge t < z\}\ P_n(\bar{e}_n)\ \{q_n\} \vdash_{tot} \\ \qquad \{p_i \wedge t = z\}\ \textbf{begin local}\ \bar{u}_i := \bar{e}_i;\ S_i\ \textbf{end}\ \{q_i\},\ i \in \{1, \ldots, n\}\end{array}}{\{p\}\ S\ \{q\}}$$

where $P_i(\bar{u}_i) :: S_i \in D$, for $i \in \{1, \ldots, n\}$, and z is an integer variable that does not occur in p_i, t, q_i and S_i for $i \in \{1, \ldots, n\}$ and is treated in the proofs as a constant.

AXIOM 14: ASSIGNMENT TO INSTANCE VARIABLES

$$\{p[u := t]\}\ u := t\ \{p\}$$

where $u \in IVar$ or $u \equiv a[s_1, \ldots, s_n]$ and $a \in IVar$.

RULE 15: INSTANTIATION II

$$\frac{\{p\}\ y.m\ \{q\}}{\{p[y := s]\}\ s.m\ \{q[y := s]\}}$$

where $y \notin var(D)$ and $var(s) \cap change(D) = \emptyset$.

RULE 16: RECURSION V

$$\{p_1\}\ s_1.m_1\ \{q_1\}, \ldots, \{p_n\}\ s_n.m_n\ \{q_n\} \vdash \{p\}\ S\ \{q\},$$
$$\{p_1\}\ s_1.m_1\ \{q_1\}, \ldots, \{p_n\}\ s_n.m_n\ \{q_n\} \vdash$$
$$\{p_i\}\ \textbf{begin local this} := s_i; S_i\ \textbf{end}\ \{q_i\},\ i \in \{1, \ldots, n\}$$

$$\{p\}\ S\ \{q\}$$

where $m_i :: S_i \in D$ for $i \in \{1, \ldots, n\}$.

RULE 17: RECURSION VI

$$\{p_1\}\ s_1.m_1\ \{q_1\}, \ldots, \{p_n\}\ s_n.m_n\ \{q_n\} \vdash \{p\}\ S\ \{q\},$$
$$\{p_1 \wedge t < z\}\ s_1.m_1\ \{q_1\}, \ldots, \{p_n \wedge t < z\}\ s_n.m_n\ \{q_n\} \vdash$$
$$\{p_i \wedge t = z\}\ \textbf{begin local this} := s_i; S_i\ \textbf{end}\ \{q_i\},\ i \in \{1, \ldots, n\}$$

$$\{p\}\ S\ \{q\}$$

where $m_i :: S_i \in D$, for $i \in \{1, \ldots, n\}$, and z is an integer variable that does not occur in p_i, t, q_i and S_i for $i \in \{1, \ldots, n\}$ and is treated in the proofs as a constant.

RULE 18: INSTANTIATION III

$$\frac{\{p\}\ y.m(\bar{x})\ \{q\}}{\{p[y, \bar{x} := s, \bar{t}]\}\ s.m(\bar{t})\ \{q[y, \bar{x} := s, \bar{t}]\}}$$

where $y, \bar{x}$ is a sequence of simple variables in Var which do not appear in D and $var(s, \bar{t}) \cap change(D) = \emptyset$.

RULE 19: RECURSION VII

$$\{p_1\}\ s_1.m_1(\bar{t}_1)\ \{q_1\}, \ldots, \{p_n\}\ s_n.m_n(\bar{t}_n)\ \{q_n\} \vdash \{p\}\ S\ \{q\},$$
$$\{p_1\}\ s_1.m_1(\bar{t}_1)\ \{q_1\}, \ldots, \{p_n\}\ s_n.m_n(\bar{t}_n)\ \{q_n\} \vdash$$
$$\{p_i\}\ \textbf{begin local this}, \bar{u}_i := s_i, \bar{t}_i; S_i\ \textbf{end}\ \{q_i\},\ i \in \{1, \ldots, n\}$$

$$\{p\}\ S\ \{q\}$$

where $m_i(\bar{u}_i) :: S_i \in D$ for $i \in \{1, \ldots, n\}$.

RULE 20: RECURSION VIII

$\{p_1\}\ s_1.m_1(\bar{e}_1)\ \{q_1\}, \ldots, \{p_n\}\ s_n.m_n(\bar{e}_n)\ \{q_n\} \vdash \{p\}\ S\ \{q\},$
$\{p_1 \wedge t < z\}\ s_1.m_1(\bar{e}_1)\ \{q_1\}, \ldots, \{p_n \wedge t < z\}\ s_n.m_n(\bar{e}_n)\ \{q_n\} \vdash$
$\qquad \{p_i \wedge t = z\}$ **begin local this**$, \bar{u}_i := s_i, \bar{e}_i;\ S_i$ **end** $\{q_i\},\ i \in \{1, \ldots, n\}$
$p_i \to s_i \neq$ **null**$,\ i \in \{1, \ldots, n\}$

$$\{p\}\ S\ \{q\}$$

where $m_i(\bar{u}_i) :: S_i \in D$, for $i \in \{1, \ldots, n\}$, and and z is an integer variable that does not occur in p_i, t, q_i and S_i for $i \in \{1, \ldots, n\}$ and is treated in the proofs as a constant.

AXIOM 21: OBJECT CREATION

$$\{p[x := \textbf{new}]\}\ x := \textbf{new}\ \{p\},$$

where $x \in Var$ is a simple object variable and p is a pure assertion.

RULE 22: OBJECT CREATION

$$\frac{p' \to p[u := x]}{\{p'[x := \textbf{new}]\}\ u := \textbf{new}\ \{p\}}$$

where u is a subscripted normal object variable or a (possibly subscripted) instance object variable, $x \in Var$ is a fresh simple object variable which does not occur in p, and p' is a pure assertion.

RULE 23: SEQUENTIALIZATION

$$\frac{\{p\}\ S_1;\ \ldots;\ S_n\ \{q\}}{\{p\}\ [S_1\|\ldots\|S_n]\ \{q\}}$$

RULE 24: DISJOINT PARALLELISM

$$\frac{\{p_i\}\ S_i\ \{q_i\}, i \in \{1, \ldots, n\}}{\{\bigwedge_{i=1}^{n}\ p_i\}\ [S_1\|\ldots\|S_n]\ \{\bigwedge_{i=1}^{n}\ q_i\}}$$

where $free(p_i, q_i) \cap change(S_j) = \emptyset$ for $i \neq j$.

RULE 25: AUXILIARY VARIABLES

$$\frac{\{p\}\ S\ \{q\}}{\{p\}\ S_0\ \{q\}}$$

where for some set of auxiliary variables A of S with $free(q) \cap A = \emptyset$, the program S_0 results from S by deleting all assignments to the variables in A.

RULE 26: ATOMIC REGION

$$\frac{\{p\}\ S\ \{q\}}{\{p\}\ \langle S\rangle\ \{q\}}$$

RULE 27: PARALLELISM WITH SHARED VARIABLES

$$\frac{\text{The standard proof outlines } \{p_i\}\ S_i^*\ \{q_i\},\ i\in\{1,\ldots,n\},\ \text{are interference free}}{\{\bigwedge_{i=1}^n\ p_i\}\ [S_1\|\ldots\|S_n]\ \{\bigwedge_{i=1}^n\ q_i\}}$$

RULE 28: SYNCHRONIZATION

$$\frac{\{p\wedge B\}\ S\ \{q\}}{\{p\}\ \textbf{await } B \textbf{ then } S \textbf{ end } \{q\}}$$

RULE 29: PARALLELISM WITH DEADLOCK FREEDOM

(1) The standard proof outlines $\{p_i\}\ S_i^*\ \{q_i\}, i\in\{1,\ldots,n\}$ for weak total correctness are interference free,

(2) For every potential deadlock $(R_1,\ldots,R_n)$ of $[S_1\|\ldots\|S_n]$ the corresponding tuple of assertions $(r_1,\ldots,r_n)$ satisfies $\neg\bigwedge_{i=1}^n\ r_i$.

$$\{\textstyle\bigwedge_{i=1}^n\ p_i\}\ [S_1\|\ldots\|S_n]\ \{\bigwedge_{i=1}^n\ q_i\}$$

RULE 30: ALTERNATIVE COMMAND

$$\frac{\{p\wedge B_i\}\ S_i\ \{q\}, i\in\{1,\ldots,n\}}{\{p\}\ \textbf{if } \square_{i=1}^n\ B_i\to S_i\ \textbf{fi } \{q\}}$$

RULE 31: REPETITIVE COMMAND

$$\frac{\{p\wedge B_i\}\ S_i\ \{p\}, i\in\{1,\ldots,n\}}{\{p\}\ \textbf{do } \square_{i=1}^n\ B_i\to S_i\ \textbf{od } \{p\wedge\bigwedge_{i=1}^n\ \neg B_i\}}$$

RULE 32: ALTERNATIVE COMMAND II

$$\frac{p\to\bigvee_{i=1}^n\ B_i,\quad \{p\wedge B_i\}\ S_i\ \{q\}, i\in\{1,\ldots,n\}}{\{p\}\ \textbf{if } \square_{i=1}^n\ B_i\to S_i\ \textbf{fi } \{q\}}$$

RULE 33: REPETITIVE COMMAND II

$$\{p \wedge B_i\}\ S_i\ \{p\}, i \in \{1, \ldots, n\},$$
$$\{p \wedge B_i \wedge t = z\}\ S_i\ \{t < z\}, i \in \{1, \ldots, n\},$$
$$p \rightarrow t \geq 0$$

$$\overline{\{p\}\ \textbf{do}\ \square_{i=1}^{n}\ B_i \rightarrow S_i\ \textbf{od}\ \{p \wedge \bigwedge_{i=1}^{n} \neg B_i\}}$$

where t is an integer expression and z is an integer variable not occurring in p, t, B_i or S_i for $i \in \{1, \ldots, n\}$.

RULE 34: DISTRIBUTED PROGRAMS

$$\{p\}\ S_{1,0};\ \ldots;\ S_{n,0}\ \{I\},$$
$$\{I \wedge B_{i,j} \wedge B_{k,\ell}\}\ Eff(\alpha_{i,j}, \alpha_{k,\ell});\ S_{i,j};\ S_{k,\ell}\ \{I\}$$
$$\text{for all } (i, j, k, \ell) \in \Gamma$$

$$\overline{\{p\}\ S\ \{I \wedge TERM\}}$$

RULE 35: DISTRIBUTED PROGRAMS II

(1) $\{p\}\ S_{1,0};\ \ldots;\ S_{n,0}\ \{I\}$,
(2) $\{I \wedge B_{i,j} \wedge B_{k,\ell}\}\ Eff(\alpha_{i,j}, \alpha_{k,\ell});\ S_{i,j};\ S_{k,\ell}\ \{I\}$
$\quad$ for all $(i, j, k, \ell) \in \Gamma$,
(3) $\{I \wedge B_{i,j} \wedge B_{k,\ell} \wedge t = z\}\ Eff(\alpha_{i,j}, \alpha_{k,\ell});\ S_{i,j};\ S_{k,\ell}\ \{t < z\}$
$\quad$ for all $(i, j, k, \ell) \in \Gamma$,
(4) $I \rightarrow t \geq 0$

$$\{p\}\ S\ \{I \wedge TERM\}$$

where t is an integer expression and z is an integer variable not appearing in p, t, I or S.

RULE 36: DISTRIBUTED PROGRAMS III

(1) $\{p\}\ S_{1,0};\ \ldots;\ S_{n,0}\ \{I\}$,
(2) $\{I \wedge B_{i,j} \wedge B_{k,\ell}\}\ Eff(\alpha_{i,j}, \alpha_{k,\ell});\ S_{i,j};\ S_{k,\ell}\ \{I\}$
$\quad$ for all $(i, j, k, \ell) \in \Gamma$,
(3) $\{I \wedge B_{i,j} \wedge B_{k,\ell} \wedge t = z\}\ Eff(\alpha_{i,j}, \alpha_{k,\ell});\ S_{i,j};\ S_{k,\ell}\ \{t < z\}$
$\quad$ for all $(i, j, k, \ell) \in \Gamma$,
(4) $I \rightarrow t \geq 0$,
(5) $I \wedge BLOCK \rightarrow TERM$

$$\{p\}\ S\ \{I \wedge TERM\}$$

where t is an integer expression and z is an integer variable not appearing in p, t, I or S.

AXIOM 37: RANDOM ASSIGNMENT

$$\{\forall x \geq 0 : p\}\ x := ?\ \{p\}$$

RULE 38: REPETITIVE COMMAND III

$$\{p \wedge B_i\}\ S_i\ \{p\}, i \in \{1, \ldots, n\},$$
$$\{p \wedge B_i \wedge t = \alpha\}\ S_i\ \{t < \alpha\}, i \in \{1, \ldots, n\},$$
$$p \rightarrow t \in W$$

$$\overline{\{p\}\ \textbf{do}\ \square_{i=1}^{n}\ B_i \rightarrow S_i\ \textbf{od}\ \{p \wedge \bigwedge_{i=1}^{n}\ \neg B_i\}}$$

where

  (i) t is an expression which takes values in an irreflexive partial order $(P, <)$ that is well-founded on the subset $W \subseteq P$,

 (ii) α is a simple variable ranging over P that does not occur in p, t, B_i or S_i for $i \in \{1, \ldots, n\}$.

RULE 39: FAIR REPETITION

  (1) $\{p \wedge B_i\}\ S_i\ \{p\}, i \in \{1, \ldots, n\}$,
  (2) $\{p \wedge B_i \wedge \bar{z} \geq 0$
        $\wedge\ \exists z_i \geq 0 : t[z_j := \textbf{if}\ B_j\ \textbf{then}\ z_j + 1\ \textbf{else}\ z_j\ \textbf{fi}]_{j \neq i} = \alpha\}$
        S_i
        $\{t < \alpha\}, i \in \{1, \ldots, n\}$,
  (3) $p \wedge \bar{z} \geq 0 \rightarrow t \in W$

$$\overline{(4)\ \{p\}\ \textbf{do}\ \square_{i=1}^{n}\ B_i \rightarrow S_i\ \textbf{od}\ \{p \wedge \bigwedge_{i=1}^{n}\ \neg B_i\}}$$

where

   (i) t is an expression which takes values in an irreflexive partial order $(P, <)$ that is well-founded on the subset $W \subseteq P$,

  (ii) $z_1, \ldots, z_n$ are integer variables that do not occur in p, B_i or S_i, for $i \in \{1, \ldots, n\}$,

 (iii) $t[z_j := \textbf{if}\ B_j\ \textbf{then}\ z_j + 1\ \textbf{else}\ z_j\ \textbf{fi}]_{j \neq i}$ denotes the expression that results from t by substituting for every occurrence of z_j in t the conditional expression $\textbf{if}\ B_j\ \textbf{then}\ z_j + 1\ \textbf{else}\ z_j\ \textbf{fi}$; here j ranges over the set $\{1, \ldots, n\} - \{i\}$,

 (iv) $\bar{z} \geq 0$ abbreviates $z_1 \geq 0 \wedge \ldots \wedge z_n \geq 0$,

  (v) α is a simple variable ranging over P and not occurring in p, t, B_i or S_i, for $i \in \{1, \ldots, n\}$.

RULE 39′: FAIR REPETITION (IDENTICAL GUARDS)

$(1')$ $\{p \wedge B\}\ S_i\ \{p\}, i \in \{1, \ldots, n\}$,

$(2')$ $\{p \wedge B \wedge \bar{z} \geq 0 \wedge \exists z_i \geq 0 : t[z_j := z_j + 1]_{j \neq i} = \alpha\}$
$\qquad S_i$
$\qquad \{t < \alpha\}, i \in \{1, \ldots, n\}$,

$(3')$ $p \wedge \bar{z} \geq 0 \rightarrow t \in W$

$(4')$ $\{p\}$ **do** $\square_{i=1}^{n}\ B \rightarrow S_i$ **od** $\{p \wedge \neg B\}$

where conditions (i)–(v) of Rule 39 hold.

Auxiliary Axioms and Rules

RULE A1: DECOMPOSITION

$$\frac{\vdash_p \{p\}\; S\; \{q\},}{\vdash_t \{p\}\; S\; \{\mathbf{true}\}}$$
$$\frac{}{\{p\}\; S\; \{q\}}$$

where the provability signs $\vdash_p$ and $\vdash_t$ refer to proof systems for partial and total correctness for the considered program S, respectively.

AXIOM A2: INVARIANCE

$$\{p\}\; S\; \{p\}$$

where $free(p) \cap change(S) = \emptyset$.

RULE A3: DISJUNCTION

$$\frac{\{p\}\; S\; \{q\}, \{r\}\; S\; \{q\}}{\{p \vee r\}\; S\; \{q\}}$$

RULE A4: CONJUNCTION

$$\frac{\{p_1\}\; S\; \{q_1\}, \{p_2\}\; S\; \{q_2\}}{\{p_1 \wedge p_2\}\; S\; \{q_1 \wedge q_2\}}$$

RULE A5: ∃-INTRODUCTION

$$\frac{\{p\}\; S\; \{q\}}{\{\exists x : p\}\; S\; \{q\}}$$

where x does not occur in S or in $free(q)$.

RULE A6: INVARIANCE

$$\frac{\{r\}\; S\; \{q\}}{\{p \wedge r\}\; S\; \{p \wedge q\}}$$

where $free(p) \cap change(S) = \emptyset$.

RULE A7: SUBSTITUTION

$$\frac{\{p\}\ S\ \{q\}}{\{p[\bar{z} := \bar{t}]\}\ S\ \{q[\bar{z} := \bar{t}]\}}$$

where $(\{\bar{z}\} \cup var(\bar{t})) \cap change(S) = \emptyset$.

RULE A8:

$$\frac{I_1 \text{ and } I_2 \text{ are global invariant relative to } p}{I_1 \wedge I_2 \text{ is a global invariant relative to } p}$$

RULE A9:

I is a global invariant relative to p,
$\{p\}\ S\ \{q\}$

$$\overline{\{p\}\ S\ \{I \wedge q\}}$$

Appendix C *Proof Systems*

For the various classes of programs studied in this book the following proof systems for partial and total correctness were introduced.

while *Programs*

PROOF SYSTEM *PW* :
This system consists of the group
of axioms and rules 1–6.

PROOF SYSTEM *TW* :
This system consists of the group
of axioms and rules 1–4, 6, 7.

Recursive Programs

PROOF SYSTEM *PR* :
This system consists of the group of axioms
and rules 1–6, 8, and A2–A6.

PROOF SYSTEM *TR* :
This system consists of the group of axioms
and rules 1–4, 6, 7, 9, and A3–A6.

Recursive Programs with Parameters

PROOF SYSTEM *PRP* :
This system consists of the group of axioms
and rules 1–6, 10, 11, 12, and A2–A6.

PROOF SYSTEM *TRP* :
This system consists of the group of axioms
and rules 1–4, 6, 7, 10, 11, 13, and A3–A6.

Object-Oriented Programs

PROOF SYSTEM *PO* :
This system consists of the group of axioms
and rules 1–6, 10, 14–16, and A2–A6.

PROOF SYSTEM *TO* :
This system consists of the group of axioms
and rules 1–4, 6, 7, 10, 14, 15, 17, and A3–A6.

Object-Oriented Programs with Parameters

PROOF SYSTEM *POP* :
This system consists of the group of axioms
and rules 1–6, 10, 14, 18, 19, and A2–A6.

PROOF SYSTEM *TOP* :
This system consists of the group of axioms
and rules 1–4, 6, 7, 10, 14, 18, 20, and A3–A6.

Object-Oriented Programs with Object Creation

PROOF SYSTEM *POC* :
This system consists of the group of axioms
and rules 1–6, 10, 14, 18, 19, 21, 22 and A2–A7.

PROOF SYSTEM *TOC* :
> This system consists of the group of axioms
> and rules 1–4, 6, 7, 10, 14, 18, 20–22 and A3–A7.

Disjoint Parallel Programs

PROOF SYSTEM *PP* :
> This system consists of the group of axioms
> and rules 1–6, 24, 25 and A2–A6.

PROOF SYSTEM *TP* :
> This system consists of the group of axioms
> and rules 1–5, 7, 24, 25 and A3–A6.

Parallel Programs with Shared Variables

PROOF SYSTEM *PSV* :
> This system consists of the group of axioms
> and rules 1–6, 25–27 and A2–A6.

PROOF SYSTEM *TSV* :
> This system consists of the group of axioms
> and rules 1–5, 7, 25–27 and A3–A6.

Parallel Programs with Synchronization

PROOF SYSTEM *PSY* :
> This system consists of the group of axioms
> and rules 1–6, 25, 27, 28 and A2–A6.

PROOF SYSTEM *TSY* :
> This system consists of the group of axioms
> and rules 1–5, 7, 25, 28, 29 and A3–A6.

Nondeterministic Programs

PROOF SYSTEM *PN* :
   This system consists of the group of axioms
   and rules 1, 2, 3, 6, 30, 31 and A2–A6.

PROOF SYSTEM *TN* :
   This system consists of the group of axioms and rules
   1, 2, 3, 6, 32, 33 and A3–A6.

Distributed Programs

PROOF SYSTEM *PDP* :
   This system consists of the proof system *PN* augmented
   by the group of axioms and rules 34, A8 and A9.

PROOF SYSTEM *WDP* :
   This system consists of the proof system *TN* augmented
   by the group of axioms and rules 35 and A9.

PROOF SYSTEM *TDP* :
   This system consists of the proof system *TN* augmented
   by the group of axioms and rules 36 and A9.

Fairness

PROOF SYSTEM *PNR* :
   This system consists of the proof system
   PN augmented with Axiom 37.

PROOF SYSTEM *TNR* :
   This system is obtained from the proof system *TN*
   by adding Axiom 37 and replacing Rule 33 by Rule 38.

PROOF SYSTEM *FN* :
   This system is obtained from the proof system *TN*
   by replacing Rule 33 by Rule 39.

Appendix D *Proof Outlines*

The following formation axioms and rules were used in this book to define proof outlines.

(i) $\{p\}$ *skip* $\{p\}$

(ii) $\{p[u := t]\}$ $u := t$ $\{p\}$

(iii) $$\frac{\{p\}\ S_1^*\ \{r\}, \{r\}\ S_2^*\ \{q\}}{\{p\}\ S_1^*;\ \{r\}\ S_2^*\ \{q\}}$$

(iv) $$\frac{\{p \wedge B\}\ S_1^*\ \{q\}, \{p \wedge \neg B\}\ S_2^*\ \{q\}}{\{p\}\ \textbf{if}\ B\ \textbf{then}\ \{p \wedge B\}\ S_1^*\ \{q\}\ \textbf{else}\ \{p \wedge \neg B\}\ S_2^*\ \{q\}\ \textbf{fi}\ \{q\}}$$

(v) $$\frac{\{p \wedge B\}\ S^*\ \{p\}}{\{\textbf{inv} : p\}\ \textbf{while}\ B\ \textbf{do}\ \{p \wedge B\}\ S^*\ \{p\}\ \textbf{od}\ \{p \wedge \neg B\}}$$

(vi) $$\frac{p \rightarrow p_1,\ \{p_1\}\ S^*\ \{q_1\},\ q_1 \rightarrow q}{\{p\}\{p_1\}\ S^*\ \{q_1\}\{q\}}$$

(vii) $$\frac{\{p\}\ S^*\ \{q\}}{\{p\}\ S^{**}\ \{q\}}$$

where S^{**} results from S^* by omitting some of the intermediate assertions not labeled by the keyword **inv**.

(viii) $$\frac{\begin{array}{c}\{p \wedge B\}\ S^*\ \{p\}, \\ \{p \wedge B \wedge t = z\}\ S^{**}\ \{t < z\}, \\ p \rightarrow t \geq 0\end{array}}{\{\textbf{inv} : p\}\{\textbf{bd} : t\}\ \textbf{while}\ B\ \textbf{do}\ \{p \wedge B\}\ S^*\ \{p\}\ \textbf{od}\ \{p \wedge \neg B\}}$$

where t is an integer expression and z is an integer variable not occurring in p, t, B or S^{**}.

(ix)
$$\frac{\{p_i\}\ S_i^*\ \{q_i\}, i \in \{1, \dots, n\}}{\{\bigwedge_{i=1}^{n}\ p_i\}\ [\{p_1\}\ S_1^*\ \{q_1\}\|\dots\|\{p_n\}\ S_n^*\ \{q_n\}]\ \{\bigwedge_{i=1}^{n}\ q_i\}}$$

(x)
$$\frac{\{p\}\ S^*\ \{q\}}{\{p\}\ \langle S^*\rangle\ \{q\}}$$ where S^* stands for an annotated version of S.

(xi)

(1) $\{p \wedge B\}\ S^*\ \{p\}$ is standard,
(2) $\{pre(R) \wedge t = z\}\ R\ \{t \leq z\}$ for every normal assignment and atomic region R within S,
(3) for each path $\pi \in path(S)$ there exists a normal assignment or atomic region R in π such that
$\{pre(R) \wedge t = z\}\ R\ \{t < z\}$,
(4) $p \to t \geq 0$

$\{\mathbf{inv}: p\}\{\mathbf{bd}: t\}\ \mathbf{while}\ B\ \mathbf{do}\ \{p \wedge B\}\ S^*\ \{p\}\ \mathbf{od}\ \{p \wedge \neg B\}$

where t is an integer expression and z is an integer variable not occurring in p, t, B or S^*, and where $pre(R)$ stands for the assertion preceding R in the standard proof outline $\{p \wedge B\}\ S^*\ \{p\}$ for total correctness.

(xii)
$$\frac{\{p \wedge B\}\ S^*\ \{q\}}{\{p\}\ \mathbf{await}\ B\ \mathbf{then}\ \{p \wedge B\}\ S^*\ \{q\}\ \mathbf{end}\ \{q\}}$$
where S^* stands for an annotated version of S.

(xiii)
$$\frac{p \to \bigvee_{i=1}^{n}\ B_i,\quad \{p \wedge B_i\}\ S_i^*\ \{q\}, i \in \{1, \dots, n\}}{\{p\}\ \mathbf{if}\ \square_{i=1}^{n}\ B_i \to \{p \wedge B_i\}\ S_i^*\ \{q\}\ \mathbf{fi}\ \{q\}}$$

(xiv)
$$\frac{\{p \wedge B_i\}\ S_i^*\ \{p\}, i \in \{1, \dots, n\},\quad \{p \wedge B_i \wedge t = z\}\ S_i^{**}\ \{t < z\}, i \in \{1, \dots, n\},\quad p \to t \geq 0}{\{\mathbf{inv}: p\}\{\mathbf{bd}: t\}\ \mathbf{do}\ \square_{i=1}^{n}\ B_i \to \{p \wedge B_i\}\ S_i^*\ \{p\}\ \mathbf{od}\ \{p \wedge \bigwedge_{i=1}^{n} \neg B_i\}}$$

where t is an integer expression and z is an integer variable not occurring in p, t, B_i or S_i for $i \in \{1, \dots, n\}$.

References

M. ABADI AND K. LEINO

[2003]   A logic of object-oriented programs, in: *Verification: Theory and Practice*, N. Dershowitz, ed., vol. 2772 of Lecture Notes in Computer Science, Springer, pp. 11–41. Cited on page **240**.

J.-R. ABRIAL

[1996]   *The B Book – Assigning Programs to Meanings*, Cambridge University Press. Cited on page **371**.

[2009]   *Modeling in Event-B: System and Software Engineering*, Cambridge University Press. To appear. Cited on page **371**.

J.-R. ABRIAL AND S. HALLERSTEDE

[2007]   Refinement, Decomposition and Instantiation of Discrete Models: Application to Event-B, *Fundamentae Informatica*, 77, pp. 1–28. Cited on pages **13** and **371**.

R. ALUR AND T. A. HENZINGER

[1994]   Finitary fairness, in: *Proceedings, Ninth Annual IEEE Symposium on Logic in Computer Science (LICS '94)*, IEEE Computer Society Press, pp. 52–61. Cited on page **455**.

P. AMERICA

[1987]   Inheritance and subtyping in a parallel object-oriented language, in: *European Conference on Object-Oriented Programming, (ECOOP)*, vol. 276 of Lecture Notes in Computer Science, Springer, pp. 234–242. Cited on page **12**.

P. AMERICA AND F. S. DE BOER

[1990]   Proving total correctness of recursive procedures, *Information and Computation*, 84, pp. 129–162. Cited on pages **150** and **183**.

K. R. APT

[1981]   Ten years of Hoare's logic, a survey, part I, *ACM Trans. Prog. Lang. Syst.*, 3, pp. 431–483. Cited on pages **124**, **125**, **150**, and **182**.

[1984]   Ten years of Hoare's logic, a survey, part II: nondeterminism, *Theoretical Comput. Sci.*, 28, pp. 83–109. Cited on page **370**.

[1986]   Correctness proofs of distributed termination algorithms, *ACM Trans. Prog. Lang. Syst.*, 8, pp. 388–405. Cited on pages **15**, **390**, and **405**.

478   *References*

K. R. Apt, F. S. de Boer, and E.-R. Olderog

[1990] Proving termination of parallel programs, in: *Beauty is Our Business, A Birthday Salute to Edsger W. Dijkstra*, W. H. J. Feijen, A. J. M. van Gasteren, D. Gries, and J. Misra, eds., Springer, New York, pp. 0–6. Cited on page **305**.

K. R. Apt, L. Bougé, and P. Clermont

[1987] Two normal form theorems for CSP programs, *Inf. Process. Lett.*, 26, pp. 165–171. Cited on page **405**.

K. R. Apt, N. Francez, and S. Katz

[1988] Appraising fairness in distributed languages, *Distributed Computing*, 2, pp. 226–241. Cited on page **455**.

K. R. Apt, N. Francez, and W. P. de Roever

[1980] A proof system for communicating sequential processes, *ACM Trans. Prog. Lang. Syst.*, 2, pp. 359–385. Cited on pages **12**, **403**, and **405**.

K. R. Apt and E.-R. Olderog

[1983] Proof rules and transformations dealing with fairness, *Sci. Comput. Programming*, 3, pp. 65–100. Cited on pages **15** and **455**.

K. R. Apt and G. D. Plotkin

[1986] Countable nondeterminism and random assignment, *J. Assoc. Comput. Mach.*, 33, pp. 724–767. Cited on page **455**.

K. R. Apt, A. Pnueli, and J. Stavi

[1984] Fair termination revisited with delay, *Theoretical Comput. Sci.*, 33, pp. 65–84. Cited on page **455**.

E. Ashcroft and Z. Manna

[1971] Formalization of properties of parallel programs, *Machine Intelligence*, 6, pp. 17–41. Cited on page **370**.

R.-J. Back

[1989] A method for refining atomicity in parallel algorithms, in: *PARLE Conference on Parallel Architectures and Languages Europe*, Lecture Notes in Computer Science 366, Springer, New York, pp. 199–216. Cited on page **370**.

R.-J. Back and R. Kurki-Suonio

[1988] Serializability in distributed systems with handshaking, in: *Proceedings of International Colloquium on Automata Languages and Programming (ICALP '88)*, T. Lepistö and A. Salomaa, eds., Lecture Notes in Computer Science 317, Springer, New York, pp. 52–66. Cited on page **455**.

R.-J. Back and J. von Wright

[2008] *Refinement Calculus: A Systematic Introduction*, Springer, New York. Cited on pages **13** and **370**.

R. C. Backhouse

[1986] *Program Construction and Verification*, Prentice-Hall International, Englewood Cliffs, NJ. Cited on page **13**.

C. Baier and J.-P. Katoen

[2008] *Principles of Model Checking*, MIT Press, Cambridge, MA. Cited on page **16**.

J. W. de Bakker

[1980] *Mathematical Theory of Program Correctness*, Prentice-Hall International, Englewood Cliffs, NJ. Cited on pages **52**, **87**, **122**, **124**, **125**, and **370**.

T. BALL, A. PODELSKI, AND S. RAJAMANI

[2002] Relative completeness of abstraction refinement for software model checking, in: *Tools and Algorithms for the Construction and Analysis of Systems*, J.-P. Katoen and P. Stevens, eds., vol. 2280 of Lecture Notes in Computer Science, Springer, pp. 158–172. Cited on page **16**.

M. BALSER

[2006] *Verifying Concurrent Systems with Symbolic Execution – Temporal Reasoning is Symbolic Execution with a Little Induction*, PhD thesis, University of Augsburg, Shaker Verlag. Cited on page **346**.

M. BALSER, W. REIF, G. SCHELLHORN, K. STENZEL, AND A. THUMS

[2000] Formal system development in KIV, in: *Proc. Fundamental Approaches to Software Engineering*, T. Maibaum, ed., vol. 1783 of Lecture Notes in Computer Science, Springer, pp. 363–366. Cited on pages **17** and **346**.

A. BANERJEE AND D. A. NAUMANN

[2005] Ownership confinement ensures representation independence for object-oriented programs, *J. ACM*, 52, pp. 894–960. Cited on page **240**.

M. BARNETT, B.-Y. E. CHANG, R. DELINE, B. JACOBS, AND K. R. M. LEINO

[2005] Boogie: A modular reusable verifier for object-oriented programs, in: *FMCO*, pp. 364–387. Cited on page **240**.

D. BASIN, E.-R. OLDEROG, AND P. E. SEVINÇ

[2007] Specifying and analyzing security automata using CSP-OZ, in: *Proceedings of the 2007 ACM Symposium on Information, Computer and Communications Security (ASIACCS 2007)*, ACM Press, March, pp. 70–81. Cited on page **406**.

B. BECKERT, R. HÄHNLE, AND P. H. SCHMITT

[2007] eds., *Verification of Object-Oriented Software: The KeY Approach*, vol. 4334 of Lecture Notes in Computer Science, Springer. Cited on pages **17, 18**, and **241**.

M. BEN-ARI

[1990] *Principles of Concurrent and Distributed Programming*, Prentice-Hall International, Englewood Cliffs, NJ. Cited on page **346**.

J. VAN DEN BERG, B. JACOBS, AND E. POLL

[2001] Formal specification and verification of Java Card's application identifier class, in: *Java on Smart Cards: Programming and Security*, I. Attali and T. Jensen, eds., vol. 2041 of Lecture Notes in Computer Science, Springer, pp. 137–150. Cited on page **18**.

E. BEST

[1996] *Semantics of Sequential and Parallel Programs*, Prentice-Hall International, London. Cited on page **266**.

E. BEST AND C. LENGAUER

[1989] Semantic independence, *Sci. Comput. Programming*, 13, pp. 23–50. Cited on page **266**.

F. S. DE BOER

[1991a] A proof system for the language POOL, in: *Foundations of Object-Oriented Languages*, J. W. de Bakker, W. P. de Roever, and G. Rozenberg, eds., vol. 489 of Lecture Notes in Computer Science, Springer, pp. 124–150. Cited on page **12**.

[1991b] *Reasoning about dynamically evolving process structures (A proof theory of the parallel object-oriented language POOL)*, PhD thesis, Free University of Amsterdam. Cited on page **240**.

[1994] Compositionality in the inductive assertion method for concurrent systems, in: *Programming Concepts, Methods and Calculi*, E.-R. Olderog, ed., Elsevier/North-Holland, Amsterdam, pp. 289–305. Cited on page **305**.

A. BOUAJJANI, J.-C. FERNANDEZ, N. HALBWACHS, AND P. RAYMOND
[1992] Minimal state graph generation, *Sci. Comput. Programming*, 18, pp. 247–269. Cited on page **16**.

J. P. BOWEN, C. A. R. HOARE, H. LANGMAACK, E.-R. OLDEROG, AND A. P. RAVN
[1996] A ProCoS II project final report: Esprit basic research project 7071, *Bulletin of the European Association for Theoretical Computer Science (EATCS)*, 59, pp. 76–99. Cited on page **406**.

S. D. BROOKES
[1993] Full abstraction for a shared variable parallel language, in: *Proceedings, Eighth Annual IEEE Symposium on Logic in Computer Science (LICS '93)*, IEEE Computer Society Press, pp. 98–109. Cited on page **305**.

S. D. BROOKES, C. A. R. HOARE, AND A. W. ROSCOE
[1984] A theory of communicating processes, *J. Assoc. Comput. Mach.*, 31, pp. 560–599. Cited on page **405**.

J. R. BURCH, E. M. CLARKE, K. L. MCMILLAN, D. L. DILL, AND L. J. HWANG
[1992] Symbolic model checking: 10^{20} states and beyond, *Information and Computation*, 98, pp. 142–170. Cited on page **16**.

L. BURDY, Y. CHEON, D. R. COK, M. D. ERNST, J. R. KINIRY, G. T. LEAVENS, K. R. M. LEINO, AND E. POLL
[2005] An overview of jml tools and applications, *International Journal on Software Tools for Technology Transfer*, 7, pp. 212–232. Cited on page **240**.

L. CARDELLI
[1991] Typeful programming, in: *State of the Art Book: Formal Description of Programming Concepts*, E. J. Neuhold and M. Paul, eds., Springer, New York, pp. 431–507. Cited on page **51**.

K. M. CHANDY AND J. MISRA
[1988] *Parallel Program Design: A Foundation*, Addison-Wesley, New York. Cited on page **370**.

E. M. CLARKE
[1979] Programming language constructs for which it is impossible to obtain good Hoare axiom systems, *J. Assoc. Comput. Mach.*, 26, pp. 129–147. Cited on pages **125** and **183**.

[1980] Proving correctness of coroutines without history variables, *Acta Inf.*, 13, pp. 169–188. Cited on page **266**.

[1985] The characterization problem for Hoare logics, in: *Mathematical Logic and Programming Languages*, C. A. R. Hoare and J. C. Shepherdson, eds., Prentice-Hall International, Englewood Cliffs, NJ, pp. 89–106. Cited on page **183**.

E. M. CLARKE, O. GRUMBERG, S. JHA, Y. LU, AND H. VEITH
[2003] Counterexample-guided abstraction refinement for symbolic model checking, *J. Assoc. Comput. Mach.*, 50, pp. 752–794. Cited on page **16**.

E. M. CLARKE, O. GRUMBERG, AND D. A. PELED
[1999] *Model Checking*, MIT Press, Cambridge, MA. Cited on page **16**.

M. CLINT
[1973] Program proving: Coroutines, *Acta Inf.*, 2, pp. 50–63. Cited on page **266**.

S. A. Cook
[1978] Soundness and completeness of an axiom system for program verification, *SIAM J. Comput.*, 7, pp. 70–90. Cited on page **125**.

P. Cousot and R. Cousot
[1977a] Abstract interpretation: A unified lattice model for static analysis of programs by construction or approximation of fixedpoints, in: *Proc. of 4th ACM Symp. on Principles of Progr. Languages (POPL)*, ACM, Jan., pp. 238–252. Cited on page **16**.
[1977b] Automatic synthesis of optimal invariant assertions: mathematical foundations, in: *ACM Symposium on Artificial Intelligence and Programming Languages*, SIGPLAN Notices 12 (8), pp. 1–12. Cited on page **449**.

O.-J. Dahl and K. Nygaard
[1966] Simula - an Algol based simulation language, *CACM*, 9, pp. 671–678. Cited on page **240**.

D. van Dalen
[2004] *Logic and Structure*, Springer, 4th ed. Cited on page **52**.

W. Damm and B. Josko
[1983] A sound and relatively complete Hoare-logic for a language with higher type procedures, *Acta Inf.*, 20, pp. 59–101. Cited on page **183**.

E. W. Dijkstra
[1968] Cooperating sequential processes, in: *Programming Languages: NATO Advanced Study Institute*, F. Genuys, ed., Academic Press, London, pp. 43–112. Cited on pages **324**, **331**, and **346**.
[1975] Guarded commands, nondeterminacy and formal derivation of programs, *Comm. ACM*, 18, pp. 453–457. Cited on pages **15**, **86**, **125**, **349**, and **370**.
[1976] *A Discipline of Programming*, Prentice-Hall, Englewood Cliffs, NJ. Cited on pages **13**, **14**, **15**, **56**, **113**, **126**, **349**, **350**, **370**, and **424**.
[1977] A correctness proof for communicating processes —a small exercise. EWD-607, Burroughs, Nuenen, the Netherlands. Cited on page **403**.
[1982] *Selected Writings on Computing*, Springer, New York. Cited on page **125**.

E. W. Dijkstra and C. S. Scholten
[1990] *Predicate Calculus and Program Semantics*, Springer, New York. Cited on page **26**.

T. Elrad and N. Francez
[1982] Decompositions of distributed programs into communication closed layers, *Sci. Comput. Programming*, 2, pp. 155–173. Cited on page **305**.

M. H. van Emden
[1997] Value constraints in the CLP scheme, *Constraints*, 2, pp. 163–184. Cited on page **455**.

E. A. Emerson and E. M. Clarke
[1982] Using branching time temporal logic to synthesize synchronization skeletons, *Sci. Comput. Programming*, 2, pp. 241–266. Cited on page **16**.

W. H. J. Feijen and A. J. M. van Gasteren
[1999] *On a Method of Multiprogramming*, Springer, New York. Cited on page **13**.

J.-C. Filliâtre
[2007] Formal proof of a program: Find, *Sci. Comput. Program.*, 64, pp. 332–340. Cited on pages **125** and **126**.

C. FISCHER

[1997]   CSP-OZ: A combination of Object-Z and CSP, in: *Formal Methods for Open Object-Based Distributed Systems (FMOODS)*, H. Bowman and J. Derrick, eds., vol. 2, Chapman & Hall, pp. 423–438. Cited on page **406**.

C. FISCHER AND H. WEHRHEIM

[1999]   Model-checking CSP-OZ specifications with FDR, in: *Proc. 1st International Conference on Integrated Formal Methods (IFM)*, K. Araki, A. Galloway, and K. Taguchi, eds., Springer, pp. 315–334. Cited on page **406**.

M. J. FISCHER AND M. S. PATERSON

[1983]   Storage requirements for fair scheduling, *Inf. Process. Lett.*, 17, pp. 249–250. Cited on page **426**.

C. FLANAGAN, K. R. M. LEINO, M. LILLIBRIDGE, G. NELSON, J. B. SAXE, AND R. STATA

[2002]   Extended static checking for Java, in: *PLDI*, pp. 234–245. Cited on pages **18** and **241**.

L. FLON AND N. SUZUKI

[1978]   Nondeterminism and the correctness of parallel programs, in: *Formal Description of Programming Concepts*, E. J. Neuhold, ed., North-Holland, Amsterdam, pp. 598–608. Cited on page **370**.

[1981]   The total correctness of parallel programs, *SIAM J. Comput.*, pp. 227–246. Cited on page **370**.

R. FLOYD

[1967a] Assigning meaning to programs, in: *Proceedings of Symposium on Applied Mathematics 19, Mathematical Aspects of Computer Science*, J. T. Schwartz, ed., American Mathematical Society, New York, pp. 19–32. Cited on pages **12** and **122**.

[1967b] Nondeterministic algorithms, *J. Assoc. Comput. Mach.*, 14, pp. 636–644. Cited on page **452**.

M. FOKKINGA, M. POEL, AND J. ZWIERS

[1993]   Modular completeness for communication closed layers, in: *CONCUR '93*, E. Best, ed., Lecture Notes in Computer Science 715, Springer, New York, pp. 50–65. Cited on pages **266** and **305**.

M. FOLEY AND C. A. R. HOARE

[1971]   Proof of a recursive program: Quicksort, *Computer Journal*, 14, pp. 391–395. Cited on pages **101**, **125**, **172**, and **183**.

FORMAL SYSTEMS (EUROPE) LTD.

[2003]   *Failures-Divergence Refinement: FDR 2 User Manual*, Formal Systems (Europe) Ltd, May. Cited on page **406**.

N. FRANCEZ

[1986]   *Fairness*, Springer, New York. Cited on page **455**.

[1992]   *Program Verification*, Addison-Wesley, Reading, MA. Cited on page **405**.

N. FRANCEZ, R.-J. BACK, AND R. KURKI-SUONIO

[1992]   On equivalence-completions of fairness assumptions, *Formal Aspects of Computing*, 4, pp. 582–591. Cited on page **455**.

N. FRANCEZ, C. A. R. HOARE, D. J. LEHMANN, AND W. P. DE ROEVER

[1979]   Semantics of nondeterminism, concurrency and communication, *J. Comput. System Sci.*, 19, pp. 290–308. Cited on page **405**.

N. Francez, D. J. Lehmann, and A. Pnueli

[1984]   A linear history semantics for languages for distributed computing, *Theoretical Comput. Sci.*, 32, pp. 25–46. Cited on page **405**.

J.-Y. Girard, Y. Lafont, and P. Taylor

[1989]   *Proofs and Types*, Cambridge University Press, Cambridge, UK. Cited on page **51**.

M. J. C. Gordon

[1979]   *The Denotational Description of Programming Languages, An Introduction*, Springer, New York. Cited on page **58**.

G. A. Gorelick

[1975]   *A complete axiomatic system for proving assertions about recursive and nonrecursive programs*, Tech. Rep. 75, Department of Computer Science, University of Toronto. Cited on page **125**.

A. Grau, U. Hill, and H. Langmaack

[1967]   *Translation of ALGOL 60*, vol. 137 of "Die Grundlehren der mathematischen Wissenschaften in Einzeldarstellungen", Springer. Cited on pages **150** and **183**.

D. Gries

[1978]   The multiple assignment statement, *IEEE Trans. Softw. Eng.*, SE-4, pp. 89–93. Cited on page **125**.

[1981]   *The Science of Programming*, Springer, New York. Cited on pages **13**, **126**, **361**, and **370**.

[1982]   A note on a standard strategy for developing loop invariants and loops, *Sci. Comput. Programming*, 2, pp. 207–214. Cited on pages **113** and **116**.

O. Grumberg, N. Francez, J. A. Makowsky, and W. P. de Roever

[1985]   A proof rule for fair termination of guarded commands, *Information and Control*, 66, pp. 83–102. Cited on page **455**.

O. Grumberg and H. Veith

[2008]   eds., *25 Years of Model Checking – History, Achievements, Perspectives*, vol. 5000 of Lecture Notes in Computer Science, Springer. Cited on page **16**.

P. R. Halmos

[1985]   *I Want to be a Mathematician: An Automatography*, Springer, New York. Cited on page **26**.

D. Harel

[1979]   *First-Order Dynamic Logic*, Lecture Notes in Computer Science 68, Springer, New York. Cited on page **125**.

D. Harel, D. Kozen, and J. Tiuryn

[2000]   *Dynamic logic*, MIT Press, Cambridge, MA. Cited on page **17**.

M. C. B. Hennessy and G. D. Plotkin

[1979]   Full abstraction for a simple programming language, in: *Proceedings of Mathematical Foundations of Computer Science*, Lecture Notes in Computer Science 74, Springer, New York, pp. 108–120. Cited on pages **14** and **58**.

C. A. R. Hoare

[1961a] Algorithm 64, Quicksort, *Comm. ACM*, 4, p. 321. Cited on pages **125** and **183**.

[1961b] Algorithm 65, Find, *Comm. ACM*, 4, p. 321. Cited on page **125**.

[1962]   Quicksort, *Comput. J.*, 5, pp. 10–15. Cited on pages **99**, **125**, **172**, and **183**.

[1969]   An axiomatic basis for computer programming, *Comm. ACM*, 12, pp. 576–580, 583. Cited on pages **12**, **65**, **68**, and **125**.

[1971a]   Procedures and parameters: an axiomatic approach, in: *Proceedings of Symposium on the Semantics of Algorithmic Languages*, E. Engeler, ed., vol. 188 of Lecture Notes in Mathematics, Springer, pp. 102–116. Cited on pages **125** and **183**.

[1971b]   Proof of a program: Find, *Comm. ACM*, 14, pp. 39–45. Cited on pages **125** and **126**.

[1972]   Towards a theory of parallel programming, in: *Operating Systems Techniques*, C. A. R. Hoare and R. H. Perrot, eds., Academic Press, London, pp. 61–71. Cited on pages **246**, **254**, **266**, and **346**.

[1975]   Parallel programming: an axiomatic approach, *Computer Languages*, 1, pp. 151–160. Cited on pages **14**, **246**, and **266**.

[1978]   Communicating sequential processes, *Comm. ACM*, 21, pp. 666–677. Cited on pages **15**, **374**, and **405**.

[1985]   *Communicating Sequential Processes*, Prentice-Hall International, Englewood Cliffs, NJ. Cited on pages **15**, **374**, and **405**.

[1996]   How did software get so reliable without proof?, in: *FME'96: Industrial Benefit and Advances in Formal Methods*, M.-C. Gaudel and J. C. P. Woodcock, eds., vol. 1051 of Lecture Notes in Computer Science, Springer, pp. 1–17. Cited on page **17**.

C. A. R. HOARE AND N. WIRTH

[1973]   An axiomatic definition of the programming language PASCAL, *Acta Inf.*, 2, pp. 335–355. Cited on page **125**.

J. HOENICKE

[2006]   *Combination of Processes, Data, and Time (Dissertation)*, Tech. Rep. Nr. 9/06, University of Oldenburg, July. ISSN 0946-2910. Cited on page **406**.

J. HOENICKE AND E.-R. OLDEROG

[2002]   CSP-OZ-DC: A combination of specification techniques for processes, data and time, *Nordic Journal of Computing*, 9, pp. 301–334. appeared March 2003. Cited on page **406**.

J. HOOMAN AND W. P. DE ROEVER

[1986]   The quest goes on: a survey of proofsystems for partial correctness of CSP, in: *Current Trends in Concurrency*, Lecture Notes in Computer Science 224, Springer, New York, pp. 343–395. Cited on page **405**.

M. HUISMAN AND B. JACOBS

[2000]   Java program verification via a Hoare logic with abrupt termination, in: *FASE*, T. S. E. Maibaum, ed., vol. 1783 of Lecture Notes in Computer Science, Springer, pp. 284–303. Cited on page **240**.

INMOS LIMITED

[1984]   *Occam Programming Manual*, Prentice-Hall International, Englewood Cliffs, NJ. Cited on pages **15**, **374**, and **406**.

B. JACOBS

[2004]   Weakest pre-condition reasoning for Java programs with JML annotations, *Journal of Logic and Algebraic Programming*, 58, pp. 61–88. Formal Methods for Smart Cards. Cited on page **240**.

W. JANSSEN, M. POEL, AND J. ZWIERS

[1991]   Action systems and action refinement in the development of parallel systems, in: *CONCUR'91*, J. C. M. Baeten and J. F. Groote, eds., Lecture Notes in Computer Science 527, Springer, New York, pp. 669–716. Cited on page **305**.

C. B. Jones
[1992]   *The Search for Tractable Ways of Reasoning about Programs*, Tech. Rep. UMCS-92-4-4, Department of Computer Science, University of Manchester. Cited on page **124**.

Y.-J. Joung
[1996]   Characterizing fairness implementability for multiparty interaction, in: *Proceedings of International Colloquium on Automata Languages and Programming (ICALP '96)*, F. M. auf der Heide and B. Monien, eds., Lecture Notes in Computer Science 1099, Springer, New York, pp. 110–121. Cited on page **455**.

A. Kaldewaij
[1990]   *Programming: The Derivation of Algorithms*, Prentice-Hall International, Englewood Cliffs, N.J. Cited on pages **13** and **183**.

E. Knapp
[1992]   Derivation of concurrent programs: two examples, *Sci. Comput. Programming*, 19, pp. 1–23. Cited on page **305**.

D. E. Knuth
[1968]   *The Art of Computer Programming. Vol. 1: Fundamental Algorithms*, Addison-Wesley, Reading, MA. Cited on page **272**.

D. König
[1927]   Über eine Schlußweise aus dem Endlichen ins Unendliche, *Acta Litt. Ac. Sci.*, 3, pp. 121–130. Cited on page **272**.

L. Lamport
[1977]   Proving the correctness of multiprocess programs, *IEEE Trans. Softw. Eng.*, SE-3:2, pp. 125–143. Cited on pages **12**, **281**, and **305**.
[1983]   What good is temporal logic?, in: *Proceedings of the IFIP Information Processing 1983*, R. E. A. Mason, ed., North-Holland, Amsterdam, pp. 657–668. Cited on page **266**.
[1994]   The temporal logic of actions, *ACM Trans. Prog. Lang. Syst.*, 16, pp. 872–923. Cited on page **371**.
[2003]   *Specifying Systems – The TLA+ Language and Tools for Hardware and Software Engineers*, Addison Wesley. Cited on page **371**.

J.-L. Lassez and M. J. Maher
[1984]   Closures and fairness in the semantics of programming logic, *Theoretical Comput. Sci.*, 29, pp. 167–184. Cited on page **455**.

P. E. Lauer
[1971]   *Consistent formal theories of the semantics of programming languages*, Tech. Rep. 25. 121, IBM Laboratory Vienna. Cited on pages **125** and **370**.

G. T. Leavens, Y. Cheon, C. Clifton, C. Ruby, and D. R. Cok
[2005]   How the design of JML accomodates both runtime assertion checking and formal verification, *Sci. of Comput. Prog.*, 55, pp. 185–208. Cited on page **17**.

D. J. Lehmann, A. Pnueli, and J. Stavi
[1981]   Impartiality, justice, and fairness: the ethics of concurrent termination, in: *Proceedings of International Colloquium on Automata Languages and Programming (ICALP '81)*, O. Kariv and S. Even, eds., Lecture Notes in Computer Science 115, Springer, New York, pp. 264–277. Cited on page **455**.

C. LENGAUER

[1993]   Loop parallelization in the polytope model, in: *CONCUR'93*, E. Best, ed., Lecture Notes in Computer Science 715, Springer, New York, pp. 398–416. Cited on page **371**.

G. LEVIN AND D. GRIES

[1981]   A proof technique for communicating sequential processes, *Acta Inf.*, 15, pp. 281–302. Cited on pages **12** and **405**.

R. LIPTON

[1975]   Reduction: a method of proving properties of parallel programs, *Comm. ACM*, 18, pp. 717–721. Cited on pages **15**, **305**, and **346**.

J. LOECKX AND K. SIEBER

[1987]   *The Foundation of Program Verification*, Teubner-Wiley, Stuttgart, 2nd ed. Cited on pages **28**, **125**, and **150**.

B. P. MAHONY AND J. S. DONG

[1998]   Blending Object-Z and Timed CSP: an introduction to TCOZ, in: *The 20th International Conference on Software Engineering (ICSE'98)*, K. Futatsugi, R. Kemmerer, and K. Torii, eds., IEEE Computer Society Press, pp. 95–104. Cited on page **406**.

Z. MANNA AND A. PNUELI

[1991]   *The Temporal Logic of Reactive and Concurrent Systems – Specification*, Springer, New York. Cited on pages **13** and **325**.

[1995]   *Temporal Verification of Reactive Systems – Safety*, Springer, New York. Cited on pages **13** and **325**.

B. MEYER

[1997]   *Object-Oriented Software Construction*, Prentice Hall, 2nd ed. Cited on page **17**.

R. MEYER, J. FABER, J. HOENICKE, AND A. RYBALCHENKO

[2008]   Model checking duration calculus: A practical approach, *Formal Aspects of Computing*, 20, pp. 481–505. Cited on page **406**.

R. MILNER

[1980]   *A Calculus of Communicating Systems*, Lecture Notes in Computer Science 92, Springer, New York. Cited on page **405**.

[1989]   *Communication and Concurrency*, Prentice-Hall International, Englewood Cliffs, NJ. Cited on page **405**.

J. MISRA

[2001]   *A Discipline of Multiprogramming: Programming Theory for Distributed Applications*, Springer, New York. Cited on page **13**.

J. C. MITCHELL

[1990]   Type systems in programming languages, in: *Handbook of Theoretical Computer Science*, J. van Leeuwen, ed., Elsevier, Amsterdam, pp. 365–458. Cited on page **51**.

M. MÖLLER, E.-R. OLDEROG, H. RASCH, AND H. WEHRHEIM

[2008]   Integrating a formal method into a software engineering process with UML and Java, *Formal Aspects of Computing*, 20, pp. 161–204. Cited on page **406**.

C. MORGAN

[1994]   *Programming from Specifications*, Prentice-Hall International, London, 2nd ed. Cited on page **13**.

J. M. MORRIS
[1982] A general axiom of assignment/ assignment and linked data structures/ a proof of the Schorr-Wait algorithm, in: *Theoretical Foundations of Programming Methodology, Lecture Notes of an International Summer School. Reidel.* Cited on page **240**.

P. MUELLER, A. POETZSCH-HEFFTER, AND G. T. LEAVENS
[2006] Modular invariants for layered object structures, *Sci. Comput. Program.*, 62, pp. 253–286. Cited on page **241**.

M. H. A. NEWMAN
[1942] On theories with a combinatorial definition of "equivalence", *Annals of Math.*, 43, pp. 223–243. Cited on page **250**.

F. NIELSON, H. R. NIELSON, AND C. HANKIN
[2004] *Principles of Program Analysis*, Springer, New York. Cited on page **16**.

H. R. NIELSON AND F. NIELSON
[2007] *Semantics with Applications: An Appetizer*, Springer, London. Cited on page **124**.

T. NIPKOW AND L. P. NIETO
[1999] Owicki/Gries in Isabelle/HOL, in: *Fundamental Approaches in Software Enginering (FASE)*, J. P. Finance, ed., vol. 1577 of Lecture Notes in Computer Science, Springer, pp. 188–203. Cited on page **345**.

T. NIPKOW, L. C. PAULSON, AND M. WENZEL
[2002] *Isabelle/HOL – A Proof Assistant for Higher-Order Logic*, vol. 2283 of Lecture Notes in Computer Science, Springer. Cited on pages **17** and **345**.

E.-R. OLDEROG
[1981] Sound and complete Hoare-like calculi based on copy rules, *Acta Inf.*, 16, pp. 161–197. Cited on page **183**.
[1983a] A characterization of Hoare's logic for programs with Pascal-like procedures, in: *Proc. of the 15th ACM Symp. on Theory of Computing (STOC)*, ACM, April, pp. 320–329. Cited on page **183**.
[1983b] On the notion of expressiveness and the rule of adaptation, *Theoretical Comput. Sci.*, 30, pp. 337–347. Cited on page **183**.
[1984] Correctness of programs with Pascal-like procedures without global variables, *Theoretical Comput. Sci.*, 30, pp. 49–90. Cited on page **183**.

E.-R. OLDEROG AND K. R. APT
[1988] Fairness in parallel programs, the transformational approach, *ACM Trans. Prog. Lang. Syst.*, 10, pp. 420–455. Cited on pages **325** and **455**.

E.-R. OLDEROG AND A. PODELSKI
[2009] Explicit fair scheduling for dynamic control, in: *Correctness, Concurrency, Compositionality: Essays in Honor of Willem-Paul de Roever*, D. Dams, U. Hannemann, and M. Steffen, eds., Lecture Notes in Computer Science, Springer. To appear. Cited on page **455**.

E.-R. OLDEROG AND S. RÖSSIG
[1993] A case study in transformational design of concurrent systems, in: *Theory and Practice of Software Development*, M.-C. Gaudel and J.-P. Jouannaud, eds., vol. 668 of LNCS, Springer, pp. 90–104. Cited on page **406**.

S. OWICKI
[1978] Verifying concurrent programs with shared data classes, in: *Proceedings of the IFIP Working Conference on Formal Description of Programming Concepts*, E. J. Neuhold, ed., North-Holland, Amsterdam, pp. 279–298. Cited on page **305**.

S. Owicki and D. Gries

[1976a] An axiomatic proof technique for parallel programs, *Acta Inf.*, 6, pp. 319–340. Cited on pages **12, 14, 15, 80, 257, 261, 262, 266, 268, 276, 292, 305, 307, 308, 311, 314, 320, 321,** and **345**.

[1976b] Verifying properties of parallel programs: an axiomatic approach, *Comm. ACM*, 19, pp. 279–285. Cited on pages **12** and **346**.

S. Owre and N. Shankar

[2003] Writing PVS proof strategies, in: *Design and Application of Strategies/Tactics in Higher Order Logics (STRATA 2003)*, M. Archer, B. D. Vito, and C. Muñoz, eds., no. CP-2003-212448 in: NASA Conference Publication, NASA Langley Research Center, Hampton, VA, Sept., pp. 1–15. Cited on page **17**.

D. Park

[1979] On the semantics of fair parallelism, in: *Proceedings of Abstract Software Specifications*, D. Bjørner, ed., Lecture Notes in Computer Science 86, Springer, New York, pp. 504–526. Cited on page **424**.

G. L. Peterson

[1981] Myths about the mutual exclusion problem, *Inf. Process. Lett.*, 12, pp. 223–252. Cited on page **327**.

C. Pierik and F. S. de Boer

[2005] A proof outline logic for object-oriented programming, *Theor. Comput. Sci.*, 343, pp. 413–442. Cited on page **240**.

G. D. Plotkin

[1981] *A Structural Approach to Operational Semantics*, Tech. Rep. DAIMI-FN 19, Department of Computer Science, Aarhus University. Cited on pages **14, 58**, and **488**.

[1982] An operational semantics for CSP, in: *Formal Description of Programming Concepts II*, D. Bjørner, ed., North-Holland, Amsterdam, pp. 199–225. Cited on page **405**.

[2004] A structural approach to operational semantics, *J. of Logic and Algebraic Programming*, 60–61, pp. 17–139. Revised version of Plotkin [1981]. Cited on page **14**.

A. Pnueli

[1977] The temporal logic of programs, in: *Proceedings of the 18th IEEE Symposium on Foundations of Computer Science*, pp. 46–57. Cited on page **13**.

J.-P. Queille and J. Sifakis

[1981] Specification and verification of concurrent systems in CESAR, in: *Proceedings of the 5th International Symposium on Programming*, Paris. Cited on page **16**.

M. Raynal

[1986] *Algorithms for Mutual Exclusion*, MIT Press, Cambridge, MA. Cited on page **346**.

J. C. Reynolds

[1981] *The Craft of Programming*, Prentice-Hall International, Englewood Cliffs, NJ. Cited on page **124**.

[2002] Separation logic: A logic for shared mutable data structures, in: *LICS*, pp. 55–74. Cited on page **240**.

W. P. de Roever, F. S. de Boer, U. Hannemann, J. Hooman, Y. Lakhnech, M. Poel, and J. Zwiers

[2001] *Concurrency Verification – Introduction to Compositional and Noncompositional Methods*, Cambridge University Press. Cited on page **406**.

A. W. Roscoe
[1994] Model-checking CSP, in: *A Classical Mind – Essays in Honour of C.A.R. Hoare*, A. Roscoe, ed., Prentice-Hall, pp. 353–378. Cited on page **406**.
[1998] *The Theory and Practice of Concurrency*, Prentice-Hall. Cited on page **405**.

B. K. Rosen
[1974] *Correctness of parallel programs: the Church-Rosser approach*, Tech. Rep. IBM Research Report RC 5107, T. J. Watson Research Center, Yorktown Heights, NY. Cited on page **266**.

S. Sagiv, T. W. Reps, and R. Wilhelm
[2002] Parametric shape analysis via 3-valued logic, *ACM Trans. Prog. Lang. Syst.*, 24, pp. 217–298. Cited on page **16**.

A. Salwicki and T. Müldner
[1981] On the algorithmic properties of concurrent programs, in: *Proceedings of Logics of Programs*, E. Engeler, ed., Lecture Notes in Computer Science 125, Springer, New York, pp. 169–197. Cited on page **266**.

M. Schenke
[1999] Transformational design of real-time systems – part 2: from program specifications to programs, *Acta Informatica 36*, pp. 67–99. Cited on page **406**.

M. Schenke and E.-R. Olderog
[1999] Transformational design of real-time systems – part 1: from requirements to program specifications, *Acta Informatica 36*, pp. 1–65. Cited on page **406**.

F. B. Schneider and G. R. Andrews
[1986] Concepts of concurrent programming, in: *Current Trends in Concurrency*, J. W. de Bakker, W. P. de Roever, and G. Rozenberg, eds., Lecture Notes in Computer Science 224, Springer, New York, pp. 669–716. Cited on page **345**.

D. S. Scott and J. W. de Bakker
[1969] *A theory of programs*. Notes of an IBM Vienna Seminar. Cited on page **150**.

D. S. Scott and C. Strachey
[1971] *Towards a mathematical semantics for computer languages*, Tech. Rep. PRG–6, Programming Research Group, University of Oxford. Cited on page **58**.

W. Stephan, B. Langenstein, A. Nonnengart, and G. Rock
[2005] Verification support environment, in: *Mechanizing Mathematical Reasoning, Essays in Honour of Jörg H. Siekmann on the Occasion of His 60th Birthday*, D. Hutter and W. Stephan, eds., vol. 2605 of Lecture Notes in Computer Science, Springer, pp. 476–493. Cited on page **17**.

J. E. Stoy
[1977] *Denotational Semantics: The Scott-Strachey Approach to Programming Language Theory*, MIT Press, Cambridge, MA. Cited on page **58**.

A. Tarski
[1955] A lattice-theoretic fixpoint theorem and its applications, *Pacific J. Math*, 5, pp. 285–309. Cited on page **448**.

Terese
[2003] *Term Rewriting Systems*, Cambridge Tracts in Theoretical Computer Science 55, Cambridge University Press, Cambridge, UK. Cited on page **266**.

J. V. Tucker and J. I. Zucker

[1988]   *Program Correctness over Abstract Data Types, with Error-State Seman-tics*, North-Holland and CWI Monographs, Amsterdam. Cited on pages **51** and **124**.

A. M. Turing

[1949]   On checking a large routine, *Report of a Conference on High Speed Au-tomatic Calculating Machines*, pp. 67–69. Univ. Math. Laboratory, Cam-bridge, 1949. See also: F. L. Morris and C. B. Jones, *An early program proof by Alan Turing*, Annals of the History of Computing *6* pages 139–143, 1984. Cited on page **12**.

J. C. P. Woodcock and A. L. C. Cavalcanti

[2002]   The semantics of Circus, in: *ZB2002: Formal Specification and Develop-ment in Z and B*, D. Bert, J. P. Bowen, M. C. Henson, and K. Robinson, eds., vol. 2272 of Lecture Notes in Computer Science, Springer, pp. 184–203. Cited on page **406**.

D. Zöbel

[1988]   Normalform-Transformationen für CSP-Programme, *Informatik: For-schung und Entwicklung*, 3, pp. 64–76. Cited on page **405**.

J. Zwiers

[1989]   *Compositionality, Concurrency and Partial Correctness – Proof Theories for Networks of Processes and Their Relationship*, Lecture Notes in Com-puter Science 321, Springer, New York. Cited on pages **125** and **406**.

Index

Author Index

498   *Author Index*

Faber, J., 486
Feijen, W. H. J., 13, 478, 481
Fernandez, J.-C., 480
Filliâtre, J.-C., 125, 126, 481
Finance, J. P., 487
Fischer, C., 406, 482
Fischer, M. J., 426, 482
Flanagan, C., 18, 241, 482
Flon, L., 370, 482
Floyd, R., 12, 122, 452, 482
Fokkinga, M., 266, 305, 482
Foley, M., 101, 125, 172, 183, 482
Francez, N., 12, 305, 403, 405, 455, 478,
    481–483
Futatsugi, K., 486

Galloway, A., 482
Gasteren, A. J. M. van, 13, 478, 481
Gaudel, M.-C., 484, 487
Genuys, F., 481
Girard, J.-Y., 51, 483
Gordon, M. J. C., 58, 483
Gorelick, G. A., 125, 483
Grau, A., 150, 183, 483
Gries, D., 12–15, 80, 113, 116, 125, 126,
    257, 261, 262, 266, 268, 276, 292,
    305, 307, 308, 311, 314, 320, 321,
    345, 346, 361, 370, 405, 478, 483,
    486, 488
Groote, J. F., 484
Grumberg, O., 16, 455, 480, 483

Hähnle, R., 17, 18, 241, 479
Halbwachs, N., 480
Hallerstede, S., 13, 371, 477
Halmos, P. R., 26, 483
Hankin, C., 16, 487
Hannemann, U., 487, 488
Harel, D., 17, 125, 483
Heide, F. M. auf der, 485
Hennessy, M. C. B., 14, 58, 483
Henson, M. C., 490
Henzinger, T. A., 455, 477
Hill, U., 150, 183, 483
Hoare, C. A. R., 12, 14, 15, 17, 65,
    68, 99, 101, 125, 126, 172, 183,
    246, 254, 266, 346, 374, 405, 480,
    482–484
Hoenicke, J., 406, 484, 486
Hooman, J., 405, 484, 488
Huisman, M., 240, 484
Hutter, D., 489
Hwang, L. J., 480

Jacobs, B., 18, 240, 479, 484
Janssen, W., 305, 484
Jensen, T., 479
Jha, S., 480
Jones, C. B., 124, 485
Josko, B., 183, 481
Jouannaud, J.-P., 487
Joung, Y.-J., 455, 485

Kaldewaij, A., 13, 183, 485
Kariv, O., 485
Katoen, J.-P., 16, 478, 479
Katz, S., 455, 478
Kemmerer, R., 486
Kiniry, J. R., 480
Knapp, E., 305, 485
Knuth, D. E., 272, 485
Kozen, D., 17, 483
Kurki-Suonio, R., 455, 478, 482
König, D., 272, 485

Lafont, Y., 51, 483
Lakhnech, Y., 488
Lamport, L., 12, 266, 281, 305, 371, 485
Langenstein, B., 489
Langmaack, H., 150, 183, 480, 483
Lassez, J.-L., 455, 485
Lauer, P. E., 125, 370, 485
Leavens, G. T., 17, 241, 480, 485, 487
Leeuwen, J. van, 486
Lehmann, D. J., 405, 455, 482, 483, 485
Leino, K., 240, 477
Leino, K. R. M., 479, 480, 482
Lengauer, C., 266, 371, 479, 486
Lepistö, T., 478
Levin, G., 12, 405, 486
Lillibridge, M., 482
Lipton, R., 15, 305, 346, 486
Loeckx, J., 28, 125, 150, 486
Lu, Y., 480

Maher, M. J., 455, 485
Mahony, B. P., 406, 486
Maibaum, T., 479
Maibaum, T. S. E., 484
Makowsky, J. A., 483
Manna, Z., 13, 325, 370, 478, 486
Mason, R. E. A., 485
McMillan, K. L., 480
Meyer, B., 17, 486
Meyer, R., 406, 486
Milner, R., 405, 486
Misra, J., 13, 370, 478, 480, 486
Mitchell, J. C., 51, 486

Symbol Index

Syntax

$=_{\text{object}}$, 187
Var, 30
$[u := t]$, 42
$[x := \mathbf{new}]$, 220
$\equiv$, 25
$\mathbf{new}$, 217
$\mathbf{null}$, 187
$\sigma(\bar{s})$, 35
$change(S)$, 57, 376
div, 30, 33
$divides$, 30, 34
$free(p)$, 41
int, 30, 34
max, 30
min, 30
mod, 30, 33
$p[u := t]$, 45
$p[x := \mathbf{new}]$, 220
$s[u := t]$, 43
$s[x := \mathbf{new}]$, 221
$var(S)$, 57
$var(p)$, 41
$var(s)$, 32
$\overset{\infty}{\forall}$, 453
$card$, 22
$min\ A$, 22
$[\bar{x} := \bar{t}]$, 46
$s[\bar{x} := \bar{t}]$, 46
$\mathbf{at}(T, S)$, 82
$\overset{\infty}{\exists}$, 410

Semantics

Δ, 34, 311
$\mathbf{mod}$, 34
$\bot$, 34
$init_T$, 218
$\nu(\sigma)$, 219
$\mathbf{null}$, 218
$\sigma(s)$, 35
$\sigma[u := d]$, 36
$\sigma \models B$, 41
$\sigma(o)$, 193
$\sigma(o)(x)$, 193
$\sigma[o := \tau]$, 194
$\sigma[u := \mathbf{new}]$, 218
$\tau[u := d]$, 194
$\mathbf{fail}$, 34, 96
$\mathcal{M}_{fair}[\![S]\!]$, 412
$\mathcal{M}_{wfair}[\![S]\!]$, 453
$\mathcal{M}[\![S]\!]$, 60
$\mathcal{M}_{tot}[\![S]\!]$, 61
$\mathcal{M}_{wtot}[\![S]\!]$, 310
$[\![p]\!]$, 42, 200, 224
$<_{com}$, 414
$\emptyset$, 21

Verification

$\models_{fair} \{p\}\ S\ \{q\}$, 430
$\models \{p\}\ S\ \{q\}$, 64
$\models_{tot} \{p\}\ S\ \{q\}$, 64
$\models_{wtot} \{p\}\ S\ \{q\}$, 311
$\mathbb{N}$, 21

501